WE TOO WERE THERE

WE TOO WERE THERE
Indians at Gallipoli

COL TEJINDER HUNDAL, VSM, PhD

MANOHAR
2025

First published 2025
First eBook edition 2025

© Col Tejinder Hundal, 2025

ISBN 978-93-6080-451-0 (hardbound)
ISBN 978-93-6080-803-7 (eBook)

Published by
Ajay Kumar Jain *for*
Manohar Publishers & Distributors
4753/23 Ansari Road, Daryaganj
New Delhi 110002

Cover design by Manoj Kumar

Typeset by Ravi Shanker, Delhi 110095

Printed and bound in India

The views expressed and suggestions made in the book are solely of the
author in his personal capacity and does not have any official endorsement.
Attributability of the contents lies purely with the author.

Contents

Figures

Maps

Tables

18   *List of Tables*

Abbreviations

AG	Adjutant General
ANZAC	Australia and New Zealand Army Corps
C-in-C	Commander-in-Chief
CO	Commanding Officer
DSO	Distinguished Service Order
FPO	Field Post Office
IDSM	Indian Distinguished Service Medal
IEF	Indian Expeditionary Force
IMS	Indian Medical Service
IST	Imperial Service Troops
MEF	Mediterranean Expeditionary Force
OC	Officer Commanding
OP	Observation Post
PM	Punjabi Musalmans
QMG	Quarter Master General
S&T	Supply & Transport
VC	Victoria Cross

Foreword

The disastrous attempt to force a naval passage through the Dardanelles Straits in early 1915 was the brainchild of the First Lord of the Admiralty, Winston Churchill. It gave rise to the ill-fated Gallipoli campaign which lasted from 25 April till 19 December 1915. The Allied force which landed on the Gallipoli peninsula not far from where the Greeks under King Agamemnon had landed to lay siege to the city of Troy in 1250 BCE, consisted of a variety of nationalities. Apart from the British and the French, there were soldiers from Australia, New Zealand, and India, which sent an expeditionary force (IEF 'G') to fight in the campaign. This consisted of an infantry and an artillery brigade along with an Indian mule corps, a medical establishment and other support services.

Apart from the fact that the GOC Mediterranean Force, General Sir Ian Hamilton, favoured Gurkha soldiers, there was also some apprehension in the minds of the British about using Muslim troops in action against their co-religionists. Two of the initial infantry battalions of the Indian brigade, the 69th and 89th Punjabis, were withdrawn from this theatre within a fortnight and sent on to fight in France. These battalions were replaced by two Gurkha battalions, and after their departure, the composition of the infantry element was mainly Gurkha, with one Sikh battalion. The artillery brigade consisted of two mountain batteries composed of Sikh and Punjabi Muslim gunners. The latter were the only combatant Indian Muslim soldiers on the peninsula. The Indian gunners were 'first in and last out' in the theatre and earned the admiration of the Australia and New Zealand Corps (ANZAC) alongside whom they served during the entire campaign. The services of the Indian mule corps were both outstanding and indispensable. Indeed, the campaign could not have been sustained without the fortitude and quiet valour displayed by them.

The Gallipoli campaign has a special place in the national identities of Australia, New Zealand and modern Turkey. While there has been an ever-growing body of literature on the campaign, study of the Indian involvement in this theatre was largely neglected until Prof. Peter Stanley's seminal work on the subject in 2015. Colonel Tejinder Hundal has carried this work forward through a detailed examination of the Sikh presence on Gallipoli. His analysis of the Indian casualties suffered during the campaign, using the detailed casualty appendices to the theatre war diaries has never previously been attempted. His examination of the organisational aspects of Indian Infantry battalions, their mobilisation, manpower replacement, as well as peculiarities of the logistical requirements of Indian soldiers on the peninsula, their postal arrangements, pay and allowances, and details of honours and awards, are all dealt with in considerable detail. The book will, therefore, appeal to military, social and community historians alike. It is an important addition to the Indian historiography of the Great War. I commend the author for his diligence and labour and trust the book will find the readership that it deserves.

SQN LDR RANA T.S. CHHINA (Retd)

Acknowledgements

The journey of research and writing about the bravery and sacrifices of the Indian troops almost 108 years later has been a long and arduous one. The predicament was further compounded by the stark reality of existence of a very limited research on the subject, which manifested very late in my journey. I had started this journey with very little knowledge and a huge domain of unknown to unravel. Rana Chhina and Peter Stanley's works have truly been a guiding light for me as I navigated the path from the familiar to the unfamiliar. Their insights have provided valuable inspiration along my journey.

I place on record my heartfelt gratitude to Rana Chhina and the Centre for Military History and Conflict Studies (CMHCS) of the United Service Institution of India in New Delhi for guidance and support in every step of this journey. The library and records held by the USI have indeed been the lifeline of this endeavour. Without this, it would have not been possible to bring the extensive research into a logical conclusion in the form of a book. The database of the National Archives of India, New Delhi is very extensive and detailed. The recent initiative of digitization of all the records in possession of the National Archives has facilitated researchers like me to remotely connect with the archives. The valuable assistance provided by the National Archives in terms of War Diaries and Casualty Appendices of Force 'G', have been the foundation of the research for this book. I am sincerely grateful to the staff of the National Archives of India for the timely provisioning of documents and records requested for digitization on demand.

The association between Australian & New Zealand Corps (ANZAC) and the Indian troops during the Gallipoli Campaign has been well researched. In my book, I have also alluded to some of the lesser known facets of camaraderie and bonhomie between the Indian troops and the Australians and New Zealanders. The collection of images and other associated data related to the Indian contribution in the Gallipoli Campaign held by the Australian War Memorial is prodigious. I take this opportunity to acknowledge the assistance rendered by the portal of the Australian War Memorial in provisioning of images in the open domain. I have taken liberty to use the open domain images available on the portal related to the Indian participation in my book.

The book discusses about the trials and tribulations of three Sikh soldiers belonging to different regiments who served at Gallipoli during the campaign. This particular part of the book would not have been possible without the active support of three families in different parts of the globe. I wish to use this platform to acknowledge the assistance rendered by them in finalising the details about their respective ancestors who fought in Gallipoli. Towards this, I appreciate the assistance and support rendered by Dr Tajinderpal Singh for filling in the gaps related to the life of Sepoy Nanak Singh belonging to the 69th Punjabis. The details along with the pictures and memorabilia shared by the family have significantly made my onerous task more manageable. In the United Kingdom, the assistance and support provided by the United Kingdom Punjab Heritage Association (UKPHA) has been wonderful. The details shared by Harbaksh Grewal of UKPHA have been greatly helpful to provide initial leads about Subadar Gurmukh Singh of Burma Military Police. The finer details along with images and memorabilia have been shared by Rani Brar, the great granddaughter of Subadar Gurmukh Singh and I am immensely grateful to her. In India, my research on Sepoy Udey Singh of the 14th Sikhs was facilitated by the support of Prof. (Dr) Charanjit Thandi Sohi, former Principal of Guru Gobind Singh College for Women, Chandigarh, the granddaughter of Sepoy Udey Singh. The family has spent long hours with me both in person and on mail to provide crucial details about the life of Sepoy Udey Singh.

I shall be failing in my duty if I fail to mention the assistance provided by archive sections of 4 Mechanized Infantry (erstwhile 14th Sikhs), 15 PUNJAB (erstwhile 1st Rajindra Sikhs) and 1 GUARDS (erstwhile 69th Punjabis). These battalions maintain elaborate records of their participation in the Gallipoli Campaign and I have extensively drawn from those resources. For the records related to the Indian Mule Corps, I have been greatly assisted by Lt Col OPN Kalyan (Retd), the Curator of the Army Service Corps Museum at Bengaluru. For the inputs on Army Postal Service, my gratitude is due to Major Mukesh Kapila (Retd) and his exhaustive collection coupled with the intimate knowledge on the evolution of the Indian Army Postal Services. Dr Narender Yadav of History Division of the Ministry of Defence, Government of India has been very supportive through the journey and has provided crucial inputs on the campaign. The help and support extended by the Library staff, in particular by Vijender Kumar Sharma of the USI, New Delhi, was very crucial in linking the dots in my research for the book. In addition, the support extended by Shravan Kumar, Gagandeep Singh, Ajay Minj, Sanjay Kumar and Naveen Kumar in carrying out the research into the casualty figures of the campaign has been phenomenal and definitely deserve mention here. I must also mention here the enthusiasm and zeal of Shri Ananya Jain of Manohar Publishers in the publication of this extensive research work. This end product of my years of research and hard work has been transformed into an alluring and elegant book by the detailed professional acumen and insight of team Manohar.

Navigating the demands of a research-oriented book alongside full-time professional commitments is undeniably challenging. The fruition of those long hours owes much to the patience, support and understanding provided by my better half, Neelam Hundal. Despite her own professional obligations, her unwavering support has been instrumental in bringing this book to life. The understanding shown by my sons Karanbir and Jaibir, during this journey is noteworthy. I would also like to express my deepest gratitude to the Almighty and my parents, without whose support, guidance, blessings and benediction, completing this work wouldn't have been possible.

Col Tejinder Hundal, VSM, PhD

Sikh Prayer of Supplication

ਹੇ ਰਵਿ ਹੇ ਸਸਿ ਹੇ ਕਰੁਨਾਨਿਧ ਮੇਰੀ ਅਬੈ ਬਿਨਤੀ ਸੁਨਿ ਲੀਜੈ ॥
ਅਉਰ ਨ ਮਾਂਗਤ ਹਉ ਤੁਮ ਤੇ ਕਛੁ ਚਾਹਤ ਹਉ ਚਿਤ ਮੈ ਸੋਈ ਕੀਜੈ ॥
ਸ਼ੱਤਰੁਨ ਸਿਉ ਅਤਿ ਹੀ ਰਨ ਭੀਤਰ ਜੂਝ ਮਰੋ ਕਹਿ ਸਾਚ ਪਤੀਜੈ ॥
ਸੰਤ ਸਹਾਇ ਸਦਾ ਜਗ ਮਾਇ ਕਿਰੁਪਾ ਕਰਿ ਸਯਾਮ ਇਹੈ ਬਰੁ ਦੀਜੈ ॥

O Sun, O Moon, O Ocean of mercy, Listen to my prayers now.
I do not beg anything else of Thee; only grant the desire of my heart
To die fighting with arms, in the thick of battle, this shall
Be my gratification, Thou supporter of devotees, the eternal
Mother of the universe, Grant me this boon through thy grace divine.[1]

---

[1] *Sri Dasam Granth*, Ang 1017.

Where Soldiers Rest

In a belated letter received from my husband, who is a nurse in the 1st Australian Stationary Hospital at Lemnos, was the following description of the cemetery at Mudros Bay, Island of Lemnos, as he saw it on the evening of Sunday, June 18. As some of our Australians are resting there, I think it might interest their relatives. A peaceful mid-summer evening is closing over the quiet ground of Mudros in the far away Aegean Sea, where lie at rest the warriors of Great Britain and of France. A boy of 19 lying side by side with men who died in the prime; men of the home countries alongside our own Australian brave; the bones of the black soldiers of France mingling with those of their French comrades in arms. At one end of the ground a little company of Sikh soldiers is tending a pile of glowing logs, among which are being cremated the bodies of two of their companions who were killed at the front.[1]

[1] Where Soldiers Rest, The *Register (Adelaide, SA: 1901-1929)*, Thursday, 14 October 1915, p. 6, https://trove.nla.gov.au/search?keyword=SikhPer cent20CremationPer cent20Lemnos.

Rest in Peace

Those heroes that shed their blood and lost their lives.... You are now lying in the soil of a friendly country. Therefore, rest in peace. There is no difference between the Johnnies and the Mehmets to us where they lie side by side in this country of ours. You, the mothers, who sent their sons from faraway countries, wipe away your tears. Your sons are now lying in our bosom and are in peace. After having lost their lives on this land, they have become our sons as well.[1]

[1] Inscription on Gallipoli Memorial put up by Turkey in 1934, also on Ataturk Memorial at Tara Kina Bay, Wellington - New Zealand.

Introduction

The previous three pages, in short tell the complete story of the death and devastation of almost 251 days in 1915, when the Mediterranean Expeditionary Force (MEF) under the command of Ian Hamilton to include Indians, Australians, and New Zealanders tried to wrest control of the peninsula of Gallipoli from the Turks. The sheer amount of loss in terms of human life suffered by both the sides may not stand the scrutiny of the contemporary concept of cost benefit analysis. The campaign has been adequately addressed in great detail by military historians across the world and the volume of literature existing on the planning of the campaign, conduct of operations and withdrawal from the peninsula is astonishing. In spite of the existence of depth and volume of research on the campaign, one dimension of the operation has been relegated to the realms of the unknown and still remains unacknowledged. Three thousand miles away from home, thousands of Indian soldiers, primarily Sikhs and Gurkhas were mobilised to fight an unknown enemy in an unknown land for an unknown cause to them.

The only time the Sikhs who fought against the Turks on the peninsula, might have heard the name *Turk* prior to landing on Gallipoli, must have been only during the recital of their holy book of *Sri Guru Granth Sahib*, wherein the word *Turk* has generally been used as a synonym for Muslims. The *Dasam Granth* of *Sri Guru Granth Sahib* while mentioning oneness of all religions, mentions about Turks, which when translated implies that, 'someone is Hindu and someone a Muslim, then someone is Shia, and someone a Sunni, but all the human beings, as a species, are recognized as one and the same'.

As late as 2015, exactly hundred years after the campaign and before Peter Stanley came up with his well-researched book on Indians on Gallipoli, even an approximate consensus on the number of Indians who fought under the British flag on the peninsula was non-existent from the narrative. Prior to this work of Peter Stanley, research on the definite number of Indian troops who were mobilised to fight on Gallipoli had largely been deficient. Peter Stanley, in his very detailed work, has been able to provide a reasonable assumption of the number of the Indian troops who went and fought on Gallipoli. As I write the introduction to this book, exactly 109 years ago, as part of the Indian Expeditionary Force (IEF), three Indian Infantry Brigades with four battalions each, were raised to fight in the Great War. Of these three brigades, the 29th Indian Infantry Brigade along with four Indian battalions, had landed on Gallipoli on 1 May 1915.

Besides being a military man myself, with an interest in military history, I must confess the existence of a personal angle to the narrative. During my teens, my grandfather Subadar Amar Singh used to tell us about the participation of our great grandfather in the Great War, the *Waddi Ladai*, as he used to allude to it. Egypt, where Sardar Ganda Singh, my great grandfather had served, was described as *Misr* by my grandfather. The service records and documents related to the military service of Sardar Ganda Singh were left behind in Narowal in present-day Pakistan, when the entire family migrated overnight to India on a hot and humid night of August 1947. As I look back into the journey for research into this book, a number of dead ends encountered during the journey can be attributed to the loss of records during the catastrophic events subsequent to the partition of our country. It also happens to be one of the primary contributing factors for the bravery of these soldiers, including Sardar Ganda Singh, being consigned to oblivion.

With no available documents to substantiate the verbal narratives of Indian troops in Egypt, as explained by my grandfather, these faint and memories of stories of the Great War in Egypt lurked in my sub-conscious till I came across the work of Peter Stanley in 2015. The spark thus rekindled, provided impetus to my efforts into further delving into the research related to the Indian participation in the Gallipoli. For the next seven years, I read about the participation of the Indian troops in the Gallipoli campaign at my own pace, with absolutely no intention of converting it into a book. The Gallipoli Campaign, being the first recorded amphibious landings, was also of interest to me in my professional capacity of being a soldier first and a scholar later. In the early part of 2022, a meeting with Rana Chhina at the United Service Institution of India, New Delhi was responsible for providing a catalyst for converting the research into a book on the subject.

The battles of Gallipoli Campaign fought by the Indian soldiers in a distant land against an unknown enemy have largely been forgotten and remain relegated to the realms of unknowable. Due to the substantial knowledge deficit in respect of Indian battalions who participated in these battles, the soldiers who participated in these battles continue to remain unknown, barring one, whose mention is explicit in Western military literature on the subject. A multitude of reasons can be attributed to this, including relative convenience, partition of the country and the loss of information which was generally passed through the generations by word of mouth.

As a cumulative consequence, there has been very few research works on the subject carried out by the Indian researchers or scholars on the subject. The First World War in its entirety though has been adequately researched by a large number of Indian scholars, detailed research on the travails of Indian battalions in Gallipoli have largely been left out. On the other hand, Western researchers have produced voluminous works on the exploits of their respective troops in Gallipoli, which has coalesced into a mode of a national military identity. Though the events of Gallipoli, in which Indians troops took an active part, occurred almost 109 years ago, the book, which I was contemplating to write, was for the contemporary generation. Recognising the gap of nearly four generations, I found it essential to conduct a thorough survey to gauge the current sentiments and perspectives regarding the essence of Indian participation in the campaign.

With an active military background, it was essential to avoid a military bias in the sample size and therefore, a large sample was considered, which could adequately represent both the military and non-military backgrounds in the survey. In spite of due care, certain biases has indeed crept into the sample size towards the military aspect, which is understandable due to the largely military aspects of the operation, which I have attempted to unravel in the book. Though, a detailed analysis of the feedback has been discussed below, to underscore a certain facet of the Indian participation, the analysis of the responses received have also been included in the relevant chapters in brief.

The background of the respondents in terms of their respective professions plays a very important role in relating to a particular construct. As Gallipoli's history is tied up with military exploits, the respondents with military background were able to clearly identify with the construct. The sample of the respondents selected for the questionnaire comprised 90 per cent of respondents belonging to the Armed Forces background. Out of the additional respondents, 3 per cent belonged to the Government Sector, 4 per cent were students, and the balance 3 per cent belonged to the miscellaneous/others background.

A credible educational background lends credence to the responses provided by the respondents. With a subject of great historical significance as the centre of the study, the educational background of the respondents assumed greater relevance. 36.9 per cent of the respondents possessed graduate and equivalent degrees, whereas 52.3 per cent of respondents possessed postgraduate degrees. Balance 10.8 per cent of the respondents possessed M.Phil and/or PhD degrees, thereby providing significance to the inputs.

The significance of Gallipoli to a military mind cannot be belittled. The campaign is significant from both historical and military perspectives. It was the first organised military landings on opposite beaches. On being asked about any previous knowledge of the Gallipoli Campaign, 77.7 per cent of the respondents replied in the affirmative, whereas 19.2 per cent respondents claimed that they have never heard of the campaign. The balance of about 3.1 per cent of respondents were not very sure, whether they had heard the term before. An interesting aspect of the analysis of the responses received for this question was that whereas almost 81 per cent of respondents with a background of Armed Forces were aware about Gallipoli campaign, only 33.33 per cent of students were aware about the campaign, thereby implying a wider knowledge deficit about the campaign in our formal educational set up.

The next question in the questionnaire was about the source of the information about the campaign. 53.8 per cent of the respondents claimed that they came to know about the campaign only during the course of their professional military education while serving in the Armed Forces. 23.8 per cent of the respondents' knowledge about the campaign originated from the self-interest in the campaign. Social media was another source of information about the campaign, which was responsible for the knowledge on the subject obtained by 15.4 per cent of the respondents. Approximately 6.9 per cent of the respondents had gained information about the campaign from family members or other veteran relatives/ friends. An interesting take away from the analysis of this question brought out that approximately 92 per cent of respondents (without background of Armed Forces) had gained knowledge on the subject through self-interest and social media, implying want of an institutionalised mechanism to impart informal education about these battles and campaigns to the youth of the country.

As compared to the Western nations, it is a well-accepted notion that there is an apparent lack of interest in the contemporary milieu about the historical battles fought by the Indian soldiers. The exploits of 21 Sikhs in the epic Battle of Saragarhi was relegated into general oblivion, except for some books, until the epic battle was made into a motion picture. In a very similar, albeit on a very large scale, the participation of Indian troops in the Gallipoli Campaign has till now not been able to capture traction in the popular imagination. To provide a definite framework for the reasons behind the general disinterest, a question in the survey was purposefully devised. In terms of response. for the 61.5 per cent of the respondents, the dearth of research material on the subject was responsible for the sparse knowledge, whereas 23.8 per cent of the respondents attributed the disinterest in historical battles / wars to the fact that the battles of those times were fought for the Imperial Army under the British flag. A meager 3.8 per cent of the respondents claimed that these battles are no more relevant to modern India, whereas 10.8 per cent of the respondents credited unspecified reasons for the general disinterest.

The Gallipoli campaign was fought by the Indian troops almost 109 years ago. As the participation of Indian troops in these battles was for reasons not Indian, the contemporary import of these battles is questionable. In order to establish an informed rationale for the present-day importance of the campaign, a question whether the campaign merits attention today, was deliberately included in the questionnaire. 79.2 per cent, which is a predominant majority of respondents, were of the view that the lessons of the campaign merit attention in the modern times. 17.7 per cent of the respondents were not very clear about the contemporary import of the campaign and therefore opted for the response of 'may be'. A very minuscule per centage of 3.1 per cent of the respondents confirmed that there is no contemporary import of the campaign. A mere 3.4 per cent respondents from an Armed Forces background dismissed the current significance of the campaign for the Indian Army. This implies a perception of insignificance in terms of deriving lessons applicable to the study and execution of similar operations in both present and future scenarios.

For carrying out research, the ease of availability and access of research material is imperative. One of the primary reasons for the general disinterest in the Gallipoli Campaign is the restricted access to research resources on the subject. As such, most of the resources have been curated from the allied perspectives, giving very little space to the actions of Indian battalions and troops; the corresponding absence of any research on the subject from the Indian perspective lends a double blow to an important subject. A mere 13.1 per cent of respondents claimed that the research resources on the subject are easily available, whereas 68.5 per cent of respondents agreed that research resources are not easily available. Another 13.1 per cent of respondents claimed that the restricted access of these resources severely impinges the research activity on the subject. Another facet of the responses to the question revealed during the analysis is that while 16.6 per cent of respondents who are graduates and below indicated the difficulty in accessing the research resources, while the proportion of the respondents who are postgraduates and above is 8.8 per cent, indicating the evidence of rigorous research methodology being adopted at higher education institutes.

It is a common refrain that the soldiers who volunteered for fighting for the British cause, did so on their own wills. A large number of factors accentuated the recruitment of Indian troops into the Indian Army of the time, as has been brought out in the book. Linking the two differing dimensions of recruitment and the subsequent fighting under the British flag with the nationalist movement is totally a different subject in itself and a deliberate effort has been made to not link the two. As part of the survey, another question has attempted to understand the dynamics in the environment about the justice and recognition served to these soldiers. To the question whether due justice and recognition has been served to these Indian soldiers in the existing historical narratives, a monumental 87.7 per cent of the respondents concurred with the notion that due justice and recognition has not been provided to these soldiers. Only 3.8 per cent of respondents were of the view that due justice and recognition has been served, whereas 8.5 per cent of the respondents opted to be neutral in answering this question.

The apparent lack of Indian literature on the subject has prevented the contemporary import and common awareness on the subject. This question was included in the questionnaire to gauge the general perception on the availability of the Indian literature on the subject. To the question that, do you know any Indian author/ military historian who has worked on the research about Gallipoli Campaign, a majority 88.5 per cent of respondents confirmed in negative. Only 11.5 per cent of respondents claimed that they were aware of Indian authors / military historians who have worked on the subject. The findings of the survey with respect to this particular question are totally in sync with the common perception on the subject prevalent in the environment.

Though the Indian youth of the time volunteered to be recruited into the Indian Army, the causes and consequences of the Great War were largely alien to the Indian nationalist movement. An effort has been made to restrict the narrative of the current work only to the recruitment and the subsequent exploits of the Indian troops in Gallipoli. The motives of the recruitment were many and adequate literature on the subject exists. To provide a contemporary hue to the existing research, a question on the motives of the Indian soldiers to recruit in the Army of the time was included in the questionnaire.

48.5 per cent of the respondents attributed the recruitment to monetary considerations, generally in line with the existing research. The balance 41.5 per cent of the respondents linked the surge in the recruitment with the then recently introduced concept of martial race and other associated caste and clan factors. Having discerned the reach, depth and availability of research on the participation of the Indian troops in the Gallipoli Campaign, one definitely concludes that the contribution of the Indian troops in Gallipoli has not been given its due. It was a difficult task, which I set out for myself by endeavouring to cover the maximum aspects of survey into the book. This holistic inclusion, though initially felt insurmountable, has been able to provide a very comprehensive and detailed outlook to the book.

The initiation and the subsequent conduct for the initial few days of the Dardanelles Campaign paved the way for the induction of the Indian troops on to the peninsula. In order to provide a context to the research, the first chapter of the book 'The Activation', attempts to unravel the decisions and strategies of the belligerents--Britain and Turkey in this case-- to capture and defend the peninsula respectively. The chapter also discusses about the origin of the various IEFs and their deployment in the various theatres of war, finally homing on to the operations of the troops of the 29th Indian Infantry Brigade in the peninsula.

The conduct of the entire campaign of Gallipoli revolved around the bravery and sacrifices of 14th Sikhs. This, however, in no way negates the contribution other battalions of the Indian Brigade to include four Gurkha battalions, two Mountain Artillery batteries, eight Mule Corps, detachments from 25 different Mule Corps, the Imperial Service Troops and three Indian Field Ambulances. For the purpose of the book, a detailed analysis of the recruitment system, patterns, incentives, the state of the Indian Army in 1914 to include the Infantry, Artillery, the Imperial Service Troops in the form of the second chapter of the book 'The Arrangements', has been included. The chapter before discussing about the operations of the 29th Indian Infantry Brigade in Qantara in Canal Defences, also briefly touches upon the oft neglected component of the Burma Military Police, which formed part of the Indian Brigade at Gallipoli, and was equal in sufferings of death and devastation.

The third chapter of the book 'The Affirmation' is dedicated to the participation and contribution of the Indian troops in the various battles, which were fought in the peninsula. Starting with the battles of Krithia, the chapter brings forth the gory and glories of the Indian troops in the August offensive and the subsequent stalemate. The privations and hardships due to the snowstorm of November 1915 and the withdrawal from the peninsula in December 1915, comprises the last section of the chapter.

Just as granularities of the Indian contribution in the various battles of Gallipoli Campaign have oft been neglected, similar or may be worse fate has awaited the preparations and activities behind these battles. Logistics of any military operation is important and can be neglected at one's peril only. The Gallipoli Campaign was distinct from several dimensions, but from the point of view of the Indian contribution, it was unique. The complete logistic support to the Indian troops was carried out from India, a distance of almost 3,000 miles. Coupled with this, the peculiar Indian food habits were not in sync with the arrangements for the provisions of rations. With the responsibility of provisioning of logistics for the entire MEF, the animals of Indian Mule Corps also required forage and water. The penultimate chapter of the book, 'The Administration', talks about the personal arms and ammunition, food, water, medical supply along with the pay and allowances of the Indian troops at Gallipoli. The sheer number of casualties suffered by the Indian units called for a continuous stream of reinforcements from India. The chapter also deals with the issues of reinforcements and reporting of casualties of the Indian units.

As discussed earlier, Peter Stanley's seminal work on the Indian troops at Gallipoli has provided a definite number to the Indian troops on Gallipoli. The names of the Indian soldiers who sacrificed their lives at Gallipoli have already been duly acknowledged by the Commonwealth War Graves Commission and even replicated in the book by Peter Stanley. What, however, stands neglected are the details of the Indians wounded at Gallipoli. The last chapter of the book 'The Acknowledgment' is dedicated to the memories of these soldiers. Intensely driven by deep research, the chapter discusses about the trials and tribulations of 16,281 Indian soldiers who served on the peninsula as part of the IEF 'G'. The chapter also painstakingly develops stories about three Sikh soldiers who participated in the campaign. The chapter is an attempt to reignite the memories of these soldiers, lest we forget.

CHAPTER 1

The Activation
Dardanelles Campaign

'Le fond de la grande question est toujours la: Qui aura Constantinople?'

The predicament over the control of Constantinople has enamored military and political leaders for centuries. This quandary was shared by Napoléon with his Ambassador in St. Petersburg, when he wrote to him, almost two hundred years back, in May 1808. But this did not help to end the quagmire and the question of tutelage of the Dardanelles, gateway to Constantinople continued to occupy military minds for the next one hundred years as well. A number of expeditions later and at the cost of thousands of lives, the solution still evaded the world. Gallipoli was one such campaign which was launched to exert control over Constantinople and resulted in a catastrophe for the Allied forces. Amongst a number of such campaigns and expeditions, Gallipoli stands out as most significant for a number of reasons. As far as magnitude of preparations and the casualties sustained by both sides are concerned, Gallipoli was a unique operation. Militaries across the world have learnt valuable lessons from the perspective of opposed amphibious landings. The granularities of the Gallipoli campaign along with the quantum of sufferings by the Allied and Turkish troops have adequately been researched by a number of scholars and military historians, thereby producing an enviable body of literature on the subject.

Like all other military campaigns and based on the experiences of the previous expeditions in the region, the Gallipoli Campaign of 1915 was also based on the premise that the geographical advantage enjoyed by Turkey was exceptional. It was believed that this advantage of Turkey, if taken over by any other power of the time, would bear catastrophic results for the Allied supremacy. As a result, a series of initiatives by the Allied powers over a period of time had ensured that this geographical advantage enjoyed by Turkey stayed singular and 'little by little it became the cardinal policy of the allies that no other power, resident or otherwise could be tolerated as Turkey's successor'.

The security of Britain's most prized jewel in the East, the Indian subcontinent, was entirely contingent upon the above proposition, and the aspect of safety of India and the whole position in the East, had kept Britain a firm adherent to this policy.[1] The domination of Dardanelles, therefore, was considered paramount and no one other power could have been allowed to take control of the Straits. The control of the Straits had also been supported by a series of conventions. The Congress of London in 1841 had acknowledged that entry of foreign war vessels shall be prohibited into the Dardanelles Straits while Turkey was at peace. For the next 73 years this convention was upheld by all the signatories. Under the provisions of the convention during times of peace, trading ships of all nationalities had the right to use the Straits without any prohibition, but the war vessels were allowed to pass the Straits and visit Constantinople, only on a case to

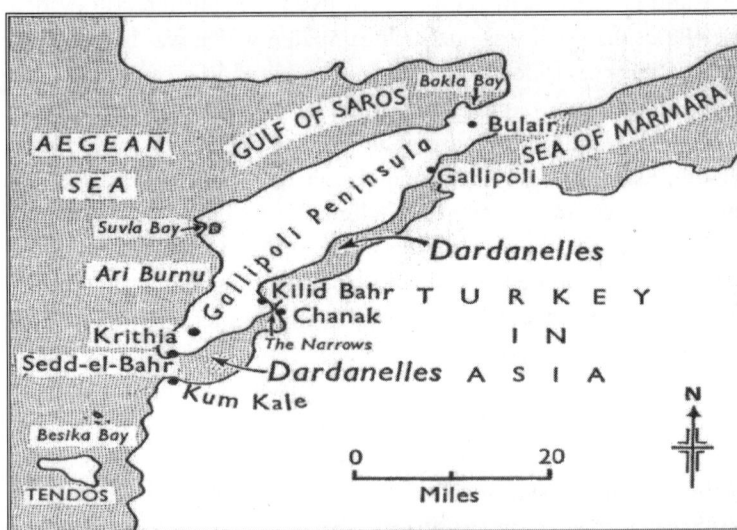

MAP 1: GALLIPOLI PENINSULA[2]

case basis and that too only with the prior permission of the Sultan. During the War, however, the Sultan had been empowered to 'intern any foreign man-of-war which remained in the Straits for more than twenty-four hours'.

After the culmination of the Crimean War in 1856, a series of concessions had been granted to Turkey by Britain. This bonhomie between the two was underscored by a factor of the strong common hostility towards Russia, which at that time was emerging as the other major player in the regional geostrategic configurations. The amiability between Britain and Turkey did not continue for long, with the Anglo-Russian agreement of 1907 playing a major role in widening of the distrust between the two. The agreement signed on 31 August 1907 in St. Petersburg firmly established an alliance between England and Russia and is also considered as one of the major contributing factors of the First World War. 'The conclusion of the Anglo-Russian Treaty gave a definite point to the Ottoman Empire distrust in British policy and confirmed the conviction that Turkey must look elsewhere for protection from the Tsarist ambitions.'[3]

These geo-strategic arrangements facilitated the entry of another major regional power, Germany, into the machinations over the control over Constantinople. Germany during this time was instrumental in raising a loan and detailing a military mission to Turkey to reorganise her army. Training courses for Turkish military officers had also been organised in Germany. The Anglo-Russian Treaty had fueled a strong sense of betrayal in Turkey. Amidst this feeling of ditching by England in Turkey, Germany had gone all out to seek the friendship of Turks. In 1913, Germany dispatched a military mission of 70 German officers under General Liman von Sanders to Turkey, which greatly ensured overwhelming German influence in the organisation, equipment philosophy and tactics of the Turkish Army. This military mission played a very significant role later in the defence of the Gallipoli peninsula against the determined attacks of the Indian troops.

Turkey was impressed by Germany in no uncertain terms that a timely alliance between the two countries would ensure a solution from the Russian threat for perpetuity and at the same time would facilitate a general uprising by the Moslem population of India and other countries, which were under 'Christian colonialism', and will ensure the restoration of the original glory and influence of the Caliphate of Constantinople. Both the countries signed a formal treaty on 2 August 1914 and Dardanelles, the quintessence of the present book, was mined by Turkey on the same day, to prevent any misadventure by Britain.

The significance of the Dardanelles Straits lay in preventing a direct communication link between Britain and France, besides ensuring that the Russians remain engaged in Caucasus through the build up of a Turkish threat. For this purpose, the straits had been mined. The next strategy of defence by the Turkish-German combine was to restrict Britain from influencing the conflict. The entry of Britain into war, if any, was to be handled by inciting a general uprising by the Moslem population of British colonies, primarily India. Any threat to the Suez Canal, which in 1914 was the fastest medium of communication to India and the shortest route for the transportation of men and material from the Indian subcontinent to the war theatres in Europe, was considered enough to entangle Britain in the region. It was assumed that due to the sensitivity of the asset, the British would largely stay away from Turkish affairs.

The Turkish inclination for neutrality was further compromised by the confiscation of two Turkish battleships under construction in the British yards by England. The loss of these battleships being constructed under a public funding programme, had further deepened the divide of distrust. The impounding of the Turkish assets by Britain coincided with another event. In display of an apparent solidarity with the Turks, two German battleships *Goeben* and *Breslau,* arrived in the waters of Dardanelles on 10 August 1914. These two events predominantly firmed the public opinion in general populace of Turkey for forming an alliance with Germany against a British-Russian build up. In a sign of events to unfold, the British naval mission in the country was closed by Turkey.

The Turkish-German alliance earnestly started preparing for an upcoming conflict. German trains had started shifting war stores into the capital through the transit from Balkan countries, which were still neutral. The Dardanelles was aimed to be made totally impregnable for any British offensive. The British and French ships already docked at Constantinople were selectively made inoperable whereas the German battleships in the waters of Turkey were reinforced with men and material. To obviate any British led offensive towards the capital, by 24 August 1914, the Dardanelles had been reinforced by three layers of mines. There were confirmed reports of part manning of the forts on the Gallipoli peninsula by the German reservists in collaboration with Turkish soldiers.

On the other side, in spite of the relatively high intensity of war-like preparations in Turkey, two compelling reasons were still keeping British polity hopeful of salvaging the situation. The peaceful and amicable solution to the imbroglio was imperative for the British interests in the region. As discussed earlier, the Suez Canal was the lifeline of British hold in the East, and Turkey was expected to interdict the waterway immediately on the outbreak of hostilities. With all available British forces engaged along the Western front, the only salvaging reality was the deployment of Indian and Dominion troops, who would have taken time to mobilise and reach Egypt. The British reluctance to accept and act immediately to the growing Turkish desperation fueled by the German instigation was primarily to ensure gaining of time by mobilising troops from India for the security of the Canal. The latter compelling factor is also linked with the former. Due to the impact of the Martial Race theory, the Indian Army of the time was heavily subscribed by two communities of the Sikhs and Punjabi Musalmans (PM). Therefore, employment of the Indian Army against Turkey was considered avoidable till extremely warranted. The British policy makers wanted to avoid a situation, wherein her actions could be interpreted as initiation of hostilities against a predominant Moslem power. The employment of Indian Army against Turks in Egypt and later on Turkey was totally fraught with apprehensions and any decision, in this regard could have manifested in massive strategic implications.

Seeing virtually no positive outcome of the peace overtures by her, the legality of sale of the two battleships to Turkey by Germany was finally not admitted by the Britain. The Turks were informed in explicit terms that the manning of these ships by the German crew was tantamount to breach of neutrality terms and these vessels would be assumed to be hostile and sunk by the British Navy at the first opportunity. In a sign of further escalation of the situation, no Turkish war vessel was to be allowed to leave the Straits and an embargo-like situation developed when the entrance to the Dardanelles Straits was blocked by the British Navy.

DILEMMA OF DARDANELLES

With a blockade-like situation firmly in place, the next stage of course was the possibility of forcing a passage through the Straits. The events leading to the blockade had confirmed that capitulation of Turkey was solely dependent on the success of the actions resulting in a passage through Dardanelles to threaten Constantinople. Historically, the question of forcing a passage through the narrows of Dardanelles and to dominate the waterway has been a vexed and complicated one. Prior to the current plan for dominating the waterway, as a prelude to the arrival of Indian troops on the scene, the history of the region had witnessed a number of plans to dominate the Straits. Unfortunately, no attempt had succeeded till now and the Indian troops were going to learn this lesson at a massive cost of their lives and limbs.

The first substantial modern endeavour to attempt a force the narrow Straits was carried out in 1807, when the British Admiral Duckworth was tasked to capture the waterway of Dardanelles with only the naval power at his disposal. This enterprise of Admiral Duckworth had some very striking similarities to the Gallipoli Campaign of 1915. The origin of the endeavour by Admiral Duckworth was also linked with the necessity of England to assist Russia against Turkey, an exact replica of the situation as it was obtained in 1915. That time also the naval expedition was considered sufficient for forcing the Straits and the requirement of troops to hold ground was relegated to the realm of non-essentials. In spite of a relatively comprehensive quantum of troops being available, the attempt to force the Straits was carried out with the naval assets alone. The operation did not succeed and failed miserably. An important lesson of the operation, reinforced the notion that the requirement of troops to hold ground along with the naval fleet was imperative for any decisive action to force the straits and threaten Constantinople.

The episode had proved beyond any reasonable doubt that the naval assets alone cannot enforce any decision on the shore, but to a power, 'whose principal strength lay on the sea, and who, in a Near Eastern crisis, would be more likely to have ships than an army available, this maxim could never be very popular'. This misplaced notion was again augmented in 1877, when the British Mediterranean Fleet was directed to be prepared to move to Constantinople for the alliance with the Turks, this time to prevent the occupation of Gallipoli peninsula by the Russians. This time also it was widely accepted that the passage of the fleet through the Straits would be fraught with danger and the Turkish hold over the peninsula would need to be reinforced to facilitate the passage of the British fleet through the Straits.

The year 1904 again brought forth a similar dilemma, but by this time the developments in the region had nearly confirmed that even a joint military naval operation to force the Straits would not be an easy enterprise. Around the same time, a joint naval and military conference to 'consider the matter for the future guidance of British diplomacy', also brought out that naval operations in isolation would not be able to force the narrows. As far as a joint naval and military operation was considered, the conference reached upon a conclusion that a near simultaneous operation to physically occupy Gallipoli and forcing of the Straits by the naval component may lead to immediate and decisive results. The British General Staff however was not convinced by the recommendation and the findings of the conference did not find much traction amongst the military polity of the time.

The dilemma again cropped up in 1911, during which time the military planners simply replicated the hypothesis of year 1906. It was opined that due to the possibility of losing surprise in the process of landing troops at Gallipoli and incurring huge number of casualties, the military option could not be recommended. With the near apparent signs of a European conflagration manifesting, it was increasingly being accepted that in the event of such a conflagration, Turkey would definitely be inclined towards the central powers. Even with an absolute clarity towards inclinations of Turkey, no apparent study to find a solution to the Dardanelles dilemma was carried out by the British General Staff.

Four precious years were lost and the dilemma continued to be relegated to the realms of indecisiveness. Considerable advances in the fields of naval gunfire, accuracy and lethality of artillery fire and the possibility of a wider conflict in which more than one front would be activated at a single point of time were not studied or planned for implementation. The option of forcing of Dardanelles was not even there on the table. Measures to ensure passive defence of Egypt along with safeguarding of British interests in Persia were the only two options on the table to open a front against Turkey. No additional measures were examined by the British General Staff and till as late as August 1914; the British Government was continuing to favour peace with Turkey. This dilemma of Dardanelles coupled with the delays in decisions was going to cost very dearly.

DECISION OF DARDANELLES

In spite of no definite action to resolve the dilemma, Dardanelles continued to occupy the minds of the polity and military alike. It was increasingly evident by now that despite the continuation of peace overtures by Britain towards Turkey, it was definitely time to take a decisive action. A series of developments in the region were forcing Britain to show her cards.

In August 1914, the Greek Prime Minister had placed all Greek naval and military assets at the disposal of the entente powers. Nearly simultaneously, the British Ambassador at Constantinople also had forwarded a proposal, recommending storming of the Straits by the British Naval Squadron already in location. The Russians, taking a cue from the gesture by the Greeks, were also contemplating an attack on the Dardanelles. As a follow-up of all these activities, Churchill asked the Chief of the Imperial General Staff to work out a plan for the capture of Gallipoli. The scope of the proposed offensive was deliberately kept very restricted and the plan was to be implemented only in case of a contingency of an imminent risk of Turkey declaring war.

Based on directions, the Imperial General Staff had prepared a plan to storm the Dardanelles. The plan was based on the premise that the peninsula which was manned by almost 27,000 troops in normal times, under the operational control of the German General Staff presently, would definitely have witnessed a surge in troop concentration. The recommendations of the British Imperial General Staff concluded that if executed, the plan would be extremely difficult and the troops requirement for the enterprise would be in excess of 60,000, duly supported by a very 'strong seize ordnance'.

In the meantime, Greece also had prepared a plan for the capture of the Peninsula. The essence of the Greek plan premised on the fact that the capture of the Peninsula was required to force the waterway of Dardanelles. Though the Greek plan was not executed, the plan had strong resemblances with the plan which was executed by the allied troops later on, albeit after unsuccessfully attempting to force a passage through the Straits with naval fleet only. The logic for the capture of the peninsula was simply based on the rationale that it was simply not possible for any fleet to enter the Straits till the clearance of the minefields was achieved. For clearing the minefields, the forts on both sides were needed to be captured, a task which could only have been completed by ensuring the physical capture of the Peninsula.

The recently implemented restructuring of the Indian and British battalions in India had suddenly brought in the prospect of an early availability of Dominion troops to protect the Suez Canal. This dimension along with the development of trench stalemate along the Western Front was instrumental in forcing an entirely new thinking process in the newly established War Council. A signal military success to strengthen the diplomatic leverage with the allies and to uplift the sagging morale of the empire had suddenly transposed into an immediate priority for the British. With massing of troops in Flanders providing no breakthrough, the thought process of the nation was slowly and surely moving against the stalemate induced by the continental warfare. It was believed that the England with its maritime dominance should not have been involved in the continental warfare in the first place. Continuous pumping of troops for the cause of France was denuding the essential component of maritime dominance, which would not hold good for Britain in the long run.

It was being felt that with the aid of available and effective amphibious prowess, under the pressing circumstances, Britain needed to strike a decisive blow elsewhere and regain the sagging prestige.

The efforts to end the stalemate along the Western front, brought about by the trench warfare, were not producing the desired results. In the words of Lord Kitchener, the trenches in the Western front would, 'render attack only a waste of men for a few yards gained of worthless ground', a statement which would play out exactly when the allied troops landed on the Gallipoli peninsula.

In the beginning of 1915, a study on the issue of forcing the straits was presented to the War Council. The study presented by Secretary of War Council, had underscored the need for scouting for a new outlet for utilising the services of additional troops under training. Western Front, it was brought out was deadlocked and no amount of additional resources pumped into the theater may provide the desired results. The study though hinted at certain options but definitely fell short of providing any concrete recommendations with respect to Dardanelles. Lord Kitchener during this time had also proposed finding new outlets for expanding the operations.

The feeling here is gaining ground that, although it is essential to defend the line we hold, troops over and above what is necessary for that service could be better employed elsewhere. The question of where anything effective can be accomplished opens a large field and requires a good deal of study.[4]

While the deliberations and discussions on identifying the new front were ongoing, a Russian intimation of situation developing in the Caucasus due to the Turkish onslaught was received in London. The intimation pleaded Britain for a demonstration of naval or military capability against Turkey 'elsewhere' so as to force them to withdraw some troops from against the Russians. Though it is claimed that the requirement of demonstration had been resolved during the time in between of writing of intimation by Russia and its receipt in London, the War Council had started in earnest, hectic parleys so as to help the Russians. With no troops available in the immediate time frame, the plan being firmed up by the British War Council to rush the Dardanelles, as a demonstration to help the Russians, involved only the maritime assets.

Admiral Carden, with the command of the British Squadron at Dardanelles, was tasked to plan for such an eventuality. By mid-January, the Admiral was ready with the plan. The plan involved

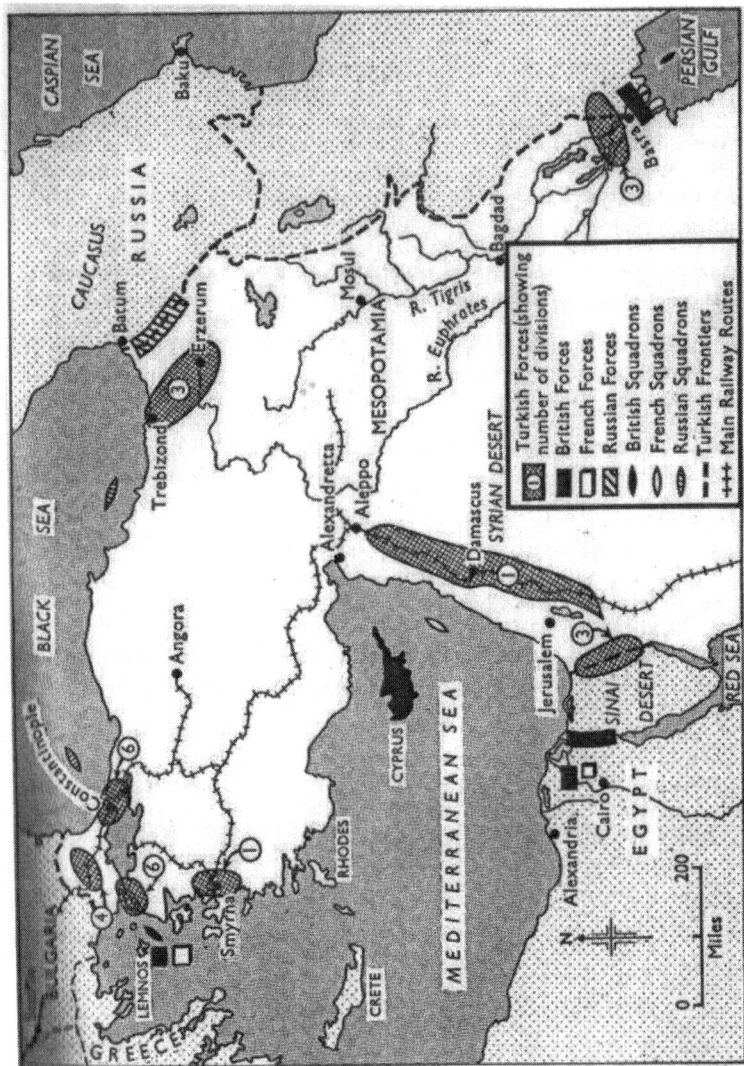

MAP 2: THEATRE OF OPERATIONS AND DISPOSITION OF FORCES[5]

execution of the plan in four phases. The first phase involved reduction of forts at the entrance, whereas the destruction of the inside of defences up to as far was to be carried out in the second phase. The third phase involved reduction of the forts at the narrows. Clearing of minefields, reduction of defences above the narrows and the final advance up to Marmara was to be executed in the final phase of the plan. The execution of the entire plan in the view of Admiral Carden could take up to a month. Though the chances of success of such an operation without the involvement of ground troops was highly questionable, the objections to the plan were brushed aside by the planners. It was explained that even if unsuccessful, the operation was being carried out as a demonstration only and could be withdrawn at any time. With no ground troops involved, calling off the demonstration at the chosen point of time was highly feasible. It was under these doubts and apprehensions, that Admiral Carden was given a go ahead to move with the plan on 15 January 1915.

In spite of the initial dissent of Lord Fisher, the First Sea Lord, who after some persuasion by Churchill, withdrew his objection, Britain's fleet was to attempt, without the aid of a single soldier, an enterprise which in the earlier days of war, was being regarded as a pure military task by both the Admiralty and the War Office. The non-availability of troops for the operation, in hindsight can be called as a compromise between the proponents of theory of sending every possible man to the Western Front and those who were proposing to conduct a severe blow to the military might of Central Powers, at an alternate place of own choosing. In fact, the French consent to the enterprise was also contingent upon the concession by the British that no existing troops would be withdrawn from Flanders. The operation was full of serious uncertainties. Besides the narrows being mined, the Turks with an active assistance from the Germans had enough time at their disposal to reinforce the defences of the peninsula.

Due to the certain geopolitical alignments, the British 29th Division meant for an alternate theatre of operations was available for employment. With the sudden availability of a division worth of troops, Dardanelles had suddenly started looking like a very viable option and concerted efforts were put in place to secure availability of the 29th Division for Dardanelles. Despite these efforts, the division was not initially allocated for the operation, however, an emergent meeting of the War Council on 16 February 1915 confirmed the dispatch of the 29th Division to Mudros at the earliest possible date, to be employed, if required.

The naval operations to storm the waterways, commenced on 19 February 1915. Though no ab-initio allotment of infantry for ground holding role was made, some parties of the Royal Naval Division were detailed for demolishing the guns on the outer forts. The artillery mustered by the allied fleet was impressive. The intense weather conditions along with the intensive mine laying in the Straits played a very decisive role in the failure of the naval enterprise. The naval bombardment though was successful up to a large extent in reducing the outer forts, the intermediate defences were still intact. By 4 March 1915, though three out of four weeks initially planned by Admiral Carden to rush through the Straits had passed, the entire operation was still lingering in the second phase only. The guns of intermediate forts and the mines were interdicting the progress of operations with impunity. The ammunition expenditure versus the availability of the same with Carden was increasingly becoming a cause of concern. It was under these circumstances, that on 9 March 1915, Admiral Carden reported to the Admiralty that no further progress was possible until and unless some air effort was dedicated for the operation.

With no headway possible for the Naval Squadron under Admiral Carden, an emergent meeting of the War Council on 10 March 1915, directed an immediate dispatch of the 29th Division to the Mediterranean. The War Council was informed that the naval enterprise had not completely failed but had been temporarily stalled and the availability of ground forces would supplement its efforts of rushing through the Straits. General Sir Ian Hamilton was appointed to lead the allied troops in the Mediterranean, with Brigadier General W.P Braithwaite as his Chief of General Staff. The Commander of the allied forces was briefed on the previously made Greek plan for the capture of the peninsula. He was assured that in spite of the Greeks having planned their operation with 150,000 troops, but with the current depleted state of Turkish troops on the peninsula, only half of that number would be required. He was also briefed that heavy bombardment by the naval component along the Straits was keeping the Turks engaged and the potential of resistance by the Turks was very limited. Hamilton, while being briefed about the ideal landing areas, was recommended to concentrate landings in the general area, from South of Kilid Bahr up to Cape Helles, where naval gun support was adequately available from the naval ships in the vicinity.

Hamilton along with his staff was directed to leave for the Dardanelles immediately and his briefings in the shortest possible time, also hinged on the premise that the support of army may not be required at all during the capture of peninsula. At most, if support at all will be required, it will be for the capture and subsequent occupation of Constantinople. It was for this reason that the convention of 10 per cent of reinforcements, which was supposed to accompany units proceeding on active service, was not moving with the units of 29th Division and was to remain in England itself. Though one French Division was also being planned to be co-opted in the enterprise, the French military hierarchy was oblivious to the overall plan for the offensive.

The naval fleet commander, Admiral Carden having been replaced by now, was of the view that his fleet would be able to rush through the Straits without any assistance from army and that the destruction of fort guns was almost complete and that only some remnants of the mobile artillery of the Turks were creating problems for him. He was still of the view that the task of the army would be greatly difficult if the naval fleet is not able to rush through the Straits, either prior to the offensive or simultaneously, because the 'Turks were working like beavers, every night and every morning new trenches and wire could be seen. All possible landing places were rapidly being prepared for defence and the ships' guns would not be able to give troops a great deal of help.'

By then it was more or less confirmed that army will not be used till the fleet had exhausted all means to get through the Straits with their own resources. With additional time available, Hamilton started looking at the logistical aspects of the employment of the division. Having arrived with his staff, he was not convinced with the Greek island of Mudros being decided upon as the base of the operations. Logistical issues to include availability of water, absence of piers or jetties would have jeopardised the operation during the initial stages itself. Alexandria, on the other hand, with all the ancillary facilities was much better equipped to serve as the base of the operation. With an active interest from Hamilton, the base of the proposed operation was changed to Alexandria.

Having taken stock of the logistical support and the reports of the Turkish defences on the peninsula, Hamilton was himself not convinced about the viability of the proposed operation. In an indication of things to come, while writing about his reconnaissance of coastline of the peninsula from Cape Helles to the isthmus of Bulair, he wrote to Lord Kitchener that, 'here, Gallipoli looks a much tougher nut to crack than it did over the map in your office'.

On the other hand, the lead time available to the Turks had been utilised well by them. The Commander-in-Chief of the force of the British Mediterranean Force was able to glean information from his first-hand reconnaissance that nearly all the possible landing places were being prepared for strong defences. Fresh dug soil and the glittering of the newly erected wire along the row of trenches provided an indication of the things to come. The advantage differential was already in favour of the Turks, and with passage of time, unless an offensive was launched immediately, the chasm of differential was going to widen only. But the decision had already been taken that the attack by army would only be launched once the naval fleet enterprise was stalled, with no further chance of success.

In an apparent resolution to resolve the continuing impasse, the British Admiralty decided to launch a general fleet attack on 18 March 1915. As per directions promulgated, the British battleships were directed to manoeuver only in those waters, which, 'were confirmed to be free of any mines'. But the British Naval expedition was to suffer catastrophically from the havoc created by the mines. The British fleet was confident about the results of an elaborate and exhaustive sweeping carried out by it. But, unknown to the British Naval fleet, a fresh row of 'twenty mines' had been laid recently. 'This line, which according to one Turkish report, was laid on the night of 7/8 March 1915 and according to another on the night of 17/18 March 1915, was placed, unlike the others, not across the Straits but lengthwise down the channel.'[6] The British naval fleet all set to launch a general fleet attack, was totally oblivious to the existence of this freshly laid minefield.

On 18 March, the first half of the day was totally in favour of the Allies. The emplacements on the forts were targeted with greater accuracy by the British and the French battleships. Due to these accurate hits, the weight of the attack was increasingly shifting towards the Allies. The Turkish guns on the forts were finding it difficult to engage the Allied battleships storming the waterway. But, by the afternoon of the day, disaster struck. The French battleship *Bouvet* was the first one to be hit by a mine and was sunk. A similar fate awaited for the other ships of the flotilla. The British battleships *Inflexible* and *Irresistible* too went down almost in quick succession. Immediately afterwards *Ocean* had also gone down, struck by a mine. Thus, within a span of a few hours, the Allied naval fleet had lost six battleships, four struck by mines and two damaged by gun fire from the forts. These few hours of 18 March 1915 along with the twenty mines laid by Turks in consultation with German General Staff had singlehandedly changed the entire course of the next nine months at the peninsula. The loss of the fleet was severe dent to the British maritime prowess and was unredeemable. It was evidently clear that the rushing in of the Straits was not possible by the Naval fleet alone and 'from this day onwards, the fleet was allowed to make no further attempts, either single-handed or in cooperation with the army, to force the Dardanelles, and the great combined operation eventually decided upon, was fated to develop into a land campaign supported by the guns of the fleet'. Though the Admiral of the fleet was in favour of renewing the attack after the setback and back in England as well, the setback was not being considered as a final failure. The British maritime prowess, it was argued, cannot be decimated by the minor setback. To affect a final solution to the imbroglio, and to supplement the fresh offensive, the Admiral was informed by London, that five new battleships are being dispatched to replace the lost assets and he should prepare for launching again.

This time, however, it was Hamilton who decided to veto the fresh proposal for the standalone assault by the naval assets. By virtue of his being in the theatre of operation for a few days by now, he had also realised the futility of launching fresh offensive by the naval fleet in isolation. The success, he viewed was possible only by the co-operation by the army and if the army had to cooperate, it would mean, not a subsidiary operation, but a deliberate advance by his whole force, to open the passage for the fleet. Lord Kitchener much against his conviction of launching a fresh attack singularly by the naval fleet could not have agreed more with Hamilton and replied to him that, 'you know my views, that the passage of the Dardanelles must be forced, and if large military operations on the Gallipoli peninsula are necessary to clear the way, they must be undertaken and must be carried through'.

The decision of using the force of Hamilton having been taken, the next dilemma facing the commanders was the timings for the amphibious landings. Turks already had a lead and had utilised that well by preparing the defences at Gallipoli. The weather conditions as obtained in March were not conducive for the landings. With the type of preparations involved for launching of almost 75,000 troops on a strongly held peninsula, Ian Hamilton had reconciled to a bare minimum requirement of a month, before the offensive could be launched.

Logistics are a very important component of planning for amphibious landings. The entire effort of the deliberations in the War Council till date was focused on the operations of the naval fleet. The sudden change of plans had caught everyone by surprise. No thought till date had been given to the likelihood of an amphibious assault on the peninsula, and therefore no planning existed. Everything had to start afresh. Notwithstanding the preparations, the die was cast for the employment of Mediterranean force for the capture of the Peninsula under the command of Ian Hamilton. As the events of the next few days would unfold, the IEF was about to join this MEF, and play a major role in the offensive for the next eight months. The history being, what it is, was going to judge the decision of Dardanelles by the British against the defence of Dardanelles by the German-Turkish combine.

DEFENCE OF DARDANELLES

While the Indian Brigade was yet to join the expeditionary force earmarked for Dardanelles, the defender was going all out to ensure that the allied troops are not able to land, and if somehow are able to land, then are not allowed to attain and subsequently retain a foothold. The maxim of the success in any military operation hinges on the preparations of the defender. More the time available with the defender to coordinate his defences, less are the chances of success of the attacker. The Dardanelles operation by the MEF of Hamilton was no different to this maxim. Before the fateful final assault by the naval fleet on 18 March, the Turks duly supported by the German General Staff, had a fair idea of the Allied intentions. The failure of the naval assault had further reinforced those assumptions. From 19 March to 25 April, the day of landings by the Allies, the Turks had 38 days with them to coordinate their defences, identify and place their reserves and they did well. The delay in the preparations by the allied forces and the resultant stalemate of the offensive was to cause much suffering to the Allied troops, as the time progressed.

Though the Turks had established an elaborate defensive system, the command and control of the roughly five Divisions at peninsula along with the placement of reserves was an immediate cause of concern. Starting from North, these Divisions were stretched along the entire length of the coast, with each division comprising three Regiments of three battalions each. In addition, some local militia (Gendarmerie) battalions had also been co-opted with the regular battalions. The coast of Gulf of Saros was the responsibility of the 5th Division. The 7th Turkish Division along with two Gendarmerie battalions was responsible for Bulair. Two divisions, 9th and 19th were responsible for the entire stretch of coast from Suvla to Sedd-el-Bahr. A portion of the 9th Division was detached for the Asiatic portion of the Straits at Kum Kale. The 11th Division along with three Gendarmerie Battalions was based along the Asiatic shore and was responsible for the entire Asiatic coast. In addition, there were troops who were manning the forts and the artillery batteries along the coast. Another Division, the 3rd, was earmarked for move to Dardanelles on 25 March and the same was also operational on the peninsula by the first week of April 1915, exactly a month prior to the landing of the allied troops. On 24 March 1915, a German officer, Marshal Liman von Sanders, who had arrived as the head of a military mission to Turkey was appointed the Commander of the Army Command of Turkish forces at Gallipoli. In order to facilitate an effective command

and control, the Turkish forces on the peninsula had been consolidated into one Army Command.

Having arrived on the peninsula, two days later on 26 March 1915, Marshal Liman von Sanders was totally not in favour of the existing state of defences at peninsula. The Turkish troops had been distributed all along the peninsula in very small-sized pockets, which, as per Sanders were absolutely inadequate to provide sustained resistance to the determined enemy. 'Quite contrary to my principles, the troops were scattered all along the coast like the frontier detachments of days gone by. Everywhere the enemy would meet with a certain amount of opposition, but the absence of reserves precluded the possibility of a sustained and vigorous defence.'[7] The arrival of the German Marshal, Sanders on the peninsula had triggered a flurry of activity with an aim to reorganise the defences on Gallipoli, which was going to transform the Turkish resistance.

As an immediate action, Sanders firstly prioritised the likely landing sites for the Allied army at the Peninsula. The landing sites on the Asiatic shore, southern side of the Peninsula, the coast on either side of Gabba Tepe and general area of Bulair, were identified by the German General Staff as likely sites. Bulair with its unique geographical layout was assessed by Sanders as the most vulnerable. Capture of this narrow strip of land would have effectively isolated Gallipoli and all future reinforcements from the mainland would have been subjected to an intense interdiction. The immediate task for the German Marshal was to prioritise the landing sites and accordingly place his troops on the entire peninsula, for which he had five Turkish Divisions with the sixth one likely to be available in future.

The concept of defensive operations in the peninsula, in terms of Sanders totally hinged on the correct placement of reserves. The reserves, depending upon the weight of the attack, once discerned, could be launched in any direction thereby being able to handle the weight of attack. In a fluid defensive battle, the reserves once committed would be very difficult to retrieve. It was, therefore, imperative that the reserves are identified and disposition of these reserves is accordingly catered for. Towards this aim, Sanders rather than deploying his available forces into the Divisions, grouped them into three distinct combat groups. These combat groups comprised troops from different

Turkish Divisions and were grouped based upon their anticipated operational roles.

As Bulair was most critical from the defender's point of view, the combat group consisting of the 5th and 7th Turkish divisions was deployed in a consolidated block. The Combat Group of 11th Division and yet to arrive 3rd Division, were made responsible for the defence of the Asiatic shore. 9th Division, commanded by Lieutenant Colonel Khalil Sami Bey was made responsible for the defence of the Southern coast of the peninsula, extending from Suvla in the north to Sedd-el-Bahr in the south. The complete complement of the Turkish 19th Division was detailed as central reserve and was placed near Boghali. The location of the central reserves was so tactically chosen, that in case required the reserve was able to move to Bulair, Gaba Tepe or the

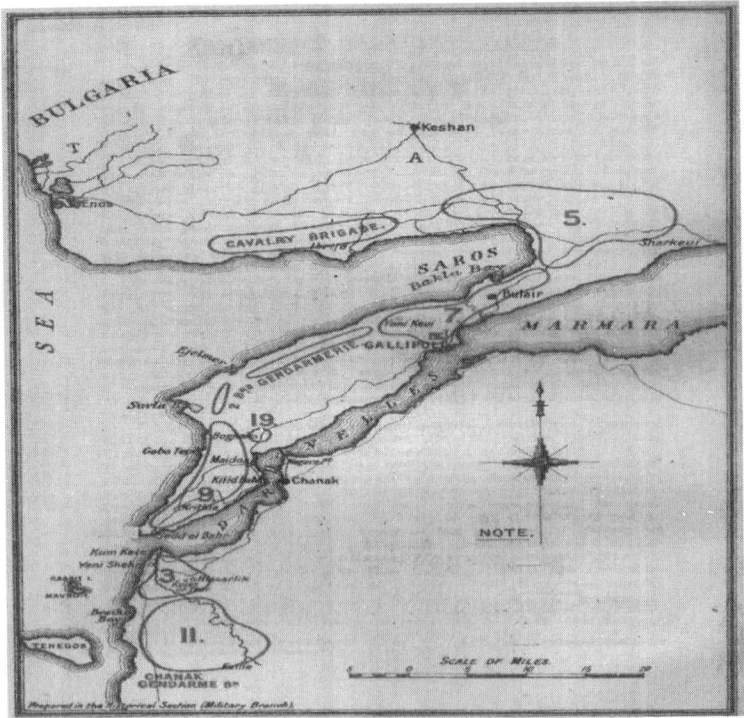

MAP 3: DEPLOYMENT OF TURKISH DEFENSIVE FORMATIONS:
25 APRIL 1915[8]

Asiatic Shore sides to beef up the defences in the shortest possible time. This reserve was centrally placed under the command of none other than the Commander-in-Chief himself.

As the plans of belligerents progressed, it was clear that the bulk of the weight of resistance by the Turkish Army at peninsula would be spearheaded by the 9th Division and the MEF was soon going to witness this in first person. The dispositions of the 9th Turkish Division bear testimony to the fact that the creation and placement of reserves was being organised not only at the central level but at every level of command. The reserves were created at the division, regiment and battalion levels. The organisation of the Division included three regiments, three field and two mountain batteries. The entire coastal front, the area of responsibility of the Division from Suvla to Sedd-el-Bahr was divided into two zones. The North Zone was the responsibility of the 27th Regiment along with the two mountain batteries of the Artillery.

The Southern Zone was the responsibility of the 26th Regiment along with one field battery of the Artillery. The 25th Regiment along with the two integral field batteries was centrally located at Kilid Bahr plateau, from where it could have moved up or down south depending upon the developing situation. The Northern Zone being commanded by Lieutenant Colonel Ali Chefik Bay had only employed the 2nd Battalion for the defenses of the coast. This battalion also had only three companies deployed, whereas one company was in reserve. The other two battalions of the Regiments 1st and 3rd along with one mountain battery of the Artillery were placed as reserve for the 2nd Regiment. In the Southern Zone, Commander (Lieutenant Colonel) Kadri Bey had deployed all three battalions. The northern-most sector of the Zone was the responsibility of the 1st Battalion of the Regiment, with three companies deployed and the fourth one held in reserve. The central sector of the Zone, Krithia, was held by the 2nd Battalion of the Regiment. The Southern sector of the Zone, being looked after by the 3rd Battalion of the Regiment had two companies each looking at 'W' and 'V' beaches respectively with two companies in reserve.

Having seen the German insistence on preventing capture of the peninsula by the Allied Forces 'at any cost', there was a rapid and dynamic movement of the Turkish forces on the peninsula and on the

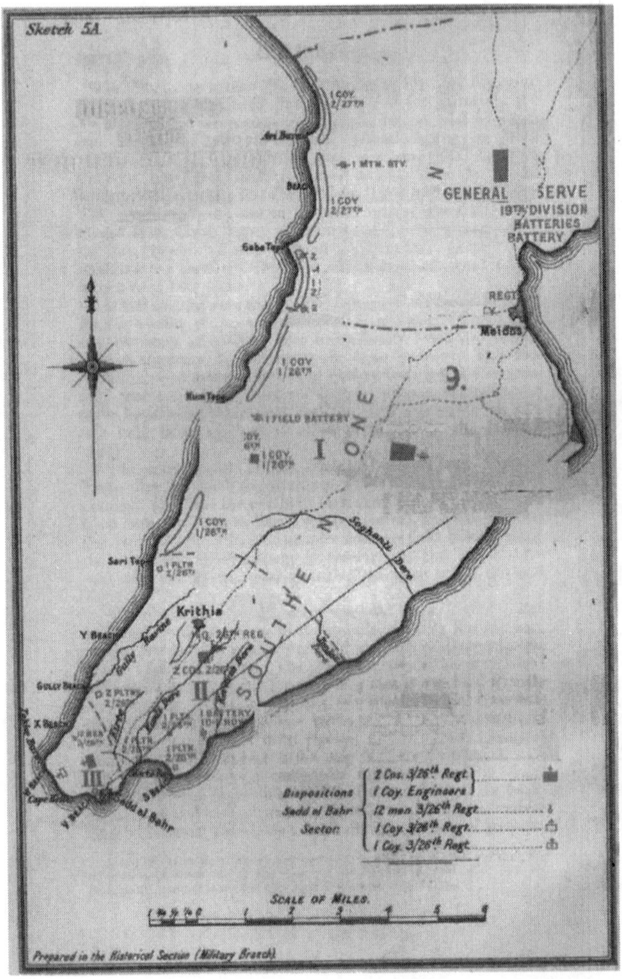

MAP 4: DISPOSITIONS OF THE TURKISH 9TH DIVISION[9]

'night before the landing, while Ian Hamilton was approaching the peninsula with 53 battalions, the Dardanelles garrison was ready to receive his MEF, by a force comprising approximately 57 battalions, of which twenty-one were at the northern end of the peninsula, nineteen on the Asiatic side of the straits and only seventeen between Suvla and Sedd-el-Bahr. Under the German offensive, the Turkish organisation and reorganisation of the existing forces at the peninsula was so rapid that by the next two days, the northern peninsula was totally drained off from all the available troops and all forces available on the Asiatic shore of the peninsula had been mobilised to the European shore. In addition, the 15th and 16th Divisions from the Turkish mainland had been mobilised and by the end of April, a complete complement of these divisions was also effective on the peninsula.

With the overall placement of the Turkish forces on the peninsula having been approximately disposed so as to counter the likely plan of the Allied Forces, the German General Staff then started working on the important facet of the improvement of the existing defences with the overhead protection and obstacle system. The Turkish defenders, under the overall supervision of German officers, worked day in and day out to improve the defences and the obstacle system. The obstacle system, primarily the wire obstacles, proved to be a very important component of Turkish resistance at Gallipoli.

These obstacles made the Turkish trenches almost impregnable and as the Allied artillery was unable to destroy these wire obstacles, the Allied troops suffered most casualties while negotiating these. In all the offensives carried out by the Allied troops, the bulk casualties were attributed to the inability of these troops to negotiate the obstacle. The Allied troops while carrying out reconnaissance of the peninsula from the sea had observed the shimmering of the newly laid out wires as obstacles against the sun. But at that point of time, the impact of deadliness of these bright shining wires was not perceptible to the attackers.

On 30 April 1915, four days after the Allied landings, a comparative analysis of the available forces at the peninsula would reveal that, while the Mediterranean Expeditionary Force had 53 battalions available, the corresponding troops available with the defenders comprised almost 75 battalions, out of which only 28 battalions had been engaged by this time. As is seen, the aspect of numerical superiority had been totally turned upside down. Though the allies had planned to storm the peninsula with an overwhelming numerical superiority, the enemy by this time, by virtue of foresight and planning of the German General Staff, had achieved complete numerical superiority. 'Were we still faced by the Divisions which originally held the Gallipoli Peninsula we would by now, I firmly believe, be in possession of the Kilid Bahr plateau, but every day a regiment or two dibbles into Gallipoli, either from Asia or from Constantinople, and in the last two days an entire fresh Division has (we have heard) arrived from Adrianople, and is fighting against us this morning.'[10]

This numerical superiority against the allied onslaught was not left unorganised and due importance was given to the command and control element of these forces by the German General Staff. As the Allied troops had already been successful in gaining a foothold on the peninsula and more reinforcements to sustain the operations further inland very likely, the Turkish and German military hierarchy had correctly anticipated the long haul of the operations on the peninsula. In a fresh reorganisation of Turkish forces in the peninsula, Marshal Liman von Sanders, on 29 April bifurcated the Turkish forces into two groups, wherein the Northern group, opposed to the ANZACs, was placed under Essad Pasha, commanding the III Corps, while the Southern, or Sedd-el-Bahr group was placed under the command of Colonel von Sodenstern, a German officer who was commanding the Turkish 5th Division.

The area of responsibility of the Southern group was also divided along the Krithia Road. The Turkish 9th Division was made responsible for the northern side of the Krithia Road and the 7th Division was made responsible for the operations along the Southern part of the Krithia Road. Giving due importance to the defence of Dardanelles, Turkey had also by this time ordered a general mobilisation of all categories, which had been excused military service till now. The defence of Dardanelles having been catered for all possible contingencies by the Turks, the time had come now for the drive for Dardanelles, an offensive strategy by the British and other Allied forces and an offensive defensive strategy by the Turks.

Drive for Dardanelles

The Turkish defences, under the directions of the German officers, were nearing completion. The reserves had been earmarked and placed accordingly. The situation at the headquarters of Limon von Sanders and Ian Hamilton were quite similar. Both the commanders were appreciating the likely landing sites available at the peninsula. The ultimate aim of both, however, were diametrically opposite. Whereas Hamilton was appreciating the landing sites for the purpose of a breakthrough, his counterpart at Gallipoli was studying the same landing sites for the purpose of checking the same. The irony of the situation happened to be that the landing sites being considered by both were common. The difference between success and failure, from the perspectives of both lay in the correct priority of the available options, based on own strengths and the appreciated weaknesses of the enemy.

Maintenance of secrecy about the impending operations was of paramount importance for the allies. The inherent challenges in maintaining secrecy while preparing for such an operation at such a scale are well known. As far as the attack by the naval fleet for rushing through the Straits was concerned, since at the initial stages the attack was supposed to be singularly naval attack alone and no troops were being planned to be used, there was no need felt for maintaining secrecy. 'The more the Turks knew about the pretended attack, and the more they feared it, the greater the chances of its objective being affected and of the pressure against the Russians in the Caucasus being relieved.' This deliberate revelation of the intended naval operations was able to provide certain dividends initially, but the failure of the attack by the naval fleet had changed the dynamics of the situation.

With decision being taken for the employment of troops for the capture of the peninsula to aid the stalled operations of the naval fleet, the requirement of secrecy was all the more important. With 75,000 troops being planned to be landed at Gallipoli, the requirement of small crafts and tugs in large numbers was suddenly acute. Time was at premium and the non-availability of these crafts in England precluded their procurement from home. The only source was in the neutral or friendly ports in the Mediterranean and a flurry of activity started to source these crafts in as many numbers as possible and as early as possible. As the number of friendly or neutral ports were limited, the intelligence of the operation was hard to conceal and when the Expeditionary Force landed in Egypt, there was virtually no possibility of concealing the intentions. As shall be seen subsequently, the Royal Naval Division and the 29th Division, when they reached

Alexandria, the sheer number of transports straightaway gave the hint of a major operation in the offing. Approximately 64 transports / vessels of varying sizes and shapes were used to transport these two divisions alone at Alexandria.

The appreciation of the number of Turkish troops at Gallipoli was also not very clear to the Allies at the moment. The intelligence reports shared with the staff of Ian Hamilton anticipated the number of troops at Gallipoli to be between 40,000 and 80,000, the difference in the margin being exactly 200 per cent. In addition, the reports cited availability of additional 30,000 troops on the Asiatic shore with the possibility of another 60,000 being available as reinforcements at short notice. Going by these reports, Ian Hamilton had to cater for enemy troops ranging anywhere between 1,30,000 and 1,70,000. These troops being spread over all over the peninsula and the very objective of the land force, at least at that time, being the reduction of coastal and mobile artillery batteries, the landings at the Asiatic shore were planned as the highest priority option. The lay of the land along with the possibility of securing the isthmus of Bulair in the north-west of the peninsula, facilitated it being selected as the second priority. The likely requirement of a Continental Campaign and the non-availability of the requisite amount of capability in terms of troops to affect such a campaign, the proposal to secure landings on the Asiatic shore were negated. Due to some major advantages being accrued, the progressing of the operations from the European side after securing landings, emerged as the most preferred option. The option if executed with precision and preparation had the potential of securing Kilid Bahr plateau and would have facilitated complete turning of the Turkish defences.

With discussion now shifting towards the European side of the peninsula, the landings at Bulair were ruled out due to a very strong possibility of interdiction of sea transports from the main Turkish positions. Similarly, landings at Suvla were also negated due to Salt Lake being impassable at that time of the year. The list of the likely landing sites was gradually getting reduced. The probable sites in the north and south of Gaba Tepe appeared to be most ideal from the technical point of view. In addition, the dead ground next to the shore provided immunity to the landing troops at their most vulnerable time, from the enemy artillery. These advantages helped landing sites at the north of Gaba Tepe, where the ANZACs ultimately landed, to be shortlisted for execution. The landing sites in the south of Gaba Tepe, though providing the shortest possible route to the plateau of Kilid Bahr were, however, negated as an 'elaborate network of trenches and wire was plainly visible from the sea; the beach was in easy reach of the Turkish batteries'.

The landing sites along the southern end of the peninsula were next in the series to be selected as would-be landing sites for the force of Ian Hamilton. A month later, the 29th Division along with the 29th Indian Infantry Brigade landed at these sites. The integrated and inherent advantages offered by these sites proved to be invaluable in facilitating their final selection. It was argued that during the landing and in the subsequent advance, effective assistance could be afforded by the fleet on both flanks. Once ashore, the army would have both flanks and rear secured by sea. The Kilid Bahr plateau does not appear to be more formidable on its southern than on its northern face.

A draft plan for the landings of the ground force had been prepared by 23 March 1915. The broad plan involved simultaneous landings of the 29th British Division supported by the French in the southern part of the peninsula and by the ANZACs in the general area north of Gaba Tepe. Apart from the dispersal of the landing forces by a huge margin as a disadvantage, the plan had a number of positives. It was believed that simultaneous landings will invoke a decision dilemma on the defenders with respect to the employment of reserves. In addition, Anzac landings would also simultaneously prevent down south movement of enemy reinforcements. With total sea control ensured by Britain, the lone disadvantage was not adversely affecting the plan in a major way. The sea control was affording enough advantages to the British for using it as a communication link between the two widely dispersed likely landing sites.

The arrival of the 29th Division meanwhile had commenced at Alexandria. The call by Ian Hamilton to shift base of the operation to Alexandria from Mudros had proven to be a great facilitator for the Allies. But the hustle created by the operational necessity had resulted in the irrational loading of the transports at the home bases. With fresh load tables under preparation at Alexandria and in sync with the disembarkation priorities, there was no option but to empty the complete transport and get the equipment of units and subunits sorted out. The transports were again loaded so as to ensure ease of access and ease of unloading of each category of stores and equipment. The issues of taking of animals along in the first phase of landing, coupled with the availability of water on the peninsula and the requirement of transport for the landing troops on the peninsula had to be weighed against individual merits and decisions taken. Too many or too less were not easily differentiated. An item or equipment left behind in the ruse of too many may in the end fall short on the shore or otherwise, too many numbers of an item which are carried may not be required at all on the shore. The planners had to carefully tread on these calculations and prepare the final tables for loading into each ship and further to tugs or trawlers. The British, French and ANZAC troops had landed on Gallipoli in the early hours of 25 April 1915, at a great human cost. The landings and the subsequent operations of these forces have been analysed in great detail by the military historians in the past 109 years. There has not been a single detail of these operations which has been missed out and not been done justice with, as deserved.

There has, however, been the aspect of the contribution of the Indian troops in the Gallipoli Campaign, which has somehow missed out the recognition it deserved. A detailed survey carried out, as discussed in the Introduction to this work, further corroborates the hypothesis. With a brief background on the initiation of the campaign, it's time now to do justice to the contribution of these 16,000 plus Indian troops, who gave an excellent account of themselves, while fighting an unknown enemy in an unknown terrain 3,350 miles away from home.

DEMAND FROM INDIA

On conclusion of spring field training in 1914, there were no rumors of war; by the end of July, speculation was rife but consensus was that the crises would blow over. Even when the war was declared there appeared small likelihood, the Indian Army would be required, then suddenly on the evening 09 August came orders for mobilization for services out of India.[11]

The rumours and the subsequent initiation of hostilities between England and Germany were hardly taken seriously by anyone in India or by the Indian Army. India was too far from the epicentre of the world and the war was unlikely to have any impact on India or the Indian Army. The general mood in the country was aligned to the fact that India and the Indian Army was never going to be mobilised for the hostilities in Europe. The requirement of the British battalions serving in India at that time to mobilise for the war in Europe, was likely but that the Indian battalions would be mobilised for war, was rarely anticipated.

A series of simultaneous but unlinked events prior to August 1914, though had given rise to the speculation of the employment of Indian Army in the World War theatres across the globe. The developments in the Persian region, increasing convergence and reaproachments with Russia, threat to the Suez Canal and other geo-political developments had germinated the idea of deployment of the Indian Army across various theatres. For the purpose of the book, it will be fair to assume that the necessary planning and war gaming of options for the constitution and the subsequent deployment of these forces must have been carried out and existed in some form. Suez Canal was of immense strategic importance. When the Ottoman Empire plunged into the Great War on the side of Germany, there was a need for a dedicated force to protect the Allied interests in the waterway. With the British troops likely to be firmly engaged in France and other theatres, the possibility of employment of Indian troops, at least for defence of Suez Canal had begun to look real. The first meeting of War Council, after declaration of hostilities on 4 August 1914, had directed the War Office to constitute an expeditionary force of a division of Indian troops for the defence of Suez Canal.

In India, however, the reluctance to pull out the regular British battalions from the western frontier of the country was quite evident. In response to a request from the War Office in London for the requirement of British battalions from India and being replaced with the Territorial's, the Viceroy in September 1914 had expressed inability to dispatch full complement of all British regular battalions being requested by the War Office and replied that, 'we have already sent or are sending overseas eleven battalions. Nine more must be retained by us for the three divisions on our frontier, since the danger zone is Afghanistan and the tribes, against whom we must always be fully prepared, and we cannot regard Territorial's as fit to cope in hill warfare with Pathans.'[12]

As far as the internal situation in the rest of the country was concerned, it was believed that the regular British battalions along with some Indian Infantry battalions could be spared. The Army Department in India was comfortable with the idea of dispatching twenty 'excellent' Indian battalions towards the cause of war effort. The void created by the dispatch of the British regular and the Indian battalions in the balance of the country was to be compensated by the arrival of 43 Territorial battalions from England. The Army Department had further put a caveat in the entire process by mandating that the regular British battalions can only be dispatched once the Territorial battalions start reaching India.

We are willing to send home the remaining 32 British regular battalions and 20 Indian battalions in addition. We think that India may be regarded as safe internally, if 32 British battalions and 20 Indian battalions are accepted and we receive 43 Territorial battalions. Before the British battalions begin to leave India, the Territorial's must begin to reach here.[13]

As discussed earlier, the British dilemma with respect to the entry of Turkey into the conflagration and its subsequent handling was multifold. The geostrategic advantage enjoyed by Turkey enabled it to threaten the Suez, the fastest waterway to India. The security of India and the rest of the Empire undoubtedly was based on ensuring the security of the Suez Canal. In addition, the apparent shortage of troops for the proposed Dardanelles campaign, envisaged some contribution from India. The Commander of MEF Ian Hamilton was asking for a Gurkha brigade to ensure capture of the peninsula by the Allies in an earlier time-frame. The War Office, at the same time, was also considering the likely implications of employing Indian battalions with composition of PMs against the Turks. A number of discussions to war game the likely scenarios emerging from the proposed employment of PM troops on Gallipoli were studied. These considerations merited that the Indian troops proposed to be employed in Gallipoli, if any, had to be carefully selected.

The mobilisation orders for twenty Indian Army Infantry battalions were issued by the Adjutant General (AG) in India on 14 October 1915. All these twenty battalions were ordered to mobilise and be prepared to embark for active service by the end of October. The instructions explicitly mentioned that all battalions had to mobilise with their respective ten per cent of reinforcements, unlike the British 29th Division, which was mobilised from England for Dardanelles without this essential component. The deficiencies of up to 120 combatants were supposed to be made up from respective reservists and the details of additional battalions provided to cater for additional deficiencies if any.[14]

TABLE 1: TWENTY INFANTRY BATTALIONS EARMARKED TO MOBILISE[15]

Unit	Formation	Deficiencies to be Provided by
14th Sikhs	1st Division	45th Sikhs
2/7 Gurkhas	4th Division	1/7 Gurkhas
23rd Pioneers	Lahore Divisional Area	32nd Pioneers
24th Punjabis	1st Division	19th Punjabis
22nd Punjabis	9th Division	19th Punjabis
3rd Brahmans	5th Division	1st Brahmans
51st Sikhs	1st Division	54th Sikhs
89th Punjabis	9th Division	90th Punjabis
2nd Rajputs	8th Division	16th Rajputs
69th Punjabis	2nd Division	67th Punjabis
93rd Punjabis	9th Division	72nd Punjabis
30th Punjabis	Meerut Divisional Area	From Own Reserves Only
1/5 Gurkhas	2nd Division	2/5 Gurkhas
128th Pioneers	8th Division	121st Pioneers
1/6 Gurkhas	2nd Division	2/6 Gurkhas
53rd Sikhs	Kohat Brigade	54th Sikhs
27th Punjabis	Derajat Brigade	From Own Reserves Only
126th Baluchistan Infantry	4th Division	124th Baluchistan Infantry
56th Rifles	Kohat Brigade	52nd Rifles

These twenty Indian Infantry battalions along with Lucknow Brigade, Imperial Service Brigade, Composite Infantry Brigade and 30 per cent reinforcements for all Indian troops of Lahore, Meerut and Indian Cavalry Divisions were clubbed into five distinct categories. The Secretary of State for India had informed the Army Department on 15 October 1915 that these forces would be dispatched to different places as under:[16]

Egypt - 8 Indian battalions
Egypt -The Lucknow Brigade
Egypt -The Imperial Service Cavalry Brigade
Egypt - The Composite Infantry Brigade
Egypt - 3 Indian Infantry brigades
France - 30 per cent reinforcements for all Indian troops of Lahore, Meerut and Indian Cavalry Divisions with 50 per cent British Officers of Indian units.

These groups were later organised into two different forces. Through an order of 23 October 1914, the Imperial Service Cavalry Brigade, the Composite Infantry Brigade along with the eight Infantry battalions was clubbed into a force, which was designated as IEF 'E'. Similarly, the Lucknow Brigade and the three Indian Infantry brigades were clubbed together to form IEF. 'F'. The force was initially organised for deployment along the lines of communications in France but the orders were changed at the last moment for deployment in Egypt.

The Lucknow Brigade was posted with one British and three native Infantry battalions, the 1st Battalion King's Own Scottish Borderers, 62nd Punjabis, 92nd Punjabis and 2/10 Gurkhas. With the Lucknow Brigade already posted with its full complement, the other three ad hoc Infantry brigades were allotted twelve battalions, out of the twenty battalions moving to Egypt. The 29th Indian Infantry Brigade with Brigadier General H.V Cox as Commander on raising, was allotted four Infantry battalions, for the subsequent tasking in the defences of Suez Canal.[17] 14th Sikhs joined the formation from the 1st Peshawar Brigade under the 1st (Peshawar) Division. 69th Punjabis joined the Brigade from the 5th Jhelum Brigade, where the battalion was serving under the 2nd Rawalpindi Division. The 89th Punjabis, the third battalion of the formation, joined the 29th Indian

Infantry Brigade from Dinapore, where they were serving under the Presidency Brigade under the 8th Lucknow Division. The last unit of the Brigade, the 1st Battalion, and the 6th Gurkhas, joined the Brigade from the 3rd Abbottabad Brigade, where the unit was serving under the 2nd Rawalpindi Division. The battalions of the 29th Indian Infantry Brigade had mobilised from their respective locations to the embarking location. The movement from these permanent locations to the designated ports of embarkation was through trains. All the battalions of the 29th Indian Brigade were to embark for Egypt from Karachi. For the Infantry component of the Brigade, three hired transports had been detailed. The transports were made available at the Karachi harbour by the end of October 1914. The battalions had also started arriving at the harbour by that time.

On arrival at Karachi, the 14th Sikhs embarked in the transport *City of Manchester*, which sailed on 3rd November in company with nine other vessels under the escort of H.M.S *Duke of Edinburgh*. The whole of the 29th Indian Infantry Brigade, under Brigadier General H.V Cox, consisting of the 14th Sikhs, 69th Punjabis, 89th Punjabis and 1/6 Gurkhas sailed for Egypt in this convoy.[18]

FIGURE 1: 14TH SIKHS AT KHANPUR RAILWAY STATION
ENROUTE TO KARACHI, OCTOBER 1914[19]

TABLE 2: MANIFEST DETAILS OF 29TH INDIAN INFANTRY BRIGADE[20]

Hired Transport	Unit	Date Ship Ready	Date Unit Arrived	Date of Embarkation	Date of Sailing
City of Manchester	HQs 29 Indian Infantry Brigade	30 Oct. 1914	1 Nov. 1914	1 Nov. 1914	3 Nov. 1914
	14th Sikhs				
	Half 69th Punjabis				
	Reinforcements				
Edavanha	89th Punjabis	30 Oct. 1914	31 Oct. 1914	1 Nov. 1914	3 Nov. 1914
	Half 69th Punjabis		1 Nov. 1914		
Teesta	1/6 Gurkhas	28 Oct. 1914	31 Oct. 1914	31 Oct. 1914	3 Nov. 1914

The battalions had embarked with their respective complement of the authorised strength. The office of the Viceroy of India also informed the Secretary of State for India on 9 November 1914 about the exact strength of the battalions of the Indian Brigade, which had set sail on 3 November 1914.

TABLE 3: TOTAL STRENGTH OF THE 29TH INDIAN INFANTRY
BRIGADE WHICH SAILED ON 3 NOVEMBER FROM KARACHI[21]

Unit	British Officers	Indian Officers	Other Ranks	Followers
HQs 29th Indian Infantry Brigade	03	-	01	5
14th Sikhs	11	18	808	40
69th Punjabis	12	19	805	75
89th Punjabis	13	18	808	60
1/6 Gurkhas	12	18	808	80
Total	51	73	3,230	260

Orders for Brigadier General Cox, Commander of the 29th Indian Infantry Brigade, IEF 'F' mandated the formation to proceed to Egypt and seek further orders from General Officer Commanding (GOC), Egypt. The Brigade as part of standard orders was required to report the arrival of transports to Chief of the General Staff, Simla and the Chief of the Imperial General Staff, London from each port of call.

With the exact information on the prospective deployment of the Brigade still not clear, adequate time available on board the transports were put to good use by the battalions. Organised physical activities by the Indian troops on board the respective transports were greatly responsible for mitigating the monotonous routine on board the transports.

Enroute to Egypt, the destination of the full complement of the 29th Indian Infantry Brigade was diverted to 'Sheikh Said', an island on the Arabian coast in the Red Sea. The tasking of the brigade involved capture of Turkish defences on the island. While, the transport carrying the troops of the 29th Indian Infantry Brigade had just sailed from Karachi on 3 November, a secret telegram was dispatched from the office of the Chief of General Staff to Brigadier General Cox and

FIGURE 2: CONVOY OF THE 29TH INDIAN INFANTRY BRIGADE[22]

a copy endorsed for the GOC Aden. The missive directed the 29th Indian Infantry Brigade to capture 'Sheikh Said' and to destroy the Turkish works, armaments and wells at the location. The operation was to be carried out by the 14th Sikhs, 69th Punjabis and the 89th Punjabis, which were on board transports of *City of Manchester* and *Edavanha*. Another battalion of the 23rd Sikh Pioneers, on board transport *Nurani*, was also detailed for the operation, under the overall command of the commander of the 29th Indian Infantry Brigade.

As the Indian Brigade had just left India and didn't have any information on the enemy, a General Staff Officer 2, Major Bradshaw, detailed by the GOC, Aden was tasked to brief Brigadier General Cox on board *City of Manchester*. The strength of the Turkish forces at Sheikh Said was expected to be in the range of 500 men supported by six or seven guns. For the proposed offensive, the naval co-operation was also planned. On 10 November, the two battalions of the 69th and 89th Punjabis carried out the landings, while the 14th Sikhs was detailed to be in reserve. The objective was captured and the major degradation of the enemy defences was carried out by the naval guns of the flotilla and 'by the time the Sikhs landed, the place was almost

FIGURE 3: PHYSICAL ACTIVITY ON BOARD THE *CITY OF MANCHESTER*, NOVEMBER 1914[23]

deserted and the field guns were abandoned by the Turks, who had fled to the mainland.' After the Turks had fled the island, the 14th Sikhs carried out the mopping up of the remnants of the Turkish defences on the island.

FIGURE 4: 14TH SIKHS DISEMBARKING FROM THE *CITY OF MANCHESTER* AT SHEIKH SAID[24]

During the mopping up, the Commanding Officer (CO) of the battalion was faced with a unique situation.

As the Sikhs were moving down to the beach, the Kot (Armoury) Lance Naik of one of the Double Company was seen carrying a flagstaff on his shoulder. He was taking it back as firewood for the company 'langar' (Cook house) as the men had been having difficulty in cooking with coal in the ship's galley and the Lance Naik had spotted the flagstaff as good material for firewood.[25]

To the query posed by the Lieutenant Cursetjee, the Medical Officer, about the flag, the Lance Naik drew out a red bunting from under his coat and said, 'Do you mean this thing? You may have it' and the Sikh continued on to the beach. By that time, Colonel Palin had also caught sight of it and, 'ordered it to be left behind, much to the regret of Lance Naik.' The flag was kept in the Adjutant's 'Yakdan' throughout the war and is now among the war trophies of the battalion.'[26]

FIGURE 5: SIKHS WITH WAR TROPHIES AT SHEIKH SAID[27]

After the successful capture of the objective, the Indian Brigade along with its battalions had reached Qantara sector on 2 December 1914. The Brigade had its headquarters at Qantara, from where the entire formation mobilised for Gallipoli in April 1915. The other two Indian brigades which were raised for the Suez Canal defences included the 28th and 30th Infantry Brigades. The 30th Indian Infantry Brigade with Major General Melliss as Commander, comprised the 76th Punjabis, 126th Baluchistan Infantry, 24th Punjabis and the 2/7 Gurkhas.

The 28th Indian Infantry Brigade with Major General Young-husband as Commander was allotted with the 51st Sikhs, 53rd Sikhs, 56th Rifles and 1/5 Gurkhas. To defend the Suez Canal and to allow uninterrupted flow of maritime traffic, the three Indian Infantry brigades under IEF 'F', were placed under the 10th Infantry Division. Another Division, namely the 11th Division was also deployed for the defence of the canal. Besides these two divisions, some additional formations of the Indian Army, to include 22nd (Lucknow) Brigade from the 8th Lucknow Division without their British battalions and an Imperial Service cavalry brigade, had also formed part of the force. The brigade and its battalions distinguished themselves while serving under the 10th Indian Division on the Canal defences. The brigade, with its four battalions and a battalion of the 22nd Brigade under command took up defences in the third sector along the Canal, with the first and second sectors being held by 30th Indian Infantry Brigade and the 28th Indian Infantry Brigade of the 10th Indian Division respectively.

With an estimated number of Turkish troops at the peninsula being in the range of 1,30,000 to 1,70,000, comparatively the Mediterranean force under the command of Ian Hamilton comprised only 75,000 troops. Out of these 75,000 also, the actual number of troops going for the offensive on the shores of the peninsula was far less. But with the primacy being given to the war efforts along the Western Front, Ian Hamilton also did not have a cause and reason to ask for additional troops for his upcoming offensive in the Dardanelles. 'At first Sir Ian Hamilton seems to have had no desire to ask for reinforcements, and the impression he gave to those around him was that of a man who is fully confident of success.'

But as D Day approached and the intelligence reports of the Allies started providing corroborated inputs on the Turkish forces on the peninsula along with the narrative of the strongly held defences with adequate troops and carefully orchestrated placement of the reserves, Ian Hamilton started having doubts on his level of preparations for the offensive. In retrospect it can be definitely confirmed that 'a definite appeal for more troops at this moment, with a full emphasis on the risks of embarking on this unexpectedly difficult enterprise, 3,000 miles from England, without an adequate reserve on the spot, might have achieved its purpose'.

A sense of mistaken loyalty prevented Ian Hamilton to ask for additional troops. He had been warned prior to moving from Britain, that the troops provided to him have been foraged from all available resources and there was no possibility at all for provisioning of additional troops. In addition, Hamilton, himself being a party to an old incident, it has been claimed, which also might have accentuated his reluctance to not ask for any additional troops. 'Sir Ian Hamilton had seen him (Lord Kitchener), in South Africa days, reply to an officer's appeal for reinforcements by taking half his troops away from him.' With such a background to the narrative, Ian Hamilton, definitely would not have wanted to be in the shoes of that officer.

In addition, the troops provided to him in form of the 29th Division, were also available to him only as a loan and they needed to be sent back to France immediately after completion of the assigned task at Dardanelles. In the meantime, ANZACs had also concentrated at Mudros in the preparation for the offensive. The two main components of the force being the 1st Australian Division, with 1st, 2nd and 3rd Australian Brigades and the Australian & New Zealand Division with the New Zealand Infantry Brigade and the 4th Australian Brigade. One complete complement of the Brigade of ANZACs comprised mounted battalions. With the type of terrain obtained at Gallipoli, totally unsuitable for the employment of the mounted battalions, coupled with the logistical issues of transporting mounts on to the peninsula, it was decided to not employ the mounted battalions at Dardanelles in the first instance. It has been recorded that,

General Birdwood (GOC of ANZAC), realising that mounted units could not be used in Gallipoli in the first instance, suggested exchanging them for an Indian Infantry Brigade, belonging to the Egyptian Garrison, in order to bring the NZ & A Division up to the normal strength of three Infantry brigades.

This was in early March 1915 and is considered as the first instance of an initial thought process of employing an Indian Infantry Brigade at Gallipoli. Ian Hamilton as discussed above was till this time shying away from asking for additional troops for his endeavor. But with D Day fast approaching, he at last took a call and asked for a Gurkha Brigade to supplement his force. In the meantime, Lord Kitchener, realising the requirement of additional troops had also earmarked 2nd Mounted Division for Egypt. By this time, it was also increasingly evident that the earmarked troops for the Dardanelles would not be adequate and there was an immediate need for identification of additional troops which can be employed in Dardanelles.

With Ian Hamilton also insisting upon the requirement of the Gurkha Brigade for the impending offensive, Lord Kitchener sent an urgent message to General Maxwell in Egypt. Having decided upon the employment of the Indian Brigade from Egypt for the capture of the peninsula, Lord Kitchener in his cable of 6 April 1915 addressed to General Maxwell in Egypt sought additional troops for the Dardanelles endeavour, 'you should supply any troops in Egypt that can be spared, or even selected officers or men that Sir Ian Hamilton may want for Gallipoli'. Having received a copy of the message from Lord Kitchener to General Maxwell, Hamilton again asked General Maxwell about the availability of the Gurkha battalions for the proposed side stepping. On inquiring from General Maxwell 'about the Gurkhas', Ian Hamilton was told that, 'he would do his best to meet his wishes'. Though all out efforts were being made to meet the requirements in terms of man power and resources, but it was an established fact that a series of simultaneous operations involving Indian troops across the length and breadth of the world was demanding too much from India.

It was one thing to conduct operations along the North-West Frontier, quite another to deploy forces where a sound infrastructure already existed such as in France and recourse to the sources of supply were near at hand. More difficult it remained to initiate and sustain campaigns where communications were poor, local support was minimal and climatic conditions governed the tempo of the operations. Each contingency supported, taxed the means available and operated against each other.[28]

Along with this, there was an additional issue of limit of the responsibilities. The Indian responsibility to meet the burden of war waged by the British was being considered as unlimited.

To these difficulties, a further remained; the expeditions were secondary operations and tangential to the greater strategy of the war which quickly devolved to meeting the German threat at its strongest point. Ironically, the greater the burden assumed by the British Army in France and Belgium, the more it fell to India to meet the needs of Britain's traditional maritime strategy.[29]

Meanwhile in Egypt, the 29th Indian Infantry Brigade was fully employed in the fulfilling of the allotted task of Canal Defences. Replying to the Lord Kitchener, through a cable of 9 April 1915, GOC Egypt had informed Commander-in-Chief (C-in-C) in India that the 29th Indian Infantry Brigade along with the 7 Indian Mountain Artillery Brigade (IMAB) was being detailed to move with the Mediterranean Expeditionary Force of Ian Hamilton. Two Mountain Batteries of 7th IMAB, landed on the peninsula along with the first wave of ANZACs on 25 April 1915, whereas the 29th Indian Brigade along with its battalions had landed on the peninsula on 1 May 1915. The troops, who fought at Gallipoli, primarily were Sikhs, PMs and Gurkhas. The attempt in the book is to underscore the stellar role played by these troops while fighting at Gallipoli. The standards of bravery set by these troops have relatively been relegated to the annals of footnotes. The subsequent chapters of the book attempt to correct the narrative and do justice to the memory of these brave hearts in line with title of the book.

NOTES

1. C.F. Aspinall-Oglander (2022), *Official History of the Great War - Military Operations: Gallipoli*, vol. 1, Naval & Military Press.
2. Ibid.
3. Ibid.
4. G.C.A. Arthur (2007), *Life of Lord Kitchener*, New York: Cosimo Incorporated, p. 85.
5. Ibid.
6. Ibid.
7. Ibid.
8. Ibid.
9. Ibid.
10. I. Hamilton (2021), *Gallipoli Diary*, vol. I & II, Complete. Independently published.
11. E. Tennant (2017), *Royal Deccan Horse in the Great War*, East Sussex England: Naval and Military Press.
12. Telegram no. 1018, 21 September 1914. Appendix I, War Diary, IEF 'D', National Archives of India.
13. Ibid.
14. Telegram Nos. 1162-7, 14 October 1915. Appendix 6, War Diary, IEF 'D', National Archives of India.
15. Ibid.
16. Telegram no. 1245, 15 October 1915, Appendix 8, War Diary, IEF 'D', National Archives of India.

17. Order of Battle of Divisions, Part 5B, Indian Army Divisions, 1st edn., South Yorkshire England: Pen & Sword Books (1993).
18. L.C.P.G. Bamford (1948), *The Sikh Regiment, The 14th King George's Own Ferozepore Sikhs*, Aldershot: Gale & Polden Limited.
19. 14th Sikhs Album
20. Quartermaster General's Table of Sailing, War Diary, Army Headquarters, India, IEF 'G', November 1914, Appendix 27, National Archives of India.
21. Total Strength of 29th Indian Infantry Brigade, War Diary, Army Headquarters, India, IEF 'G', November 1914, Appendix 35, National Archives of India.
22. 14th Sikhs Album.
23. Ibid.
24. Ibid.
25. Bamford, *The Sikh Regiment*, op. cit.
26. Ibid.
27. 14th Sikhs Album.
28. A. Jeffreys (2022), *Indian Army in the First World War: New Perspectives (War & Military Culture in South Asia)*, rpt., Helion and Company, Warwick, England.
29. Ibid.

CHAPTER 2

The Arrangements
Indian Army on the Eve of the Great War

When we asked some of the prisoners if they had had enough of fighting, and if they were tired of it, they said they were not – they should fight yet again; and if we fought fair, they should beat us.[1]

The transition of the Sikh army from an exclusive religious entity to an all-encompassing military outfit, who at its pinnacle challenged the British supremacy, is an historian's delight. The very fact that the same Sikh soldier later on transformed into a most trusted ally of the British military, makes this transition all the more interesting, requiring additional introspection, research and analysis.

The military evolution of the Sikhs can be traced back to the religious bigotry of Muslim Emperor Aurangzeb. This religious persecution against the Sikhs though witnessed a relative decline during Aurangzeb's era, the military rise of Sikhs was an important milestone of the times. The rise of Sikhism as a religion and later as a State was not against a particular religion or caste but was largely guided by an urge to suppress the oppressor. Corroborating above, Griffin in his work on Ranjit Singh posits that, 'had the Moslems been tolerant to the Hindus there would have been no Sikhism'. Along similar lines another historian quotes:

If the mighty Mughal government had left the Sikhs in peace, free to sing their hymns and to develop their *langars*, it is quite probable that Sikhism would have remained a comparatively obscure provincial cult. Persecution brought it to the stage of Indian history. Through blood, sweat and tears it walked to political power: the peaceful sect established by Guru Nanak developed into the invincible Khalsa.[2]

Military prowess alone would not have provided the credibility and recognition to the respective military bands. Coalescence under a political entity was imperative for the leaders of these bands. The arrival of Ranjit Singh provided a much-needed political legitimacy to the Sikhs, which was instrumental in changing the dynamics of military and polity in the Punjab. He merged the strong political will with the available military machine and carved out an unparalleled identity for the Sikhs and, 'found the military array of his country a mass of horseman, brave indeed but ignorant of war as an art and left it mustering 50,000 disciplined soldiers, 50,000 well-armed yeomanry and militia and more than 300 pieces of canon for the field'.[3] The establishment of Sikh state by Ranjit Singh was not based on the premise of any divine or heredity rights. He was a self-made man and the monarchy forged by him was purely based on his personal courage and prowess:

The popular obedience is willingly given to the great captain, the leader of men, who seems in the dazzled eyes of the people to embody the spirit and glory of the country. But the glamour is personal to the man on the throne and does not transfigure his heirs and successors. Then the throne founded by genius is seen to be a poor, tawdry thing, on the steps of which stand a crowd of greedy, unscrupulous parasites, who have no thought but of enriching themselves at the expense of the people. Discipline and obedience give place to conspiracy and revolt; enthusiasm is succeeded by contempt.[4]

Unfortunately, his successors were not able to provide a continued strong political leadership to the military might and the state soon withered away and dismembered itself. The mercurial rise and fall of Sikh kingdom were phenomenal. 'The Sikh monarchy was Napoleonic in the suddenness of its rise, the brilliancy of its success, and the completeness of its overthrow.'[5] True to the above, the successors of Ranjit Singh were not able to follow the ethics and traditions propounded and implemented by Ranjit Singh and soon fell into the vices of vile, conspiracy and greed. The military might of Khalsa strong as it was, found itself orphaned without a strong political and military leader. The army was uncontrollable and the resultant political vacuum did not help. With his military and political acumen, Ranjit Singh was also alive to the advantages of symbiotic relationship with the

British and the relationship was mutually beneficial to both. Ranjit Singh continued to respect this relationship throughout his lifetime, even at the cost of antagonising his powerful generals and a host of foreign military advisers. Though many of his generals and military chieftains were not happy with the closeness of Ranjit Singh with the British but the charisma and personality of Maharaja had kept these generals within the realms of obedience.

Immediately after the demise of Ranjit Singh, these generals found their voices and an opportunity to derive much desired freedom from the policy directions given by the erstwhile Maharaja. The process of military development was completely stalled after the demise of Ranjit Singh. With political leadership being weak, the soldiers started their machinations with the respective political masters, who happened to be too many. The services of the army started being auctioned to the highest bidder, who could pay better wages and spoils of the loot. It was in the middle of this total treachery, plunder and disloyalty that the Sikhs had entered into a war with the English and the English were quite confident of the victory against the rag tag military of Khalsa:

Unwarned by precedents, uninfluenced by example, the Sikh nation has called for war, and on my word, Sirs, they shall have it with a vengeance. The rebellion of Raja Sher Singh, followed by his army, the rebellion of Sardar Chatter Singh with Durbar army under his command, the state of troops and of the Sikh population everywhere, have brought matters to that crisis, I have for months been looking for, and we are now not on the eve but in the midst of war with the Sikh nation and the kingdom of Punjab. I have drawn the sword and have thrown away the scabbard, both in relation to the war immediately before us, and to the stern policy which that war must precede and establish.[6]

The brave and gallant army of the Khalsa fought valiantly but was led treacherously with greed and vile by its most corrupt and coward generals and thus lost the wars and the state. As a result, this brave army was disbanded and Punjab state annexed by the British. The rise and the subsequent fall of the Sikh state do not provide any significant political lessons but the military lessons are very hard to miss by an adept eye. With an exception of a brief political expediency during the times of Ranjit Singh, the story of Sikhs is essentially and only about military. The British were witness to this military prowess of the Sikhs very intimately during the two Anglo Sikh wars and they were deeply impressed by the attitude and the exploits of Sikhs during these two wars. The British realised that the Sikhs happen to be the best fighting material available in the country at that point of time and a careful handling of this resource had the potential to produce immense dividends for the British:

As military materials they are admirable. Possessing strong individuality, inured to hard labour and exposure from their early youth – leading a healthy open-air life in their hamlets and villages. They combine a fine physique with energy, due to climate, occupation and the Northern strain in their character, the legacy of the old stock from which they sprang. Freedom from the trammels of superstitious caste ceremonies as inculcated by their spiritual guides, the stern and warlike nature of the iron creed of Guru Govind, the baptism of fire through which the nation passed in its early days, and the coherent rule of Ranjit Singh have undoubtedly stamped them with a national character.[7]

The short history of Sikhs had produced another very pertinent lesson for the British. The British had realised that it is the battle which brings out the best in the Sikhs. The martial nature of the Sikhs withers during peace time and it is during the times of crises that the inherent warrior in a Sikh starts dominating:

War is a necessary stimulus for Sikhism. In the reaction of peace, the Sikh population dwindles. It was in the struggle with Islam, during the ascendancy of Ranjit Singh, in the two wars against the British, and after in the Mutiny, when the Sikhs proved our loyal allies, that the Khalsa was strongest.[8]

The development of a relationship between the Sikhs and the British has also been claimed to have nurtured the ideal of Sikhism. It has also been brought out that had Sikhs not been enrolled into the Indian Army, the relatively new religion and society might not have been able to retain its distinct characteristics. It was with these views about the Sikhs in general and Jats in particular, that the British had gradually started looking at a grand role for Punjab in the British Army. The capitulation of Punjab had brought the British in direct contact with the lawless tribal regions of Afghanistan. With the buffer state of Punjab not being there any more, the period was also marked by the first ever delineation of the so called boundary between India and Afghanistan.

To man this new frontier, there was an immediate need of a force, which was loyal to the British. As a result, the period immediately after the Anglo Sikh wars, witnessed raising of several new Corps, which were primarily manned by the troops of the erstwhile Sikh army. The Punjab Irregular Force was the first such force which was raised in 1851. This force owed its Irregular suffix to the fact that this force was outside the jurisdiction of the Regular British East India Company and the Presidency armies of the three Presidencies of Bengal, Bombay or Madras. In order to facilitate a decentralised decision-making process, this irregular force was placed under the command and control of the British Chief Magistrate of Punjab, known as the President of the Board of Administration from 1849, a designation which was changed to the Chief Commissioner from 1853. In sync with the name of Irregular, the soldiers of these entities were not supposed to be regular soldiers and leaned more towards the definition of 'guerrilla force'. The force was re-designated as Punjab Frontier Force in 1865 and on the eve of the Great War was rechristened as Frontier Force.

The role of the army during the first Indian War of Independence in 1857, had necessitated a complete review of the recruitment process. On the other hand, the role played by troops from Punjab in quelling the rebellion was much appreciated. The overwhelming ascendancy of martial races enjoyed by the Bengal Army over others in the overall composition was one of the derived lessons of the Mutiny. 'The Mutiny was the Bengal Army's homogeneous fusion into one huge body of soldiers.'[9] During and immediately after the Mutiny, the elements of the disbanded Khalsa Army being readily available, were recruited at a much faster pace, which in turn had helped British quell the flames of rebellion. In 1857, the Punjabis constituted about 44 per cent of the Bengal Army and the Punjab Frontier Force, but only a quarter of the entire armed forces.

Due to the massive recruitment of Punjabis immediately after the Mutiny, by June 1858 the composition of the Bengal Army was flipped totally and out of the total 80,000 native troops in the Bengal Army, 75,000 were Punjabis. The recruitment from Punjab and Nepal increased so much in the immediate aftermath of the mutiny that by 1893, the Punjab, and Nepal jointly represented almost 44 per cent of the entire Indian armed forces, which had further increased to 57 per cent by 1904. As a result of the domination of troops from Punjab in the overall composition of Indian Army, it was feared that the homogeneous dominance of troops from Punjab, may lead to a repetition of the situation of 1857. To avoid a repeat and also for the purpose of management of boundary issues with Afghanistan, the Viceroy Lord Curzon divided the Punjab province into Punjab and North-West Frontier Province in 1901 and the administration of the newly created province was placed directly under the Government of India.[10]

As far as Sikhs recruitment in Punjab is concerned, the recruiting pattern of Sikhs in Punjab primarily was related two distinct regions of *Majha* and *Malwa*. The entire area between Beas and Ravi rivers was known as *Majha* and included the areas of Amritsar, Taran Taran, Kasur and certain parts of Lahore. When the Punjab was annexed by the British after Anglo Sikh wars, the entire area north of Sutlej River was colloquially started to be known as *Majha*. However, within this tract the distinctions between regions falling between different rivers in the area, was known as *Doabs* or the area between the two rivers. It has been officially recorded that, 'the *Majha*, though a small tract of country, gives more men to the service than any other portion of the Sikh recruiting ground. The men of the *Majha* rank equally with those of the Malwa as the best Sikh material for military purposes.'[11]

For recruitment purposes, the existing definition of the Malwa region was used by the British recruiting officers, as per which, all the area lying in the south of Sutlej River was defined as Malwa. The area included the districts of Ferozepore, Ludhiana, and the native states of Patiala, Nabha, Jhind, and Maler Kotla. The area known as Malwa was the most fertile ground for recruitment due to being the largest sub-region of Punjab and hence was adequately addressed by the recruiting officers nominated for the purpose. In addition, since the region was also the primary catchment area for a host of native states, the competition to get the best stock of recruits by both the agencies was a norm rather than an exception. Besides competition, the youth of the region had a choice of selecting an option of serving in the Native State or in the then Indian Army. These conditions of willingness and availability of Punjabi youth, fully supported by the policy decisions was an ideal prelude to the recruitment from Punjab preceding and during the Great War.

CONSTRUCT OF MARTIAL RACES

Prior to the onset of hostilities of the Great War, the proportion of Punjabis in the standing army of the time had already reached very high. Due to massive skew, Punjab was a major contributor in the war efforts of the empire during the Great War. A number of reasons, explanations and hypothesis have been put forward by various eminent historians to explain and justify the exponential increment in the recruitment from Punjab of the time with the progress of the war:

A total of 14,40,437 Indians were recruited for the British Empire's war effort between August 1914 and December 1919. Of the total number of Indians recruited, 4,80,000 men, of whom 4,08,000 served as combatants, came from Punjab. By the war's end, Punjab had provided over forty per cent of the total number of Indian combatants and nearly one-third of all Indian recruits. Most of these Punjabi soldiers were recruited from the semi-literate peasant-warrior classes of North India in accordance with the 'martial race' theory.[12]

As far as recruitment into the Indian Army was concerned, when compared to the population size at that point of time, Punjab was ahead of all other provinces. The state during the First World War supplied more than 40 per cent of all the combatants, both enlisted and mobilised and out of all the recruits, Punjab alone supplied almost one-third of the Indian recruits. The state was also at the forefront by supplying more than one-third of the total numbers who served. These efforts of the state, besides justifying the concept of Martial Race theory was duly recognised as well. 'When we remember that the province contains only a thirteenth part of the population, and of the area of India, and that all the provinces were avowedly doing their best, the Punjab may well be proud of its effort.'[13]

A comparison of the contribution from Punjab, into the Indian Army, the primary catchment area of British recruitment during the First World War underscores the pre-dominance of the state. In the British districts of Punjab, one man in every 26 male residents of the district recruited himself; whereas the corresponding figure for the rest of Indian was 150, leaving the state just behind the contribution from the United Kingdom itself.

TABLE 4: PUNJAB: POPULATION *VS* MOBILISATION[14]

State	Total Male Population	Numbers Mobilised	One Man in Every
United Kingdom	2,27,00,000	61,54,000	3.5
British Districts (Punjab)	1,09,92,000	4,15,000	26
Indian States (Punjab)	23,23,000	65,000	33
Rest of India	14,70,00,000	9,77,000	150

In the state of Punjab during the course of the Great War, two types of agencies were functioning for the recruitment. Central Recruiting Board, being responsible for direct enlistment and the divisional recruiting officers, who were generally working at the respective Divisions. Another peculiar arrangement of the time was the establishment of Depots of the Regiments in the heartland of the province. These depots served as the motivational centres for the Punjabi populace. The establishment of these Depots was also responsible for providing a massive fillip to the recruitment trends:

It was an accepted maxim of all the best authorities that the best possible recruiter in the wavering districts was the newly joined recruit. It was a common experience to find a youth who had but a short while before been hardly prevailed upon to leave his village, coming back full of enthusiasm and self-esteem, and persuading his friends to follow his example.[15]

The establishment of Regimental Depots in hither-to-fore inexperienced districts in the recruitment, were instrumental in providing a very positive glimpse of military life, which in turn positively impacted recruitment. It was an ideal opportunity for the young men of the region to first-hand witness military life. Over a period of time and spread due to word of mouth, these Depots slowly turned into an ideal destination for the:

Shy young men and over fond parents to see for themselves what life in a regiment meant, before committing themselves or their sons to it. It also meant that for the first few months of their service, recruits were able to pay frequent visits to their homes, and to exhibit to their relations what regular exercise and a soldier's diet could do in the way of converting a country bumpkin into a well set up young man.[16]

An analysis of the religious denomination of the recruits supplied by the Punjab state in the Great War also provides certain very interesting analytics. Prior to the commencement of the Great War, the Sikhs contribution in terms of recruitment of soldiers at levels was much above their proportionate share, which was at the cost of the share of the other two major communities in the province. During the course of the war, situation changed and the number of Sikhs, Hindus and Mohammedans in the combatant ranks multiplied by more than 2.5, 4 and 5.5 times respectively, thereby providing an edge to the hitherto unrepresented communities. But at the onset of hostilities of the Great War, Punjab continued to be the leading provider of the recruits. 'At the outbreak of the war, it was found that the Punjab supplied about half of the Indian soldiers in the Indian Army. In 1914, of the total 1,096 Infantry companies, 431 companies were wholly Punjabi and 221 were partly Punjabi.'[17]

Within the overall denomination of Punjabis, the Sikhs were overtly dominating in the representation from Punjab in the Indian Army. The contribution of Sikhs in the overall composition of the Indian Army, throughout the Great War has been phenomenal and the recruitment trends continued to witness a constant upward trajectory, during the course of the Great War.

The overwhelming dominance of the Sikhs can be attributed to many reasons, but primarily due to the reason that the population percentages of Hindus and Muslims as such were higher than of Sikhs. As the war progressed the recruitment pattern gradually shifted towards the other communities, while Sikhs continued to contribute more than their share. As a result of these, the overall representation of the

TABLE 5: RECRUITMENT OF SIKHS DURING THE GREAT WAR[18]

Total obtained during the first year (31 July 1915)	12,293
Total obtained during the second year (31 July 1916)	14,973
Total obtained during the third year (31 July 1917)	16,234
Total obtained during the fourth year (31 July 1918)	31,265
Total obtained during the fifth year (30 November 1918)	14,160
Total	88,925

Sikhs in the Indian Army witnessed a steady decline throughout the duration of the war. The decline of the percentage of Sikh soldiers over a period of four years was in two-digit percentage terms. Thus, while on 'the 1st January 1915, the Sikh soldiers were 39.6 per cent while at the end of the war they were 26 per cent'.[19] The concept of Martial races, which initially was meant for Sikhs only in the Punjab, had gradually widened the scope for inclusion of other races in the concept, leading to more Muslims getting recruited in the later phases of the war.

TABLE 6: PERCENTAGE SHARE OF DIFFERENT COMMUNITIES FROM PUNJAB IN THE INDIAN ARMY[20]

	Mohammedans	*Hindus*	*Sikhs*
Combatants in the Indian Army on 1 Jan. 1915	38.2 per cent	22.2 per cent	39.6 per cent
Combatants recruited during 1915-18	55.4 per cent	22.6 per cent	22 per cent
Total Share	51.4 per cent	22.6 per cent	26 per cent

The contribution of Sikhs in the Indian Army was overwhelming, but the similar trend was evident in the Imperial Services also. As per an estimate, on 1 January 1918, the Sikhs were forming approximately 13 per cent of the Imperial Service Troops. When we juxtapose this figure against another fact that Patiala district in Punjab sent the highest number of Punjabis in the war, an enviable figure of 37,020 men, it becomes fair to assume that Sikhs contributed equally predominantly in the Imperial Services as well. With an excess of

6,000 troops of Imperial Services contributing in the First World War, the domination of Sikhs was absolute.

The concept of general economic betterment, the upward trajectory of social mobility along with the standing of the community in the overarching nomination of 'Martial Race', were instrumental in the recruitment of Sikhs in large numbers in the Indian Army. A perpetual indemnity against frequent famines and rising debts have also been credited by the historians as responsible for the massive tilt in the Sikh recruitment in the Indian Army of the time. Chaudhry Hameed in his seminal essay on Punjabi Recruitment in the First World War, posits that the concept of *izzat* was equally, if not more responsible in sustaining the recruitment drive through the Punjabi heartland during the Great War. This concept of *izzat* was of the individual, family and in the larger framework transcended to the clan. This concept, when linked with the then prevalent social system in Punjab, the understanding becomes relatively easy. The Punjabi villages were predominantly based upon particular castes and in majority of cases the names of the respective villages were based upon the caste. The phenomenon of *izzat*, therefore, transformed into a primemover for recruitment and the subsequent retention of Sikh soldiers in the army.

Corroborating the above, as a precursor to the present work, I conducted an extensive survey about the compelling reasons for the Indian youth of the time to get recruited into the British Army. A relative overwhelming percentage of respondents (48.5 per cent) concluded that pecuniary considerations were the main influencers, which swayed the decision of the youth of the time to get recruited into the British Army of the time. The second most influencer as assessed by the respondents towards swaying the decision towards recruitment was the Martial Race considerations (at 24.6 per cent). The Cast & Clan factors along with other non-specified factors were considered by the respondents as the third most important influence for recruiting into the British Army (26.9 per cent). It can, therefore, be posited that more than 50 per cent of the respondents attributed the recruitment trends of Punjab populace to the Martial Race concept and the cast/clan dimensions:

Only certain ethnic and religious groups – such as the Pathans, Dogras, Jats, Garhwalis, Gurkhas and Sikhs, among others – were deemed fit to fight; incidentally, these were men from rural backgrounds who had traditionally been *'loyal'* to the government. Various strands – from Victorian interest in physiognomy and Darwinism to indigenous notions of caste and political calculation – combined to form this elaborate pseudo-scientific theory. Forged in the aftermath of the Sepoy Uprising of 1857, it was enormously influential and shaped the formation of India's armed forces.[21]

Though responsible for the infamous Jallianwala Bagh massacre which killed hundreds of innocent civilians in 1919, credit for the massive scale recruitment in the Army from Punjab during the Great War, is also attributed to Lieutenant-Governor Michael O'Dwyer, the head of the government in Punjab from 1913 to 1919. The period of governorship of O'Dwyer broadly coincides with the First World War. The modus operandi of Michael O'Dwyer included formally addressing a series of well attended large gatherings and making repetitive emotional appeals to the rural populace in different cities, regions and communities to stimulate the recruitment. In these meetings O'Dwyer would repeatedly and deliberately invoke comparisons:

Rawalpindi, Jhelum, Rohtak, and Ludhiana are reminded of their own high reputation, of the valour of their men and the spirit of their women; it is only necessary to urge them to endure to the end. Karnal, Lahore, Gujranwala, Ferozepore are reminded of bygone traditions of bravery; they are urged to emulate the best districts and the neighbouring States. Backward tracts and tribes are contrasted with their more spirited neighbours. The 'educated' are implored not to lag behind Bengal. In one case the number of casualties is dwelt on as an incentive to brave avengers; in another their slightness in comparison with the toll of fever and plague is brought out. Battle honours are held out as bait for some: rewards of pay or land for others.[22]

Michael O'Dwyer compared the recruitment statistics in these public gatherings and used to maintain that it's only by recruitment in the army that one's clan's and the society's *izzat* can be maintained or rather earned. He once scorned the people of Gujranwala in 1917 about the very poor statistics of the district as compared to other districts of the state in providing manpower for the war effort:

Your neighbours in Gujarat, Amritsar and Gurdaspur will point the finger of scorn at Gujranwala, and say, 'that is the district which stood aloof in the Great War when we gave our manhood in tens of thousands to fight for the Sarkar'. It will be said that you were either too cowardly or too well off to do your duty. If those things are said, and they certainly will be said, what Izzat will you have with Government or your neighbors? You have still a chance – a last chance – of making good the lost ground, of coming into line with your neighbors and of redeeming the good name of your clan, your race and your district.[23]

System of Recruitment

Till the effects of First World War started manifesting in terms of tremendous strain on the existing recruiting system and as a result certain major changes were envisaged and implemented, the age-old regimental system of recruitment had stood the test of time. The system had been able to supply the recruits required by the battalions as vacancies or special recruitment drives. All the battalions or sub-units of the Indian Army who participated in Gallipoli, had all men recruited through the Regimental system. In Punjab, each Regiment of the Indian Army of the time had one Recruiting Officer, usually posted at a central place of the catchment areas for the regiment. The headquarters for PMs, for example was at Rawalpindi, but the Recruiting Officer or his assistants had the liberty to examine potential recruits at any other place within the catchment areas also, provided the station had a Civil Surgeon posted, in order to carry out the medical inspection of the recruits. Generally, each Recruiting Officer was assisted by two Assistant Recruiting Officers and explicit instructions existed as to the time of employment of these assistants, so as to equally divide the period of summer and winter months between both. The role of these officers was very important, both for the Regiment and themselves in their personal capacity. While the officers provided a good recruit to his class of battalions, it also afforded an opportunity for them to visit the catchment areas of the battalions, meet pensioners of the regiment and professionally develop themselves. The service with the recruiting parties offered all these to the officers of the battalion:

To a keen young officer who takes an interest in his men and who is fond of camp life, these tours are both profitable and enjoyable. He obtains first-hand knowledge of the country and the tribes, he meets the influential men of those tribes, and he learns from pensioners and others who come to see him, other aspects of regimental concerns than those to which he has been accustomed. In cases of doubtful verification, and it may be here remarked that 'verification rolls' are not always dependable, he can, with judicious examination of the village 'Patwaris' books, obtain conclusive proof as to the status and tribe of any man on whom suspicion rests. Indian soldiers always appreciate the fact that an officer has visited their country, has probably stayed in their village and has received hospitality from their kinsmen. This will always in future be a bond of union between the officer and his men. If the right stamp of young officer is sent as Assistant Recruiting Officer, it is both an advantage to himself and to his Regiment.[24]

These officers were therefore carefully chosen at the Regimental levels. The Recruiting Officers and the Regimental Parties worked in unison to get the best available recruits for their respective regiments. The exact requirement in terms of numbers of recruits to be selected or any other specific requirements of the battalions were communicated by the Regimental Parties to the office of the Recruiting Officer in advance. The system in vogue required dispatch of Regimental Parties only on receipt of confirmation from the office of the Recruiting Officer. There were explicit directions on the modalities of dispatch of recruiting parties. 'The party should be given an advance of pay, they are entitled to an advance of two months' pay and sufficient funds to cover all recruiting expenses, which will include railway fares, subsistence of recruits, Sarai charges, etc.'[25]

The Regimental Parties were mandated to operate in only those tehsils, where the members of these parties belonged. They were also supposed to be from same tribes / castes from which the prospective recruits were to be enlisted. The experience of the enlistment through the recruiting parties has been that, a good stock of recruits cannot be recruited if the recruiting parties worked outside their districts or tehsils. The scales of enlistment for each member of the recruiting party required each member to round off to an 'all round average is about 7 or 8 "passed" recruits to each recruiter, for one month's work'.[26]

In spite of these directions, the members of the recruiting parties used to get recruits for enlistment who suffered from diseases, were medically unfit, under age or belonged to different castes / tribes as mandated. In such cases, Regimental Parties was supposed to maintain the men brought for enlistment at their own expenses, if the Recruiting Officer declared these individuals as unfit for enlistment due to a variety of reasons. As a further deterrent, the Regimental Parties were also denied railway warrants for the railway journeys of the individuals, who have been declared unfit, thereby making these parties to even pay for back home journey of these 'unfit individuals'. For the subsistence of recruits selected for enlistment, but not yet moving to the Recruiting Officer, the responsibility was of the recruit only. The subsistence by the Regimental Parties, of the individual selected for enlistment, started from the day of journey to the Recruiting Officer. An average expenditure of three and a half to four annas per day was considered sufficient for the subsistence of a recruit.

On the date fixed for their inspection the Recruiting Officer examines the recruits brought up by the recruiting party, rejects those whom he considers unsuitable and sends the remainder for their medical examination. After the medical inspection the Recruiting Officer completes I. A. F. K.- 164 in respect to each 'passed' recruit, settles the account for each 'rejected' recruit on the same form, provides the 'passed' recruits and their escort with a railway warrant to the regimental headquarters and the 'rejected' recruits with warrants to the nearest station from their homes.[27]

To cater for wastage due to rejections on the basis of medical and other grounds by the Recruiting Officer, the Regimental Parties were mandated to get generally between one and a half times to double of the existing requirement. After taking out the men not selected by the medical officer, only the bare minimum number of men were left, which were more or less required by the concerned battalion. If any case, a greater number of men were available for going to the battalion then originally required, then only the required strength of men was dispatched to the battalion and balance of the men usually remained as *umeedwars* (applicants) for the concerned battalion / regiment till the occurrence of vacancies in that particular unit. In these cases, normally the CO of the concerned battalion informed the Recruiting officer about the addresses of the *umeedwars* for the subsequent action. The Recruiting Officer then coordinated the movement of these men from their residences to the Recruiting Officer and further movement to the battalion. These *umeedwars* were not supposed to get any travel concessions to reach Recruiting Officer again on occurrence of vacancies in the battalion and had to pay for their respective fare. Sometimes it happened that a smaller number of recruits were available then required in the battalion due to reasons of medical rejections and less availability of recruits due to sowing or harvesting seasons. Under these circumstances, one representative of the Regimental Parties was sent with the recruits selected to the battalion and balance of the recruiting party was again sent to the catchment areas for selecting more men for enlistment.

Generally, fairs were considered as suitable and convenient places to get recruits for the enlistment, and the recruiting parties under normal circumstances used to visit these places for selection. For the purpose, a calendar of annual or seasonal fairs being conducted in the various parts of the catchment areas was also percolated to the battalions and the Recruiting Officer to plan for movement accordingly. In order to provide a rough yardstick to the Recruiting Officers, a list comprising the various tehsils of Punjab was mapped with the potential 'quality and quantity' of recruitment. The value of each tahsil of the district was differentiated into six categories of Very Good, Good, Fair, Bad, Very Bad and Indifferent, depending upon the aptitude of the local populace to serve in the Indian Army.

Again, the recruiting parties were adequately warned to not overtly rely on the fairs only, for selection of recruits. Due to the short window of interaction at the fair, the recruiting party was not able to exercise due discretion in the selection of the person, hence recruiting parties were supposed to go to the respective village after the fair and then verify the antecedents of the shortlisted men, make more inquiries and satisfy themselves in totality prior to finalising the shortlisted men for enlistment. Sometimes the personal of the battalions who were on leave, also used to get recruits for enlistment as *umeedwars*. The system in vogue, in fact motivated leave parties to get recruits for enlistment. But the onus of maintenance and subsistence of these recruits till the time they were selected or in case they were not selected, rested on the leave party. 'As the railway fares of "rejected" recruits who are brought up for enlistment by furlough and leave men (to regimental headquarters or the Recruiting Office) cannot be recovered from Government, it has to be paid by either the Regiment, the' rejected' recruit, or the man who has brought him up for enlistment.'[28]

This system over a period of time, developed into a well-oiled system which catered for the requirements for the Indian Army units. It will be appreciated that, the system could have worked only for the time, the battalions were in India and not deployed on active services for a very long period of time. The system came under severe stress, when it had to supply recruits to the battalions deployed in active service in Gallipoli. In addition, the sheer number of casualties suffered by these battalions in Gallipoli almost made it impossible for the Recruiting Officer to select personal for active service and the system was soon overwhelmed by the demand of reinforcements.

An analysis of the recruitment carried out by both the sources highlights the recruitment by both the agencies. For instance, in 1905-6, the Recruiting Officers had recruited 10,275 recruits whereas for the same period the Regimental Parties accounted for 13,814 recruits for their respective regiments, thereby bringing a total of 24,089 recruits to the Indian Army during the period. The comparable figures for the period 1913-14, however, tell a different tale. The percentage of recruits, handled by the Recruiting Officers reduced to almost 70 per cent of the figures of 1905-6, whereas the strength recruited by the Regimental Parties reduced to almost 50 per cent of the comparable figures. In 1913-14, the Recruiting Parties recruited only 7,517 rmen and the Regimental Parties 7,686 recruits. The effects of this reduction snowballed into a major crisis for the Indian Army when the recruiting process came under severe stress in view of the massive number of casualties suffered by the Indian battalions in the initial phases of the World War.

With the Battalions themselves being in active service, the Regimental Parties could not be dispatched to recruit youngsters. The non-availability of Regimental Parties in turn had an adverse effect on the efforts of the Recruiting Officers, as over a period of time the Recruiting Officers had also become dependent on the Regimental Parties to fetch suitable recruits for the respective battalions. Thus, a vicious cycle started, where in the respective Depot, battalions were denuded of available manpower due to the dispatch of reinforcements overseas. With the Depots being no more in a position to spare manpower for the Regimental Parties, the recruiting strength reduced over a period of time which in turn had further debilitating effect on the process of dispatching of reinforcements to the battalions indulged in action overseas.

In the later part of the Great War to facilitate the extensive recruitment, an extensive arrangement of Provincial and the District Recruiting Committees was established in 1917 and a quota was fixed for each district and province to be met. Though this system has been alleged to have similarities with conscription but due to 'variety of legal and administrative tools to contain dissent, there was no serious unrest during the war'. The scheme was aptly named as Territorial Recruitment and replaced the class system of recruitment existing till now. Each division in the state was posted with a Divisional Recruiting Officer and a corresponding authority at the district level was christened as District Assistant Recruiting Officer. At the state level an agency to coordinate the efforts of these officers, known as Provincial Recruitment Board, also came into being. The mandate of this board was 'to assess the amount of manpower which the province as a whole and each district individually might be expected to contribute and thus an attempt was made to adjust the burden of war equally over all classes'.[29] The results of a coordinated and well-established mechanism to recruit soldiers from the Indian dominion were very promising and by 1918:

All these commitments had ballooned the 1914 army to 3 Cavalry and 13 Infantry Divisions, a force larger than the combined total raised by all the dominions. To do this India had enlisted 8,77,068 combatants and 5,63,369 non-combatants in support units. It was a remarkable war effort wrung out of a country rich in little but manpower. It was also one that was relegated rapidly to the historical attic.[30]

INCENTIVISING THE RECRUITMENT AND RETENTION

Due to the peculiar recruitments of enlistment from India, it was a sincere endeavour from the British that the enlistment terms were as favourable as possible to the potential recruits. This was particularly more evident in the recruitment post the mutiny of 1857. The incentives to the Indian recruits were pitched at two distinct levels. An initial incentive aimed to make recruitment into the army as luring as possible, whereas the subsequent incentives aimed to motivate the ranks to conform to the standards expected out of them. The quantity and quality of incentives also proportionally increased with the length of service put in by the men in uniform.

An initial example of introduction of incentives can be referred back to the concept of grant of 'Good Conduct Pay' introduced in 1837. A clean personal conduct sheet for a continuous period of two years would make a person eligible for an extra rupee per month after sixteen years of service, an amount which was doubled to two rupees additionally per month after twenty years of service. This criterion was further relaxed in 1877, when an obedient Sepoy was eligible for a grant of an extra rupee per month after three years of service, two additional rupees after nine years of service and an additional three rupees per month after fifteen years of service.

The pay scales of senior Indian soldiers were enviable. A Havildar in the Indian Infantry Battalion was entitled to a pay scale of fourteen rupees a month. Similarly, four senior Subadars of an Infantry Battalion each earned not less than a hundred rupees a month, a very handsome figure by the standards of those days. No other profession in the country offered this kind of influence, honour and financial incentives. Due to these perks and privileges, Indian officers of the Indian Army were quite successful in achieving the recruitment targets. In addition, the promotional prospects were bountiful, coupled with the prospects of the land grants, and incentives for the distinguished performance during the active service.

The pension regulations of 1864, were instrumental in promulgating pension at the full scale of seven rupees a month, after completion of 40 years of service. These regulations also had allowed pension at a reduced scale of four rupees a month if the soldier was rendered invalid after fifteen years of service. The experience during the active service made for a case to reduce the qualifying service to become eligible for full pension. Accordingly, to reduce malingering, the qualifying service for full pension was reduced from forty years to thirty-two years in 1876. 'Even this proved to be too long. Only about one hundred men of the Bengal Army and the Punjab Frontier Force served on to their full pension every year; but about 4,600 – many of them malingerers – left with the benefits due to invalids.'

The promotion to the rank of Indian officer was strictly based on seniority and not on merit. The seniority-based principle definitely helped to maintain discipline in the army. The system also ensured that genuinely interested soldiers stayed in the army and got rewarded for their loyalty by way of promotion. A large number of soldiers who were interested in short-term economic upgradation to ward off immediate danger of economic collapse or to stave off famine, went back home immediately the requirement was met. This used to leave off soldiers who were required to stay in army for longer period due to economic compulsions. The numbers of these soldiers were not large though. 'In 1885, veterans with 20 years' service made up only 3 per cent of the Bengal Infantry and 7 per cent of the Bombay Army. Only in the Madras Army, where 14 per cent of men had served for 20 years or more, was long service at all,' indicating the widespread differential in the reasons and effects of long-term engagement across the various armies in the country. This skewed ratio could also be attributed to the fact that the Bengal Army was frequently deployed in the internal security duties and limited foreign expeditions prior to the First World War, whereas the Madras Army was relatively left out of such opportunities, leading to its soldiers not becoming eligible for incentives and accelerated upgrades due to active service.

Other incentives offered to the soldiers included enhancing the social status of soldiers in the society for their unique contribution. An executive order granting precedence to the soldiers in hearing and disposal of civil suits involving them was promulgated in 1899. The order provided the much needed boost to the perception of military service amongst the rural populace and was instrumental in fast tracking the recruitment drive. The gallantry and sacrifice of Punjabi soldiers in operations even before the Great War had been unparalleled and due recognition of these sacrifices was imperative.

Individual awards though recognised bravery and sacrifice, but a larger message to the society could only be given by due recognition to the society in general and extended family in particular. A series of well thought out initiatives made sure that society at large was aware of these sacrifices, thereby ensuring a wider connect and generating a message for consumption by a wider audience.

The Great War induced further measures to win respect for soldiers. They and their relatives gained preferential treatment in Punjab government appointments; the children of the dead and disabled received free primary education. Those who had marched with the Indian Army were to walk tall when they went back to their villages.[31]

A Punjabi soldier is deeply attached with the land. As discussed earlier, the enlistment strategy of a Punjabi soldier generally revolved around the factor of land. The limited and gradually decreasing per capita land holding has been cited as a major factor in the decision of a soldier and his family to support recruitment. Towards the end of the nineteenth century, the average per capita land holding had reduced to 8 acres. There was no shortage of land, but the land holdings of irrigable land were very limited. A major part of the available land was totally dependent upon unreliable monsoon to support the farming. The once flourishing settlements in the valleys of the Doabs, as obtained in Punjab, had gone dry, resulting in the restriction of the people in the areas watered by the well system. Wells though, a reasonable source of water for the parched land, were labour intensive and the quantity of water extracted was also limited, thereby restricting the area under irrigation.

It was during this time that the British came up with a concept of development of canals for irrigation. With a carefully planned and executed network of distributaries and sub-distributaries, the system soon developed a fancy with the populace of Punjab.

From the 1880s, large tracts were restored to agriculture and repopulated. The lower Chenab Canal was built between 1892 and 1905, and the area watered by the Lower Bari Doab Canal, completed in 1917, was colonised in 1922. The increase in the irrigated area was prodigious. In 1880 there were a little over one million irrigated acres in the Punjab, but by 1917 more than four million were artificially watered.[32]

With mere statistics of the development being overwhelming, within 37 years almost four times increase in the land under irrigation, was a major socio-economic change, which affected the lives of the rural peasantry, a major catchment area for the British Indian Army. Soldiers belonging to the rural heartland of Punjab, like any other soldier, though desired gallantry awards and incentives during the active service, and performed accordingly, but the incentives in the form of parcels of canal irrigated land, happened to be the pinnacle of desires. Though the system of grant of land parcels to the soldiers who distinguished themselves, was in vogue even prior to the development of Canal Colonies and after the Great Mutiny, yet the scale of allotment after the development of Canal Colonies was humongous. Seeing the massive response to the project, in 1911, an order was passed which ensured that every Canal Colony scheme will invariably have the provision for the military personnel. With the provision in place, 'the Canal Colonies were gradually militarised, as the government sought to bind the enlisted classes closer to the Raj'.[33]

The overwhelming representation of troops from Punjab in the Indian Army ensured that the demand for the grants was unending. The officers from the Infantry battalions who were part of the Regimental Parties deputed to recruit soldiers from the heartland of Punjab also mentioned about this high demand, in their reports after completion of the tour. In one such instance, Lt F.A. Jacques of the 14th Sikhs, who also later on served with the battalion at Gallipoli, emphatically talked about the positives of the scheme of land grants and the views of pensioners of the battalion with whom he interacted during the tour,

The old pensioners are very anxious to know whether Government will give them grants of land in the new canal colony when it is opened, and I fear there will be great disappointment unless a certain portion of land is allotted to those who have served the *Sirkar* during the best years of their life. This will do more to make the service popular than anything I can suggest.[34]

In Punjab, the effect of the scheme was very apparent. With the state already leading, in terms of proportion of population enlisted as compared to the rest of India, the share of rewards and distinguished performances in the active service was naturally more with the soldiers from Punjab. With a greater number of claimants for these parcels of land, the competition was accordingly higher as a result of which, 'during and after the Great War, far more land was set aside for soldiers'. The Governor of Punjab reserved almost 1,78,000 acres in the Lower Bari Doab for the men, both officers and soldiers, who had distinguished themselves in various battles. 'For the ordinary Punjab peasant, the unit of allotment is to be 12 and 1/2 acres, but for military pensioners and other special grantees it is to be 25 acres. As regards this, it might be left to Regimental Commanders to distribute some of their grants in half rectangle allotments (12 and 1/2 acres) so as to make provision for a large number of grantees.'[35]

Thus, each officer allottee was entitled to two parcels of land, measuring 25 acres each, whereas a soldier allottee was awarded with one parcel only, measuring same 25 acres. 'Given that the average holding in the Punjab was a mere eight acres, the plots were highly desirable. Between 1919 and 1939, the Punjab Government gave one-third of a million acres of prime irrigated land to military grantees.'[36] In addition to the benefits to the serving soldiers and officers, these land grants served as perfect motivators to other soldiers for distinguishing themselves during the active service. The Canal Colonies also gradually started developing into a collective and distinct military identity. The ties with the Raj, even after retirement of the individual stayed strong and cohesive. With limited opportunities of labour available to cultivate the allotted grant, the grantee had to invariably look towards his extended clan to look after the grant. As a result, the grant besides incentivising the soldier also facilitated the bonding with the Raj of the extended family of the soldier. The land grants in the designated Canal Colonies to the soldiers were an award for the distinguished service. As these awards were granted at the will of the Raj, they stood a very high chance of being revoked also, based on some specific criteria. There were numerous instances of these grants being revoked, on reporting of some specific incidents against the grantee.

In another type of incentivisation for the recruitment, keeping in mind the sudden surge in the requirement of reinforcements due to the onset of hostilities of the Great War, the colonial administration also granted a general amnesty to all the deserters. The Indian Army Order of 19 December 1914 granted a general amnesty to all the deserters. The Army Order permitted all deserters from the Indian

Army, who were in a state of desertion as on 5 August 1914 and who surrender themselves at any place in India on or before 15 January 1915 or at any station outside of India, where there were regular forces on or before 15 February 1915 to join back. The Army Order further promulgated the forfeiture of all service duration prior to the desertion but left open the option of regularisation of the absence period under the conditions of restoration. The general amnesty was not applicable for the recruits who had enrolled themselves in the regular army under any conditions, which were considered as improper.

The effect of these largesses was visible in the recruitment patterns across the entire length and breadth of Punjab. The disproportionate and highly skewed ratios of recruitment from Punjab over the years are a clear indicator of the strong influence of the above and a cumulative effect of considerations of 'Martial Races' theory and economic / administrative incentives.

TABLE 7: PERCENTAGE OF PUNJABI SOLDIERS IN
THE NATIVE ARMY[37]

Year	Total Native Army	Total from Punjab	Per cent of Punjabis
1880	1,37,299	25,810	18.8
1890	1,47,852	30,548	20.7
1900	1,44,095	50,952	35.3
1910	1,76,455	69,458	39.4
1919	8,13,607	3,62,027	44.5
1925	2,19,523	99,113	45.1

During and after the Great Mutiny of 1857, the social composition of the Indian Army witnessed multifarious changes. The recruitment weight had gradually started shifting from higher castes of Awadh towards the Punjab and North-Western Frontier region. In addition, recruitment of lower castes also started manifesting in the recruitment trends. Under the stewardship of Major General Peel, the Secretary of State for War, a Commission was appointed in July 1858, with a mandate, to study the existing structure of the Indian Army and to recommend changes if any in the existing system. The Commission included officers from the forces of the British Crown and from the

East India Company, and it heard evidence from the 47 witnesses in London between August and September 1858.[38]

As the Commission was constituted in the immediate aftermath of the Indian Mutiny, inevitably, the existing and future recruiting strategy of the Indian Army came under severe scrutiny during the meetings of the Commission. The caste factor in the recruitment strategy was discussed animatedly by the proponents of the opposite schools of thought:

Most agreed that less deference should be shown to caste when selecting recruits. Beyond this there was little consensus. Many witnesses wanted the higher castes to be excluded from the army; others believed that they made the best soldiers, and should not be alienated. Some believed Sikhs or Muslims to be the most trustworthy and efficient recruits: others warned that it would be an enormous risk to depend on them.[39]

The Commission though gave wide ranging recommendations with respect to the recruiting strategies but fell short of recommendations as far as castes / regions of India for potential recruits were concerned.

INDIAN INFANTRY ON THE EVE OF GREAT WAR

In a major policy shift, post the mutiny of 1857, the Indian Army promulgated certain checks and balances which impacted the recruitment from Central India, with the Bengal Army getting most affected. The state and predicament of Bengal Army at this stage was aptly summed by Lord Ripon, 'The Bengal Army was a mere fortuitous congeries of regiments, raised in haste, brought together in haste, reduced in haste.'[40] As a result of these paradigm changes, the regional origin of the Indian Infantry battalions witnessed major changes. The four primary catchment areas for recruitment in the Indian Army, accordingly moved up or down in the slider scale. A glance at the state of number of Infantry battalions belonging to different catchment areas, over a period of time actually corroborates the British policy.

As a result of the continuous improvements in the recruiting system, on the eve of the Great War, the Indian Army was much better organised then its earlier *avatars*. The old decrepit system of Presidency Armies having been relegated to oblivion, the Indian Army of the day

TABLE 8: NUMBER OF INFANTRY BATTALIONS BELONGING TO
DIFFERENT REGIONS[41]

Region	1862	1885	1892	1914
Nepal	5	13	15	20
Hindustan East of Yamuna River	28	20	15	15
Punjab & NWFP	28	31	34	57
Madras	40	32	25	11

was a distinctive *Unitary Institution.* As far as the role of this newly crystallised force was concerned, it primarily revolved around domination over the restive region of the North-Western part of the country, with certain secondary tasks to include assistance to the civil authority and also be prepared to move overseas as part of expeditionary forces, if required. As part of the reforms, though a planning body for military operations in the form of Indian General Staff, was conceptualised, it was still in infancy and was not trained or equipped to plan and control the ferocious intensity of operations, the Great War was about to unleash. The scale of devastation and casualties suffered by the Indian battalions during the initial stages of war was unprecedented, thereby making the demand for reinforcements for these battalions singularly unheard of.

The system of depots and reservists, carefully nurtured by the Indian Infantry battalions over a period of time was first to burst under the stress. Indian Infantry battalions were used to carry out recruiting themselves, a system which had stood the test of time as long as casualties were limited. The 'Martial Race' concept was able to sustain the reinforcements of the Indian Army only till when the casualties were limited and the reinforcements were required to be dispatched within the country. The system of reserves and reinforcements carefully nurtured by the battalions was suitable only for operations in the North-West or overseas with limited mandate. The sheer number of casualties suffered by the battalions in the initial phases of the Great War severely tested the system.

In addition, unlike the operations in the North-West, the distances involved from India to the various theaters of operations in the First World War were colossal. The logistics of move of the reinforcements had never been tested before and coupled with the recruitment process taking severe blow, the Indian battalions in the active service started operating with severe deficiencies in man power. The calls for reserves in form of reinforcements were desperate. 'The Indian Army was 1,59,000 strong in 1914, with 35,000 reservists – a figure that turned out to be less impressive than it seemed. It had never been designed for extensive, lengthy, overseas deployments.'[42]

With the Indian Army of the time being a service for life and the qualification service for pension being 25 years, there was hardly a requirement of reservists in excess of the routine wastage. The absolute lack of scarcity of the means of employment outside the domains of the army deterred the men to leave, in spite of hardships. On the one hand, this arrangement provided an Infantry battalion with a trained manpower for the serving life of a soldier, it also provided the soldier and his family monetary security and the much-needed respect in the civil society. But the advent of the Great War changed the situation drastically.

With extensive, lengthy, overseas deployments not witnessing a downward trend throughout the duration of the war, there was an immediate need to find an alternative to the Depot system. The 'Martial Race' theory underwent tweaking and a large number of other classes and castes started getting recruited. During the course of the Great War, 75 new classes were recruited into the Indian Army which adversely affected the domination of Sikhs in the overall composition of the Indian Army. In the aftermath of the Mutiny of 1857, the Bengal Army witnessed complete reorganisation. 'The regiments which had either revolted or been disbanded were replaced by the regiments raised in Punjab, composed of the Sikhs, Dogras, Punjabis and Pathans.'[43] As a result of this repositioning, the number of troops from Punjab witnessed a massive increase, whereas a corresponding decrease in the representation from other areas was witnessed and 'in 1892, the number of Infantry battalions from Punjab was 34 and by 1914 it had increased to 57 while the number of units from Madras decreased from 25 in 1892 to 11 in 1914.'[44]

On the eve of the Great War, there were 51 British Infantry battalions stationed in India with an authorised establishment of 28 officers and 1,008 other ranks with each battalion. Due to the outbreak of hostilities and the subsequent deployment of these battalions into the various theatres across the world, the strength of the British Infantry battalions in India had been reduced by 45. Along with the recommendations of the Indian Retrenchment Committee, the authorised establishment of each Infantry battalion was further reduced.

As far as Indian battalions were concerned, each Indian Infantry battalion was posted with 12 European officers. In addition, there were 17 Indian officers in each Indian Infantry battalion, who held the Viceroy's Commission and the authorised strength of an Indian Infantry battalion was 882 other ranks. British officers of the battalion included CO, Second-in-Command, Adjutant and Quarter Master along with the four Double-Company Commanders and four Double-Company Officers. Indian officers included a Subadar-Major, sixteen Subadars and Jemadars, each responsible for a half-company. In addition, there used to be a mix of followers, both private and public. The system of followers has been discussed in the subsequent part of the book.

The evolution of an Infantry battalion in various armies across the world had followed different trajectories, depending upon a host of factors, peculiar to each country. One thing, however, has bonded these different trajectories with a common factor that the Infantry battalion has remained a primary fighting tactical unit of any army. The building block of a battalion has been the companies. The number of companies in a battalion and the bayonet strength of a company have also evolved over a period of time. With the advent of firepower in terms of Artillery weapons and its integration with Infantry coupled with development in the modes of transportation, it was gradually realised that for better command and control in a fluid battlefield, it is better to reduce the number of companies in an Infantry battalion, which can facilitate better command and control. In spite of major armies in the world transforming to a leaner structure of an Infantry battalion, the British Infantry battalion, till as late as 1912, continued to support an eight company Infantry battalion. 'By 1912, the one European army that had yet to adopt the four-company battalion was that of Great Britain. At a time when German, French and Russian battalions consisted of four large companies, battalions of the British

Army were divided into eight small ones.'[45]

After a number of studies and reports of various committees and in an acknowledgment of the changing environs, the British War Office brought about a major change in the composition of a British Infantry battalion in October 1913. The Infantry battalion was henceforth to comprise of only four companies. These directions, how-ever, were not applicable to the Indian Infantry battalions, whose organisation in the beginning of the First World War, continued to be based on eight companies. With an effective strength 882 other ranks, the Indian Infantry battalions though, were at par with the British Infantry battalions, the bayonet strength of the Infantry battalion, however, was divided into eight companies. Each company of the Indian Infantry battalion comprised on an average of only 120 other ranks.

On the eve of the Great War, though the British Infantry battalions were stabilised under the fresh command and control structure, the Indian Infantry battalions were going to the war with a bulky command and control structure. Just prior to the onset of the Great War, there were ongoing discussions about the actual composition of an Infantry battalion. Since the origin of eight company battalions, this was going to be the first time when the Infantry battalions were going to be actually engaged in large-scale conventional operations. These discussions led to a paradigm shift in the structure of the Infantry battalions. There were some very convincing arguments put forward by the proponents of a four company Infantry battalion:

Owing to the number of men who were always absent from their companies, on specialist or other duties within the Battalion, or were never, even approximately, at full strength. Companies at home were particularly weak when at training, owing to a large number of men being always at recruit drill or recruit's musketry. Abroad, the actual strength of a company at training was seldom more than 80, while at home it was sometimes as low as 20 or 30. It was thus frequently difficult for a company commander to exercise his junior officers and noncommissioned officers, owing to lack of men for them to command.[46]

At the same time the proponents for retention of eight company Infantry battalions contested the issue on the basis that it will be very difficult for a company commander to command a strength of 240 men in operations. Due to these raging discussions, although eight company organisation was maintained, two companies were joined together under one company commander for training purposes and a unique concept of 'Double Company' concept was implemented for Indian Infantry battalions in 1914. The Indian battalions, when landed at Gallipoli in May of 1915, had been organised on the basis of the concept of Double Company.

Another far reaching change implemented in the structure of an Infantry battalion just prior to the World War was the introduction of actual Headquarters and a Headquarter Wing in the Infantry battalion. Till now, though a battalion comprised a Headquarters and four Double Companies, but in actual fact there was no personnel posted with Headquarters. There being no dedicated manpower posted with the Headquarters of an Infantry battalion, the problem at hand had a very important connotation, particularly when the battalions were being mobilised for an active duty outside the country.

Every man of the battalion belonged to a company, whether employed in headquarter duties or not. In peace time there are always many men who do not do duty with a company, such as those who are employed on service with a battalion as a whole, i.e. quartermaster stores personnel, police, sanitary personnel, specialist personnel like machine gunners, signalers, bandsmen and buglers or drummers.[47]

During active operations, since the Headquarters and the companies were invariably dispersed with adequate spatial disconnect, it was not feasible to arrange accommodation and messing arrangements for the personnel required at Headquarters at the respective company location. A need was therefore felt to post personnel to Headquarters, separately from companies and to provide a distinct identity and permanency to the Headquarters.

The war organisation of an Infantry battalion, therefore, now comprised a headquarters, a headquarter wing and four companies. The headquarters comprises only the four headquarter Officers – Commanding Officer, Second-in-Command, Adjutant and Quartermaster. The headquarter wing is divided into four groups, composed of Number 1 Group as Signalers, Number 2 Group as Machine gun personnel, Number 3 Group as Administrative personnel and the Number 4 Group as Band.[48]

The introduction of a Machine Gun section in an Infantry battalion was a significant change, which was going to provide an inherent and dedicated fire support alternative to the CO. This step institutionalized the role and organisation of a Machine Gun section in the Infantry battalion. Prior to this development, the personnel of the section were divided into the Companies and did not have a definite and structured role in the battalion operations. This was very common in the initial stages of the First World War.

As the trench warfare got established in the war, the Machine Gun section also found a very prominent role for itself. The Indian Infantry battalions, earmarked for Gallipoli were to realise this at a great peril at the peninsula. The Machine Gun section assumed such an important role in the trench warfare generally and at Gallipoli particularly that at one point of time; it was also conceived by the War Office to double the number of machine guns in an Infantry battalion from the existing two to four.[49] But with an exponential increase in the number of troops getting mobilised, the production capacity of the guns was not able to catch up with the requirement,[50] and the authorisation of the machine guns to an Infantry battalion continued at the scale of two only, at least during the Gallipoli operations.

Post the Mutiny of 1857, a series of measures were also undertaken to change the composition and recruitment patterns of the Indian Army. The narrative here was slightly complex because though the need for the Indian Army was quite well established, but with the memories of 1857 still fresh in mind, the new regimental system had to be fool proof. Therefore, on the eve of the Great War, changes were not only introduced in the organisation and equipping philosophy of an Infantry battalion, but the composition of the battalions was also impacted. The aim of these changes was to retain the fighting efficiency, while at the same time not allowing a repeat of the situation of 1857.

Broadly speaking, three primary models for the organisation of an Infantry battalion were implemented at different times for the Indian battalions. The foremost and basic model stipulated the mixing of all religion, caste and linguistic biases into a single company. Though the underlying concept and practice of 'General Mixture' was good and offered a number of advantages, but the system suffered from the disadvantage of not being time tested. It was difficult to forecast the prognosis of the adaptation of the model in an actual combat situation. The popular thought of the time was aligned to the fact that the different races if mixed together, 'do not long preserve their distinctiveness; their corners and angles, and feeling and prejudice get rubbed off'. It was believed that over a period of time, the regimental identity would subsume all other identities and biases. With respective identities no more being there, repetition of a mutiny like 1857 was very much possible.

To obviate the recurrence of the situation of 1857, a consensus therefore emerged, to replace the 'General Mixture' system of regimentation with the Class Company system. In this system an entire Company or Companies in a unit were endeavoured to be drawn from different communities, as a result of which the Class Company regiments at the company level, conformed to the identical caste equations. 'The companies therefore mutually competed in military excellence, since the pride of each one reflected that of the community which it embodied.' It was also believed that since the religious and political grievances would not affect a Class Company regiment in a same way as it would affect a Class Company, therefore, in a case of a serious grievance, only a portion of the regiment would be affected. Eden Commission of 1879, had also recommended gradual transformation of 'General Mixture' regiments into Class Company Regiments and by the end of the nineteenth century, generally all the Infantry battalions were based on the 'Class Company' system. The system though generally good, also suffered from some serious drawbacks. It became difficult to employ a complete battalion in internal security duties without offending the sensibilities of some of the Class Companies, one of whom invariably had some soft corner for the rebels. Discipline issues also started to increase disproportionately in some of the Class Companies. Two of the battalions, which were initially deployed as part of the 29th Indian Infantry Brigade, the 69th Punjabis and the 89th Punjabis, were the 'Class Company' battalions.

Out of eight companies in the 89th Punjabis, three companies were Sikhs, three companies of PMs, one company of Rajputs and one company of Brahmans. The peculiar composition created certain apprehensions regarding their employment in the initial phases of employment of the 29th Indian Infantry Brigade at Gallipoli. The apprehension of the senior military hierarchy of Gallipoli campaign bears testimony to the statement. The MEF commander, Ian Hamilton had discussed about this dilemma with Brigadier General Cox, the commander of the 29th Indian Infantry Brigade, 'Cox is not going to take his Punjabi Mohammedans into the fighting area, but will leave them on 'W' Beach. He says, if we were sweeping on victoriously, he would take them on, but that, as things are, it would not be fair to them to do so.'[51] In actual fact, 29th Infantry Brigade did not deploy three PM companies of each of these two battalions before both the battalions were deinducted from the peninsula on 15 May 1915. The Class Companies of PMs in these two battalions were deliberately not employed in any of the operations against the Turks, but rather were kept in reserve. The War Diary of 29th Indian Infantry Brigade also makes a mention that, 'remaining three Companies, 69th Punjabis will remain in reserve in their present position. The 89th Punjabis, less three companies will move back to the rear trenches now held by the 14th Sikhs in line with Brigade Headquarters and will also be in reserve.'[52]

A third type of system, therefore, emerged as a panacea of all problems afflicting the regimentation issues of the Indian Army of the time, the 'Class Regiments'. The Class Regiments were downright configured on a single caste basis. In a Class Company Regiment, the Companies used to be caste based, but in a Class Regiment, the entire Regiment was caste based. Out of the battalions which took part in Gallipoli, 14th Sikhs was a Class Regiment, whereas two Punjabi battalions were Class Company regiments as discussed above. Religion and caste-based differences in a Class Company Regiment were not good for regimentation, but the same between two Class Regiments were perfectly acceptable from the point of view of maintenance of supremacy of the Raj. The Class Regiments ensured that the respective social identities on a larger scale were merged and overlapped with the regimental identities as a result of which the stronger identities were forged and these battalions performed very well in the operations.

A homogeneous regiment was also more of a known quantity than a class company unit during civil unrest, for its simple composition was a ready index of its reliability in the event of an internal disturbance. Jealousy between different companies might interrupt the working of a class company unit;

but tension between different class regiments was useful to the Raj, since it caused few discipline problems and hampered mutinous combinations.[53]

The system in vogue for recruitment during those days also favoured the Class Regiment system. The senior soldiers of the regiment used to get their own kith and kin to be recruited in the class regiments. The system worked out to mutual benefits for all three stakeholders in the process, with the regiments getting fit recruits belonging to the same caste with known antecedents, the recruiting party used to get respect and influence by getting greater number of fit recruits and the families of the recruits also used to have a sense of gratitude and attachment with the Raj. These kinships induced networks worked to a great advantage to the soldiers of the Indian Army in the lonely trenches of Gallipoli and were a source of much needed psychological support.

Based on the intake patterns, the matrix for promotion in these regiments also differed. The Class Regiments followed a system wherein the promotion was based on the overall seniority list in the battalion, whereas in a Class Company Regiment, the seniority was based on the vacancies in the respective companies. The system by virtue of its composition provided faster promotional avenues in the class regiments as vacancies were calculated overall for the battalion, but the same was not true for Class Company regiments where vacancies were strictly company based. In spite of these advantages, the Class Regiments, in the views of the senior British military hierarchy suffered from some fundamental flaws:

By 1914, 52 of the 136 battalions in the Indian Army belonged to Class Regiments and 84 to the Class Company ones. Homogeneous regiments did have one slight disadvantage. It could be difficult for British officers to discover what was happening in the ranks, since men of a single community were unlikely to inform on one another. A conspiracy was therefore easier to foment and more difficult to detect.[54]

The system slowly and steadily caught the fancy of the senior British military hierarchy. The system was much better than the earlier systems. The system stood the test of time in the First World War, wherein the Class Regiments performance was much better than the Class Company based regiments. From 1864 to 1897, there was a steady increase in the Class Regiments at the expanse of 'Class Company' and 'General Mixture' battalions. The recruitment in Punjab during the period was also accordingly distinctly divided into two classes and fed the two different types of units as existing in the Indian Army of the time, the Class Regiments and Class Company Regiments.

TABLE 9: INTERNAL STRUCTURE OF BENGAL INFANTRY REGIMENTS FROM 1864 TO 1897[55]

Composition	1864	1883	1890	1891	1893	1897
General Mixture	20	-	-	-	-	-
Class Company Regiments	16	32	43	39	23	22
Class Regiments	07	12	21	25	41	42
Total	43	44	64	64	64	64

The underlying basis of composition of Infantry battalions being caste and region based, the vernacular dialect had assumed the role of a major binding factor of homogeneity. With the attempts and success of the British officer cadre in learning the language of men, this bonding had developed further. 'In contrast to most European armies which expected their native soldiers to learn the European's language, in the Indian Army every officer had to learn to speak to his soldiers in their vernacular, not least because he was regarded as the neutral arbiter in any local disputes.'[56]

Even prior to mobilisation for the Great War, Indian soldiers had proved their mettle again and again in the various campaigns in India and abroad. Accordingly, the appeal of commanding the Indian troops, had also reached its zenith by this time. More and more British officers wanted to command this finest body of troops and the 'appeal of command in the Indian Army was so high that, in 1913, of the top 25 cadets at the Royal Military Academy Sandhurst, 20 of them opted to join the Indian Army'.[57]

As far as tactics was concerned, in the late part of nineteenth century and early part of twentieth century, since the sole focus of the Indian Army was the defensive warfare in the restive regions of North-West, the manning and equipping of the Infantry battalions was accordingly managed. Almost complete training of men was carried out on job only. There were no specialised schools of instruction for imparting training on the nuances of hill warfare. The responsibility of training their men rested with the battalions themselves and the restive regions were the constant source of training of the Indian troops in the warfare:

As such there was no formal learning process for the men who defended the frontier; knowledge of how to fight on the frontier simply passes on. Firstly, the ways and means of hill warfare were passed on and learnt on the job during periods of fighting against the local tribesmen who inhabited the frontier. Alternatively, when there was a lull in the fighting, mock battles would be arranged, one regiment would attack as if a native lashkar (war party) and another would defend using their usual tactics.[58]

Before deployment at Gallipoli, the British Army had an experience of trench warfare gained during the battles of the Boer War. The equipment profile and battlefield tactics of the British Army in the pre-War period was largely modeled on the experiences of the Boer War. In the planning phase of the Gallipoli operations, it was never thought by the planners that the initial foothold by the allied troops on the peninsula would result into a never-ending stalemate which would consume thousands of lives. It was assumed that after landing, the Infantry will be able to easily overwhelm the Turkish defences, duly supported by the naval Artillery. Thus, the organisation, equipment, tactics and the composition of the Indian Infantry battalions had a decisive role to play in the operations at Gallipoli. The Indian Infantry battalions prided themselves with their conduct and exemplary display of valour and dedication to the cause. With mounted battalions of ANZACs also being employed as foot Infantry, the contribution of Infantry troops, both allied and Indian, in terms of casualties suffered and inflicted, remain unparalleled.

INDIAN ARTILLERY IN 1914

The Sikhs are considered as pioneers as far as the initiation of use of the small guns known as Zamburas or Swivels in the warfare is concerned. During the initial period of reorganisation of the Sikh Army under Ranjit Singh, the heavy pieces of Artillery were never the forte of Sikhs and the unshakable faith of Sikhs on the cavalry was irreplaceable. Like Infantry, Ranjit Singh with his military mind and foresightedness had correctly identified Artillery as another arm of the future. After putting Infantry into the path of modernisation and reforms, Artillery was the next to be put into the reformation cycle by him. During the initial phase, with a resolute conviction of the Sikhs in the capabilities of cavalry, the recruitment trends were not very promising for the Artillery. In fact, the, 'pay rolls of the first few years reveal that the bulk of the personnel of Artillery consisted of non-Punjabis, mostly the Poorbias'.[59]

Fortunately for Ranjit Singh, the Sikhs were not as averse to reformation in Artillery as they were to reforms in Infantry. Innovative and versatile as they are, the Sikhs under the supervision of European officers like Claude Auguste Court and Alexander Gardner, became adept in handling the artillery pieces in a very short time. The mastery in the manning of heavy artillery demonstrated by Sikhs during the two Anglo-Sikh wars was exemplary. 'Sir C. Gough and Cunningham both bear testimony to the fact that the Sikh guns were served with great rapidity and precision during the Anglo-Sikh wars.'[60] A closer examination of strength of the Sikh Artillery at different periods of Sikh rule, reveal a very rapid rise in the ranks of both men and material, which had reached culmination point by the end of the Sikh rule.

TABLE 10: THE EXPONENTIAL INCREASE IN THE STRENGTH AND CAPABILITIES OF SIKH ARTILLERY[61]

Year	Strength	Number of Guns	Number of Swivels	Total Monthly Salary (Rs.)
1819	834	22	190	5,840
1829	3,778	130	280	28,390
1839	4,535	188	280	32,906
1844	8,280	282	300	82,893
1846	10,524	376	300	89,251

The British Army was witness to the expertise of the Sikh Artillery, under not very friendly circumstances, during the Anglo-Sikh wars. But the specialisation and the proficiency achieved by the Sikh gunners prior to the Anglo-Sikh wars was also appreciated by the British officers. In the words of Lieutenant Barr, who had witnessed the drill of a Sikh battery in January 1839:

On our arriving in front, they (gunners) saluted us, and the general (court) then directed the native commandant, a fine soldier-like looking man, handsomely accoutered, to put them through their drill. This they performed with great credit; their movements being executed with celerity and precision that would have done honour to any army. The orders were given in French, and the system of gunnery used by that nation has also been adopted.[62]

Post the rout of the Sikh Army in the Anglo-Sikh wars, the British raised three Horse Light Field Batteries on 18 May 1849. Number 1 Battery was raised at Kohat, Number 2 at Bannu and the Number 3 at Dera Gazi Khan. All these Light Field Batteries drew Sikh Artillerymen, who had been disbanded after the second Anglo-Sikh war. The Number 1 Light Field Battery was renamed as Number 1 Kohat Mountain Battery in 1879, probably linking the designation with the place of raising. In another re-designation exercise carried out in 1903, the Battery was renamed as 21st Kohat Mountain Battery (Frontier Force).

The movement of heavy artillery pieces over the difficult terrain has always been a serious logistical issue. Gunners have since time immemorial, grappled with the issue of move of Artillery pieces over a rough country, where wheeled columns cannot traverse. Coolie transport, elephants, bullocks and camels have all been experimented over a period of time to haul artillery guns. Camels were extensively used by Charles Napier's famous camel corps in 1845, an experiment which was adversely commented upon by Napier himself, 'An animal more unfitted for military purposes cannot be imagined.'[63] None of the experiments carried out to tow the guns in the rough country were successful and almost all of them suffered from inherent disadvantages. The most probable solution to this problem had its origins in Spain, a country famous for mules.

Their efficiency and endurance, combined with an intelligent and often endearing nature, provided the Mountain Artillery with a very faithful servant for a century. The mule is sure footed, and no other animal can compare with him for carrying a load in the rough and precipitous country of the frontier hills. He is not too particular about his rations, provided that he gets good water.[64]

The experimentation of Indian Artillery with mules to haul the artillery pieces over rough terrain had been relatively successful, and gradually, mule became an inseparable part of any Indian Mountain Battery. The existence of a Mountain Battery and its performance in the battlefield was up to a large extent dependent on the surefooted mules. For the uninitiated drivers, who joined the battle at Gallipoli in the later stages albeit without their mules, the experiences at Gallipoli were revealing. Watering of the mules was a major logistical nightmare for the commanders at Gallipoli. Existence of a combination of animals in terms of horses and mules coupled with the scarcity of water created many problems for the drivers of these animals. Since mule was a primary mode of transportation of the guns, ammunition and rations of the Mountain Batteries, the watering of these animals was a recurring and perpetual quandary for the drivers of Mountain Batteries. Though not directly related to the operations at Gallipoli, an interesting anecdote on the process of watering of horses and mules by a veterinary officer bears striking resemblance with the conditions on Gallipoli.[65]

> *Horses are more*
> *Particular about their food and less*
> *Particular about their water than mules*
> *Mules are less*
> *Particular about their food and more*
> *Particular about their water than horses;*
> *Hence,*
> *If you have to water*
> *A mixed force*
> *Of horses and mules*
> *Water your Mules first*

Another mountain train, namely Jacobabad Mountain Train was raised by General John Jacob in 1858. This train was subsumed into Number 2 Company of Bombay Mountain Battery and thus was renamed as Number 2 Bombay Mountain Battery in 1876. Bombay

Mountain Battery had its origin in the *Golandauz* Battalion, which was raised in 1826. After the Indian Mutiny of 1857, the battalion was re-raised as Number 2 Company Bombay Mountain Artillery. The unit was re-christened as Jullundur Mountain Battery in 1901. In 1903, another change of designation took place, when by including the name of the founder of the battery, the battery was re-designated as the 26th Jacob's Mountain Battery.

The timings of the raising of these Mountain Batteries had coincided with the era of a shift in the equipment of the artillery. 'The batteries were formed at the tail end of the long era of the cast, smooth bore, muzzle loading pieces which had then been in service for three hundred and fifty years.'[66] The newly introduced guns of these batteries included 3 pounder (pr) guns and brass 42/5-inch howitzer. The composition of each battery in terms of these guns was based on various permutations and combinations, till a standard authorisation of three guns and three howitzers came into being for each battery. With an approximate range of 800 yards, both armaments served Mountain Batteries very well. The employment of these batteries in the period was primarily in the restive region of North-Western Frontier and the overseas deployment of these guns in an expeditionary role was neither envisaged nor planned. 'In those days of short-range small arms and close-range fighting one of the most menacing targets was the Pathan's deadly *ghazi rush* when a horde of tribesmen, clad in their waded clothing which acted like an armour, and armed with the long knives which could outreach a bayonet, would pour down the hill side to overwhelm their enemy.'[67] The case shot fired by the guns of the Mountain Battery, with each tin case consisting of thirty to forty heavy musket bullets was the most overwhelming response against the raging hordes of tribals and was extensively used during these operations.

1865 was another historic year in the development of the Indian Artillery, when the first rifled guns got introduced. The equivalent gun for the Mountain Artillery comprised 7 pr Rifled Muzzle Loading gun. This gun boasted of a range of 3,000 yards and proved its mettle during the now famous *ghazi rushes*. As part of the continuous development process, by 1899, the 7 pr gun was replaced with a 2.5-inch screw gun. These guns of Mountain Batteries due to their propellant produced dense clouds of white smoke, which was a quick give away to the location of these guns. On the other hand, by this time both the Horsed and Field Artillery had graduated to the smokeless propellants providing tremendous advantages. To resolve the anomaly, 1901 witnessed the introduction of a new 10 pr Breech Loading gun with the Mountain Artillery. Armed with a range of almost 6,000 yards, this was a very powerful and multifaceted weapon. The increased mass of its projectile, ensured greater lethality. But with an increased weight of the gun and of the projectile, the gun was prone to rolling backwards in the low-lying grounds. A column of five mules was required for the carriage of the various components of the gun with the distribution of loads for the gun line mules including axle, wheels, carriage, breech and chase.

Both Kohat and Jacob's Batteries which distinguished themselves in the Gallipoli Campaign, witnessed an active and intense action by the 10 pr guns. During these operations, the guns also witnessed some modifications, which brought about fixing of shields in the front. In addition, certain modifications and innovations were also carried out in the accessories of the guns and, 'in accordance with the developments of that time, it was provided with a dial sight and sight clinometers and could be laid indirectly. At this point, also, though the old case shot was still retained, short fused shrapnel was found to be a more effective substitute.'[68] In another change in the equipment profile, Gunners of Mountain Batteries were issued with Carbines M.E Artillery, which used to be carried slung along with 70 rounds in a bandolier. The Indian officers and trumpeters of the batteries were issued with the Webley pistols. Indian officers wore brown Sam Browne belts, carrying pistols, like their British counterparts. In a major increase in the monthly emoluments, just prior to the First World War, the monthly pay of all ranks witnessed an upward revision, with effect from 1 January 1909.

In order to cater for war time wastages in the authorised establishments, all the Mountain Batteries used to maintain reservists under their respective arrangements. These reservists were called to the respective battery location for training at specified intervals for specified durations. The strength of reservists for each battery had also witnessed an increase, reaching a maximum figure of 30 gunners and

TABLE 11: MONTHLY PAY RATES OF SOLDIERS OF THE MOUNTAIN
ARTILLERY BATTERIES[69]

Rank	New Monthly Pay (Rs.)
Subadar	100
Jemadar	50
Gunner Havildar	20
Gunner Naik	16
Gunner and Trumpeter	12
Driver Havildar	20
Driver Naik	18
Driver	11

49 drivers in 1908 for each Mountain Battery. The Mountain Battery
on its move to a location for active service left behind a small
detachment of all personnel which were in addition to its authorised
establishment. The history of the Mountain Artillery Training Center
closely followed the formation of establishment of these detachments.
The men of these Mountain Batteries in very rare instances belonged
to a different background than a military one. The camaraderie between the men of these batteries can be attributed to the common
catchment areas for recruitment. As there was no concept of common
recruitment process, the fresh recruits were invariably related to the
personnel already serving in the batteries. This feature was not restricted
only to the Mountain Batteries, but was a very common phenomenon
in all types of units/ sub units.

On the eve of the Great War, in July 1914, there were twelve
Mountain Batteries in the Indian Army, out of which six were grouped
at the rate of two Mountain Artillery Batteries each under the 1st, 5th
and 7th Indian Mountain Artillery Brigades. One battery each was
located in Burma and Hong Kong and four batteries were located in
North-Western Province of India. A major common characteristic of
all these batteries was related to their composition. The composition
of all these batteries was half Punjabi Mohammedans and half Sikhs.[70]
The training and morale of the troops of these Mountain Batteries
was recorded at highest possible levels:

When mobilisation was ordered, all Batteries were trained to a high pitch of efficiency in so far as their equipment permitted, and all were eager for the coming test of a world war against the Germans and their allies. There was no lack of enthusiasm amongst the men, and many who were on furlough paid their fares in order to get back to their units without delay.[71]

In August 1914, the 7 Indian Mountain Artillery Brigade (IMAB) was located at Dehradun and was being commanded by Lieutenant Colonel J.L Parker. The brigade consisted of two Indian Mountain Batteries to include the 21st Kohat (FF) and the 26th Jacob. On 7 August 1914, 7 IMAB was designated as a component of IEF 'A', which was earmarked for operations in Europe. The IEF, comprising two Infantry Divisions (Meerut and Lahore) and two Cavalry Brigades (Ambala and Secunderabad), had disembarked at Marseilles on 26 September.

For the impending operations, 7 IMAB, along with its two batteries had received general mobilisation orders on 9 August. The complete formation concentrated at Karachi, the nominated embarkation port in the first week of September 1914 and had set sail from Karachi on 19 September 1914 on board H.T. *City of Poona*, with sealed orders, to be opened only after sailing. During this time, the entire Brigade staff was totally unaware of the destination of the formation and the orders when opened on 21 September, directed the Indian Artillery Brigade to disembark at Suez.

The strategic importance of the waterway of Suez could not be belittled. The 120-mile waterway, trims the route between Europe and South Asia by almost 4,300 miles. In the early part of twentieth century, the Suez Canal was central to the Allied plans in the region. The entry of Ottoman Empire in the war, in alliance with Germany, had complicated the matters for the Allied troops in the region and defence of the waterway assumed prime importance. It was under these circumstances that 7 IMAB had disembarked at Suez on 3 October 1914. The formation further entrained for Ismailia and was placed under the 9th Infantry Brigade of the 3rd Division for operational control. The MEF under Hamilton while preparing for the landings for the capture of the peninsula was facing severe shortage of artillery. The typical terrain as obtained on the peninsula required the mountain guns which were able to take on Turkish targets. The availability of two Indian mountain batteries in the vicinity triggered the orders for attachment of the 7 IAMB with the ANZACs.

After a very interesting tenure at the Canal Defences, the 7 IMAB had received orders in April 1915 to move to Alexandria. The Indian Artillery Brigade along with its two Mountain Batteries entrained for Alexandria on 3 April 1915. On 4 April 1915, the formation was placed under command of GOC ANZAC. On the same day, the complete formation had found itself on board transport ship *A - 7*, destined for Mudros Bay in Lemons Island. The formation with its complete battle loads disembarked at Mudros Bay on 8 April 1915. In order to cater for the sustenance on the peninsula post landings, while at Mudros Bay, the Brigade was directed to be self-contained for the first three days of the operations. Under the extant of the orders, both men and animals were to be self-contained and the landing of the subsequent supplies was planned only after three days. On 12 April 1915, the detailed orders were issued to the 7 IAMB and the specific landing locations of the individual units and sub units were promulgated. British 29th Division was to land in the south of the peninsula at Cape Helles, the French component of the landing force was to land at the Asiatic coast and the ANZACs duly supported by 7 IAMB were to land at Gaba Tepe. Upon landing at Gaba Tepe on the morning of 25 April 1915, the equipment profile of both the Indian Mountain Artillery Batteries consisted of six 10 pr guns with each.

1 Royal (Kohat) (FF) and 6 (Jacobs) Mountain Batteries were the only units of the Indian Artillery which fought in the European Theatre (Gallipoli in Turkey), being in support of the ANZAC, while the rest of the Indian Artillery operated in the other theaters of war, to include East Africa, Mesopotamia, Palestine and Persia. Indian Mountain Artillery was then the only Artillery which the Indian Army had possessed for 56 years (1858-1914), the other Artillery in India during this period being the RA (including RGA, who manned the British Mountain Batteries also, as distinct from Indian Mountain Batteries). In a brief narrative, it is not possible to relate the story of each action of the Indian Mountain Gunners on the Anzac beach and beyond, during eight months of fierce fighting, but sustained gallantry, fortitude and professionalism of the men and their officers is evident from the

farewell message sent by the GOC, ANZAC to their Brigade Commander in January 1916:

I want to thank you, both your batteries, and all your officers and men for the really magnificent work they have done for us during the months when, I am glad to say, we were all together at Anzac, what a high regard the Australian troops have for your two batteries, and I am delighted this is the case, for they have thoroughly deserved their high reputation.

Both Mountain Batteries, i.e. the 26th Jacob's Mountain Battery and the 21st Royal Kohat Mountain Battery along with the 23rd Peshawar Mountain Battery (Frontier Force) combined to raise the 21st Mountain Regiment in the aftermath of the First World War. Post-Independence of India and partition of the sub-continent, the regiment was awarded to the Pakistan Army. Today the regiment, known as First Self-Propelled Regiment (Frontier Force) is the senior-most artillery unit of the Pakistan Artillery.

IMPERIAL SERVICE TROOPS

Prior to the mutiny of 1857, the Indian Princely States were maintaining two types of forces, with the first category being those forces which were totally maintained by the State rulers but were officered by the East India Company and later on by the Crown. The second category solely comprised East India Company troops totally funded by the state rulers. The troops in this case were primarily maintained for the personal protection of the state rulers. The mutiny of 1857 had witnessed an almost abolition of the second category.

The state raised forces maintained by the princes were not limited by treaty but they were not regarded with favour by the Government of India. It was the accelerating technical development of warfare which gradually deprived these forces of any serious military value and rendered them just adequate for ceremony and local security.[72]

Due to the geopolitical situation developing in the region and the apprehensions of a Russian threat, some of the state rulers, offered to 'make elements of their state forces available to the paramount power in time of war or emergency'. In the first fallout of the threat, the designation of these troops was changed from State Forces to Imperial Service Troops. In order to bring these forces at par with the regular Indian forces, the equipment of these forces was to be provided by the British Army. The British who till now, had deliberately stayed away from royal machinations, found this as an ideal opportunity to be in know of things in the respective states. The norms finalised by the two sides at that time included common standards for the Imperial Service Troops and the Regular Indian Troops, besides establishment of schools of instructions in the respective states. The officers of these forces were also deputed on attachments with the regular Indian units, basically belonging to the same ethnic composition.

On the eve of the outbreak of hostilities of the Great War, twenty-nine Indian states were participating in the Imperial Service Troops arrangements. A combined strength of 22,749 troops, of these states was available to the British Army for application in the Great War. The Infantry component of the Imperial Service Troops available to the British was almost 10,298 troops, about 50 per cent of the total available strength. The other components of these troops comprised Cavalry at 7,673 troops, Artillery at 373 troops, Sappers at 741 troops, Signals at 34 and joint Camel and Transport Corps at 3,360 troops. Out of these, 22,749 troops, a staggering 80 per cent (almost 18,000 troops) served overseas.[73] In 1910, the contribution of Imperial Service Troops in the various operations within India and outside was recognised in the form of an institutionalised increase to the separate establishment of the Order of British India for Imperial Service Troops from 10 First Class and 20 Second Class appointments to 12 First Class and 25 Second Class appointments.

With troops of Patiala State Infantry reinforcing the 14th Sikhs at a critical juncture during the Gallipoli Campaign, in this section, the origin and composition of Patiala State Infantry is being discussed briefly. The Patiala state of Punjab belonged to the Cis-Sutlej group and the major portion of the state was in the plains of south of Sutlej River. Some portions of the state also included the portion up to Simla and Narnaul district in the vicinity of Shekhawatti district of Jaipur. The state owed its origin to the founder Sardar Ala Singh in 1752. When in 1814, the then Government of India launched operations against the Gurkhas, the Infantry of Patiala state was part of Colonel Ochterlony's force in the operations, while some cavalry of the state was also deployed in a purely defensive role. Thereafter in a series of operations, the Patiala state continued to aid Government of India in terms of men and material.

In the latter half of 1897, due to the impending outbreak of a war on North-West Frontier, the Imperial government offered an espousal of convenience, wherein the state was required to maintain a specially trained column of 600 cavalry and 1,000 numbers of foot Infantry fully equipped and prepared for mobilisation at very short notice. In September 1891, taking this agreement a bit further, the state approached the Imperial government to prepare two Regiments of Infantry of 600 strength each by an increment of 200 men to an already sanctioned strength of 1,000 men. Due to the history of close cooperation and engagements between the state and the Imperial government, the proposal was approved. In a further improvement in the equipping philosophy of the three regiments (one Cavalry and two Infantry), a system of allotment of integral transport to each regiment was evolved, which further reduced the mobilisation differential of the state forces. The forerunner of the 1st Infantry (Rajindra Sikhs) was raised by Baba Ala Singh on 13 April 1705 and was organised as an Infantry Battalion on the French model in 1709. The Battalion was further reorganised as part of the Imperial Service Troops on 1 May 1889.

On the eve of the Great War, the Battalion was organised into six companies, with an average strength of 600 troops. Due to the excessive requirement of reinforcements during the course of the war, an experiment of raising three additional companies of three hundred troops was carried out. The experiment did not pass the muster of the demands of the war and by the end of the Great War the experiment was dropped. At the outbreak of the Great War, both the 1st and the 2nd Infantry of Rajindra Sikhs had been mobilised. Since both battalions were short on the authorised manpower, both the units were combined for mobilisation and renamed as 'The Patiala Imperial Service Infantry'.[74] The composition of the battalion was overwhelmingly Sikhs, with a sprinkling of other castes and religions.

TABLE 12: COMPOSITION OF RAJINDRA INFANTRY
ON THE EVE OF THE GREAT WAR[75]

Caste	1900	1914
Pathans	5	-
Punjabi / Hindustan Musalmans	131	3
Sikhs	448	561
Rajputs	2	2
Gurjars	-	3
Other Hindus	14	1
Total	600	570

As part of the Great War effort, the Patiala state was at the forefront in recruiting personnel for the war and also for assistance in kind. In this furtherance of the war efforts, the state recruited 28,022 men, an envious figure by the standards of the day. Discounting a figure of 8,870 personnel, who were already serving in the Patiala Imperial Service Troops serving in the field, the total fresh recruitment carried out by the state exclusively for the First World War was 19,152 men.[76] The distribution of these 28,022 personnel was not only restricted to Infantry but was wholesomely encompassing all the dynamics of warfront to include supplies. As part of mobilisation for the First World War, the 1st Patiala Rajindra Sikhs had left Patiala for Bombay on 12 October 1914 under the command of Lieutenant Colonel Gurbuksh Singh. The battalion had set sail from Bombay on 29 October, reaching Ismailia on 21 November. While at Ismailia, the battalion was brigaded under the 32nd Imperial Service Brigade, under the 11th Division with effect from 1 January 1915. The battalion as part of the brigade was deployed on the defences of Suez Canal.

As far as Gallipoli is concerned, with severe depletion in the strength of the 14th Sikhs after the Third Battle of Krithia on 4 June 1915, two companies of Patiala State Infantry were mobilised as reinforcements for the beleaguered 14th Sikhs. 'A' Company of the Battalion, with 180 troops, under the command of Major Hardam Singh along with two British officers as Special Service Officers, joined the 14th Sikhs in July 1915 at Imbros. In September 1915, 'C' Company of Patiala Sikhs, again with two British Special Service

Officers, had also reinforced the 14th Sikhs at Anzac Cove. Both the companies had rejoined their parent battalion of Patiala Sikhs after the withdrawal from Gallipoli, in January 1916. These two companies of the battalion, while in support of the 14th Sikhs had given an excellent account of themselves.

Prior to the joining of the two companies of the Patiala Infantry with the 14th Sikhs, the C-in-C India in a correspondence to GOC, Canal Defences, Egypt of July 1915, had agreed to the contention that Double Company of Patiala Infantry attached with the 14th Sikhs should stay as a homogeneous entity and not mixed with other components operating in the peninsula. In the same correspondence, it was directed that casualties of the Patiala Infantry be separately mentioned and not subsumed under the list of casualties of the 14th Sikhs. An analysis of the casualty returns of the 29th Indian Infantry Brigade also reveals that casualties of the Patiala Sikhs were endorsed as separate entities and the details were not merged with those of the 14th Sikhs.

Not only in the case of the Patiala Sikhs, but with all other components of the State Forces, which participated in the First World War, the casualty figures speak about themselves. An analysis of the casualty figures of state forces, both in the First and Second World Wars, provide a very clear insight into the level of participation and contribution of the troops of state forces. Similarly, the quantum of participation of state forces, in terms of units/subunits in the active operations is also relatively very high during the First World War.

The overwhelming action and support of the Patiala State was backed by a large number of background actions to support the war

TABLE 13: CASUALTIES OF IMPERIAL SERVICE TROOPS
IN THE WORLD WARS[77]

	Killed in Action		Died of Wounds	
	1914-18	*1939-45*	*1914-18*	*1939-45*
Second Officers	18	14	–	5
Indian Officers	25	13	3	3
Indian Soldiers	556	330	142	103
Total	599	357	145	111

effort. On the first anniversary of the Great War in 1915, a huge gathering of Sikhs was organised at Simla, which was presided over by the Maharaja of Patiala, who requested the gathering to join him in his earnest prayers to *Sat Sri Akal* for the speedy victory of British Arms. The speakers during the meet also exhorted the gathering by referring to the lives and teachings of the Sikh Gurus, to donate generously for the common cause in terms of men and material:

At Abchal Nagar, when the great Guru was on the point of leaving this earthly frame, he solemnly advised his followers as follows: Practice the art of war, be gallant and bravely face the foe, you will gain all the worldly wealth, enjoy yourself and let others enjoy it, die in the battle field and enter the gates of heaven to enjoy all bliss there. The Sikhs who believe and act according to the above teachings, feel confident that the victory of their government is the victory of their faith, totally identifying themselves with the British rule and the progress and prosperity thereof.[78]

In spite of the brilliant performance of these troops in the distant battle-fields, the differences in the establishments, strengths of the Imperial Service Troops with the regular Indian units contributed to several problems in the actual operations as has been discussed subsequently. In order to obviate these problems, a holistic review of the prevalent terms of employment of Imperial Service Troops was undertaken by the Indian Army. Though this revision was carried out after the First World War, the experiences of the war were the dominating factors which facilitated this revision. As part of this revision, a selected number of Field Service Units were nominated from the Imperial Service Troops. These units were supposed to be immediately available to the Crown in case of emergency. The overall responsibility of arming and equipping of these units, on the lines of the regular Indian Army units, was vested with the Crown.

As part of this overhaul, the balance of the Imperial Service Troops were nominated as General Service Units, arming and equipping of which again was to be carried out by the Crown albeit from the cost to be provided by the respective states. The final category of units being maintained by the states included militia units, which were not permanently embodied and had reduced standards of establishment and arms as compared to regular Indian army units. The popularity of the scheme can be gauged from the fact that a total of 49 princely states opted for this and the strength of troops under the scheme almost doubled from 22,749 troops during 1914-18 to 50,000 troops by 1920.

BURMA MILITARY POLICE

The origins of police in colonial Burma is closely linked with the British rule in neighbouring India. For the first two extensions of the British rule in Burma, the requirement of the Military Police was not felt so acutely and neither did any actions were undertaken to establish the same. The concept of military police gained traction during the process of pacification of Upper Burma, wherein a prominent role was assigned to the outfit, surprisingly at the cost of regular army, to suppress the hordes of dacoits operating in the areas. The nature of political agitation in Burma and civil disturbances in Burma were quite different from the same as obtained in India. As a result, the civil police in Burma had an earmarked role in containing the agitations in the urban areas of the country where the Military Police had a very limited mandate. The primary role of the Military Police was more prominent in the rural areas, where the civil police had been found ineffective against the organised gangs of dacoits operating in the hinterland.

The unarmed civil police were responsible for the prevention of crime, with a focus on crime committed by local criminals in the villages and towns. More serious crime, across wider territories and involving dacoits and robbers, or when riots became rebellion, called for the deployment of the military police.[79]

The first step towards the creation of a Military Police in Burma was taken in 1886, with the arrival of almost one thousand plus recruits from India. Initially, the outfit was also termed colloquially as Special Police or the Armed Police. The introduction of Military Police Act of 1887 had further legitimised the raising of a Burma Military Police. The broader organisation of the police force was based on battalions which were commanded by the British officers. As was prevalent in the colonial army of the time, the major composition of the Military

Police comprised either Sikh or Gurkha soldiers. The exploits of these troops were well known in the empire by the time. The Burmese administration of the time was also of the view that as far as possible, only troops belonging to Sikhs or Gurkhas should be recruited in the Military Police.

'Men of races other than Sikh, Garhwali, Punjabi-Mohammedan or Gurkha should be gradually eliminated from the Battalion, as they block promotion. They are, as a rule, unable to deal with the men they are brought into contact with. The system should be purely 'caste company' or freely 'mixed company.'[80]

Thus, by the end of the nineteeth century, in Burma Military Police, out of the total of 388 military officers, 105 were Sikhs and 90 were Muslims. There was virtually no Christian military officer. But by 1915, the number of Christian officers and men had risen to 1,141 but still just half the number of Sikh officers and men. Following the First World War, the number of Muslims in the Burma Military Police fell, from 2,239 in 1915 to 1,283 in 1921. But there was increased recruitment of Kumaonis, Garhwalis, Brahmins, Dogras, Karens, and Kachins, while the number of Sikhs and PMs fell by half.

But in the beginning of the Great War, the Sikhs comprised the major composition of the Burma Military Police. Anticipating a likely requirement of additional Sikh and PM troops, the Government of India had forewarned the Burmese Government to be prepared to provide strength of 400 Sikhs and 1,200 PMs as reinforcements. The request for additional reinforcements was placed to the Burmese Government in January 1915, much prior to the break-out of hostilities in the peninsula.

Based on the recommendations of the Indian Government, the training of these earmarked troops had commenced in the respective locations, prior to the dispatch. The musketry training was being carried out on charger loading rifles, which had recently been supplied for this purpose by the Ordinance Department to the Burma Military Police. As part of this training, the troops of the Burma Military Police were to carry out training for 18 days, in which they were to fire 70 to 80 rounds on these newly supplied rifles. The first lot of Sikh troops from the Burma Military Police was supplied to the 15th Sikhs and 58 Rifles, at their respective depots in India at Multan and Ferozepore respectively. In spite of the very brief training carried out in Burma, it was felt that these reinforcements should carry out additional musketry practices in the respective Depots of the nominated battalions, prior to moving out for active service. As all the Sikh troops coming from Burma belonged to Punjab, there were requirements of War Furlough, when they were to join the depots of respective units. With a very critical and urgent requirement of reinforcements, the directions promulgated, required these troops to report to the respective Depots for training and to proceed on furlough thereafter, provided there was a time lag between completion of training and the embarkation dates.

For equipping these troops, directions had been received in May 1915, which allowed issue in kind of uniform and boots at par with the regular soldiers of the Indian Army. Though the initial lot of Sikh reinforcements was not meant for the 14th Sikhs, the massive casualties being suffered by the battalion required a constant source of reinforcements. With a precedent being set already, additional reinforcements were further requisitioned by the Government of India from Burma, this time for the 14th Sikhs. As a response, on 24 June 1915, a missive was sent by the Burmese Government, which informed that a strength of one Indian officer along with 78 other ranks will be dispatched from Rangoon by 1 July 1915. Out of these, one Indian officer along with 72 other ranks and two followers had embarked from Karachi in August 1915 to reinforce the embattled 14th Sikhs. The ill-fated transport of these reinforcements, while moving from Alexandria to Dardanelles was torpedoed by a German submarine on 19 September 1915, in which 48 Sikh troops of Burma Military Police along with 229 other Indian troops lost their lives.

Supply and Transport Corps

The Indian Army on the eve of the Great War was dependent upon a host of animals as the primary means of mobility. Sufficient animals of each variety were essentially required in the suitable class and configuration for the specified roles as per the requirements of the terrain. With the anticipated theaters of operations of Indian Army at that time being spatially dislocated, the modes of transportation of these animals were being worked out in advance. These arrangements were working very fine, till the time Indian Army was operating within the country, including the restive North-West Frontier areas. As far as the deployment of the IEFs in the First World War was concerned, it was initially anticipated that only a Cavalry Brigade and two or three Infantry Divisions would be required to mobilise from India for the war effort. For the mobilisation of these troops and animals the appropriate quantity and quality of shipping had been requisitioned. The orders to the concerned were passed accordingly, 'At once consider the arrangements, required to meet the above contingency and any enquiries he may have to make from shipping companies should be made very confidentially. A Cavalry Brigade would require seven ships and each division 23 ships of about 5,000 tons.'

The shipping requisitioned from trade for mobilisation could be easily modified into troopships. But for these merchant vessels to carry animals over huge distances, necessary preparations were mandatory. In the prewar period, only 620 mule and 700 horse fittings were available in India. By invoking the provisions of emergency, these quantities were further enhanced and a sanction was given to requisition 1889 fittings for mules and 4,114 for horses. The availability of far less numbers of shipping transport then required further allowed the distance between two adjacent animals to be reduced while in transit, much against the provisions of the existing Army Regulations on the subject. 'No objection was raised provided sufficient air space was provided and there was no overcrowding.'[81] The situation was, however, very different on ground. The overcrowding of animals became a rule rather than an exception. The deficiency of space combined with cleaning materials, tools for fixing of boxes for animals and brooms were woefully inadequate:

When shipping troops on board transports for a voyage of any length, it was essential that a scale of cleaning materials was allowed. This had not been sanctioned on the present voyage. Spanners and saws for refining horse boxes, shovels and brooms for litter removal were also required together with an ample supply of cresol disinfectant. The harness and saddle rooms should be provided. Ports or openings could be placed in the ship's side giving direct access of light and air to troop decks, also enabling litter to be thrown directly overboard instead of being brought up on deck first.[82]

The Indian Mule Corps along with Lahore and Meerut Divisions had performed brilliantly in France. Though the results of the battles fought by the Indian troops were largely mixed, 'yet it was in some measure a success, for it showed that long lines of trenches could be taken, and it proved conclusively for all time the splendid fighting capabilities of Indian troops'.[83] The adaptability and innovativeness of the Indian Animal Transport had been a major contributor to these successes.

The story of Gallipoli Campaign from the Indian perspective would never be complete without the mention of animal transport columns, which by the way, were the only supply element which participated in the entire campaign. These elements were part of the 29th Indian Infantry Brigade in the campaign. Initially, the animal transport column was not considered essential for the campaign as it was felt that the troops would have to just march across the narrow peninsula after the landings with no opposition. In the records of the time, there is a mention of an apparent tussle between Lord Kitchener and the office of Supply and Transport in the War Office regarding the requirement of animal transport for the impending operations:

By the simple analogy of the impracticality of a Battalion of the Guards encamped in St James Hyde Park drawing their water from the lake, if it was drinkable, by means of their mess tins, reinforced by the reminder that on active service a properly organized supply of ammunition was essential, Lord Kitchener was persuaded to agree to a quota of transport accompanying the troops. The requirement for the impending operation at Gallipoli was purely sought as 'emergency ration' and some Indian Mule Transport was asked 'just in case British Transport should prove unsuitable.[84]

After having arrived at Marseilles, on receipt of orders, the Indian Mule Corps was informed that Dardanelles was going to be the next destination of Mule Corps. Without any clear directions to plan, the requirement was anticipated only 'just in case' and no firm plan was in place for its actual usage. A purely mathematical distribution of the available assets was carried out and 138 carts along with the staff were allocated to the 29th Indian Infantry Brigade, which was expected to arrive shortly at Alexandria having been relieved from the Canal defenses. The new organisation carved for the expedition was purely ad hoc. It was created by pulling out the components from different units and comprised 'superior establishment', thereby implying that the disproportion of officers to men was going to be greater than ever. During the campaign, as we further go along, it shall be seen that this disproportion gets amply addressed by the gallant actions of the Indian muleteers.

The administrative planning was completely detached and isolated from the operational plans. As a result, the proposed new organisation was purely based on carts and the planners of the operation did not foresee the requirement of mules being used in the pack role. The pack animals of the corps, in the first instance therefore, did not accompany the Mule Corps from France. The Indian Mule Corps was organised into four Mule Cart Corps and each corps consisted of ten troops each of 108 mules, 50 carts and 60 drivers. Including the conductor and administrative staff, the strength of each Mule Cart Corps worked out to be 650 men and 1,086 mules. On the eve of departure from Marseilles for Alexandria and further to Gallipoli, these four Mule Cart Corps were combined to form an 'Indian Mule Train'. This Mule Train had set sail for Alexandria on 3 April 1915, in a 3500-ton merchant vessel owned by the Liverpool Shipping Company, *Ramazan*, the ill-fated vessel, which was sunk by a German U Boat in September 1915, with hundreds of Indian troops on board.

The Indian Mule Train commanded by Col. C.H. Beville arrived at the port of Mudros on Lemnos Island on 22 April 1915. Carts formed an essential component of the Mule Corps, but since loading of carts and mules had taken place separately and no forethought was applied as to the movement of the carts post-landing at Gallipoli, it was decided at the last moment that the carts would not be landed first and that the mules would swim across to the beach without the carts. Since the carts would take time to come ashore, the mules till that time were to be employed in pack role. This was another last-minute direction for which no preparations whatsoever had been carried out earlier. The conversion of saddlery was required to use the mules in pack role. Indian muleteers, not to be left behind, came up with an innovative solution for modifying the existing drought saddlery of mules to make it suitable for pack role:

The saddle was convertible. It is primarily a pack saddle; but, with the addition of a pin to secure the curricle bar, a different pattern of breast piece and a pair of traces and swingle trees, it can be adapted for drought work. All these extras are carried by the driver in his bundle of gear.[85]

The saddlery modification allowed the use of mules in pack modes, but the cause of much concern, the transportation of water to the forward troops continued to torment the muleteers. The non-availability of water containers, appropriate for carriage on mule back continued to be a serious handicap for the Indian Mule Corps till suitable water containers had been made available, which was possible only by July 1915.

While the preparations for the August offensive were on, it was realised by the staff that the scale of stocking and dumping envisaged for the offensive cannot be undertaken by the mules in pack role alone. For this the carts were definitely required and hence mule carts were planned to be used for stocking. The limited availability of space, which could be identified by the Turks along with the creaking and squeaking of mule carts during the movement at night, gave Turkish snipers and Artillery observers ideal targets and during these one-sided duels, it was the Indian Mule Corps which suffered the most.

INDIAN MUSLIMS AND GALLIPOLI

As per an estimate, the population of Muslims in the world was 270 million in 1914. Strachan, in his book on the First World War, goes on to say that, out of these only 30 million Muslims were the subjects of Muslim rule and the balance, a massive figure of 89 per cent, were subjects of other states. The British Empire alone had, 'about 100 million Muslim subjects in Egypt, the Gulf States and above all India'. Before the commencement of allied landings on Gallipoli, in early March 1915, an Indian officer in France had incited 22 followers of the 58th (Vaughan) Rifles and had deserted to the German side. As all these 22 followers were Pathans, the remaining 120 Pathans of the battalion were immediately disarmed and were placed under the British Guard.

With a dominating component of the Indian Army being composed of PMs, the incident was viewed very seriously by the British Army. A diversionary front against the Turks, under active consideration, further compounded the predicament. As the plan for storming the Straits with Naval assets had failed miserably and with the physical assault on the peninsula under final stages of deliberations, the desertion by the Muslim troops in France was not a very good news for the MEF. The incident underscored the potential fragility of Muslim-dominated Indian battalions in active service in the various theatres across the world. The seriousness of the situation can be gauged from the fact that the Commander of the British Expeditionary Force had to discuss the issue with the Commander of the Indian Corps in France, General Sir James Willcocks:

I told him to consider the question and let me know tomorrow, whether the Indian Corps is fit to attack on Wednesday or not. If he has any doubts about their advancing, I won't employ them. It is a serious matter for the future of the Native Army, if the Imperial Commanders judge the regiments here unfit for offensive operations.[86]

During the time of the deployment of the 29th Indian Infantry Brigade at the Canal defences in the Qantara sector, in order to gauge the potential undercurrents in the Indian Muslim populace, particularly due to alliance of Turkey with the Axis Powers, in 1915, a survey was carried out by Sir Theodore Morison, a former Principal of the Muslim College Aligarh. As an inference of the survey, Morrison was able to make a case that:

Islamic law enjoined India's Muslims to be 'loyal and obedient subjects' of the Government of India. Allegiance to the Government of India, therefore legally precluded allegiance to any other Power. On the other hand, he observed, Indian Muslims had a passionate sympathy for the Turks, and there was some danger that this might sweep all other considerations aside.[87]

While the above happened to be a generalised survey, more specific region and province-based surveys to identify the leanings of the Muslims had also been underway. The general Muslim opinion on the subject of operations against Turkey ranged from, 'unsettled and conflicting' in United Province to 'good deal of secret satisfaction at the continued retreat of the Russian' among Muslims of Punjab.

On the other hand, India with its major component of Muslim

populace could not be left unattended by the German strategists, who were working in close cooperation with Turkey. The joining of the First World War by Turkey further emboldened the planners in the German side. The Kaiser, taking cognizance of Muslim dominance in the Indian society and correspondingly Indian Army, had planned to use this to the German advantage. The worries of the British military hierarchy were further increased when Shaikh-ul-Islam proclaimed *jihad* against the entente powers by issuing a *fatwa* on 14 November 1914. The *fatwa* promulgated that, 'Muslims living under British, French or Russian rule would merit the fire of hell, if they fought against the soldiers of Islam; they would merit painful torment, if they took up arms against Turkey's allies Germany and Austria.'[88]

Due to these developments, the British found themselves at a loss to explain to the Muslims of India regarding the future of holding of holy places of Islam. Pains were taken to clarify that the sanctity of Muslim holy places would continue to be respected as hither-to-fore and the control of these holy places would continue to remain in the hands of Muslims, if not Turkey. In India, however, the newspapers had continued to support the Indian Muslim's participation in the war against the Turks and Turkey was projected as responsible for the turmoil among the Indian Muslims:

Turkey's gratuitous intervention at the present moment is all of her own seeking and she must reap the full consequences of her mad act. So far as we, the Muslims of India, who have always displayed a profound interest in the welfare of people, who are our co-religionists and also the guardians of the Holy Places of Islam, are concerned, we have discharged our duty in time and in the clearest language possible. That duty having been discharged, Turkey's future fate ceases to have any concern for us. We are the loyal subjects of His British Majesty, and his flag is the only one under which we mean to live and prosper.[89]

Another very prominent vernacular daily of Lahore, clearly differentiated between the Muslim populace of Turkey and the Muslims of India. The editorial went on to exhort the Indian Muslims to fight against the Turks:

God alone knows what the consequences of the mistake of Turkey will be. No doubt, Turkey is a Mohammaden power and Mohammadens sympathise with her, but the present war, into which Turkey has deliberately chosen to plunge, is a political war, and there is no reason why Musalmans as such should have any sympathy with her.[90]

As far as Muslims and Gallipoli are concerned, in 1906, exactly nine years before the actual Gallipoli landings, the future conduct of operations in the Dardanelles were studied by the British General Staff. The imperatives of the operations in terms of backlash from the Muslim world were indeed given a serious consideration. 'There would be a grave risk of a reversal, which would have a serious effect on the Mohammedan world.'[91] The repercussions of Gallipoli landings for the Muslim populace of India were anticipated to be grave, through which 'the repulse of a British landing might be followed by a general uprising against British authority throughout the East'.

But the machinations at higher levels apart, the sentiments of Indian Muslims serving in the Indian Army were visibly not in sync with the designs of Germany. One Indian Muslim officer had written home in December 1914, supporting the fight against Turkey, 'What better occasion can I find than this to prove the loyalty of my family to the British Government. Turkey, it is true is a Muslim power, but what has it to do with us. Turkey is nothing at all to us.'[92] Just as the advent of operations against Turkey was judged against the opinion of Muslim population in India, the planned evacuation from the peninsula in the later part of 1915 had been anticipated with more dread, particularly in view of the opinion of Muslim population in India. There was a general anticipation in the government circles that an allied retreat from Gallipoli would embolden the trust of Turkey amongst a wider proportion of Indian Muslim population. 'Defeat in the Dardanelles would be absolutely fatal in India, since Mohammedans would then undoubtedly turn their eyes to danger.' Lord Hardinge, being in the know of the ground situation and the underpinnings, had vehemently opposed the planned evacuation from Gallipoli against all odds. 'From an Indian point of view, our policy should be to hang on to our positions at the Dardanelles even if there is no likelihood of being able to push forward.'[93] It was assumed that any withdrawal from Dardanelles would not help the cause of the Indian Muslims against the British Empire and will result in a general uprising.

In retrospect, though the two Punjabi battalions, the 69th and 89th Punjabis were withdrawn from Gallipoli within 15 days of landings, with no close combat with the Turks being carried out by the Muslim components of these battalions. However, post their withdrawal, the Muslim gunners and drivers of the 21st and 26th Indian Mountain Artillery Batteries continued to take part in active operations against the Turks from 25 April 1915 onwards till the time of their withdrawal from Gallipoli in December 1915. During these operations, there were numerous casualties amongst the Muslim drivers of the Indian Mule Corps, who continued to provide administrative support to the allied troops against all odds during the time they were there. The casualties amongst these drivers were disproportionately higher and the analysis of the casualty figures as covered in the last chapter of the book substantiates the hypothesis.

Canal Defences of Suez

The safety of Suez Canal was of primary importance to the British. Any sort of interdiction by the Turks to the canal would have jeopardised the shortest route to India and in fact the complete portion of empire in the east would have been threatened. The battalions of the 29th Indian Infantry Brigade, had taken over the responsibility of the canal defences in the Qantara Sector of the Suez Canal by the first week of December 1914. The Indian troops, initially witnessed with a lot of enthusiasm the convoy of ships carrying cargo of men and material, passing through the canal on their way to France. But this enthusiasm soon turned into monotony as no signs of enemy appeared. 'The monotony was whiled away with training, periods in the outposts, and games of soccer, which the Sikhs began playing, as hockey was not possible in the sands of Qantara.'[94]

In December 1915, all the available Indian troops on the Suez Canal were ordered to be reorganised into two divisions, the 10th and 11th Divisions. The 10th Division was to consist of the following troops:

28th Brigade
29th Brigade

30th Brigade
7th Mountain Artillery Brigade
105th Field Ambulance
108th Field Ambulance
135th 5th Field Ambulance
Supply Column from Brigade Supply Units
33rd Mule Corps for 1st Line Transport

The 11th Division was to consist of the following:

22nd Brigade
31st Brigade
Imperial Service Infantry Brigade
10th Company Sappers & Miners
110th Field Ambulance
122nd Field Ambulance
137th Field Ambulance
Supply Column from Brigade Supply Units
7th & 26th Mule Corps for 1st Line Transport

FIGURE 6: DEFENCES OF THE 29TH INDIAN INFANTRY BRIGADE
ALONG THE CANAL[95]

On 25 January 1915, a mounted patrol of the 14th Sikhs had established contact with the Turks almost two miles east of the forward positions. Though the contact was called off later, the necessity of operational preparedness was realised and the Indian brigade started taking the threat of a Turkish attack seriously. In a follow up, on 28 January, when a two hundred strong contingent of Turks was preparing to attack the 'E' Company of the 14th Sikhs, the Regimental Scouts was able to decipher the intentions of the enemy. The scouts of the Sikhs:

fell back silently and warned the company in the outposts. Captain Channer immediately informed Brigade Headquarters, who passed on the information to HMS Swiftsure, which was tied up in the Canal. Officers and men had established a liaison with the Navy and the men called the ship their 'Bada Bhai'. The Swiftsure switched on her searchlights on the enemy column and opened fire, as did the Sikhs.

FIGURE 7: SCOUTS OF THE 14TH SIKHS: QANTARA[96]

Barring a few minor incursions by the Turks along the canal defences, the situation was very well handled by the 29th Indian Infantry Brigade and the battalions had settled to an established routine in defence, when the orders were received to mobilise in the first week of April 1915. The requirements of troops for the Western Front along with the unfolding situation at Gallipoli, placed mutually opposite demands on the planners of the operations. It has also been claimed that, 'with nearly every officer whose opinion counted was now on the Western Front and that there was scarcely an influential person in England who had not some friend or relation fighting in Western Front, it is easy to gauge the tremendous opposition that was likely to be roused by any attempt to strengthen the Mediterranean Force at the expense of British Expeditionary Force (BEF) in France'. It was against these conflicting requirements that the last few days of April were spent at Gallipoli by the British and Allied forces.

On the other hand, from the German perspective, the importance of Dardanelles was never lost sight of. The Turkish preparations under the German supervision had continued unabated. The German General Staff had their priorities sorted out. 'The forcing of the Dardanelles would be a severe blow to us, we have no trumps left.'[97] The initial footholds notwithstanding, the situation was entirely not in favour of the Allied troops. the General Staff of the MEF in Gallipoli was requesting only for small arms ammunition, whereas seeing the situation, the corresponding French staff had already started asking for reinforcements from their respective channels. Towards this the French Admiral had written to his superiors on 26 April, that 'all goes well, but in order to ensure continued success it is of utmost importance to reinforce immediately the Expeditionary Force which is insufficient for such extensive operations'.

NOTES

1. Words of a British soldier as he wrote in his diary after the Battle of Gujerat, Anglo-Sikh War
2. J.D. Cunningham and A.C. Banerjee (1949), *Anglo-Sikh Relations*.
3. J.D. Cunningham (1990), *History of the Sikhs: From the Origin of the Nation to the Battles of the Sutlej*, Low Price Publications, Delhi.
4. Ibid.
5. L. Griffin (2018), *Ranjit Singh*, Srishti Publishers & Distributors, Delhi.

6. Statement of Lord Dalhousie on 5 October 1848 at a Public Banquet at Barrackpore (Calcutta).

7. E. Candler (2020), *The Sepoy*, Writat, London.

8. Ibid.

9. The Imperial Gazetteer of India, *The Indian Empire*, vol. IV: Administrative, New Edition (Oxford, 1907), pp. 347-53.

10. Report on The Administration of the Punjab and Its Dependencies. Palala Press.

11. C.A.H. Bingley (1899), *Handbooks for the Indian Army Sikhs*, Government Central Printing Office, Calcutta.

12. Quoted in *Empire of Honour: Punjabi Recruitment in the First World War*, Chaudhry Hameed.

13. M.S. Leigh (2022), *The Punjab and the War*, Government Printing Punjab, Sang-e-Meel Publications, Lahore, Punjab.

14. Ibid.

15. Ibid.

16. Ibid.

17. S.D. Pradhan (1978), 'The Sikh Soldier in the First World War', in D.E.C. Ellinwood (ed.), *India and the World War 1* (1st edn., pp. 213-25), Manohar, New Delhi.

18. Ibid.

19. Leigh, *The Punjab and the War*, op. cit.

20. Ibid.

21. M. O'Dwyer (1925), *India as I Knew It 1885–1925*, Unistar Books, Chandigarh, 2015.

22. Leigh, *The Punjab and the War*. op. cit.

23. Michael O'Dwyer, 'Speech Delivered by His Honour the Lieutenant-Governor at a Darbar held at Gujranwala on the 8th August 1917', in War Speeches, 62.

24. L.C.J.M. Wikeley (1915), *Handbooks for the Indian Army, Punjabi Musalmans*, Superintendent Government Printing, Calcutta.

25. Ibid.

26. Ibid.

27. Ibid.

28. Ibid.

29. Pradhan, 'The Sikh Soldier in the First World War', op. cit.

30. B. Gudmundsson (2005), *The British Expeditionary Force 1914-15* (*Battle Orders*) (1st edn.), Osprey Publishing, Oxford.

31. D. Omissi (1998), *The Sepoy and the Raj: The Indian Army, 1860-1940*

(Studies in Military and Strategic History), Palgrave Macmillan, London.

32. Ibid.
33. Ibid.
34. Scheme for the Colonisation of the Area Commanded by the Lower Bari Doab Canal in which 1,03,000 acres were allotted for Military Pensioners, Sanctioned, 1914, p. 10. Digitised Public Records, Abhilekh Patal, National Archives of India.
35. Ibid.
36. Omissi, *The Sepoy and the Raj*, op. cit.
37. By the author, from different sources.
38. Report of the Peel Commission, pp. 5-7.
39. Omissi, *The Sepoy and the Raj*, op. cit.
40. Ibid.
41. Ibid.
42. Gudmundsson, *The British Expeditionary Force 1914-15*, op. cit.
43. Pradhan, 'The Sikh Soldier in the First World War', op. cit.
44. Ibid.
45. Gudmundsson, *The British Expeditionary Force 1914-15*, op. cit.
46. X. (2022), *The Army in India and its Evolution 1924*. Generic.
47. Ibid.
48. Ibid.
49. Gudmundsson, *The British Expeditionary Force 1914-15*, op. cit.
50. Ibid.
51. I. Hamilton (2022), Ian Hamilton/Gallipoli Diary, 2 vols. 1920. Generic, (ibid., p. 193).
52. Brigade Major. Gallipoli Diaries: Headquarters 29th Indian Infantry Brigade 1915 (p. 29). Great War Diaries Ltd., Sussex.
53. Omissi, *The Sepoy and the Raj*, op. cit.
54. Ibid.
55. Ibid.
56. Ibid.
57. C.C. Trench (1988), *The Indian Army and the King's Enemies, J1900-1947*, Thames & Hudson, London.
58. T.R. Moreman (1998), *The Army in India and the Development of Frontier Warfare, 1849-1947*, Basingstoke: Macmillan, pp. 19-23.
59. S.N. Singh (1970), *Maharaja Ranjit Singh*, Languages Department, Patiala.
60. Ibid
61. Ibid.

62. Ibid.
63. C.A.L. Graham (2014), *The History of the Indian Mountain Artillery*, Naval & Military Press Ltd., East Sussex.
64. Ibid.
65. C.H.T. Macfetridge (1974), *Tales of the Mountain Gunners: An Anthology.*
66. Ibid.
67. Ibid.
68. Ibid.
69. Ibid.
70. Ibid.
71. Ibid.
72. J. Gaylor (1996), *Sons of John Company: Indian and Pakistan Armies, 1903-1991 (Into Battle)* (new edn.), Parapress Ltd., Kent.
73. Ibid.
74. R. Head and T. McClenaghan (2013), *The Maharajas' Paltans: A History of the Indian State Forces (1888-1948)*, 2 pts., Manohar, New Delhi.
75. Ibid.
76. Punjab State Archives. (1920), Records Patiala State, Ijlase Khas, File No. 1556, Part I (vol. 120).
77. Head and McClenaghan (2013), *The Maharajas' Paltans*, op. cit.
78. Punjab State Archives (1920), Records Patiala State, op. cit.
79. Lalita Hingkanonta (2013), 'The Police in Colonial Burma', PhD thesis. SOAS, University of London http://eprints.soas.ac.uk/17360
80. *Report on the Police Administration of Burma for the Year 1898*, Rangoon: Government Printing, 1899, p. 79.
81. H.M. Alexander (2017), *On Two Fronts, Being the Adventures of an Indian Mule Corps in France and Gallipoli*, Van Haren Publishing, The Netherlands.
82. G. Winton (2018), 'The Mobilisation and Supply of India's Equine Army 1914', in A. Jeffreys (ed.), *The Indian Army in the First World War*, pp. 52-90), Helion & Company Limited, Warwick.
83. Alexander, *On Two Fronts, Being the Adventures of an Indian Mule Corps in France and Gallipoli*, op. cit.
84. Ibid.
85. Quoted in David Omissi in 'The Greatest Muslim Power in the World: Islams, the Indian Army and the Grand Strategy of British India, 1914-1916', in *The Indian Army in the First World War* by Allan Jeffreys.
86. Ibid.
87. Geoffrey Lewis, 'The Ottoman Proclamation of Jihad in 1914 in Arabic and Islamic Garland: Historical, Educational and Literary Papers

presented to Abdul Latif Tibawi', London: The Islamic Cultural Centre, 1977, p. 159.

88. *Observer*, Lahore, 4 November 1914.
89. *Jhang Siyal*, Lahore, November 1914.
90. Starchen, *First World War*, p. 113. French, 'Origins of the Dardanelles Campaign', p. 211.
91. 'Muslim officer to his brother' (Central India), December 1914 (Urdu) in Omissi (ed.), *Indian Voices of the Great War*, p. 25.
92. Hardinge to Chamberlain, 12 November 1915.
93. P.G. Bamford (1948), The Sikh Regiment, The 14th King George's Own Ferozepore Sikhs, Gale & Polden Limited, Aldershot.
94. 14th Sikhs Album.
95. Ibid.
96. German Admiral von Tirpitz, quoted in Aspinall-Oglander, *Military Operations, Gallipoli*.

CHAPTER 3

The Affirmation
Indian Troops on Gallipoli

> I found in brief, that all great nations learned their truth of word and
> strength of thought in war, that they were nourished in war and wasted
> by peace, taught by war and deceived by peace; in a word that they
> were born in war and expired in peace.[1]

Prior to the commencement of hostilities on the Gallipoli peninsula,
by virtue of experience of the Boer War, the British Army had some
experience of trench warfare. On the eve of the Great War, therefore,
the equipment profile and battlefield tactics of the British Army had
been largely modeled on the experiences gained during the Boer War.
A careful analysis of deliberations preceding the launch of amphibious
landings by the MEF troops, does not provide any indication that the
thought of a stalemate which would consume thousands of lives,
would have crossed the minds of the military planners. On the
contrary, it was a widely held belief that after the landings have taken
place, the infantry duly supported by the allied naval artillery would
be able to overwhelm the lightly held and uncoordinated Turkish
defences.

The initial naval attacks without any troops in ground role were
carried out on Turkish defences at the peninsula on 19 February 1915
whereas the first Allied troops had physically landed on the beaches
of Gallipoli on 25 April 1915. During this period, the Turks had a
window exceeding two months to figure out the anticipated plan of
operations of the Allies. With time at their disposal, the Turks had
fortified and coordinated their defences. These defences had been
further strengthened by barbed wire entanglements. The defenders

knew their ground and under the guidance of the German General Staff had executed a coordinated plan for defence. The barbed wire obstacles were duly covered by observation and fire from machine guns and artillery. The likely concentration places of allied infantry were marked in advance and identified as likely artillery targets besides covering the likely advancing grounds of infantry with the killing zone of machine gun fire. The near perfect coordination of defences was going to be a tough and obstinate obstacle for the MEF initially and later on for the IEF.

Much against the experiences imbibed by the British Army during the experiences of the Boer War, this time, the Turks on the peninsula did not withdraw in the face of a strong offensive and held their ground against all odds. As the Turkish defences on Gallipoli were being coordinated by the German General Staff, the manifestation of striking resemblances with the operations along the Western Front against the BEFs was imperative. The onset of trench warfare along the Western Front had brought about a stalemate with obvious advantages to the defender. This type of warfare also precluded success of a large-scale offensive against a well-entrenched defender. Imbued by the stalemate obtained on the Western Front, the German General Staff on Gallipoli had attempted to replicate the similar defensive template on Gallipoli also. Sanders was of the view that with supply lines of MEF over-stretched, it was a matter of time before the offensive was petered out, provided the Turks continued to hold their defences and were able to launch strong counter attacks to evict the enemy from the captured localities.

The initiation of the trench warfare along the Western Front had ensured that the defences of belligerents were almost hugging each other. The No Man's Land was gradually being nibbled by each, slowly and steadily. Reduction of No Man's Land was creating more problems at least for BEFs. The Allied forces in the Western Front did not have a faintest idea as to how to break the stalemate and 'the first British solution to the problem of how best to attack German fortified positions was suggested by the German themselves'.[2] Under the innovative practice, with the futility of mass offensives in the trench warfare having been adequately witnessed, the Germans discarded offensives with massive objectives and replaced it with the concept of limited objectives. 'The objective of the attack was to improve the German defences in a given area by seizing a discrete piece of terrain. More specifically, the idea was to seize terrain that allowed the Germans to hold a given area with fewer troops, thereby releasing forces for decisive employment on other fronts.'[3]

The objective in this case was carefully chosen, the main criteria being the ability of the objective to facilitate the defensive potential of the existing defences. As a result of these small-scale offensives, the gradual nibbling of the Allied defences had begun. With the objective being compact, the availability of artillery support was not an issue any more. The Germans were able to carpet the target with the limited artillery available followed by the infantry assault. With this concept, a number of small-scale offensives could be launched across the front.

Though the Allied forces had landed on the peninsula on 25 April 1915, but with no forward movement possible in view of the fierce Turkish resistance, the situation on the peninsula was gradually approaching a stalemate. Without any initiation of decisive action by the Allied military hierarchy, there was an imminent threat of being thrown into the sea by the weight of the Turkish counter attacks. But a serious deficiency of the additional reinforcements for the MEF had stalled further operations. During the six fateful days of 25 to 30 April, the primary course of action for commanders at all levels had shifted from offensive to survival and holding on to the gained ground, which had been captured at great human cost. It was important to hold on to the captured footholds, howsoever tactically unsound they may have been and simultaneously ensure the survival of the troops on ground until fresh reinforcements could arrive. 'The heavy casualties suffered by the Australians and New Zealanders on the 25th of April, the strength of the Turks now opposed to them, and the extraordinary difficulties of the Anzac country, all tended to show on 26 April that no further advance inland could be made in the northern zone till General Birdwood was reinforced.'

The Turkish defenders were also prepared to launch strong counter attacks and dislodge the troops of MEF from the captured localities. On 30 April 1915, an Operation Order of Turkish forces was recovered from the dead body of a Turkish soldier, which talked about the importance of not letting the Allied forces to gain a foothold on the peninsula. The content of the order provided some indication of the foreboding for the IEF:

Be sure, that no matter how many troops the enemy may try to land, or how heavy the fire of his Artillery, it is absolutely impossible for him to make good his footing. Supposing he does succeed in landing at one spot, no time should be left to him to coordinate and concentrate his forces, but our own troops must instantly press in to the attack and with the help of our reserves in rear, he will forthwith be flung back into the sea.[4]

It was therefore imperative for the MEF to not lose the captured ground to the incessant and vigorous Turkish counter attacks. The sustenance of the troops already on the peninsula, was a pressing requirement under the circumstances. The immediate priority for the allied troops was survival and they had been engaged in continuous digging to prevent being thrown back into the sea and any subsequent operation inland would have to wait for fresh reinforcements. 'Till some of these new formations arrived he could do little but remain on the defensive, resting his battered battalions, consolidating the ground already won, beating back hostile attacks, and seizing every opportunity for local offensive action to improve his existing positions.' In the long run, this inescapable delay was going to prove disastrous for the Gallipoli campaign. There was an inescapable requirement for the fresh reinforcements if the MEF had to regain the almost lost initiative.

Ian Hamilton was aware of this sensitive requirement and was constantly in touch with the War Office. After lengthy discussions, some reinforcements for the MEF were nominated by the War Office to augment the offensive capabilities of MEF. These included an Indian Infantry Brigade from Egypt, a British Territorial Division, a French Division and two dismounted brigades of ANZACs. In the order of priority, the 29th Indian Infantry Brigade from Egypt was the first one to land on Gallipoli and to provide the much needed succor to the MEF.

On 29 April 1915, making a mention of Indian troops, Ian Hamilton informed Kitchener that a fresh offensive is being planned to end the stalemate, immediately on the arrival of the Indian brigade in the peninsula. Indian troops of the 29th Indian Infantry Brigade were the first reinforcements which landed on the peninsula on 1 May 1915. The military hierarchy of the time had a phenomenal belief in the capabilities of the Indian troops who were about to land on the peninsula. The arrival of the Indians was being eagerly awaited. The day 29th Indian Infantry Brigade was landing, Ian Hamilton wrote in his diary that with the Indian troops landing at the peninsula, the Turks are going to have a tough time:

> Better late than never is all I could say to him: he and his Brigade are sick at not having been on spot to give the staggering Turks a knock out on the 28th, but he is going to lose no more chances; his men are landing now and he hopes to get them all ashore in the course of the day.[5]

By the time the Indian troops were getting reorganised after landing on the peninsula, the Turks were fully prepared to launch small-scale offensives to capture limited territory and the Indian Brigade was to face the full force of the impending counter attack by the Turks immediately on landing. The situation was difficult from at least two perspectives, first, that the foothold established by the Allied troops was very limited and there was no option but to move inside the peninsula against the Turks. Second, with the success of the Turks in the tactics of nibbling, the Allied troops were staring at a possibility of being thrown back into the sea. The first five days of the campaign at Gallipoli had not brought any substantial success to the Allies and the danger of being thrown back into the sea was looking very real, when the 29th Indian Infantry Brigade had landed.

The Indian brigade and its battalions had distinguished themselves while serving under the 10th Indian Division along the canal defences. The Brigade, with its four battalions and a battalion of 22nd Brigade under command had taken defences in the Qantara (Third) Sector along the canal, with the first and second sectors being held by the 30th Indian Infantry Brigade and 28th Indian Infantry Brigade of the 10th Indian Division respectively. The Brigade had its headquarters at Qantara from where the entire formation had mobilised for Gallipoli in April 1915.

The Indian Brigade immediately on landing was placed under command of the British 29th Division, with effect from 1 May 1915. Due to the composition of the 69th and 89th Punjabis, as discussed earlier, both these battalions were withdrawn from the formation on 15 May 1915. While the 69th Punjabis was allotted to 21st Bareilly Brigade under the 7th Meerut Division, the 89th Punjabis saw themselves posted to 7th Ferozepore Brigade under the 3rd Lahore Division. The Indian brigade in Gallipoli continued under the command of the 29th British Division till 7 July 1915, when it was placed under command GOC ANZAC for subsequent operations on the peninsula at Anzac Cove.

After the move of two Punjabi battalions from the command of the 29th Indian Infantry Brigade, for a limited time three British infantry battalions to include the 1st Battalion Royal Inniskilling Fusiliers, 1st Battalion Lancashire Fusiliers and 1st Battalion Royal Munster Fusiliers of the 29th Division had been placed under the command of the formation. In the later part of the campaign at the peninsula, the brigade was posted with three additional Indian infantry battalions. The 1st Battalion, 5th Gurkha Rifles (Frontier Force) joined the formation from the 28th Indian Brigade, 10th Indian Division in June 1915. Another Gurkha battalion, the 2nd Battalion, 10th Gurkha Rifles also joined the formation in June 1915 from the 22nd Lucknow Brigade of the 11th Indian Division. Towards the end of the campaign at the peninsula, the 1st Battalion, 4th Gurkha Rifles had joined the Indian Brigade in October 1915 from the 9th Sirhind Brigade of the 3rd Lahore Division.

Indian Troops on Gallipoli

The Indian Infantry had landed on the peninsula on 1 May 1915, but on 25 April 1915, two batteries of the Indian Mountain Artillery had already landed along with the initial waves. Like the Indian Infantry Brigade, these Mountain Batteries had also been part of the canal defences, prior to being mobilised for Gallipoli. The troops of Indian batteries had embarked on troopship *Pera,* and had sailed from Mudros for a 'secret rendezvous' in the afternoon of 24 April 1915. Though the officers of the Indian Mountain Batteries had a fair idea about the likely location after sailing from Mudros, the actual location was revealed to the Indian troops on board only.

During the briefing, it was revealed that the 26th Mountain

Battery was to land first at the shores of Gallipoli at 0600 hours on 25 April 1915 and the same boats were then required to come back for the 21st Mountain Battery. It was expected that after dropping the 26th Mountain Battery on the shores of the peninsula, the boats for the gunners of 21st Mountain Battery will be back by 0800 hours. Due to the fluid situation during the landings as obtained on the shores of the peninsula on the morning of 25 April, the boats for the first Battery itself were delayed, leading to the troops of both the Mountain Batteries to continue to wait for the boats to arrive. Due to the intense shelling by Turks, the first boats of the 26th Battery were able to reach only by 0800 hours and the boats for the gunners of the 21st Battery had not arrived till 1600 hours on 25 April 1915:

The day wore on, I was continually trying to make the officers and men sit down, so as not to start dead tired. We went down to every meal very early and ate hugely. Troops were ordered to land with three days' rations, first day 'in the stomach' and we tried to comply. At last about 4 p.m. our tow arrived, we set to work and got men and animals on board in very quick time and without incident. The men had to climb down rope ladders to the boats with bare feet and carrying all the various side arms of the guns, signaling equipment etc. We had practiced this a lot in Mudros, but by this time it was quite rough and none too easy to get from the ladder into the boat.[6]

The next challenge for the 21st Mountain Battery was to arrange a tow for the flat-bottomed boats, so as to be able to tow the boats to the shore. Tow was finally available almost two hours later and by this time nearly all the troops were suffering from sea sickness. Another challenge being faced by the acutely sea sick gunners of the battery was to prevent the loaded boats from striking the sides of the ship due to the severe sea waves. Amidst this, by the time the gunners of the Battery were on shore, it was dark. Both these batteries were directed to dig for the night at the assigned locations. The actions of the Indian gunners during that time were inspired by the directions of the GOC, which the Officer Commanding (OC) of the 21st Mountain Battery recalled later on, 'remember three things, fire always, husband your ammunition and rations and Dig, Dig, Dig'. Though the troops had dug in and the 10 pr Mountain Guns emplaced, the harassing fire from the Turkish snipers was causing a number of casualties to the gunners and drivers of the Indian Mountain Batteries. Both sides resorted to the application of innovative solutions to cause and prevent the sniping casualties respectively. One of the innovative and improvised solution by the Indian gunners is worth reproducing here:

After we had been ashore quite a long time and were well dug in at '*Pifferpore*' we always had at least one casualty per night which always occurred in the same place, just opposite our Mess. One night at dusk just after our Doctor had been talking about it; I noticed something white beside the road, just where the casualties occurred. I sent a man to see what it was and he came back with a piece of white cloth. That night there were no casualties at that spot, but next night there was a piece of white paper there. I had this taken away, again no casualties. After that it was the Mess Orderly's job to look out for and clear away marks from there every evening at dusk and casualties ceased. The modus operandi apparently was, the sniper laid his rifle on or a little to one side of the mark. When he saw it obscured, he pulled the trigger, if the target was going one way he missed, if the other, he hit. There was so much rifle fire going on all round, he was not likely to be spotted from his firing within our lines.[7]

As the Indian gunners had landed amongst the first waves, the trenches were not deep enough to let a soldier pass without crouching. The probability of being hit by a sniper was real and was a major cause of a number of casualties to the ANZAC troops. To avoid sniper fire, the troops had to crouch while passing through the trenches, either for administrative or operational tasks. The situation in the trenches during those initial days was further compounded by the presence of a large number of troops.

For the Indian gunners passing through a trench, full of soldiers who were lying to rest and saving oneself from the Turkish snipers, at the same time was an extremely difficult proposition. Even a minor peep outside the parapet of the trenches was inviting bullets from the Turks. The CO of the 21st Battery did not like the task of moving through trenches full of own troops. 'I did not like it as the trench was only about two feet deep. On my way back a polite Australian got up a little to let me pass and promptly got a bullet through his head, and I received many bits of his skull in my face and pagri.'[8]

While the professionalism and determination of the Indian Mountain gunners was being tested on the peninsula, the 29th Indian

Infantry Brigade, still at Qantara had also received orders for general mobilisation on 10 April 1915. For the Indian Brigade also, due to the secrecy of the impending operation, the location of the fresh deployment of the formation was not disclosed to the troops. Immediately on receipt of orders, the Indian Brigade had started preparations for the impending move. A stock of the available manpower with each battalion of the brigade was organised and the respective home depots were intimated to make up the existing deficiencies in terms of authorised strength of the battalions.

From Qantara, the mobilisation of the battalions of the Indian Brigade to Port Said was carried out through the train transport and by 20 April 1915, the entire formation was able to concentrate at Port Said. On 25 April 1915, when the initial landings of the Indian Mountain Batteries along with the 29th Division and the ANZACs were taking place on the shores of Gallipoli, the allotted transport for the battalions of the Indian Brigade had started arriving at Port Said. For the transportation of the Indian Brigade, five 'Hired Transports' had been made available. These included, HT *Umfuli*, HT *Ajax*, HT *Japanese Prince*, HT *Dunluce Castle* and HT *Ismailia*. The 'Order of March' mandated for the move, had involved the moveout of the components of the Indian Brigade in a similar order.

HT *Umfuli* had on board Number 1 and 2 Double Companies of the 69th Punjabis, whereas HT *Ajax* was allotted to the 89th Punjabis and HT *Japanese Prince* had on board the 69th Punjabis less Number 1 and 2 Double Companies along with first line transport of the battalion, The Machine Gun sections of the 89th Punjabis, 14th Sikhs and 1/6 Gurkhas along with their first line transport. In addition, the vessel had also onboard Number 1 Section of the 108th Field Ambulance. The total manifest of the ship for the operation included 12 British officers, three British Non-Commissioned Officers (NCO), 15 Indian officers, 426 Indian rank and file, 108 followers, 148 transport followers, 398 mules and horses and 60 carts. HT *Dunluce Castle* was allotted to Headquarters 29th Indian Infantry Brigade, 14th Sikhs and 1/6 Gurkhas, whereas HT *Ismailia* had on board the entire second line transport of the formation. The stores and rations of the battalions were to be loaded along with the troops of the battalion in the respective transport.

FIGURE 8: INDIAN ANIMAL TRANSPORT EMBARKING FOR
GALLIPOLI[9]

With HT *Dunluce Castle* being allocated to the 14th Sikhs, the
battalion had started embarking on the transport on the night of
26 April 1915. Due to the maintenance issues in the sewage disposal
system of cook houses and lavatories of *Dunluce Castle,* the loading
of the transport of the battalion suffered a delay, which was possible
to be repaired only by the early hours of 27 April. Due to the time
taken in the restoration, the 14th Sikhs was split into two parts, with
one part on board the transport and the other at the port.

The orders for the exact location of the move of the Indian Brigade
had still not been divulged to the Brigade Headquarters. The complete
transport of the 29th Indian Infantry Brigade less transport of the
14th Sikhs sailed out from Port Said at 0700 hours on 27 April 1915.
With an unknown destination and virtually no information about
the impending operations, the Indian troops on board the ships were
quite apprehensive. HT *Dunluce Castle* after the immediate restoration
work, was able to sail only by the noon of 27 April. The routine of
the troops from different battalions on board the different transports

FIGURE 9: NUMBER 4 DOUBLE COMPANY OF THE 14TH SIKHS
EMBARKING ON HT *DUNLUCE CASTLE* AT PORT SAID[10]

did not differ much. A strict regimen of organised Physical Training, within the constraints of available space on board was being organised by all the Indian battalions on board.

In the late evening of 29 April 1915, a message was received on board HT *Dunluce Castle* from the Headquarters of the 29th Indian Infantry Brigade that the formation will disembark at Cape Helles, the southern tip of the Gallipoli peninsula and will be placed under command of the 29th Division for further operational control. The Operation Order for the formation had also provided detailed administrative instructions for the landing troops. The order required all troops on disembarking from the respective transports to carry on person three days of rations and two hundred rounds of ammunition of personal weapons. In addition, all battalions had to ensure that another one hundred and fifty rounds of ammunition per rifle, three thousand rounds per machine gun and additional seven days of ration was to be landed under the arrangements of the respective battalions on the peninsula. During the early hours of 30 April 1915, the entire complement of the formation had arrived and the transport was anchored at Cape Helles in the Gallipoli Peninsula. As the British and French troops had already landed by this time, two

FIGURE 10: FLOTILLA OF THE 29TH INDIAN INFANTRY BRIGADE
ENROUTE TO DARDANELLES[11]

beaches on the southern tip of the peninsula had been identified for
landings.

The arrival of the Indian Infantry Brigade at the southern end of
the peninsula, was witness to a near simultaneous naval fire support
to the British and French troops on ground. The action happening
on the peninsula, right at that time was a welcome distraction for the
Indians on board, bored by the monotonous routine being followed
on transports till now. The general impression one obtained from the
enthusiasm of the Indian troops, towards the impending landings,
highlighted the eagerness to join the action at the earliest.

It was an inspiring sight approaching Cape Helles, where they arrived on the
30th of April. A large fleet of warships, transports and trawlers lay off the
Gallipoli Peninsula, and the guns of the warships were continuously in action
bombarding various Turkish forts on both sides of the straits or supporting
the Allied troops on shore.[12]

Though having anchored at Cape Helles by the first light of 30 April, the orders for disembarkation for troops of the Indian Brigade did not come for another 24 hours, as a result of which the Indian troops continued on board the respective transports. HT *Umfuli*, with the two Double Companies of the 69th Punjabis on board, meanwhile was still to reach. The disembarkation orders for the troops on board the anchored transports were finally received at 0200 hours on 1 May and the first troops of the Indian Brigade started landing at Gallipoli Peninsula by the first light of 1 May in what was going to be a supreme selfless and bravest contribution to the cause of the British Empire in the annals of military history. Starting from the first light, the complete troop component of the Brigade was at the shores of the peninsula by afternoon. The stores and other material to include animals, however, continued to be transported from ships to lighters and from lighters to shores during the balance of the entire day and night as well. The 'W' beach, where the Indian troops landed, was reeling under the immense pressure of the logistical build up. The ammunition and other stores of the British troops already landed during the previous five days, were still on the shores. Further movement of these stores had been hampered due to the reverse movement of casualties and the shortage of troops to carry these stores further inland.

For the Indian Brigade, the troops, stores and animals landing at the same place, the restoration and retention of command and control of the troops by the respective battalions was an immediate challenge. During this time, the continuous shelling by the Turkish artillery on the beaches and beyond further impacted the landing process. During this confusion, the Brigade was allotted a camping location, which was just north of the light house on Cape Helles. In the meantime, the Indian Brigade had also been nominated as the reserve formation to the 29th Division.

By the last light of 1 May 1915, with an exception of the two Double Companies of the 69th Punjabis, which were still to arrive, the entire formation along with the stores and animals had landed at Gallipoli. Having been earmarked as reserve of the British Division, which was embattled in consolidating its positions on the peninsula, the immediate task of the Indian Brigade involved construction of a road and breakwater at the 'W' beach. The responsibility was further

FIGURE 11: SITUATION AT 'W' BEACH ON 1 MAY, DURING THE
LANDINGS OF THE 29TH INDIAN INFANTRY BRIGADE[13]

delegated by the Indian Brigade to the 89th Punjabis and a portion of the 69th Punjabis. The reasons for the particular nomination of these two battalions for the fatigue duties on the beach are discussed in a subsequent section of the book. On the morning of 1 May, the troop strength of the Indian Infantry Brigade is depicted in Table 14.

As the Sikh troops belonging primarily to the 14th Sikhs and in some proportion from 69th and 89th Punjabis, started approaching the shore after disembarking from transports, the Turks from their vantage positions were surprised to see the bearings and attire of the Sikh troops. Though Sikhs as part of Indian Mountain Artillery Batteries had landed in the initial waves on 25 April, but those landings happening further away at Anzac Cove and the Sikh troops of the Artillery Batteries being not involved in close combat, this was perhaps the first time the Turks were observing Sikh troops from such closer quarters.

It has been documented that; a very strong rumour was circulating amongst Turks that the newly inducted Indian troops on the peninsula were 'man eaters'. The body language, the strong rustic built along with the long beards and turbans with steel rings was indeed depicting a formidable image of the Sikhs:

In the initial stages when landed at Cape Helles under the cover of a grounded Transport Vessel and faced the enemy, the Turks were terrified as if we were

TABLE 14: COMPOSITION OF THE 29TH INDIAN INFANTRY BRIGADE AS ON 30 APRIL 1915[14]

Units	British Officers	Indian Officers	NCOs & Men	Public Followers	Private Followers	Clerks/ Orderlies	Horses/Mules
HQ 29 Indian Infantry Brigade	4	-	-	1	5	5	7
14th Sikhs	13	18	735	24	9	-	23
1/6 Gurkhas	13	17	738	66	17	-	87
69th Punjabis	13	18	735	24	14	-	87
89th Punjabis	13	17	736	24	9	-	23
108 Field Ambulance	4	8	13	165	7	-	23
S&T Corps	1	-	36	52	-	-	100
Total	61	78	2,993	356	61	5	350

cannibals! Our bushy beards, big turbans and shining steel quoits frightened them. Since the shining steel quoits gave out to the enemy our positions, they were covered with khaki pugree cloth and eventually discarded for the duration of the war.[15]

As the campaign progressed, it was increasingly realised that the apprehensions of the Turks were not entirely unfounded. Except for the fear of cannibalism, the Sikhs proved every apprehension of the Turks true to the core. As discussed earlier, prior to the landings of MEF on 25 April, the Turks in consultation with the German General Staff had made elaborate arrangements for denying the initial foothold to the allied troops. Though at a great human cost, but despite such elaborate arrangements, the initial foothold along the specified beach heads had been obtained by the troops of MEF. With time at premium, the next challenge was to move inland from the beaches. Any further delay by the allied troops on ground, to wait for additional re-inforcements, was advantageous to the defenders. Every hour delay by the MEF to progress the advance further inland was increasing the chances of success of Turkish counter attacks and the subsequent dislodgement of the MEF foothold. The Turkish intended to launch a formidable counter attack, before the Allies were able to get re-inforcements, while the Allied strategy hinged on to the efforts to hold a likely strong counter attack from the Turks, prior to the arrival of reinforcements.

It was in the midst of such conflicting designs of opposing troops, when the 29th Indian Infantry Brigade was landing on Cape Helles on the morning of 1 May 1915. Though the Turks were very much alive to the possibility of arrival of Allied reinforcements, the exact nominated landing place of these troops had been difficult to anticipate during the disorientation, as obtained on the peninsula on the night of 30 April and 1 May. Simultaneously, Marshall von Sanders, the German officer responsible for the Turkish defence, had also received an operationally immediate message from the Turkish warlord, Enver Pasha. The communication directed Sanders, 'to drive the invaders back into the sea'. With limited available Artillery and the absolute dominance enjoyed by the allied naval fleet from the three sides of the southern portion of the peninsula, the mandated operational task of Sanders was not easy. But a strong counter attack by the Turkish forces was imperative to deny enemy the use of footholds to launch major offensives into the heartland of the peninsula.

The German Marshall Sanders, directed Sodenstern, another German and the GOC of the Turkish Division, to launch the offensive on the Allied positions on 1 May. With almost twenty-one battalions at his disposal, the GOC of the Turkish Division planned to drive the invaders back into the sea with a substantial majority of troops. He planned to launch all available troops into this massive attack. During the past five days, the Turkish troops had given a tough fight to the Allied troops as defenders. This was going to be the first major offensive by the Turks on the peninsula against the Allied troops. The order for the offensive planned for a total annihilation of the Allied invaders and the allegiance to the religion and country was invoked to completely annihilate the invaders. 'Attack the enemy with bayonet and utterly destroy him. We shall not retire one step; for if we do, our religion, our country, and our nation will perish.'[16] The plan of the Turkish High Command was not to let any of the invaders escape unscathed. For this purpose, the troops had been directed to carry inflammable materials to burn down 'everything' of the infidels.

On the night of 1 May, as the troops of the Indian batalions were in the process of settling down, the massive Turkish counter attack manifested. Tremendous pre-attack bombardment by the 56 guns of Turkish Artillery, gave an inkling of the infantry assault to follow. Immediately afterwards, masses of Turkish soldiers had assaulted the hastily prepared and uncoordinated defences of the 29th and the French Divisions. Immediate internal readjustments of defences by the 29th Division and the French Division were instrumental in holding of the captured ground by the MEF and by the first light of 2 May, the Turkish troops had taken a terrible beating.

As the troops in the defences of the Turkish front line were busy in collecting their injured and coordinating the defences, the Commander of the 87th Brigade of the 29th Division carried out a local attack with a mix of troops available with him. The initiative was successful and the Allied line had moved 500 yards ahead along the eastern edge of the Gully Ravine, a no mean achievement considering the situation on the peninsula that day. Though the Turkish offensive had been beaten back, but it had been achieved at a great cost. The French Division had lost 58 officers and 2,064 other ranks, whereas the British losses included 37 officers and 641 other ranks. The losses were huge and '29th Division had lost a disproportionate number of senior officers, including five Battalion commanders, four adjutants and the commander of an Artillery Brigade'.

While the British and French Divisions were involved in actual fighting, the troops of the Indian Battalions, continued to be on standby for the support of the 29th Division, which bore the brunt of the Turkish attack. Amidst a very heavy gunfire through the entire night, the entire Indian Brigade was prepared for induction into the battle at a very short notice. The very first night of the Indian troops of the 29th Brigade on the peninsula was not easy:

The first night on the peninsula was a nerve-racking experience for the 14th Sikhs, for the Turks first broke through a part of the French line and then through a sector held by the 29th Division. On occasions the situation was critical and the 14th Sikhs were ordered to 'stand to' and be prepared to move at a moment's notice. However, the situation was restored by local reserves and the services of the 29th Indian Brigade were not required.[17]

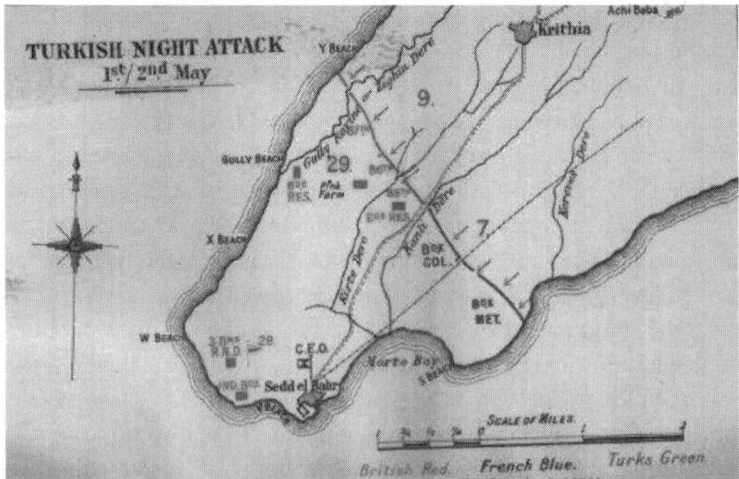

MAP 5: DISPOSITIONS OF THE INDIAN BRIGADE
ON THE NIGHT OF 1/2 MAY 1915[18]

The terrible losses suffered by the French during the Turkish attack on 1 May, forced the GOC of the French Division to seek help from Ian Hamilton. As an immediate measure, two battalions from the Royal Naval Division were put under operational control of the French. Though casualties had been suffered by the 29th Division as well, but Hamilton was in favour of an immediate launch of an offensive into inland. The recent failed offensive by the defender had resulted in a great number of Turkish casualties, which could prove beneficial in an early launched offensive by the MEF. With nearly no hope of an immediate arrival of further reinforcements, except for the recently arrived 29th Indian Brigade, launch of an attack now would definitely put the Turks on a back foot. From England also, the pressure of an early resolution of stalemate had started building up. On 4 May, Lord Kitchener had specifically asked Hamilton about the proposed offensive. 'I hope, the 5th will see you strong enough to press on to Achi Baba. Any delay will allow the Turks to bring up more reinforcements and to make unpleasant preparations for your reception.'[19]

The Indian Infantry Brigade on 2 May had received orders to move up to the junction of the British and French held defence lines. The Brigade, led by 1/6 Gurkhas, had moved up with the OCs of the battalions carrying out initial reconnaissance and orientation with the areas held by its own troops and the enemy. In the absence of any orders for subsequent action, the Brigade had fallen back to the general area of the stone bridge just north of 'W' beach by the evening of the day. The shelling by the enemy was continuing unabatedly. With no covered positions available, the troops of the Indian Infantry Brigade were deployed in very basic and hastily dug trenches.

For the next couple of days the Indian Infantry Brigade was kept on standby on several occasions, sometimes to act as reserves for the attack by Allied troops and sometimes in anticipation of attack by the enemy. The Indian troops, who had boarded the ships on 26 April 1915 were already in a bad state as far as sanitation was concerned. The availability of sea shore at 'W' beach was a welcome opportunity for the Indian troops, who were very particular about taking baths regularly. During one such outing into the welcome relief of sea water, on 4 May, the 69th Punjabis had 7 men wounded from a bomb dropped by an enemy, probably German aircraft flying over the peninsula.

By 4 May, three additional brigade size groups had also arrived at Gallipoli, in addition to the 29th Indian Infantry Brigade. The losses suffered in the initial days of landing by the British forces had necessitated an immediate reorganisation of the available forces. The battalions of the 86th Brigade of the 29th Division, which had borne the brunt of Turkish counter attacks, were divided into two other brigades of the 29th Division. The newly arrived 29th Indian Infantry Brigade and 125th Brigade of the 42nd Division were put under command of the 29th Division. In addition, with the arrival of two dismounted brigades of ANZAC, a composite division with the Headquarter of Royal Naval Division was established. The Royal Naval Division now had three brigades under its command. As the reorganisation of the Allied troops was underway, irrespective of the original affiliations, the Turkish reinforcements were also being rushed into the southern portion of the peninsula. As per an estimate, by 5 May, there were 31 Turkish battalions in the south of Achi Baba. Based on these inputs, the Turkish strength in the vicinity of MEF defences was estimated to be in the range of 18,000 to 20,000 troops. Simultaneously, with the reorganisation of formations of MEF, a redistribution of defensive line held by the British and French troops also took place.

During the redistribution, there was a continuous shelling by Turkish artillery. The Indian troops during this time being in open, with no definite defensive positions, continued to suffer casualties. The balance of the 69th Punjabis on board transport *Umfuli* had also landed during this period. Since the landings of 25 April, except for an initial foothold, nothing substantial had been achieved by the Allied troops. It was imperative to shake the inertia and capture dominating areas immediately in front of Allied defensive positions, before the enemy was able to reinforce it. With readjustments being carried out both in command and control and the defences, it was now the time to launch attack and facilitate inward movement of the MEF. 'General Sir Ian Hamilton considered it essential to gain ground before the enemy had time to strengthen his defences and bring up reinforcements. He therefore ordered a general advance on the 6th of May.'

Catering for a lot of reorganisation and artillery support, detailed orders for the battle of 6 May were issued at 1345 hours on 5 May. The orders specifically mentioned about the morale of the enemy. The enemy had suffered massive losses in their failed attack of 1 May and with the moral ascendancy and numerical superiority, the Allied forces could easily overrun the Turkish front line. The objective of the entire enterprise was the capture of the enemy strong point at Achi Baba, failing of which would make the entire Turkish front line redundant, with no means of supply from the north.

Though in the initial phases the plan of the offensive involved the French Division, but the primary weight of the attack was to be spearheaded by the reorganised 29th Division. The three Brigades of the Division, namely 125th, 87th and 88th, were to be engaged in the offensive of the 29th Division. The 29th Indian Infantry Brigade was to be employed in the reserve and was located almost one mile south-east of the mouth of Gully Ravine. A realistic assessment of the troops being launched into the offensive would reveal that except for the 125th Brigade which had recently arrived, the 87th and 88th Brigades were a poor shadow of their earlier selves. The number of casualties suffered, particularly in the officer ranks in these formations, was serious and was having a detrimental effect on the morale of the troops. Coupled with this, the anticipation of Turkish counter attacks every night along with the digging activity and a very poor state of administrative support, were seriously sapping the available effective manpower. The wounded casualties having been evacuated, the re-inforcements for these formations were still a distant dream.

The Indian Infantry Brigade, though relatively fresh, again was in reserve. Non-utilisation of the Indian Brigade in the second battle of Krithia on 6 May can only be attributed to the factor of composition of the Indian Brigade in terms of troops. Both the 69th and 89th Punjabis of the Indian Brigade had three companies each of PMs. Though Ian Hamilton had time and again requested for a complete Gurkha Brigade from GOC Egypt, the nomination of 29th Indian Brigade for the operations on Gallipoli, if seen from the perspective of GOC Egypt would appear to be logical. The other two brigades of Indian battalions at Egypt, namely the 28th and 30th Infantry Brigades also didn't have the complete composition of the Gurkha Battalions.

Changing the homogeneity of the Indian Brigades at Egypt and reorganising one complete Gurkha Brigade, was against the basic tenets of military tactics. GOC Egypt also had a Composite Imperial Brigade at its disposal, but the regulations in vogue at that time prohibited the mixing of the regular troops with the Imperial troops. With no feasible permutation and combination possible, the War Office had made the 29th Indian Infantry Brigade available to MEF, with two Punjabi, one Sikh and one Gurkha Battalions. The composition of the Indian Brigade kept on changing during its stay in Gallipoli, and by the end of operations at Gallipoli in December, the 29th Indian Infantry Brigade consisted of four Gurkha battalions and one Sikh battalion.

For the proposed offensive, the operation order of the Indian Brigade was issued by Brigadier General Cox on 5 May. The success signal nominated for the troops of the Brigade included a red rocket for the infantry when it was halfway across the ground towards enemy trenches, white rocket when it was close to the trenches and the green rocket when the enemy trenches had been captured. The operation order specified that the complete complement of the 29th Indian Infantry Brigade was to include 14th Sikhs, 1/6 Gurkhas less 69th Punjabis while half the Battalion of the 89th Punjabis will be prepared to move at short notice. To cater for two routes of induction for the advance, both the battalions were allotted separate areas for the night.

For the logistics support, each battalion was allotted 93 mules on pack basis for the advance. As part of the mobilisation each man was to carry on person 200 rounds of ammunition, one day of cooked meal and two days of emergency ration. For animals, the scale involved two days of grains in addition to the current day. For the supply beyond specified three days, an officer under the Brigade arrangements was detailed to organise this move with the respective battalion Quartermasters and mule carts from the second line Cart Corps and an escort from the 69th Punjabis.

The Brigade continued to be in reserve for the entire day on 6 May while a determined attack was launched on the Turkish trenches by the French, 88th and 87th British Brigades, Lancashire Fusiliers Brigade and Composite Naval Brigades. The allies made great efforts to advance on the 6th, 7th and 8th May, but success eluded them and

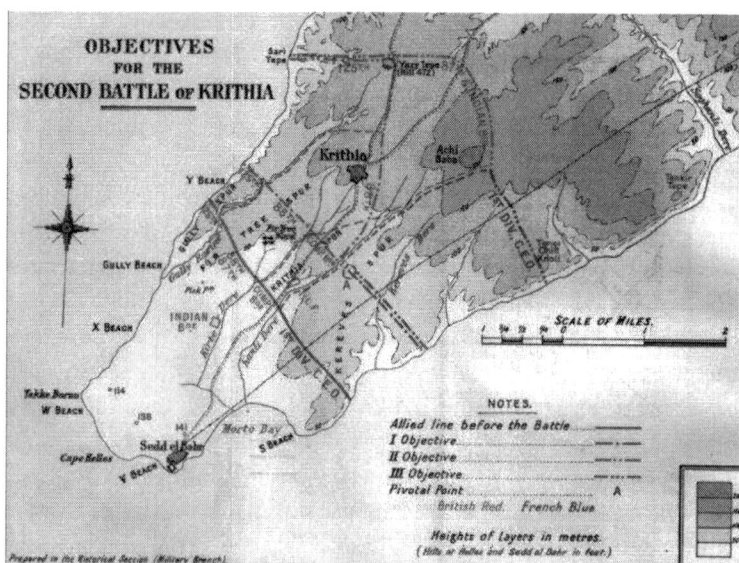

MAP 6: OBJECTIVES FOR THE SECOND BATTLE OF KRITHIA
AND THE DISPOSITIONS OF THE INDIAN BRIGADE[20]

the battle ended with the Allied line advancing nowhere more than six hundred yards.' Though the Allied troops fought bravely under the circumstances, the lack of inherent Artillery support had made the task difficult. The planned offensive began at time on 6 May, but the limited artillery support did not let the troops to cross the wire obstacles of Turkish forward posts itself. The 29th Division was not able to locate the main defences of the enemy and was actively engaged by the advance positions. By evening there had been no change in the front lines of either, and the status quo as on morning of 6 May continued.

Realising the necessity of retaining the momentum of the initiative, fresh orders for the resumption of offensive in the forenoon of the next day had been issued by the evening of 6 May. In an exact repeat of the situation, of the previous day, the assault did not achieve much, except for causing more casualties in the MEF. Due to continuous assaults being initiated by the MEF, the artillery ammunition was depleting day by day and the replenishment of the same was nowhere in sight. While the sustained operations by the allied troops continued on 7 and 8 May as well, the Indian Brigade was still in reserve. Another Operation Order of 7 May, directed the Indian Brigade to continue in reserve and when ordered to move, the battalions were to leave all surplus kits at the present positions and the troops were to advance with personal weapons and entrenching tools only. The artillery shells of the Turks, were still inflicting damage and casualties. The mules and drivers of the Indian Mule Corps were the most affected due to this intense shelling by the Turkish artillery. With casualties to mules due to shrapnels, all mule transport was ordered to immediately move back. 'The Brigade remained in reserve in the same position throughout the morning and evening while the New Zealanders and Australians attacked the Turkish trenches in its front and the 87th Infantry Brigade further to the left.'[21] When the Indian Brigade was in reserve, some components of the formation were continuing to provide manpower for the fatigue duties on the beach. The supplies being dumped at the shores needed to be moved up. Almost complete component of the 69th Punjabis was deployed for these beach fatigues.

On the same night, reorganisation of defensive positions took place, in which 14th Sikhs and Battalion less two Double Companies of 89th Punjabis occupied trenches in conjunction with British troops. As the operation was in the initial stages itself, the number of trenches were limited. With frequent turnover of troops due to changes in area of responsibility of operations of various battalions, the limited space available in the trenches was getting dearer by the day. The 89th Punjabis trenches were overcrowded due to the presence of troops of South Wales Borderers of the 88th Brigade who were sent back from the front line for rest and recoup. Meanwhile, 1/6 Gurkhas and the 29th Indian Infantry Brigade Headquarters had occupied positions in the reserve, slightly behind the forward line.

In another turn of events, the Indian Brigade was directed to take over another set of defences, when the orders were received that the formation will relieve troops of the 87th Brigade on the northern flank by 1900 hours on 9 May. As a result, 1/6 Gurkhas took over the defences held by the King's Own Scottish Borderers, extending from coast to the ravine. The 89th Punjabis relieved the troops of Royal Inniskilling Fusiliers along with the Machine Gun section of the 69th Punjabis and the 14th Sikhs was deployed from ravine to sea coast along the erstwhile front line. Brigade Headquarters was deployed along the eastern edge of ravine, in line with the deployment of the 14th Sikhs. During this time, there being no protection from enemy shelling, trenches were the only saviours. For the next four days the Indian Brigade continued to hold the front line. This was the time when the trench warfare was beginning to get hold at Gallipoli. The intent on both sides was to move forward inch by inch on a daily basis and capture as much ground as possible, however, least it may be. 'Trench warfare had now begun and all efforts were directed to consolidating and strengthening the front and to raiding small sections of the enemy's line.'[22]

With an aim to break the stalemate and capture the maximum possible territory, the plans for offensive were in the process of being crystallised. In this series of offensives to regain momentum, a limited offensive was planned by the 29th Indian Infantry Brigade. As part of the operation, a massive artillery tirade was launched against Turkish defences. A Double Company of 1/6 Gurkha silently moved along the sea shore very skilfully and scaled a 300-foot-high bluff. By 0430 hours on 13 May with fire support provided by the Machine Gun section of the battalion, the second Double Company of the Gurkhas had reinforced the first Double Company and by the first light of 13 May 1915, the bluff was firmly in the hands of the Gurkhas. The bold and brazen maneuver by the troops of the Indian Brigade provided the much needed momentum to the stalled offensive. By virtue of this action of Indian troops, the forward line of the formation was able to move forward by about 600 yards, a significant distance in the terrain and conditions of those times on the peninsula. This dashing and very skilfully executed move came at the cost of very limited own casualties. The bravery and determination in the face of heavy odds was duly recognised in the General Routine Order, number sixteen of 17 May 1915. 'In order to recognize the good work done by the 1/6 Gurkha Rifles in capturing the bluff on the coast west of Krithia, the General Officer commanding has ordered that this bluff will in future be known as the Gurkha Bluff.'

Due to the advance of 1/6 Gurkhas, there was a requirement of readjustment of own defences again. Number 1 and 2 Double Companies of the 14th Sikhs in the morning of 13 May immediately moved ahead to support operations of Gurkhas. In the afternoon, another set of orders had directed 14th Sikhs to take over defences from the 89th Punjabis and the right half of ground held by the Gurkhas. Number 3 and 4 Double Companies of the Sikhs relieved the 89th Punjabis, whereas the first and second Double Companies took over the right half from the Gurkhas. Due to the freshly captured areas in and around the Gurkha Bluff, the consolidation of the position was imperative to prevent Turkish counterattacks. The enemy was continuously interdicting the consolidation and induction of fresh troops into the area with shelling and some weak counter attacks. In order to provide relief to the embattled troops of the 14th Sikhs, one Sikh Company of 69th Punjabis under the command of Subadar Ganga Singh, was placed under the command of the 14th Sikhs. Ultimately the Machine Gun section of the Sikhs was moved ahead along with a company of Royal Fusiliers to support the consolidation, which the Sikhs were able to complete. The entire next day, 14th Sikhs continued to improve the defensive posture while the enemy also continued to shell the area with intermittent artillery fire.

By the evening of 14 May, both the Punjabi battalions of the Indian Brigade had started receiving indirect messages to be prepared to move out from Gallipoli peninsula at a very short notice. The exemplary work initiated by the brave troops of these two battalions was left in between when the firm orders for the withdrawal from the peninsula were received in the early hours of 15 May. As the orders specified for immediate move out, both the battalions after getting relieved from the front line, had concentrated at 'V' beach by evening. The urgency to deinduct both 69th and 89th Punjabis from the peninsula was so severe that the complete complement of 89th Punjabis along with two Double Companies of 69th Punjabis had boarded HT *Suffolk* on the same night and moved out from the peninsula for France. Similarly, after a very limited, but a significant contribution towards the war effort by the Indian troops of the battalions, the balance two Double Companies of 69th Punjabis, had also boarded HT *Hymettus* on the same evening. Four British officers of 69th Punjabis were left with the 29th Indian Infantry Brigade. These officers, after the departure of the battalion, were posted with 108th Field Ambulance, 29th Brigade Signal Company, 29th Brigade

Ammunition column and as the 29th Brigade Transport Officer, respectively.

When these two battalions moved out of the Order of Battle of the 29th Indian Infantry Brigade, two British battalions, namely, the 1st Lancashire Fusiliers and the 1st Royal Inniskilling Fusiliers were temporarily placed under the Order of Battle of the 29th Indian Infantry Brigade. With the change in composition of the Brigade, the GOC of the formation ordered a fresh redistribution of troops to hold the Brigade defences. In addition, a stock of the casualties' figures of the formation as on 15 May was also carried out. All the four battalions of the formation had suffered the first blood on Gallipoli. This, however, was just the initiations and the situation were going to get repeated, day after day and month after month, while the Indians stayed in Gallipoli. By 15 May 1915, the Indian Infantry Brigade had already suffered 39 personnel killed, 224 wounded and 5 missing, but the pinnacle of sacrifice, grit and determination was yet to come. In the meantime, through Operation Order Number 7, the 29th Indian Infantry Brigade ordered the redistribution of defences, among the battalions of the Brigade.

TABLE 15: CASUALTY FIGURES OF THE INDIAN INFANTRY BRIGADE: 15 MAY 1915[23]

14th Sikhs			69th Punjabis			89th Punjabis			1/6 GR		
Killed	Wounded	Missing	Killed	Wounded	Missing	Killed	Wounded	Missing	Killed	Wounded	Missing
8	58	2	1	17	0	7	78	3	23	71	0

While in the southern peninsula, the Indian Brigade was getting baptized by fire on landing, in the northern part, in support of ANZACs, the two Indian Mountain Batteries were providing an excellent account of themselves. Both the batteries were under command of ANZAC during the time. On 19 May 1915, the enemy launched a massive offensive at about four in the morning on the ANZAC defences. When the attack by the Turks was unfolding, the CO of the 21st (Kohat) Mountain Battery was with the guns of the Battery. The central section of the Battery was drawing heavy fire from the Turkish artillery. The conduct of the men of the Battery was exceptional on this day and the CO being the first hand witness to this, was full of praise for the men and animals of the Battery. Timely replenishment of ammunition at the gun position was imperative for offensive or defensive fire support by the artillery. The entire action of the Battery was dependent on the loads carried by mules and their drivers and these did not let the *Naam, Namak* and *Nishan* of the Battery to go down:

Now leading a mule was very different from proceeding by bounds as I did. A mule does not take cover when it hears a shell, but on the contrary probably stops to bray, or whatever a mule's song is called, yet not a man jibbed and not a mule broke loose from its driver. Altogether, if the Battery had never done another good thing, they had earned my eternal gratitude for their work this day.[24]

A noteworthy peculiarity of the section was that, in spite of the continuous interference by the enemy, this particular section continued to support the Allied infantry from same position till the ultimate withdrawal was realised in December 1915. The gun position of the section was largely the same, from the time of the arrival of the Battery on Gallipoli to its departure. The Observation Post (OP) of the section had been very cleverly camouflaged position and the Turks were never able to accurately pinpoint the location of the post. It has been claimed that the post of the section was finally identified by the Turks during the Suvla operations in August 1915, when an Australian artillery battery had tried to construct the position of its OP very next to the OP of the central section of the Kohat Battery. When the Turks shelled the OP of the central section, the OP officer of the Kohat Battery along with his radio operator was buried.

On 21 May, the GOC of the 29th Indian Infantry Brigade visited the location of the 14th Sikhs and a plan for the move forward of troops of the battalion by about 200 yards was discussed. The plan involved moving forward of Sikhs defence line to include a small nullah emanating from the gully ravine into the battalion defences. Prompt and swift action by a Double Company of the battalion ensured successful advance by the battalion. A very prompt and dashing action by the Sikhs ensured the linking of the new defensive

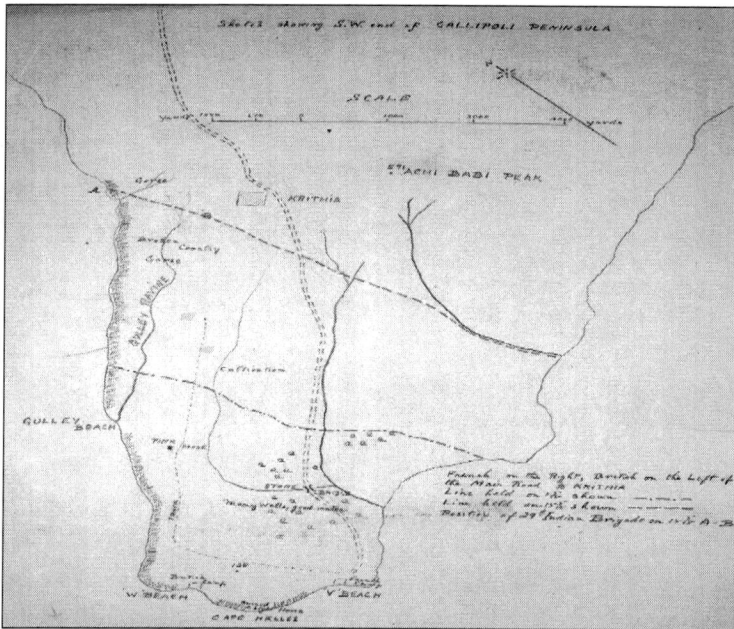

MAP 7: DISPOSITIONS OF THE 29TH INDIAN INFANTRY BRIGADE
AS ON 15 MAY 1915[25]

line with Lancashire Fusiliers on the left and 88th Brigade on the right
of the 14th Sikhs.

During this period, another important series of events had started
to unravel. In an improvised and modified tactic, in the front held by
each battalion, the troops were directed to advance by digging forward
in the night leading to a process of continuous digging. During day
time, the troops of the 29th Indian Infantry Brigade were digging and
improving their existing defences to make them more defensive and
safer. During the night, the same troops moved ahead of the defensive
line into the No Man's land in the front and were digging smaller
trenches with little or no commotion so as not to arouse the suspicion
of the Turks. This new line of trenches was abandoned by the first
light, troops used to fall back to the own line and continuous improvement of the same was resorted to during the subsequent nights.

The next in line were the communication trenches to link these
trenches. After the new system of trenches was stabilised, the troops

FIGURE 12: IMPROVING THE DEFENCES: 14TH SIKHS[26]

used to occupy these and their own defensive line used to move forward. The new trench line was occupied after two or three nights of improvement. The process continued through the entire defensive line held by the 29th Indian Infantry Brigade, until the troops were within 50 yards of Turkish defences. Sometimes the Turks used to occupy these newly dug trenches in the night, against which the troops of the Indian Brigade had to use force of firing by weapons or bayonets to move out the Turks. These were, however, small-scale affairs, as the dimensions of the newly created defences didn't allow occupation of these trenches by a major force of the enemy and only a few soldiers of enemy were able to occupy them. During this time, in a major flare up, the enemy one night, infiltrated in strength and occupied an extensive portion of these newly created defences. The Sikhs were surprised to see the trenches being occupied by the Turks:

On the night of 22 May, Captain Engledue (attached from 69th Punjabis), moved out with B Company of the Battalion (14th Sikhs), to occupy trenches constructed the previous night, he found that a section of trench on his right which had been dug by the 2nd Royal Fusiliers was occupied by the Turks.[27]

Taking advantage of the captured launch pad, occupied in the defences of Royal Fusiliers, the Turks were planning a counter attack. The enemy tried to exploit the gap in defences between 'B' Company of the 14th Sikhs and the Royal Fusiliers. 'A' Company of the 14th

Sikhs covered the gap and further inroad by the enemy into the Brigade defences was halted. Simultaneously, another attack was launched by the enemy on the defences held by the 1st Battalion Royal Inniskilling Fusiliers and 1/6 Gurkha Rifles. The ferocity of the attack by the enemy resulted in abandoning of a machine gun by the 1/6 Gurkha Rifles in the trenches. 'Later in the evening, about 18:00, a counter-attack by the 1st Bn Royal Inniskilling Fusiliers and 1/6th Gurkha Rifles recaptured the old King's Own Scottish Borderers trench and retook the abandoned Machine Gun. All the Turks in the trench were killed.'[28]

On the other side, the Sikhs had launched a ferocious counterattack on to the Turkish line and ejected the enemy from the occupied trenches and reclaimed the trench line during the same night itself. The attack by the battalions of the 29th Indian Infantry Brigade was a great success. An estimated 700 of enemy troops were dead in front of the Brigade defence line. With weather conditions unbearable, the varying degree of death and decay of enemy troops lying in the No Man's land in front of Indian Brigade sector was a major health scare. The war diary of the 29th Indian Infantry Brigade of 22 May 1915, talks about this apprehension. 'Many unburied dead are lying in our front. Those will cause a serious nuisance in a day or two and as things are, it is impossible to bury them.'

This was a first major engagement of Indian Infantry Brigade in the operations in the peninsula. With only two Indian Battalions and two British Battalions, the actions of the Brigade were indeed very determined and resulted in the overall objectives of the GOC 29th Division being achieved. The camaraderie and the integration achieved between the Indian and British Battalions, while under the overall command of the 29th Indian Infantry Brigade was a major take away of the operation:

For the prompt action by the 14th Sikhs in relieving the pressure on Royal Fusiliers, the Sikhs received the thanks of the commander of the Royal Fusiliers. A pleasant sequel followed six years later, when both battalions being stationed at Khyber Pass, the officers of the Royal Fusiliers presented the officers of the 14th Sikhs with a silver grenade inscribed: *In Memory of Gallipoli 1915, and the Khyber Pass, 1921.*[29]

On 24 May, the 1st Battalion of Royal Munster Fusiliers was placed under the command of the 29th Indian Infantry Brigade, with an aim to relieve 1/6 Gurkha Rifles for a much-needed rest and recoup. The relief of troops was completed by last light on the same day. The Gurkha Battalion moved as reserve on the "Y" Beach. In another planning of relief of troops in contact with the enemy, Royal Inniskilling Fusiliers which was in reserve till date was directed on 26 May to relieve the troops of the 1st Battalion Lancashire Fusiliers in the centre of the Brigade defence line. After two days, the Gurkha Battalion was ordered to take over operational responsibility from Royal Munster Fusiliers.

The Operation Order Number 8 dated 27 May issued by the 29th Indian Infantry Brigade, directed Royal Munster Rifles to move back under command of the 87th Infantry Brigade. The Operation Order also included some fresh readjustments in the own defence line. The Indian Infantry Brigade was on this day occupying a frontage of approximately 800 yards on the extreme left of the British defences. The dispositions of the battalions of the Brigade included Gurkhas holding the defences on a series of small cliffs along the Aegean Sea. The 1st Battalion of Lancashire Fusiliers was holding the centre of the Brigade line across the Gully Spur. The Sikhs were on the extreme right of the formation and were in coordination with the 4th Worcestershire Battalion of the 88th Brigade on the right. The Brigade Headquarters along with 108th Indian Field Ambulance and the 1st Royal Inniskilling Fusiliers as reserve continued to be located in the general area of the "Y" Beach. Due to the recent ferociousness of the attack by the enemy and to cater for the sufficient time allowance for the reserves to move out at short notice, the reserves were well placed at three different locations. Along with the Brigade Headquarters, the complete Battalion of Lancashire Fusiliers less one company was located, whereas one company of the battalion was located in the vicinity of Gurkha Bluff. Half battalion of the 14th Sikhs was placed as reserve in Gully Ravine. In addition, the extent of defences allotted to each unit was deliberately kept small to ensure regular relief of troops from within the respective battalion resources:

The length of line allotted to each unit permits of the firing line being held in sufficient strength to withstand attack by day and night and allows for about 2/3 of each unit being in close and more distant support, enabling at least half the strength of each corps to obtain regular rest and sleep and permitting of reliefs of firing line and close support within units at short intervals.[30]

The casualty returns of 29th Indian Infantry Brigade Headquarters of the time reveals the intensity of the battles and the quantum of the casualties suffered by the battalions of the formation with maximum casualties in the list being suffered by the battalions on the night of 22/23 May 1915.

TABLE 16: CASUALTIES INDIAN INFANTRY BRIGADE: 30 MAY 1915[31]

14th Sikhs			1/6 GR			1st Lancashire Fusiliers			1st Royal Inniskilling Fusiliers			1st Royal Munster Fusiliers			108 Field Ambulance		
Killed	*Wounded*	*Missing*	*Killed*	*Wounded*	*Missing*	*Killed*	*Wounded*	*Missing*	*Killed*	*Wounded*	*Missing*	*Killed*	*Wounded*	*Missing*	*Killed*	*Wounded*	*Missing*
17	60	8	21	51	0	3	19	0	52	91	14	2	13	0	1	3	0

Apart from launching counterattacks and defending against the desperate counterattacks by the enemy, the battalions of the Indian Infantry Brigade were also deeply involved in the digging, in order to create additional space and making these trenches slightly more liveable. The weather conditions during this time were very warm and humid. These conditions warranted a continuous supply of water to the frontline troops. Along with this, in view of the number of casualties being suffered, there was a never-ending requirement to find replacement of casualties to man the defences.

Though the mules with drivers of the Supply Corps were allocated to the battalions of the Indian Brigade, there was a need to provide guides and escorts for these in order to reach the locations wherever possible and also for the purpose of inherent protection. Wherever the mule tracks were not there or reaching of mules was not possible due to tactical reasons, the dumping of stores and water was carried out at the track head and further carriage of stores, ammunition, water and rations was organised under the arrangements of the respective battalions. Some of the troops of Indian Brigade were also deployed on the administrative duties associated with the operations and the tasks entrusted to these troops included looking after the landings of stores, equipment, arms and ammunition meant for the battalions of the Indian Brigade. As some British battalions were also forming part of the 29th Indian Infantry Brigade during this period, the Indian troops were also performing the task of guiding the reinforcements joining these battalions to the respective operational locations. One British officer of Royal Munster Fusiliers had an unexpected face off with a Sikh Subadar during one such reception:

I was one of 18 of the unattached officers posted to the 1st Battalion Royal Munster Fusiliers, 29th Division and told to report to them forthwith on Gallipoli itself. We had already packed our kit, all 30 lb. of it: and so, we at once proceeded with it to the gangway to which we were directed. This led us down to a fleet sweeper of some size, already partly loaded with troops, of whom many were Indians. At the foot of the gangway, as we stepped aboard, there stood a Sikh Subadar, a magnificent specimen of a man with a long black beard, who must have stood six feet four or five and was broad with it. As each of us officers came abreast of him, he gave him a quick glance and then peered into his face, and either stepped back or gave him an obviously approving pat on the shoulder. I was not one of those approved of; I was still too lanky.[32]

THE PUNJABIS DURING THOSE FIFTEEN DAYS

When Hamilton wrote his Diary on 1 May 1915, the 29th Indian Infantry Brigade along with four of its battalions was in the process of landing on the peninsula. Hamilton initially had requested for a 'Gurkha Brigade' to provide momentum to the operations at Gallipoli, which were almost stalemated after the initial landings by the Allies on 25 April 1915. When the Indian Brigade was finally ready to be employed in the operations at Gallipoli, the composition of the battalions of the Brigade was another cause of concern for Hamilton. At this time, the 29th Indian Infantry Brigade was composed of 69th and 89th Punjabis, besides the 14th Sikhs and 1/6 Gurkhas. In the immediate aftermath of certain desertions by the Muslim troops of the empire in other theatres and a series of reverses being faced by the

MEF on the peninsula, Hamilton was not going to take a chance. Even if the situation warranted for the employment of troops of the 69th and 89th Punjabis in close combat with the Turks, Hamilton had taken a word from Commander of the Indian Brigade, that these two battalions will not be used in the fighting area:

Cox is not going to take his Punjabi Mohammedans into the fighting area, but will leave them on 'W' Beach. He says, if we were sweeping on victoriously, he would take them on, but that, as things are, it would not be fair to them to do so.[33]

Though these two Punjabi Battalions stayed on Gallipoli only for 15 days, prior to their withdrawal, these troops were instrumental in establishing the initial foothold on the southern peninsula for the 29th Indian Brigade. Due to obvious reasons, the research and discussion about their stay on Gallipoli has generally eluded the popular consciousness.

89th Punjabis was raised at Machilipatnam by Captain A. Macleod in 1798. The battalion had undergone a series of transformations in designations and composition in its history by the time it had landed on Gallipoli. The battalion was designated as 29th Burma Infantry in 1901 and the designation of the 89th Punjabis was adopted by the battalion in 1903. After a very demanding tenure at Meiktila, Burma the 89th Punjabis had arrived at Dinapore on 17 April 1914. As the Indian Battalions were still operating on an eight-company structure, out of eight companies in the 89th Punjabis, three companies were Sikhs, three of PMs, one company of Rajputs and one company of Brahmins.

As part of the mobilisation for the Great War, the battalion received general orders for mobilisation on 11 October 1914 and had left India for Egypt on board the HT *Edavana* on 2 November 1914 from Karachi. The battalion had disembarked at Suez and occupied defences along the canal by the first week of December 1915, after destroying the Turkish defences at 'Sheikh Said' on 10 November 1914 in a major operation. A Turkish attack on the canal in February 1915 was repelled by the battalion, without any allegations or incidents of mutiny on religious grounds.

The 89th Punjabis landed on Gallipoli along with the other

battalions of the 29th Indian Infantry Brigade on 1 May 1915. The employment profile of the battalion for the next fifteen days, generally confirm to the prophecy of Hamilton, which he had inscribed in his Diary on 1 May 1915. The troops had started disembarking by the first light on 1 May and by evening the battalion established itself in bivouacs, on the cliffs between "V" and "W" beaches on Cape Helles. With all the outposts of Allied troops under heavy attack throughout the night, and 89th Punjabis in reserve, the battalion had rested in its accoutrement's. Similarly, for the next day as well, the battalion again stayed as reserve. On 2 May, though the entire Indian Brigade was ordered to move ahead and 89th Punjabis as third battalion in the Order of March had moved out for front line early in the day, but after moving out for a while, the entire formation halted and continued to stay in reserve for the whole day. The Indian Brigade had returned to their earmarked places by the evening of 2 May.

For the next few days, the entire battalion was employed to improve the trenches along the second line from "Y" beach eastwards. A fatigue party of almost 400 troops from the battalion was also employed for making shelters for the 87th Brigade of the 29th Division. On 6 May, with the French ordered to move further ahead, the battalion was tasked to occupy a line of trenches vacated by the French. The 'E' Company of the battalion moved further ahead to occupy some advance isolated trenches. A 'flurry of orders, changing at the last moment', continued to engage the battalion for the next few days. The battalion by this time was occupying positions from the sea to the ravine running up from Gully beach.

The 89th Punjabis continued to improve trenches and observation positions. A party of engineers from Anzac was also working with the battalion to place barbed wire obstacles across the bottom of the ravine in the gaps between picquet posts in the ravine. From 10 May onwards, the battalion had faced mass attacks from the enemy, with reinforcements at some point being detailed from troops of the 88th Brigade. Two machine guns of the 69th Punjabis attached with the battalion were recalled on 12 May and in their place two machine guns of Armoured Motor Company attached with the Naval Division arrived for support of the battalion.

A series of counter attacks by the Turkish coupled with incessant

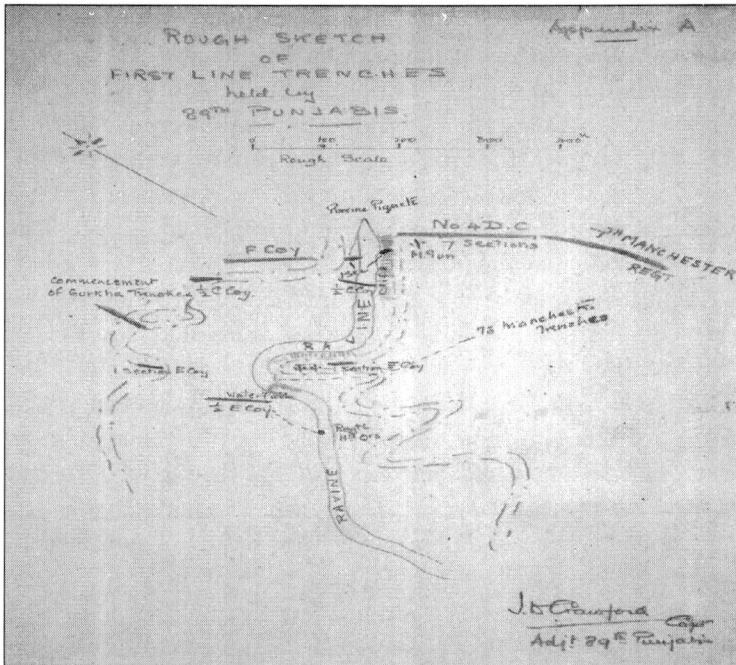

MAP 8: DEPLOYMENT OF THE 89TH PUNJABIS: AS ON 6 MAY 1915[34]

shelling during this time had resulted in severe casualties of the battalion. The Medical Officer of the battalion, besides providing medical attention, to its own casualties also took care of the casualties of the neighbouring Manchester Regiment, which was also in the thick of battle. When 89th Punjabis was relieved by the 14th Sikhs on 13 May, the casualties of the battalion included one British officer and three Indian officers wounded, five other ranks killed and 35 wounded. On the last day of fighting by the battalion on Gallipoli, a total of 46,108 rounds were fired by the troops, bespeaking of the ferocity of the Turkish counter-attack.

By this time a string of rumours had started floating, which talked about withdrawal of the battalion along with the 69th Punjabis from the peninsula. True to these, the orders for the evacuation of the 89th and 69th Punjabis were received. On 14 May 1915, the battalion had reached in its bivouacked location next to the beach and spent the whole day waiting for transport. The orders for embarkation were received very late in the evening and the embarkation on board S.S *Suffolk* was able to commence only in the early hours of 15 May. The battalion within 15 days of its arrival on the peninsula was further enroute to Alexandria, leaving behind a saga of bravery and sacrifice of the highest order. The battalion had arrived at Alexandria by 0930 hours on 18 May and was allotted to the 7th Ferozepore Infantry Brigade of the 3rd Indian (Lahore) Division earmarked for operations in France along the Western Front.

Similarly placed, like the 89th Punjabis, the 69th Punjabis also had a class company composition, in which three companies were of PMs and the other companies were of Sikhs and Brahmins. The battalion was raised in 1759 as the 10th Battalion Coast Sepoys and had joined the 29th Indian Brigade from the 5th Jhelum Brigade, where the battalion was serving under the 2nd Rawalpindi Division. From the deployment of the canal defences, the battalion had embarked on board HT *Japanese Prince,* along with the 89th Punjabis and anchored at Cape Helles at 07:00 hours on 30 April 1915. Like the 89th Punjabis, the battalion was also very rarely employed in the close combat with the Turks. All the four Double Companies of the battalion were bivouacked in a camp immediately above the 'W' beach by afternoon. The battalion as part of the Brigade was on standby for the entire night as breakthrough by the Turks through the lines held by the British and French troops was highly expected.

With every Turkish attack, the entire formation was kept ready to reinforce the threatened localities at short notice. On 6 May, a general attack on Turkish held line was planned to commence by 10:30 hours. The offensive was launched by a composite brigade sized force. The 29th Indian Infantry Brigade less '69th Punjabis and half a battalion of 89th Punjabis' was in reserve. The Machine Gun section of the battalion was attached with the 14th Sikhs for the offensive. In spite of not being in reserve, both 69th and 89th Punjabis were left in the trenches itself and were tasked to provide beach working parties for the newly arrived East Lancashire Division for unloading stores and clearing the beach.

The process of detailment for providing beach fatigue parties by the battalion continued for the next few days. With almost no protection from enemy shelling, the battalion continued to suffer casualties while working at the beach. On 13 May, the battalion was tasked to occupy support trenches in the third line between the sea on the left and gully ravine on the right. The cooking pots, rations and the kits of the men arrived later on with the pack animals. The battalion on 14 May had provided a company under Subadar Ganga Singh to the 14th Sikhs as reinforcements. The orders for evacuation from peninsula were received on 14 May and the battalion embarked on board S.S *Suffolk* and sailed out on 15 May 1915 for Alexandria from the V Beach.

In spite of complement of two full battalions of the Indian Infantry Brigade, being available in combat ready situation, the resource was not employed by the 29th Division. This was the time, when the 29th Division and its battalions had suffered massive casualties in their efforts to gain a foot hold on the peninsula. Within five days of the landings of the 29th Division, a full complement of the Indian Brigade was available, ready to be employed. The internal machinations and deliberations, however, obviated its employment and the MEF in spite of having additional battalions, on 15 May 1915 was relatively in similar situation as they were on 30 April 1915.

Battles for Krithia

Worn out by their exertions of the past week, inadequately supplied with hand- bombs and other equipment vital for this type of fighting, and almost completely without effective Artillery support, the allied soldiers could make little progress against their hidden enemy. The pitiless sun, already hot enough to cause discomfort, was another burden on the shoulders of the dogged but exhausted Infantry.[35]

When the Indian Brigade was embarked on respective transports towards Gallipoli, the offensive, also known as the first battle of Krithia, for the capture of Achi Baba ridge was launched by MEF on 28 April 1915. The offensive was a total failure and with almost 2,000 plus casualties among its men and officers, 29th Division was on its edge. Along with virtually no possibility for additional re-inforcements in the immediate future, the Achi Baba was too far to be a reality for the MEF.

As discussed in the earlier part of the chapter, regaining the initiative was imperative for both sides to avoid the situation slipping into a stalemate. The stakes here were higher for the MEF, as a situation of stalemate as obtained along the Western Front, would not have augured well politically and diplomatically. The Turks on the other hand, also were eager to seize initiative and dislodge the invaders as early as possible. With this as an aim, the Turks had launched an offensive on 1 May, when the Indian Brigade was in the process of settling down on the peninsula. The second battle of Krithia, for capturing the Achi Baba ridge was launched by the allies on 6 May. In spite of the operation getting extended into the second and third day, no tangible outcome was achieved by either side, except for suffering of severe casualties by the both.

To end the stalemate existing on the peninsula, another offensive, the third battle for the capture of Krithia was being planned by the MEF. The aim of the proposed offensive was to gain tactical advantages in front of the entire own defence line. With a sufficient supply of shells ensured on the peninsula, unlike the first and second battles of Krithia, this time a 'heavy Artillery barrage' was assured. The availability of troops, to the tune of almost 30,000 this time also was weighing heavily in the mind of General Hunter Weston, the commander of newly formed VIII Corps. Towards this a meeting, on 1 June 1915, was held by the GOC of the 29th Indian Infantry Brigade with the GOC of the 29th British Division.

Immediately after return of GOC from the Divisional Headquarters, a conference of the Commanding Officers was called for. The continuous demand of a Gurkha Brigade by Hamilton, in the meantime, had also found favour with the military planners by now. With both the 69th and 89th Punjabis having moved out; a deficiency was created with the 29th Indian Infantry Brigade. So, while the preparations for the planned offensive were going on, two additional Gurkha battalions arrived from Egypt on 3 June to reinforce the Indian Brigade. The 2nd Battalion, 10th Gurkha Rifles and 1st Battalion, 5th Gurkha Rifles on arrival were, however, placed under command of the 87th Infantry Brigade of the 29th British Division. Sikhs while in defences and improving the defensive posture also witnessed a series of high-level visits to the defences of the 'Red tabbed staff officers'. With an experience of almost a month at the peninsula,

FIGURE 13: TROOPS OF THE 14TH SIKHS JUST PRIOR TO THE
THIRD BATTLE OF KRITHIA[36]

the Sikhs had the premonition of an offensive developing through their defences or they themselves going for an offensive, with the second option being closer to the reality.

As part of the overall plan, the attack plan of 29th Indian Infantry Brigade was issued through the Operation Order Number 9 of 3 June 1915. The troops tasked for the attack was supposed to advance uphill up the spurs and contest the occupancy of the nullahs at the same time as maintaining an approximately straight line. The operation order specifically provided detailed plan for the preparatory artillery bombardment for softening of the target prior to the launch of Infantry. The wire obstacles erected in front of the enemy trenches had proved to be a formidable obstacle for the Allied infantry, particularly in the second battle of Krithia. To have a reasonable chance of success, it was therefore, imperative that the wire obstacle was destroyed just prior to the attack being launched. To keep the enemy head down during the launch of assault by troops and for the purpose of degradation of wire obstacles, an increased belief on the capabilities of MEF was absolutely in order:

It was arranged that on 4th of June an Artillery bombardment would be carried out from 0800 hours to 1120 hours all along the allied front. The guns would then cease firing for ten minutes, during which the forward troops would cheer and show fixed bayonets above their trenches to induce the enemy to man his parapets. From 1130 hours to 1200 hours in the noon, the guns would bombard the enemy's front line heavily. At 1200 hours the batteries would increase their range and the first Infantry wave would rush out of their trenches to the assault, followed at 1215 hours by the second wave.[37]

The attack plan of the 29th Indian Infantry Brigade involved capturing the assigned objective in two succeeding waves. Surprisingly, the Operation Order Number 9 of 3 June 1915 did not provide any specific details about the objective, with the actual objective being referred to as the objective only. The battalions may have been given specific objectives verbally or through other means as copy of the above-mentioned Operation Order was endorsed to all the battalions. The first wave of the brigade was to capture a series of Turkish defences along the trench line referred to as J11 and consolidate the position after capture. The troops allocated in the first wave included battalion less two Double Companies of 1/6 Gurkhas, 1st Battalion Lancashire Fusiliers and two Double Companies of 14th Sikhs. Second wave of the attack, following immediately behind, was to capture the subsequent Turkish trench line, known as J13. Troops for the second wave included two Double Companies of 1/6 Gurkhas, 1st Battalion Royal Inniskilling Fusiliers less two companies and battalion less two Double Companies of the 14th Sikhs. Two companies of Royal Inniskilling formed the brigade reserve for the offensive.

The designated objective of the 14th Sikhs was at the far end of an open ground which sloped upwards in the north-east direction. The objective of Gully spur dropped abruptly into the Gully Ravine, which was about 75 yards wide and 40-50 feet deep. The lay of the ground was very ideal for defender and offered numerous advantages to him for contesting the advance of troops of MEF. The three gullies to be used for attack by VIII Corps to include Gully Ravine, Krithia Nullah and Achi Baba Nullah/ Kanli Dere divided the Gallipoli Peninsula into three equal sectors.

The approach along these gullies besides being dominated from both sides of the approach and providing an ideal killing ground for the Turkish also provided the defender very vital communication lines through which troops

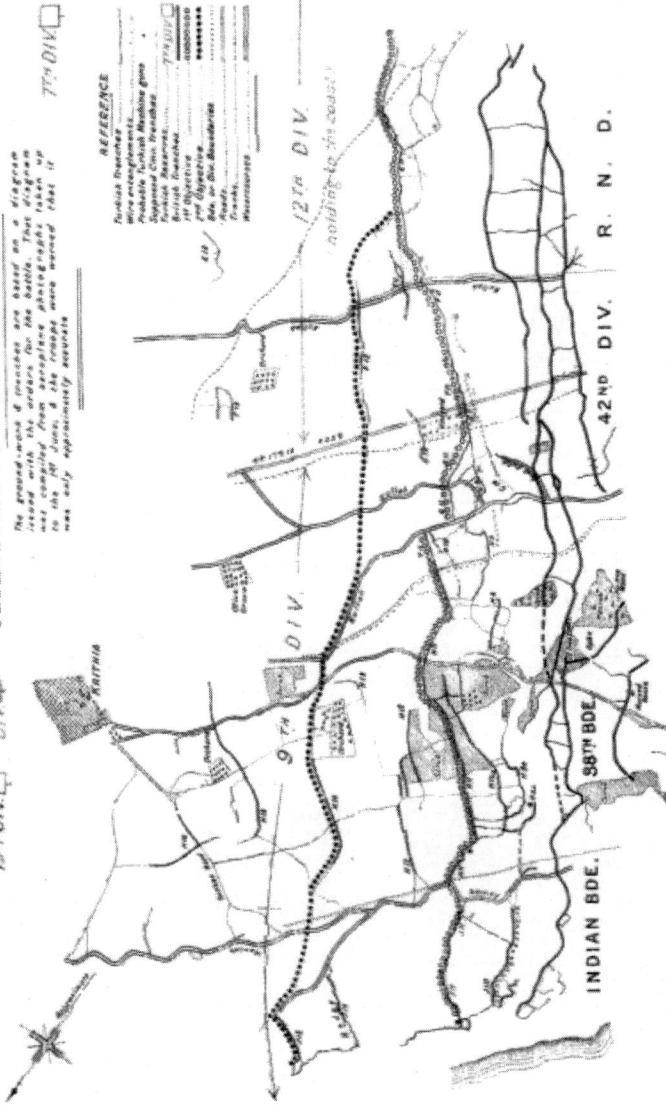

MAP 9 : OBJECTIVES OF THE INDIAN INFANTRY BRIGADE FOR THE THIRD BATTLE OF KRITHIA[38]

could pass without detection by the Allied troops or suffering the bombardment by the allied Naval fleet.[39]

The approach along the Gully Ravine itself was anticipated to have been manned by several small trenches, besides being covered by the fire of machine guns deployed along the few but dominating heights along the ravine. The objective of the 14th Sikhs was not an easy one as it was dominated by two tiers of trenches of Turks, known as J10 and J11.

The Gully Ravine which divided the Sikhs defence line into two parts was central to the entire operation of the 29th Indian Infantry Brigade on that fateful day. The ravine was very steep, with sides generally extending beyond 40 feet on both sides. The slopes of the ravine were interspersed with small nullahs / dry rivulets merging into the ravine at regular intervals. The slopes were thickly covered with low bushes and scrub almost up to 2 feet high. On the east side of the ravine, the ground gradually moved up towards a crest line towards further east. The trenches of Sikhs and Turks were separated here by approximately 250 yards of No Man's Land. Both the adversaries here, Sikhs and Turks, were using the Gully Ravine for backward movements towards respective rear echelons.

AUSTRALIAN WAR MEMORIAL   G02127

FIGURE 14: THE STEEP SLOPES OF GULLY RAVINE[40]

On the western side of ravine, the ground was relatively higher, with a spatial differential of approximately 200 to 250 yards between the trenches of the two adversaries. The lay of the ground on the eastern side of the ravine lent a definite advantage to the Turkish defenders. The trench line of the enemy was so disposed that besides bringing effective fire on the front, the enemy was able to dominate by observation and fire any forward movement in the eastern side of the ravine. Besides, the enemy side of the ravine was adequately covered by fire of machine guns. Thick undergrowth of shrubs in the ravine was instrumental in obviating any possibility of visual confirmation of enemy defences prior to the physical assault by the Indian troops.

This being the first deliberate offensive by the Indian troops at Gallipoli, the plan was made in great detail. In consonance with the overall plan of 29th Indian Infantry Brigade, the CO of the 14th Sikhs, Colonel Palin gave Battalion Commander Orders in the evening of 3 June. The orders nominated Number 2 and 4 Double Companies for the attack in the first wave. Number 2 Double Company was tasked to assist the attack of Lancashire Fusiliers on the left flank by capturing the trench line J10 of the enemy. In the next stage of the same phase, the Double Company was to assist the Lancashire Fusiliers in their capture of Turkish trench line of J11. Number 4 Double Company of the battalion in the first wave on the right flank was tasked to align themselves with the advance of the battalion of the 88th Brigade. The Double Company of the 14th Sikhs was also given a task to ensure that no gap existed between the advance of the 29th Indian Infantry Brigade on the left and 88th Brigade on the right.

The Number 1 Double Company of the 14th Sikhs was to follow the advance of Number 4 Double Company on the right in the second wave, whereas Number 3 Double Company was to follow the advance of Number 2 Double Company in the Gully Ravine. The two Machine Guns of the 14th Sikhs were tasked to provide covering fire to the advance of Lancashire Fusiliers for capture of J10 and J11. These machine guns were not to move forward till the time of capture of J11 trench line. Only after the capture of J11 trench line, the machine guns were to move forward for supporting the subsequent exploitation. Gully Ravine was the most imposing geographical feature in the entire scheme of things of the 29th Indian Infantry Brigade. The role of the

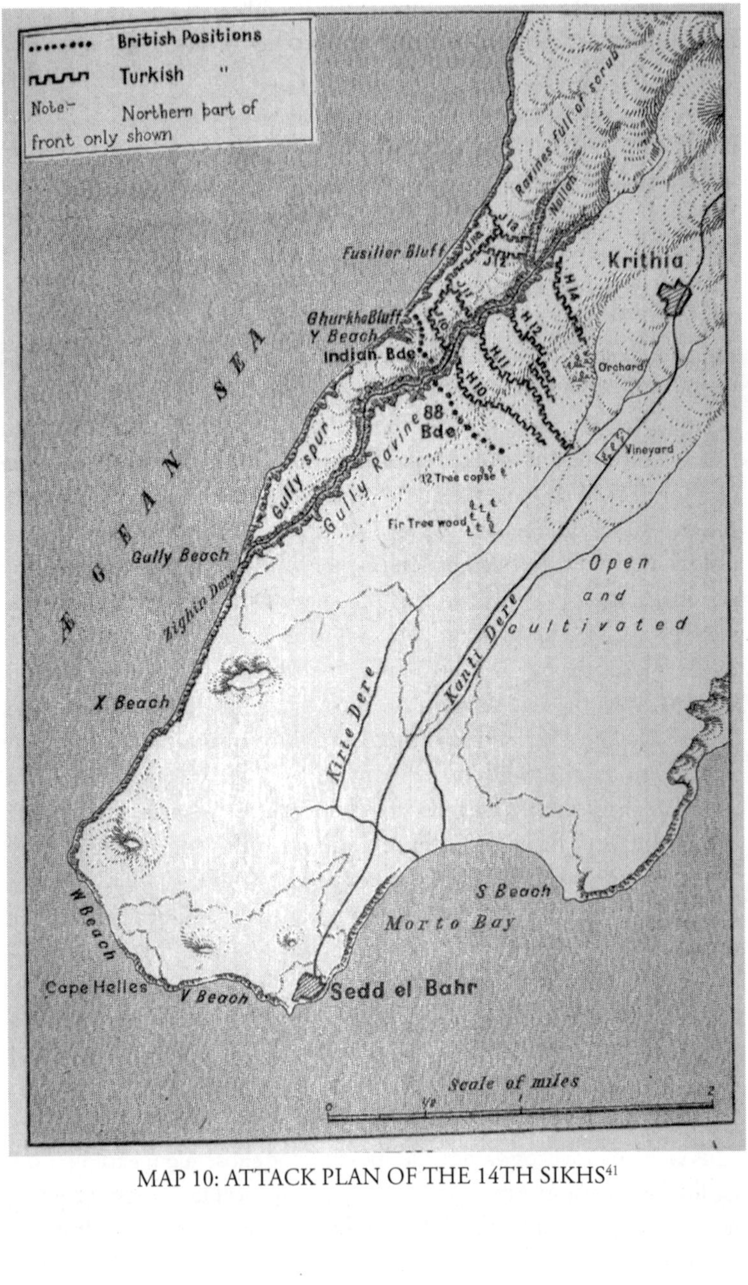
British Positions
Turkish "
Note:- Northern part of front only shown
Ravines full of scrub
Nullah
Fusilier Bluff
Krithia
Ghurkha Bluff
Y Beach
Indian Bde
88 Bde
Orchard
Vineyard
12 Tree copse
Fir Tree wood
Gully spur
Gully Ravine
ÆGEAN SEA
Gully Beach
Zighin Dere
Open and cultivated
Kanli Dere
Kirte Dere
X Beach
S Beach
Morto Bay
W Beach
Cape Helles
V Beach
Sedd el Bahr
Scale of miles

MAP 10: ATTACK PLAN OF THE 14TH SIKHS[41]

14th Sikhs was very crucial in the entire operation and 'the Battalion formed a connecting link between the two brigades to operate forward with the ravine in its center'.[42]

On 3 June 1915, the forward line of defences held by the 14th Sikhs was straddled along the Gully Ravine on the right flank of the formation. The defences of the battalion were slightly uncoordinated due to the presence of Gully Ravine in between. On the eastern flank of the ravine, the defences of the battalion extended by another 150 yards towards the left most battalion of the 88th Brigade. The defences itself were not yet complete from a defender point of view. The co-ordination between the two edges of the defences, with Gully Ravine in between was still to be worked out. With the uncoordinated own defences, the battalion was going onto a full offensive next day. In spite of these serious problems, the actions of the battalion on 4 June 1915 speak for themselves and are unparalleled in terms of terrain, resources, casualties and the intricacies of own defences.

The entire day of 3 June was spent by the Sikhs in cleaning and final inspection of personal weapons. In spite of assured artillery support prior to the offensive by the Infantry, the emphasis on the importance of personal weapon in the last hundred yards cannot be negated. The preparations for attack by the Indian Brigade went on undeterred by the complexities of supply lines of logistics. With the supply of additional ammunition contingent upon the supplies reaching the forward most trenches, for the impending attack, the redistribution of ammunition was organised by the Sikhs under the arrangements of the respective Double Companies. Over a period of time, the own trench line had been dug deeper and wider to provide protection from the Turkish rifle and artillery fire, the Sikhs in the night carved out steps towards the enemy in their own trench line, to facilitate easy move out of their own troops for the assault on the enemy defences at the designated time.

The preparatory bombardment by the allied artillery commenced at the designated time of 0800 hours on 4 June 1914. The Indian troops, in their own trenches, waited to witness the 'assured' destruction of the enemy defence line by the own artillery. The troops were briefed in no uncertain terms about the preponderance of own artillery for the offensive, which will result into the complete annihilation of the

FIGURE 15: WEAPON CLEANING PRIOR TO
OFFENSIVE IN A TRENCH OF THE 14TH SIKHS[43]

enemy defences, leaving only the mopping up to be carried out by the own troops:

At 08:00 on 04 June the British bombardment begun, pounding the Turkish lines continuously until 10:30. Following a half hour break, to give the Turks the idea that an attack was coming so as to catch them in the open, the barrage recommenced. The allied troops in the front-line fixed bayonets and opened rapid fire on Turkish trenches, in another ruse to get the Turks to man their trenches, and again they were delivered another Artillery installment.[44]

The actual situation at the Turkish defences, however, was totally divergent from what was expected. The overhead protection, a relatively stronger constitution of the enemy trenches along with the lack of own artillery observers had precluded any significant damage to the enemy defences. The plan to induce the enemy to occupy their trenches through cheering by their own troops and causing casualties by the subsequent artillery bombardment to follow, was taken with apprehension by the officers and men of the 14th Sikhs:

> It all seemed simple enough, but we were rather skeptical as to the cheering, and wondered if the sound of our voices would not be drowned in the general noise of battle. We were also skeptical as to whether our Artillery would be sufficiently accurate to hit a single line of Turks, manning their front-line trenches, had our cheering induced any of them to man them at all. However, it was all part of the game, orders were orders and there was nothing for it but to do the best we could.[45]

Under the circumstances, it was increasingly hoped that own artillery fire will result in the substantial damage to the Turkish defences. As was anticipated by their own troops, the allied artillery fell short of destroying the wire obstacles and the enemy trenches. The carefully concealed machine guns of the Turks in the thick shrub undergrowth and along the forward edges of defences did not suffer any major damage and laid in wait for the advancing columns of Sikhs,

FIGURE 16: 14TH SIKHS IN THE GULLY RAVINE[46]

to open up with deadly and precision spray of lead. Though the almost negligible effect of the pre-assault artillery bombardment on the wire entanglements in front of the enemy trenches, particularly along the Gully Spur and the area around was quite apparent, but by then it was already the time for the assault by the Infantry. The Company Commanders had already briefed their respective Companies and the Sikhs, totally oblivious to the actual impact of the preparatory bombardment were prepared to launch the offensive on the relatively intact enemy defences at the designated time of 12:00 hours. As part of the coordination prior to the attack, the Company Commander of the Number 4 Double Company of the Sikhs and his Subaltern had carried out liaison with the British Battalion of the 88th Brigade on right and own Number 2 Double Company on the left and the own Number 1 Double Company, which was to follow in the wake of the advance of the Number 4 Double Company.

A severe artillery bombardment targeted at the Turkish defences on the morning of 4 June, though had taken the Turks by surprise, but the intensity of the shelling could have surely provided the defender, a fair idea about the impending assault. By now, the Turkish Artillery had also started retaliating and the Indian troops while still being in their own defences, were subjected to an intense assault by the enemy artillery. It was around 11:45 hours on 4 June when the troops of Number 4 Double Company of the 14th Sikhs, who were leading the assault of the battalion, had completed their meal and were waiting for the assault signal. The Indian officers of the battalion had already completed the last-minute checks of the company and were in the process of giving the final report to the Company Commander. With limited space available in the trenches and every man with a definite role in the trenches to be prepared for an assault by the enemy, the Indian officers had personally visited each and every man in the company and confirmed the individual preparations for the offensive.

Just then, the Turkish artillery shells had started hitting the trench line held by the 14th Sikhs. The hastily constructed and uncoordinated defences of Sikhs suffered damage during this shelling by the Turks. The direction to the Turkish artillery fire by their OP officers were quite accurate. In the trenches of the 14th Sikhs, both the officers of the Company, to include Company Commander, Maj Fowle and the company Officer, Second Lieutenant Reginald Savory, were almost buried in the collapse of one of the trench walls due to the intense shelling. The shelling also resulted in some injuries to the Sikhs, who were lined up for the assault. With these injuries, there was a need to again have a check on the status of each man and to find replacements for the injured troops. The Indian officers carried out an immediate check about the status of each man of the company and there being no serious injuries, the company was all set for the assault at the nominated time.

For the impending assault, in order to avoid bunching up while moving towards the offensive, each soldier of the company was allotted his space for the assault at the rate of one yard per person. The entire exercise had been coordinated and conducted by the Indian officers of the battalion. Each man was standing next to the steps carved out in own trenches for smooth moving out from their own trenches. Within the defences, the location of the two British officers was earmarked and both officers were at their respective places by this time. Major Fowle, the Company Commander was in the right half of the company, with an aim to coordinate progress of the attack with the 4th Worcestershire Battalion on to the right. Second Lieutenant Savory, the Company Officer was in the centre of the left half and was entrusted with the task of coordinating with the flanking company of the battalion on to the left of the assault line.

Those last few minutes before zero hour made no deep impression on me, except possibly the familiar feeling of waiting for the pistol before a sprint with a void in the pit of one's stomach and anxiety as to the result. And, then … twelve noon … blow the whistle scramble over the top … off you go.[47]

At the nominated time, the Sikh war cry of *Jo Bole So Nihal, Sat Sri Akal* reverberated amidst the din of artillery, machine gun and rifle fire. While, the Turks were retaliating with the intense artillery and machine gun fire, the assault by the troops of the 14th Sikhs was entirely being led by their personal weapons. The moment the troops were out of the own trench line, in a dash towards the enemy front line, entire control was lost and every soldier was on his own. The intense fire by the carefully concealed machine gun nests was not able

FIGURE 17: JUST BEFORE THE OFFENSIVE[48]

to stop the assault by the Sikhs and the glistening wire of the obstacles under the afternoon sun, in front of the enemy trenches, seemed to be beckoning the Sikhs.

Every step of the advance of the Sikhs towards the Turkish frontline was causing casualties to the Sikhs. The British Artillery had fallen silent, which had allowed the Turks to take aimed shots at the approaching mass of Sikhs from behind the parapets of their trenches. The ferocity and the masculinity of this converging horde would indeed have been a deadly sight for the enemy. The entire battlefield was reverberating with the war cries of *Jo Bole So Nihal* and *Waheguru Ji Ka Khalsa, Waheguru Ji Ki Fateh*. However, with the enemy obstacles largely unscathed and coupled, 'with little artillery and no howitzer support these units were all brought to a standstill in front of the uncut Turkish wire, taking heavy casualties from the intense rifle and machine gun fire thrown at them from the Turkish trenches.'[49]

During the advance of the Sikhs towards the Turkish defences, the intensity and aimed enemy fire and the pumping adrenaline rush had resulted in every soldier's single point focus to be the enemy trenches. No sideways glance was possible and the focus of every soldier was in the front, the aim being to reach there as early as possible, 'the sooner, I could get across No Man's Land and reach the cover of the enemy trenches the better'. The Company Officer of the company, Second Lieutenant, Reginald Savory, mentions that the din of the battlefield had subdued all sounds except of guns:

The nearest man to me was a yard away, and even then, I could not see him. Soon I found myself running on alone, except for my little bugler, a young handsome boy, just out of his teens, who came padding along behind me and whose duty it was to act as runner and carry messages.[50]

On the other hand, the advance of troops of the flanking the 4th Worcestershire Battalion of the 88th Brigade was relatively successful. These advancing troops of the 88th Brigade on the right flank of the 14th Sikhs were safe from the enfilading fire from the western side of the ravine as their advancing movement was on a slightly higher ground. The Sikhs, however, faced the entire onslaught of these machine guns from the western side of the ravine. The assault of Number 4 Double Company of the Sikhs was being severely hindered by the flanking fire from the Gully Spur.

As a result of this, whereas the advance by the 4th Worcestershire Battalion of the 88th Brigade was relatively smooth, the casualties of Sikhs were very heavy. Incidentally, there was very less opposition to the assault of the Sikhs from the enemy trenches in front. During the frontal assault, both the officers of the Double Company were hit by the enfiladed fire during the initial stages of the assault itself. While Lieutenant Fowle was killed, Second Lieutenant Savory was wounded badly. The evacuation of Second Lieutenant Savory amidst the intense fire, by Sepoy Udey Singh of Number 4 Double Company is a legendary epic and has been discussed in detail in the last chapter of the book.

The Sikhs of the Number 4 Double Company, who survived the massacre in the short distance to enemy trench line, had soon found themselves at the parapet of the Turkish trenches. The Turks were equally bewildered to see the determination of these Sikhs, who in spite of suffering huge losses in their dash, were pouncing on to the Turks with their bayonets drawn. Though, no definite record exists of these visuals, it can be fairly assumed, that the moment would definitely have been a dream for every soldier going for an assault and a nightmare for every soldier whose duty was to defend the trenches.

The shock of seeing these burly, tall and ferocious Sikh soldiers in the trenches was too much for the Turks.

And then, before I could realise it, I found myself standing on the parapet of a Turkish trench and looking down at a Turk inside it. He was not even firing, but was leaning against the back of his trench. Yet, if I had given him time, he would have shot me and there were others on either side of him. I jumped in and skewered him to the back of his trench with my bayonet.[51]

The mention of the bravery and the composure of the Sikhs during the assault of 4 June are not restricted to the records of the 14th Sikhs or those of the 29th Indian Infantry Brigade. The entire 29th Division was proud of the exemplary display of bravery and sacrifices of Sikhs. Major Cripps of the 1st Royal Dublin Fusiliers, the battalion which was closely following behind the advancing Sikhs, writes about the losses suffered by the Sikhs in his memoirs and the grit and determination with which the injured Sikhs, in spite of being mowed down, continued to help the following on troops going for the assault:

We were in the first battle of the 4th June in the nullah with the Dublin's following up behind the Sikhs. I was sent forward to contact the Sikhs and got within, say, 30-40 yards of the Turkish fire trench on my tummy, wriggling through the scrub and dead and wounded Sikhs in great numbers. Thank Goodness I was not discovered and a very friendly still-alive handsome Sikh did his best to make me keep my head down.[52]

The sacrifices of the Sikhs were not in vain. In spite of these huge losses, wherein the entire rank and file of the company was decimated, the Sikhs had delivered in terms of their bravery and faith. The task allotted to the Double Company may not have been accomplished in full, but the very determination in the face of heavy odds had created a legend in the name of these *Khalsa* warriors:

In spite of very heavy losses on the slope, the 14th Sikhs managed with the greatest determination to keep pace with the British Brigade to their right, carrying the trenches facing them very gallantly and putting the Turks to the bayonet as they turned to escape into the ravine. The two Companies here maintained the touch ordered with the Worcestershire Regiment during the whole advance, held the left of the trenches gained by the 88th Infantry Brigade.[53]

The magnitude of the casualties suffered by the Double Company in this phase can be gauged from the fact that on the next day when relief of troops in contact was carried out, the number of the fit personnel (who were not wounded or dead) of the Number 4 Double Company was only one British officer, one Indian officer and fourteen other ranks.

On the other hand, the attack of Number 2 Double Company on to the left flank also did not proceed as per plan. The machine gun nests very carefully camouflaged in the thick undergrowth of ravine had played havoc with the advance of Sikhs. The enemy defences on the western flank of the ravine were very strong and the repeated attacks by Lancashire Fusiliers on the left had completely failed to evict the enemy. With the attack on the eastern flank of the ravine being effectively interfered by the enfiladed machine gun fire, the Turks were able to effectively stall the assault of the Sikhs along the narrow gorge:

In Gully Ravine, Lieutenant Colonel Jacques led Number 2 Double Company moved forward with great gallantry in face of a very high fire. They encountered numerous machine guns in hidden positions on both sides of the ravine and both officers of the company were killed immediately. The Double Company pushed on but suffered very heavy casualties while trying to cut its way through the enemy wire.[54]

The heavy machine gun fire along with the rifle fire from the enemy positions proved calamitous for the advancing Indian troops, who were massacred in dozens during the advance by the Turks, deployed behind the protection of still intact barbed wire entanglements. Just like Sepoy Udey Singh in the Number 4 Double Company, the action of Number 2 Double Company on the left flank cannot be discussed without the mention of Havildar Maghar Singh, who later on became the Subadar-Major of the Training Battalion in the Sikh Regimental Centre.

Havildar Maghar Singh was leading one of the Sections of Number 2 Double Company in this advance. The wire obstacle in front of the enemy trench was hindering the forward movement of the Sikhs, while at the same time, the enemy machine guns were wreaking havoc on the surviving Sikhs. Delay of every moment was mounting the casualties and there was no time to negotiate the wire obstacle. Any attempt to manoeuvre through the wire obstacle would have caused more casualties to the Sikhs, who happened to be in the open with absolutely no cover. The situation was more critical, as their own artillery fire had already abated and the enemy trench just across the wire obstacle was spewing fire. With forward movement not possible and no option of a status quo, the section was fast running out of viable alternatives. Havildar Maghar Singh being in the lead of the troops, truly lead by own personal example under these trying circumstances. The sight of Maghar Singh going over the wire obstacle and reaching to the enemy trench with bared bayonet must be the dream run of any soldier in offensive. 'Havildar Maghar Singh suddenly leapt over the obstacle, as if it was a hurdle, and, followed by his Section, captured an enemy trench.'[55]

FIGURE 18: HAVILDAR MAGHAR SINGH IN A TRENCH[56]

While moving in the ravine, the Sikhs had some limited advantage of dead ground, but that advantage was totally negated by the hidden machine guns. The charge of the Sikhs on to the Turkish defences, with little or no artillery support, cross fire from the hidden machine guns and intact wire obstacles was nothing but a pure exhibition of guts, glory and determination. The intensity of Turkish resistance was such that the Number 2 Double Company immediately had lost four officers and almost 25 per cent of its bayonet strength. With frontal assault having failed miserably, the brave Sikh troops tried to launch a flanking attack from the western side of the ravine. Under a very effective command of the Indian officers under terrible losses, the Sikhs were able to establish a lodgement in the ravine but this small piece of ground was captured at a great cost. The serious interference by the Turkish machine guns and rifle fire in the first phase of the operation and the number of casualties suffered by the phase one troops notwithstanding, the second wave of the assault had also been launched. The almost complete wiping out of Number 2 and 4 Double Companies in the first wave and the inability of the Allied Artillery to destroy the Turkish wire obstacles and the trenches, did not invite any review or holding back of the assault by the planners.

As the time for the launch of the second wave had already passed, the balance two Double Companies of the Battalion also dashed forward towards their respective obstacles. The Number 3 Double Company accompanied by the Commanding Officer and the Battalion Headquarters had started moving forward to consolidate the gains of Number 2 Double Company. The so-called remnants of Number 2 Company, who were far and few, were valiantly holding on to the minor lodgement, achieved at a great cost. The flanking attack by the Lancashire Fusiliers also having been stalled, the J10 and J11 trench lines of enemy were bringing very effective fire on to the advancing Sikhs. The CO, Colonel Palin, appreciated that without the neutralization of both the trench lines, further advance by the battalion was futile and therefore launched an offensive by the Number 3 Double Company to capture these. But under command of the Commanding Officer, Number 3 Double Company was able to consolidate only on a small spur just south of the J10 trench.

During this assault, the Sikhs lost three officers, to include their Adjutant and Quartermaster from the Battalion Headquarters. The losses amongst troops and the Indian officers were also unparalleled. With no support from their own machine guns, it was getting difficult to hold on to the position. The initial orders had promulgated the moving forward of the two machine guns of the battalion only after the consolidation of the position subsequent to the capture of J10 and J11. The interference by the Turks to the advance and the amount of losses being suffered by the Sikhs forced the CO to modify the orders and the two machine guns were ordered to be brought up. 'Nevertheless, the Sikhs held on and entrenched the position, while later in the afternoon, the battalion's two machine guns, as well as two machine guns from a Royal Navy unit joined Colonel Palin and helped to strengthen the position.'[57]

In spite of machine guns having been deployed at the hastily prepared positions, the much-needed fire support from these weapons was not able to help the beleaguered Sikhs, presumably due to the absence of any preparatory reconnaissance. The Turks, by virtue of holding the dominant ground, were totally in control of the situation and an immediate assault by them could have decimated the foothold established by the Sikhs. This foothold of Sikhs, was being held by the CO, the Regimental Doctor and only 47 men, many of them already wounded. This was the only strength which was left out of the combined strength of a Double Company and the Battalion Headquarters. These brave Sikhs under the command of their CO, continued to hold on to the ground the entire night. On the other hand, the Turks having identified the precariousness of situation of Sikhs did not let their guard down and continued to bring heavy fire on to the group:

Colonel Palin and his men were attacked time and time again from Gully Spur and subjected to almost continuous fire. This party suffered further casualties during these attacks and the two naval Machine Guns and one of the Sikhs guns were knocked out by enemy bombs, but it held on stubbornly to its trenches.[58]

During the defence of this foothold, this small detachment of Sikhs did not waiver even for a single moment during the entire night. In spite of the Turks sitting on a higher ground and the position being subjected to continuous fire, never a thought came in the mind of anyone to abandon the position. With only CO and the Regimental doctor available at the position, the doctor was the de facto Adjutant of the battalion. The tremendous amount of fire being drawn by the position was not letting any Sikh to move about. At around midnight, a young Sikh soldier in the makeshift trench, next to the doctor, suddenly fell down. The soldier informed the doctor about him taking a bullet hit in the head. The doctor, within the confines of the trench, checked him and since there was no mark on the turban with no bleeding, he ordered him to go back to his position. The soldier, being a simple soul as he was, obeyed orders and went back to his trench, took up his position and started engaging the enemy with his rifle:

The next afternoon, when the Sikhs were washing in the stream that flowed through the gully, the man ran up to Lieutenant Colonel Cursetjee, the Battalion Doctor who was shaving nearby and said; 'Look; you said I was not hit last evening', and he held up his 'kangi' (comb) with a bullet embedded in it.[59]

In the meantime, the holding of position by the CO and his men was getting precarious minute by minute as Turks were planning to encircle the position and isolate it. Sensing the situation to be irretrievable, a decision was taken by the GOC, the 29th Indian Infantry Brigade, to withdraw the small party. Out of the four machine guns in the position, three had been destroyed by the enemy bombs. During withdrawal of the party, one of the machine guns was left behind as there was no crew left to operate or lift it.

Leaving behind of weapon was not acceptable to the Sikhs. On arrival of the CO and the wounded men back to the location, the Sikhs under the command of Lieutenant Mathew, the battalion Machine Gun Officer, decided to get the battalion machine gun back. In spite of Sikhs having withdrawn, the Turks were still dominating the position and any attempt to lift the machine gun, amongst the seriously wounded and dead of the Sikhs was being interfered with by the enemy. The lifting of the weapon was difficult under the circumstances. 'As each man carrying the gun was hit, another took his place until Mathew alone was left unhurt and he too tried to bring the gun back, but he was almost immediately hit in seven places.'[60] The indomitable Sikhs, in spite of severe losses were not able to get the machine gun back but they carried their officer back to safety, who eventually died of his wounds in the hospital.

Meanwhile, on the right, Number 1 Double Company of the battalion under Captain Engledue moved behind the Number 4 Double Company and tried to exploit the success. In spite of heavy losses, the Double Company was able to capture the second and third lines of enemy trenches on to the east of ravine. The continuous and murderous fire from the enemy positions on the western flank of ravine continued to rain death and misery upon the Sikhs. The Sikhs, however, never slowed down and continued to move ahead and a time came when by late afternoon of 4 June, the Number 1 Double Company was left with only Captain Engledue, Jemadar Narain Singh and thirty men. 'This small party held on to the captured trench in spite of continuous efforts by the enemy to bomb their way back from Gully Ravine.'[61] The Turks carried on relentless attacks but the Sikhs continued to hold on with Captain Engledue. Due to the severe casualty rate of the Double Company and as only twelve men were left with him, seeing the precariousness of the situation Captain Engledue and his men were also ordered to withdraw on the afternoon of 5 June.

The casualties of dead and wounded of Sikhs were so high that no resources were available for retrieving the wounded from the No Man's Land. The enemy trenches and the area in front were brown over brown, with the brown colour of scrub having mixed up with the brown of Khaki of uniforms and yellow of turbans. With virtually no possibility of any further advance or gains by the Sikhs under the circumstances, the battalion was ordered by the 29th Indian Infantry Brigade to withdraw to own defences on 5 June 1915. The survivors of the battle of the previous day, though in very little numbers, got along with them some of their own walking wounded.

On the afternoon of 4 June, the 14th Sikhs had moved out with strength of 15 British officers, 14 Indian officers and 514 other ranks. When the withdrawal was affected the next afternoon, the battalion was left with only 3 British officers, 3 Indian officers and 134 Other ranks and within a span of 24 hours had lost 80 per cent of its officer strength and 74 per cent of its rank and file. The battalion had only three British officers left, who were unwounded to include the Commanding Officer, the Battalion doctor and Captain Engledue. The serious losses suffered by the battalion in the Third Battle of Krithia, invited some introspection. The plan for the assault of the Brigade and of the Division did come under serious scrutiny from the officers and men of the battalion. The plan to launch the offensive without catering for adequate artillery support and move of the massed Infantry into the incoming hail of bullets was questioned by the then Second Lieutenant Reginald Savory of the 14th Sikhs, who later on rose to become Adjutant General of the Indian Army:

Methods here seem to be based on a theory that all tactics are rot, and that the only way to do anything at all is to rush forward bald headed, minus support, minus reserves, and in the end probably minus a limb or two. Hence causing the almost total wiping out of the 14th Sikhs on 4th June. We had as our own special task, to advance up a nullah (a thing which one has learned should never be done until all the ground commanding it is first seized) against the Turks who were in a wired trench at the end, and also on both sides and at the top, and their machine guns took us in front and rear and from practically every side.[62]

In spite of all the odds heavily stacked up against them, the rush for the Turkish trenches by the Sikhs in the afternoon of 4 June has become a legend. Lieutenant Reginald Savory, who himself was wounded on that day, while writing about the exploits of the battalion writes:

Well, at 12 noon, we got up out of our trenches, got through their barbed wire (the only regiment that did) and bagged their first trench: total time taken, roughly twenty minutes. We hung on there all right, unable to go forward because of having only two British officers left, and also because of their machine guns, not a single reinforcement did we get after repeated messages had been sent, and at about 9 am next day we had to come back having had nine officers killed and three wounded out of fourteen, and the regiment being 135 strong. So, bang goes one of the finest regiments of the Indian Army, and certainly the best on this old peninsula.[63]

The exploits of bravery and sacrifice of the Sikhs didn't go totally unnoticed. General Ian Hamilton wrote to the Commander-in-Chief in India praising the heroism and bravery of the Sikh troops. I would not be able to do justice to the sacrifice of those brave men of the 14th Sikhs, if I do not quote the passage from the letter of General Sir Ian Hamilton:

In the highest sense of the word extreme gallantry has been shown by this fine Battalion. In spite of these tremendous losses there was not a sign of wavering all day. Not an inch of ground gained was given up and not a single straggler came back. The ends of the enemy's trenches leading into the ravine were found to be blocked with the bodies of the Sikhs and the enemy who died fighting at close quarters, and the glacis slope is dotted with the bodies of these fine soldiers all lying on their faces as they fell in their steady advance on the enemy. The history of the Sikhs affords many instances of their value as soldiers, but it may be safely asserted that nothing finer than the grim valour and steady discipline displayed by them on the 4th June has ever been done by soldiers of the Khalsa. Their devotion to duty and their splendid loyalty to their orders and to their leaders make a record their nation should look back upon with pride for many generations.[64]

The bravest conduct on the battlefield by the troops of the 14th Sikhs on that day has no parallel in the annals of the history. Unfortunately, the saga of bravery and sacrifice has not received its due recognition due to a number of reasons, which are beyond purview of the instant work. The spirit of sacrifice depicted by the Sikhs on that day came under praise from the neighbouring battalions who were involved in the attack on that day. The brave men of the Lancashire Fusiliers who held on with the Sikhs on the left and the 4th Battalion Worcestershire Regiment whom they fought alongside on the right of the ravine, were full of admiration for the gallantry of their Indian comrades. 'The defence of the point gained in the ravine itself with an enemy entrenched on both sides above it speaks for itself and is a very fine example of the character the Sikh bears as a stubborn fighting man.'

During the coordinated offensive launched by the MEF and IEF, to capture Krithia, the lay of the ground provided distinct advantages to the defender as enemy, besides taking care of the frontal assault, was also able to bring down effective enfiladed fire on to the advancing Indians. The failure of the assault to proceed on one side also impacted the subsequent operations of the Indian Brigade and 'because the Lancashire Fusilier attack failed in the middle of the Indian Brigade, this neutralized the success of Gurkhas nearer the coast and that of the 14th Sikhs in Gully Ravine.' Though minor successes were achieved by the Indian troops but the overall tactical advantage still eluded the MEF. The failure of the coordinated attack by the 29th Indian Infantry Brigade of 4 June in turn affected the advance of the neighbouring 88th Brigade on to the right flank as it found its left flank wide open and enfiladed from across the ravine.

Except for some local level tactical successes, at the cost of very heavy casualties, their own defence line only moved forward by a few hundred yards and the number of casualties suffered by the Allied troops was in no way conformance with the gains achieved.

With such a massive quantum of casualties suffered, the process of evacuation of the wounded from the peninsula was almost impossible. The 14th Sikhs had so many wounded that there were not enough men with the battalion to move the casualties to the beach for evacuation. The scene on Gully beach was desperate on 5 June and not counting dead, the number of wounded itself was overwhelming:

The place was full of wounded, who were being got off on boats as quickly as possible. The left had been held up, unable to advance. The casualties were heavy. The whole situation was terrible – no advance, and nothing but casualties, and the worst was that the wounded had not been got back, but lay between ours and the Turks firing line. It was impossible to get at some of them. The men said they could see them move. The firing went on without ceasing.[65]

The casualties of the Indian Brigade overwhelmed the entire formation. The quantum of casualties, both dead and wounded, had wiped out entire battalions. At one point of time, the situation in the Indian Brigade was so desperate that the Sikh and Gurkha battalions had to be merged so as to maintain some sort of combat worthiness of the formation. The staff of the 29th Indian Infantry Brigade, was horrified when a staff check on the number of casualties suffered by the battalions of the formation was carried out. The brigade had suffered 951 casualties, including killed, wounded and missing in the first five days of the month, the majority of which had occurred on 4 and 5 June 1915.

TABLE 17: CASUALTIES OF THE INDIAN INFANTRY BRIGADE IN FIRST FIVE DAYS OF MAY 1915[66]

Date	14 Sikhs	1/5 Gurkhas	1/6 Gurkhas	Lancashire Fusiliers	Royal Inniskilling Fusiliers
1 to 3 June	7	-	7	3	1
4 to 5 June	364	116	88	342	23
Total	371	116	95	345	24

An in-depth analysis of the casualty figures provided by the War Diary of the 29th Indian Infantry Brigade provides some very interesting insights. The casualty figures above as mentioned, combines the numbers of killed, wounded and missing. The proportion of missing soldiers out of the total casualties suffered by the British battalions is much more than the Indian battalions, particularly the 14th Sikhs. The casualties suffered by the 14th Sikhs and the Lancashire Fusiliers during the third battle of Krithia, being almost identical; the percentage component with respect to missing is very glaring. The casualties suffered by the Indian battalions of the formation were primarily killed or wounded. For a comparable number of casualties suffered, 14th Sikhs and the Lancashire Fusiliers have distinct differential between the percentage of killed and wounded and the percentage of missing.

TABLE 18: COMPARABLE FIGURES OF DEAD, WOUNDED & MISSING OF THE 29TH INDIAN INFANTRY BRIGADE (THIRD BATTLE OF KRITHIA)[67]

Battalion	Total Number of Casualties	Per cent of Killed & Wounded	Per cent of Missing
14th Sikhs	371	90.55	9.43
1/5 GR	116	87.06	12.93
1/6 GR	95	91.57	8.42
Lancashire Fusiliers	345	33.90	66.08
Royal Inniskilling Fusiliers	24	91.66	8.33

On the morning of 5 June 1915, the 29th Indian Infantry Brigade was responsible only for 230 yards of frontage, which was being held by the 1/6 Gurkhas. The just arrived battalion of 1/5 Gurkhas was in close reserve to the 1/6 Gurkhas. From 5 June till 14 June, the 14th Sikhs, having been withdrawn from the forward line were put into the rear as reserve. But with the effective manpower available, the battalion was not fit even to act as reserve. The other two British battalions of the Brigade were also moved to the other British Brigades in the 29th Division. As part of these changes, the 1st Battalion Royal Inniskilling Fusiliers was ordered to join the British 87th Brigade on being relieved by South Wales Borderers and the 1st Battalion

Lancashire Fusiliers moved to the 87th Brigade. Meanwhile, the third Gurkha Battalion, 2/10 Gurkhas, which had reported at Gallipoli on 3 June, was also placed under the command of the 29th Indian Infantry Brigade. As a result of these changes, the 29th Indian Infantry Brigade was now consisting of three Gurkha battalions and the 14th Sikhs. With an enhanced combat strength, the Brigade was now tasked to take over additional frontage on the right flank of 1/6 Gurkha. 1/5 Gurkhas moved forward and took up this additional responsibility from the South Wales Borderers of the 88th Brigade. With these changes, by the evening of 6 June, a complete complement of 2/10 Gurkhas and a depleted 14th Sikhs were available as reserves to the 29th Indian Infantry Brigade.

While the reorganisation of the 29th Indian Infantry Brigade was being carried out, the local counter attacks with an increased emphasis on throwing of bombs on the unprepared Allied defences were being exploited to the hilt by the Turks. The aim of the enemy was to gain as much as territory lost by them in the recent Allied offensive. Efforts

FIGURE 19 : MACHINE GUN DETACHMENT OF A GURKHA BATTALION[68]

wherever possible to retrieve the bodies of their own soldiers lying in the No Man's Land were taken by the 14th Sikhs and the 1/6 Gurkhas. The enemy, however, did not allow it by resorting to heavy firing wherever these efforts were taking place along the defence line. With 1/6 Gurkhas also having suffered casualties, it was decided that 2/10 Gurkhas will relieve the 1/6 Gurkhas. With two freshly arrived battalions, the 1/5 Gurkhas and 2/10 Gurkhas holding the frontage now, both 1/6 Gurkhas and the 14th Sikhs were now the reserves of the formation.

By 9 June 1915, the changeovers having been implemented, the dispositions of the 29th Indian Infantry Brigade included 2/10 Gurkhas (Left) and 1/5 Gurkhas (Right) in the front holding complete frontage, approximately 100 yards short of Gully Ravine. The 1/6 Gurkhas and the 14th Sikhs were in reserve at Y Ravine and Gully Ravine respectively. With a large number of casualties suffered by the British officers in this battle, some re appropriations of the available British officers was also carried out during this period. As part of these changes, the CO of the 14th Sikhs, Colonel Palin was temporarily posted to the 126th Brigade to assume the command of the Brigade. As a result, the next available senior-most officer of the battalion, Captain Engledue took over the command of the battalion.

During this time, the Indian Infantry Brigade was also tasked to provide flanking fire support to the troops of the neighbouring 88th Brigade on the right in their attempt to retake some H11 trenches which had been captured on 4 June but abandoned later. In spite of fire support and loan of 200 bombs to the 88th Brigade by the 29th Indian Infantry Brigade, it was possible to retake only a portion of the H11 trenches. With a severe paucity of fresh troops, it was again decided to put the battle-hardened 14th Sikhs and 1/6 Gurkhas again in to the front line. The day of 14 June witnessed the 1/6 Gurkhas replacing the 2/10 Gurkhas and the 14th Sikhs and three companies of 2/10 Gurkhas taking over the front line defences from the 1/5 Gurkhas.

With these changes, as on 14 June 1915, 1/6 Gurkhas was the left-most battalion of the Indian Brigade with responsibility from cliff picquet onwards for about 150 yards. From the right most, troop of 1/6 Gurkhas to the right of the line for approximately another 100

FIGURE 20: SOLDIERS OF THE 1/6 GURKHAS IN A TRENCH[69]

yards was responsibility of three companies of 2/10 Gurkhas. Further right, for about another 100 yards the responsibility was devolved to the 14th Sikhs. Thus, the entire 29th Indian Infantry Brigade was holding a frontage of approximately 350 yards, which was about 100 yards short of Gully Ravine on to the right. 2/10 Gurkhas less three companies and 1/5 Gurkhas was in reserve. During this time, due to the serious interference by the Turkish Artillery, the movement of Indian troops to take over the reorganised defences resulted in a number of casualties to the Indian troops. The enemy shelling and sniping from 6 June to 15 June, was responsible for almost 68 casualties on to the Indian soldiers.

TABLE 19: CASUALTIES OF THE 29TH INDIAN INFANTRY BRIGADE:
1 TO 15 JUNE 1915[70]

14th Sikhs	1/6 GR	1/5 GR	2/10 GR	108 Field Ambulance
7	12	18	30	1

The depleted strength of Indian battalions in the 29th Indian Infantry Brigade was causing concerns in India. All out efforts were being made by the respective Depots to recruit more soldiers from the respective catchment areas to recoup the deficiencies in the respective battalions. 15 June 1915 was an important day for the

Indian Brigade, as the day brought some immediately scrounged reinforcements for the Indian Battalions. These reinforcements were primarily mobilised from Egypt for immediate deployment on Gallipoli.

By this time the military planners of the operation at the peninsula had realised that with the type of resistance being offered by the Turks in active collaboration with the German General Staff, the capture of Gallipoli was not a possibility in a near time frame. Till that time, the Indian Infantry Brigade was operating at Gallipoli under the mandate of IEF 'E'. The peculiarities of operating in a hostile terrain against a well-entrenched enemy and with extended logistical lines, it was imperative that a separate Force Headquarter was created for Indian forces operating on the peninsula. In order to streamline the process, on 18 June 1915, Secretary of State for India directed that the Indian troops with the MEF be designated as IEF 'G'. As part of this change, the Indian troops with IEF 'E' as on 18 June 1915 were designated as IEF 'G'. The troops included the Headquarters of the 29th Indian Infantry Brigade, 14th Sikhs, 1/5 Gurkhas, 1/6 Gurkhas, 2/10 Gurkhas, 7th Indian Mountain Artillery Brigade, 21st Mountain Battery, 26th Mountain Battery, 108th Indian Field Ambulance, 110th Indian Field Ambulance (Clearing Hospital) and C Section of the 137th Combined Field Ambulance.

Leaving behind the debacle of the Third Battle of Krithia and with redistribution of defences within the Indian Brigade and the receipt of drafts by the battalions of the formation, fresh offensive plans had started to crystallize to gain more ground from the enemy. During this period, the 1/6 Gurkhas of the formation tried to raid the beach picquet of the enemy on 25 June. But the assaulting party

TABLE 20: REINFORCEMENTS JOINING THE 29TH INDIAN
INFANTRY BRIGADE: 15 JUNE 1915[71]

Battalion	Recruits
14th Sikhs	109 Other Ranks
1/6 Gurkhas	28 Other Ranks
1/5 Gurkhas	1 Gurkha Officer, 91 Other Ranks
2/10 Gurkhas	2 British officers, 2 Gurkha Officers, 87 Other Ranks

of the Gurkhas was observed by the Turks and the assault was aborted. By 27 June the offensive plans having been finalised, the front-line troops of the Indian Brigade were once again relieved by the 2nd Battalion of South Wales Borderers of the 87th Brigade and the Indian Brigade concentrated in the general area of Y ravine for the impending task. The Operation Instructions for the Indian Brigade were issued on 26 June and the overall offensive plan envisaged the capture of H and J series of enemy trenches. The plan envisaged that trench lines of H11, H12 and H12A were to be captured by the156th Brigade. The trench lines on the left of the Gully ravine being heavily fortified and held in strength by the enemy were allotted a greater number of troops for the capture. For the capture of J9, J10 and J11 series of trenches the responsibility was given to the 87th Brigade and the 86th Brigade was made responsible for the capture of J12 and J13 series of enemy trench lines.

The Indian Infantry Brigade was tasked to provide necessary assistance to both the brigades for the capture of their respective objectives. Learning lessons from the previous debacle, the artillery bombardment this time was specifically tasked to concentrate on the enemy wire obstacles. The preparatory bombardment of Artillery Batteries and Machine Gun Sections was to start by 0900 hours on 28 June and was to continue for two hours with intermittent breaks in between. Following up immediately after, the Infantry assault was to commence at 1100 hours. As follow up of the initial assault, the task of Indian Brigade was to take over the captured defences of J11A, so as to facilitate consolidation by the 87th Brigade.

As preparatory bombardment was being given its due emphasis in the operation, the 14th Sikhs was tasked to provide two sections strength for the local protection of Royal Artillery forward observers. This time the attack was relatively successful. 2/10 Gurkhas was able to take over J11A while 1/6 Gurkhas and 1/5 Gurkhas moving in the second wave of assault were able to take over portions of J13. The enemy made violent counter attacks to take over J13, the first of which was repelled by the Gurkhas but the second was successful. The Gurkhas however, were able to re-take J13 from the Turks by the morning of 29 June. The 14th Sikhs also by this time had moved forward and occupied the area in the vicinity of J9 and J10.

FIGURE 21: SIKHS IN THE DEFENCES[72]

The objectives of the Brigade in the latest offensive were achieved and the casualty figures were relatively under control as troops were not directly involved in the capture of the enemy defences. However, conversion of enemy defences taken over from the 86th and 87th Brigade in the minimum time possible and repelling enemy counter attacks with success did cause some casualties in the Brigade. Enemy artillery fire along with the snipers continued to extract toll of Indian troops in these operations and the period between 16 and 30 June 1915, added another 500 casualties to the battalions of the Indian Brigade.

The position held by the 1/6 Gurkhas at J13 was again counter attacked by the enemy in the night of 30 June. A strong repulsion by the Gurkhas facilitated retention of the position by the Indian Brigade. On the other hand, the position along J11A held by 2/10 Gurkhas was precarious. The battalion had suffered a large number of casualties, thereby inducing a decision to relieve the defences held by the Battalion by troops of the 87th Brigade on 2 July. After the capture of the Fusilier Bluff by the Allied troops in the last week of June, a salient had been created in the enemy defences. The eastern end of J13 was still with the enemy and therefore the British front line was running along the back of J11A. The enemy recoiled by the capture of Fusilier Bluff,

TABLE 21: CASUALTIES OF 29TH INDIAN INFANTRY BRIGADE:
15 TO 30 JUNE 1915[73]

Battalions	14th Sikhs	1/5 Gurkhas	1/6 Gurkhas	2/10 Gurkhas	108 Field Ambulance
Casualties	17	100	155	203	6

launched a massive counter attack. On 2 July, a massive preparatory bombardment was launched by the enemy on the positions held by the 14th Sikhs and 1/6 Gurkhas in J13. 'The Turks charged forward with great determination, but they were repulsed with heavy losses all along the front. Shortly after 9 p.m. the enemy again launched an attack on the Sikhs and Gurkhas after an artillery concentration of fifteen minutes.'[74]. The valiant efforts of the Turks were checked by even more determined and valiant Sikhs and Gurkhas in the defences and the enemy suffered major losses and later on withdrew. 'The Turks left very many dead on the ground and contended themselves with digging in a line between the cliff edge and Gully Ravine about 250 yards from our line during the night.'[75]

The 14th Sikhs now was commanded by Captain H.G. Wilmer, who had recently been posted to the battalion from the Headquarters of the 29th Indian Infantry Brigade, where he was posted as Staff Captain. In the evening of 3 July, the Indian Brigade was tasked to capture the enemy held portion of J13. In spite of all the arrangements to ensure the artillery and Engineer support for the offensive by the 14th Sikhs and the bravado of the Sikhs, the status quo persisted:

All arrangements made for rushing the enemy's barricade in J13 at 07:15, Artillery and Engineers co-operating; the actual rushing being done by parties of the 14th Sikhs under Capt. Wilmer's directions. The scheme failed, the men were got on to the barricade once and brought up to it again five times by Capt. Wilmer only to be bombed off again by the Turkish bomb throwers situated in a small side sap (a bayonet charge also came under machine gun fire and failed). Eventually our barricade was re-established in its original position and the Turks' remained also in its place.[76]

In this operation, though the overall command was of the 14th Sikhs but bombers were also drawn from the 1/5 and 1/6 Gurkhas.

In spite of five determined attempts, the enemy held portion of J13 could not be retaken. Unfortunately, resistance by the enemy was too strong and, in the process, the Indian Brigade suffered a large number of casualties. By 5 July all four battalions of the 29th Indian Infantry Brigade had been decimated and the sheer numbers of casualties suffered by the battalions were beyond redemption. Independent existence of the Indian units was neither feasible nor desirable. The consolidation of the remnants under a cohesive command and control structure was need of the hour. 'The 14th Sikhs, with little more than ninety men was amalgamated with the 2/10 GR, who themselves had only a subaltern in command. The 5th and 6th Gurkhas were in a like state and were also combined.'[77] With severe depletion in the strength of British officers in the battalions, the merging of remnants of the Indian battalions on the peninsula was able to facilitate the regaining of much-needed command and control.

In the meantime, with so much wear and tear of the Indian Brigade, the 29th Division offered to withdraw one battalion of the Indian Brigade in the rear so as to provide the much needed refit and recoup. In a memorandum dated 3 July, the staff of the 29th Division, offered the 29th Indian Infantry Brigade to hold the allotted 450 yards of defence line with two battalions and with one battalion in reserve, the fourth battalion could be taken off from the defences and sent to the rear in the general area of Y Beach. The GOC, 29th Indian Infantry Brigade, though agreed that his battalions were overstretched and needed time for rest and recoup, the immediate tasks at hand did not allow him the opportunity to relieve his troops for refit. The strength of the Indian battalions of the Indian Brigade on 3 July 1915 was just a proportion of their authorised strength. Against an authorised establishment of almost 735 men, the present manpower of the Indian battalions was far less.

Thus, the 14th Sikhs was holding just about 30 per cent of the authorised strength of the establishment, which was after including the fresh draft of 109 other ranks, received by the battalion on 15 June. The magnitude of huge losses of the 14th Sikhs therefore can be ascertained and put into perspective. Even with the precarious state of the battalions, the GOC of the Indian Brigade, had requested the

TABLE 22 : PERCENTAGE OF AUTHORISED ESTABLISHMENT HELD
BY THE INDIAN BATTALIONS AS ON 3 JULY 1915[78]

Indian battalions	Available Strength	Per centage of Authorised Establishment held on 3 July 1915
14th Sikhs	220	29.97 per cent
1/5 Gurkhas	450	61.22 per cent
1/6 Gurkhas	400	54.42 per cent
2/10 Gurkhas	420	57.14 per cent

29th Division that with the type of tasking at hand and the imminent danger of fresh counter attacks by the enemy, he was no position to spare any manpower for rest and recoup. As a last resort, the GOC agreed that he can relieve only half the battalion of 2/10 Gurkhas in three days' time and no troop withdrawal should be carried out before that.

If, as I anticipate the enemy after the failure of his 3rd counter-attack (last night), adopts defensive tactics, half the 2/10 Gurkhas could be sent back, say in 3 days' time (the sapping will then be finished), but I strongly recommend that this should not be done till we are more sure than we are now that enemy's offensive is played out and until our line is a more satisfactory one.[79]

The justification provided by the Indian Brigade convinced the 29th Division that in spite of severe losses, the 29th Indian Infantry Brigade was still a cohesive fighting unit and left the decision of pulling back of formation or reorganisation of the dispositions of the Indian Brigade upon the discretion of the GOC 29th Indian Brigade. As a result, the Indian Brigade continued to hold defences in the general area east of Gully Ravine and so continued the counter attacks and shelling by the Turks, albeit at relatively smaller levels.

In the early hours of 5 July, the Turks had again launched a strong attack on the defences held by the Sikhs and the Gurkhas. 'The greatest pressure was against the right flank of the Sikhs and wave after wave of Turks surged forward from the dead ground in the Nullah. The Turks were thrown back by rifle and machine gun fire and in spite of many gallant attempts to get forward, they could make no progress and suffered very heavy casualties.' Though the Sikhs were able to withstand the attack, but unfortunately lost their officiating CO, Captain Wilmer in the battle. The area in front of the defences of Sikhs was already strewn with the dead bodies of the previous skirmishes, so it was not possible to approximately estimate the number of dead of enemies in the latest battle. However, conservative estimates, deduced from the number of fresh bodies lying in the No Man's Land, pegged the enemy losses in this battle to be over one hundred dead. While the CO of the Sikhs was lost in the battle and one British officer of 1/6 Gurkhas wounded, the Sikhs lost 20 men in the operation. The 1/6 Gurkhas lost another 20 men and 1/5 Gurkhas lost 15 men in the battle. By this time, the Indian Brigade had already suffered 280 additional casualties from 1 July onwards, again with the Sikhs having all their casualties as dead or wounded with no missing, whereas other battalions of the formation had their share of missing soldiers in these battles.

TABLE 23: CASUALTIES OF THE 29TH INDIAN INFANTRY BRIGADE: 1 TO 15 JULY 1915[80]

Battalion	Killed/Wounded	Missing
14th Sikhs	104	-
1/5 Gurkhas	105	3
1/6 Gurkhas	45	1
2/10 Gurkhas	21	1
Total	275	5

REGAINING THE MOMENTUM

The quantum of losses suffered by the Indian battalions, reignited the thought process that there was an immediate need for taking a stock of the situation and take corrective actions. With tremendous losses both in rank and file, it was being increasingly being felt that the Indian Brigade strongly needed rest, refit and recoup. The Headquarters of the Indian Brigade was very much aware of these considerations. The previous opportunity of withdrawing from the active front for getting reorganised, had already been declined by the Indian Brigade. The losses amongst the troops and the Indian officers were very high along with the British officers of the respective battalions. The successes of the Brigade in the Gully Ravine were many, but unfortunately with no dedicated reserves and inherent artillery support, the consolidation was being interfered with by the enemy. With no consolidation being possible, the enemy was able to re-take occupied positions from the Indian troops in many instances. GOC of the Indian Brigade in his memorandum of 9 July addressed to the Headquarters of the 29th Division, discussed these concerns and wanted his formation to be sent to a location for rest and refit, from where they could still contribute to the overall cause:

I am quite sure that I represent the feelings of the whole Brigade when I say that I hope we may be sent somewhere where we can still do good work for those at the front. The men are very well and we can give them sufficient rest and still find 600 men a day for fatigues etc. Labour must be much wanted at various places such as Mudros. Also, after a short period of rest I suggest that we might send back to the front a small corps of highly trained scouts, say 100 men with 2 British Officers. I think that they would do useful work on our flank at any rate.[81]

The 29th Division concurred with the recommendations of the GOC, 29th Indian Infantry Brigade, and by the evening of 9 July, the defence line held by the Indian Infantry Brigade was taken over by the troops of the 156th Infantry Brigade and the battalions of the Indian Brigade had started withdrawing from Gully Ravine:

We spent four days awaiting transport, while we bathed, washed and slept. It was not all bathing and sleeping, however. There was time in which to take stock ourselves. We had been on the peninsula for two months and had scarcely had a rest. Twice, our numbers had been reduced to less than a hundred men, and now we were little more than a band of survivor. Our men, all Sikhs, had never turned, never wavered, never complained.[82]

Continuous fighting of almost two months without any relief, had taken a terrible toll on all the men. 'To state that their morale was high would be an overstatement; but it was certainly not low.' The troops did not show any impairment in the spirits and they lived and went about their daily tasks in good spirits. The feelings of camaraderie and brotherhood, developed between the British officers and the Sikh troops were mutual. The sufferings of the battalion in the peninsula, though only a part of what was yet to come had formed an unparalleled bond between the men and their officers. Reginald Savory was the most vocal proponent of this inseparable bond between the troops and the British officers:

Our paucity of numbers gave us a feeling of community. We had been through dangers and discomfort together. I was the sole person to whom they could refer and who could speak their language, however imperfectly. They looked after me as if I were one of their younger brothers. I shall never forget, one night when we were still in the trenches and I was trying to snatch some sleep, being woken up by one of them bending over me in the cold of early dawn, and covering me with a blanket, possibly his own.[83]

On the evening of 9 July, the complete 1/5 Gurkhas, 1/6 Gurkhas and Battalion less two companies of 2/10 Gurkhas embarked for Imbros. The elements of the 29th Indian Infantry Brigade embarked on the morning of 10 July 1915, whereas the 14th Sikhs along with the balance of 2/10 Gurkhas had embarked on the evening of 10 July for Mudros.

While at Imbros, the Indians battalions started to take stock of men and material. The frequent change of responsibilities, while at Cape Helles, had resulted in the maintenance of equipment being neglected. In addition, the battalions had to take care of the equipment and personal belongings of the men who had died, wounded and shifted to hospitals and of those who were missing. At Imbros, the reinforcements of the battalions had also started arriving and joining the respective battalions but with the magnitude of the losses suffered by the battalions being so high, the quantum of reinforcements being received was not able to match up.

In the true sense of refit and recoup, a Double Company of the 1st Patiala Infantry joined the depleted 14th Sikhs at Mudros on 12 July. A number of British officers posted to the battalions of the 29th Indian Infantry Brigade also started joining the respective battalions while at Mudros. With the actions and tasks of the formation

FIGURE 22: INDIAN TROOPS DISEMBARKING FROM A TRANSPORT
ON THE GREEK ISLAND OF LEMNOS[84]

in the immediate past and the impending operations, the GOC
Brigadier General Cox was in constant touch with all the battalions
of his formation and was visiting his battalions daily to speak with
the officers and men of his command. On 14 July the GOC met the
men and officers of the recently arrived Double Company of the 1st
Patiala Infantry.

The primary task, while at Imbros, of the battalions of the Indian
Infantry Brigade was to incorporate these newly joined reinforcements
into the drills and procedures of the respective battalions. With the
new reinforcements being received at an enhanced pace, it was
imperative that they get absorbed into the training activities as early
as possible. With the limited number of recruits available in the
respective depots, the entire losses could not have been recouped. The
period of training and the memories of the hardships faced while at
Gallipoli with the other soldiers of the company and Battalion, were
too much to endure for some. While at Imbros, when the reinforcements
were being absorbed, the new Subadar Major of the 14th Sikhs also
assumed appointment. Subadar-Major Sham Singh was promoted in

place of Subadar-Major Lal Singh, who was killed in action of 4 June 1915. The new incumbent was equally competent and professional like his predecessor:

He was a tower of strength. Tall, soldierly, dignified, strict, he was the beau-ideal of the Sikh (or any other) soldier. He retired in 1918, to rest on his well-earned laurels, as Honorary Captain Sham Singh; Sardar Bahadur; Order of British India; Indian Distinguished Service Medal; and recipient of the French Medaille Militaire.[85]

In addition to these reinforcements, the men of the battalions who were lightly wounded and were hospitalised also started to report back to their units. One of the notable and much awaited returnees to the 14th Sikhs was their CO, Colonel Palin. He had been detached temporarily while the battalion was at Cape Helles, to command a Brigade. The battalion was overjoyed at his arrival back in the midst the troops. 'His arrival was greeted with joy. The men were transported. Here at last, was someone whom they really know and whom they would follow to the death.' Some new drafts and the wounded personal having recuperated also started to join the battalions of the Brigade.

With new drafts and fresh reinforcements joining the Indian battalions, it was imperative that these troops were put into a training regimen so as to create homogeneity. The 14th Sikhs had received one company strength of 1st Patiala Infantry from the State Forces of the Maharaja of Patiala. The training standards of both the forces were naturally different and the short period available at Imbros was supposed to iron out these differences and result in a homogeneous fighting unit which was fit to fight another battle. It has been recorded that while 'the men of Patiala State Forces were magnificent material, but had not the same standards of training as those from the regular depots. There was much to be done'.

One of the novelties of training during this period was the receipt of a new variety of bombs. The importance of bombs in the trench warfare at Cape Helles had adequately been witnessed by the troops of the Indian Brigade. While at Cape Helles, the battalions were using a crude contraption, infamously known as Jam Tin, as it was made from the discarded tins of apricot jam being received in rations. The empty tin was filled with explosives. But the new type of bombs was different and required practice. The brief interlude at Imbros was effectively utilised to make the troops habitual to the use of new bombs. These bombs were also not free from problems and the troops started learning the use of these at the cost of suffering casualties during the training. 'It took us many hours, and not a few casualties, before we became proficient with these.' To provide adequate firing practice to the troops, the Indian Brigade improvised a firing range at Imbros.

With the low hills at Imbros matching the terrain obtained at the Gallipoli Peninsula, the troops engaged in long marches in the night with full battle loads. In any military operation, the importance of marching in the night and ensuring that the surprise is maintained are difficult propositions and continuous practice in the field craft makes the men perfect. In the night, the command and control are the first casualty and a constant practice by both the soldiers and the commanders is required to avoid loss of surprise. For the impending operations, while at Imbros, the Indian troops had started to practice the night marches with full battle loads. Maintenance of surprise during these long night marches was an essential component of all the briefings of the Indian battalions. The Indian battalions had passed strict orders to refine the drills for passing of messages from the front to the back of the column and in reverse order and the troops were expected to, 'fall in once during the night in any close formation and to remain so closed up for a period of at least half an hour, during which passing of commands (messages from front to rear and back again and to the flanks) is to be practiced'.[86]

With the surprise element being imperative, it was also required that all the troops were accustomed to starlight. Explicit instructions were passed to ensure that the troops get used to the move under starlit conditions. The proposed operation was planned on moonless nights and the troops were expected to get adapted to move on starlit nights. In order to prepare the Indian troops for the impending operations, orders were passed for the issuance of maps of the area, to the Indian battalions in advance. 'The troops must be accustomed to the starlight, which may be expected during the night operations. Troops landing should be provided with Maps 1/20,000 of the areas in which operations are to take place. These maps were to be in bulk, and not issued till after landing.'[87] These night exercises provided excellent opportunity to the troops to develop closeness and camaraderie with the newly joined reinforcements and provided avenues to the officers of the battalions to know their troops.

While at Imbros, the Indian troops came across a totally new dimension of the warfare on Gallipoli, the probability of which was quite high. The military planners of the MEF, were anticipating the use of gas by the Turkish defenders under the overall command of German General Staff. The use of gas by the Germans at the Western front was a strong indicator of things to follow. The troops of the Indian Brigade were also briefed about the possibility of use of gas by the enemy.

To counter the probable threat and to ensure the retention of combat effectiveness, the Indian Brigade troops were to practice wearing of gas masks. The supply of gas masks being limited, the troops at one point of time were also briefed to, 'urinate in a sock or if one was lucky and near a field hospital into a pad of cotton wool and lint and tie it over our mouth and nostrils'.[88] The Indian troops, particularly the Sikhs, were not comfortable with the idea of wearing gas masks. The design of the gas mask did not facilitate the wearing of it by the Sikh troops. The Sikh troops, however, were able to find a solution to the problem and a contraption was devised by them, which made possible wearing of mask even on top of the turbans. 'These introduced an altogether new element into our ideas of warfare. They were flimsy things and we had no great faith in them, but they were better than nothing, and we did our best to learn how to put them on with all possible speed.'[89]

While at Imbros, in the midst of all the intense training activities, the Commander of MEF, Ian Hamilton visited the troops of the Indian Infantry Brigade. Writing about the event, Reginald Savory mentions that the parade was supposed to be a ceremonial one but the existing tactical conditions did not allow the conduct of a full-fledged ceremonial parade. With troops in no condition to march in ceremonial attire and considering the existing tactical conditions, a compromise formula was adopted. The Sikhs, in spite of suffering serious casualties in the recent past were upbeat about the future operations of the battalion and they put up a spectacular show to receive their Commander. 'There is a point below which turns out and drill cannot be allowed to fall without men becoming dirty and slipshod. They then lose their self-respect and their value as fighters.'[90]

As a result of a large number of casualties of the British officers posted with the Indian battalions, the British officers had now started to join the Indian battalions from other British battalions also. These freshly arrived British officers naturally were not well versed with the vernacular and traditions of the troops with whom they were now posted. Though sincere efforts were being made by these officers to know their rank and file but the time available was at a premium. With the type of preparations underway, it was well known that the tenure of the Indian Brigade at Imbros was going to be a very short one. Simultaneously, the Indian battalions had also suffered a disproportionate number of casualties amongst the Viceroy Commissioned Officers of the Indian battalions as well. These Indian officers had served with the respective battalions for a long time and were thoroughly aware of the pulse of the Battalion. The replacements of these officers were difficult to come by and even after the receipt, the required homogeneity and knowledge was deficient. Recent losses had denuded the Indian battalions of this important asset. With the senior Indian officers having been evacuated, the freshly arrived British officers and the recent reinforcements having been received from the varied units / sub-units and catchment areas, the cohesion and homogeneity of the Indian battalions and the sub units was under serious threat.

Meanwhile, the reinforcements for the Indian battalions were still being foraged from the Indian countryside. The combat effectiveness of all the Indian battalions, in particular the 14th Sikhs was below par due to the monumental casualties having been suffered in the previous battles on the peninsula. Towards these efforts, on 25 July, the Chief of General Staff had informed G.O.C. Egypt that the delicate situation of the 14th Sikhs for the reinforcements is being given due importance and urgency. Accordingly, following drafts for the embattled battalion are being dispatched from India during August 1915.[91]

Depot of the 14th Sikhs: 38 Men
87th Punjabis: 100 Men
Burma Military Police: 117 Men

In addition, the Company strength from the 82nd Punjabis was also being planned to be dispatched as reinforcements for the 14th Sikhs in September.

The day of mobilisation from Imbros for the next operational task of the Indian Brigade was near. A number of clear signs of the impending operations had started manifesting. The Indian battalions were witness to the conferences of the COs almost on a daily basis. The staff officers of the 29th Indian Infantry Brigade along with the nominated officers of the battalion had been nominated for the reconnaissance of the peninsula from the vantage positions in the sea. The troops were being actively engaged in the embarkation and disembarkation drills from the transports at the harbour while the long night marches with full battle loads continued. When the Indian battalions had moved out from the peninsula in July 1915, the spare baggage and kits of the battalions were dumped at Cape Helles. These kits were also now brought to Imbros to be with the respective battalions. By the end of July 1915, the Indian Brigade had received fresh instructions, providing command and control structure for the impending operation. The 29th Indian Infantry Brigade was to be attached with Australia & New Zealand Army Corps (ANZAC) during the upcoming operation. These instructions provided some inkling for the Indian battalions for the impending operation. By the end of July 1915, the Indian battalions had also been reinforced by a reasonable number of reinforcements. As on 30 July 1915, the strength of fresh reinforcements which had joined the Indian battalions included the following (Table 24).

In spite of the clear directions by Hamilton, to provide maps of the intended area of operations prior to the landings, and 'not after landings', the 14th Sikhs, at least was issued with the maps of Beshika Bay in the vicinity of Kum Kale, along the Asiatic shore of the peninsula. At hindsight, this may be attributed to the aspect of maintenance of secrecy, but the fact remains that troops were issued with the maps of an area which was totally opposite to the area where

TABLE 24: FRESH REINFORCEMENTS FOR 29TH INDIAN INFANTRY
BRIGADE: 30 JULY 1915[92]

Battalion	British Officers	Indian Officers	Rank & File	Followers
14th Sikhs	1	-	53	-
1/5 Gurkhas	5	3	203	12
1/6 Gurkhas	-	1	61	-
2/10 Gurkhas	2	3	137	7

the Indian troops were going to land. As far as the Indian troops and officers of the 14th Sikhs were concerned, the battalion was going to be launched for operations along the Asiatic Shore of the peninsula, whereas the actual landings were planned on the opposite side. As the subsequent events were going to unfold, the Indian Brigade was going to land at Anzac and play a substantial role in a major operation being planned by the MEF, to regain the initiative.

WITH ANZACS FOR THE AUGUST OFFENSIVE

The old battle tactics have clean vanished, I have only quite lately realised the new conditions. Whether your entrenchments are on top of a hill or at the bottom of a valley matters precious little: you may hold one half of a straight trench and the enemy may hold the other half, and this situation may endure for weeks. The only thing is by cunning or surprise, or kill, or tremendous expenditure of high explosives, or great expenditure of good troops, to win some small tactical position which the enemy may be bound, perhaps for military or perhaps for political reasons, to attack. Then you can begin to kill them pretty fast. To attack, all along the line is perfect nonsense- madness.[93]

Even after three months of intense fighting and countless casualties, no headway to break the stalemate was in sight for the MEF. The trench warfare had firmly set in and the Turks, operating under the directions of German General Staff, were quite comfortable with the existing situation. With extended logistical lines to support the troops on the peninsula, it was imperative that an early solution to the impasse was realised by the MEF. In spite of launching a series of offensives in the southern portion of the peninsula, the Allied troops were still very far from linking the two footholds at Cape Helles and Anzac. To gain additional terrain on the peninsula and to facilitate the link up, the Allied troops had to move out of protection afforded by the trenches.

Amidst all this, the tactical intelligence, very crucial for the operations at Battalion and Company level was restricted by the vicinity of the enemy. The rifle and carefully concealed sniper positions of the Turks were not allowing any observation beyond the enemy trenches. Only limited tactical intelligence was available from the documents recovered from the captured Turkish prisoners of war. The corroboration of this intelligence from alternate sources, a very essential facet of intelligence collection was virtually missing. In addition, the traditional maneuver warfare tactics of the battle had virtually been dominated by the static trench warfare, being witnessed on the peninsula. As a result, the headlong massed attacks by the Infantry were failing repeatedly with no positional advantages being accrued.

To break the stalemate of static warfare, some planning was already underway. Some probing activities by the Allies along the shores north of Anzac in the months of May and June had hinted at the relative weakness of enemy defences along the shore. Repeated intelligence inputs had also substantiated the claims. At the same time, the enemy positions between Anzac and Cape Helles were found to be strongly held and the terrain obtained in the area had also foreclosed any possibility of an offensive through the area. The intelligence of a possibility of a wider sweeping maneuver from the right flank of the enemy had opened up wide ranging possibilities.

It was increasingly being thought possible that a sweeping and overarching maneuver by the MEF and the subsequent capture of Sari Bair would definitely unhinge enemy defences and would also isolate enemy holding defences in the south, providing very crucial opportunity to allied forces to launch offensive from the south of the peninsula. Coupled with this, there were reports that the motivation and morale of the Turks was on the brink of a collapse and a large-scale offensive, if properly executed will definitely yield results for the MEF:

When confronted with the reality of a positional war of attrition, both

Hamilton and Birdwood reverted to the comforting notion of a decisive battle through maneuver as a means by which to escape the morass of trenches. For Hamilton and Birdwood, news that the enemy's flank was open, offered a tantalizing opportunity for a return to a comfortable mode of thought and action, an open warfare away from transformation to static warfare of trench.[94]

The omnipresent belief in the advantages of maneuver warfare as against the impasse of trench warfare coupled with a very positive conviction of allied forces, 'being structurally, physically and morally stronger than their foe', was influencing the minds of allied commanders to grab the opportunity being afforded. The sentiment that the action would also force the enemy to move out from the relative protection of trenches, which can be subsequently decimated by the superior allied Infantry, further cemented the idea:

In a maneuver battle of old style our fellow here would beat twice their number of Turks in less than no time but, actually, the restricted peninsula suits the Turkish tactics to a 'T'. They have always been good at trench work where their stupid men have only simple straightforward duties to perform, namely to stick on and shoot anything that comes up to them. They do this to perfection; I never saw braver soldiers in fact than some of the best of them. When we advance, no matter the shelling we give them, they stand right up firing coolly and straight over their parapets. Also, they have unlimited supplies of bombs, each soldier carrying them, and they are not half bad at throwing them.[95]

It was in the midst of these comforting thoughts that the plan for the Suvla offensive germinated. The Suvla plan owed its origin to the restriction of space in Anzac, which did not allow holding of more than one additional division. Gabe Tepe, in the south of Anzac, being strongly defended, Suvla Bay in the north was considered an ideal landing ground for fresh divisions being summoned from England. The crowded situation at Anzac was not conducive for accommodating additional divisions, which were planned to be landed at Suvla Bay with an objective to capture a very troublesome Turkish Arty Battery and also the dominating heights in the vicinity of the bay.

The Suvla Bay towards the north of the Anzac positions had always been an enigma for the Allied troops in general and for the Australian and New Zealand troops deployed at Anzac, in particular. With the MEF concentrated in the south of the peninsula, the focus of the ANZACs had rarely been towards the north to include Suvla Bay, except for being a beautiful geographical feature. Though the continued fighting did not provide a relief to the ANZAC troops, but still for the past three months, the ANZAC troops had wondered about this silent and serene piece of land. 'For months the ANZAC troops had looked across the Suvla plain, surrounded on three sides by formidable hills, like an enormous amphitheatre, the Salt Lake glistening harshly, and the yellow aridity of the ground, which looks deceptively flat and uncomplicated, broken here and there by a few stunted olive trees.'[96] The relative openness of the terrain in the vicinity of Suvla Bay was in total contrast with the compactness of defences as obtained at Anzac. The terrain in this country, in its entirety was devoid of any cover and the hills surrounding the plain were harsh, hostile and aggressive. 'Towards the hills, as the ground begins to rise, there are belts of scrub, thickening at the foot hills, and there one can detect a patch of greenish cultivation among the dreary dusty brown of the Plain.'[97]

By the time the August offensive was being planned, the mammoth proportion of casualties vis-à-vis the objectives achieved in the Gallipoli campaign till date had achieved gigantic publicity. The planners of the operation had to tread on this debatable subject very cautiously. The selection of fresh troops for the operation being planned, there-fore, had to be planned taking into consideration a multitude of factors. The emotional issue of relative mutual importance between the France and Gallipoli and accordingly the prioritisation of troops for these two theatres had subsumed the due primacy of logic and tactics. The selection of fresh divisions for the respective landings at Gallipoli, therefore took time. The complexity of the proposed operation was further accentuated by the fact that besides the main operation through Anzac, Helles in the South and Suvla in the north required a very high level of coordination to obviate a repeat of situation of 25 April 1915.

Between Helles and Suvla, the priority of Helles was higher because a holding operation at Helles was very much required and therefore planned to prevent Turkish reinforcements towards Anzac. The debate on whether to get experienced troops for the impending operations or to use fresh divisions from England, weighed heavily on the minds of the planners. With GOC Egypt also having his requirements of troops along with the never-ending requirements of troops for the Western Front, the only option left to the planners was to get fresh troops from England. 'The new Army divisions now on their way from England were unbloodied and inexperienced, but as the Suvla landings were regarded as the easiest part of the whole operation, it was eventually decided to use them, grouped into an army corps numbered IX Corps.'[98] General Stopford was nominated as the commander of the IX Corps. The operational plan of the IX Corps involved complementary operations to the main attack from Anzac. The operational instructions for the IX Corps explicitly mentioned complementarity of the Suvla landings with the main Anzac offensive. Whatever was being done at Suvla was to support the main operation at Anzac and the primacy of Anzac considered to be supreme:

Your primary objective will be to secure Suvla Bay as a base for all the forces operating in the northern zone. Owing to the difficult nature of the terrain, it is possible that the attainment of this objective will, in the first instance, require the use of the whole of the troops at your disposal. Should, however, you find it possible to achieve this object with only a portion of your force, your next step will be to give as much assistance as is in your power to the GOC ANZAC.[99]

The history of the April landings at Gallipoli, still fresh in the mind, the GOC of the IX Corps was not very much in favour of extending support to the main offensive through the Anzac. The so-called subsidiary operation of the Suvla landings, for the GOC was the primary operation and he did not see the viability of supporting the ANZAC under the existing circumstances. This foreboding is quite evident in his letter to Ian Hamilton of 3 August. 'I fear that it is likely that the attainment of the security of Suvla Bay will so absorb the force under my command as to render it improbable, that I shall be able to give direct assistance to the GOC ANZAC.'[100] It has been argued by various military historians that the Suvla operation being complementary to the main Anzac operation was in isolation, devoid of relevancy. The capture of Kiretch Tepe and Tekke Tepe by the IX

Corps, even if materialised would not have had any substantial effect on the capture of Sari Bair ridge line, as it dominated both the features. The overarching importance of the Anzac operation, therefore, required much greater preparation and even the minutest details required final confirmations and reconfirmations. With these conflicting and mutually divergent views on the nature of proposed operations, the Indian troops of the 29th Indian Brigade were about to embark on another offensive operation in a bid to capture the peninsula.

With the moon in in waning crescent, the D day of the offensive was fixed for 6 August 1915. In order to maintain the element of surprise and to avoid a repetition of the April landings, it was decided that the newly arrived 10th and 11th Divisions would be landed at Suvla before the rise of the moon on the day. The freshly arrived third division, 13th, was to land at Anzac Cove a day prior and stay concealed until the scheduled break out the next day. For this purpose, 'On the nights of August 3rd- 4th, 4th- 5th and 5th- 6th the 13th Division was to be smuggled ashore at Anzac and hidden until the evening of August 6th.'[101] At Anzac, preparations were started in the second fortnight of July for the August offensive. Though no mention of the details of the incoming formation was revealed, as early as 24 July 1915, New Zealand and Australia Division had directed the 4th Australian Infantry Brigade to commence the work for terracing of gullies. No details of the launch of the impending operation were shared with the 4th Australian Brigade, when it was directed to complete the work of terracing by 2 August. The availability of troop labour being a concern, the directions allowed the 4th Australian Brigade to use the troops of the Army Corps. 'Terracing of gullies should be resumed. Work to be completed not later than second August. Troops in Army Corps reserve may be utilized.'[102] By utilising all the available resources at the disposal of the 4th Australian Infantry Brigade, work for construction continued in full frenzy for the arrival of troops of the 29th Indian Infantry Brigade. The paucity of space and the crunch of resources coupled with the term of reference of strict maintenance of secrecy played its part. But in spite of all this, accommodation for about 10,000 troops in the form of terraced bivouacs had neared completion by 31 July. 'The work has not produced such extended accommodation in these areas as might have been anticipated, owing to the general steepness of the slopes, involving much waste space for the reception of the spoil from the excavations.'[103] It was ensured that no terrace should be in the direct view of the enemy and the earth from the excavation was also accordingly disposed. At Anzac besides resources, the space was also at a premium. The bivouacs provided for the troops of the Indian Infantry Brigade were small, cramped and the danger of enemy shelling was omnipresent:

The average terraces measure from 8 to 10 feet wide and accommodation has been estimated at 27 inches per man; in cases where terraces are wider accommodation has been estimated proportionately. In all cases troops will be very closely bivouacked, and heavy casualties may be expected should the terraces be subjected to shell fire. Latrine spaces will be very limited, but small spaces have been left. No accommodation has been made for stores except in Rest Gully.[104]

The Indian Brigade fresh after the recent stint of reorganisation at Mudros, was to land at Anzac a night before the offensive and was to stay hidden in these numerous terraces, tunnels and hideouts which had been engineered into the cliffs by the 4th Australian Brigade. The obsession with secrecy with respect to the impending operation also took a toll on the preparations. The operation was planned for the first week of August and even by 30 July 1915, the senior officers were not privy to the actual plan. As a high level of secrecy was maintained, the commanders of the columns involved in the operations were inordinately delayed in reaching out to their respective troops. 'General Cox, commanding the Indian Brigade, who was to command the operations of the Left assaulting column, only arrived at the beginning of August and when he urged reconnaissance scouting parties to find the best route to the summit, was peremptorily told this was impossible.'[105]

The involvement of the Indian troops in the August offensive was being treated as the panacea for all the ills of the Gallipoli Campaign so far. The very involvement of an Indian Brigade in the offensive was premised on the fact that the terrain as obtained in Gallipoli was very similar to the one in the frontier province of India. The drills, knowledge of the terrain and combat experience of the Indian troops was being considered as supplementing the difficult operation. This notion, however, was repudiated by the GOC of the Indian Brigade and he maintained the importance of reconnaissance prior to the launch of any offensive. 'I find there is an idea in some high places that you have only to show a Gurkha (officer or men) a bit of the country, however, difficult, and he can at once say the best way to tackle any proposition regarding it.'[106]

The idea of his troops being launched into an offensive on an unknown terrain without the essential and pre-required component of reconnaissance was not liked by Brigadier General Cox. He was not very much satisfied with the plan of operation. Troops of any ethnicity, including Indians would require a careful study of the outlay of the land prior to the actual launch of operations. 'I am sure that you do not share this idea, and know that to get the real value out of their special knowledge they must have time to look about them and to study the lay of the land.'

Therefore, though by the end of July, while the Indian Brigade was still not aware of its potential deployment on the peninsula, the preparations were in full swing at Anzac to induct the Indian Brigade. Starting 3 August 1915, ships had started to disembark men and material of the Indian Brigade at Anzac. On three successive nights, almost 20,000 additional troops along with their supplies and guns landed at Anzac and were hidden away in the 'labyrinths of new caves, trenches and dug outs. By dawn the sea was empty again.' For the reconnaissance of the proposed area of operations, the officers of the Indian Infantry Brigade had boarded a destroyer of Royal Navy and carried out confirmatory reconnaissance from the Aegean Sea. The Indian Brigade had by this time, been posted with a number of new British officers due to a large number of casualties of officers of these battalions in early offensives. The 14th Sikhs alone by this time had lost 13 officers. The officers who had been with the battalion earlier were well versed with the traditions/customs of the battalion and had learnt language of the men. The new officers joining the battalion came with no experience of Indian troops, and didn't have any knowledge of the language of these men. With the newly joined British officers yet to adapt to the vernacular of the men, in the meantime the Indian officers were supposed to interpret the orders as per their little knowledge of English. The battalions of the Indian Infantry Brigade having been recently recouped with the tranches of reinforcements had witnessed the carefully nurtured class composition of the units undergoing changes. The British officers joining the battalions had virtually no idea about the men they were going to command in the battles ahead. The CO of 1/6 Gurkhas was quite apprehensive of these newly joined reinforcements. 'The more the plan was detailed and as the time got nearer the less I liked it, especially as in my own regiment there were four officers out of seven who had never done a night march in their lives.'[107]

The everlasting dual of relative importance of Infantry vis-à-vis Artillery, was quite evident in the run up to the August offensive as well. At least during the initial phases of the Great War, the British military doctrine had outweighed the Infantry over the Artillery. For a considerable period of time, Artillery was supposed to be an accessory only to the operations by the Infantry. 'In 1915 British doctrine and operational theory viewed Artillery as an accessory (and subsidiary) to the Infantry, rather than an autonomous arm.'[108] Supported by this notion and the employment philosophy, most of the time, the Infantry was able to make its operational plans without consultation with the Artillery and in turn Artillery was also planning and operating its fire support plan in a totally independent manner. At least Gallipoli was witness to this independent way of functioning. The requirement of an integrated fire planning, with the involvement of the assaulting troops was realised by the planners towards the end of the Great War. 'Indeed, it was not until 1917 that the British realized the full potential of Artillery and adapted their plans and planning processes accordingly fire plan of the Artillery.'[109]

Though, the initial, and of course, the subsequent reverses could be attributed to a plethora of reasons, the lack of essential fire support was one of the important reasons for the reverses suffered by the MEF. 'As the war progressed it became clear that fire support was much more than an accessory. It was 'the lord of the battlefield' and it was essential for success.'[110] The reasons of maintaining secrecy had prevented the New Zealand & Australian Artillery to register targets on the Sari Bair ridge and the neighbouring ridge lines. So, when the offensive commenced and the ANZAC and Indian troops were approaching the objectives, the Artillery support failed miserably. The advance registration of targets would have definitely helped the Indian and ANZAC troops to reclaim the objectives as shall be seen in the later part of the chapter. As far as integral fire support for the advancing columns, within the Anzac sector was concerned, it was grossly insufficient. The integral machine guns of the battalions were not able to provide the support against the unopposed artillery shelling by the enemy. 'The minimal covering fire available from within the Anzac sector was not sufficient, with troops having to rely on Maxim Machine-Gun fire to protect their local advances.'[111]

Naval gunfire from the two destroyers anchored off the coast was available for intricate support but with no on call support arrangements, the fire from the Naval Destroyers was completely at the discretion of Royal Navy. The collateral damage in such type of situation was inevitable, and this is exactly what happened, when the Indian troops who had captured the allotted objective with their ingenuity and bravery had to vacate it, due to the intense shelling by the own Naval guns. In addition, to the above, eight, near obsolete guns of two batteries of the 7th Indian Mountain Artillery Brigade were providing fire support to the advancing columns in Anzac. The orders for the Order of March of each advancing column, had earmarked the location of these two Batteries. Four guns of Kohat Mountain Battery (21st) along with the four guns of Jacob's Mountain Battery (26th) were to move along with their respective columns. As these Batteries were moving with the columns, it was technically not possible to provide support for the troops of respective columns:

Because of their close proximity to the troops, these mountain batteries were forced to employ crossfire techniques, firing in support of their flanking column rather than their own. There was little communication or cooperation between the two batteries, which as a consequence of their physical separation caused them to fire on those targets they presumed to be of importance to the other column, rather than what was necessarily required.[112]

The possibility of an impending stalemate during the initial stages of the August offensive, was weighing heavily on the minds of the military planners. The Naval fire support along with the fire support

AUSTRALIAN WAR MEMORIAL   C02192

FIGURE 23: INDIAN GUNNERS WITH THEIR GUN AT ANZAC[113]

of the Indian Mountain Artillery Batteries was not finding traction. 'Realizing that eight obsolete mountain guns were insufficient to protect the exposed troops, all Batteries of the Australian Divisional Artillery that could fire in a north easterly direction were ordered during the afternoon of 7 August to register fire on the Sari Bair Ridge.'[114] Though the Divisional Artillery of the Australian Division along with the New Zealand Divisional Artillery continued to provide indirect firing on the objectives and approaches to Sari Bair, there were never enough guns to provide the requisite fire support, had troops been able to capture the objectives. 'There were not sufficient guns to support them on their objective. The planners of the offensive should, he believed, have recognised this and landed more guns at Anzac as a precaution in case the attack did not succeed in the first instance.'[115]

THE ASSAULT FOR SARI BAIR

It was almost three months, when the allied troops had landed at Gallipoli. A series of offensives, both at large scale and small scale had failed to produce any worthwhile results. With winters approaching, the window available to achieve a breakthrough was getting compressed day by day. Cape Helles, having had its share of offensives launched by the MEF, it was time to turn north. The stalemate at Cape Helles was more or less stabilised. With very limited chances of success at Cape Helles, the military planners planned to launch an offensive through the north of Anzac cove. After three months of intense fighting, the ANZACs had consolidated their position in an approximate semi-circle, with sea coast at both the edges, with the centre of the semi-circle protruding into the Turkish territory. The enemy positions were separated from the defence line held by the ANZACs, by an average distance of one hundred yards. In the areas where the advantages accrued to ANZACs, due to flanks being protected by the sea, the Turks were at a disadvantage. In the absence of flank protection, both edges of the Turkish defences were continuously being dominated by observation and fire by two Destroyers of Royal Navy anchored at each end. This domination was unsuccessfully contested by the Turks several times but the heavy fire power of the Allied Naval guns was overwhelming. The Turks also had reconciled to the domination of the Destroyers and cauterized the ends of their defence line by digging a series of parallel trenches to the sea, as far as possible from the arc of fire of the Destroyers.

The resultant No Man's Land between the sea and the Turkish trenches was being totally dominated by the Royal Navy. In the night, the powerful lights of these vessels obviated any attempts by the Turks to extend their trench lines. Prior to the launch of the August offensive, a sort of routine had developed, wherein the lights of the destroyers were being switched off at regular intervals to be followed by severe shelling by the guns of the destroyers. This routine had invariably set a pattern in the minds of the Turks, that switching off of the lights of the Destroyers would definitely be followed by severe shelling. Therefore, the moment lights used to be switched off, the enemy used to take cover in the trenches to be safe. This phenomenon had totally been drilled into the minds of the enemy, prior to the launch of the August offensive. 'This became routine; the Turks became accustomed to it and, scenting a trap, stayed safely in their dug-outs. Thus, these two flanks, instead of being part of No-Man's-Land became virtually Anzac Land.'[116] The entire plan of the August offensive, hinged on this basic template as obtained in Anzac. The strip of undulating ground, with shrubs and thick undergrowth, between the sea and the

Turkish defence line, was going to be the focus of the offensive. In order to provide a reasonable chance to this offensive to succeed, a couple of feign attacks were also planned by the MEF, so as to draw Turks away from the defences:

The general plan is, while holding as many of the enemy as possible in the southern theater, to throw the weight of our attack on the Turkish forces now opposite the Australian and New Zealand Army Corps. It is hoped, by means of an attack on the front and right flank of these forces, to deal them a crushing blow, and to drive the remnants south towards Kilid Bahr. It will then be the object of the General Commanding to seize a position across the peninsula from Gaba Tepe to Maidos with a protected line of supply from Suvla Bay.[117]

The success of the plan was contingent the two aspects of, capture of Hill 305 and the capture and subsequent retention of Suvla Bay as a base of operations for the Northern army. The directions for the offensive were explicit and the operation was planned to be launched with multiple objectives:

The operations from within the present Anzac position will begin during the day immediately preceding your disembarkation (the reinforcements for General Birdwood's force having been dribbled ashore in detachments at Anzac Cove on the three previous nights). The operations will begin with a determined attack on the Turkish left centre, with the object of attracting the enemy's reserves to this portion of the line. At nightfall, the Turkish outposts on the extreme right of the enemy's line will be rushed, and a force of 20,000 men will advance in three or more columns up the ravines running down from Chunuk Bair. These advances which will begin about the same time as your first troops reach the shore; will be so timed as to reach the summit of the main ridge near Chunuk Bair about 2.30 a.m.[118]

The attack involved capturing of Sari Bair ridge and was planned to be a two-pronged attack with two columns of Infantry, the right and the left assaulting columns. The right assaulting column was directed to capture Chunuk Bair while advancing through Rhododendron Spur. The Left assaulting column was mandated to achieve twin objectives. The column was directed to split at Aghyl Dere into two separate columns. The first column was to move eastwards, through the Damakjelik Spur, Azma Dere and Abdul

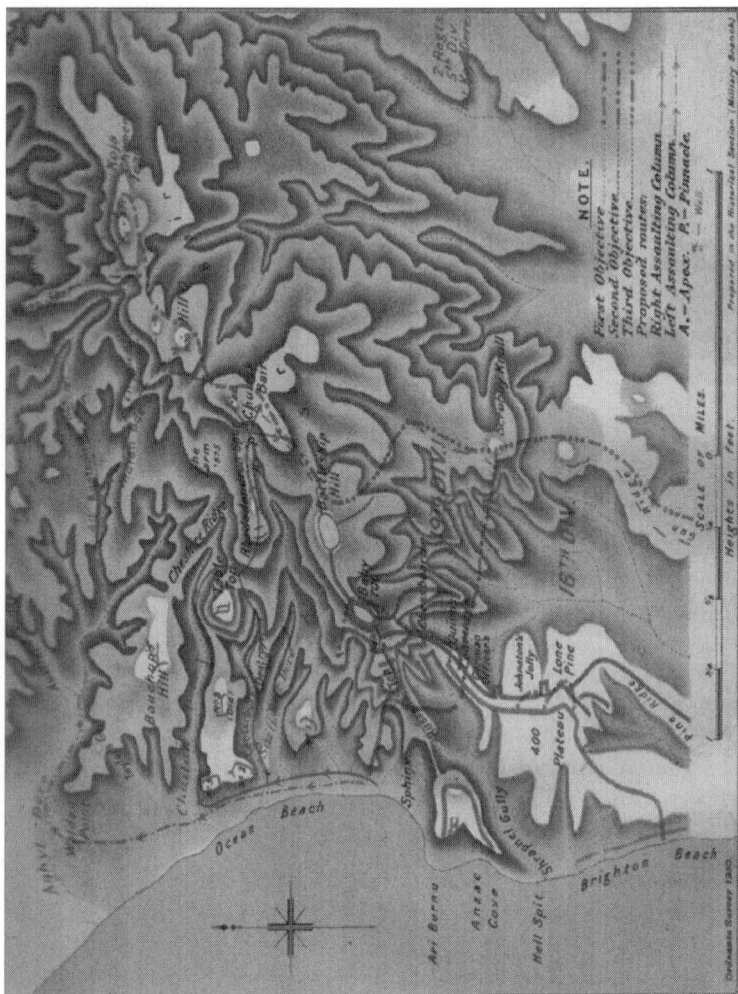

MAP 11: ROUTE AND OBJECTIVES OF THE TWO COLUMNS[119]

Rahman Spur to Hill 971. The second column of the left assaulting column was to capture Hill Q, while moving through the Damakjelik Spur.

In order to prevent any interdiction to the move of Right and Left Assaulting Columns and to facilitate their unhindered approach to the objectives, two covering force columns were also detailed. The right covering force was tasked to capture enemy held positions on Destroyer Hill, Table Top, Old Number 3 Post and Bauchop's Hill, whereas the left covering force was to move along the beach to Walden Point, cross Aghyl Dere and further occupy the heights of Damakjelik Bair. The subsidiary task of the left Covering Force also involved providing flank protection to the right flank of IX Corps as the troops of the Corps landed at Suvla.

The right assaulting column comprised troops of New Zealand Brigade along with a Battery of Indian Mountain Artillery. The column was tasked to capture Chunuk Bair while moving along the route from Anzac Cove to Rhododendron Spur. The other column comprised the 4th Australian Brigade, 29th Indian Infantry Brigade and the second Battery of the Indian Mountain Artillery. Both the columns while moving in the prescribed Order of March would move out from the Anzac Cove and were supposed to move along the coast line for approximately two miles, before turning towards inland. In the same Order of March, the column was to split into two sub columns under respective Brigades after covering a distance of about three miles of a total inhospitable terrain.

The column of the 4th Australian Brigade was tasked to capture Koja Chemen Tepe (Hill 971) and the 29th Indian Infantry Brigade was tasked to capture the central height of the Sari Bair Ridge, Hill Q. The strategic aim of the operation revolved around division of the Turkish forces on the peninsula. Sari Bair Ridge was the dominating ridge line in the peninsula and its capture would have clearly and cleanly bifurcated the enemy forces. It was believed that, 'in capturing these three main points along the ridge (Chunuk Bair, Hill Q and Koja Chemen Tepe), the Turkish forces to the south would be cut off, the Dardanelles forts taken from the rear and the campaign as good as won'.[120]

LANDINGS AT ANZAC COVE

As part of the overall landing plan at Anzac, the troops of the Indian Brigade were to be landed at Anzac on the night of 3/4 August 1915. All the disembarkations were planned to be carried out at night. 'It will be necessary to carry out these disembarkations at night and the movements can begin as soon as it is convenient to the Naval Transport authorities.'[121] The detailed plan of disembarkation, involved the landings of almost 2,350 men and 1,300 animals over a window of four-day period.

As the Indian troops were landing at Anzac for the first time as part of the 29th Indian Infantry Brigade since the initiation of the campaign, the administrative orders for the landings were quite exhaustive. Coupled with the secrecy concerns and the constraints of keeping almost 2,000 plus men concealed at the Anzac prior to them being launched into the offensive, required promulgation of detailed administrative instructions. All the Indian troops earmarked for landings, were to be equipped with the individual Field Scale equipment, including respirators and were mandated to carry pack and waterproof sheets. The orders specifically mentioned about no carriage of blankets and the officer's kit was reduced to what they could carry on an individual basis. No transport of any kind was to be made available to move any baggage or equipment, and accordingly everything was to be carried on man pack basis.

As far as ammunitions weres concerned, Small Arms ammunition was to be carried @ 200 rounds per rifle or person. 3,500 rounds per machine gun in belt boxes and guns, limbers and wagons were to be filled with fuse shells. All individuals were to land with their respective filled water bottles. The battalions were directed to ensure that iron rations, one day meat and biscuits and two days groceries sufficient to provide breakfast were carried. Fuel for cooking was planned to be issued on shore. All Infantry tools were to be carried at twin levels of Regimental and Brigade. Regimental reserve was distributed to individuals and carried in person; whereas the Brigade reserve entrenching tools were distributed to the units, and further by them to individuals and carried in person.

The Affirmation 251

TABLE 25: ORGANISATION ORDERS FOR INDIAN TROOPS LANDING AT ANZAC[122]

Date	Unit	From	Men	Animals	Remarks
Before the Morning of 3 August	Mule Corps	Helles	50	200	
Night of 3/4 August	29th Indian Infantry Brigade	Imbros	2,000	-	Machine Guns & other equipment carried by hand
Night 6/7 August	Mule Corps	Helles	150	300/150 Mule Carts	New Beach
Dawn 7 August Onwards	Mule Corps	Mudros	-	400	Sufficient Personnel to look after Mules
Be prepared to land immediately after above	Mule Corps	Mudros	150	300/150 Mule Carts	Anzac Cove/ New Beach

On disembarking, troops will be met by staff officers and guides, and will be marched off direct to the ground allotted to them, in no case more than 1,200 yards from the beach. All kit brought must be removed by the troops, and must be taken out of the lighters at the same time as the troops leave.[123]

The places were earmarked for the Indian troops by the battalion. In order to obviate any possibility of Turks coming to know about landing of additional troops at Anzac, strict orders were promulgated to restrict movement during day time. 'No troops are to leave the area allotted to them between 4 a.m. and 8 p.m. except on special duty with the authority of the Brigade Commander. Picquets will be placed under area arrangements at intervals around the area to prevent men straying independently.'[124] As the operation was planned to be launched immediately after landings, it was directed that the emergency ration and water will not be consumed. Water was to be issued to all troops at the rate of one gallon per person per day. 'This includes water for all purposes. For bathing, the sea is available, but may only be visited after 9 p.m. daily.'[125]

Emergency ration was not to be used under any circumstances. 'Troops are not to use any portion of the iron ration with which they land. Issues will be made under Brigade arrangements of rations and extras to last the period of their stay.'[126] The space being restricted; specific orders were issued for the use of latrines. The 4th Australian Brigade had done a commendable work for the Indian troops under the existing conditions. The hygiene and sanitation issues were anticipated to be a concern, keeping in mind the limited space available and the number of troops planned to be inducted. The 4th Australian Brigade, however, had planned for the same. 'Latrines for immediate use are dug and marked in each area; additional latrines are to be prepared by units and the strictest orders issued to prevent fouling the ground. Latrines are to be made very deep, as space is much restricted.'[127]

The orders for the proposed offensive were briefed to these officers of the battalions of the Indian Infantry Brigade on the evening of 2 August 1915. 14th Sikhs as part of the 29th Indian Infantry Brigade was issued with the mobilisation orders on the morning of 4 August 1915. The destination however, was still a secret. On the same night, the Commander of the 29th Indian Infantry Brigade along with his staff and the COs of the battalions had left for an unrevealed location. The 14th Sikhs in line with the operational plan, had embarked on the trawlers from the Kephalo harbour of the island. With the destination still not known, each soldier was very apprehensive about the things to come. With full battle loads, each company was allotted two trawlers for the journey. Though, the destination was still a secret, it was briefed to the troops that the proposed journey will take about two hours. The trawlers had set sail at 1900 hours and by 2100 hours had slowed near a:

black mass rising out of the sea, silhouetted against the deep blue of the sky and twinkling with countless lights, the sound of an occasional shot, followed at times by a burst of fire; and the plunking of bullets as they dropped spent, into the sea around us; lamps moving on shore; and the sounds of distant shouting, interrupted now and then by a fiery spray of shrapnel as it burst over the beach, or the muffled boom of a bomb.[128]

With the entire Indian Brigade still in the respective trawlers, waiting for orders to disembark, the entire area was teeming with confusion. The darkness and silence of the sea coupled with the activities on the peninsula was very conflicting. With no orders forthcoming, the anticipation for the upcoming operation was outweighing everything in the minds of the Indian troops. 'Around us were the forms of numerous other trawlers, as they too waited their turn-to discharge their cargoes of troops; without lights, save for an occasional spark from a funnel or the· glow of a forbidden cigarette.'[129]

The troops spent the whole night in the trawlers, waiting for orders. With very limited space available, the men and the battle loads jostled for a place to rest. No one had the faintest idea about the plans. Though by this time, the officers of the battalion had assumed a fair idea about the intended area of operations. The maps supplied to the battalion were an absolute means of deception. The battalion was going to land in area of Anzac, an area one-hundred-and-eighty-degree opposite of Kum Kale, for which the maps had been provided to the Indian troops. While keeping one sentry for look out, the troops had adjusted themselves along with their weapons and battle loads in the limited space available. The orders for disembarkation were finally received sometime during the latter part of the night and the men had started disembarking. The enemy sitting on heights of the peninsula and in full observation was able to make out some sort of activity near Anzac.

The troops of the Indian Infantry Brigade started landing at Anzac Cove in the night of 5 August 1915. Adequate preparations were already in place to accommodate these troops in the terraces and fox holes. The troops continued to land throughout the night of 5 August and on the next day also. The troops of 1/6 GR, 'were ferried over on the night of August 5th- 6th, arrived exhausted from the effects of a bad crossing and were disposed of in little rabbit holes in a steep cliff'.[130] In the case of the 14th Sikhs, only half of the battalion had disembarked, when the interference by the enemy in the landing operations increased to dangerous levels. The landing operations of the balance battalion were accordingly put on hold and the trawlers carrying these troops went back into the sea. The orders specified that balance of the battalion was to disembark only after the last light. 'There we spent an exceedingly uncomfortable day, as the wind had got up, and the trawlers tossed about like corks. We tossed about in lighters all day; hot; men all sick; sea rough.'[131] The balance of the troops while being on trawlers were literally at sea. There was no information at all about the orders for the operation. There was no senior officer of the battalion with the troops. The junior officers were equally clueless. The battalion was supposed to get further orders while at shore, after landing. But in this case no landing had happened and half of the battalion was at shore, with the other half literally at sea.

FIGURE 24: VIEW OF Anzac FROM TRAWLER OF THE 14TH SIKHS[132]

Unknown to the troops still in trawlers, however, this was the beginning of the fiercest fighting the peninsula had witnessed till date. With no visuals, the sounds of the battle raging at the peninsula were an adequate indicator of the things to come. This half of the battalion was finally able to land at Anzac after the last light on 6 August. Amidst intense shelling by the enemy, who by this time also had developed a fair idea about the impending operation, this half of the battalion was also tucked into the maze of terraces and tunnels developed along the beach for the very purpose.

The troops of the battalion were without their backpacks. The mountainous terrain in conjunction with the earmarked role for the troops of the Indian Brigade at Anzac had precluded any possibility of getting heavier baggage with them for the offensive. The very basic minimum carried by the troops was not sufficient to cater for the temperature drop in the night. 'We have no kit with us, not even a pack, as it is too hilly to carry them; so we are not over comfortable and it gets infernally cold at nights, just before dawn.'[133] Maintenance of surprise also required that unnecessary movement by the troops should be avoided. Immediately after the landings, the troops were sent to the holes dug in the hills:

An improvised Brigade cook-house and ammunition dump had been established there. I found our men working like beavers. They had dug themselves into a small re-entrant in the side of the ravine, lit their fires and were preparing the first cooked meal we were to taste for four days.[134]

Coupled with the lack of equipment and sufficient clothing, a continuous three months of inactivity at the Cape Helles had not done much good to the battalions of the Indian Brigade. The trench warfare, in which the battalions were engaged while being at Cape Helles, was going to change at Anzac. The designated role for the troops of the Indian Infantry Brigade at Anzac now involved offensive operations. The Officers' of the Indian battalions were also apprehensive of the physical capabilities of the troops:

None of us are very hard after three months enforced inactivity in the trenches and consequently when attacking up a very steep rough slope, which rises 900 feet in a very short distance. We all get so done, that we have to stop for a bit to rest and though partially hidden by the scrub, the bullets come whistling through all night.[135]

ASSAULT PLAN OF THE 29TH INDIAN INFANTRY BRIGADE

First detailed briefing of the Company and Platoon Commanders of the battalion was held on at 2100 hours on 7 August. The simplicity and boldness of the offensive were mutually divergent. The aim of the offensive was the capture of height of Sari Bair, the most dominating geographical feature of the peninsula. By infiltrating through the gap between, the enemy held defence line and sea, the Infantry would not only have been able to turn the enemy defences at Anzac but also would have cut off the enemy held positions at Cape Helles in the south, thereby facilitating the operations of the 29th Division and the French towards the north. The Brigade Major of the Indian Brigade, while briefing the troops of the formation on the night of infiltration, reiterated the importance of the mission. The stalemate of trench warfare firmly set in the peninsula could only be subjugated by the results of the impending offensive.

If Sari Bair were captured and consolidated, the Turkish position at Anzac would be outflanked and the Turks at Cape Helles cut off. Here was a plan which appealed to the imagination. Here was the chance of breaking away from trench warfare and operating in the open. It was to be 'Gurkha Bluff' on the grand scale.[136]

The 29th Indian Infantry Brigade, initially while being part of operations conducted by the 29th Division and now Anzac, was the crucial component of force levels in both the operations. With both the 69th and the 89th Punjabis, the initial component of the 29th Indian Brigade, having moved out of the formation and fresh Gurkha battalions now being part of the Indian Brigade, the14th Sikhs along with the 1/6 Gurkhas was the only constant feature of the Brigade and both of them were going to play a very important role in the entire plan. The Indian Infantry Brigade was tasked to march along the northern edge of the Anzac defences. The troops allotted for this mission included the 29th Indian Infantry Brigade, 4th Australian Brigade, 21st Kohat Mountain Battery and a company of New Zealand Engineers. The objective of the column was the capture and subsequent occupation of Point 305.

With the terrain and enemy dispositions along the route being largely unknown, strict security measures were taken to prevent the enemy from coming to know about the objectives of the column. Passwords for the identification of friends and foe were circulated separately. The Operation Order of the 29th Indian Infantry explicitly mentioned that anyone not able to provide counter to the password or without identifiable distinguishing marks was to be treated as enemy. The order also directed COs to send covering parties ahead to seek exploitation of the ground as far as possible and also to ensure that the parties of the battalions turning the enemy defences or preparing fresh defences are adequately protected by these covering parties from anticipated counter attacks by the enemy. For success signals, the battalions were instructed to light green flares to indicate the most advanced positions secured by them. The battalions were to light these flares at specific intervals at 0345 and 0355 hours on 7 August. Within the overall order of march of the column, a subset of order of march for the troops of the Indian Infantry Brigade involved move of 1/5 Gurkhas, 2/10 Gurkhas and 1/6 Gurkhas in that order after the Brigade Headquarters. The 14th Sikhs was directed to provide an escort to the guns of the 21st Kohat Mountain Battery with a Double Company. The balance of the 14th Sikhs was to move as a rear guard to the entire column. The distance of the Sari Bair objective from the assembly point was only 3 miles and it was anticipated that even with a very conservative estimate, the column will be able to reach in the vicinity of the objective by three in the morning.

THE ASSAULT

Reconnaissance of the area of the intended operations is a basic military tenet. The broad plan of the operation was kept a secret as far as possible. The secrecy, however, cannot obviate the need for a proper reconnaissance prior to the operations. Striking a balance between two competing terms of reference, officers of New Zealand Mounted Rifles Brigade had been tasked to carry out a reconnaissance on behalf of the entire formation, thereby letting only a selected lot to do the rather than every formation carrying out their own parallel reconnaissance in the same area, a cardinal error in the military operations. An officer of Canterbury Mounted Rifles of ANZAC, Major Overton had been entrusted with the responsibility of navigating the entire column to the objective. Overton along with a few other officers, assisted by a selected lot of Greek civilians carried out elaborate reconnaissance sorties into lower foothills of the peninsula. The COs of the battalions going for attack were also given opportunities to do respective reconnaissance from some vantage points selected for the purpose in Anzac

With the first light of dawn expected by around 04:00 hours, it was expected that forming up place on Abdul Rahman Spur would be occupied by about 02:00 hours, catering for enough cushion to capture the summit by first light. For an approximate distance of 3.5 miles, time allotted was three hours, which considering the length of column, an unpredictable route which was not pre-reconnoitered and the physical state of troops was far too ambitious. One of the Battalion Commanders of the 4th Australian Brigade, was quite apprehensive of the overall plan:

Our physical condition was very poor, and we had heavy loads to carry. We had too many untrained reinforcements who, though keen and willing, had not the unit esprit-de-corps. Most of our men were very weak, and I doubt if they could have marched the distance required in the time, given day light, proper guides, and no opposition. It was the worst 48 hours I can recollect in Gallipoli.[137]

Keeping in mind the number of troops involved along with the limited availability of space the preparatory activities prior to the move of columns for the objective took much of the time and it was only after 23:00 hours, when the 4th Australian Brigade led by the 13th Battalion started moving out of No. 3 post. As per given order of march, 14th Battalion followed the 13th, after which Brigade Headquarter was moving, followed by the 15th and 16th battalions in that order. 'The advance was checked almost at once, and progress soon became so slow that it was not until four hours later that the rear of the column filed past the starting point. The success of the operation had thus been gravely imperiled almost before it began.'[138]

The troops of the Indian Brigade following closely behind the 4th Australian Brigade virtually had no idea as to the direction and objective of the advance. With limited ground available for the assembly, which was safe from shelling by the enemy, confusion prevailed. The dark night, with no moon light further compounded the problems of the commanders of the units and sub units. The subunit commanders were finding it difficult to identify their men in the confusion and get them to the right place for marching. The confusion and panic were evidently visible. The CO of the 1/6 Gurkhas, while narrating the events of the night said:

There was a feeling of panic and doubt in the air as to where we were and where we were going. It was pitch black night. Suddenly I heard a rush in front; I thought it was Turks and drew my revolver and was almost at the same moment knocked down. Captain Dallas behind me fixed bayonets and stopped the rush. It was only a panic of a few men in the regiment in the front.

Meanwhile, the advance guard of the column, Major Overton was influenced by the advice of a local guide who insisted upon taking a short cut to Aghyl Dere through a narrow gorge, which according to their guide was a normal practice during peace time. With the complete route of the left assaulting column having not been reconnoitered earlier, putting the entire column through the gorge was a cardinal mistake. The gorge was overgrown with prickly scrub, through which the movement of the Infantry was very difficult. Pioneers in the column were moved ahead to cut the undergrowth and make some path for the Infantry. In addition, the sniping action from the heights along both sides of the gorge caused severe casualties to the column. Due to the delay in clearing action in the gorge, the tail of the column, comprising Indian troops was still at No. 2 Post and had not moved ahead. The entire column being misguided by a native guide lost its way in the initial stages of the advance itself:

The troops stumbled along in the dark, already tired and apprehensive. A few Turks snipers caused great confusion as the troops groped their way down the valley in the dark, and by 2 a.m., when half of the column should have been on Abdul Rehman spur and the other half on its way to Hill Q, the head of the column had only reached the Aghyl Dere. When units had been sorted out, Overton and the guides found it extremely difficult to fix their positions.[139]

Even leaving out the aspect of getting misguided, the advance was in very difficult conditions and the progress of the advance was very slow. The length of the column was too long to be able to be managed under a single commander with different units and sub units forming part of it. 'There were numerous delays owing to the difficult country, the pitch-black night and the enemy snipers who harassed the column from both flanks.'[140] With no clear-cut demarcation between the different components of the infiltrating column, the confusion had started the moment; the column commenced its march. A single halt of minor duration by anyone in the column was cascading into huge delays for the entire column. One of the Company Commander of the 14th Sikhs, while describing the unfolding of the events of the night has written about the bafflement and disorientation prevailing amongst the troops:

Rest of our Battalion had gone ahead and were now somewhere behind the Turks. The sooner we could catch them up the better. We were given a guide and before long were winding our way along the· beach. Soon we joined the tail of another column which had preceded us and the pace slowed down to that of a snail, with many long halts. It was very dark. Led by our guide, we shuffled forward a few paces at a time, and by the time it was getting light, we had only reached the-exit from the Anzac position.[141]

The combined effects of difficult terrain, carefully concealed Turkish snipers and the tired troops had an adverse impact on the operations of the 29th Indian Infantry Brigade. At 06:30 hours on 7 August 1915, the 14th Sikhs was directed to come under the command of the 4th Australian Brigade for the capture of Hill 971. 'But the Australian Battalion commanders had to point out that their men were too exhausted to move again that day, and Cox cancelled his order.'[142] With the delay in advance, by the early morning of 7 August, the column had dispersed far and wide. The Australian Brigade by 04:30 hours in the morning had just reached Damakjelik Bair. The War Diary of the Indian Brigade mentions that the orientation of the guide allotted to the column was also affected during the advance and the objectives for the battalions were confused with each other. The column comprising the Indian battalions, by this time was in a complete chaos. The troops were exhausted to the limit with total loss of orientation. Most of the troops and officers of the battalions had not been in a state of night march before. The previous three months having been spent in the trenches with very little movements being carried out at the cost of one's peril played havoc. The troops had no idea of the terrain. Coupled with this, the enemy snipers were further adding to their panic, though the Indian troops were not new to the sniping actions by the enemy, as they had witnessed the action while being in the defences. The present situation was a bit different and difficult, as the troops were being sniped at while in movement. The combined sense of disorientation, panic and enemy sniping was too much for the men. The remnants of the previous actions in the area in form of dead and decaying mortal remains of the soldiers, own and enemy, and the groans of the wounded did not help the situation either.

FIGURE 25: HUMAN REMAINS OF
THE DEAD AT DEMEKJALIK BAIR[143]

The officers and men of the Indian battalions were virtually in the same position as far as panic, loss of direction and total disorientation was concerned. 'The place was covered with the dead and dying. Many in great pain were throwing themselves about. One began to know again what war was.' While, if one compares the casualty figures of the period with the previous figures, while in defence, the casualty figures were not much, but enemy snipers and the sight of the dead and wounded along with an anticipation of enemy artillery actions in the morning wreaked havoc on the psychology of the troops and officers alike. The commander of the party responsible for navigation, Major Overton had also lost his life while guiding the troops of Indian Infantry battalions to their revised objectives.

With absolutely no movement forward, any remaining hopes of moving forward to Hill 971 on 7 August 1915 quickly evaporated. On the other side, all three Gurkha battalions of the 29th Indian Infantry Brigade were very widely scattered and there was no possibility of regaining of command and control of these scattered battalions to be able to be launched again to capture Hill Q. The only hope was the use of available reserves. At this time, the Commander of the Indian Brigade asked for and received permission to employ the 39th Brigade of the 13th Division for the capture of Hill Q in the available time, before the arrival of Turkish reinforcements. Like the Indian battalions, the battalions of the 39th Brigade were also having orientation issues and had embarked along a totally different direction. 'On returning to Cox's Headquarters, the Commander of 39th Brigade realised that through some misunderstanding all four of his Battalions had started south of Chailak Dere,'[144] thereby making the situation irretrievable.

The rear column of 14th Sikhs, till now detached from the main column, was also carrying the administrative requirements of the battalion. Water, a very essential commodity on the peninsula, was being carried by the column in *pakhals*, two of which were generally composed of one mule load. In an unknown country, with a guide who himself was lost; the prognosis of the operation seemed poor. This column continued to look for the main body of the battalion, which had moved ahead and was now nowhere to be found:

We spent the whole of the 7th August trying to find the 14th Sikhs. Our guide had no idea where they were. We wandered up a valley leading to the right and getting steeper each moment. We found ourselves among the back areas of the troops in the front line but there was no sign of the regiment.[145]

The column was not able to find the battalion, but the water load being carried by it was reduced considerably in the process. Water was a precious commodity and all troops, including ANZACs, marching since the previous night were totally dehydrated and the water being carried by the Sikhs seemed a godsend:

One of the scouts we had sent ahead had spotted the regiment in the Aghyl Dere, a valley a mile or two further north. A Sikh is a Sikh, and easily seen, with his beard and his turban. So off we went again, down to the beach and along the coast, and at seven in the evening, tired and hungry, rejoined at last.[146]

The Company Commander of the Sikhs was at last able to locate his battalion. But the battalion, like others, was equally tired:

'We found the regiment tired too; they had been marching all night. They had got right behind the Turks, some of whom they had captured in their bivouacs; a German officer had been surprised in his tent, clad only in his pajamas; a Turkish field-Battery had been seen in the early light, limbering-up and moving off, just in time to escape capture. The Turks had shinned up the sides of the valley in the darkness and shouted to each other, trying to find out what was happening below. The maps were bad; it was difficult to find one's position; regiments had been mingled; there was no one to give orders; the men were tired out.[147]

On 7 August, two Gurkha battalions of 1/5 and 2/10, were ordered to go up along the two spurs immediately next to the halted column. Both the battalions, totally unaware of the terrain and enemy positions along the spurs came across a very strong opposition and suffered a large number of casualties. The seriousness of the opposition can be gathered from the fact that reinforcements from 14th Sikhs were sent to consolidate the gains and reinforce one of the Double Companies of 1/5 Gurkhas which was isolated. 14th Sikhs in the meantime, by 10:30 hours was also ordered to advance and capture the feature of Koja Chemen Tepe in a combined offensive with the troops of the 39th Infantry Brigade. With the delay in the arrival of the 39th Brigade, the orders were retracted. The troops of the battalion, who had moved up to reinforce 1/5 Gurkhas, were also under tremendous opposition from the enemy. With casualties mounting, the complete Double Company of the battalion was ordered to supplement the operations of the 1/5 Gurkhas. By afternoon, with no relief expected from the Turkish resistance, the Double Company of Patiala State Infantry had also moved up to support the 1/5 Gurkhas.

With no relief in sight, the balance of the 14th Sikhs and 1/6 Gurkhas also were ordered to move along a spur and capture the maximum ground possible. The War Diary of the29th Indian Infantry Brigade, further goes on to say that, 'All units went up spurs different to those allotted to them in orders, owing to the guide having completely lost his bearings and mistaken the gullies and spurs in the semi darkness.' With different objectives than the original ones and amidst the confusion of Turkish counter attacks, the battalions of the Indian Infantry Brigade had performed reasonably well. 1/5 Gurkhas along with some troops of 2/10 Gurkhas and reinforcements provided by the 14th Sikhs had captured a portion of the subsidiary spur of Chunuk Bair by 07:30 hours.

Along a parallel spur, 1/6 Gurkhas and a portion of the 14th Sikhs along with some elements of the 2/10 Gurkhas had climbed Chunuk Bair and were facing tremendous fire from the top of the main Chunuk Bair ridge and the spurs leading to it. The Indian troops were in a continuous battle for the past three days by now. The scarcity of drinking water was afflicting troops badly and the heat of the day along with the frequent orders of move in the midst of enemy fires was drawing a heavy toll on the Indian troops. The twin, almost simultaneous activities of bringing down the wounded and fetching up water and ammunition to the troops engaged in bitter fighting along the spurs, was too much, for the Commander of the Indian

FIGURE 26: 2/10 GURKHAS DURING ATTACK ON SARI BAIR RIDGE[148]

Brigade, Brigadier General Cox, who himself was a veteran of several battles along the north-western India. In his words, 'Gallipoli heat was worse than anything he had ever experienced.'

As far as the operation of the 1/6 Gurkhas was concerned, the allotted objective to the formation had still not been reached and the troops in a state of total disarray were still entangled in the foothills only. The Gurkhas during the firefight had landed upon an abandoned Turkish position with considerable defence potential. But due to the ongoing confusion, the success of the battalion was not exploited. The reinforcements required for holding the position did not move ahead and ultimately the Gurkhas were ordered to fall back and to entrench themselves at their previous location itself. The Gurkhas continued to be in entrenched location for the whole day and waited for orders for advance. Thus, the occupation of a tactically advantageous position by the Gurkhas was not exploited and had orders been received on time, the initiative of the Gurkhas would have greatly contributed to the objective.

With a very strong possibility of enemy counter attacks and imminent effective artillery fire on the troops in open, it was decided that the troops will entrench themselves at their respective current locations. The tiredness of the troops due to the continuous operations coupled with the extensive prevalence of disease had made troops lost entire sense of direction. The absence of guides and the dense scrub obtained in the area further had disoriented the troops. In another change of plans in the dynamic and confused situation, 1/6 Gurkhas was also directed to be placed under command of the 4th Australian Brigade for their offensive. The CO of the battalion mentions that in compliance with the fresh orders, he left the battalion in a defiladed position and proceeded to meet the commander of the Australian Brigade along with a few men of his battalion:

I discovered him hopelessly tied up, it seemed to me, in the low hills, a lot of shooting seemed to be going on, and there were some wounded lying about, but what I mostly saw were men hopelessly exhausted lying about everywhere, all movement and attempt to advance seemed to have ceased.[149]

The experience of the CO of the 1/6 Gurkhas while meeting with the Brigadier General Monash of the 4th Australian Brigade was not a very pleasant one. The CO of the Gurkhas mentions in his memoirs that commander of the Australian Brigade flatly refused to take the services of the Gurkha Battalion. The Gurkha CO returned back to his location, dejected by the sights along the way and at the Headquarters of the 4th Australian Brigade, which later on, he documented:

I went up and told him that my Battalion had been placed in reserve at his disposal, but he said to me, what a hopeless mess has been made of this, you are no use to me at all.[150]

The CO apprised the commander of the Indian Brigade, about the development and ordered the Battalion to be prepared to move up, apparently without any support from the the 4th Australian Brigade. 'It was useless to lie in cover in the low hills, when every minute counted, and I knew rests of my Brigade were on the move forward.'[151]

Overall, the day of 07 August in the history of 29th Indian Infantry Brigade did not prove to be very successful. The other formation in the column, namely the 4th Australian Brigade was also done for the day as brought out above. The orders given to the 29th Brigade for the balance of the day included reconnaissance in the balance day light hours of the day in the immediate vicinity of respective battalions and to bivouac at respective places for the night. Fresh orders for the next day were drafted at about 1800 hours on 7 August 1915, in which the 29th Indian Infantry Brigade was again earmarked for a decisive push into the Turkish defences.

For the proposed operation, the overall command was with the commander of the 29th Indian Brigade. The objective being, capture of Hill Q and Hill 971, the troops earmarked included the 4th Australian Brigade, the 39th Brigade and the Indian Brigade. The predicament of General Cox on the morning of 8 August 1915 was unenviable. Out of almost 13 battalions under his command, only the battalions of the 4th Australian Brigade were in a compact location, thanks to the efforts of the previous day. All battalions of the Indian and the 39th Brigade were spatially dislocated and in no way could have got together in the time available for the planned assault. As Commander of 29th Indian Brigade, General Cox still believed that the Indian battalions could be launched in the given time frame but the whereabouts of the elements of the 39th Brigade were absolutely not known.

Reconciled to launch the assault with the available elements only, General Cox drew up a plan for a general assault to commence at 0415 hours on the morning of 8 August 1915. The instructions for the move of the columns and for the subsequent attack were issued separately and the troops were directed to reach within the assaulting distances of the respective objectives by 0415 hours on 8 August, the objective being Hill Q and the spurs emanating from it. The available troops were divided into four columns, which in turn required breaking down the homogeneity of the formations:

No. 1: Column (Under Lieutenant Colonel F.G.H Sutton)
6th South Lancashire (39th Brigade)
9th Warwickshire (39th Brigade)
2/10th Gurkhas (29th Indian Infantry Brigade)
Objective: Northern Slopes of Chunuk Bair

No. 2: Column (Lieutenant Colonel T.A Andrus)
7th North Staffordshire (39th Brigade)
9th Worcestershire (39t^h Brigade)
1/6 Gurkhas (29th Indian Infantry Brigade)
Objective: Southern peak of Hill Q

No. 3: Column (Lieutenant Colonel P.C Palin)
14th Sikhs (29th Indian Infantry Brigade)
1/5 Gurkhas (29th Indian Infantry Brigade)
Objective: Northern peak of Hill Q

No. 4: Column (Brigadier General J. Monash)
4th Australian Brigade
6th King's Own (39th Brigade)
Objective: Abdul Rahman Spur & Hill 971

The cohesion of units and sub units having been already compromised, it was quite difficult for the commanders at all levels to get their troops together for the impending attack. The darkness and the active enemy snipers made the task more difficult. For the capture of spur leading from the farm, 2/10 Gurkhas along with two battalions from the 39th Infantry Brigade were nominated. For the attack, the overall command of the sub operation was with the CO of the 2/10 Gurkhas. All three battalions were directed to be prepared for the offensive by 0300 hours on 8 August. Similarly, under the command of the CO 1/6 Gurkhas, two more battalions of the 39 Infantry Brigade were directed to capture Hill Q, by advancing from the Chamchik Punar spur. The column was to start from their concentration point by 0315 hours. For the capture of Hill Q, a third column of the 29th Indian Infantry Brigade was also tasked. Comprising of the 14th Sikhs and 1/5 Gurkhas, the column was to operate under the overall command of the CO 14th Sikhs. Interestingly the time of concentration of troops and the time for the start of advance were left to the discretion of the respective Column Commander. The column was also instructed in the Operation Order to leave one company behind to watch the enemy activities on a nearby spur. As per these orders, 1/5 Gurkhas was to advance straight to the objective in a straight line. The 14th Sikhs on the other hand, with two Double Companies was ordered to infiltrate behind enemy lines and to outflank the Turks from the north. The balance 14th Sikhs was kept in reserve.

Both the battalions had commenced advance for the attack at 0415 hours on 8 August 1915. The advance was immediately contested by the enemy. Enemy snipers and Machine Gun fire continued to harass the advancing columns of these two battalions. As a result, 1/5 Gurkhas was not able to move forward and was totally tied down by the massive opposition. Sikhs on the other hand, took advantage of the lay of the ground and were able to successfully evade the Turkish defences. The column of the Battalion succeeded in moving approximately 300 yards, before they were stopped in their tracks by the wall of machine gun fire, which had been meticulously camouflaged in the scrub.

As far as move forward of No 4 Column was concerned, the attack plan involved advance by the 14th, 15th and 16th battalions of the 4th Australian Brigade, whereas the 13th Battalion along with 6th King's Own were tasked to hold the current position of the formation. The advance was not unopposed. Severe Turkish resistance firstly through fire and subsequently a strong counter attack by the Infantry tested the resolve of the Australians, which impacted the 14th and 15th battalions very badly. Both the battalions suffered a large number of casualties. The situation of No 1 and No 4 Sub Columns formed for the operations of 8 August, was quite different from that of No 3 Column. The dispersal of components of these columns affected during the previous day was way beyond the control of the respective commanders. Both the columns were not able to achieve anything substantial on 8 August. Only achievement of the day, if any, was by the troops of the 1/6 Gurkhas.

The Battalion besides being exhausted from the march of the previous day was combating severe extremes of weather during day and night. Whereas, the heat of the day was unbearable, the nail biting cold in the night was equally worse. Describing the conditions in the Battalion on 7-8 August night under the summit of objective of the Battalion, the CO of the Battalion wrote that, 'We had been heavily shelled that evening and I had been much frightened. We had no blankets and no coats, and when I got the orders, I was so shivering with cold that I could with difficulty read them.'[152] The battalion was ordered to attack the top of Hill Q, in support of two British battalions of the 39th Infantry Brigade. The two British battalions were dispersed all along the base of the hill and were not able to rendezvous with the CO of the Gurkhas. As the time passed, the chances of the Turks getting reinforced and putting up a coordinated resistance were increasing. The CO decided to take a calculated risk by commencing the attack forthwith and exploit the advantages being offered by the early dawn rather than waiting in vain for any reinforcements.

The 1/6 Gurkhas was alone in this assault on the Hill Q. The brave Gurkhas had reached almost 300 feet below the top of the hill, when they came under severe Machine Gun fire from the top. The Gurkhas had dug in at the instant location and later on, with some support from the remnants of two other battalions of the 39th Brigade, clubbed within the No. 2 Column were able to move further near to the summit. Within 100 feet of the summit of the Hill, the Gurkhas dug in again and that was the nearest they could reach to summit of Hill Q.

The news of this determined and daring advance of Gurkhas was not able to reach the Headquarters of ANZAC amid the din and

FIGURE 27: TROOPS RESTING AFTER SUCCESSFUL ATTACK
ON 8 AUGUST 1915[153]

confusion of battle and the 29th Indian Infantry Brigade was ordered
to abandon any plans for the fresh offensive on the same day. It was
further directed to collect the remnants of scattered formation and be
prepared to launch another offensive on Hill Q, the next day. Giving
the stalled offensive another chance of success, the next day, on 9
August, the 1/6 Gurkhas with the three companies of 1st Battalion
South Lancashire Regiment commenced advance to capture the
objective of Sari Bair. The thoughts of the Battalion Medical Officer,
of the Gurkhas, Captain E.S Phipson, just prior to the commencement
of advance provide a vivid backdrop to the offensive:

The period to which my thoughts turned so vividly was the 8th and 9th
August 1915, when lying alongside Allanson and Cornish in Battalion
Headquarter, a rough dugout or foxhole some 300 yards from the summit,
timed to begin about dawn, and preceded by a bombardment by the Navy
of the area beyond ridge.[154]

By this time 1/6 Gurkhas had suffered serious casualties and the
foreboding of the Medical Officer of the Gurkhas was not very off the
mark. The objective of Sari Bair, was appearing very formidable to the
troops of 1/6 Gurkhas, as they were sitting just at the foot of the
summit. The summit being totally infested with the rough scrub, duly

interspersed with rocky ravines and deep nullahs was a perfect battle ground for a defender, but offered a very difficult proposition for the attacker. The march for the offensive by the Gurkhas, along with the three companies of Lancashire's commenced at the designated time of 0515 hours on the sultry morning of 9 August.

The bitter cold of the night was about to turn into the intense heat of the day. The troops, being on a continuous march since they landed at Anzac, almost five days back, were also nearly at the end of their endurance. The emergency food and water being carried by troops was long over. As the Gurkhas gathered their weapons and equipment to launch another advance for another attack, the enemy was waiting for this moment. While the Gurkhas had started moving up towards the enemy trenches at the anointed time of 0515 hours, the critical artillery support was another half an hour away. The supposedly artillery fire came at exactly 0525 hours. In the meantime, the furious battles for the trenches at the summit had already commenced along the neighbouring ridges as well.

The so called 'own Artillery support' had nothing own about it. To the horror of the Gurkha officers and the men alike, the aimed artillery fire had resulted in the shells exploding amongst them. It has been claimed that amidst the din of battle that, six massive explosions of shells were fired by the Royal Navy, who evidently mistook Gurkhas for Turkish troops. The origin of the fire of these shells has been attributed to the 12-inch guns of a Monitor of Royal Navy anchored in the bay. The CO of the Gurkhas, Allanson also attributed the origin of these devastating shells to the Monitor. In the words of the CO:

the results of those six mighty explosions were ghastly at such close quarters, and led to a sudden retreat of the troops to the line from which they started. The blast was so tremendous that, although protected by the ridge, I was blown backwards heels over head out of the fox-hole, but I was not hurt.[155]

When the Gurkha CO was evacuated after getting injured, an officer from the 53rd Sikhs was nominated to take over command of the battalion. The CO of the battalion being injured and the new incumbent yet to arrive to assume the appointment, and no other British officer left to assume the command of the battalion, in an exact replica of the situation of the 14th Sikhs, two months back, the

Medical Officer (MO) of the battalion was directed to take over the command of the Gurkhas. When all this was happening with the Gurkhas, the Turks were getting together to launch a counter attack on the remnants of the Gurkhas. The last words of the CO to the MO, just before retreating assisted by two stretcher bearers were very inspiring for the newly appointed ad hoc CO of the battalion, the MO, 'Well, Phippy, there's no one left to hand over to but you. Do all you can to help Gambirsing Pun (the Subadar Major), and he will never let you down.'[156] The MO of the battalion had not yet gained commission in the army to command combatants, but the seriousness of the situation demanded him to take over the reins:

My first thought, oddly enough, was that I must cease to claim the protection (if any) of the Geneva Convention, and so I removed my Red Cross Brassard, and put it in my haversack. I might, I thought, have to do with combatant officers of other units, and although at that time, I held no combatant commission myself.[157]

The MO met the Subadar Major of the battalion, who just reinforced and reiterated the dire situation of the outfit, in terms of the losses of British Officers, Indian Gurkha Officers and Gurkha other ranks. The three days of intense battles had cost the battalion 38 killed, 154 wounded and four missing. It was pretty evident that the battalion will not be able to hold against a determined counter attack by the Turks. The MO as the officiating CO of the battalion, did his level best to find reinforcements at his own level by speaking or sending messages to the neighbouring battalions, but with everyone nearly in same state as far as troops were concerned, the MO was not successful in getting any reinforcements for his beleaguered battalion. The MO later on reminisced:

The troops on our flanks, when I wrote to them in the capacity of CO - the South Wales Borderers, the 9th Worcester's and the South Lanes - replied that they had either retired, or expected to retire, and themselves needed reinforcements or were momentarily expecting an attack, so it was evident that we were out on a limb and in no shape to hold a determined Turkish counter-attack which indeed, seemed imminent.[158]

The whole night, the battalion suffered more casualties from the

Turkish sniping and rifle fire. But the Gurkhas somehow held on to their positions. On the early morning of 10 August, the battalion received the much awaited orders for withdrawal to the next main position being held by the Allied troops. The inexperience of the officiating CO of the Battalion in these matters was at the fore. Captain Phipson, the officiating CO of the battalion, was really surprised at the depth of experience, knowledge and the situational awareness of Gambirsing Pun, the Subadar Major. It is claimed by the MO, that entire withdrawal operation was conducted under the total command and control of the Subadar Major:

Fortunately we could both converse in Hindustani of a sort, and it soon became apparent, to my relief, that he knew the drill from A to Z, and I marveled at the precision with which he described the different phases of the retirement and the proper precautions to be taken, such as the removal and disposal of the bolts of rifles which could not be taken; the disposal of surplus ammunition, collection of stores, destruction of equipment which could not be carried, and the timing of the movement itself and what a movement. To retire 900 feet down a rocky decline, intersected by deep and narrow gullies, many of them choked with corpses, and the infinitely difficult job of carrying down the wounded - all these problems, insoluble to me, presented little difficulty to Gambirsing Pun, whose knowledge and competence seemed complete and indefeasible. I recalled Allanson's words, He'll never let you down.[159]

When the 1/6 Gurkhas were preparing for a withdrawal from the untenable position, the Turks launched a heavy counter attack. Duly supported by Artillery, the enemy was determined to annihilate the remnants of the Allied troops dispersed all along the spur, without any coordinated defences. The dispositions along the ridge primarily consisted of battalions of the 39th Infantry Brigade and two battalions of the 29th Indian Brigade. With shape of the ridge, in this particular sector almost in a horseshoe shape, the troops were being fired from three sides and with reduced bayonet strength due to casualties amongst all battalions, the trench lines were being held by a very limited number of Indian troops.

The heavy shelling by the enemy Artillery on the positions held by the Indian troops had resulted in the thick undergrowth catching fire. With a number of casualties, both dead and wounded still lying where they had fallen, from both sides, the results of the fire were not very pleasant to the soldiers on ground. The attack on the 8th August morning had faltered but the thick and dry undergrowth had caught fire due to the combination of the machine gun and the Artillery fire:

I watched the flames approaching and the crawling figures disappear amidst dense clouds of black smoke. When the fire passed on little mounds of scorched khaki alone marked the spot where another mismanaged soldier of the king had returned to the mother earth.[160]

As the enemy troops were coming down the slope, the forward most positions of the Allied line held by the remnants of 1/6 Gurkhas and 2/10 Gurkhas were in the process of almost getting encircled. Seeing the desperate situation, the 39th Infantry Brigade sent a distressed signal to the Headquarters of 29th Indian Infantry Brigade. The message reiterated the situation of 1/6 Gurkhas and asked for immediate Artillery support to cover the withdrawal of battalion. The efforts and professional acumen of Subadar Major of the battalion however carried the day for the Gurkhas and they were successful in effecting a withdrawal along the previously held line at the base of the Sari Bair ridge.

The confusion and conflict had taken a terrible toll during the offensive. The short stint of recent training with the newly arrived reinforcements by all the battalions of the Indian Infantry Brigade, though had tried to absorb the freshly arrived reinforcements into the drills and procedures of the respective battalions, but the limited time available for the officers and troops alike, to know each other, a very essential component of Infantry operations had fallen short of expectations. With so many fresh troops and officers in the Battalion, the bonhomie and camaraderie existing in the operations carried out by the battalion in June and July was clearly found lacking:

To say that there was considerable confusion is to use a phrase which is meaningless to those who have never seen fighting. The sheer terror of some men, the bewilderment of others; none of whom had slept for four days; all of whom were at the end of their physical tether; all mixed up together; with strange officers trying to control men whom they had never seen before; with men looking for officers they could not find; with shouted orders merely adding to the uproar.[161]

Despite a large number of reinforcements already in the battalions, the mammoth losses of the June offensive were still not recouped. The 14th Sikhs were still short of the authorised bayonet strength. The fighting in the August offensive had further depleted the strength of the battalion. As a result of the Sari Bair battles, the 14th Sikhs, for instance, had been reduced to six British officers, one Viceroy's commissioned officer and two hundred and twenty-three other ranks. The process for recouping the losses was ongoing. During the next few weeks, the battalion had received several large drafts to include, 'one under Major Earle, one from the 87th Punjabis, one from the Burma Military Police and a second Double Company of Patiala Imperial Service Infantry.'[162]

Immediately after the Sari Bair offensive, when the battalion was consolidating itself at the new location, a company of Sikhs from the Burma Military Police joined the depleted ranks of the battalion. The nuances of war fighting at Gallipoli being what they were, it has been claimed that the troops of the Burma Military Police were totally misfit for the operations due to lack of training and weapons. The bare minimum training of 14 days being provided in musketry before their dispatch as reinforcements was simply not enough. 'Good men, but lacking in training. However, they settled down and were fortunate in not being sent straight into battle.'

With the Sari Bair offensive having failed to yield the desired results, the Indian Brigade had again found itself in the defenses. With new configuration of the fresh location, the trenches for the defence were not there. The battalions of the Indian Brigade had again started to dig. 'Our Brigade was given the task of consolidating Gorse Hill, and of gradually prolonging the line northwards to link up with the right flank of the troops at Suvla.'[163] The surrounding heights of Sari Bair were still in the possession of the enemy. Every activity of the Indian troops was being closely observed by the enemy, who were still shaken and surprised by the daring August offensive launched by the Indian Brigade.

With no covered or defiladed space available at the newly designated location of the Indian Brigade, the troops were directed to stay in the defiladed location of Aghyl Dere during the day and the task of digging trenches was carried out during the hours of darkness.

At the new location of Gorse Hill only the 'fighting patrols' were left by the battalions during the day, whose task was to ensure that the freshly dug defences were not occupied by the enemy:

This went on for a week. It was good training and we became proficient at night advances and withdrawals, though not without trial and error. Night marches are tricky it is so easy for the head of a column to go too fast and for the tail to lose its way.[164]

FIGURE 28: VIEW OF W HILL FROM GROSS HILL[165]

The rear elements of a company at the last of the column of the 14th Sikhs during one such night move had got detached from the main body of the battalion and wandered towards the No Man's land and further towards the enemy trenches. With situations of holding defences changing hands so frequently and the induction of fresh troops to new locations becoming a daily routine, the troops were not getting enough time to reconnoiter and identify locations during the day time. The situation was further compounded by the enemy localities being so close that the concept of No Man's land had virtually become redundant. Incidents like this were many, and were on the rise due to the fresh lot of troops and officers joining the battalions of the Indian Brigade at an enhanced pace:

On the night of the 13th August, a Friday, we heard plaintive cries coming' from no-man's-land "14th Sikhs - 14th Sikhs!". It was from our second-in-command, just out from India. He and a large party of men had wandered on and got lost, but we managed to recover them, after they had been fired at by both sides.[166]

The incidents of the bravery of the Sikhs continued even after the failure of the August offensive for the capture of the Sari Bair. As the Sikhs were settling down in the defences and linking up with the right most portion of XI Corps at Suvla, the Turks had established a sniper post, by putting some sand bags across a sunken track. The post location was carefully chosen by the Turks, which afforded a continuous observation of the operational and administrative movement of the Sikhs. In addition, the enemy snipers would have used this post to harass and cause casualties to the battalion. The destruction of the post, still under construction was important for the unhindered movement of the Sikhs. The CO of the Sikhs, one day directed one of the Second Lieutenant of the battalion to take a party of men from battalion and 'demolish the block'. The operation was supposed to be a tactical operation to be launched in the night with complete preparations and reconnaissance of the area and the fire support was to be planned and coordinated.

The Sikhs however, were able to convince the relatively inexperienced Second Lieutenant to launch an immediate patrol to destroy the post. The party of the battalion went across, demolished the post and even got empty sand bags back with them for the usage at its own defences: 'It was one of the coolest pieces of cold-blooded gallantry known. Colonel Palin, however regarded it as a gross breach of discipline as he had imagined that he ordered to do this at night as a tactical operation'.[167]

Though most of the Turks were unaware of the religious denomination of Sikhs, the outwardly appearances of Sikhs were creating confusion for many Turks. In an interesting incident on 21 August 1915, the Turks misinterpreted Sikhs to be Mohammedans. The Sikhs were tasked on that night to relieve the troops of Canterbury Mounted Rifles, who had also been digging fresh trenches along with them. In the thickness of the night, when the New Zealanders had started to move out from their trenches for fresh deployment, some Turks entered in the trench in the far end. As a result, when the last man of the Canterbury Mounted Rifles had moved out and Sikhs started filling in the vacated trenches, suddenly they faced the Turks who were already in the trenches:

> How they got there I have never been able to discover. The result was that the leading men of my regiment, as they took over from the Canterbury Mounted Rifles, and were about to occupy their trench, found themselves looking down on a large party of Turks, estimated later at three hundred men.[168]

The Turks completely bewildered to see the tall, burly Sikhs, though did not immediately open fire but on the contrary evinced interest that the Sikhs give themselves up in surrender. Maintaining a very tight grip on their weapons with their left hands, the Turks raised their right hands in unison to greet the Sikhs with the cries of Mohammedan greetings. The Turks were also equipped with bombs, which were tied to their belts. An officer of the Turks, who was behind the hordes of enemy was beseeching his soldiers for an immediate action to kill the Sikhs. The Sikhs, on the other hand, through sign language also indicated the enemy to surrender their weapons before any further action. When the Turks refused to give up their weapons, there were incidents of the Sikhs and Turks wrestling for the possession of the weapons of each other. The limited space available within the confines of the trench did not prove to be deterrent for the spirit of the Sikhs and hand to hand jostling had commenced.

By this time, when the Turks were still in a dilemma, whether to seek surrender of the Sikhs or to open fire, the Sikhs in the front took the initiative and opened fire. Some of the Turks surrendered, but majority of the enemy retreated from the trenches in the darkness, leaving their wounded and dead behind, in the Sikh trenches. With no interpreter available, the Sikhs were not able to interrogate the captured Turks, but it was assumed that newly inducted Turkish troops on the peninsula had misconstrued Sikhs to be co-religionists and had attempted to induce Sikhs to desert their battalion and join the Turks.

The Stalemate

Slowly and steadily, the Sikhs settled into a routine in the defences. With the real danger of Turkish attacks lurking, the regulation 'Stand

To' drills in the morning and evening and at odd hours continued to occupy the time of the troops. The continuous efforts of the battalion over a period of time had resulted in the increase in the extent of the defences. The greater extent required greater observation of the front. Accordingly, the troops in the night were detailed for patrolling the perimeter of the defences, to prevent a surprise attack by the Turks:

Otherwise, the life was almost of a domestic nature. The maintenance of the trenches; the improvement of dug-outs, with shelves and sleeping-ledges; the regular reliefs; the daily medical inspections; orderly room; the drawing of rations, the cooking and fetching of food; the clearing out of latrines; the occasional inter-company competition for a cup, made from a biscuit-tin, for the cleanest trenches; and, most important of all, the inspection of arms.[169]

Other than the enemy, the boredom of the trenches was killing literally. With a very active recent past, the troops were finding it really difficult to sustain. With the defences of the battalion now contiguous with the defences of Suvla Bay of XI Corps, the troops and officers of the battalion found an outlet for recreation. Those who were not required on duty were able to go the beach and take bathe. The opportunity to take bath regularly, a ritual very close to the Sikh troops, had beckoned after a long time. The troops made full use of the opportunity. Besides, fresh water well was also located close to the

FIGURE 29: SIKHS IN TRENCHES[170]

defences of the battalion. This had eased out the requirement of fetching of water by the mules, reducing further the requirement of fatigue duties by the troops. The maintenance of long unshorn hair and beards of the Sikhs, long neglected due to the paucity of water for drinking and bathing purposes at the previous locations, had suddenly found an outlet:

There was also a fresh water well where the men would gather 'to wash their long. black hair, and their beards, and anoint them with Sarson-Oil, which was now beginning to be sent out to them regularly from India. The long unshorn hair of the Sikh was a source of wonder to the British troops, most of who had never been to India. It was part of the outward and visible sign of their religion.[171]

The reinforcements for the 29th Indian Infantry Brigade were continuing to be dispatched from India. In a fresh tranche in the month of November, new reinforcements for the Indian Brigade deployed at Gallipoli peninsula were dispatched. These troops comprised fresh drafts of the battalions along with troops earmarked from other battalions to be attached with the battalions of the Indian

AUSTRALIAN WAR MEMORIAL   C00805
FIGURE 30: SIKH TROOPS WASHING THEIR CLOTHES IN THE SURF
AT Anzac COVE, GALLIPOLI PENINSULA[172]

TABLE 26: STRENGTH OF REINFORCEMENTS FOR THE 29TH INDIAN BRIGADE (EMBARKED AT BOMBAY & KARACHI)[173]

Details	Troops			Port of Embarkation	Vessel	Date of Embarkation	Date of Sailing
	Officers	SASs	Rank & File/ Followers				
Supply			1	Bombay	Bandra	14th November 1915	14th November 1915
14th Sikhs from 82nd Punjabis	2	-	106	Karachi	City of Glasgow	16th November 1915	16th November 1915
14th Sikhs from 14th Sikhs	-	-	1	Karachi	City of Glasgow	16th November 1915	16th November 1915
2/10 Gurkhas from 1/7 Gurkhas	2	-	100	Karachi	City of Glasgow	16th November 1915	16th November 1915
1/6 Gurkhas from 2/6 Gurkhas	2	-	98	Karachi	City of Glasgow	16th November 1915	16th November 1915
Porter Corps	4		617	Karachi	Thongwa	18th November 1915	18th November 1915

Brigade. The 14th Sikhs received reinforcements from their own battalion and attached troops from the 82nd Punjabis. Similarly, 1/6 Gurkhas had reinforcements of attached troops from 2/6 Gurkhas and 2/10 Gurkhas had additional troops attached from 1/7 GR. These reinforcements had sailed from Ports of Embarkation at Bombay and Karachi. Besides, seven British officers, one British Warrant Officer and two NCO's, the details of the reinforcements included the following as shown in Table 26.

By November 1915, additional Infantry battalions had starting arriving in Egypt from France. The C-in-C in India, already facing severe problems in making up the critical deficiencies in terms of reinforcements for the Infantry battalions at Gallipoli, directed G.O.C. Egypt to sidestep additional troops from the Infantry battalions arriving in Egypt from France to the Infantry battalions deployed in the peninsula.[174]

Under these arrangements, all troops of 5 Gurkhas serving with 1/1 Gurkhas were to join 1/5 Gurkhas at Gallipoli. Similarly, all troops of 4 Gurkhas with 1/1 Gurkhas were to report to 1/5 GR. All troops of Burma Military Police were to report to 2/10 Gurkhas at Gallipoli. Under these arrangements, 229 rank and file of Burma Military Police was transferred to 2/10 Gurkhas. As on 10 November 1915, the details of effectives present and enroute to join Force 'G' at Gallipoli included the following as shown in Table 27.

The state of fighting strength was forwarded by G.O.C. Egypt to the C-in-C in India through a cable on 16 November 1915. The state did not include the details of additional reinforcements, if any, which had departed from India after 10 November 1915.[175] On 21 October 1915, GOC, Canal Defences, Ismailia had sent the details of casualties amongst British and Indian ranks of units of Force 'G' up to and inclusive 20 October 1915.[176] It may be noted that by this time, major battles of the campaign were already over but after this occasional casualties due to enemy sniper or shelling and also due to the adverse climatic conditions had also been there.

From the analysis of the above two tables, one overbearing conclusion can be drawn. As on 16 October 1915, the total effectives of I.E.F. (Only Indians), present on the Gallipoli (less British Officers) were 4,033. While templating the same figure on to the next table

TABLE 27: STATE OF EFFECTIVES OF THE 29TH INDIAN INFANTRY
BRIGADE AS ON 16 NOVEMBER 1915[177]

Unit	British Officers	Indian Officers	British Troops	Indian Troops	Followers
Mountain Battery Reinforcements en route	-	-	-	63 Gunners 98 Drivers	4
21st Mountain Battery	1	4	-	96 Gunners 167 Drivers	19
26th Mountain Battery	5	4	-	91 Gunners 1,150 Drivers	18
Headquarters 7th IMAB & Ammunition Column	2	-	-	21	2
Indian Mule Train	13	12	33	209	3,425
03 Sections, 137th Ambulance	3	3	15	8	124
108th Indian Field Ambulance	6	7	-	10	169
110th Indian Field Ambulance	5	4	1	24	173
2/10th Gurkhas	13	19	-	748	48
1/6th Gurkhas	11	17	-	651	42
1/5th Gurkhas	7	20	-	679	42
1/4th Gurkhas	10	21	-	943	40
14th Sikhs	10	15	-	833	39
Patiala Infantry	2	5	-	207	17
Total	88	131	49	5,996	4,121

(Table 28), which depicts the total number of Indian casualties on the peninsula till 20 October 1915, it manifests that by that time Indian troops had already suffered casualties almost equal to the state of effectives on that day (4,031). With a situation of stalemate having nearly stabilised, towards the end of October, permission was granted to the 7th Indian Mountain Artillery Brigade to dispatch half of the strength to Mudros for rest and refit.

The authorised establishment of each Indian Mountain Battery

TABLE 28: TOTAL CASUALTIES OF THE 29TH INDIAN INFANTRY BRIGADE AS ON 20 OCTOBER 1915[178]

Details	7th IMAB	14th Sikhs	69th Punjabis	89th Punjabis	1/4 Gurkhas	1/5 Gurkhas	1/6 Gurkhas	2/10 Gurkhas	Indian Mule Cart Train	108th IFA	107th IFA	137th CFA	Miscellaneous	Total
British Officers														
Killed	1	10	-	1	-	10	04	04	01	-	-	-	03	34
Died of Wounds	01	02	01	-	-	03	02	01	-	-	-	01	01	12
Wounded	05	12	02	04	01	12	13	09	01	01	-	-	06	66
Missing	-	03	-	01	-	-	01	02	-	-	-	-	-	07
Indian Officers														
KIlled	01	05	-	-	-	06	02	09	-	-	-	-	-	23
Died of Wounded	01	-	-	-	-	-	01	-	-	-	-	-	-	02
Wounded	05	15	-	06	-	12	09	11	02	-	-	-	-	60
Missing	-	-	-	-	01	-	-	-	-	-	-	-	-	01
Rank & File														
Killed	12	176	03	06	03	136	93	101	35	01	-	01	01	568
Died of Wounds	19	37	-	01	01	24	30	51	28	05	01	03	01	201
Died	03	02	-	-	02	05	01	06	08	-	-	-	-	27
Wounded	303	715	24	97	24	485	533	520	292	43	-	10	-	3,046
Missing	-	51	-	03	-	01	08	39	01	-	-	-	-	103
Total	351	1,028	30	119	32	694	697	753	368	50	01	15	12	4,150

was four Indian Officers, 276 Rank & File and 25 Followers. When the first half of the Brigade strength had left the peninsula on 24 October 1915, there was still a considerable strength of the Indian Batteries which had not left the peninsula for any reason since 25 April 1915, the day of landing. 21st Mountain Battery had three Indian Officers, 149 Rank and File and 17 followers who were still continuing on the peninsula, whereas 26th Mountain Battery had four Indian Officers, 76 Rank and File and 18 followers. These soldiers and followers primarily comprised the troops who had either not been wounded or had been wounded, but joined back and were not evacuated. The grit and determination of the Indian gunners and drivers had ensured that by the end of October 1915, there were 88 per cent of Indian Officers, 54 per cent Rank and File and 70 per cent followers who had never been evacuated from the peninsula, in spite of the casualties.

THE SWIRL, SNOW AND SQUALL

The battalions of the 29th Indian Brigade had witnessed a terrible and humid summer in Gallipoli, through which the majority of operations had been conducted to include the three battles of Krithia and the famed August offensive. By November 1915, the Indian troops had settled down to a routine in defence. With no major offensive planned, the troops had established a system of trench living. Though, casualties due to enemy Small Arms fire and Artillery shelling were still occurring, overall Indian troops had established a relatively stabilised routine in defence.

It was in the second half of November that the weather underwent a sudden and drastic change on 26 November 1915. In the morning on that day, the weather was absolutely fine, with bright sunshine. The troops had gone about their routine tasks. The fatigue parties for ration and water had returned back to the respective company trenches. The drivers and mules of the Indian Mule Corps had also returned back to the respective mule lines when suddenly the entire skyline turned black. A thunder- storm was building up and rain was imperative. Battalion War Diary of 2nd Royal Fusiliers, co located with the 14th Sikhs, mentions about the after effects of the downpour:

Fine day until 5 pm when it started to rain heavily, soon developing into a regular tropical downpour. Water stood 2 feet deep in the trenches after one hour's rain. A tremendous flood of water poured into our trenches from the hills behind the Turks, washing away our barricade completely and drowning several men. A mule, a pony and three dead Turks were actually brought into our trench by the water. In the space of about 2 minutes our entire section was converted into a regular lake, communication trenches being transformed into swirling streams of muddy water.[179]

With the sudden gush of water, the entire trench lines, both of Indians and Turks, were inundated with water. There was no separation now, and water was everywhere. In the trenches, the equipment of the battalions along with the clothings and weapons of the troops had been washed away. With the dimensions of the trenches having been increased gradually, to make lives of the soldiers comfortable, the water had found an ideal outlet. The bodies of troops, of both sides along with those of mules were floating in these trenches. Though the complete Indian Infantry Brigade had borne the brunt of vagaries of the rain on the two days starting from 26 November 1915, but the Sikhs were the ones who were most affected. The War Diary of the 29th Indian Infantry Brigade explicitly talks about the havoc caused by the rains during those two days:

Very heavy rain commenced to fall this evening, turning trenches into streams of water in places several feet deep. Rain continued throughout the night. A volume of water came down the Azmak Dere carrying everything before it, in places coming over the top of the parapet of the fire trenches. The 14th Sikhs on our left and nearest this Dere suffered most, the men being flooded out, many kits being washed away.[180]

But this was not the end of the inclement weather. The suffering of the troops was to continue. As if the intensity and ferocity of the rains was not enough, the rains on the next day, the 27 November, was substituted by very high winds. The day also brought along a snow blizzard, this resulted in 'hard frost and a two-day freeze'. The troops who were in the open due to the rain of the previous day, suffered more due to the hard frost. 'Known as the Great Storm, many men froze to death, especially those in exposed positions in and around Suvla.'[181]

FIGURE 31: A VIEW OF THE 14TH SIKH TRENCHES
AFTER THE SNOW BLIZZARD[182]

The sequential actions of rain, snow and freeze brought much discomfort to the troops. The defences of the Sikhs were in the low-lying ground and all the water from the hills had come down and collected in the trenches of the Sikhs:

A 'tidal wave' waist-high had rushed through washing all before it. Ammunition, food, bedding and all the paraphernalia of the regiment had been swamped. By the time it had drained away and subsided, the men were living in a sea of stinking, glutinous mud.[183]

FIGURE 32: HEADQUARTERS OF THE INDIAN BRIGADE
AFTER THE STORM[184]

The troops with everything wet and a tremendous loss to the personal equipment had started working on improving and cleaning the trenches almost immediately. The work of cleaning had not yet finished, when snow came. With these conditions prevailing, the weather-induced hostilities had nullified the hostilities against each other. The weather was playing havoc with everyone and no discrimination whatsoever on any basis was being played up. Everyone was equally affected by the adverse weather:

It was as much as flesh and blood could stand. No human, Indian, British or Turk, could stay in trenches in such conditions. They clambered out on to the top and existed miserably in the open, within a hundred yards or so of each other; both sides were too concerned with keeping warm and salvaging such things as they wanted, to bother about firing at each other.[185]

By 5 December, the 14th Sikhs was almost recouped to the authorised strength, with additional reinforcements having been joined. The after effects of the recent squall and gale were very much evident in the Battalion. The troops were issued with winter clothing and also one additional blanket per man had also been issued to cater for the extreme cold conditions prevalent in the peninsula by that time.

FIGURE 33: RETRIEVING MESS PROPERTY AFTER
THE BLIZZARD[186]

This was not, however, the end of sufferings. The troops had to suffer more while being at the peninsula. The bodily ailments caused by these weather conditions had started afflicting the troops now. The severe frost started causing frost bite to the troops. With basic minimal medical support available to cater for the entire Indian Brigade, the troops were left to themselves to manage these conditions. The newly joined British officers as reinforcements had previous experiences in locally managing the symptoms of trench foot and the Battalion saved a large number of casualties through the guidance rendered by these officers. Men were told to take precautions to avoid exposure and the men who were exposed had their condition managed with the help of these officers: 'We, in the 14th Sikhs, were fortunate in having some officers who had recently come from France and knew about "trench-feet" and their treatments, and surprisingly, suffered only eighteen cases of frost-bite'.[187]

In spite of these, there were casualties in the battalions of the Indian Brigade due to severe frost bite conditions. The details are discussed in the next chapter of the book. The telephone orderly of

FIGURE 34: INDIAN TROOPS AFFLICTED WITH FROST BITE
DURING THE SNOW STORM[188]

the 14th Sikhs was found dead one morning frozen to death as his
duty required him to man the post. The maximum number of casualties
during those days can be attributed to the frost conditions:

The cases of frostbite during the last 4 days number 332 in the Brigade
evacuated to the Field Ambulance (10 on November 28th, 56 on November
29th, 67 on November 30th, 199 on December 1st). There still remain about
150 slight cases being treated regimentally.[189]

The demand for gum boots, braziers of fuel for drying clothing
had increased manifolds due to prevailing weather conditions. The
logistical concerns of demand and supply had totally let down the
troops again at the peninsula. The repeated requests for these basic
essentials for survival at the peninsula in those days didn't manifest
into supplies. Thankfully, the 14th Sikhs had enough stock of rum
which was shared equally with the Gurkhas of the Brigade and the
wintry days were drowned. 'Fortunately, there was no shortage of rum;
and the Sikhs, and our friends the Gurkhas, took full advantage of
the generous issues which were made from the large stock which had
accumulated.'

The availability of wood was also very limited in the location of the Indian Infantry Brigade. The enemy being so near also obviated any probability of parties moving out in the open for collection of fire wood. As a result, the Indian troops managed their conditions within their trenches. The sudden assertion of extreme weather conditions had not only affected the men and animals but also put the functioning of weapons and equipment under severe stress and strain. An entry in the War Diary of 29th Indian Brigade mentions about employment of innovative means to keep the weapons functional. 'Water in machine gun froze and was replaced by a mixture of rum and ethanol.' The sudden onset of winter conditions along with severe gale and windy conditions had also affected the movement forward of essential supplies and equipment. Glycerin and petroleum reserves having been totally exhausted, no fresh supplies were in the pipe line. Thinner rifle oil an essential supply for the maintenance of personal weapons had run out of supply, adversely affecting the maintenance and cleaning of rifles.

It was the Indian Mule Corps during these critical times which did not let down the soldiers fighting the brunt of weather and enemy together. The mules, carts and their drivers continued their dangerous sojourns. These administrative journeys became more important after the snow storm as the requirement of administrative stores had peaked and survival against the inclement weather had turned out to be the most important part of the campaign during those few days.

EVACUATION AND ENDING

The weather induced harsh conditions had brought forth a speculation on the future of the allied operations at Gallipoli. A series of storms during those few days had destroyed a number of piers, through which the troops at the peninsula were being sustained. Though at the battalion level, there was an apparent vacuum as far as strategic discussions with respect to the future of the campaign was concerned, there was a sudden influx of very strong rumors regarding the withdrawal of the Allied troops from the peninsula. Slowly and steadily the Allied troops had started retreating from the peninsula. The deception measures to simulate the presence of forces in original continued in full measure. The field hospitals inducted in the wake of the August offensive had started to be deinducted:

A hospital camp, near Fisherman's Hut was found to be empty, save for a skeletal personnel, whose duties lay in keeping fires and lights burning at night and of walking about, by day, giving the impression of normal activities.[190]

After the snow storm, the Artillery guns had also relatively fallen quiet. At this stage, the reasons which can be attributed to the silence can range from strategic to administrative. In addition, the requirement of these precious guns was also being acutely realised in the other theaters. Using adequate deceptive means, these guns had slowly started to withdraw from Gallipoli. These guns of the Field Artillery were being traded with the guns of the mountain batteries, which had limited requirements in the other theatres. The deception measures included firing of four rounds of rapid fire in quick succession from the mountain guns so as to simulate the fire of complete batteries, thereby letting Turks know about the normal state of affairs and providing alibi for the Allied Artillery field guns being still on the peninsula.

The Indian troops at Gallipoli, with the exception of Artillery guns and Indian mule carts were mostly on man pack basis. The Infantry was able to carry all their essentials on man pack, but the Indian Mule Cart Corps, had accumulated a large number of voluminous stores over a period of time, which could not be taken back under the prevailing conditions. These stores could not be left behind and needed to be turned into unserviceable, lest they were captured by the Turks. With the orders to the effect that all non-essential stores will be left behind, the Mountain Artillery mules were also clubbed into the category of non-essential stores.

Orders were received that only Supply & Transport (S&T) mules and carts were to leave the shore. The logic behind the decision was based on a premise that, 'mules of an ordnance stamp were more easily procurable in Egypt than those of an S & T stamp.'[191] With great difficulty the CO of the 21st Mountain Battery was able to get the orders reversed, at least for his Battery and no ordnance mule of the Battery was left behind. Sultan Ali, the Pay Havildar of the 21st Mountain Battery had been credited with ensuring that nothing was left behind on the peninsula: 'He sat at the beach near a pier with all our heavy kit, with orders to shove the stuff on any old barge he could get permission for. He did this with such success, sending a few men with each consignment that we lost nothing'.[192]

With a very large strength of horses and mules on the peninsula, the transport effort being provided was simply not enough. With the limited availability of the shipping effort being made available, it was not possible to take back all the stores and the animals on the peninsula:

It was obvious that large quantities of stores would have to be abandoned, and it was accordingly planned that as many of these as possible should be burned, to prevent their falling into the enemy's hands. One unpleasant task fell to my lot in assisting to carry out the destruction of large number of mules and horses. We had to shoot them with revolvers as they stood in their standings. I hope never to have to participate in such wholesale slaughter again.[193]

The Indian Mule Cart Train also played an important role in the creation of deception, while the evacuation of the Allied troops from the peninsula was taking place. The Indian mules and drivers simulated the actual dumping of stores and equipment to the forward locations as was the practice till now, whereas actually the dumping of stores and equipment was happening in the reverse order, from the forward defences to the beaches:

AUSTRALIAN WAR MEMORIAL   PWDJ0152

FIGURE 35: INDIAN MULE CART TRANSPORT DRIVERS
AND MULES EMBARKING FROM A PIER AT Anzac[194]

On the 'big night' my pal and I were ordered to commandeer some Indian Gharries, which were carrying petrol cans (used for carrying water) and we took them to as near as we could to 'Johnny Turks' trenches, to kid him that we were bringing goods up. We made as much noise as we could by running the Gharries around and then quietly strolled back to Brigade Headquarters.[195]

The 14th Sikhs were provided a subtle hint on 12 December 1915, that a withdrawal was imminent. The orders were passed on 12 December afternoon that the battalion had to report at Anzac beach, with complete personal kits by the last light of 14 December 1915. The battalion was ordered to mobilise for the movement with all the sick, attachments, medical personnel and any other men not required to man the defences at the front-line trenches. The manifest of the battalion had to account for each and every man posted or attached with the battalion. The battalion was relieved by the troops of 1/4 Gurkhas before the first light of 14 December.

The 14th Sikhs concentrated at the reserve trenches before the fore-noon of 14 December 1915. The entire day was spent by the troops in packing up of the battalion and personal stores and by the end of the day, the battalion was ready to move, but not before dispatch of some heavy baggage to the earmarked beach, to be loaded in the trawlers. The battalion discarded the stores and equipment which was not needed or was too heavy or voluminous to be carried in the location only and it was ensured that those stores and equipment were made unserviceable prior to the move of the battalion for the beach.

As per the orders of the Indian Brigade, the battalion left behind two officers and eleven other ranks to be attached with the Headquarters and deinducted with the balance of the Indian Brigade. The move of the battalion commenced at last light and the troops 'fell-in' behind the troops of 2/10 Gurkhas, which was just ahead in the planned Order of March. The withdrawal was also a tactical move and was carried out by the battalion in an absolute tactical manner:

The timing had been admirable. We had fitted into our place in the long column with no halt, no delay. There was complete silence, except for the sound of shuffling feet; the occasional bump of a rifle-butt; or a muffled cough.[196]

The battalion was able to concentrate at the Anzac beach by eight in the evening and was directed to move to the Walkers Pier, where two lighters were placed at the disposal of the battalion. Reginald Savory of the battalion mentions in his memoirs that the lighters at the beach, even after every one had boarded waited for 'some stores' to be loaded, which:

included some cases of whiskey. We were determined to leave none behind. We were equally determined that the Australians should not lay their hands on them. Some of them had been seen eyeing them and had been heard to remark that it would be a 'pity not to 'salvage' them.[197]

In order to salvage these 'precious stores', the battalion had nominated, some not so sick and wounded troops, to retrieve as many bottles from their cases and keep on handing them to the rank and file of the battalion as they embarked on the nominated lighters:

This minor operation was carried out with the smooth efficiency which marked the whole of the evacuation. As I was waiting to step over the gunwale, a mysterious figure sidled up in the gloaming, and with a, *"Sahib; Hujoor di Veesky",* (Sir, Your Honor's whiskey), handed me four bottles. Two of these I passed to my orderly. The other two I crammed into my greatcoat pockets. The others were similarly distributed. We then went aboard, and left the soil of Anzac behind us.[198]

These two lighters shifted their cargo to the two steamships, *Redbreast* and *Snaefell*, which were at sea. The entire battalion was able to embark these two steamships after several trips by the two lighters to and fro, from Anzac beach. By around midnight of 14 December 1915, the two ships had sailed for Mudros. At Mudros, the battalion had shifted to two larger transports *Tunisian* and *Lake Michigan* and finally sailed from Mudros on 19 December 1915. While sailing away from the peninsula, the thoughts of the men of the battalion were with the men who were not there with them now. They had sailed together towards Gallipoli in April, but after nine months the composition of the battalion had totally changed as a result of the massive losses suffered on Gallipoli:

On 23rd December, we disembarked at Alexandria, and took the train for Suez. Our Gallipoli chapter was finished. We had acquitted ourselves to the best of our ability, and lost in the process no less than twenty-eight British officers, seventeen Indian officers and one thousand five hundred and sixty-three men, killed, wounded or missing. It was a heavy price.[199]

FIGURE 36: SORTING OUT THE KITS ON ARRIVAL AT SUEZ
FROM Anzac[200]

The battalion was leaving Gallipoli with an unparalleled reputation, 'and their gallantry and devotion to duty had added further laurels to its good name'. The men of the battalion were awarded thirty-five Indian Distinguished Service Medals for the display of unflinching bravery in the face of heavy odds. The details of these awards are included in the last chapter of the book. All these awards were promulgated in one Gazette, of 28 July 1916. 'The award of thirty-five decorations in one gazette is understood to be a unique record.'[201]

NOTES

1. R.R. James (2018), *Gallipoli* (1st edn.), Harper Collins, London.
2. B. Gudmundsson (2005), *The British Expeditionary Force 1914-15* (Battle Orders) (1st edn.), Osprey Publishing, Oxford.
3. Ibid.
4. Ian Hamilton, 30 April, p. 187. I. Hamilton (2022), *Ian Hamilton / Gallipoli Diary*, 2 vols., 1920, Library of Alexandria, Egypt.
5. Ibid.
6. Gallipoli, 1915, Maj. A.C. Fergusson, *Gallipoli Journal*, Winter 1997.

7. Ibid.
8. Ibid.
9. Australia War Memorial.
10. 14th Sikhs Album.
11. Ibid.
12. L.C.P.G. Bamford (1948), *The Sikh Regiment, The 14th King George's Own Ferozepore Sikhs*, Gale & Polden Limited, Aldershot.
13. 14th Sikhs Album.
14. Major B. & M. Gillott, eds. (2017), *Gallipoli Diaries: Headquarters 29th Indian Infantry Brigade 1915*, Great War Diaries Ltd., Sussex, UK.
15. Sikh seeks Sikh, Maj Dhanna Singh, *Gallipoli Journal*, Autumn 1978.
16. History of the Great War, *Military Operations Gallipoli* (1st edn., vol. 1, Inception of the Campaign), 1935, p. 317, William Heinemann Limited, London.
17. Bamford, *The Sikh Regiment, The 14th King George's Own Ferozepore Sikhs*, op. cit.
18. C.F. Aspinall-Oglander (1929), *Military Operations, Gallipoli* (History of the Great War Based on Official Documents, by Direction of the Historical Section, Committee of Imperial Defence), W. Heinemann Ltd., London.
19. Ibid.
20. Ibid.
21. Major B. & M. Gillott, eds. (2017), *Gallipoli Diaries: Headquarters 29th Indian Infantry Brigade 1915*. Great War Diaries Ltd., Sussex.
22. Bamford, *The Sikh Regiment*, op. cit.
23. Adapted from Casualty Database by the author.
24. Colonel A.C. Ferfusson in C.H.T.M.W.M. (1974), *Tales of the Mountain Gunners. An Anthology, Compiled by Those who Served with Them, and Edited by C.H.T. MacFetridge and J.P. Warren*, Blackwood, Alexander Books, ON, Canada.
25. Dispositions of the 29th Indian Infantry Brigade on 15 May 1915. From War Diary 69th Punjabis.
26. 14th Sikhs Album.
27. Bamford, *The Sikh Regiment*, op. cit.
28. Major B. & M. Gillott, *Gallipoli Diaries*, op. cit.
29. Bamford, *The Sikh Regiment*, op. cit.
30. Major B. & M. Gillott, *Gallipoli Diaries*, op. cit.
31. Ibid.
32. Lt-Col. R.F.E. Laidlaw, *Gallipoli Journal*, Autumn 1915, p. 23.

33. I. Hamilton (2022), Ian Hamilton / *Gallipoli Diary*, 2 vols., 1920, Library of Alexandria, Egypt, p. 193.
34. Disposition of 89th Punjabis on 6 May 1915, *War Diary 89th Punjabis* (Capt J.D. Crawford, Adjutant 89th Punjabis).
35. R.R. James (2018), *Gallipoli*, Harper Collins, London, UK.
36. 14th Sikhs Album.
37. Bamford, *The Sikh Regiment*, op. cit.
38. S. Chambers (2003), *Gully Ravine: Gallipoli*, Casemate Publishers, Hovertown, USA.
39. James, *Gallipoli*.
40. Major B. & M. Gillott, *Gallipoli Diaries: Headquarters 29th Indian Infantry Brigade 1915*.
41. Australian War Memorial.
42. Bamford, *The Sikh Regiment*, op. cit.
43. 14th Sikhs Album.
44. Chambers (2003), *Gully Ravine*, op. cit.
45. R. Savory (2016), *A Subaltern of the Sikhs*, Abhishek Publications, Chandigarh.
46. O. Creighton (1915), *With the 29th Division in Gallipoli*, Longmans Green, London.
47. Savory, *A Subaltern of the Sikhs*, op. cit.
48. 14th Sikhs Album.
49. Ibid.
50. Savory, *A Subaltern of the Sikhs*, op. cit.
51. Ibid.
52. *Gallipoli Journal*, Spring 1975, p. 27.
53. Ibid.
54. Bamford, *The Sikh Regiment*, op. cit.
55. Ibid.
56. 14th Sikhs Album.
57. Bamford, *The Sikh Regiment*, op. cit.
58. Ibid.
59. Ibid.
60. Ibid.
61. Ibid.
62. Savory, *A Subaltern of the Sikhs,* op. cit.
63. Chambers (2003), *Gully Ravine*, op. cit.
64. Bamford, *The Sikh Regiment*, op. cit.
65. Chambers, *Gully Ravine*, op. cit.
66. Major B. & M. Gillott, *Gallipoli Diaries*, op. cit.

67. Ibid.
68. 14th Sikhs Album.
69. Ibid.
70. Major B. & M. Gillott, *Gallipoli Diaries,* op. cit.
71. Ibid.
72. 14th Sikhs Album.
73. Major B. & M. Gillott, *Gallipoli Diaries,* op. cit.
74. Bamford, *The Sikh Regiment,* op. cit.
75. Major B. & M. Gillott, *Gallipoli Diaries,* op. cit.
76. Ibid.
77. Savory, *Gallipoli Journal,* op. cit., p. 11.
78. Adapted from Casualty Database by the Author.
79. Savory, *Gallipoli Journal,* op. cit., p. 11.
80. Major B. & M. Gillott, *Gallipoli Diaries,* op. cit.
81. Ibid.
82. Savory, *Gallipoli Journal,* op. cit., p. 12.
83. Ibid.
84. Australian War Memorial.
85. *Gallipoli Journal,* Spring 1974, p. 21.
86. I. Hamilton (2022), *Ian Hamilton / Gallipoli Diary,* 2 vols. 1920. Library of Alexandria, Egypt.
87. Ibid.
88. Savory, *A Subaltern of the Sikhs,* op. cit.
89. Ibid.
90. Ibid.
91. War Diary, Army Headquarters, India, *IEFG,* vol. I, 21 to 31 July 1915. National Archives of India.
92. Major B. & M. Gillott, *Gallipoli Diaries,* op. cit.
93. Hamilton to Kitchner, 2 July 1915.
94. R. Crawley (24 June 2015), *Climax at Gallipoli: The Failure of the Augustust Offensive* (vol. 42) *(Campaigns and Commanders Series),* University of Oklahoma Press.
95. Hamilton to French, letter, 17 June 1915, Hamilton Papers, LHCMA, Hamilton /2, in R. Crawley (24 June 2015). *Climax at Gallipoli: The Failure of the Augustust Offensive* (vol. 42) *(Campaigns and Commanders Series),* University of Oklahoma Press, Norman, USA.
96. James, *Gallipoli.*
97. Ibid.
98. Ibid.
99. Ibid.

100. Ibid.
101. Ibid.
102. Australian War Memorial (July 1915), *Australian Imperial Force Unit War Diaries*: 4th Infantry Brigade (23/4/1, Part 2).
103. Ibid.
104. Ibid.
105. Ibid
106. Ibid.
107. James, *Gallipoli.*
108. S. Bidwell and D. Graham (2004), *Fire-Power: British Army Weapons and Theories of War, 1904-1945*, Barnsley: Pen and Sword, pp. 61, 72.
109. P. Griffith & P.G. Griffith (1994), *Battle Tactics of the Western Front: The British Army's Art of Attack, 1916-18*, Yale University Press, Connechcut, USA.
110. D. Bidwell & D. Graham (2004), *Fire Power: The British Army Weapons & Theories of War 1904-1945*, Pen and Sword, South Yorkshire, 4.
111. Evidence of Brigadier-General G.N. Johnston to the Dardanelles Commission, 2 May 1917, TNA, CAB 19/33, 1396.
112. Ibid.
113. Australian War Memorial.
114. Australian War Memorial, *Narrative of Operations*, 6–9 August 1915, 1st Australian Div. Artillery WD, AWM 4, 13/10/12, pt. 1.
115. Ibid.
116. *Galipoli Journal*, Spring 1974.
117. Hamilton, *Gallipoli Diary.*
118. Ibid.
119. Aspinall-Oglander, *Military Operations,: Gallipoli.*
120. Quoted in Cat Wilson in 'The Dark Shadow of the Dardanelles: Churchill's World Crisis and his Portrayel of the Indian Army at Gallipoli', in *The Indian Army in the First World War* by Allan Jeffreys.
121. Hamilton, *Gallipoli Diary.*
122. Ibid.
123. Ibid.
124. Ibid.
125. Ibid.
126. Ibid.
127. Ibid.
128. *Gallipoli Journal*, Spring 1974.
129. Ibid.
130. James, *Gallipoli.*
131. *Gallipoli Journal*, Spring 1974.

132. 14th Sikhs Album.
133. *Gallipoli Journal,* Spring 1974.
134. Ibid.
135. Savory, *Gallipoli Journal,* Christmas, 1974, p. 11.
136. Ibid.
137. Aspinall-Oglander, *Military Operations, Gallipoli.*
138. Ibid.
139. Ibid.
140. Bamford, *The Sikh Regiment,* op. cit.
141. *Galipoli Journal,* Spring 1974.
142. Aspinall-Oglander, *Military Operations, Gallipoli.*
143. 14th Sikhs Album.
144. Ibid.
145. *Gallipoli Journal,* Spring 1974.
146. Ibid.
147. Ibid.
148. 14th Sikhs Album.
149. James, *Gallipoli.*
150. Ibid.
151. Ibid.
152. James, *Gallipoli.*
153. 14th Sikhs Album
154. C.E.S. Phipson (1970), 'With the Gurkhas on Sari Bair', *Gallipoli Journal,* 3(1970), pp. 15-19.
155. James, *Gallipoli.*
156. C.E.S. Phipson (1970), 'With the Gurkhas on Sari Bair', *Gallipoli Journal,* 3(1970), 15-19.
157. Ibid.
158. Ibid
159. Ibid.
160. James, *Gallipoli.*
161. *Gallipoli Journal,* Autumn 1975, p. 11.
162. Bamford, *The Sikh Regiment, The 14th King George's Own Ferozepore Sikhs.*
163. *Gallipoli Journal,* Autumn 1975, p. 13.
164. Ibid.
165. 14th Sikhs Album.
166. *Gallipoli Journal,* Autumn 1975, p. 12.
167. Bamford, *The Sikh Regiment, The 14th King George's Own Ferozepore Sikhs.*
168. *Gallipoli Journal,* Autumn 1975, p. 14.

169. Savory, *Gallipoli Journal*, Autumn 1915, p. 14.
170. 14th Sikhs Album.
171. Savory, *Gallipoli Journal*, Autumn 1915, p. 14.
172. Australia War Memorial.
173. War Diary, National Archives of India (1915), Army Headquarters, India, 14(1915).
174. Ibid.
175. Ibid.
176. Ibid.
177. Ibid.
178. Ibid.
179. On this Day, *Gallipoli Journal*, 26 November 1915.
180. Major B. & M. Gillott, *Gallipoli Diaries: Headquarters 29th Indian Infantry Brigade 1915.*
181. On this Day, *Gallipoli Journal*, 26 November 1915.
182. 14th Sikhs Album.
183. Savory, *Gallipoli Journal*, Autumn, 1975, p. 11.
184. 14th Sikhs Album.
185. Ibid.
186. 14th Sikhs Album.
187. Savory, *Gallipoli Journal*, Autumn, 1975, p. 11.
188. Australian War Memorial
189. Major B. & M. Gillott, *Gallipoli Diaries: Headquarters 29th Indian Infantry Brigade 1915.*
190. Savory, *Gallipoli Journal*, Autumn 1976, p. 12.
191. Alexander (2017). *On Two Fronts, Being the Adventures of an Indian Mule Corps in France and Gallipoli,* Van Haren Publishing, The Netherlands.
192. Gallipoli 1915, Maj A.C. Fergusson, *Gallipoli Journal*, Winter 1997.
193. Alexander (2017). *On Two Fronts*, op. cit.
194. Australian War Memorial.
195. Suvla Memories, W.T Cowley, RAOC, *Gallipoli Journal*, Spring 1978, p. 29.
196. Savory, *Gallipoli Journal*, Spring 1977, p. 9.
197. Ibid.
198. Ibid.
199. Savory, *Gallipoli Journal*, Spring, 1977, p. 11.
200. 14th Sikhs Album.
201. Bamford, *The Sikh Regiment, The 14th King George's Own Ferozepore Sikhs.*

CHAPTER 4

The Administration
Logistics of the Indian Troops at Gallipoli

The importance of administration of an invading force, particularly during amphibious operations, needs no introduction. A body of fighting troops cannot sustain itself after a particular time if the logistic follow up does not turn up or gets delayed. The existing research on the Gallipoli Campaign by the Western military historians have resultantly laid a significant emphasis on this crucial aspect. The inadequacies of the planning in the subsequent sustenance of the MEF on the peninsula have been adequately researched and the relevant lessons drawn, analysed and implemented for future operations.

For the IEF on the peninsula, the intricacies of provisioning of logistics were more intricate and complicated. Though the strength of the Indian troops on the peninsula was just a small sub set of the overall availability of the MEF, the dynamics of the provisioning for the Indian troops were relatively more elaborate. As discussed in length in the second chapter, a very high quantum of casualties suffered by the Indian battalions had resulted in the disintegration of the depot system back in India.

The dynamics of the Indian battalions of the time, required reinforcements from the same class composition as obtained in the intended recipient. With very limited sources available, with identical class composition, the reinforcements were scrounged from the Burma Military Police, other police battalions and the Infantry battalions of a similar class. Selection, collection and the subsequent dispatch of these reinforcements to Gallipoli, almost 3,000 miles away from India, was a logistical nightmare. The reinforcements did not only mean the troops, but also included replenishment of arms, ammunition and supplies. As a result, there were delays in replenishment. The replenishment of Artillery ammunition specifically has come under a lot of criticism from military historians. The commander of MEF, Ian Hamilton himself has been very critical about the manner in which logistics was handled on the peninsula:

Indian troops, being part of the larger picture were not unaffected by the shortage of the critical commodity (ammunition). The whole story of the Artillery at Helles may be summed up in the following sentences: insufficiency of guns of every nature; insufficiency of ammunition of every nature, especially of HE; insufficient provision made by the Home Authorities for spare guns, spare carriages, spare parts, adequate repairing workshops, or for a regular daily, weekly or monthly supply of ammunition; guns provided often of an obsolete pattern and so badly worn by previous use as to be most inaccurate; total failure to produce the trench mortars and bombs to which the closeness of the opposing lines at Helles would have lent themselves well – in short, total lack of organisation at home to provide even the most rudimentary and indispensable Artillery requisites for daily consumption; not to speak of downright carelessness which resulted in wrong shells being sent without fuse keys and new types of howitzer shells without range tables. These serious faults provoked their own penalties in the shape of the heavy losses suffered by our Infantry and Artillery, which might have been to a great measure averted if sufficient forethought and attention had been devoted to the 'side show' at the Dardanelles.[1]

A survey and the subsequent review of literature on the subject, emphasises the point that, though the entire range of weapons and equipment in possession of the allied troops on Gallipoli, has been given due emphasis and has been discussed in great detail by the Western historians, side by side, there has been a relative lack of research and existing literature on the holding of arms, ammunition and equipment with the Indian troops and its subsequent replenishment.

With no previous precedence of time-tested system of reporting of casualties, on active service, the ad-hoc system of reporting of casualties, devised for the campaign, broke down under the information overload or the lack of it. The challenges were overbearing, but by the end of the campaign in December 1915, a reasonably working system had been put in place to report the numbers and details of the casualties to India. Aligned with this aspect, was the crucial role played by the Indian Field Ambulances during the campaign. In the subsequent sections, an attempt has been made to analyse the gradual developments in the system of reporting of Indian casualties on the peninsula and the crucial role played by the Indian Field Ambulances while on Gallipoli.

Supply and Mule Corps was an inalienable aspect of the participation of the Indian troops in the campaign. The rations for the average strength of 3,000 plus Indian troops and forage for the animals of eight Mule Corps, 22 detachments of Mule Corps and three Imperial Services Transport Corps, was a mammoth task involving coordination and cooperation of all agencies. The peculiar food habits of Indian troops, coupled with underlying caste equations made the system more complex. Availability and provisioning of water to the forward-most trench occupied by any MEF or IEF troop on the peninsula was another challenge, which the Indian Mule Corps, performed very professionally. Two sections of the present chapter are dedicated to these important but forgotten details of provisioning for the Indian troops.

Other associated aspects of logistics on the peninsula include the functioning of the Indian Field Post Offices, the practice of religion by the Indian troops while stationed on the peninsula along with the system of field allowances developed for the Indian troops on the peninsula, have also been attempted to be addressed in the chapter. In order to ease off the burden of logistics, deployment of a Coolie and Labour Corps from India was also mulled during the later stages of the campaign. Though the dispatch of this Corps from India was implemented during the period of deployment of the 29th Indian Infantry Brigade on the peninsula, ultimate application of this Corps on the peninsula did not actualize and the Indian Coolie and Labour Corps was not able to go through this unique experience.

Weapons and Ammunition

During the first decade of the nineteenth century, the Indian Army was supplied with a short, magazine-loaded Lee-Enfield (Mark I). The rifle with a length of 44.5 inches was relatively shorter in length and was equipped with a magazine with a capacity of five-rounds. The rifle had apparent advantages over the previous rifles and was able to fire at a faster rate of fire. Indian troops on Gallipoli had been equipped with the Lee Enfield as the standard personal weapon. The rifle was famous for its short magazine and was ranked much above its contemporaries existing at that time.

With each weapon having been authorised 500 rounds, 300 rounds were carried with the soldier / battalion, whereas balance 200 rounds were classified as Ordnance reserves. An analysis of the War Diaries of the battalions of the 29th Indian Infantry Brigade, reveal that the troops for all the major Gallipoli operations to include the Third Battle of Krithia and the August Offensive had been directed to carry 200 rounds of ammunition on person. When the Indian troops landed on Gallipoli on 1 May 1915, each soldier was supposed to carry 200 rounds of ammunition of the rifle on his person.

Very large and frequent turnover of casualties of the Indian battalions had given rise to a peculiar problem for the military planners in India. The accelerated pace of recruitment and dispatch of the reinforcements for the battalions of the Indian Infantry Brigade was not able to match up with the production and supply of personal weapons to equip these fresh drafts. It was practically impossible to equip the reinforcements being dispatched from India with the required arms, ammunition and equipment prior to them boarding the respective transports at the nominated Ports of Embarkation.

In order to ease out the crucial deficiency of personal weapons, a decision was taken in July 1915, which required all fresh drafts proceeding to reinforce Indian Infantry battalions with IEF to not proceed with rifles, bayonets and the bandolier equipment. Therefore, all drafts which were dispatched to IEF in August 1915 and later were not provided with arms and ammunition. The arms and ammunition for these soldiers was provided by Ordnance channels prior to the deployment at Dardanelles, which had been collected from the Indian casualties since evacuated from the peninsula.

Further amplifying the directions, in a separate communication related to the dispatch of reinforcements for the battalions of the 29th Indian Infantry Brigade, the Director General of Ordnance in India had informed GOC Egypt that 570 Indian Infantry drafts proceeding to Dardanelles from India in August 1915, will not take rifles, bayonets or bandolier equipment. GOC Egypt was further requested that arrangements be made for equipping these reinforcements in Egypt itself. The above directions were the result of a similar direction by the AGs Branch to the General Officers of the 2nd, 8th and Burma Divisions in July 1915 that the drafts proceeding as reinforcements from India to all these forces will move without arms, ammunition and equipment and will be supplied with these on arrival. The shortage of arms and ammunition was such that even for the reinforcements proceeding to Dardanelles in the month of September 1915, the GOC Egypt was informed that the details of arms and ammunition were being worked out and will be intimated in due course of time.[2]

FIGURE 37 : BRITISH OFFICERS OF THE 14TH SIKHS WITH A SIKH TROOP IN THE TRENCH ALONG WITH PERSONAL WEAPON[3]

The Gurkha troops of the Indian Brigade carried Khukris as one of the additional weapons on person. Khukri is a multipurpose weapon and tool, which besides being used as a close quarter weapon also can be used for shaping wood, clearing foliage or used in the cook house. MK-1 is believed to be the first mass produced Khukri for use by the Gurkha troops:

The blade is of tempered steel, slightly curved and exceedingly sharp. The handle is usually of wood or buffalo horn. A nick in the blade close to the handle serves the purpose of preventing blood from reaching the handle and is also symbolic of the Hindu Trinity of Bramha, Vishnu and Shiv. The blade is enclosed in a scabbard of wood and leather and the whole weapon is some sixteen to eighteen inches long.[4]

FIGURE 38: GURKHA TROOPS OF THE INDIAN BRIGADE (MOST LIKELY 1/6 GURKHAS) IN A TRENCH CARRYING KHUKRIS[5]

As discussed in Chapter 2, the institutionalisation of the Machine Gun Section in the Indian infantry battalions just prior to the mobilisation for the Great War, was a much-needed reform. Both the Machine Gun Sections of the Indian battalions were equipped with Vickers Machine Gun. The machine gun being supplied to the Indian battalions was of superior standards as far as other competitors were concerned:

The Vickers gun was considerably lighter than both the older Maxim guns and the newer French machine guns. The German Maxim (Model 1908) tipped the scales at 64 kg (141 lb) and the standard French machine gun (the St Etienne, Model 1907) weighed 51 kg (112 lb). The Vickers gun weighed only 38 kg (83 lb). Thanks to its water jacket, the Vickers could maintain a high rate of fire, long after the air-cooled St Etienne had overheated.[6]

These sections played a pivotal role in providing crucial support to the advancing columns of the Indian Infantry during various operations. All four Infantry battalions of the Indian Infantry Brigade, which landed on the peninsula on 1 May 1915, had their machine gun sections with them. The administrative orders for the landings had mandated carriage of 3,000 rounds per machine gun. These machine guns proved very valuable in breaking the determined enemy assaults and for harassing fire on the enemy positions.

FIGURE 39: A SIKH REGIMENTAL MACHINE GUN
POST ON THE PENINSULA [7]

While at Imbros, as replacements for the innovative *Jam Tin* bombs, a new type of bomb was supplied to the Indian battalions. The troops, at a cost of several casualties, during training in July 1915, mastered the use of these bombs. Some improvisations were carried out by the troops of the Indian battalions to ensure the increased reach of these bombs into the Turkish trenches. The constraints of the trench warfare notwithstanding, the contraption did ensure keeping the Turks at bay during the campaign. The bomb catapult prepared by the Sikh troops of the 14th Sikhs was another improvisation which was very effective in ensuring the defence of the Indian trenches from the Turkish counter attacks.

Like the Jam Tin bombs and bomb catapults, trench mortar was another weapon which was fully exploited by the Indian troops on Gallipoli. The exploitation of the Japanese Trench Mortar in the defensive operations had still not been institutionalized when the

FIGURE 40: IMPROVISATION OF A BOMB CATAPULT BY
THE 14TH SIKHS IN GALLIPOLI[8]

curtains came down on the Gallipoli campaign, but the weapon, named because of its origin in Osaka was used almost to perfection by the troops of the Indian battalions. The adaptiveness of the Sikhs in learning the new weapon system had been particularly amazing.

The authorised establishment of each Indian Brigade included an

FIGURE 41: A SIKH TROOP WITH A JAPANESE TRENCH
MORTAR AT GALLIPOLI[9]

Ordnance Officer attached along with the support staff to cater for the ordnance requirements of the formation. The 29th Indian Infantry Brigade, while on Gallipoli was also posted with an Ordnance detachment. The movement of ammunition and stores from the beaches to the forward trench lines was entirely carried out by the Indian Mule Corps under the overall supervision of the Ordnance Officer. The extraordinary role played by the Indian Mule drivers along with their mules and carts came under appreciation many a times from the British officers and men who had an opportunity to utilise the services of the Indian Mule Cart Train. One officer, Captain W.T Cowley of Royal Army Ordnance Corps, attached with the 32nd Brigade wrote about the precarious conditions of terrain and shelling at the peninsula, under which the drivers and mules of the Indian Mule Cart Train performed their duties.

Each afternoon the Staff Captain would hand me a list of stores to be collected from the Ordnance depot on the Beach and which were handed over to the Units next morning. So off we went on the long trek, and if ammunition was to be collected, I had to contact the Sgt-Major of the Battalion on duty for an armed escort. As you can imagine my requests were not received with much enthusiasm.[10]

From the beach, after the necessary clearances the Indian mule carts and the pack animals were allotted for the subsequent transfer of the stores from the beach to the forward locations of the battalions. 'On arrival at the beach, I requisitioned the necessary Indian Mule Gharries and pack mules from the compound and loaded up for the journey 'home'. We had plenty of exciting trips and once we had a Garry load of ground sheets disappear over the cliff edge to the sea, including mules and driver.[11]

The initial operations on the peninsula immediately after the landings had resulted in a very fast pace of expenditure of ammunition. The initial demand of the ammunition was so high that the first accurate stock of usage of ammunition and the balance state of the allied forces was possible to be compiled only by 9 May 1915, 15 days after the first landings. The fluid operational situation coupled with the very high rate of casualties had not allowed the concerned staff to accurately predict the requirement of ammunition:

AUSTRALIAN WAR MEMORIAL   C01461

FIGURE 42: INDIAN MULE CORPS TRANSPORTING AMMUNITION
TO THE FORWARD LOCATIONS[12]

Now, today (the 9th), I have at last been able to send the Ordnance a statement
(made under extreme difficulty) of our ammunition expenditure up to the
5th May. We were then nine million small arms still to the good having spent
eleven million. We had shot away 23,000 shrapnel, 18 pr., and had 48,000
in hand. We had fired off 5,000 of that (most vital), 4.5 howitzer and had
1,800 remaining.[13]

Continuation of operations on all fronts on the peninsula had
ensured that the ammunition expenditure remains exceptionally high
during the initial days. There was likely to be a severe shortage of
ammunition, if the expenditure was not controlled. The extended
supply lines for the ammunition forced an inherent delay which was
imperative to be figured into the entire scheme of things. Hamilton
was aware of the sensitivity of the situation. The lines of communication
on the Western Front and in the peninsula were markedly different
and no comparison between the two widely dispersed theatres was
practical. Ian Hamilton in his dispatch to the War Office reiterated
this point,

With reference to your No. 4432 of 5th instant, please turn to my letter to you of 30th March, wherein I have laid stress on the essential difference in the matter of ammunition supply between the Dardanelles and France. In France, where the factories are within 24 hours distance from the firing line, it may be feasible to consider and reconsider situations, including ammunition supply.[14]

The requirement of ammunition in the ongoing operations at Dardanelles was higher for obvious reasons. Hamilton also justified the increased pace of expenditure of ammunition and requested the War Office to cater for the increased requirement:

Faced by heavy Artillery, machine gun and rifle fire our troops, made a fine effort. Our troops have done all that flesh and blood can do against semi-permanent works, and they are not able to carry them. More and more munitions will be needed to do so. I fear this is a very unpalatable conclusion.[15]

The Indian Mountain Artillery Batteries had continued to support the Infantry operations since the time of the landings. Due to the initial confusion, the transportation of the ammunition to the respective gun positions was also taking time.

On arriving at Cape Helles during the first week in May, I found that heavy fighting had occurred without ceasing from the time of the disembarkation. The greatest difficulty was experienced in obtaining figures of expenditure from the units, so constant had been the fighting, which still continued, and so great the casualties, and consequent confusion in reckoning expenditure. Yet after some delay, sufficient information was obtained to enable me to demonstrate with certainty that, if such severe fighting continued, the Force would soon be in danger of losing their Artillery support.[16]

Both the Indian Mountain Batteries were equipped with the vintage 10-pounder guns. The efficiency of the guns was under serious question mark but the efficiency, professionalism and detailed knowledge of the Indian gunners was never questioned:

When I assumed command of the Artillery at Helles, there were two Batteries of mountain guns (10-prs) in action, but they were of a prehistoric pattern. In 1889 the Khedive of Egypt possessed in his Army, in which I was then serving, mountain guns which were more up to date in every respect. So inaccurate were these 10-prs that they had to be placed close behind the front

FIGURE 43: INDIAN MOUNTAIN BATTERIES IN ACTION[17]

trenches lest they should hit our own Infantry, the result being a very heavy casualty list in officers and men. These obsolete old guns wore out so quickly that the two Batteries melted into one Battery, and when they finally left Helles for Anzac at the end of July, I believe only 3 guns and their detachments were left in being.[18]

The peculiar terrain obtained in Gallipoli was not suitable for mountain guns. The features of the gun did not facilitate identification of a suitable Gun Position on the peninsula. 'Gallipoli was a Howitzer country, but England in those days possessed no Mountain Howitzer though the specifications for them had been out for years.' The professionalism and the inherent ingenuity of the Indian Mountain gunners had converted the existing 10 pr Mountain guns to Howitzers:

After a bit we made our own Howitzer, first by cutting down full charges for the gun, and later by using the Star Shell charges. Of course, we had no Range Tables for this and it was all guess work, and like so many makeshifts at the commencement of the War a disgrace to the nation to send men to do jobs improperly equipped. Another disgrace was that our shrapnel shell broke up so badly that we had to boil them before using.[19]

The problems being faced by the Indian gunners did not relate only to the shells, but was also related to the vintage guns. The repair chain for the guns was quite long and arduous. The fast rate of firing from the vintage guns used to erode the vents of the gun. With the nearest repair facility being available only at Mudros, the turnaround time for the repair did not keep pace with the requirement. The Indian gunners found an innovative solution to this problem. All the spare breach blocks were collected and used to be sent to the section of the Battery, which was witnessing the action on that particular day. The frequent change of breach blocks in between the intense Artillery duel deeply impacted the morale of the Indian gunners and was very frustrating. It was amidst one such intense action day that 'fire-eating', Lance Naik Prem Singh had rushed to the make shift Officer's Mess and had literally thrown the breach block on the table. The NCO was in such anguish and pain due to not being able to match the rapidity and ferocity of the Turkish Artillery with the vintage guns of the Indian Battery. Though the abuse was in chaste Punjabi, the CO of the Battery produced a translated version of the same in his memoirs, 'what the devil is the use of supplying things like this, the other gun is getting off many more rounds than us because our breech blocks are bad'.

The Australian Artillery on the peninsula was also in awe of the ingenuity of the Indian Mountain gunners. Lieutenant Colonel Charles Rosenthal, Commander of the 3rd Australian Field Artillery Brigade, 1st Australian Division, while commenting on the professionalism of the Indian gunners had commented, 'In the meantime, the Indian Mountain Battery attached to 1st Australian Division, which had landed early in the day, was in action, doing splendid work though suffering severe casualties.'[20] The ammunition supply to the deployed guns at the respective gun positions was a very difficult task, which the Indian drivers and gunners, under the intense Artillery and small arms fire by the enemy performed excellently. 'The delivery of the ammunition was very difficult. It had to be delivered by hand to the guns over a bullet swept area, the distance from the beach to the guns being about half a mile, while in this distance the hills rose 400 feet.'[21]

The gunners of the Indian Mountain Batteries had carried out a splendid work in making their gun positions safe from enemy Artillery,

FIGURE 44: FOUR UNIDENTIFIED GUNNERS OF THE INDIAN
MOUNTAIN BATTERIES AT GALLIPOLI[22]

while simultaneously engaging the Turkish defences. 'Our Batteries
were of necessity in many cases under direct observation of the enemy,
and only the splendid work of the detachments in building earthworks
for their protection made it possible to carry on.'[23] The issue of the
frequent jamming of the tubes was resolved by placing a *mistri*
(repairman) in battle ready condition available with all his tools in
the vicinity of the Gun position. With no support in terms of repair
of the damaged guns, the ingenuity of the Indian gunners had also
resulted in the establishment of a makeshift workshop, where minor
repairs of the mountain guns were carried out. 'Under the protection
of the banks of a small ravine near the beach, our artificers established
a workshop, and the extraordinary ingenuity and skill displayed in
the repairing and replacing of damaged guns earned for the artificers
our most grateful appreciation and thanks.'[24]

The signalers of the Indian Mountain Batteries were not to be left
behind in the entire scheme of things. A Signaler has an immense role
in the coordination of Artillery fire. The quantum of casualties suffered
by the troops of Artillery Batteries had also adversely affected the
availability of signalers in the Batteries:

Owing to the losses among signalers, and the Battery being split up in three
bits, each with a distant O.P., we were very soon reduced to one signaler per

FIGURE 45 : INDIAN GUNNERS WITH THEIR GUN[25]

phone who was on duty day and night, always sleeping with his instrument in his ear. The headquarter phone was run by Pyara Singh, a mess orderly, in addition to his other duties.[26]

Narain Singh, a lineman in the 21st (Kohat) Battery was another dare devil, who without caring for his personal safety was always out repairing the lines damaged by the enemy shelling. 'We had one lineman only, who managed to keep alive during the whole war in some wonderful way. He was always out repairing lines in dangerous places, and two or three times brought back chits from Australian officers to say they had seen him repairing lines under heavy fire.' The individual was later on awarded the IDSM for his conspicuous bravery and display of professionalism of highest order.

The wonderful display of extreme professionalism by the Indian gunners was marred with an allegation about own troops being hit by their own artillery fire. These allegations were substantiated by findings of the bodies of 10-pounder shells of the Indian Mountain Artillery, 'in places where they could not possibly have put them'. As it was technically not possible to shell these areas by the Indian Mountain sections, these allegations could not be verified. One day, however, one of the Section Commanders of the 21st Mountain Battery, during the period of shelling by the Turks was directed, by an Australian, towards the body of a 10 pr shell which had just burst, overshooting the target of the trench:

Campbell went and looked at it and found a shell with marks to show that it had been made at Cossipore and filled at Rawul Pindi, and the scoop of the shell showed that it had come from right outside our line. He phoned down to me and I went and satisfied myself that it could not possibly be ours. I then went and asked Corps to wire and ask if Helles had lost any Mountain guns. The answer came back 'No' so the matter remained a mystery, but the Australians were still suspicious that we were doing it.[27]

The issue was creating a rift between the Indian Mountain Batteries and the ANZAC, whose operations the guns of these Batteries were supporting. The mystery of guns of Indian Mountain Batteries firing at own troops was however, resolved much later. It has been claimed that before the commencement of the hostilities of the Great War, the New Zealand Artillery had ordered a Battery of Mountain guns from England. 'England sent our old 10 pdrs and New Zealand refused to accept delivery. After a lot of correspondence England told to sell them and credit them with the proceeds. New Zealand sold them to Turkey and here they were being used against us'.[28]

UNIFORM AND CLOTHING

The wear and tear of travel from the Canal defences to Gallipoli and the intense action on the peninsula immediately on arrival had resulted in the severe stress to the clothing of the Indian troops. The conditions of fighting at Gallipoli in general and particularly in the initial days of war were demanding and the corresponding toll on the soldiers and equipment was massive. Corroborating the state of clothing, an entry in the War Diary of the 69th Punjabis, dated 6 May 1915, mentions about the poor quality of trousers material which had been supplied to the Indian troops. 'The cloth trousers supplied to Indian troops were of bad material and quickly wore out.'[29]

A review of the personnel equipment, specifically the web equipment was carried out by the British Army in the immediate aftermath of the Boer War. As the Indian Army was technically part of the British Army, the changes introduced in the webbing equipment of the British Army were percolated to the troops of the Indian Army as well. Prior to 1908, when changes were introduced in the webbing equipment, the standard issue of the British Army was composed of leather Slade-Wallace equipment. The equipment had been introduced in service in 1888. The leather web equipment was proving unsuitable for longer use as the conditions of modern warfare demanded. The leather webbing definitely wouldn't have survived the trench warfare of the First World War. In addition, with the introduction of clip-based cartridges as compared to individual rounds of the earlier era, the webbing equipment certainly required up-gradation.

The Royal Commission on the war in South Africa set up in 1903, recommended changes in the standard issue web equipment of the British army. In 1906, a British army officer, Major Burrows of the Royal Irish Fusiliers, in collaboration with a US based company designed a new pattern webbing to be issued as a standard issue to the British soldiers. The design of the new equipment after a series of trials was finally adopted for pan British army roll out in December 1907. On the eve of the Great War, the Indian Army was equipped with the webbing equipment introduced in 1908. The entire equipment resembled wearing a jacket when fully assembled. Two ammunition pouches were in front for the ease of taking out ammunition clips. These pouches were held together with the help of two straps which crossed each other diagonally in the back. In front, these pouches were attached with a belt. The backpack was at the back, as the name suggested, and was attached with two diagonal straps on the back. With so many cross connections and attachments, the buckles and the ends of straps had brass components. One full complement of a single webbing equipment comprised a belt with a width of three inches, two braces of two inches width each, two pouch sets, with capacity of each pouch set to hold 75 rounds of rifle ammunition, one carrier to attach the bayonet scabbard with the belt, a water bottle, a backpack, a haversack and an entrenching tool.

The type of order, marching or battle, guided the wearing sequence of haversack and backpack. The marching order required wearing of both haversack and backpack, whereas the battle order required wearing of only backpack with the essentials. The Royal Commission, while studying the lessons of Boer War, had also commented upon

the weight carried by each Infantry soldier. With the introduction of
the new web equipment, each Infantry soldier of the Indian Army
was carrying 25.9 kilograms in full marching order and 22.3 kilograms
in battle order. This, however, did not include the personal weapon,
rations, additional ammunition, which invariably increased the likely
load to be carried by the soldier much more than the laid down limits.
But the loads carried by the troops of the 29th Indian Infantry brigade
during the operations at Gallipoli, particularly during the August
offensive, were much greater than the laid down scales.

With no overhead protection available on the peninsula, digging
was imperative for the Indian troops. The frequent change in the
deployment of the Indian units and sub units had ensured that the
process of digging never stopped. The improvement of defences to
include catering for additional space for the reinforcements, weapon
emplacements made the possession of entrenching tool compulsory
for the Indian troops and was a most prized possession of a soldier,
sometimes more important than a personal weapon itself. The tool
came with a combination of separate carriers for the head and heave.
The entrenching tool was a lifesaver amidst the intensive requirements
of tunneling and digging. 'The defensive dugout yielded by the
entrenching tool was a fundamental refuge for soldiers and was often
their only form of shelter and protection.' The authorisation of these
tools was, however very limited for the Indian troops on Gallipoli.
An entry in the War Diary of the 69th Punjabis, discusses about the
authorisation of entrenching tool, 'Experience in the Gallipoli
peninsula proved that the number of large entrenching tools as well
as the Sirhind Entrenching tool supplied to the battalion was too
small.'[30]

The Sirhind pattern of entrenching tool was the man portable
equipment issued to the Indian troops. The peculiar name of the
entrenching tool owes its origin to the name of a place in Punjab
where the tool was developed. When the 1908 pattern of equipment
was being adopted by the army, the entrenching tool was also adopted
as a universal tool for entrenching across the British Army. This two-
piece combination was an indispensable equipment for the type of
trench warfare witnessed on Gallipoli.

The tool consisted of two parts, the head and the helve, with the head being made up of cast iron. The design of the head was versatile, with one end meant for broad shoveling, while the other end worked like a miniaturised pick. The helve was made of wood, wherein one end was fitted with cast iron ferrule where the head was supposed to fit in. Besides being used for digging the fortifications and latrines, the entrenching tool was also modified to be used as a close combat weapon. The limited availability of space in a trench resulted in extremely close combat with the enemy. These closed spaces obviated the use of rifles and bayonets as weapons of close combat. These entrenching tools therefore became the favourite weapons of Indian troops inside the trenches for close quarter battles. This improvised usage required the edges of these tools to be kept sharpened at all times, which the Indians ensured. The intensive amount of digging carried out by the Indian troops in the hard and rocky terrain had been made possible only due to the availability of the Sirhind entrenching tool.

With no clarity on the likely termination of the campaign, the approaching winter season was a cause of concern for the Indian troops. With rains and no overhead shelters available in the gun positions, the gunners of the Indian Mountain Batteries were wet most of the time. The approaching winters were expected to make survival even more difficult. Though there were ongoing deliberations regarding the withdrawal of MEF from the peninsula, the troops on ground were oblivious to these machinations. The shortage of warm clothings was a perpetual for the Indians. In order to overcome the problem of shortage of warm clothing, the 21st Mountain Battery had, 'started collecting Turkish clothing left in unfrequented and dangerous gullies'.[31] In order to avoid and friendly casualties due to mistaken identities, specific orders were passed that these warm coats and blankets were not to be used outside of the designated areas of the Battery. This acquired apparel came in very handy and ensured that every soldier had some dry clothes available to change into after a 'wet outing'. The chief architect of the entire enterprise was Gunner Phuman Singh of the Battery, 'a real bad hat but priceless at that sort of thing and was the chief acquirer of stolen goods and chattels'.[32]

The innovativeness of Phuman Singh did not end here and he was further instrumental in improvising a tunnel drying room in the trenches. As the troops came from gun positions or other allocated tasks in wet clothes and used to sleep in the same, the incidences of illness were increasing in the Battery. The tunnel drying room innovated by Phuman Singh was being used as a check point where the Havildar Major of the Battery was made responsible to check the dryness of clothes worn by the troops, before proceeding for rest.

A contraption of two discarded drums of paint converted into stoves was prepared. The contraption was such that fumes of the stoves were made to pass outside the tunnels and kept the tunnel warm throughout the night. The warmth of the stoves not only made the troops comfortable in the night, but also helped to dry the wet clothings. The comfort, however, came with the associated problems and invited unwanted guests in the trenches, 'the tunnel funk pits for shelling, tunnels for keeping rations and firewood dry etc. made the place a regular rabbit warren'.

Though the weather had turned cold suddenly in November 1915, but prior to that Indian troops on the peninsula had innovated means to take bath in the tunnels. In the Headquarters of the 7 Indian Mountain Artillery Brigade, a tunnel bathing room had been engineered in September 1915. The Brigade Havildar Major Amar Singh was responsible for the assembled bathing room. The roster for taking bath was such created by Havildar Major Amar Singh, that it was ensured that turn of every soldier will come up at least once in a week:

It was a work of art, beautifully sloped towards the longitudinal axis and towards the door. A thick sacking purdah under the door with a Soyer stove inside for hot water, and recesses for clothes when water was being chucked about made it very popular. Days were allotted so that every man could have one hot bath a week. I happened to pass this in the middle of the cold snap when it was really too cold for words and saw a crowd waiting their turns to go in. I asked if they were doing it on their own or by order, and they said on their own, they would not lose their weekly bath for anything.[33]

Though the Indian Labour Corps was never employed at Gallipoli, but the genesis for the creation and subsequent employment of the

Corps, in the other theatres of the Great War, can be attributed to the actions of IEF 'G'. The terms of conditions of service of the Corps,[34] mandated that Indian officers of the Corps will be provided with free field service clothing and other ranks will be provided with the winter scale of clothing along with free boots. Each individual of the Corps was to be supplied with one free identification disc. In fact, most of the casualties of the Indian battalions were identified with the help of identification discs found on the mortal remains. The Labour Corps being dispatched in the latter part of the campaign were being provided with maximum possible amenities. All Indian ranks except the Indian officers were to get free rations from the date of enrolment. For cooking purposes, 40 sets of aluminum cooking pots were also authorised to each Corps.

RATIONS AND WATER

Lieutenant General George MacMunn in his epic work on the Colonial Indian Army correctly emphasised upon the importance of administration. The food habits of the Indian soldiers being very peculiar, differing from company to company within a battalion, in class company regiments and from battalion to battalion in class regiments, had to be factored in, while making the administration plans. Up to a large extent, the very peculiar food habits of Indian soldiers had been ensured when the battalions were in the active service within the country. As earlier described, the dearth of sources and reference material on the Indian troops at Gallipoli has deterred many Indian military historians to further research the subject. But the importance of supply of essentials to the army, whether marching or deployed cannot be understated. This factor assumes more importance, if the army is deployed in a stalemate-like situation, as was obtained in Gallipoli.

Since an army crawls on its belly, and masses of battalions and regiments and Batteries do not make an army, or even divisions of it, administrative troops are an essential component. A quarter column of bakers' carts does not convey the pomp of war. . . . Yet these are the services that make men with muskets into an army, and should not be forgotten in the tally for their more outwardly effective comrades.[35]

There has been extensive research on the aspects of supply and availability of rations along the Western Front, where also the Indian troops were at the forefront. The cooking habits of Indians troops whether at Gallipoli or Western Front, or for that matter anywhere at the world, wherever they fought remained generally the same. The exclusivity and almost religious like fervor linked with the activity of cooking of food even at the forward-most trench lines remained the specifiable trait of Indian food habits. Even during the visit of German Senator Beveridge's visit to a Prisoner of War (PoW) camp at Jossen, which housed almost 12,000 PoWs, primarily Russian and French with a sprinkling of British and Indians, it has been mentioned that conversation with the Indian PoWs provided a definite peep into the psyche of the Indian martial races. 'In the barracks occupied by the prisoners from India there is an unusual feature: every Hindu cook and, in every way, prepares his own food, for he will not eat anything touched by Christian hands. Many of them were observed at this private and religious culinary occupation.'[36] A little bit of history of the method of procurement and supply of rations to the Indian troops in active field has been attempted to put the perspective in context.

The system of Commissariat, a typical western administrative concept, was introduced by the British to take care of the administrative requirements of the Indian troops, during the latter part of the nineteenth century. The Commissariat system was instrumental in regulating the availability and sale of provisions from the nominated markets. These markets, later on developed into so called 'Regimental Bazaars'. The poor quality of merchandise along with reports of fleecing of soldiers by these bazaars was increasingly being found to be difficult to curtail. With poor salary structure, a soldier was not able to buy vegetables from the market in peace time and during active service, the nominated vendor was not able to supply them, which in turn gave birth to the concept of 'Regimental Gardens'. The composition and charter of the Indian Army's Service Corps was peculiar as it used to provision for both the British and Indian troops in India:

The Indian Army's Service Corps was composed of two branches: Supply and Transport. The Supply Branch was responsible for purchase and distribution of rations for the British soldiers at all times and at all localities, grain and fodder for the regular Indian cavalry regiments and all the British cavalry regiments. Under special circumstances did this branch undertake to supply food to the Sepoys. In addition, the Supply Branch had the responsibility to provide fuel to the Indian soldiers for cooking, and utensils to both the Indian and British troops.[37]

Not only in the Indian Army, the issue of rations, whether paid by the soldier or free, was also a cause of concern for the Indian troops serving in the Burma Military Police. These soldiers later on proved their mettle on Gallipoli also, as reinforcements for the 14th Sikhs and Gurkha battalions. The prevailing conditions of disease and the provisioning of dry rations for the troops located at remote locations in the countryside of Burma was having an adverse effect on the morale of the troops particularly belonging to Punjab. Feeding of the military police in the hills was proving to be a considerable challenge for the authorities. The remoteness of the locations allowed only monthly delivery of the rations for the men. The vegetables, considered as an essential part of the rations for these troops, were generally missing from the delivered rations. The ration therefore was invariably a scarcity of rations for the Indian troops of the military police. The condition of Sikh troops with respect to the supply of rations at the far-flung places in the country, was therefore, not conducive to the general military morale. The Sikh troops had also reported about the poor state of rations being supplied in the Burma Military Police.

Men of the battalion, with due respect, have reported that they are losers by serving in the Chin Hills under present arrangements, and when one considers the nature of the Sikhs(of what the battalion is very largely composed) one recognizes that he must either be allowed to go, or his position improved, or he will not serve at a loss in the Chin Hills when there are numerous regiments in Burma which would gladly welcome him, especially as the men are of very fine physique and appearance and have the right at the termination of three years' service to cut their names and re-enlist in any other police battalion in Burma.[38]

With all the problems associated with the supply of essential commodities to the soldiers on active service, the clamor for free supply of rations to the soldiers was increasing. The military hierarchy of the time was also aligned with the idea that a soldier should not be worried about provisioning of his supplies and he should singularly focus on the task at hand. The Adjutant General of the Indian Army, while favoring the issue of free rations to the troops had also recommended that:

the Native Army of the present day in a great measure consists of men of northern races of greater physique than the Sepoy of the old army previous to 1857; that animal food whenever procurable, forms a portion of their diet, and that the men eagerly secure such diet; that the climate of the north stimulated the appetites and requires men exposed to it to be better fed than in more tropical climes, and that to maintain soldiers in work on a campaign demands a ration rather fuller than that found sufficient for warmer regions.[39]

As a result of these directions and due to the problems of supply of rations in the field along with the need to avoid hardships to the soldiers in the field, the facility of free rations as per laid down scales was granted to the Indian troops on active service. The scales of ration for the Indian troops had also developed over a period of time, before getting stabilised by the time the Indian troops had reached Gallipoli. The British operations on the Northwest Frontier in 1890 can be credited with laying down comprehensive scales of ration for the Indian troops and followers on active service. During the campaign, though *dal* (pulses) was authorised to troops, but the process of cooking *dal* used to be afflicted with problems due to poor quality of water and the dearth of firewood.

The force commander of the operations in North-West Frontier had recommended certain scales of rations for the Indian troops and followers. This was probably the first time when the Force Commander had recommended the extension of authorisation of *masalas* (condiments) to the followers. The reason for authorisation of the commodity to the followers was justified by the Force Commander with the medical necessity. 'At present the follower gets no *masala* and his food is consequently unpalatable and gives him dyspepsia.'[40] It has been claimed that the troops were mandated to compulsorily eat *amchur* (mango powder), as a precaution against the widespread menace of scurvy.

As a result of this authorisation in the First World War, the authorisation for the Indian soldiers also included quarter of a pound of meat for the non-vegetarians, whereas for the vegetarians, 3 ounces

TABLE 29 : SCALES OF RATIONS FOR INDIAN TROOPS[41]

Item	Indian Troops	Followers
Atta (lb)	2	2
Ghee (oz)	2	2
Dal (oz)	2	-
Firewood (lb)	3	3
Meat (thrice, oz)	8	-
Amchur (oz)	1/2	1/2
Gur (oz)	2	-
Chilies (oz)	1/6	1/6
Turmeric (oz)	1/6	-

of milk was scaled. Some of the special items in the ration included two ounces of *gur*, a variation of unrefined sugar developed from raw sugar cane juice or sugar. Additional items authorised to Indian troops on a daily basis included half a quarter of a pound of potatoes, one-third ounce of tea, half an ounce of salt, one and a half pounds of flour and four ounces of *dal* (lentils) or peas or beans, In addition, troops were also authorised one-third ounce of ginger.

Emergency (Iron) rations of Indian troops in the First World War included one pound of biscuit, eight ounces of *gur*, one ounce of tea and six ounces of condensed milk or two and a half ounces of dried milk in lieu, if available. The troops of the Indian battalions of the 29th Indian Brigade when landed at Gallipoli had been directed to carry the Emergency rations on self. On receipt of orders for mobilisation, the Indian troops were to embark with 60 days of rations, whereas for animals, grain and fodder was to be carried for 30 and 45 days respectively.

The Indian troops when landed on the shores of the peninsula were having centrally cooked meals on board the respective hired transports. With bare minimum emergency ration on person and that too not available with all troops, the troops had started to land on the ill-fated shores of the peninsula in the early hours of 1 May 1915. With no possibility of availability of cooked meals on shore, in the near term, the Indian troops had carried with them the spare *chapattis* and *dal*, which was available in the transport vessel. Sepoy Nanak

Singh of the 69th Punjabis has recounted the experience of having the stale and smelly *dal* along with the hardened *chapattis* for a few days, following the landings.

The specificities of rations of Indian troops were quite peculiar. *Gur* was an essential part of the ration for the Indian troops. There were competing requirements of provisioning of sugar or *gur* to the Indian troops. The Indian troops had overwhelming preference for *gur* over sugar. There was a possibility of provisioning of sugar from Egypt, but the procurement of *gur* was possible from India only. In October 1915, the Supply Department in Egypt had written to the Quartermaster General (QMG) in India for provisioning of 3,500 maunds (a unit of weight in India, roughly equivalent to about 37 kg) of *gur* for the men and camels.[42] At that time the cost of sugar sourced from Egypt was 0-2-9 (Re, A, P) for a pound.

The Supply Department further amplified that the *gur* had to be procured from India only if it is cheaper than the cost of the locally sourced sugar from Egypt, after including all additional costs of procurement and transportation. Then also, 1,000 maunds of *gur* was required to be procured from India. In a reply to this request, the QMG had replied that in any case the cost of *gur* to be sourced from India was more than the cost of sugar procured from Egypt, but the preference factor of the Indian troops being for *gur*, being what it is; *gur* will be required to be procured.

The balance of the dry rations was also being procured from India and then dispatched to Alexandria for further transportation to the peninsula. There was a constant correspondence between India and Egypt regarding procurement and transportation details of the rations from India. On 13 November 1915, C-in-C in India intimated GOC, Egypt through a cable about the dispatch of dry rations from India. The ration dispatched was meant for both Indian troops and animals under the command of GOC Egypt, including the troops and animals at Dardanelles. Two transports, *Hartington* and *Ozada* had sailed from India to Egypt and the ration on board comprised the following[43] (all in *maunds*):

Flour: 4,000
Atta: 15,000

Barley: 10,000
Bran: 11,800
Gram crushed: 119,400
Firewood: 14,200
Ghee: 4200
Dal, rice & gur each: 2800
Chilli & turmeric each: 280
Ginger: 140

The conditions as obtained at the peninsula did not facilitate central cooking at the company level. With the concept of *bhai-bundh* (being from same caste/clan/village), being strongly entrenched at the company level, the Indian soldiers cooked their own food. The cooking was delegated to the sub company levels and a group of soldiers cooked their food themselves in the respective trenches. *Chapattis* were made from the flour supplied in the rations, which were then baked over a fire. During the initial days on the peninsula, there was a severe shortage of firewood for cooking. The availability of firewood was scarce and the Indian troops had to manage the firewood from the washed off wood along the beaches of the peninsula for cooking purposes. Fire wood was authorised to a soldier at the rate of 2 *seer*

FIGURE 46: TROOPS OF THE 14TH SIKHS HAVING MEALS IN THE TRENCHES[44]

(unit of measurement) per day. The availability of firewood being an issue, and it also being not readily available at all places, just prior to the onset of hostilities of the Great War, it was started being supplied to the Indian troops at free of charge. But as the time passed the firewood started coming as part of the rations on the peninsula and the situation improved.

As far as operational situation allowed, the food habits of the Sikhs manifested in preparing fresh food for each meal during the campaign. The delegation of arrangements of cooking and consumption to the level of trenches was also very beneficial in the murderous climes of Gallipoli, wherein any extra movement was inviting sniper fire. Food was therefore prepared and consumed within the defences. Sometimes, the barter system of exchange was resorted to break the monotony in the food pattern. 'They cooked *chapattis* on iron sheets laid over wood-fires, and traded them now and again with British soldiers for a loaf of bread.' With supply of fresh vegetables generally not materializing on the peninsula, *dal* along with the flat bread was generally the staple diet of Sikh troops on the peninsula.

FIGUREN 47: MEALS IN THE TRENCHES ON GALLIPOLI[45]

During the times of intense action, the Sikh troops were more than eager to share their rations with their British officers and other Allied troops at the peninsula. During and immediately after the landings for the August offensive, it was realised that the cook house was difficult to establish. All the dry rations were being carried by the soldiers in small quantities distributed among them. Therefore, as far as the troops were concerned, the cooking had started wherever possible along the defiladed positions. But for the British officers of the 14th Sikhs, the cook house of the Officers Mess, even by last light was yet to be established. An intense opposition by the Turks to the landings along with the lack of space on the shores did not allow the establishment of the cook house.

Though the Emergency Rations in the form of tinned beef was there with the British officers of the 14th Sikhs, but sea journey combined with the factors of tiredness and darkness had made sure that the tinned food was totally unpalatable. 'We had of course our bully beef and on that we had been subsisting for the past four days or more; but it was lukewarm and not palatable.'[46] In addition, there was a requirement of warming the tins of beef, but with no means available, the British officers had no resort but to subsist on this severely unpalatable food. The Sikh troops, helpful as they are, were immediately ready to share their food with their officers.

Simultaneously, the religious beliefs of Sikhs also did not allow them to part with their religious compulsions about touching beef. Reginald Savory of the Battalion has commented on this predicament about the conditions of the food as prevalent in the peninsula, that a Sikh would go hungry but would not touch beef. 'Our men would have been only too happy to have shared their rations with us. There was plenty to spare; there always is, when casualties are heavy. But there are limits to which a European stomach can absorb chapattis, dhal, ghee, and, when available, goat.'[47] On the other hand, the rations of the officers of the Battalion had enough bully beef and, it would be better warmed up some way or another. But no Sikh would touch the sacred cow.[48]

The utter shortage of tobacco ration was a great cause of concern for the other Allied troops, but the Sikh troops were not bothered by the shortfall. Their religious fixations forbade any consumption of tobacco. 'They were non-smokers, to a man, and so were not worried by the shortage of the tobacco ration. A tot of rum, however, they appreciated.'[50]

FIGURE 48: MAKESHIFT MESS OF THE 14TH SIKHS
ON THE PENINSULA[49]

The supply of milk for the Indian troops at Gallipoli remained a
cause of concern throughout their stay at the peninsula. The Sikh
troops particularly were used to a diet of milk and the deficiency of
milk in the rations being supplied to the Indian troops was clearly
getting evident through the side effects day by day. Tea being an
essential component of Punjabi culture had also lost its flavour due
to an absolute lack of milk. Colonel Fergusson, the CO of the 21st
Kohat Battery, about the deficiency of milk in the rations and the
corresponding medical side effects of the deficiency of Vitamin C,
'Punjabi is usually an indefatigable walker, but GHQ refused to give
them a milk ration for a long time and they were all showing signs of
scurvy.'[51] The cases of scurvy amongst the drivers of the Indian Mule
Cart Train had also been rising. To increase the intake of Vitamin C,
the OC of the B Section of Indian Hospital at Suvla had recommended
that the scale of fresh vegetables authorised to an individual be
increased to 4 oz from the then existing authorisation of 2 oz, with
immediate effect.

The troops of the Indian Mountain Artillery Batteries and the
Indian Mule Corps being both Sikhs and Mohammedans were issued
with the live animals so they can be slaughtered in accordance with
the respective religious beliefs. Due to the distances involved, the sheep

and goats were not sourced from India, but were locally sourced and supplied. The delivery of the animals was generally carried out at the beaches by the Greek/ Egyptian traders.

FIGURE 49: A LIGHTER WITH A LOAD OF SHEEP ABOUT TO BE TAKEN ASHORE AT THE BEACH NORTH OF Anzac COVE[52]

These animals, after receipt were kept near the slaughter yards and followers took them for grazing in areas safe from shelling on the peninsula. The Indian trench lines in the rear generally had separate slaughter yards erected, by both Sikhs and Mohammedans to slaughter the animals as per their respective religious customs. Though initially not followed, but due to the intense menace of flies, the Indian troops started to keeping the area clean and disposing the offal daily and ensuring the burial at a distance.

At Anzac the supply of water to the front-line troops was being carried out by the Indian Mule Corps. The drinking water from the water ships to the shore was transported through specifically customised water containers known as 'lighters'. The Turkish seemed to have developed a particular liking for these lighters as they had distinctly identifiable colour scheme. A lot many of them were destroyed by the Turkish Artillery during the journey from water ship to the shore and then at the beach itself. The severe shortage of these containers induced

C01614

FIGURE 50: A SIKH FOLLOWER TENDING SHEEP SUPPLIED
FOR RATIONS[53]

a reduction of authorised scales of water per man per day. 'More than once the supply ran short, and the daily water ration had to be reduced to half a gallon a man -- quite insufficient, considering the heat and hard work.' To obviate the frequent reduction of water scale, a scheme for the piped distribution of water was also innovated but was not successful due to frequent breakdowns caused by shelling and sniping of the repair teams. As a result of which, Indian muleteers continued to supply water to the trenches amidst heat, humidity, disease, sniping and shelling.

As the weather turned warm and humid, the existing wells on the peninsula started drying up. The troops in the forward trenches required a continuous supply of drinking water and the supply of water over the distance was feasible only through the mules. Due to the severe shortage of water, further induction of mules on the peninsula also would not have served the purpose. As a cumulative result of all these factors, the existing Indian animal transport on the peninsula was working round the clock without any rest.

The round trips for supply of water from the shore/source to the

AUSTRALIAN WAR MEMORIAL   J02732

FIGURE 51: TRANSPORTATION OF THE STORES BY THE
INDIAN MULE CORPS[54]

forward most trenches involved a dangerous trek. With the mules of
the Indian Mule Corps being responsible for supply of water to the
entire complement of allied troops on the peninsula, the drivers and
mules were traversing the treacherous treks on the peninsula many
times a day. With the continuous movement, most of which was in
open terrain, the casualties amongst Indian drivers were manifold and
these casualties amongst men were gradually becoming harder to
replace.

The existing accommodation for the drivers was very minimalistic
and prone to frequent shelling. The space crunch coupled with death;
disease due to insanitary conditions took a heavy toll on the morale
of the men. In addition to these hardships, the speed and intensity of
water supply to the forward trenches was impacted due to the lack of
suitable water carriers which could be carried by pack mules and when
the sealed water containers for pack mules arrived, the quantity
received was far less than what was required. The severe water scarcity
had made sure that the water supply to the forward line of trenches
continued by the Indian Mule Corps even during the day times. The
men and animals of Indian Mule Corps suffered numerous casualties
in the process, but the water convoys carried on regardless.

FIGURE 52: INDIAN MULES TRANSPORTING WATER IN PAKHALS[55]

The watering of the mules of the Indian Mountain Artillery Batteries was an activity with an almost religious fervour. Indian drivers of these mules could themselves go without water but will not in any case, let mules go unwatered. The Kohat Mountain Artillery Battery was managing a mules well, which was sufficient to water the animals twice in a day. With the passage of the time, the well had started going dry. The water expert of ANZACs informed the OC of the Indian Mountain Battery, that with the depleting water in the mule well, it would be advisable to water the mules only once in day. The intense heat and humidity, however required that mules were watered minimum two times a day.

The OC of the Battery, in turn, tasked Havildar Major, Parkhar Singh to scout for alternate sources of water in the vicinity for the mules of the Battery. The ingenuity and resourcefulness of the Battery Havildar Major was for everyone to see, when the OC returned in the afternoon. The OC later on commented on the innovativeness of the Havildar Major, 'That morning I left Parkhar Singh, to look for water instead of coming around with me. When I came back, he had started a well which watered an average of 200 animals twice a day till November, in spite of the water expert doing his best to tap our source by digging wells all round it.'

SUPPLIES AND TRANSPORT

For the landings at Gallipoli, it is a known fact that initially no transport was envisaged to be attached with the landing troops. The assumption was based on a premise that no transport will be required by the troops on the peninsula as the operation for the capture of the peninsula would be a very swift one and the first wave would be able to capture the Turkish defences with relative ease. But, in hindsight, the hypothesis was far from the truth. The Allied troops including Indians, were not able to capture the peninsula, even after more than eight months of continuous operations and the Indian Mule Corps was an inalienable and indispensable part of the whole operations.

The Indian Mule Transport on the peninsula was the primary mode for the transport of ammunition, equipment and supplies from the shore up to the forward-most trenches. A number of units and sub units of the Indian Mule Corps were deployed on the peninsula during those eight months. The peninsula was witness to the deployment of 1st, 2nd, 9th, 11th, 15th, 28th, 31st and 32nd Indian Mule Corps. Each Mule Corps consisted of ten troops each of 108 mules, 50 carts and 60 drivers. Including the conductor and administrative staff, the strength of each Mule Cart Corps was 650 men and 1,086 mules. Taking this as a baseline, the total strength of the full complement of eight Indian Mule Corps on the peninsula was approximately 5,200 men and 8,688 mules. But this being the authorised strength, the actual strength varied from time to time as reinforcements kept on joining throughout the campaign while the sick and injured were evacuated. In addition, the peninsula also saw the deployment of detachments from the 3rd, 6th, 7th, 8th, 10th, 12th, 14th, 18th, 19th, 20th, 21st, 22nd, 23rd, 24th, 26th, 27th, 29th, 33rd, 34th, 35th, 36th and 37th Indian Mule Corps. Besides these, the detachments from Gwalior, Bharatpore and Indore Imperial Service Transport Corps also served on the peninsula.

At Mudros, just prior to the landings of 25 April 1915, firm orders had been received for the Indian Mule Corps. As per these orders, 150 carts along with the 324 mules and staff were allocated to the 29th Division which was landing at Cape Helles. Balance of the corps was allocated to the ANZACs, who were landing up north of Cape

Helles. The overall distribution of the Indian Mule Corps involved landing of five troops of Mules Corps at Anzac and the balance two at Cape Helles. The ANZAC commanders were happy to note that the Indian Mule Corps was accompanying them at the Anzac as they were also perturbed by the uncertainty of ammunition and water supply for the subsequent operations inland.

The distribution of the Indian Mule Corps into two components, to be landed separately at two spatially distanced shores of the peninsula was questioned by the OC of the Mule Corps. He was informed by the staff of Hamilton that a linkup between the two distinct forces, one landing at Cape Helles with the 29th Infantry Division and the Anzac at Gaba Tepe was part of the planned operation and therefore the Mule Corps was going to be an important component of both the operations. As the link up was already planned, therefore, troops of the Mule Corps were landed with only three days of rations for men and animals. Seven days of rations for both men and animals were left on ship only as the operation and the subsequent link up was not expected to go beyond three days. 'I asked whether the two detachments of my Corps were likely to link up again, and was told that if they did not do so in three days the campaign would have failed.'[56] From the planned three days, it took almost 240 days, a massive 8,000 per cent of the initial estimate, for the planners to call withdrawal of the troops from Gallipoli and not before hundreds of Indian troops gave the ultimate sacrifice.

The Indian muleteers on board ship for landing at Anzac were tasked to deal with another contingency prior to actual landing. Another transport earmarked for Cape Helles, having gone aground, the ship carrying the Indian Mule Corps was tasked to take on board a portion of Zion Mule Corps which had already been allocated to the 29th Infantry Division for landing at Cape Helles. 'The whole of the night of 24 April was occupied in transferring the Zionists. It was to our own interest, as well as to the interest of the expedition, to render every assistance in our power, and all the work in the ship was done by the Indians, who were kept hard at it the whole night.'[57] On the morning of 25 April, the situation was totally different from the expected. Allied Naval guns were bombarding Kum Kale on the Asiatic side and the hill of Achi Baba with tremendous intensity. Landings at Sedd-el-Behr and the V beach had failed initially due to unanticipated presence of Turkish machine gun detachments. All this while Indian Mule Corps was waiting in the transport to disembark the Zionist Mule Corps. Having watched the landings, death, despair and determination from the transport itself, finally the Zionist Mule Corps was ordered to disembark on the morning of 26 April. To facilitate the landing of the Zionist Mule Corps, the help of the Indian Muleteers was sought. When the mules of Zionist Mule Corps were being lowered into lighters to get them ashore, eight Indian drivers were detailed to go along with each lighter.

All my drivers wanted to be the first to land. The selection fell on a Dogra, Naik Narain Singh and men of his troop. Led by Driver Bir Singh, a splendid little Dogra, with four mules, they leapt into the sea which was about up to their necks. The men knew they would land under fire: they would have been disappointed if there had been none.[58]

After completing the disembarkation of the Zionist Mule Corps, the next day, the Indian Mule Corps turned towards Gaba Tepe for the actual landing of Indian Mule Corps. Here also, though the landings had taken place two days back, the deficiency of follow on support in terms of ammunition and stores had led to ANZACs falling back to the original position which was quite firmly secured by now. Indian muleteers formed a supply depot at the base of Mule Gully, named as such because of the mules itself. The accommodation for the men was dug into the mountains, with only criteria of necessity of saving lives. The craftsmanship of the Indian carpenter and the culinary skills of the cook of the Mule Corps is legendary in the annals of ANZACs. In several books on Gallipoli, the exploits of both of them have been adequately emphasised.

Brown had an orderly, Kangan by name, whose fame as a cook soon spread. It was really wonderful what appetizing dishes he succeeded in serving up with only ordinary army rations to work upon. It was a long time before any bread or fresh meat rations were issued, but plain bully beef or Maconochie rations were good enough for Kangan: he used some of the spices issued amongst the Indian rations and produced stews and curries of quite extraordinary excellence.[59]

340   *We Too Were There*

AUSTRALIAN WAR MEMORIAL   J02706

FIGURE 53 : INDIAN MULE CORPS AT MULE GULLY[60]

The Initial work at Anzac primarily involved use of mules in pack role only. Entire night was spent by men and animals of the Mule Corps in transporting the critical ammunition and stores from the beach to the forward trenches through treacherous hill tracks. Though the distance was not that much, the sniping and shelling by the enemy had extracted a heavy toll in the process. Due to slow pace of transportation by use of mules in pack role only, there was a strong case to make use of carts, which were already available on the peninsula. With limited availability of existing tracks suitable for the use of Indian mule carts, on an experimental basis, it was decided to recoup the advance supply and ordnance depot situated through the Shrapnel valley towards the Courtney's Post with the Indian Mule carts.

AUSTRALIAN WAR MEMORIAL   A00882

FIGURE 54: UNLOADING AND TRANSPORTING OF SUPPLIES FROM BARGES ON THE SHORE[61]

In the middle of May, three columns of 20 carts were planned to be run on the route. The carts had joined the Indian Mule columns by end of May 1915. Though, with the use of carts, lifting of additional quantity of stores had become possible, on the other hand the Turkish snipers also seemed to have mastered the art of listening to the groaning and creaking of carts, and accordingly adjusted their routine to interdict the movement of Indian Mule carts:

It was very dark; rifle fire, always heavy at night, seemed worse than ever; carts kept tipping off the road, and every time there was a halt the bullets seemed to come closer and to be hitting the ground all round us. The road was commanded by the enemy snipers, and it seemed as though they could hear the carts, and opened fire whenever the noise ceased.[62]

AUSTRALIAN WAR MEMORIAL   C01460

FIGURE 55: INDIAN MULE CART AT Anzac[63]

The experience of the experimental move taught invaluable lessons to the Corps. As the newly carved track was very narrow, there was no turning place for the carts, resulting in the manhandling of carts for turning. As a result, the Engineers dug out a suitable turning place for the carts near the advance supply and ordnance depot. Along the track also suitable crossing places were engineered to allow carts of up and down convoys to pass through. In the meantime, four troops of Number 3 Mule Corps also had landed at Anzac. These included two troops of the 9th Mule Corps, commanded by Kot Duffadar Bahawal

Din and Kot Duffadar Ghulam Rasul, and consisting entirely of men who had been in France with the Lahore Division.'[64]

The climate of Gallipoli was warm and harsh for both the troops and the animals. Due to constant shelling and sniping by the Turks, the staging forward of stores was assuming difficult propositions. As day time movement was causing casualties to the animals and men, and the primary task of the animals, the supply of ammunition, rations and stores to the forward troops from the landing beaches could only be accomplished at night. On the other hand, the watering of animals, a basic survival necessity for animals was also possible only during the night time, putting severe strain on the existing resources.

A balancing act was therefore required through which both the activities could be carried out without prejudicing the other. The supervisory and conductor staff of the Indian Mule Corps deserves complete credit for the same. No unit or formation of allies, which served at Gallipoli, was left untouched by the bravery of these muleteers and their mules. The cheerful disposition and demeanor of the drivers of the Indian Mule Corps, in spite of the hardships is a legend in the history of the contribution of the Indian troops at Gallipoli.

On Anzac, when one was not dealing with the sniping and shelling by Turks, he was dealing with the flies. The menace of flies at Anzac had reached epic proportions and there, 'seemed to be more flies to the square inch at Anzac than are found to the square mile anywhere else'. The trenches were affected by the menace and the Mule Gully due to the presence of mule lines and supply depot was worst affected. Sometimes, the mules were completely covered by the flies making the colour of their skin from brown to black. The mules were totally discomforted by this plague of flies. Some respite for the mules was arranged by the Indian muleteers by burning dried dung and putting the improvised veil on the eyes of the mule, but the menace could only be contained partly.

The food was equally affected by the fly menace. This menace was more applicable to Indian food as Indian food is invariably cooked and the flies used to completely overwhelm the cooking process. The cooking area was virtually black. One could not eat their food without having a bite of flies in between. 'All one's food was black with them:

AUSTRALIAN WAR MEMORIAL   P02649.028

FIGURE 56: A CHEERFUL INDIAN MULE CORPS DRIVER[65]

it was practically impossible to avoid eating them.' This issue further manifested in dysentery and jaundice as shall be seen in another section of this chapter. As most of the work by the Indian Mule Corps was in the night, the drivers were not able to get rest during the day due to the infestation of flies. The intensity of the menace virtually rendered all measures to include mosquito netting and fly papers totally ineffective. 'They were a veritable plague which rendered any attempt to sleep in the day time quite futile: this was particularly trying because there was of necessity so much night work.'

With the passage of time, the Indian Mule Corps was posted with increased staff at command and control level. The understanding of Hindustani by the frequently changing British staff was a problem for the Indian drivers. In order to facilitate smooth functioning of the

AUSTRALIAN WAR MEMORIAL   C01642

FIGURE 57: A MULE OF INDIAN MULE CORPS WITH AN
IMPROVISED VEIL OVER ITS EYES[66]

Mule Corps, interpreters from the men of the battalions deployed on trenches were sought. 'These interpreter billets were rather sought after, because they meant getting out of the trenches and diving in greater comfort; moreover, interpreters had the rank and pay of corporals.'

In comparison to Anzac, the situation at Cape Helles was much better. Here due to the distances involved, the rifle fire and sniping was subdued but was adequately compensated by the high explosive shells. Mules of the corps had suffered hugely because of these shells but the casualties amongst men were reduced. The totally indifferent attitude of the Indian muleteers in the face of heavy shelling was a much-discussed subject amongst the officers and men of the Allied battalions. 'Except for an occasional joke, the men took absolutely no notice of the shell fire, nor did the Indian muleteers, who carried away the stores when landed and, although it took me some time to get used to it, I found the men's nonchalance a great help and hope I did not show the fear I felt.'[67]

By the end of July, plans were afoot to launch another offensive on to the Turkish defenses. Indian Mule Corps, like the previous operations in the campaign on the Peninsula, was again going to play a central role in the scheme of things. 'The planning involved transportation of twenty million rounds of small arms ammunition and thousands of shells and bombs to various advanced points where dumps were going to be formed. Three thousand sealed tins containing water had to be taken out for the use of the troops during the advance. Innumerable sand bags had to be carted to the trenches and substantial advance dumps of rations were required.' The terms of reference for the planning for the upcoming offensive included use of existing resources in terms of men and animal as no more reinforcements were expected. For the impending operation, the forward dumping of ammunition, stores and rations was required to be completed by 3 August 1915.

The plan of the operation envisaged Number 2 outpost as an important communication centre in the scheme of things. The outpost was manned by the troops from Otago Mounted Rifles of New Zealand Mounted Brigade. A freshwater source of approximate 6,000 gallons was the pride of the post. The post was to act as Headquarters of the staff of the Left Assaulting Column for the August offensive. Till this time on the peninsula, carts had been used only along the right flank from Anzac. The left flank had been serviced by pack mules only. But the quantum of the proposed dumping necessitated the use of carts along this route as well and the Indian Mule Cart Corps was up and running for the task.

The repeated move of carts along this track, made it operational and the resultant smoothness reduced the resultant groaning and creaking of the carts during movement. The secrecy of the intended operation did not allow movement of carts along this route during the day, lest enemy gets to know about the direction of advance. 'One night one of the destroyers inadvertently gave the show away. A convoy was well on its way when the destroyer turned her searchlight right on to it for several minutes, with the result that machine-gun fire opened on the convoy and caused severe casualties.' This incident really must have warned the enemy as the very next day the Turkish Artillery Batteries started to register the route taken by the Mule Cart convoy on the previous day as a potential target. 'A Turkish gun fired three rounds of shrapnel. The first burst on the beach, beyond the

AUSTRALIAN WAR MEMORIAL   C03404
FIGURE 58: LOADING OF SUPPLIES ONTO INDIAN MULE CARTS[68]

track made by the mule carts on their way to Number 2 post; the second pitched a little short of the track and the third right on it. Brother Turk seemed to be "bracketing" on the track with a view to strafing it later in the evening.'

Another issue for the drivers of the Mule Corps was the carriage of bombs by the pack mules. Bombs were not a very convenient load for a pack mule owing to the size of the bomb and the modified carrier harness of the pack mule. Coupled with the terrain obtained in the Anzac on peninsula and constant shelling by the enemy, the bombs loaded on the pack mules tended to fall off and explode on impact with the ground and, 'one night two drivers were killed and an interpreter and five men wounded in this way'.

In the first week of August, the Indian Infantry Brigade had started concentrating at Anzac for the August offensive. The respective camps were established in the Reserve Gully. The supply depot of the Brigade was established in the Mule Gully, co located with the location of the Indian Mule Corps. As part of the August offensive, the further sub allotment of mules to the formations, involved sub distribution to the New Zealand Division, the 13th Division and the Indian Infantry Brigade. As the Australian Division on the right flank of Anzac was not involved in any forward movement, no sub allocation of Indian

Mule Corps to the Australian Division was envisaged. The Supply Officer of Indian Infantry Brigade, Captain Rebsch was responsible for the management of the component of the Indian Mule Corps sub allocated to the formation for the August offensive. The preparations for the move of the mule columns involved cutting of a series of long and deep trenches along the existing dugouts to prevent enemy interdiction. All along the gullies, where mule columns were to move, supply of several days of hay was dumped in advance and 'each animal was provided with a small bag tied to its saddle containing three days' grain. Each man was served with three days of emergency rations'.

FIGURE 59: INDIAN MULE CORPS TRANSPORTING HAY
FOR THE ANIMALS[69]

It was during this period only that the Indian Mule Corps had received the news that Rissaldar Hashmet Ali, Lance Naik Bahadur Singh and Driver Bir Singh of the Indian Mule Corps had been awarded the Indian Order of Merit for their exemplary conduct and self-less service in the operation of 6 May 1915 on the peninsula. The effort and dedication put in by the Indian Mule Corps for the August offensive also didn't go unnoticed by the commanders at all levels. Gen. Birdwood, GOC, ANZAC visited the Corps during the preparations and complimented the men for their efforts. Referring to the inspection, the OC of the Indian Mule Corps reminisced, 'the feeling we all had after his inspection was that mule transport was the most important thing in the whole of Anzac'. The failure of the British and Allied troops to break the impasse in the August offensive required a further change in the organisation and composition of echelons of the Indian Mule Corps on the peninsula.

Post the August offensive, the Indian Mule Corps at the peninsula was consolidated and further divided into four groups, known as 'A', 'B', 'C' and 'D' groups. To sustain the troops in and around Outpost Number 2. 'A' group of 500 first line pack mules along with their drivers and associated staff were deployed at Outpost Number 2. 'B' group comprising another 500 mules of first line along with drivers and staff was deployed as base transport at Mule Gully to cater for the movement ahead of the Mule Gully. 'C' group comprising almost similar numbers of mules was nominated as the beach transport and located at Anzac Cove on the beach. The 'D' group detachment was mandated to be redeployed for supporting the operations of the Australian division on the southern flank:

All along this period, out of all the groups, 'A' group transport was shelled continuously day in and out in its camps and performed perilous journeys every day. It was the lot of Kot Duffadars like Bahawal Din and Ghulam Rasul, to have their troops always as far forward as transport could go.[70]

Post the August offensive, situation at the Anzac had changed to the effect that due to the capture and loss of some positions and ground, the tracks and communication trenches earlier used by the Indian Mule Corps were no longer tenable. All the four groups besides carrying out their primary duties also contributed to the construction of additional communication trenches along with personnel from Engineers and fatigue parties from the battalions. As the offensive in August was not able to facilitate the capture of the dominating feature of Baby 700, the supply operations along the route from the Mule Gully to Outpost Number 2 were continuously interdicted through enemy fire. As a result, the transport of 'B' and 'C' groups suffered tremendous losses during this period. But the display of courage, single

FIGURE 60: DUGOUTS OF THE INDIAN MULE CORPS[71]

minded focus on the operational task and the innovations by the
drivers of the Indian Mule Corps had metamorphosed into a legend
at Anzac:

One night when there was a full moon, this journey was particularly bad,
but the behavior of the drivers was such as to command universal respect.
They treated it as a joke. The carts were sent off one at a time, the driver,
protected on the exposed side by the boxes and bags which formed his load,
being ordered to cross the open space at full gallop. Usually they are forbidden
to go out for a walk, and they quite enjoyed this unaccustomed license. But
the return journey, when there were no boxes to protect the men, was a
hazardous one. The drivers would arrive breathless at the foot of Mule Gully
shouting, *Bachgia, Sahib* with a broad grin on their faces, except those (and
there were many) who had not escaped.[72]

In the August offensive itself, the Indian Mule Corps at Anzac
had lost 63 men and 296 mules killed, implying the intensity of the
operations. In terms of tangible gains, the August offensive was
successful in making the parts of the north beach safe from enemy
sniping. This had been made possible by the advance of Allied troops

on the northern flank of Anzac Cove. This advance had further facilitated establishment of a direct link between the ground held by the troops landed at Suvla Bay and the northern positions at Anzac along a sliver of land strip.

Though other gains of the Allied operation were not very much substantial, but the morale of the enemy had received a fillip from the stalemate reached. Amidst the floating rumours of an impending evacuation of the Allied troops from the peninsula in wake of failure of offensive, preparations for the approaching winters were going on. In spite of sustaining serious losses in terms of men and material, the transport columns of the Indian Mule Corps continued to operate with the same enthusiasm and zeal. The weather in the approaching autumn was comfortable and the relatively longer duration of darkness was supplementing the efforts of the Indian Mule Corps. With the arrival of large quantum of stores, rations and ammunition for winter stocking, the drivers and animals of the Indian Mule Corps were working day in and out amidst the continued shelling and sniping activities by the enemy. 'Hospitals were established in tents to hold large numbers of sick, in view of the probability of bad weather making it impossible to evacuate them for days together. Material arrived for improving dug outs and roofing them in, and large reserves of rations and ammunitions were brought ashore.'[73]

The situation at Suvla bay for the Indian Mule Corps was slightly different, though operational tasks remained the same. Relatively longer period of stay at Anzac and Cape Helles had allowed the drivers of the Indian Mule Corps to identify the routes and places to avoid and accordingly a maze of dug outs and communication trenches had been developed. The relative openness of terrain at Suvla Bay, something akin to Cape Helles, facilitated the enemy to shell the bay continuously. The freshly landed Infantry troops were still struggling to develop a system of dug outs and trenches and for the time being were deployed in the open. As a result, both the Infantry and the Indian Mule Corps continued to suffer from frequent shelling. The impact of shells landing on the troops and mules in the open had disastrous results.

There was a detachment at Lala Baba, three miles south of Suvla where mules were picketed on the cliff above the beach. One day an 8-inch shrapnel shell burst in the middle of these lines with the most appalling effect. Sixty mules were killed, or had to be shot, and fifty-five more received wounds. It seemed almost inconceivable that one shell could do so much damage.[74]

The food prepared by the Indians was fresh and invariably was a welcome change from the dull routine of bully beef, the standard ration of the allied troops. The freshness of the *chapattis* prepared on ad hoc arrangements by the Indian troops was favourably looked at and opportunities to partake these were awaited equally by the officers and troops of Anzac. 'For a few days I was sent on detachment to take charge of an ammunition dump which was kept supplied by an Indian unit with mule transport. Their chapattis were a great treat and these 'they cooked very skillfully in their mess tins'.[75] The relative lull in the fighting post August offensive, had allowed certain new innovations to be experimented. As part of these innovations, the Indian Mule Corps had endeavoured to deploy a light railway at Anzac.

The interpersonal relationships among different ethnic groups form a very strong foundation of any military outfit, particularly Infantry. This template of a strong interpersonal relationship has stood the test of time since times immemorial. The template further gets strengthened if the troops belong to a similar background. Like Infantry battalion in the Indian Mule Corps also, the endeavour was to have men of the same caste in one troop, whereas the NCO's and other key personnel invariably belonged to other castes. As the Indian Mule Corps was going to play a major role in the impending operations, similar class composition of the Mule troops was endeavoured to be implemented as far as possible. For the same, even the order of berthing of ships was changed at Alexandria. 'I should have liked to detail the four troops of the 15th Mule Corps from the latter; these were all men of the same caste, and it would be a good plan to keep them together.'[76]

MEDICAL AND CASUALTY EVACUATION

The medical components in support of the Indian troops fighting at Gallipoli included, the 108th Indian Field Ambulance (with the 29th Indian Infantry Brigade), 110th Indian Field Ambulance with a convalescent depot which also acted as a clearing hospital, 'C' Section (Indian) of the 137th Combined Field Ambulance which was attached with the 7th Indian Mountain Artillery Brigade and 'C' Section

(British) of the 137th Combined Field Ambulance on a transport. Another Section of 137th Combined Field Ambulance, namely, the 'C' Section, was specifically earmarked for the Indian Mule Cart Train located in Suvla in October 1915. The section of the Indian Combined Field Ambulance attached with the 21st Kohat Mountain Battery, was commanded by Lieutenant Colonel Thomas Carey Evans of Indian Medical Service. With the Batteries of the Indian Mountain Artillery being the sole Indian contingent in the entire Anzac during the initial part of the operations, the services of a dedicated section of the Ambulance were available to the Indian troops of these Batteries. The seriousness of the quantum of casualties was never anticipated by the planners of the operation, and the arrangements for medical treatment and evacuation were found to be completely inadequate:

Though there was no other wounded man in sight, the whole valley was resounding with that ghastly cry - 'stretcher bearers / stretcher bearers' and awful curses. All day when the din of firing sank a little, I had heard it. It went on all night until dawn. The valley was full of groaning. No stretcher bearers came; there were not enough.'[77] The situation was worse at Anzac, where wounded men were rowed in small boats in a rising sea from ship to ship, suffering terribly, until they found a ship which could accommodate them.[78]

If at last, any fortunate soul was able to find a berth on a hospital ship, the conditions on the hospital ship were terrible. The same ship was being used for multifarious tasks and the basic requirements for casualty handling in these ships were totally lacking:

The conditions on the transports once the wounded got on board, which in itself was a difficult and hazardous operation as few of the ships had proper tackle, were execrable. On one transport, an army surgeon found mules on the fore deck. The ship had been left dirty, the latrines were choked, the food bad, ventilation very imperfect; actual hospital accommodation not provided.[79]

But the services of the Indian Ambulance attached with the 7 IMAB came under immense praise from the CO of the 21st Kohat Battery. The casualty evacuation and subsequent treatment by the Indian Ambulance here was very professionally handled.

The CO of the Indian Field Ambulance ran a wonderfully good show, assisted by two priceless Hospital Assistants, Adjudhia Pershad and Daulat Singh. We lived at the bottom of Shrapnel Valley, and were being constantly crumped. When this was going on, these Hospital Assistants kept a look out, and whenever they saw a man hit, gave a shout of *Challo Bhai* to the stretcher bearers and dashed out to bring in the casualty, no matter how heavy the shelling was.[80]

FIGURE 61: INDIAN STRETCHER BEARERS CARRYING CASUALTY[81]

The popularity of the Hospital Assistants was not limited to the Indian Troops of these two batteries only. The Australians and New Zealanders of ANZAC were equally in awe of the professionalism and helpful nature of these two Hospital Assistants. Not only the treatment part, but the cooking of fresh food by the Indian troops of the Field Ambulance had the ANZACs overawed. The rations of the ANZACs was primarily consisting of bully beef, which was repeated day after day. Coupled with the existing state of sanitary conditions and the outbreak of cholera and dysentery amongst the troops, the bully beef dominated ration supply was not at all a very good option for the ANZACs, whereas the Indian food, in these trying times, happened to be a welcome break. 'The Australians used to come to Evans in preference to their own hospitals, especially with stomach troubles, and our men used to feed them on *dal* and *chapattis* when their insides refused bully beef.'[82]

A very professional handling of the situation by the 137th Combined Field Ambulance also helped to keep the percentage of sick troops in a very remarkable way. 'In spite of dysentery, which was pretty bad, the percentage of men invalided per month for our eight months on Gallipoli was on an average only 3.6 per month for the Battery and 5.5 for the whole Brigade.'[83] The overwhelming magnitude of casualties, which had not been anticipated, had resulted in the shortage of both trained orderlies as well as stretchers. Troops who had no experience in handling of casualties, perforce had to join in the evacuation of these. 'The unskilled orderlies refused to lift badly wounded cases from the stretchers, with the result that stretchers were in desperately short supply on shore.'[84] The stretcher bearers of the 'C' section of 137th Combined Field Ambulance did their best to evacuate all casualties on the peninsula.

'B' Section of the 137th Indian Combined Field Ambulance was located at Mudros Island, when it received orders on 3 October 1915 to proceed to Suvla to provide medical care to the wounded and sick of Cart trains of Indian Mule Corps located at Suvla. The section after disembarking from the transport ship in the early hours of 4 October and in the backdrop of an apparent paucity of space at Suvla, established the hospital in the area very next to the Indian Mule train location. The process of digging of dug outs for the wards of the hospital, though commenced right away was hampered by the deficiency of manpower with the section and also the relative hardness of ground.

The section placed the demand for 'fatigue parties' with the higher headquarters. The mandate given to the section was to treat only minor cases of 'constipation and abrasions' wherein troops were able to perform their duties without leaving the peninsula. The serious cases were required to be sent to the affiliated Field Ambulance; wherein adequate medical facilities were available. At the time of arrival of the section of Ambulance at the peninsula, five Indian Sub Assistant Surgeons were attached to the Indian Mule Cart train at Suvla. These Indians were going to be very helpful and significant contributors to the success of operations of section of Field Ambulance at Suvla:

1st Grade SAS Ghous Mohammed
1st Grade SAS K.G. Alikar
2nd Grade SAS Sampuran Singh
3rd Grade SAS V.S. Panjre
3rd Grade SAS Mahomed Din

When the dedicated section of Field Ambulance for Indian Mule train at Suvla had landed, the sanitary conditions prevalent in the camp of the Indian Mule Train were very deplorable. As mentioned earlier, the ground being very hard was not at all helping the efforts. Amongst the first things the section ensured in the lines was the digging of sullage pits near the cook houses. In addition, empty tins as receptacles for the miscellaneous trash were erected at convenient places. The rocky conditions prevalent in the area had made the latrine system redundant. The area allocated to the latrines being very small and compact, there was very limited scope for expansion.

The Field Ambulance ensured that the hygiene and sanitary conditions, which were in bad shape due to the latrine system in vogue, was improved upon. The Field Ambulance improvised a new system of latrines, which were built with empty kerosene oil tins as receptacles. Strict orders were passed to all Indian troops to close the trenches applying the Creole solution. Slaughter houses along the cook houses were inspected on a regular basis. To ensure the proper disposal of skin and other discards from the slaughter house, a sentry was placed, with an order to burn all the discards from the slaughter house. Locally developed incinerators were installed by the section to burn the excreta. In addition, to prevent the unnecessary movement of troops, urine pits were prepared and night urinals near dug outs and sentries were placed, which were removed during the next morning. The mule litter was being thrown over the cliffs into the beach area. These dispersed mounds of mule excreta were a source of many sanitation problems in the camp including the infamous fly menace. The arrival of section heralded a new chapter in the disposal of the dung. The dung heaps were put on fire, the smouldering dung didn't allow the flies to breed and the resultant smoke up to a large extent inhibited the free movement of flies.

The Mule Cart train was without the services of a dedicated section

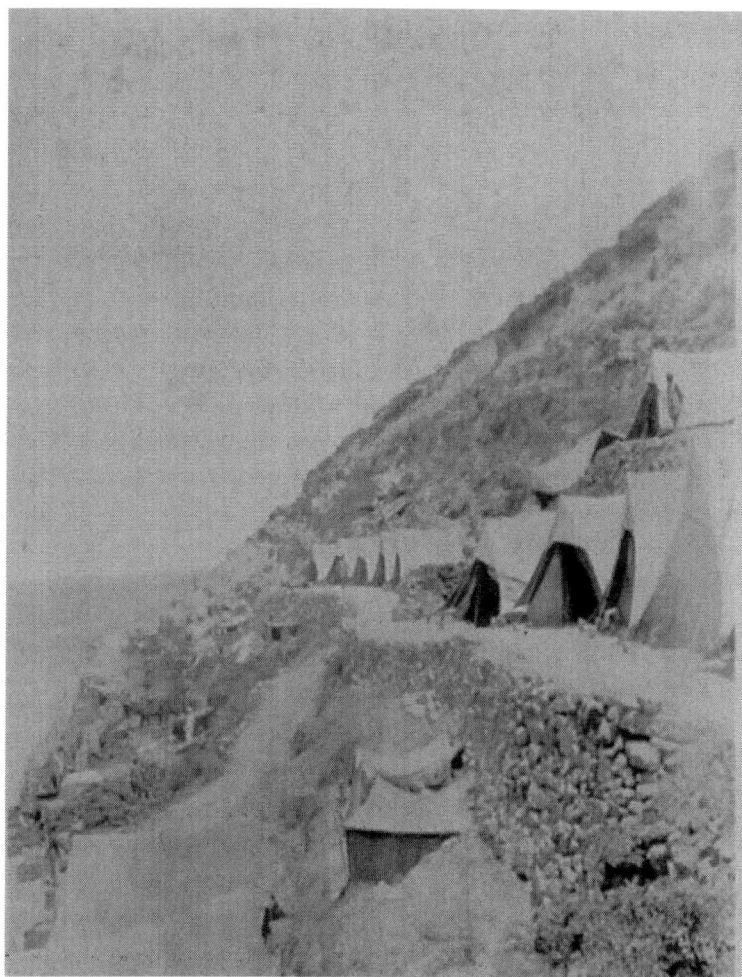

FIGURE 62: INDIAN FIELD AMBULANCE Anzac[85]

of Field Ambulance for a long time. The requisitions of medicines and comforts were till now being handled by the respective Sub Assistant Surgeons. This practice was centralized by the section of Field Ambulance and all the requisitions and medicines were now being centrally processed through the section hospital. Though the Indian Mule Cart train was posted with a sanitary officer, but the said officer being unable to understand the language and 'also being largely unaware of the Indian sanitary methods' was not able to positively influence the sanitary system prevalent at the camp.

The perennial requirement of sandbags for the creation of hospital wards has been repeatedly highlighted in the war diary of the section hospital. Coupled with this, the non-availability of wood for the overhead protection of the wards also delayed the progress of work. In the meantime, the section received, '3000 sandbags out of 10,000 demanded, and 14 lbs of nails against a requisition of 50 lbs'. The system of provisioning of rations for the troops though was relatively stabilised by the time of arrival of section hospital, but there was still a scope of improvement. When the Section Hospital started checking the drivers of the Indian Mule Cart train, symptoms of scurvy were rampant. A large number of Indian troops from the train were found to be suffering from the initial symptoms of vitamin deficiency. As a first step, to arrest the rising cases, an immediate increase in the fresh vegetables in the ration supply was recommended. In addition, an order was passed that all the drivers and other staff of the Indian Mule train will be paraded to the OC of the Section Hospital once in a week and will be administered concentrated lime juice in the presence of the OC. In spite of all the above problems the morale of the drivers of the Indian Mule Cart train was very high and, it has been recorded that 'the health of mule corps drivers in this area is excellent and all the men are in the best of spirits. The callousness of the mule corps drivers under heavy fire is admired by everybody.'[86]

The intake of contaminated water and food by the drivers of Mule Cart trains was also resulting in the cases of cholera amongst the Indian troops. 'Anti Cholera' serum, supplied by the Red Cross, therefore, was started for the drivers. By this time, the wards of the section hospital were relatively well established. With the admission of drivers in these wards, another problem of provisioning of utensils for these patients was being suffered by the staff of the section hospital. 'Mule drivers have not got separate utensils of their own but eat in messes. So, when men came to hospital, they have no utensils to eat from. Red Cross depot supplied ten plates and 50 mugs for use of patients in hospital.' In the meantime, the weather had also started to change. With change of weather, the menace of flies was on the wane. But the change of weather was about to bring its own peculiar challenges.

In the meantime, the Indian section hospital was witness to a large number of violations of the existing orders on hygiene and sanitation. With no institutionalised system of enforcement of hygiene and sanitation measures in the British Lines, the efforts of the Indian Section hospital in the Indian Mule Cart train lines were getting adversely impacted. The situation at one point of time had reached such a flash point that the OC of the Indian Section hospital had to visit the designated Camp Commandant of the area and request for the positioning of a British guard to keep an eye on the defaulters. In addition, a large number used toilet papers from the British lines due to not being disposed properly were blowing into the lines of the Indian Mule train due to strong winds. To curb this menace and to keep the area clean, the Indian Section hospital specifically deployed cleaners, whose sole task was to collect and incinerate the scraps of such toilet papers.

With the supply of anti-cholera vaccine increasing, all the drivers of the Indian Mule Cart train were vaccinated. Scurvy check was being carried out regularly by the staff of the section hospital. With a relative increase in the content of fresh vegetables in the rations, the 'scurvy cases amongst the drivers have greatly diminished of late'. Another menace apart from flies, dysentery, cholera and numerous others, which was debilitating for the Indian troops was lice. With limited water available for personal bathing purposes, the washing of clothes was a dream. The overwhelming stench of lice-infected clothes was an absolute deterrent for wearing them. But with bare essential clothing available with the troops, there was hardly an option. As a result, troops were wearing the same clothes day in and day out.

With no washing facilities possible, centralised or otherwise, disinfection of lice-infected clothes of troops was an improbable task. The lice covered clothes had started infecting the skin and scalp of Indian troops. A field innovation by Colonel W. Hunter in Serbia to disinfect the lice infected clothes of the troops, transformed the entire medical landscape of the Indian Mule Cart Train at Suvla. The B section of 137 Indian Combined Field Ambulance was the pioneer in the introduction of this innovation at Suvla and may be at Gallipoli. The war diary of the section hospital mentions in an entry of 21 October 1915 that the hospital had started work to install the disinfector for the troops of Indian Mule Cart Train. The contraption for the disinfector was not very complex and involved very basic engineering skills. The functioning principle of the disinfector had adequately been explained by the innovator:

A sound wine or water barrel is taken, through the bottom of which one large central hole is made, with a circle of five or six holes around it, through which the steam can enter the barrel, which stands on a circular boiler of cast iron or galvanized iron. To prevent any escape of the steam between the boiler and the bottom of the barrel a narrow sausage ring filled with sand is placed between the boiler and the barrel. The weight of the barrel presses this down, forming an efficient valve. To keep the clothes in the barrel away from the holes in the bottom through which the steam enters a small frame made of two or three crossed thin bars of wood or wicker-work is placed inside the barrel over the holes and about 9 inches above the holes. The barrel is provided with a wooden lid, purposely made heavy, with an edge which fits inside the barrel or overlaps it. The object of the lid is not to prevent entirely the escape of the steam, but to retard its escape, the purpose being disinfection by current steam, which escapes slowly and with some difficulty around the edges of the lid.[87]

During the Gallipoli operations, the logistics being neglected as such did not provide for disinfectors. The rudimentary version of the contraption was being installed by the Indian Section hospital for its dependency of troops. The requirement of a barrel was met by a request to the Field Engineers and the newly installed disinfector was very much appreciated by the Indian troops. The popularity and success of the disinfector was so much that the authorisation of the same was recommended at the scale of one disinfector per company, thereby making it four disinfectors per battalion.

The installation of the disinfector for the Indian troops was a novelty for the Allied troops. Orders were passed for all sanitary officers and medical officers of all the Divisions to visit the Indian Section hospital at Suvla and to gain firsthand knowledge of the disinfector. Diary entry in the War Diary of the Indian Section Hospital for 24 October, makes a mention of the familiarisation visit by the concerned staff to witness the working of the disinfector. 'The next day, sanitary officers and ADMSs of Divisions started visiting, to see the clothes which were lice free due to the disinfector.'[89]

AUSTRALIAN WAR MEMORIAL   P11155.011.001

FIGURE 63: INDIAN MULE LINES AT SUVLA[88]

Meanwhile, for the battalions of the Indian Infantry Brigade, the 108th Indian Field Ambulance was providing the medical cover. For the 14th Sikhs, with the Battalion medical officer, Lieutenant Cursetjee, himself getting wounded badly at Cape Helles on 28 June 1915, the battalion was without any dedicated Medical Officer. The same situation was to continue even during the August offensive, in which the battalion was taking part. But the troops had never felt the absence of a Medical Officer. Immediately after the completion of the landing of the complete battalion at Anzac, the Regimental Aid Post was established at the beach itself, with whatever little camouflage was possible, within the constraints of the existing conditions. With no Medical Officer posted with the battalion, the aid post was run very efficiently by the sub assistant surgeon of the battalion. SAS Bhagwan Singh was in-charge of the post:

A thickset Sikh, Bhagwan Singh, was of priceless worth. Fearless, efficient, cheerful, indefatigable, he was more than a tower of strength. Sikhs, Gurkhas, New Zealanders. Australians and British, all were in his dressing-station. He was not a trained doctor, but had passed an army course and knew his work. Many a wounded man owed his life to him.[90]

FIGURE 64: CASUALTY EVACUATION BY TROOPS OF THE
14TH SIKHS[91]

The peculiar food habits of Hindu and Mohammedan troops required separate cook houses for both of them. The intensity of battles and shelling till now had not allowed creation of separate cooking and dining facilities based on religion. The relative lull in the battle facilitated 'B' Section of the Indian Field Ambulance to create separate cook houses and dining rooms for the Hindu and Mohammedan troops at Suvla. Due to the long and open area between the hospital wards and the newly established latrines, a number of casualties were happening due to shell fire. Creation of communication trench from the wards of the hospital to the latrines by the section hospital also reduced the number of casualties, as the exposure of the troops/patients significantly decreased. Another interesting aspect related to the Section Hospital was the dissonance between the OC of the hospital with the DDMS of the division. Orders were received by the section hospital from the office of the DDMS to fly the Red Cross flag over the Section Hospital. Whereas, the OC of the Section Hospital was of the view that since the hospital is located too close to the mule lines, therefore as per ruling of the General Staff, the Red Cross flag should not be hoisted.

Around 26 October 1915, due to the sudden rainstorm, followed by hailstorm, the weather turned incredibly cold. Warm clothes were drawn from the ordnance but the stores held by the ordnance were not enough to cater for the complete strength. The Serbian disinfector was working overtime to disinfect the warm clothes and the waiting period for the disinfection had suddenly increased. The rain and sleet continued unabated throughout the next day. With no overhead protection, the trenches were flooded with rain water, leading to the damage to the clothing and stores of the troops in the trenches.

As if this was not enough, a very heavy snowfall commenced by 29 November 1915 and the situation at Suvla turned desperate. The Indian Section Hospital was intimated to be ready to receive a large number of casualties due to the exposure of the troops to the cold. The casualties amongst the troops due to the prolonged exposure to the cold started rising and all field hospitals on the peninsula were full to their capacity. The War Diary of the Indian Section Hospital talks about receiving 77 casualties in terrible shape and 'none of them could walk and some of them were comatose'. Every available space in the hospital was taken over to accommodate the additional casualties, so much so that patients were accommodated in the cook house of the hospital. The weak composition of the patients due to months of deficiencies in rations was further compromising the condition of the troops.

By this time the entire hospital premises were full with patients, exposed to the cold. During the treatment, in the Indian Field Ambulances, all the patients, including ANZACs, were treated with additional nutrition and the typical Indian diet and food habits came to the rescue of these patients. Traditional healthy Indian recipes to include hot soup and hot chicken curry along with rice for all the patients was arranged by the staff of the Indian Section Hospital.

The entry in the War Diary for the day of Indian Section Hospital, specifically mentions the role played by SAS, First Class Abdul Ghafoor, SAS Third Class A.K Sarkar, Naik Genoo and Dhobhi Mansur Ali. The efforts of the staff of the section hospital were duly recognised by the officers in the chain of command as well. The congratulatory message from the Corps Commander of the XI Corps, acclaimed the role of the Section Hospital in these words:

His very special thanks are also due to the doctors and attendants of B Section 137 Field Ambulance, whose assistance during the last few days has been invaluable. By their voluntary effort and skill, they have undoubtedly contributed to the saving of many lives.[92]

Hospital Ships were an important part in the chain of casualty evacuation. The evacuation of Indian casualties from Dardanelles to Indian Hospital in Alexandria and back to India was possible only through these ships. With a number of Indian Expeditionary Forces deployed in the different parts of the world, the demand for these ships was naturally very high. As the casualties of Force 'G' were already extreme, there was a definite requirement of a dedicated Hospital Ship for evacuation of the Indian casualties from Dardanelles to Alexandria. The dedicated shipping effort was not being provided to the Force 'G' on the pretext that such an allocation would reduce the availability of ships on the Bombay-Suez route, impacting the overall availability of shipping effort on the route.

The C-in-C in India on 21 July 1915 had provided a detailed update on the state of availability and serviceability of these ships to the Secretary of War Office in London. It was brought out that with only four Hospital ships available, GOC of Force 'D' immediately requires the services of *Madras* and *Takada*. With the demand of *Guildford Castle* for Force 'G', the Bombay-Suez run will only be left with the services of *Syria*. It was further highlighted that the IEF deployed in East Africa was without the service of a Hospital Ship since 2 April 1915. The availability of a dedicated transport for the Indian casualties, it was claimed was possible only at the cost of overall reduction of ships on Bombay Suez route. 'I do not recommend withdrawal of *Guildford Castle* but the Ship can be withdrawn, if arrangements can be made in Egypt for Indian sick. No additional ship is available for Bombay Suez run.'[93]

With an impending reduction in the availability of ships on the Bombay-Suez run and to plan the withdrawal of wounded and sick back to India, the C-in-C in India asked the GOC Egypt to provide details of Indian wounded and sick requiring evacuation to India on a monthly basis in two categories. The two distinct categories were meant for casualties essentially requiring Hospital Ship for evacuation and those who failing availability of Hospital Ship could be accommodated in normal transport and the possibility of provisioning of another ship on the Bombay-Suez run was to be decided based upon the details.[94]

The *Guildford Castle* was about to be nominated as a dedicated Hospital Ship for the Indians on the Dardanelles-Alexandria run.

With the availability of a dedicated ship likely, the Surgeon General of the allied forces wrote to the Chief of General Staff that with the requirement of medical staff for other forces also being there in the similar time and space, it was difficult to source the staff for Indians from the force in Egypt. Accordingly, the following staff medical staff, specifically for the Indian casualties being transferred on the Dardanelles -Alexandria route was requested:[95]

10 Temporary Lieutenants: Indian Medical Service
16 Sub Assistant Surgeons
20 Ward Orderlies
40 Bearers, Army Bearer Corps
02 Hospital Store Keepers
02 Hospital Store Keeper Assistants
04 Cooks
04 Bhisties
12 Sweepers
20 Dhobies

The Hospital Ship *Guildford Castle* was detached from the Bombay-Suez run with effect from 1 August 1915. The orders for the ship to run on Dardanelles-Alexandria run specified that the ship is not well fitted for work in hot climates and the crew is not able to withstand the climate and another ship was nominated by the Secretary of War Office in London to replace *Guildford Castle* on the Bombay-Suez run.[96] Dedicated Medical cover for the Porter Corps and two Labour Corps proposed to be sent from India for operations in Dardanelles was also imperative. More so, after the setbacks of casualty treatment and evacuation during the initial stages of Dardanelles campaign had raised serious questions on the provision of medical cover for the landings and the subsequent operations.

The initial lot of Indian Porter Corps was ready to be dispatched from India by November 1915 for Dardanelles. The planning process for the dispatch of the Porter Corps had catered for the dedicated medical support.[97] The Army Headquarters expressed their inability to provide three Indian Medical Service officers for the Corps and suggested that in order to provide dedicated medical support to the troops, three temporary Lieutenants of Indian Medical Service (IMS) and recruited at home may be sent directly to the destination. As a result, the medical establishment earmarked to move along with the Porter Corps and the two Labour Corps included the following:

Sub Assistant Surgeons: 5
Ward Orderlies: 5
Bearers, Army Bearer Corps: 18
Sweepers: 6
Dhobies: 3
Cooks: 6
Bhisties: 3

By the mid of December 1915, the B Section of the 137th Field Ambulance had received orders for locking up and be prepared to embark. The hospital embarked from Suvla Bay on 16 December 1915. With very limited space available on board, the cooking space and accommodation was virtually not available. In addition, the transport did not set sail for the entire day and continued to be on harbour for the next three days. The hospital in a very short time frame available for embarkation was able to load their entire equipment on the transport. The tentage of the hospital was deliberately left erected at the peninsula to deceive the enemy about the actual presence of elements. The Section Hospital finally disembarked at Mudros on 23 December 1915, awaiting further directions.

POSTAL ARRANGEMENTS

Field Post Office (FPO) was an integral part of a brigade level formation on the eve of the Great War. When the 29th Indian Infantry Brigade sailed from Port Said for Gallipoli in April 1915, it was accompanied by the 34th Indian FPO. After the landings of the Indian Brigade, the Indian FPO continued to operate from the anchored ships due to the paucity of space on the shores. Though the troops of the Indian brigade were baptized with fire on their landing at the peninsula on 1 May 1915, with the limited availability of trawlers, the elements of the Indian FPO, were able to land on the peninsula only by 6 May 1915.

By this time, the Indian Brigade was operationally deployed as reserve to the limited offensives being launched by the 29th Division and the battalions of the Indian Brigade were operating with orders on a day to day basis. With no definite location of the Indian Brigade having been decided by this time, the FPO when it came on shore on 6 May, it was established at 'W' beach itself under the command of Lieutenant A.G. Gillespie. While the process of establishment of the FPO was on, the location was heavily shelled by the Turkish Artillery on the same day. Later on, it was realised that the Turkish Observation Officer had misinterpreted the flag of FPO with that of 'Divisional Commander' of the Allied forces.

Before 29th Indian Infantry Brigade was placed under the operational command of Force 'G', the Brigade with all its battalions was still under the operational control of IEF 'E', therefore, the FPO was also functioning under the overall operational control of Force 'E'. After the establishment of IEF 'G', for the operations on the peninsula, the operational control of FPO was shifted to the newly formed force. Along with this change, Base 'H' for the overall co-ordination of postal facilities for the Indian troops of Force 'G', was established at Alexandria on 28 June 1915. Three sub FPOs, to include the 65th FPO, 66th FPO and 325th FPO were established at different physical points on the peninsula to look after the postal needs of the Indian troops.

In an effort to provide better postal facilities for the Indian Brigade and its units, another echelon for the purpose of sorting and acting as Advanced Base Office for the four FPOs located at the peninsula, in the form of 33rd FPO was established at Mudros Island on 13 July 1915 and Lieutenant K.C. Sen was posted as Assistant Director to look after the functioning of all four Indian FPOs functioning on the peninsula and the office of the Assistant Director operated from the anchored transport HT *Arragon*. Before the establishment of Advance Base Office of the 33rd FPO at Mudros, the mail meant for the Indian battalions at the peninsula was directly being transported from Alexandria along with the mails of the British and Australian troops to the 34th Indian FPO, functional on Gallipoli. From the FPO, the mail of different Indian units was then collected by the respective unit post orderlies. The unit post orderlies were also employed by the units for multifarious tasks. Sometimes due to non-availability of these orderlies, it was not possible for the units to depute other troops for

J02443

FIGURE 65: INWARD MAIL AT ANZAC AWAITING
DISTRIBUTION TO THE UNITS[98]

collection of mail and during these times it was a staff of the Indian FPOs who himself used to deliver the mails to the respective units in the forward trenches. 'It often happened that on account of more pressing needs it was not possible to detail a post orderly for mails and on such occasions the Inspector would, at considerable risk to himself, personally deliver them to the units in the first line of trenches.'

The requirements of the censoring mandated that all mails from India meant for units at Gallipoli will be first consigned to Base 'H' at Alexandria, whereas the English and Australian mail was directly received at Mudros. After sorting at Alexandria, the mail was then re-directed to 33rd FPO, from where it was further directed to the Indian FPOs located on the peninsula. During the reverse process, the mail initiated from the peninsula by the Indian units was forwarded by the Indian FPOs on the peninsula to the FPO at Mudros for detailed sorting:

Mails received for delivery were accordingly scrutinized and those for 'in-effectives' returned at once to the Base Post Office with a suitable endorsement. Thus, each Field Post Office worked also as a Returned Letter Office for the units attached to it.

All mail meant for India and Egypt was further consigned to Base

FIGURE 66: AN INDIAN MULETEER PREPARES TO LEAVE A FIELD
POST OFFICE, HIS MULE HEAVILY LADEN WITH MAIL[99]

'H' by the 33rd FPO, whereas the mail for England was handed over
to the local British Base Army Post Office. The mail was transported
from Alexandria to Mudros through transports, where after being
sorted out, the postal bags were transferred through trawlers to the
four FPOs on the peninsula and this transfer primarily used to take
place under the cover of darkness:

The job was a most dangerous one as, apart from floating mines, the enemy
gunners kept the points of landing under intense Artillery fire by day and
night. The terrible dangers and difficulties encountered and cheerfully
endured by the gallant little postal band on Gallipoli cannot be exaggerated,
one relaxation being to test the efficacy of the fire of the Turkish snipers by
holding an envelope on a stick over a trench and having it (the envelope)
shot away. This usually caused much amusement and gave rise to a few side-
bets.

Each Indian FPO, in addition to the posted list of British and
Indian officers in the various units operating in the peninsula, was
also maintaining a list of Indian Rank and File, which had become
ineffective. Though an effort was made by the Indian FPOs to update
the list on a daily basis, the magnitude of casualties amongst the Indian
troops sometimes hindered the process. In addition, the continuous

arrival of reinforcements to replace the casualties further compounded the problems for the postal staff. But under the circumstances as obtained on the peninsula, during those fateful eight months, the postal staff of the Indian FPOs gave an excellent account of themselves, 'the Indian Post Office shared in all the danger and glory of Gallipoli and its Field Post Offices remained on the shell swept beach till the peninsula was finally evacuated at the end of the year, when the curtain on this splendid failure was rung down'. During the later stages of the operations at Gallipoli, the FPOs had also started accepting money orders meant for families back home from the Indian troops and, 'it is needless to say that a great boon was thus conferred on the Indian soldier who found a safe outlet for his petty savings'. For making the correspondence of the Indian troops easy with the families back in India, the system of free postage to India was also sanctioned by the C-in-C in India on 25 November 1914. 'With time two IEFs being deployed in the region, the provision was made applicable for the Indian troops serving with both the Expeditionary Forces, Force "E" & Force "F".'[100]

THE INDIAN LABOUR CORPS

An intrinsic study of the military recruitment pattern during this period in Punjab, brings forth an important inference. By the later part of the nineteenth century, the military recruitment had started to compete with other fast emerging modes of employment, which were not restricted to limited employment opportunities in the agricultural sector. The military recruitment as sepoys beyond doubt had retained the primacy of the primary choice of the rural youth, but the engagement as followers in the Army was not same as sepoys and was considered as the second rung. It was during this period that extensive laying of railway lines in the Punjab province was picking up. With maximum recruitment happening in the follower's trade, the Punjabi rural youth started preferring work in the avenues like laying of railways. Coupled with this, the near simultaneous development of Canal Colonies in the hinterland of Punjab was being considered as more honourable than the engagement as followers. The overwhelming dominance of the concept of martial races, the higher echelons of the Military in India were still not ready to explore other regions of India for the recruitment/ engagement of followers.

A large number of privileges bundled with the rank in the Army, facilitated in making the appointment of a sepoy very lucrative. But along with the passage of time and with the experience of many campaigns, Indian Army besides enrolling the combatants was also very much interested in engaging the services of a large number of non-combatants. Also known as followers, these non-combatants, in the roles of stretcher-bearers, mule-drivers, cooks, Bhisties (water-carriers) and other routine works for which combatants were not to be used, had performed excellently in active service, both in India and outside.

The followers formed the backbone of the functioning of military entity in the Colonial India. Though uniform and ration were provided to them during the active service, the issues with respect to the peace time provisioning had not been resolved for a long time. It was also increasingly being realised that the services provided by these non-combatants during the active service were invaluable and supported the contribution of the combatants in no less way. As the discussion progresses, it will be realised that these followers and mule drivers exposed themselves equally, if not more, during the deployment at Gallipoli and their contribution in the overall gambit of the operations, indeed has been denied its due.

The term 'follower' is very closely linked with the Coolie Corps, which in reference to the Colonial Indian Army has a long and chequered history. Long before the advent of the Great War, the Indian Coolie Corps had mobilised with the various expeditionary forces moving out from India. 'Coolie units accompanied many expeditionary forces sent from India: for instance, to Abyssinia (1868), China (1900), and Somaliland.'[101] Prior to the breakout of the First World War, Indian indentured labour was being sent to various parts of the empire. Though there was opposition to this system, the supply and demand dynamics of the labour, however, was instrumental in sustaining the system. 'This was a labour regime structured by five-year contracts which bound the emigrant to one employer at remarkably stagnant wages, and used a grid of penal provisions to enforce work and punish desertion.'[102] It was also being increasingly believed that the Indians being subjugated within the country by an Imperial empire were also very much impacted by the standing of the Indian indentured labour on the foreign shores. The instance was associated with serious implications in the newly formed colony of Australia. The settler colony was afflicted with the serious labour shortages. The human resources available to work on the land were much below the datum of land available. The initial enthusiasm to select only the 'right sort' of European immigrants and access to land had vastly outstripped the manpower available to work it. Schemes to attract only the 'right sort' of European immigrants was not providing the quantum of labour required. As the settler colony was envisaged as a 'penal settlement', the imminent completion of the convict obligations was going to further deteriorate the situation. The idea to import indentured labour from India to compensate for the serious labour shortage in Australia was directly based upon the experiences of getting labour from India by the Mauritian government in 1834. After a lot of discussion and overcoming the opposition from the supporters of 'White Australian' policy', there was some finally some forward movement on the proposal:

The Legislative Council also initially seemed open to the idea, and minutes of evidence were collected and published by the Committee on Immigration into New South Wales in 1837. As the debate progressed, however, concerns about the social, political and racial implications of importing non-white workers into the colony emerged, while the upsurge in humanitarian opposition to indenture among abolitionists in Britain from 1838 onwards soon soured the appetite of many colonists for the scheme. In the end only, a handful of Indian labourers were imported, and these by independent settlers without government subsidy or support.[103]

The concerns on the mistreatment of Indian labour in the colonies of the empire, whether indentured or otherwise, was a serious issue. The apparent equivalence of the indentured labour with the 'Coolie' or the 'Coolie Corps', meant for supporting the operations of the Indian Army was very natural under the circumstances. The decoupling of the concept of indentured labour from the Coolie Corps was very much required. 'The dilemma which therefore confronted government was how to distance the sending of labour "for military work overseas" from this now stigmatised system of migration.'[104]

To create a distinction between the two, an institutionalised system of formal enrolment of the Coolie Corps into the Indian Army was opened up. 'The formal enrolment of labour under the Indian Army Act and the label of "war service" not only served this purpose, but also facilitated the imposition of a blanket of censorship over conditions of work and treatment in Mesopotamia.'[105] Radhika Singha in her work has used a comprehensive term of 'Coolie Corps' for all the non-combatants being engaged during the active service. As per her, the terminology, besides introducing an element of non-combatant in the combative environs of war fighting, also brings about the generally backgrounded social fabric, particularly relevant in the colonial army and the colonial society, as obtained in India during the time.

A singular focus on the combatants in the First World War, cannot be in any way be studied in isolation from Punjab, whereas, an inclusion, however of the contribution of the Indian Labour Corps to include followers both private and public completely balances out a Punjab-centric approach. As one treads into the role and contribution of the followers in the First World War, one also moves away from the Punjab. United Provinces was instrumental in providing the second largest share of combatants in the Great War and were the singular highest contributor of the followers, both public and private in the war. Moving into the Gangetic valley, we find that the United Provinces supplied the largest number of non-combatants, and came second in terms of combatants.[106] The ratio between the combatants and non-combatants, for an all India figure of the time, is in the range of 1.65. But in spite of a general disinterest in the populace for engagement as followers, Punjab provided 3.59 combatants for every non-combatant, whereas the United Provinces were able to muster only 1.39 combatants for every non-combatant recruited. Slowly and steadily the recruitment for the Coolie Corps, at least in Punjab, had been delinked from the concept of the Martial Races.

While the role of combatants in the war has generally been adequately covered by the various military historians, both foreign and Indian, the significance of the role played by the followers in supporting these battles has largely been relegated to the imagination, with the role of IEF in Gallipoli being no exception. On the mob-

TABLE 30: SHARE OF EACH PROVINCE IN OBTAINING COMBATANT AND NON-COMBATANT RECRUITS UP TO THE ARMISTICE[107]

Province	Non-Combatants	Combatants	Total
Punjab	97,288	3,49,688	4,46,976
United Provinces	1,17,565	1,63,578	2,81,143
Madras	41,117	51,223	92,340
Bombay	30,211	41,272	71,483
Bengal	51,935	7,117	59,052
Bihar & Orissa	32,976	8,576	41,552
North West Frontier Province	13,050	32,181	45,231
Burma	4,579	14,094	18,673
Assam	14,182	942	15,124
Central Provinces	9,631	5,376	15,007
Ajmer-Merwara	1,632	7,341	8,973
Baluchistan	327	1,761	2,088
Total	4,14,493	6,83,149	10,97,642

ilisation of IEF 'G', all the battalions of the 29th Indian Infantry Brigade had moved with their share of public and private followers. The uniformity of the proportion of followers with each battalion, just like the proportion of combatants, was simply missing. As the catchment areas for the engagement of followers were different for each battalion, the differential might be attributed to the availability of followers with each battalion in November 1914:

TABLE 31 : STATE OF PUBLIC & PRIVATE FOLLOWERS IN THE 29TH INDIAN INFANTRY BRIGADE AS ON 30 APRIL 1915[108]

Unit	Public Followers	Private Followers	Total
HQ 29 Indian Infantry Brigade	1	5	6
14th Sikhs	24	9	33
1/6 Gurkhas	66	17	83
69th Punjabis	24	14	38
89th Punjabis	24	9	33
108 Indian Field Ambulance	165	7	172
S&T Corps	52	-	52
Total	356	61	417

Apart from 1/6 Gurkha, all other three Infantry battalions of the Indian Brigade had 24 public followers @ six followers per Double Company. The number of private followers in respect of the 1/6 Gurkha is also relatively on a higher side as compared to the other three battalions. The authorisation of public and private followers was however institutionalised in the same year, when the 29th Indian Infantry Brigade was fighting on Gallipoli. The Indian Army Order 351 of July 1915 laid down the limit of authorisation of followers, both Public and Private, for each Infantry battalion. The specific Army Order authorised 39 Public Indian followers and 48 Private Indian followers for each battalion. Thus, each Infantry battalion was authorised 87 followers. Each Double Company of the battalion was authorised to hold six public followers to include Chowdhri-one, Tindal-one, Lascar- three, and Weigh man-one. In addition, 14 bearers were authorised for the medical establishment in the battalion, thereby making a total of 38 followers for an Indian battalion. In addition, the shoemaker was authorised an assistant, thus totaling up to 39 public followers in the battalion. As far as private followers were concerned, each officer above the rank of subaltern was authorised two private followers each. The subalterns were authorised one public follower, except the Machine Gun officer who was authorised two followers. The Battalion Medical Officer was authorised three private followers.

By 31 August 1915, the campaign in Gallipoli had witnessed un-precedented casualties amongst the battalions of the Indian Infantry Brigade. While, the MEF and the IEF 'G' did not engage in any major battles on Gallipoli after this time, yet the military planners, both in England and in India ,were involved in hectic preparations to reinforce the troops on the peninsula. The impending winters at Gallipoli would require a large number of porters and coolies to sustain the inbound logistics. In addition, there was requirement of labour for the improvement of roads / tracks on the peninsula.

The likely non-availability of Greek and Egyptian labour along with the anticipated reduction in combatant manpower for the move-ment of stores and construction / improvement of roads / tracks, provided by the Indian battalions due to the impending winter, were instrumental in finalising a decision to induct an organised corps of Indian Coolies for these tasks in Gallipoli. In a communiqué dated

1 September 1915, the Secretary of State for India informed the Viceroy in the Army Department that an organised Corps of Indian Coolies from Punjab to serve with the IEF 'G' would be required.

The proposed force was to be employed for work on roads and railways along with the unloading on beaches. 'For work on roads and railways 2,000 Hazaras and for unloading on beaches 1,000 workers would be required.'[109] Drawing parallel with the supervisory staff of 'Spedding and Company', the company engaged for the construction of the Gilgit Road, the requirement for Gallipoli was of a semi-military organisation and provisions of recruitment were accordingly drafted. Working under operational conditions was anticipated for this Corps, 'Liability to work under fire must be included in the indentures of the men selected. All soldiers are required to fight and imbroglio goes on many beaches.'[110] The precondition of recruitment of 2,000 Hazaras only, for the proposed 'Corps of Indian Coolies', was difficult to manage by the Viceroy of the Army Department in India. The non-availability of Hazaras in view of the competing requirements of the same caste for recruitment of combatants in the Indian Army and the proposed homogeneous Mohammeden composition of the proposed Coolie Corps was quite apparent:

It is most improbable that we can procure anything like 2,000 Hazaras. Men of this class are required for the Indian Army and we are unable to obtain sufficient for that purpose. In our opinion, the policy of having such a homogeneous corps of Mohammedens to face the Turks is a most doubtful one, as the Hazaras are by no means free from objection to oppose their co-religionists.[111]

The response also made a mention of the withdrawal of 69th Punjabis and 89th Punjabis from the peninsula in the initial stages of the campaign attributable to the same reasons. 'We would like definite instructions as regards the permissible proportion of Mohammedens, in view of the fact that two Indian battalions with some of this class have already been removed from Force "G" by the War Office.'[112] The issue of competing requirements of both combatants and non-combatants from the similar catchment areas was a problem for the Army Department in India. As the war in Europe continued to rage, coupled with the ever-increasing requirement of reinforcements for the beleaguered Indian battalions, the twin conditions of state and class/caste were becoming difficult to comply. The Army Department was by no means capable to meet these twin conditions, at least for the proposed Indian Coolie Corps in Gallipoli.

The involvement of followers in some of the campaigns within the country, had highlighted the need to have both combatants and non-combatants from the Martial Races. A school of thought, therefore, was still of the view that it was imperative to retain the maintenance of 'martial, nature of these and therefore, required strict adherence to the state and class/ caste regulations for the recruitment of these'. Maybe it was due to this school, that a compromise in at least one condition for the raising of Coolie Corps was proposed by the Army Department:

If you desire, we can endeavour to raise 3,000 coolies both Mohammaden and Hindus from the Punjab provided that the classes acceptable by the War Office will not be the classes those enlisting for the Indian Army and the Supply and Transport Corps; we still require constant large recruiting for both these purposes and cannot afford competition.[113]

With the proposed divergence from the preconditions, the Army Department in India also highlighted the fact that it will not be possible to guarantee that, 'men of the classes we are prepared to endeavour to obtain for the Coolie Corps will, unarmed, stand fire or be suitable for such imbroglios as you describe'. The difficulties of meeting all the pre-conditions were increasingly being taken note of and was realised that the concerns of the Army Department were indeed genuine: As a result, the pre-condition of requirement of only Hazaras was relaxed, but it was reiterated that the recruitment for the Coolie Corps was to be realised from Punjab only. '3,000 Punjabis will do excellently, the proportion of Mohammedans to Hindus is quite unimportant.'[114]

However, the question of indemnity bond from the men recruited for the Corps was important and was impressed upon in no uncertain terms. The experience of the fighting in Gallipoli till now had brought out an important lesson about the casualties. The followers, both of the battalions and of Supply and Transport Corps had formed a significant component of casualties amongst Indian troops till date.

The War Office was not ready to negotiate this aspect and reiterated the requirement of indemnity. 'It should be noted that the essential condition is that the men are liable to come under fire and must be willing to take this risk. It is essential that the organisation should be of a semi-military nature. We are unable to give any guarantee that the men will not come under fire.'[115]

The followers, both private and public, had played a commendable role in the Gallipoli. The casualty analysis of the Indian troops in the last chapter of the book succinctly highlights this oft ignored fact. The followers were an inseparable part of the functioning of the Infantry battalions and Artillery Batteries on the peninsula. These personnel demonstrated as much esprit-de-corps, if not more as the fighting men in every combat situation. 'Humble men they were, doing humble work, but proudly maintaining a high standard of their work. Most of them seem to have no civil background.'

PAY AND ALLOWANCES

To compensate for difficult living conditions outside of the cantonments, all Indian army soldiers were entitled for *batta* (allowance). The element of *batta* was invariably a pre-decided percentage of the monthly pay of each soldier. Prior to the mobilisation for the Great War, the system of *batta* was in force and was being drawn by the rank and file of the Indian Army for the duration of the active service. A soldier was eligible for the grant of *batta* from the date of leaving a cantonment in India and was applicable till the date of arrival back to the cantonment.

On mobilisation of the various IEFs in August 1914, a case was taken up by the Secretary of State for India with the Viceroy (Army Department) that the Indian officers and men should be granted an European Field Allowance of Rs. 15 and 3 per month, a demand, which was later on reduced to Rs. 10 and 2 respectively. After much deliberations, the increase of pay for the Indian troops of IEF 'A' was notified through the release of Indian Army Order 429 of 1915. Since, the IEF 'A' was deployed in the most sensitive sector of the time, hence the increase of pay and allowances for the Indian troops of the force was also notified for the same. As IEF 'D', was not deployed along the Western Front, it was left out from the proposed increase. On the other hand, all the regular Indian troops serving at Dardanelles as part of IEF 'D' were being provided with a field allowance at the rate of 25 per cent of the authorised pay. The aspect of discrimination in the Field Service Allowance for the Indian troops deployed at France and in other Expeditionary Forces was a vexed one and took a lot of time and correspondence to resolve. At the time of deinduction of IEF 'G', it was possible to resolve only a portion of the problem.

The office of the Adjutant General in India informed GOC, Canal Defences, Ismailia in August 1915 that the proposal to grant to the troops serving with the IEF 'G' the increase of pay notified in the Indian Army Order 429 of 1915 for Indian combatants and non-combatants of IEF 'A' is under consideration by the Secretary of State for India. In addition, with a large number of casualties being suffered by the Indian troops, the casualties being dispatched to Egypt and Malta for treatment and recuperation also were being declined the grant of the subject field allowance. In order to ensure the universal implementation of the provision and to ensure that the casualties under treatment and are likely to reinforce the battalions struggling with the reduced bayonet strength are given their due, the Secretary of State for Indian informed the Viceroy (Army Department) in December 1915, that War Office has agreed to the contention and henceforth all Dardanelles casualties sent to Egypt and Malta will continue to receive the allowance so long as they form part of the MEF.[116]

Another issue, with respect to the pay and allowances of the Indian troops at Gallipoli, came to the fore when 1/4 Gurkha joined the IEF 'G' from IEF 'A' in France. The Indian troops of some of the Indian Mule Corps who had earlier been moved from France to Dardanelles were also in similar situation. As a consequence of the re-deployment of 1/4 Gurkha from the IEF 'A' to the IEF 'G', the troops of 1/4 Gurkha and Indian Mule Corps were being denied the grant of additional pay granted by the Indian Army Order 429 of 1915. The GOC of the 29th Indian Infantry Brigade took up a representation with the GOC of Canal Defences regarding this anomaly.[117] The representation underscored the need to avoid the financial hardships to the Indian troops on being transferred from France to the Dardanelles as technically the troops were still serving in Europe only with the change in the 'sphere of operations'.

Secretary of State for India in his correspondence with the Viceroy (Army Department) in November 1915 again reiterated the issue that, with Indian troops now being transferred from France to the Dardanelles, the resolution of the matter is important. He further suggested that the ibid allowance should be made general and should not be linked with a particular force. Due to the sensitivities involved, the withdrawal of the subject allowance was strictly not recommended:

Withdrawal might have bad effect, but if continued, I suppose allowance should be extended to all Indian troops serving in Force 'D' and perhaps elsewhere out of India, but without retrospective effect. Could this allowance be made general instead of ordinary batta?[118]

The solution to the problem had become convoluted and the military planners had to look at both the angles now. The Viceroy underscored the dilemma when he wrote to the Secretary of State in India, 'withdrawal of allowance from troops already in receipt would cause grave discontent. On the other hand, to continue the allowance to troops transferred from Europe, while withholding it from those with whom they will in future serve, would provoke grave and just discontent on the part of the latter.'[119] With troops in France being granted allowance, substitution of allowance with the *batta* would have in certain cases resulted in actual reduction in the emoluments and 'this would practically defeat the objective of allowance besides affording grounds for discontent'.[120]

As a middle path the recommendation of the Viceroy, included the uninterrupted continuance of the field allowance to the troops of IEF 'A' and its extension with effect from 1 December 1915 to all the Indian troops serving with all the IEFs. For the Indian non-combatants, the proposal recommended, restriction of the field allowance to only those non-combatants drawing Rs. 100 and less a month. The recommendations at last were able to resolve up to some extent the long outstanding anomalies in the field service allowances of the Indian troops of IEF 'G'.

The question of the clothing allowance and the disposal of the kit and personal belongings of the deceased Indian soldiers of various

Expeditionary Forces also impacted the Indian troops at Gallipoli. The IEF 'G' with a large number of fatal casualties was the most affected due to the lack of clear directions. By 31 September 1915, the IEF 'G' had suffered severe number of fatal casualties, and the clarity on the issue of the disposal of kits had still not been forthcoming. After a lot of discussions and deliberations, in October 1915, detailed instructions with respect to the disposal of kits and personal belongings of the deceased Indian soldiers on the peninsula were promulgated. According to these, the disposal of kits was to be carried out at the discretion of GOC of the force and the proceeds of the same were to be deposited in the Government fund. In the case of Indian ranks and permanent followers, who had drawn clothing allowance in peace time and who had completed three years of service by the date of death, the heirs to the estate were to receive from Government of India, reimbursement at the following rates:

Indian Officers (Combatants):	Rs. 60
Non-Commissioned Officers & Men:	Rs. 30
Indian Officers (S & T Corps):	Rs. 45
Non-Commissioned Officers & Men (S &T Corps):	Rs. 25
Army Bearer Corps & Army Hospital Corps, Lascars & Followers:	Rs. 12

The provisions of the above-mentioned promulgation were not made applicable for the temporary followers, who were provided with outfits by the Government on field service and hence were not eligible to receive any compensation. All the articles of sentimental value and money of the deceased Indian troops were to be dispatched to the respective depots, from where it was to be further transported to the respective heirs.

The Indian Medical Service (IMS) played an exemplary role while serving with the IEF 'G' on the peninsula. Initially the medical personnel deployed with the 29th Indian Infantry Brigade had no separate instructions for the payment of field allowance. In an order of February 1915, the Viceroy office in India had authorised the grant of active service pay to the personnel of the IMS deployed with the Expeditionary Forces. The promulgation, provided for the following rates of active service pays and field allowance:

TABLE 32 : RATES OF ACTIVE SERVICE PAY AND FIELD ALLOWANCE
OF INDIAN MEDICAL SERVICE[121]

Appointment	Pay (Rs./ Month)	Field Allowance (Rs./Month)	Total (Rs./Month)
1st Grade Sub Assistant Surgeon	70	10	80
2nd Grade Sub Assistant Surgeon	50	5	55
3rd Grade Sub Assistant Surgeon	35	5	40
Ward Orderly	11	1-2-0	12-2-0
Cooks	10	5	15
Water Carrier	10	5	15
Sweeper	8	4	12

As discussed in the earlier section, the Indian Labour Corps was being recruited for the deployment on the peninsula as part of IEF 'G'. The concept, being the first of kind initiative, required detailed deliberations and the issue of instructions on every singular aspect of the Corps. Though the Corps did not witness the deployment on the peninsula, and served in the other theatres of the war, but the proposed pay scale for the troops of the Labour Corps included the following:

TABLE 33: PROPOSED PAY SCALE OF INDIAN LABOUR CORPS[123]

Appointment	Pay Scale (Rs/Month)
Head Clerk	100
Second Clerk	80
Quarter Master Clerks (Pay & Pension)	80
Pay Clerks	50
Store Keeper	60
Writer	60
Havildar	40
Naik	35
Carpenter	50
Smith	50
Hammerman	25
Bellows Boy	20

Mason	40
Labourer	20
Bhisti	12
Sweeper	12
Langri	12

The specialised task of the Corps in the intended area of operations required specialised scales of pay and allowances. An analysis of the pay scales of the Indian Labour Corps reveals that, carpenter and smithsmen, a traditionally higher skills job, were given higher scales of pay than the basically supervisory type of role envisaged for Havildars and Naiks in the Labour Corps. Pay and allowances of the soldiers of the Indian battalions on the peninsula were an important factor in the pain, misery and death being suffered by these brave men from India. The economic conditions of the time, being what they were, a career in the Army definitely provided with prestige and means to sustain the vicious cycle of droughts and drudgery.

PRACTICE OF RELIGION

As discussed in the Chapter 2, the disciplined life in the Army provided a very balanced outlet to the Sikh troops to express, maintain and celebrate the spirit of Khalsa. The initial arrival of Sikhs on the peninsula in May 1915 was watched with much apprehension by the Turks. The appearance with the unique religious symbols was a source of much dread for the defenders. The reverberation of the battlefield with the religious cries of, *Jo Bole So Nihal, Sat Sri Akal* on 4 June 1915 during the Third Battle of Krithia almost achieved a folklore status.

On Gallipoli, while the bravery of the Sikhs has been the part of a folklore, the administrative requirements of Sikh troops were equally simple and elementary. It is fact that, a Sikh being a devoted disciple of his faith takes an ultimate pride in his outwardly appearance, with which he has been anointed by his master. Sustained fighting on the peninsula, without a break significantly impacted the routine of his maintenance of the semblance. Continuous engagements with the enemy on the peninsula resulted in no time for the troops to look after their physical appearances and 'their long hair and long beards had become gray and grubby with the dust and dirt of the trenches'.[124] The maintenance of the facial hair is a matter of great pride for a Sikh and with limited availability of water for drinking and that too on a reduced scale, the Sikhs had virtually no means to maintain their outwardly appearances. In those times, the primary mean of maintenance of beard was either clarified butter or *sarson* (mustard) oil. With no possibility of availability of clarified butter, the only alternative available to the Sikhs for maintaining the beards was *sarson* oil. Therefore, the primary and only request from the men in the battalion, as also highlighted by Reginald Savory in his memoirs was the *sarson* oil, 'their chief request was for *sarson*-oil, with which to anoint their long hair and their beards'.[125]

As the time passed on the peninsula, the limited availability of *sarson* oil available with the troops was exhausted. With no provisions or facilities for procurement of the commodity through own sources, the Sikhs were totally dependent on the official supply channels for the provisioning. In addition, the supply of local herb *reetha* (Indian soap-berry/wash-nut), an essential commodity for washing of hair back home in Punjab was also scarce. Both, *reetha* and the *sarson* oil were a must for a Sikh to take care of the facial hair. Being aware of the acute requirements of these two commodities, the Maharaja of Patiala in May 1915 offered the essentials to be supplied to the Sikh troops, serving in the various Expeditionary Forces to include:

Khaki Shirts of Cawnpore Twill:	10,000
Short Underwear for Sikh Troops, *kachha* (another essential for Sikhs):	10,000
Towels:	10,000
Combs and Ornamental Swords (*kirpans*):	10,000
Religious Books (pocket size):	2,000
Reetha (Indian soap-berry/wash-nut):	worth Rs 1,500
Sarson oil:	worth Rs 700

These commodities were dispatched through a goods train on 10 June 1915 to the Embarkation Commandant, Bombay. The supplies included, '1489 tins containing sweetmeats (*panjiri* @ 2 lbs per Indian soldier), 195 drums of *sarson* oil, 110 bags of *reetha* and three boxes containing books, combs and *kirpans*'. In April 1915, the Maharaja of the Princely State of Jind had also supplied 10,000 combs for the Sikh soldiers at the front, along with 1,000 Sikh prayer books, 'to be distributed among the sick and wounded'.

The overwhelming proportion of the Sikh troops serving in the various Expeditionary Forces across the world required facilitation for maintaining their religious connect. Preservation of the religious connect was imperative during the prolonged deployment of these troops in the harsh and difficult terrains. A Sikh deployed far away from home for the motherland takes inspiration form the religious congregations. The scattered deployment of the battalion had not allowed holding and conduct of central religious functions on a regular basis. Even before the Gallipoli landings, a need was felt to procure the pocket sizes Sikh religious books for the Sikh troops deployed on the Canal defences. With there being no possibility of sourcing of scriptures from Egypt, on 5 January 1915, one hundred copies of Sikh scriptures for the Sikh troops stationed in Egypt were demanded by the Secretary of State for India from the Viceroy.[126]

The extensive pace of operations being conducted by the 14th Sikhs was slowly denuding the religious connect of the troops with their holy book, *The Guru Granth Sahib*. A series of operations at the peninsula, in which the battalion had participated, the daily and the weekly rituals of the Gurdwara (Sikh temple) had been overtaken by the operational exigencies. After the August offensive, while at the defences at the new location, the troops were able to install their holy book in a make shift Gurdwara along the rear trenches. 'A Gurdwara (Sikh temple), was set up in a dug-out in the reserve trenches, and there the men could come to worship before the Guru Granth Sahib, their Holy Book, with the regimental *granthi*, or priest, in attendance'.[127]

The battalion celebrated the birthday of the first guru of the sect, Guru Nanak Dev on 21 Nov 1915, while being in the trenches only. The British officers of the battalion were invited by all ranks of the battalion to participate in the festivities:

on special occasion of the birthday of Guru Nanak Dev Ji, we British officers were invited to attend and, leaving our boots at the door and entering in stockinged feet, were allotted places in the front row, taking our part in the service and our share of the holy *Karah Parshad*. It was a family existence.[128]

The Sikh troops of 14th Sikhs, the Mountain Batteries and the Mule Corps had given an excellent account of themselves on the battlefields of peninsula. These Sikhs while battling the enemy under most trying conditions had also made sure to maintain their religious connect as mandated in Sikhism.

REPORTING OF CASUALTIES

When the IEF, comprising troops of the 29th Indian Infantry Brigade had embarked for Egypt in the first week of November 1914, the system of reporting of casualties had not been institutionalised. The sheer magnitude of casualties suffered by the Indian Brigade on Gallipoli in 1915 overwhelmed the casualty reporting system. Considering the magnitude, number of agencies and the distances involved, a reasonably robust system developed over a time for reporting the casualty returns. With the involvement of a number of troops of Infantry battalions, belonging to different units and sub units, majority of them joining as reinforcements, the correctness and authentication of details was a colossal task. The two Mountain Artillery Batteries from India, which were first to land, had their composition changed rapidly with the arrival of fresh reinforcements.

The eight Mule Corps operating with full complement of drivers and mules, spread in the different parts of the peninsula further complicated the data collation. Besides, these eight Mule Corps, detachments from 22 Mule Corps also were deployed on the peninsula in varying strengths of drivers and mules. In addition, mule transport from Gwalior, Bharatpore and Indore Imperial Service Transport Corps with different compositions also found themselves on the peninsula.

The previous works on the subject have provided a general magnitude of substance of participation of the Indian troops at Gallipoli along with the details of casualties in terms of killed only. A detailed and deeper analysis of the Indian participation at Gallipoli acknowledges the quantum of Indian casualties which were wounded or died of natural reasons / diseases inflicted during their tenure on Gallipoli. Before coming on to estimate the Indian troops killed, wounded or died due to the natural causes at the peninsula, it would be in order to discuss about the system of reporting of casualties, which was in vogue at that time.

When the Indian Brigade formed part of the Canal defences in Egypt in December 1914, the system of casualty returns was in infancy. With the operations of the Brigade in Qantara still some time away, the initial casualty returns reported about the casualties due to natural causes. On 12 December 1914, the GOC, Canal Defences, Ismailia in Egypt had intimated the Chief of General Staff in India about the death of Sepoy Gujar Singh of 69th Punjabis on 1 December due to Malaria.[129] An analysis of the subsequent returns, reveal that with the increase in number of casualties of the 29th Indian Brigade due to action or natural causes, the details started becoming sketchy. The casualty details did not have regimental numbers in the returns, resulting in problems for the respective Depots back in India to reconcile the details, leading to the confusion about the actual details of casualties. The problem was further compounded by the similar names of the Indian soldiers, a system more applicable to the Sikh and Gurkha troops and in case of the 29th Indian Brigade, all the battalions of the Brigade happened to be comprising of troops, which were either Sikhs or Gurkhas. The regimental numbers, in these cases were the only definite source which could differentiate between the similar looking names. In one of such instances, when the Regimental Number of a casualty was not specified, the OC of Depot of 14th Sikhs in India, on 6 February 1915, inquired from the Adjutant General in India about two similar names mentioned in the casualty return. 'Two Jemadars Partab Singh's in Regiment - One in "D" Coy, One in "E" Coy. Please inquire which casualty is referred to.'[130] Based on the above, the office of the Commander-in-Chief in India, had further inquired about the status of the casualty from the GOC, Egypt.

The agencies in Egypt, which were responsible for compiling the details of casualties, were classifying all the injured as 'wounded', without any further division based upon the severity of the wounds. Without any details of the degree of severity, the AGs Branch in India was in dark about the status of wounded soldiers' status with respect to joining back of duty or deinduction from the deployment areas. It also had adverse cascading effect on the planning for reinforcements from India to replace the severely injured casualties. To have a better visibility of the status and degree of severity of wounds, the Chief of General Staff in India asked the GOC, Canal Defences that, 'in future when reporting casualties please specify, whether men are dangerously wounded, severely wounded or slightly wounded'.[131] Another peculiar problem being faced during the initial stages of the deployment of IEF 'G' with respect to the returns was that the consolidated returns were being forwarded to India, with the casualties not being classified as per date of occurrence of incident, but rather were being consolidated over a period of time. In one such telegram dated 4 February 1915, the GOC, Egypt intimated the Commander-in-Chief, in India about the casualties of 89th Punjabis, having occurred at Qantara.

As the military personnel entrusted with the responsibility of preparing and reconciling the casualty returns in Egypt were not familiar with the typical rank structure of the Indian Army and more so when the same rank had different connotations in Sikh and Gurkha Battalions, the rank of Sepoy and Rifleman were often exchanged. To correct the anomaly, the OC of Depot of 2/10 Gurkhas in India had written to AG in India to correct the discrepancy, 'in all cases already reported, rank should be Rifleman and not Sepoy'. During the deployment of the 29th Indian Infantry Brigade at Canal Defences,

TABLE 34: CASUALTY RETURN OF THE 89TH PUNJABIS[132]

Number	Rank	Name	Casualty
2217	Sepoy	Bachan Singh	Killed
1232	Sepoy	Lakim Singh	Killed
2607	Sepoy	Bachan Singh	Killed
2583	Sepoy	Sucha Singh	Died of Wounds
2281	Lance Naik	Banea Singh	Died of Wounds
2150	Nk	Mohammed Khan	Severely Wounded
1187	Lance Naik	Kishan Singh	Severely Wounded
2109	Sepoy	Kirpal Singh	Severely Wounded
2514	Lance Naik	Harnam Singh	Severely Wounded
2286	Sepoy	Wazir Singh	Severely Wounded
2451	Sepoy	Hari Singh	Severely Wounded

the casualties due to natural reasons were also affecting the operational efficiency of the Indian battalions. As early as 8 December 1914, the casualties not related to action were reported from the Indian battalions. The telegram dated 26 January 1915 initiated from the office of GOC, Canal Defences, Egypt to the Chief of General Staff in India intimated about these casualties.

As a result of all the efforts to reduce the shortcomings in the system of reporting of casualties, the subsequent casualty returns had started including all possible details about the casualty in the return. This resulted in the development of a better and an efficient system of reporting of casualties. A memorandum[133] from the GOC of Canal Defences addressed to the Chief of General Staff in India, giving

TABLE 35: PHYSICAL CASUALTIES OF THE 29TH INDIAN
INFANTRY BRIGADE

Number	Rank	Name	Unit	Casualty	Reason
777	Rifle man	Radharaman Rai	2/10 Gurkhas	Died	Pneumonia
222	Sepoy	Sarup Singh	Patiala Infantry	Died	Rheumatic Fever
1507	Driver	Kakee	7th Mule Corps	Died	Pleurisy

Adapted from casualty database by the author.

detailed information about the casualties can be termed as near ideal.

Similarly, a well-defined system for reporting the casualties not attributed to the action in battlefield had also developed. The details for the non-operational and operational casualties had also started including the granular details. A series of telegrams[134] from the GOC, Canal Defences to the Chief of General Staff in India had incorporated these finer details about the casualties.

The OCs of the respective Depots, though not directly in contact with the GOC of the Canal defences, developed a system of inquiring about the details of the casualties from the office of the AG in India. This was particularly more relevant in respect of the casualties which have been reported as missing or required further corroboration of details in respect to the Regimental Numbers. A telegram dated

TABLE 36 : DETAILED CASUALTY RETURN (OPERATIONAL) OF THE 29TH INDIAN INFANTRY BRIGADE[135]

Number	Rank	Name	Unit	Casualty	Date	Type	Location
1078	Rifleman	Karka Gurung	1/6 Gurkhas	Wounded	26 Jan. 1915	Bullet, Scalp Right	Qantara
3386	Sepoy	Mangal Singh	14th Sikhs	Killed	28th Jan. 1915	Killed	Qantara
346	Lance Naik	Nania Thapa	1/6 Gurkhas	Wounded	28th Jan. 1915	Bullet Shoulder, Slight	Qantara

TABLE 37 : DETAILED CASUALTY RETURN (NON-OPERATIONAL) OF THE 29TH INDIAN INFANTRY BRIGADE[136]

Number	Rank	Name	Unit	Casualty	Date	Type	Location
112	Sepoy	Hira Singh	Patiala Infantry	Sick	10 Feb. 1915	Enteric Fever	No. 8 Indian Gen Hospital, Cairo
305	Rifleman	Joglal Rai	2/10 Gurkhas	Dead	9 Feb. 1915	Died of Wounds	No. 8 Indian Gen Hospital, Cairo
216	Sepoy	Prem Singh	Patiala Infantry	Dead	1 Mar. 1915	Dysentry	No. 8 Indian Gen Hospital Cairo

11 October 1915, by the the OC of the Depot of 2/10 Gurkhas and addressed to the AG in India asked about the status of two soldiers of the battalion:[137]

The following casualties have been reported from the Officer Commanding 2/10 Gurkha, from Mediterranean through Regimental Battalion Orders, but nothing has been heard from you as yet about these casualties - No. 783 Rifleman Kirpadhoj Rai, A Company, died from acute peritonitis on 23rd July in No. 108 Indian Field Ambulance and No. 2529 Rifleman Birkabahdur Limbu, A Company, killed in action on 7th August 1915.[138]

The battalions of the Indian Infantry Brigade, engaged on Gallipoli also intimated their respective Depots about the casualties suffered, through the respective Regimental Battalion Orders. As discussed above, these telegrams also solicited information from the AG about the status of the soldiers reported as missing in the previous correspondence. In such a telegram,[139] the OC of the Depot of 2/10 Gurkha asked the office of the AG about the status of almost 30 soldiers of the Battalion, reported as missing in the previous Regimental Battalion orders.

With almost 4,000 plus personnel of the Indian Mule Corps on the peninsula, coupled with very frequent turnover due to casualties and reinforcements, it was getting very difficult to reconcile the details of the casualties amongst these troops. The situation was further compounded by the fact that these troops belonged to a mix of Corps and Cadres. The system of allocation of Regimental Numbers to the troops of both the types of entities was different. There were eight Mule Corps with full complement of troops and mules, supporting the operations of the 29th Indian Infantry Brigade. In addition, there were detachments from 22 different Mule Corps along with elements from three Imperial Services Transport Corps. As a result, for the initial months of Indian troops being on the peninsula, the system of reporting of casualties in respect of troops and followers of the Indian Mule Corps suffered from serious handicaps. In order to resolve the difficulties being encountered, the Central Casualty Bureau in Simla wrote to the 3rd Echelon in October 1915 about the changes recommended in the policy of reporting of casualties in respect of Indian Mule Corps. 'When reporting casualties amongst Indian personnel of Supply and Transport Corps and followers, please state station of entertainment or division from which proceeded on service, in addition to number allotted at station of entertainment.'[140] For the troops and followers of the Army Bearer Corps and Army Hospital Corps, it was directed that details of number of peace company to which belonging in addition to field unit with which serving, should invariably be forwarded.

Though the details of British officers of the 29th Indian Infantry Brigade and its battalions, who were admitted to the various hospitals in Egypt subsequent to the injuries sustained or due to sickness are available in records, the details with respect to the Indian troops injured and subsequently admitted to the Hospitals in Egypt have been difficult to locate. The Commander of the 29th Indian Brigade was admitted in a hospital in Malta on 23 September 1915 due to the reasons of Diarrhea and debility, details of which are available in the records. In the absence of the details of the Indian troops, with respect to admission and discharge from these hospitals, it is a difficult proposition to corroborate the details of sick and wounded Indian troops as available in the casualty appendices of the National Archives.

The nominated agency for reporting the casualties of the force 'G' back to India was the GOC, Canal Defences, Ismailia. Due to the non-availability of the updated nominal rolls with the office of GOC, sometimes the details forwarded were not correct and this also resulted in the generation of additional correspondence, between Canal defences and the Central Casualty Bureau in India, in form of errata's and corrigenda. A relatively large number of these corrigenda do not facilitate the near real measure of the quantum of the casualties suffered by the Indian troops in the Gallipoli campaign. For instance, in a Telegram dated 30 October, the GOC, Canal Defences, Ismailia issued corrections to the details of casualties reported earlier. '1662 Junima, 1st Mule Corps erroneously reported died of wounds was invalided on Hospital Ship 'Madras', 26th September. 1-4th Gurkha casualties reported as received cannot be verified pending receipt nominal rolls here.'[141]

The initial period of engagement of the Indian Brigade on the peninsula was heavy in terms of suffering of casualties. Though, the Indian troops were in reserve for the first and second battles of Krithia, their involvement in the third battle for Krithia was monumental. The casualties suffered by them were also equally monumental if not more. With a flurry of telegrams intimating the Commander-in-Chief in India about the severity of the casualties, it was very clear to the military planners in India that an immediate action was needed to supplement the vacuum created by the quantum of casualties was required. While simultaneous actions were initiated for the provisioning of reinforcements for the embattled Indian battalions at Gallipoli, the OC Depots of the battalions in India and the office of Commander-in-Chief in India went into an overdrive in the immediate aftermath of the third battle of Krithia to confirm the status of the casualties. The telegram dated 8 June 1915, asked about the status of 29 troops of 14th Sikhs from the GOC, Canal Defences, Ismailia.[142] Prior to this telegram, the OC Depot of the 14th Sikhs at Multan had already forwarded a query to the AG in India regarding the correct Regimental Number (3234) of Sepoy Mit Singh of the battalion, in lieu of 2,234 being intimated.[143] In a detailed reply, the details of these casualties were forwarded by the GOC of the Canal Defences, Ismailia to the office of the Commander-in-Chief in India (Table 38):[144]

When the Indian battalions of IEF 'G' had mobilised from India in October 1914, there were a good number of private servants from India who had accompanied the British officers of these battalions. As most of these servants were personally arranged by the respective officers, the records of these were rarely available centrally by the concerned battalions or in India. So, when the casualties occurred in respect of the personal servants, the specific details of these were not available either with the records in India or with the respective battalions. But the casualty bureaus in India continued to ask the details from the respective battalions, 'Reference your M-70 of 5th June, please wire name of officer whom syce Sukhlal served and station of enrolment of syce.

As per existing provisions the injured troops of the Indian battalions from the peninsula were being invalided to India. When these men reached their respective villages, people from nearby villages also visited them and enquired about their relatives serving outside the country. The news about the injuries sustained by the relative often sparked intense anxiety about the status of casualty. With no other

TABLE 38: CASUALTIES OF THE 14TH SIKHS AS REPORTED BY
THE GOC, CANAL DEFENCES[145]

Regimental Number	Name	Details (15 June 1915)
4234	Chanan Singh	Severely Wounded
4209	Harnam Singh	Wounded
3886	Arjan Singh	Slightly Wounded
3698	Pakhar Singh	Severely Injured
2414	Battan Singh	Slightly Wounded
4039	Sarwan Singh	Severely Wounded
3260	Dalip Singh	Severely Injured
4467	Bachan Singh	Severely Injured
4471	Chur Singh	Slightly Wounded
4348	Arjan Singh	Severely Injured
3783	Dasaunda Singh	Slightly Wounded
4142	Sher Singh	Slightly Wounded
4468	Harbaksh Singh	Invalided to India
4566	Ganga Singh	Slightly Wounded
Subadar	Tilok Singh	Slightly Wounded
Jemadar	Partab Singh	Severely Wounded
4382	Pall Singh	Died of Wounds
4574	Sant Singh	Died of Wounds
3234	Mit Singh	Invalided to India
3835	Bhola Singh	Slightly Injured
2847	Nihal Singh	Severely Injured
4450	Nikka Singh	Severely Injured
4135	Gajindar Singh	Severely Injured
4305	Ranjit Singh	Slightly Wounded
3799	Kartar Singh	Slightly Wounded
4474	Bhagwan Singh	Slightly Wounded
3865	Hari Singh	Slightly Wounded
4271	Bakhsh Singh	Missing
4225	Arjan Singh	Severely Injured

means available to find the status, the next of kin had no other option but to visit the Depot of the Battalion. The OC Depot also had no wherewithal to confirm the status of the casualty and had to ask the office of the Commander-in-Chief in India or the Central Casualty Bureau. In one such correspondence, the OC Depot of 87th Punjabis in Dera Ismail Khan had requested the Central Casualty Bureau:

Make further inquiries on Number 2435 Sepoy Uttam Singh attached to 14th Sikhs as some men and a Havildar of this unit, who have returned from unit to villages injured, have informed that this man died in their presence as they were being taken from Dardanelles to Alexandria. They state that he received a bad bomb wound in the Dardanelles and died from the effects on the ship. The man's father has been told this story by some men in his village and he is anxious to find out whether it is correct.[146]

The casualties of the Imperial Service Troops when invalided to India due to injuries or any other reasons were dispatched to the Depot of the battalion, regular or Imperial Service, to whom they were attached during the operations. The ration requirements of these troops while in field were being taken care by the battalion with which they were attached, but when back in India, the Depot of the battalion with which they were attached in field, did not provide them with rations or warrants for the return journey to their home states.

This anomaly in the system was creating great difficulties and inconvenience to the Imperial Service Troops who had returned from active service. In July 1915, a proposal was mooted by the GOC, Canal Defences, Egypt to the QMG in India, wherein it was proposed that Imperial Service Troops (IST) when invalided to India due to injuries or any other reasons should be dispatched from respective Ports of Embarkation straight to the Headquarters of their units in India rather than to the Depots of the battalions, with which they were attached while in active service. The merit of the case found favour with the QMG in India and the ISTs returning to India started moving straight to their respective battalions in India. In order to ensure the implementation of order with immediate, the orders were passed to Commandants of Ports of Embarkation at Bombay and Karachi.

The Aftermath

To defend the Suez Canal and to allow uninterrupted flow of maritime traffic, IEF 'F', comprising of the 10th Indian Division and the 11th Indian Division was raised in Egypt in 1914. Besides, these two divisions, some additional formations of the Indian Army, to include 22nd (Lucknow) Brigade from the 8th Lucknow Division without their British battalions and an Imperial Service Cavalry Brigade, also formed part of the force. The 10th Indian Division comprised of three Indian Infantry Brigades, which were raised along with the division.

After performing the task of defence of the Canal, the 10th Indian Division was disbanded in 1916 and the three formations under it were re distributed to other divisions. 28th Indian Infantry Brigade of the formation, in 1915 was assigned to 7th (Meerut) division. The 29th Infantry Brigade in 1915 took part in the Gallipoli campaign as an independent formation and later on was disbanded in 1917. The 30th Indian Infantry Brigade of 10th Indian Division was assigned to 6th (Poona) Division in September 1915.

On the raising of 29th Indian Infantry Brigade, for the subsequent tasking in the defences of Suez Canal, four infantry battalions were allotted to the formation. As discussed earlier, 14th Sikhs from Peshawar, 69th Punjabis from Jhelum, 89th Punjabis from Dinapore and 1/6 Gurkha Rifles had joined the formation from Abbottabad. After the withdrawal of the formation from the peninsula by the end of 1915, the battalions of the formations gradually were reallocated to different formations. 14th Sikhs was detached to Tor in February 1916 and later on was transferred to Bushire in May 1916. 1/4 Gurkhas was allotted to the 31st Indian Brigade of 10th Indian Division for the Canal defences in December 1915, whereas 2/10 Gurkhas had also joined the Canal defences in January 1916. 1/5 Gurkhas and 1/6 Gurkhas left 29th Indian Infantry Brigade in February 1916 to join 1st Peshawar Brigade of 1st Peshawar Division in February 1916.

NOTES

1. I. Hamilton (2022), *Gallipoli Diary*, 2 vols. 1920. Generic, p. 287, vol. II, Library of Alexandria, Egypt.

2. War Diary, Army Headquarters, India, IEFG, vol. I, 21 to 31 July 1915. National Archives of India.
3. 14th Sikhs Album.
4. Website Gurkha Brigade Association.
5. 14th Sikhs Album.
6. B. Gudmundsson (2005), *The British Expeditionary Force 1914–15* (Battle Orders) (1st edn.), Osprey Publishing, Oxford.
7. 14th Sikhs Album.
8. Ibid.
9. Ibid.
10. W.T. Cowley, RAOC, Suvla Memories, *Gallipoli Journal*, Spring 1978, p. 29.
11. Ibid.
12. Australian War Memorial.
13. Hamilton, *Gallipoli Diaries*.
14. Ibid.
15. Ibid.
16. Statement on Artillery by Brig Gen Sir Hugh Simpson Baikie, Ex Cdr of the British Arty at Cape Helles, quoted in Hamilton (2022). Ian Hamilton / Gallipoli Diary Two Volumes 1920. Generic. 279, Vol II.
17. Australian War Memorial.
18. Ibid.
19. Gallipoli, 1915, Maj A.C Fergusson, *Gallipoli Journal*, Winter 1997.
20. Hamilton, *Gallipoli Diaries*.
21. Ibid.
22. Australian War Memorial.
23. Hamilton, *Gallipoli Diaries*.
24. Ibid.
25. Australian War Memorial.
26. Gallipoli, 1915, Maj A.C. Fergusson, *Gallipoli Journal*, Winter 1997.
27. Ibid.
28. Ibid.
29. War Diary, *69th Punjabis* (no. 4272).
30. Ibid.
31. Gallipoli, 1915, Maj A.C. Fergusson, *Gallipoli Journal*, Winter 1997.
32. Ibid.
33. Ibid.
34. War Diary, Army Headquarters, vol. 13, IEF 'F' and 'G'. 1st to 31st October 1915. National Archives of India.

35. Lt-Gen. George MacMunn (1991), *The Armies of India*, Forgotten Books, New Delhi.

36. Andrew Tait Jarboe (April 2013), *Soldiers of Empire, Indian Sepoys in and beyond the Imperial Metropole During the First World War 1914–1919*, North-Eastern University Boston, Massachusetts.

37. Feeding the Leviathan: Supplying the British Indian Army, 1859-1913, Kaushik Roy Source: *Journal of the Society for Army Historical Research*, Summer 2002, vol. 80, no. 322 (Summer 2002), pp. 144-61.

38. From B.S. Carey, Political Officer, Chin Hills, to the Chief Secretary to the Chief Commissioner, Burma (through Inspector-General of Military Police), nos. 67-35, dated 25 March 1895, quoted in Lalita Hingkanonta (2013), 'The Police in Colonial Burma', PhD thesis. SOAS, University of London.

39. Quoted in Feeding the Leviathan: *Supplying the British Indian Army*, 1859-1913, Kaushik Roy Source: Journal of the Society for Army Historical Research, Summer 2002, vol. 80, no. 322 (Summer 2002), pp. 144-161.

40. A.J. Mohair, *History of Army Service Corps*, pp. 255-6.

41. Ibid.

42. War Diary, National Archives of India (1915), Army Headquarters, India, 14(1915).

43. Ibid.

44. 14th Sikhs Album.

45. Ibid.

46. Reginald Savory, *Gallipoli Journal*, Christmas 1974, p. 9.

47. Ibid.

48. Ibid.

49. 14th Sikhs Album.

50. Savory, *Gallipoli Journal*, Christmas 1974, p. 9.

51. C.H.T. MacFetridge (1974), *Tales of the Mountain Gunners*, An Anthology, Compiled by Those who Served with Them, Blackwood.

52. Australian War Memorial.

53. Ibid.

54. Ibid.

55. Ibid.

56. H.M. Alexander (2017), *On Two Fronts, Being the Adventures of an Indian Mule Corps in France and Gallipoli*, Van Haren Publishing.

57. Ibid.

58. Ibid.

59. Ibid.
60. Australian War Memorial
61. Ibid.
62. Alexander, *On Two Fronts.*
63. Australian War Memorial
64. Alexander, *On Two Fronts.*
65. Australian War Memorial.
66. Ibid.
67. Lt-Col R.F.E. Laidlaw, Royal Munster Fusiliers, *Gallipoli Journal*, Autumn 1977, p. 9.
68. Australian War Memorial.
69. Ibid.
70. Alexander, *On Two Fronts.*
71. Ibid.
72. Ibid.
73. Ibid.
74. Ibid.
75. Lt-Col M.B. Hancock MC, *Gallipoli Journal*, no. 40. 1986, p. 17.
76. Alexander, *On Two Fronts.*
77. R.S. James (2018), *Gallipoli* (1st edn.), Uniform Press.
78. Ibid.
79. Ibid.
80. Colonel A.C Fergusson in *Tales of the Mountain Gunners.*
81. Australian War Memorial.
82. Fergusson in *Tales of the Mountain Gunners*, op. cit.
83. Gallipoli, 1915, Maj A.C Fergusson, *Gallipoli Journal*, Winter 1997.
84. James, *Gallipoli.*
85. 14th Sikhs Album.
86. War Diary, B Section, 137 Field Ambulance.
87. C.W. Hunter (September 1918), 'Lice Borne Diseases and Disinfection', *The Lancet*, 378-81.
88. Australian War Memorial.
89. War Diary, 'C' Section, 137th Indian Field Ambulance.
90. Savory, *Gallipoli Journal*, Christmas 1974, p. 11.
91. 14th Sikhs Album.
92. War Diary, B Section, 137 Indian Combined Field Ambulance.
93. War Diary, Army Headquarters, India, IEFG, vol. I, 21-31 July 1915. National Archives of India.
94. Ibid.

95. Ibid.
96. War Diary, Army Headquarters, India, IEFG, vol. II, 1-31 August 1915. National Archives of India.
97. War Diary, Army Headquarters, India, National Archives of India, 14(1915).
98. Australian War Memorial.
99. Ibid.
100. War Diary, IEFF, vol. 6, Army Headquarters, India, National Archives of India.
101. Radhika Singha (2019), *The Coolie's Great War: Indian Labour in a Global Conflict, 1914-1921*, C. Hurst & Co., London.
102. Prabhu P. Mohapatra (2004), 'Assam and the West Indies, 1860–1920: Immobilising Plantation Labour', in Douglas Hay and Paul Craven (eds), *Masters, Servants and Magistrates in Britain and Empire, 1562–1955*, Chapel Hill: University of North Carolina Press, pp. 455-80.
103. A. Major (2 January 2017), 'Hill Coolies: Indian Indentured Labour and the Colonial Imagination, 1836–38', *South Asian Studies*, 33(1), 23–36. https://doi.org/10.1080/02666030.2017.1300374.
104. Radhika Singha, 'The Great War and a "Proper" Passport for the Colony: Border-Crossing in British India, *c.*1882–1922', *Indian Economic and Social History Review*, vol. 50, no. 3 (2013), pp. 289-315.
105. Singha, *The Coolie's Great War: Indian Labour in a Global Conflict*.
106. Ibid.
107. Ibid.
108. Major B. & M Gillott, eds. (2017), *Gallipoli Diaries: Headquarters 29th Indian Infantry Brigade 1915*, Great War Diaries Ltd., Sussex.
109. War Diary, Army Headquarters, India, vol. 3, 1 to 30 September 1915, Appendix 4, Dy No. 20077, National Archives of India.
110. Ibid.
111. Ibid.
112. Ibid.
113. Ibid.
114. Ibid.
115. Ibid.
116. War Diary, Army Headquarters, IEF F & G, vol. 15, 1 to 31 December 1915, National Archives of India.
117. War Diary, Army Headquarters, India, National Archives of India, 14(1915).
118. Ibid.
119. Ibid.

120. Ibid.
121. Various Sources.
122. Ibid.
123. Ibid.
124. Savory, *Gallipoli Journal*, Christmas 1974, p. 9.
125. Ibid.
126. Appendix 51, *General War Diary*, vol. 13, Army Headquarters, India, 1 January to 31 January 1915, National Archives of India.
127. Savory, *Gallipoli Journal*, Autumn 1915, p. 14.
128. Ibid.
129. Memorandum 31/5, 12 December 1914. National Archives of India.
130. Telegram no. 171-D, 6 February 1915. National Archives of India.
131. Telegram no. S-113, 16 January 1915. National Archives of India.
132. Adapted from Casualty database by the author.
133. Memorandum no. 31-8, 2 February 1915. National Archives of India.
134. Adapted from Casualty database by the author.
135. Telegram nos. 31-15 & 31-21, 23 February and 1 March respectively. National Archives of India.
136. Adapted from the Casualty database by the author.
137. Telegram no. 9301-XA, 11 October 1915. National Archives of India.
138. Ibid.
139. Ibid.
140. Telegram no. 30515-1, 3 October 1915. National Archives of India.
141. Telegram no. 196-197, 30 October 1915, National Archives of India.
142. Telegram no. S-11846, 8 June 1915, National Archives of India.
143. Telegram no. 71-31 D, 5 June 1915. National Archives of India.
144. Telegram no. M-181, 15 June 1915. National Archives of India.
145. Ibid.
146. Telegram no. M-133, 28 January 1916. National Archives of India.

CHAPTER 5

The Acknowledgement
Lest we Forget

The contribution of Indian troops in The Great War is an oft ignored concept. Except for a few researchers in India who have attempted to trace the granularities of the involvement of these brave men in the war effort, the research on the contribution has largely been carried out by the military historians from the West. The available research on the First World War, has also generally been confined to the Western theatre, thereby relegating the Indian contribution in the other theatres of The Great War to the realms of ignorance and ignominy. As a result, the efforts, bravery and sacrifices of thousands of Indian soldiers, primarily from undivided Punjab have been lost to the younger generations of the country.

In terms of initiation, conduct and effect, the First World War was largely Eurocentric. The participation and contribution of the Indian troops in Europe during the course of the Great War has witnessed significant research and a reasonable quantum of literature on the contribution exists. During the war, the Indian troops also participated and contributed gallantly in the other theatres of war to include Egypt and Africa. The necessary recognition and acknowledgement of the sacrifices of Indian troops in these theatres has generally eluded the public consciousness and the limited research in this domain has fallen short of expectations. As a cumulative impact of the above, the Indian contribution in the War effort, particularly in Egypt and Africa, has been denied its rightful place in history.

Between the intervening period of the First and Second World Wars, Indian nationalism also was also simultaneously witnessing an increased traction. Up to some extent the primacy of Indian contribution in the First World War can also be attributed to the anticipation of grant of self-governance by the British, subject to the success of Britain in the Great War. In spite of no significant progress in the accord of promised self-governance to the Indians after the First World War, the Indian contribution towards the war effort in the Second World War, was in no way less consequential.

In the aftermath of the Second World War, the subsequent Independence of the country further accentuated the deviation of the narrative from the Indian Army of pre-Independence era to the Indian Army of post-Independence era. The Indian soldiers, who were recruited and fought as Indian Army under the British flag in the various theatres of world, suddenly realised that their sacrifices were not for India but for Britain. 'Indian soldiers who served "have been doubly marginalized" by Indian nationalist history which has largely focused on the heroes of the Independence movement and by the grand narrative of the war which still remains largely Eurocentric.'[1]

These brave men had volunteered to fight against an enemy of which they knew nothing and didn't have any idea about the terrain on which they were going to fight, yet they went, fought bravely, sacrificed their lives but the deserving acknowledgement and recognition has eluded them. The records of these men and the battalions to which they belonged, under whose *nishan* and *namak*, they fought desperate battles for their and Battalion's *naam*, have very rarely been written about. This selective amnesia about the contribution of Indian soldiers in the Great War from the Indian perspective has been a major detrimental factor to the cause of the recognition for these brave men.

These men were undoubtedly heroes: pitch forked into battle in unfamiliar lands, in harsh and cold climatic conditions they were neither used to nor prepared for, fighting an enemy of whom they had no knowledge, risking their lives every day for little more than pride. Yet they were destined to remain largely unknown once the war was over: neglected by the British, for whom they fought, and ignored by their own country, from which they came.[2]

Supporting the thought process, another survey carried out by me in the run up to the present work, adequately corroborated the feelings. The survey carried out was quite contemporary, both from context and environment perspectives and therefore does not subsume the biases apparent in the immediate aftermath of the Great War, either for soldiers who fought for the Imperial Britain or the Indian nationalists. A massive 96.9 per cent of the respondents in the survey have agreed that the battles fought by the Indian soldiers in the Great War merit more research and study. Over a period of time these battles have been researched and written about in great details by the military historians of Britain, Australia, Canada and New Zealand. The Indian research on these themes, however, has not achieved the requisite depth and breadth.

In the earlier chapters of the book, an effort has been made to put into context an Indian perspective of a small but an important campaign of Gallipoli. Due to the overwhelming presence and action of British and ANZAC troops, the narrative of the campaign has prominently been deflected away from the Indian contribution. A very apparent lack of research on the Indian troops on the peninsula which followed subsequently was primarily responsible for eluding due recognition to the Indians who served and fought on the Gallipoli peninsula.

Having adequately discussed the nuances of the Indian contribution in the previous chapters from the enemy, formation units and sub unit's perspective, in the last chapter of the book, I have attempted to provide a realistic journey of few of the Indian soldiers from their respective personal perspectives. In addition, the dimensions of operating with the ANZACs, the journeys of reinforcements meant for the Indian units fighting on the peninsula, the sinking of an Indian transport along with the reinforcements by a German U Boat have also been covered in the subsequent sections of the chapter. The total number of Indian troops which served on the peninsula and the details of the Indian casualties during the campaign have generally been approximated. In the last section of the chapter, an attempt has been made to calibrate the total number of Indian troops which served on the peninsula, the details of the casualties suffered and total number of reinforcements received by the various Indian battalions, during their deployment on the peninsula.

In all the research carried out till date on subject, the Indian troops who were deployed on the peninsula, during the conduct of campaign have always been equated with the battalions with which they served on the peninsula. The individual identities of these faceless and nameless souls have been subsumed into the collective identities of units and sub-units. Towards an attempt to correct the aberration, the life stories of three Indian troops, who served in the campaign have been endeavoured to be co-related with the operational aspects of the campaign. Out of more than 16,000 Indians who served on the peninsula, the actions of three nameless souls on the peninsula have been attempted to be recreated with an active assistance from the respective descendants.

Sepoy Udey Singh, 14th Sikhs

The exploits of the Number 4 Double Company of the 14th Sikhs on 4 June 1915 can never be complete without the mention of Number 3767, Sepoy Udey Singh. The saga of bravery of Udey Singh, during the third battle of Krithia, has been immortalised by the memoirs of Reginald Savory. The present exposition has been made possible due to the assistance provided by Prof. Charanjeet Sohi, the granddaughter of Sepoy Udey Singh.

Udey Singh was born in 1886 in the dusty and rustic environs of Manakwal village in the Ludhiana district of Punjab. Having been born in a family of farmers and like other youngsters of the village, Udey Singh also had started helping in the farming. During those days, the farming-based subsistence, was a difficult proposition and coupled with the limited availability of irrigable land along with the over dependence on rains did not help the sustenance. Growing up in these circumstances, Udey Singh was fast turning up into a tall and handsome Sikh young man.

The Punjab in those days was a land of fairs. With no other modes of amusement available, attendance in the fairs provided a sole source of gaiety and hilarity for the populace. The young, aged and children, all used to look forward to these fairs, when people in groups flocked to these fairs. The atmosphere in these fairs was electrifying, with all sorts of competitions to include rooster fighting, bullock cart racing, martial arts, wrestling, kabaddi, etc., being conducted. Udey Singh being over 6 feet tall, and endowed with the good physique and strength, had developed a liking towards the sport of wrestling and over a period of time had become a permanent fixture in these tourneys. The schedule of fairs in the Punjab of those days was decided, upon the availability of farmers, either post-harvest or during the relative comfortable weather conditions. As a result, the schedule of these fairs was spread over evenly throughout the year. Most of these fares were organised immediately after the crop cutting, thereby ensuring both, relative availability of farmers to attend and also availability of money/ grains to induce spending / bartering during these fairs.

Village Manakwal in the later part of the nineteenth century was part of the Ludhiana tahsil (Revenue Unit). In the tahsil, with bountiful fairs being organised throughout the year, the entire year was colourful. Termination of one fair at a particular village used to lead to the anticipation of another one in a different village. The participation of young Udey Singh in the village level competitions of wrestling was inviting fame. The strength and expertise of Udey Singh in these wrestling events was responsible for a great deal of acknowledgement and recognition for the young man in the nearby villages. Having participated in such events for almost two years by now, Udey Singh had achieved some sort of professional level in the game.

In the month of August 1907, young Udey Singh was participating in one such competition, in a fair in the nearby village in the tahsil. Weather conditions in Punjab during the month of August are very hot and humid, yet the festival atmosphere in the fair was attracting people from the nearby villages. In the fair, people wearing their best clothes were checking the merchandise being offered at the various stalls. Sugary cups of tea along with sweetmeats and fritters were flowing. This festive and cultural bonanza was an ideal ground for the Recruiting Parties of the various Regiments to scout talent for the respective battalions. On that day also, a Recruiting Party of 14th Sikhs under an Indian Jemadar was looking for prospective recruits for the battalion in the same fair.

The wrestling bout of Udey Singh was about to start, when the Recruiting Party also reached the corner of the dusty ground, where the fair was being organised. With a fine athletic body, over 6 feet tall and coupled with physical prowess, Udey Singh prevailed and the duel was over even before it started. The Recruiting Party of the 14th Sikhs was witness to this one-sided display of raw power and the show of strength by the young man, instantly found favours with the Recruiting Party.

On the termination of the bout, Udey Singh was asked some basic questions by the Indian officer-in-charge of the Recruiting Party which was immediately followed by a visit to village Manakwal where certain additional inquiries were made by the team. The turn of events was so fast that young Udey Singh who was playing a bout of wrestling in the morning found himself shortlisted for recruitment and in a couple of days, was on his way to become an *umeedwar* (candidate) in the 14th Sikhs. From village Manakwal in Ludhiana, Udey Singh, relocated to the Depot of the 14th Sikhs in Multan. After the basic formalities and a very short initial training at the Depot, Sepoy Udey Singh had reported to the battalion, '14th Prince of Wale's Own Ferozepore Sikhs', then stationed at Ferozepore.

Immediately after the joining of Sepoy Udey Singh, the 14th Sikhs had marched from Ferozepore to Hangu in North-Western Frontier and further to Fort Lockhart. Like Udey Singh, the balance of the battalion was also endowed with exceptional physical characteristics. A touring member of British Parliament was witness to the march of this exceptional show of martial bearing, when he happened to, 'see the Regiment on the march near Lahore.' The lasting impressions of the Member of Parliament were profound and remarkable, which later on, also found a mention in one of the English newspapers of the day.

The other day during our morning ride, we passed a Regiment, the 14th Sikhs, in Marching order, on their way from Ferozepore through Lahore to the frontier, and a finer lot of men it has never been my lot to see... Without exception they were much above middle height and their sergeants, as the elders of the corps, were models of dignity. They kept perfect rank and stepped out in perfect time, but at the same time with an easy long swing that it would be hard for any European regiment to rival.[3]

Sepoy Udey Singh served with the battalion at Fort Lockhart, the place of exceptional display of bravery by the 21 Sikhs of 36th Sikhs at Saragarhi, nine years ago. From Fort Lockhart, Sepoy Udey Singh moved with the battalion to Quetta, which was a, 'very long and interesting march along the edge of the Frontier, through Kohat, Bannu, Tank, the Gomal valley, the Zhob valley, Fort Sandeman and Hindubagh'. The 14th Sikhs had moved from Quetta to Loralai and further to Peshawar, where it was located under the 1st Peshawar Brigade of the 1st (Peshawar) Division. As part of the mobilisation for the Great War from India to Egypt, Sepoy Udey Singh had mobilised with the battalion from Peshawar in October 1914 and embarked on the HT *City of Manchester* from the Karachi Port.

The association between the then Lieutenant Reginald Savory (later General) and Sepoy Udey Singh is long and cherished by the battlefield camaraderie on Gallipoli between the two. Lieutenant Savory had joined the 14th Ferozepore Sikhs, seven years later then Udey Singh, while the battalion was at Peshawar. Both had come across each other for the first time, on the train, during the move of the battalion from Peshawar to Karachi, for the subsequent move to Suez. The first meeting itself had resulted in an immediate acknowledgment of each other. 'Sepoy Udey Singh saluted smartly and the Sahib asked smilingly, *Thik Hai*, and in the words of Harbans Singh Thandi (son of Sepoy Udey Singh), "my father replied, *Thik Hai*", thereafter, whenever they came face to face, these words were repeated and thus they became friends.'[4]

This association was further strengthened, when both men served the battalion on Gallipoli in the Number 4 Double Company. While getting ready for assault against the enemy trenches on the fateful day of 4 June 1915, both again came across each other in own defences and 'Reginald Savory said, Hand to Hand fight – *Thik Hai*?[5] and Sepoy Udey Singh had replied in affirmative, *Thik Hai*.

On 4 June 1915, though the Sikhs were able to reach the Turkish parapets, a very small numbers of these individual soldiers were not adequate to dislodge the Turks from their strongly established and well-coordinated defences. The Company Commander of Number 4 Double Company of the Sikhs suffered fatal injuries during the advance. The British subaltern of the Sikhs, Second Lieutenant Savory was also seriously injured during this advance. Savory, when groggily gained senses, had realised to his horror, that his near lifeless body was being used at the parapet of the Turkish trenches as a sandbag, from the top of which the Turks were firing at the advancing reserves of the Sikhs. General Savory writes in his memoirs that, with no energy left after having taken a severe injury from a shrapnel/ bullet on his head, he had again lost his senses immediately afterwards. It has been mentioned by him, that before he lost consciousness for the second time, he did not see any Sikh troop, who was alive in the vicinity. 'When I woke up, there was silence and the Turks seemed to have gone. I began to look around me, and saw my little bugler lying dead, brutally mutilated. No one else was near. My head was bleeding and I was dazed. I could find none of my men.'[6] Back in the trenches, the miniscule survivors of the company were aware that the Company Commander Major Fowle was dead. But there being no confirmation on the status of the subaltern, worst was expected. The injured troops, who were returning back to own trenches after harrowing experiences, also couldn't recollect having seen the Lieutenant. In the meantime, the Turks thinking Savory to be dead amongst the masses of lifeless, also had retired to their trench line.

Upon gaining senses and still dis-oriented, Savory was not able to recollect the incidents of the afternoon. Totally ignorant of his surrounding, Savory got up and had started moving back in the general direction of own defences. The dead and wounded of the Sikhs were lying all over the No Man's Land. No survivor of the Company was able to recollect having seeing Savory dead, but the amount of losses suffered by the Sikhs and with the entire No Man's Land being littered with dead and wounded of Sikhs, no one was aware about the fate of Savory. Even after the conduct of reorganisation drill, post the assault, with a small number of survivors, the Number 4 Double Company of the Sikhs was still not aware of the status of their Subaltern.

After considerable time, in the words of Harbans Singh Thandi, 'my father said to his colleagues that Sahib has not returned. They said leave him to his fate, but my father decided to go for his search.'[7] Sepoy Udey Singh who himself had just returned from the No Man's Land, much against the advice of his surviving Indian officer, immediately moved out from the safety of his trench to look for Savory. After walking some distance amidst the dead, Udey Singh found

Savory in a dazzled and injured condition, who unable to walk back
had again fallen amongst the dead and injured of the Sikhs. Savory
later on mentioned in his memoirs that, he didn't recollect anything
except for being picked up by Udey Singh.

I was picked up by a great burly Sikh, with a red beard; he looked like a
Greek wrestler, Udey Singh by name. He was one of our battalion wrestlers.
He slung me over his shoulder and took me back. Where he took me, I do
not remember, all the time we were being shot at. But my next recollection
was of walking by myself down the Gully Ravine with my head bandaged.[8]

Udey Singh continued to serve with his battalion on the peninsula, before being evacuated in December 1915. The difficulties and
privations of the stay at peninsula had taken its toll on Sepoy Udey
Singh and he was frequently suffering from the bouts of Diarrhea.
On the move of the 14th Sikhs from Gallipoli to Suez defences in
January 1916, Sepoy Udey Singh had moved out with the battalion.
The Sikhs had subsequently embarked from Suez again, for the move
to Bushire. With his physical well-being getting deteriorated day by
day, Sepoy Udey Singh had nearly made up his mind to leave service.
Due to the frequent illnesses coupled with the requirement to look
after his ancestral land in Manakwal, Sepoy Udey Singh applied for
discharge from service. The sudden change of mind by Sepoy Udey
Singh to take discharge had surprised Lieutenant Savory, who did not
want to let him go and requested him to reconsider his decision. He
told Udey Singh, in no uncertain terms that, 'I want to do something
big for you.' To this, Sepoy Udey Singh had replied in that case he
may be allowed to proceed on discharge to his village. Though much
against his wishes, the discharge process of Sepoy Udey Singh was
recommended by Reginald Savory and the discharge from service of
Sepoy Udey Singh was finally sanctioned on 10 October 1916. During
the period of Indian Independence, the only surviving son of Sepoy
Udey Singh, Harbans Singh Thandi had enlisted in 11th Sikhs in
1947 and had served the battalion till March 1951.

Though Sepoy Udey Singh expired on 9 December 1947, the
connect between General Savory and Harbans Singh Thandi continued,
much against the anticipations of family of Udey Singh. 'I had a
lurking feeling that the General may not offer the same love and

FIGURE 67: HARBANS SINGH THANDI DURING
HIS SERVICE (SON OF SEPOY UDEY SINGH)[9]

affection to the family as before; but love grew with each passing day.'[10]
The family of Sepoy Udey Singh were the special guests in the British
National Memorial Service in June 1915, which was conducted, 'to
honour the memory of General Sir Reginald Savory for his involvement
in the Gallipoli campaign during the First World War'.[11]

Sepoy Nanak Singh, 69th Punjabis

Sepoy Nanak Singh was one of the Indian soldiers who landed on the
shores of Gallipoli on the morning of 1 May 1915 along with the
69th Punjabis. Though, the 69th Punjabis stay on the peninsula was
a very short one, a brief narrative on the life and times of Sepoy Nanak
Singh brings into perspective the preparations and the subsequent
landings of the Indian troops on the peninsula. For the inputs on life
and times of Sepoy Nanak Singh, I am grateful to the assistance
provided by Dr Tajinderpal Singh, the great grandson of Sepoy Nanak
Singh.

Nawanshahr, was one of the four tahsils of the Jullundur district
in the later part of the nineteenth century, the other three being
Jullundur, Nakodar and Phillaur. The riverine villages of Nawanshahr,

Nakodar and Phillaur were generally divided into uplands and lowlands by the older north bank of Sutlej River. In Nawanshahr tahsil, the upland tract was known as *dhak* (Palash) country, deriving the name from the fact that the area was earlier infested with *dhak* trees. Though by this time, large tracts had been cleared of the jungles, adequate infestation of the area with the jungles of *dhak* was still preponderant.

Amongst these uplands, out of 274 villages in the revenue records of the time, in the Nawanshahr, there existed a small village of Naura. The average population in the villages of the time being 300-400, Naura was also an average village by the standards of population. Like in any other village of Punjab, the children were put to work in an early age. The young boys were tasked to take the cattle for pasteurizing or drive the bullocks at the Persian well or cane mill. As they grow older, the young men were graduated to the tasks of weeding and turning the water into irrigation beds. The common profession of the youth of the village was to join the family profession of rearing the cattle or to join the cultivation. With frequent floods along with the very demanding taxation regime, the agriculture-based survival was not very attractive proposition and the people had started looking for jobs either in Canal colonies, upcoming railways or the Indian Army.

Nanak Singh was born in a rustic family in the village in 1876, and when he grew up, like other youth of his age, was also destined to join the family profession of rearing cattle and look after the small holding of land of the family. Though at that point of time, some young men of the nearby villages had recruited themselves in the Indian Army, Nanak Singh was still in two minds, whether to join army or to continue helping his family in the rearing of cattle head and look after the small family land holding. The severe floods of 1900 in the area had a major bearing on his decision to join the Army. The lure of the assured salary along with the other associated benefits of service, were instrumental in swinging the decision.

During the same time when Nanak Singh had decided to enroll himself into the Army, the State Gazetteer of Jullundur, came out with an interesting observation. Commenting upon the increasing population pressure on the available irrigable land, the Gazetteer referred to the emigration of Indians from the region to Australia for living.

The hope of relief for the congestion of the District population lies in continued and increased emigration, and it is satisfactory to notice that it is becoming quite a common thing for men from the District to emigrate to Australia. Some six or seven years ago a few adventurous spirits returned from Australia with substantial proof of the fact that money could be earned there, and since then it has become quite the thing for one of a large family of brothers to be sent off. The cost of getting there is about Rs 200. The sugar plantations find work for many of these emigrants and some trade as peddlers.[12]

As discussed in detail in the earlier part of the book, the recruitment patterns for the Regiments in Punjab, by the turn of the century had achieved a reasonable stability. The Recruiting Parties in active collaboration, with the nominated Recruiting Officer of the district were visiting fairs and common places to recruit the potential soldiers. The recruiting party of 9th Madras Infantry, a precursor of 69th Punjabis was also visiting Jullundur in the summer of 1901, where Nanak Singh was also one of the potential candidates.

As far as Jullundur was concerned, the Cantonments at Jullundur and Nakodar were established after the capture of *Doab* by the British in the aftermath of first Anglo Sikh war. The cantonment at Nakodar being later on discarded by the British, Jullundur was under the command of Lahore Division of Northern Command. In the early part of the twentieth century, the Jullundur Garrison comprised of a one (Field) Battery of Artillery, one British Infantry battalion, a native Infantry battalion and a native Regiment of Cavalry. As part of assigned mandate, the Jullundur Cantonment during those days, was also responsible for the bulk recruitment of the Sikh component of 67th, 69th, 90th and 92nd Punjabis.

Nanak Singh, tall, lanky and handsome young men of 25 years found his destiny in Jullundur, when he was recruited into the 9th Madras Infantry. After the completion of the recruitment paperwork, the young recruit was dispatched to the battalion. In an ongoing process of reformation and reorganisation, the 9th Madras Infantry was converted into 69th Punjabis in 1903. At the time of conversion, the battalion comprised of a Company each of Sikh, Dogra Brahmins, Dogra Rajputs. In addition, there was a mixed Company of Punjabi

Hindus and two Companies of PMs. On recruitment Sepoy Nanak Singh had joined the Sikh Company of the Battalion.

After having served in various parts of the country, Sepoy Nanak Singh, then with about 13 years of service, was posted with the 69th Punjabis, under the 5th Jhelum Brigade, where the battalion was serving under 2nd Rawalpindi Division. 69th Punjabis had received the orders for mobilisation on 14 October 1914 and Sepoy Nanak Singh along with the battalion had reached Karachi on 1 November 1914, from where he along with half of the battalion had embarked on board HT *City of Manchester*. Before reaching the assigned destination, the battalion along with the complete Indian Brigade was directed to carry out an offensive on 'Sheikh Said'. Both 69th and 89th Punjabis were launched in the first phase of the operation whereas the 14th Sikhs was in reserve. The company of Sepoy Nanak Singh was launched in the initial stages of the offensive, wherein he also participated in the assault to storm the Turkish defences. After the successful capture of the objective, the battalion had re-embarked on the transport and had occupied the allocated defences at Suez Canal by 2 December 1914.

In the Qantara Sector, where the Indian Brigade occupied defences, the Company of Sepoy Nanak Singh was tasked to patrol the hinterland of Canal, to prevent any buildup of attack by the Turks. Like the neighbouring battalion of the 14th Sikhs, the 69th Punjabis had also established a robust system of scouts, who used to patrol the huge stretches of the hinterland, to obtain any information about the enemy. During the first fortnight of April 1915, the 69th Punjabis had received orders for mobilisation. The destination being still not clear, the Companies of the Battalion had started winding up their equipment and stores at Qantara and the Company of Sepoy Nanak Singh had reached Port Said on 20 April 1915.

Even while the Hired Transport had started marshaling at the harbour of Port Said on 25 April 1915, the battalion still had no inkling about the prospective destination. The first two Double Companies of the battalion were allotted HT *Umfuli* and the other two Double Companies had embarked on HT *Japanese Prince*. The Sikh Company of Sepoy Nanak Singh had embarked on HT *Umfuli*. Though the entire flotilla had set sail for an unknown destination, the

Umfuli had somehow slowed down due to some mechanical issues. As a result, while the entire flotilla had moved in the open seas, the *Umfuli* started lagging behind. 'Transports *Ajax, Japanese Prince* and *Ismailia* came in sight and joined *Dunluce Castle*. They reported that *Umfuli* had dropped behind at 16:00 on 27/4/15 and not been seen since.'[13]

Though the entire transport of 29th Indian Infantry Brigade had reached in the vicinity of the Gallipoli peninsula in the early hours of 30 April 1915, the orders for disembarkation were issued only by 0200 hours on 1 May 1915. By this time HT *Umfuli* had also anchored near the Cape Helles. The Sikh Company of the 69th Punjabis had started disembarking from the transport in the early hours of darkness. The boat in which Sepoy Nanak Singh along with his half company had disembarked, also was having few horses, belonging to the battalion, which had been transported on board *Umfuli* itself.

A British Sergeant Major from the landing organisation, who was detailed to guide the boat to the designated landing beach, was with the boat. The Turks, deployed at relatively higher ground, were on high alert due to the impending offensive being launched by them on the night of 1 May 1915, with the directions to drive the 'invaders back into the Sea'. The boat carrying the half Company of Nanak Singh was wobbling heavily due to the waves and also due to the continuous movement of the horses on board. These horses had been in the confines of a very restricted space on board the transport for the past couple of days, and the first opportunity of movement was being fully exploited by them. The Jemadar of the Company had deputed few men of the Company to keep the horses still. The boat had not yet covered half the distance to the shore, when suddenly bursts of small arms fire from the shore had started hitting the waters around. The horses on board, already craving for movement, with no control of respective handlers, had bolted from the boat into the waters.

By this time, the boat had started receiving aimed fire from the Turkish defenders. With first light fast approaching, the task of Turks was becoming easy minute by minute. The situation all around was similar with all boats, even of other battalions receiving aimed small arms fire. Due to the cumulative impact of fire and the bolting of horses, the side panels of the boat broke, and boat was about to capsize. The horses along with their handlers were in the water and were 'flapping like fish'. The British Sergeant Major ordered balance of the troops on board to jump into the water and disperse to avoid getting hit by the hail of fire being delivered by the defenders.

After jumping into the water and surviving the terrible fire being received from the beaches, Sepoy Nanak Singh somehow reached the assigned 'W' beach on the peninsula. The battle drills for regaining command and control both at Company and battalion levels, had commenced forthwith. The half Company of Sepoy Nanak Singh, along with the other remnants of the Company, who didn't receive bullets were still trickling in ones and twos.

By late evening, the entire battalion was on the beach and was bivouacked on a slightly raised ground for the night. Though the troops had been ordered to carry emergency rations, but the capsizing of boat of half Company of Nanak Singh had resulted in the loss of every equipment and stores, including dry rations loaded on to the boat. While on board, HT *Umfuli*, the *langar* (cook-house), for the troops on board was functional. The leftover stale *chapattis* and cooked *dal* was being carried in limited amount by some of the troops which was the sole alternative available for dinner that evening. Sepoy Nanak Singh, later on reminisced with his son that the *chapattis* were so hard and *dal* so stale and smelling, that nobody wanted to eat that ration.

FIGURE 68: SEPOY NANAK SINGH DURING
HIS LATER YEARS WITH HIS MEDALS[14]

In the midst of this melee, a small Turkish detachment had started firing at the encampment of the Company. The immediately available troops of the battalion were mustered, and were directed to clear the Turkish position. Sepoy Nanak Singh happened to be one of the members in the assault group. The night was pitch dark, and the sounds of the bullets and shells were ringing as they whizzed past overhead, when the orders for the assault were passed. As the group had started moving up, in the words of Sepoy Nanak Singh, 'we realised we were walking over the dead bodies of Sikh troops, with turbans all over the place. We took care to not step over the turbans. It was a very touchy moment for us and I cannot forget that moment.'[15] The group was able to reach the identified location of Turkish defenders, but the position was found abandoned when the Punjabis reached there, the Turks having fled.

The next few days on the peninsula were quite hectic for the Company of Nanak Singh. With the PM Companies of the Battalion being used for fatigue duties on the beach itself, all actions involving the Battalion on the peninsula were the responsibility of the balance Companies. Due to the reasons, discussed in detail in the earlier chapters, the 69th Punjabis for the entire duration of their deployment on the peninsula, were not employed in any significant operational tasking. Most of the time, the Battalion continued to be in reserve for the operations of the 29th Indian Infantry Brigade.

The logistics of the entire Gallipoli campaign were still being pushed forward from the bases in the rear. With Turks, targeting the beach parties, there was requirement of additional troops at the beach to work as beach parties and to unload the continuously arriving ammunition and stores. At one point of time, the 69th Punjabis had provided more than half of the battalion for beach duties. In addition, the work on the construction and improvement of defences was an ongoing activity. With no trenches available, the battalion continued to provide fatigue parties for the construction and improvement of the existing defences.

At the end of their stay on peninsula, 69th Punjabis provided a Sikh Company under Subadar Ganga Singh to reinforce the 14th Sikhs, with Sepoy Nanak Singh being one of the soldiers of the Company during this relocation. Having been with the 14th Sikhs, for a period of less than a day, fresh orders were received by the battalion, to be prepared to move to an undisclosed location. On receipt of orders, Sepoy Nanak Singh with his Company detached themselves from the 14th Sikhs and started moving back towards the beach in the early hours of 15 May 1915. By the late evening of 15 May 1915, the entire battalion was embarked on SS *Suffolk* and had started moving towards the next destination. The battalion was tasked to move to Flanders along the Western Front. In the latter part of the Great War, Sepoy Nanak Singh again got a chance to serve in Egypt, with the battalion. Having served the Indian Army for twenty plus years, Sepoy Nanak Singh had returned to his native village, Naura in the middle of 1920s. A veteran of the *Waddi Larai* now, Sepoy Nanak Singh started looking after his land in the village.

FIGURE 69: SERVICE MEDALS OF SEPOY NANAK SINGH[16]

Nanak Singh continued to look after his ancestral agricultural land in his native village, till he bid adieu to this world on 9 June 1976.

SUBADAR GURMUKH SINGH, BURMA MILITARY POLICE

The previous sections of the book have discussed the life and times of the two soldiers belonging to the 14th Sikhs and 69th Punjabis, the

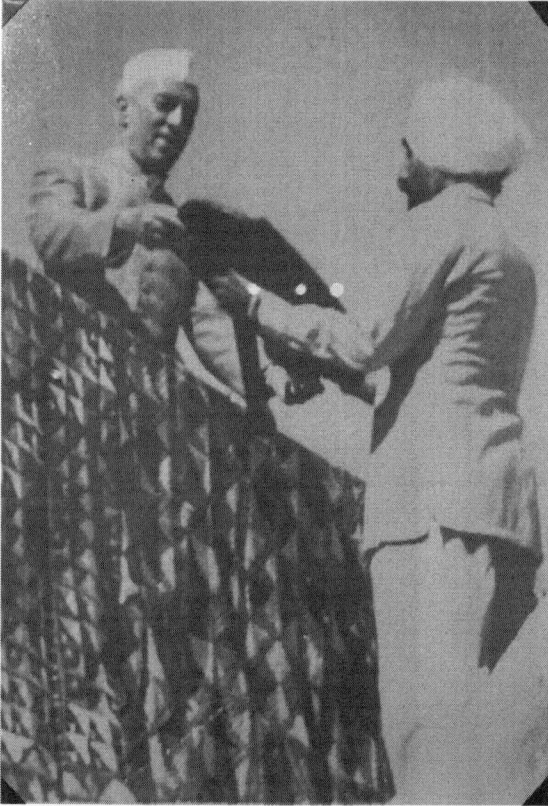

Providing a contrast of sorts, just like Sepoy Nanak Singh served in the Indian Army, and was a proud veteran of the Great War, his son, Captain Shiv Singh had served in the Indian National Army (INA) and fought for the Independence of India. Captain Shiv Singh was incarcerated in the Red Fort and was sentenced to be hanged for being actively involved with the INA. The sentence was held in abeyance, due to the impending Independence of India in August 1947. The contribution of Captain Shiv Singh in the freedom struggle of India was acknowledged by the then Prime Minister of India, when he visited the native village of Sepoy Nanak Singh in 1953.

FIGURE 70: CAPTAIN SHIV SINGH (INA) BEING
FELICITATED BY THE THEN PRIME MINISTER[17]

two battalions of the Indian Army which fought on the peninsula. Besides, the battalions of Sikhs, Punjabis and Gurkhas on the peninsula, there were a large number of troops belonging to lesser known detachments, which went as reinforcements for these beleaguered battalions on the peninsula. In spite of an intensive effort to research on the troops of these battalions, it was practically not possible to find any credible leads.

The 14th Sikhs as part of reinforcements had received a considerable number of troops from Burma Military Police. A large number of these reinforcements perished during the sinking of SS *Ramajan*. In addition, there were large numbers of casualties suffered by the troops of the Burma Military Police, while operating on the peninsula with the 14th Sikhs. The troops of Burma Military Police not only served with the 14th Sikhs but were sent to other Sikh battalions serving in the other theatres of the Great War as well. In fact, the first lot of Sikhs which were requisitioned from Burma Military Police were meant for the 15th Sikhs and the detachment was sent to the Depot of the battalion located at Multan in April 1915.

The travails of the Sikh troops of the Burma Military Police being almost similar, in this section of the book, I have attempted to recreate the journey of another Sikh soldier belonging to the Burma Military Police, Gurmukh Singh who went as part of reinforcements to the 15th Sikhs and later on joined 14th Sikhs. Though Subadar Gurmukh Singh did not serve on Gallipoli, but he died during the later phases of the Great War, on 26 October 1918, while being attached with the 14th Sikhs during operations leading up to the battle of Sharqat in Egypt.

In the league of Sepoys Udey Singh and Nanak Singh, Subadar Gurmukh Singh is like another name in the long list of the casualties of the Great War. But behind the facade of the rank and name, there is a story of every soldier who fought in the Great War. The efforts to bring forth the life and times of Subadar Gurmukh Singh have been feasible, only because of the assistance rendered by the Project Empire, Faith and War being steered by the United Kingdom Punjab Heritage Association (UKPHA). For the personal inputs on the life of Subadar Gurmukh Singh, I stand indebted to the help and support rendered by Sukhpal Kaur Brar, the great granddaughter of Subadar Gurmukh Singh.

In the latter half of the nineteenth century, a large number of Sikh troops had recruited into the Burma Military Police. Subadar Gurmukh Singh, born in 1870s, in a remote village of Akalia Jalal ka, in the present-day Bathinda District of Punjab was also one of the young men of the Malwa region, who had volunteered to be enlisted in the Burma Military Police. This region of undivided Punjab was the second largest contributor of troops for the Indian army of the time, only behind the Majha. Being the only child of his parents, the journey of joining the Military Police was a difficult one for him. As discussed in the second chapter, Burma Military Police by the end of the nineteenth century was largely composed of Sikh troops and the deployment of these troops was predominantly in the hinterland of the country. Gurmukh Singh was also one of those hundreds of Sikh troops who were deployed in the remote areas of the country.

At the onset of hostilities of the Great War, once all the established resources for the provisioning of reinforcements fell short, the Burma Military Police was identified as one of the potential sources for reinforcements. On 8 January 1915, the Army Department in India had requested the Burma Government for 400 Sikhs, 1,200 PMs and 50 Mounted Infantry to be sent as reinforcements for the various Indian battalions deployed in the various theatres of war. To the above request, the Burma Government had confirmed that as a first installment, only 200 Sikhs will be available by the end of March 1915. These 200 volunteers from the Burma Military Police, Gurmukh Singh being one of them, were put on a short and intensive musketry course on charge loading rifles and were dispatched from Rangoon through a British India steamer on 12 April 1915. Out of these 200 Sikh troops, 150 troops were earmarked to proceed to the Depot of the 15th Ludhiana Sikhs at Multan and the balance 50 Sikhs were to move to the Depot of the 58th Rifles at Ferozepore. The party of 150 Sikhs, including Subadar Gurmukh Singh, had joined the depot of the 15th Sikhs at Multan on 19 April 1915.

As all these reinforcements were to join the battalions which were on active service in the various parts of the world, the issue of war furlough came up during the transit of these troops from Rangoon to Multan. War furlough was authorised to these troops as existing regulations but due to the operational requirements, these troops were directed to proceed to the respective depots first and then proceed on leave after completion of the second phase of training, with the first part of the training having been carried out in Burma.

The 15th Ludhiana Sikhs was deployed in France in the initial phases of the Great War as part of the IEF 'A'. Strength of two Indian officers along with 152 Rank and File of Burma Military Police along with 25 drafts for the 15th Sikhs had boarded the transport *Elephanta* from the Port of Karachi on 16 May 1915.[18] Gurmukh Singh was one of the soldiers from the Burma Military Police who was on board *Elephanta*. Prior to the departure of reinforcements, the effective strength of the 15th Ludhiana Sikhs had been reduced below par due to a large number of casualties and the Battalion had required a minimum strength of 225 additional troops as reinforcements.[19] It was proposed to make up this deficiency from the variety of re-inforcements being collected and dispatched and the reinforcements from Burma Military Police, including Gurmukh Singh, had joined the 15th Sikhs on 5 June 1915 in France.

FIGURE 71: MEDALLION OF SUBADAR GURMUKH SINGH
(PRESERVED BY HIS FAMILY)[20]

Three days later, a major decision with respect to the move of the 15th Ludhiana Sikhs was proposed. The status of the 15th Ludhiana Sikhs, along with certain other Indian battalions in France had turned precarious due to the reinforcements not being able to keep pace with the rate of occurrence of casualties. In order to find a one time solution to the vexed issue, the Viceroy in India took up a case with the Secretary of State for India on 8 June 1915 for replacing some battalions in France from Egypt, which had suffered severally or for which it was difficult to supply drafts. The 15th Ludhiana Sikhs along with the 59th Scinde Rifles, 58th Vaughan Rifles and 41st Dogras were nominated to be reverted to Egypt.

These battalions were selected based on the criteria that the nominated battalions had a link in Egypt, which was proposed to be used as a, 'half way house for drafts which must largely consist of young soldiers in future. This would result in their being more matured by the time of their arrival in France.'[21] The entire contingent of Gurmukh Singh's Burma Military Police who was now attached with the 15th Ludhiana Sikhs had reached Egypt for the subsequent tasking in the August 1915, where Gurmukh Singh was promoted to the rank of Jemadar on 17 August 1915.

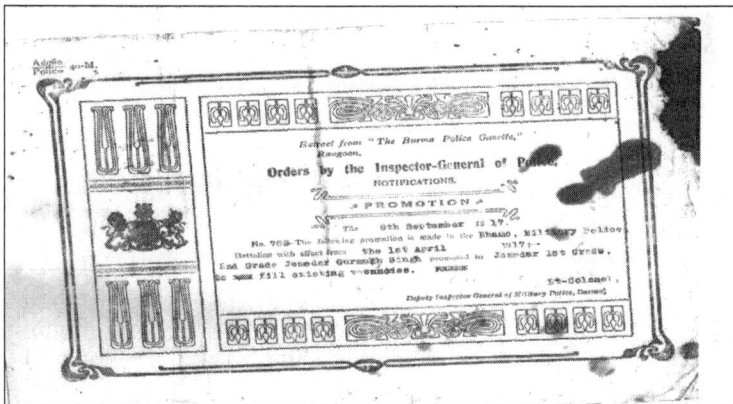

FIGURE 72: PROMOTION PARCHMENT OF SUBADAR
GURMUKH SINGH[22]

As the 14th Sikhs was the link Battalion of 15th Sikhs, some reinforcements comprising of Burma Military Police from the 15th

Ludhiana Sikhs had started reporting to the 14th Sikhs, Jemadar Gurmukh Singh being one of them. Though no exact date is available, it is most likely that Jemadar Gurmukh Singh had joined the 14th Sikhs during the latter stages of the Gallipoli campaign.

FIGURE 73: SUBADAR GURMUKH SINGH SITTING IN
THE MIDDLE ROW, *THIRD FROM THE LEFT*[23]

After the deinduction from Gallipoli, the 14th Sikhs was detached to Tor in February 1916 and later on was transferred to Bushire in May 1916. Jemadar Gumukh Singh continued to serve with the 14th Sikhs in Bushire until February 1917. On 6 February 1917, the 14th Sikhs was directed to proceed to the Tigris front. The company of Jemadar Gurmukh Singh had embarked on the Transport *Bamora* on 8 February 1917 and had reached Basra by the last light on 9 February 1917.[24] In Basra, the 14th Sikhs was to replace 36th Sikhs of 37th Brigade which had suffered serious casualties.

At the last moment, however, the orders were changed and the 14th Sikhs was deployed to secure line of communication as a replacement for 2/9 Gurkhas. 'This change was necessary, as there were no Sikh reinforcements available and that casualties in the 14th Sikhs could not be made good. It was therefore unwise to send the

Regiment to the front line at that time.'[25] From Basra, Jemadar Gurmukh Singh had moved to Baghdad in October 1917, 'where in they joined 1st Battalion the Highland Infantry, 2nd Rajputs and the 1/10 Gurkhas.' From Baghdad the battalion was further dispatched to 'Samarra to guard the aerodrome and ordnance dumps there.' While in Samarra, Jemadar Gurmukh Singh was promoted to the rank of Subadar on 11 January 1918. In October 1918, the battalion was ordered to pursue the Turks and destroy the Turkish forces south of Mosul and then secure the town. For capturing Sharqat, the reduction of the Turkish position at Mushak was imperative.

The Turkish position at Mushak was very strong, especially the left flank near the river. On the west of the road there was a tangled mass of (precipitous hills, and the ground was quite flat between the river and the road. Since it was expected that the Turks would withdraw during the night the 14th Sikhs were ordered to move up on the right of the Highlanders and carry out a rapid attack across the flat ground east of the road.[26]

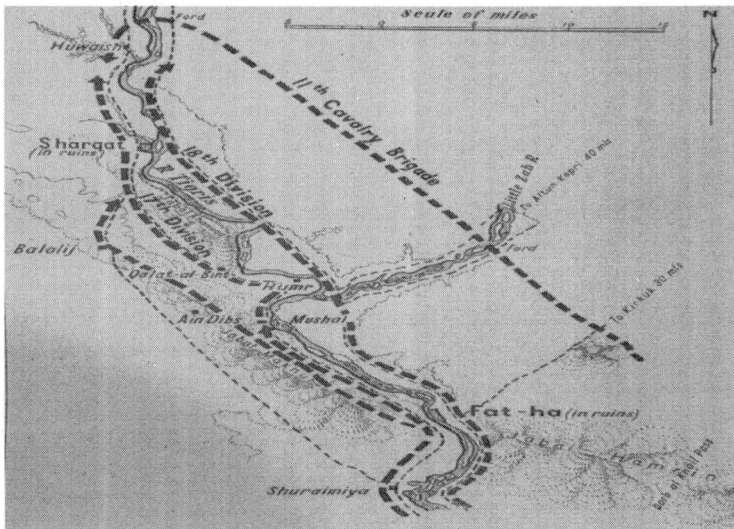

MAP 12: OPERATION OF THE 14TH SIKHS ON TIGRIS[27]

The 14th Sikhs had commenced to advance at 0625 hours on 25 October 1918 and was targeted with a very high volume of incoming artillery fire from Turks. As the Sikhs neared the defences, the carefully concealed machine guns wreaked havoc on the advancing Sikhs. The absence of any cover further exacerbated the situation for the Sikhs.

The men continued to press forward very gallantly with great determination and in spite of increasing casualties, including three company commanders. By 7.30 a.m. the forward companies, which had been reinforced by 'D' Company, had almost reached the enemy's wire and 'A' Company on the left had joined up with the Highland Light Infantry, when they were held. Companies re-formed as best they could and. took up a line three hundred yards south of the enemy's wire, where they remained for the rest of the day. After dark the 14th Sikhs were withdrawn and placed in reserve behind the Highland Light Infantry. They had suffered serious losses. Second-Lieutenant Irving and sixty-six men were killed, while Major Channer, Captain Bunbury, Lieutenants O'Connor, Church and Humphreys and two hundred and fifty-one men were wounded.[28]

The wounded were being taken care of by the Gallipoli fame medics of Captain Cursetjee and Sub-Assistant Surgeon Bhagwan Singh, who continued to do a very good work against all odds here as well. 'In the ten days' fighting the 14th Sikhs suffered 352 casualties, which was the highest number suffered by any unit in the Division.' Amongst the dead was Subadar Gurmukh Singh who lost his life on 26 October 1918.

The memory of Subadar Gurmukh Singh is commemorated on the Panels 59 and 68 of the Basra Memorial. Subadar Gurmukh Singh, when died in action left behind his widow Asso Kaur and three young children, the youngest of who was just three years old. A letter of sympathy and deep regrets from the king was received by the family of Subadar Gurmukh Singh in December 1918.

WITH THE ANZACS

Another facet of the Indian participation in the Gallipoli campaign was the development and the subsequent maintenance of a very close and intimate relationship between the Indian troops and the Australians. The Indian and Australian troops fought under the British

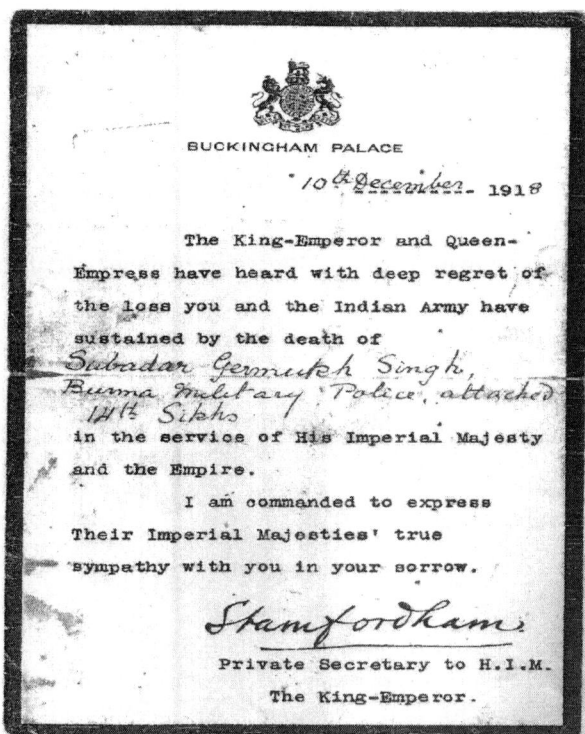

FIGURE 74: A LETTER EXPRESSING DEEP REGRETS AND
SYMPATHY FROM THE KING ON THE DEATH OF
SUBADAR GURMUKH SINGH[29]

flag for a common cause and the association of eight months under
the trying and testing conditions of Gallipoli further strengthened the
bond between the two. The bond between the two countries is very
strong today and the Geo Strategic relationship between India and
Australia is dominating the strategic narrative of the region. The people
to people relationship between the two countries is at its peak leading
to the Indian diaspora going to become the largest in Australia in the
years to come.

By April 1915, it was apparent that Australians were going to
fight alongside British troops in the capture of Gallipoli. At the same
time, Australians were also aware that they were going to fight alongside

Indians in the endeavour to capture Gallipoli. The Australian newspaper, *The Daily News* in its edition of 23 April 1915, broke the news that Indians after their exploits in France and Flanders were going to help 'our boys' in Turkey. The paper went on to give basic traits of the Sikhs, Gurkhas and Mohammedan troops, who the Australians were going to find amidst them, in their battles to capture the peninsula of Gallipoli. Though the Sikhs and Mohammedan troops, as part of the Indian Mountain Artillery Brigade were with Australians since 25 April 1915 and it will be fair to assume that by 23 April, the day of publication of news, the information was in the public domain.

The Indians have distinguished themselves fighting for their Emperor on the battlefields of France and Flanders, they are of especial interest to Australians just now because they will be fighting alongside our boys under General Sir Ian Hamilton. In Turkey, where they are to help the Allied fleets in the conquest of the Dardanelles forts and the conquest of Constantinople. The Sikhs (pictured on the left) are members of the famous warrior community of Northern India, whose ascetic creed originated their name. They neither smoke nor eat beef.[30]

SOLDIER TYPES IN THE INDIAN CONTINGENT—SIKH, GURKHA AND MOHAMMEDAN.

The Indians have distinguished themselves fighting for their Emperor on the battlefields of France and Flanders. They are of especial interest to Australians just now because they will be fighting alongside our boys under General Sir Ian Hamilton in Turkey, where they are to help the Allied fleets in the conquest of the Dardanelles forts and the conquest of Constantinople. The Sikhs (pictured on the left) are members of the famous warrior community of Northern India, whose ascetic creed originated their name. They neither smoke nor eat beef. The middle figure is a Gurkha, another race of Rajput ancestry, but now of mixed blood. The third, an Indian Mohammedan, belongs to a people from whom our Punjab regiments are recruited. The Pathan (or Afghan) tribesman in the Indian Army come under the same religious category. Urdu is their common tongue on duty, but otherwise each set uses its own language—Sikhs, Punjabi; Gurkhas, Gurkalli; Pathans, Pushtu.

FIGURE 75: HELPING OUR BOYS IN TURKEY[31]

Prior to the landings of 25 April 1915, two Indian Mountain Artillery Batteries were waiting for almost three weeks at Mudros. As the guns of these Batteries were to be in support of operations of ANZAC, the initial interaction and subsequent familiarisation amongst the Indians, Australians and New Zealanders had already commenced at Mudros. The bonhomie thus created in the initial phases of operation was to continue during the balance of the operation. 'We received many visits from Australians and New Zealanders to look at the Indians and there commenced an entente which afterwards became most remarkable.'[32] The differential in the compatibility of language was an impediment between the Indians and ANZACs. With no interpreters available, 21st Indian Mountain Artillery Battery came to know about an Australian gunner, who was the son of an Indian Missionary who, 'talked Urdu fluently'. The efforts of the CO of the Indian Battery to entice Meyer (Australian Gunner) to switch were not successful and, in the meantime, the 14th Sikhs was able to rope Meyer for the translation purposes and 'would not part' with him.

Before, discussion of the relationship between Indian troops and the ANZACs, it will be prudent to discuss about the Sikhs in the Australian Army prior to both of them meeting again in the trenches of Gallipoli. As part of Australian Imperial Force (AIF) and the New Zealand Expeditionary Force (NZEF) in the First World War, at least 19 Sikhs had enrolled themselves. Out of these 19 Sikhs, the name of 'Gurbachan Singh' is of particular interest, as far as Sikhs, Australians and Gallipoli is concerned. The name probably resonates equally for all three in some proportion or other.

Regimental Number 1414, Private Gurbachan Singh was enlisted in the Australian Imperial Force on 3 October 1914. As per official records, Private Gurbachan Singh was unmarried and 40 years old when he was enlisted. The individual had stated his profession as hawker and the original address documented in the records, mentions about him belonging to Jullundur in Punjab, India. After enlistment, on 20 October 1914, along with the G Company of 3rd Infantry Battalion, the individual had embarked Sydney for the Middle East on board Transport *Euripides*. The enlistment of a Sikh in the AIF was

A SIKH IN AUSTRALIA.

An unusual recruit for the Austra-lian Imperial Expeditionary Force was found in a wiry-built, brown-skinned man, who made his application in full khaki kit, forage cap, and leather put-tees. On his tunic dangled the South Africa and Tirah campaign medals. "I'm a Sikh," he exclaimed proudly. "Two years I fought in South Africa, and two years I was with the Mala-kand Field Force. I came from the Punjab, and I would fight again. I am not too old, only forty, and I have my papers. Here I have been hawking, but I am a Sikh, and when I put on my uniform I forget I have been a trader, and become a soldier. We Punjabis make good fighters."

FIGURE 76: A SIKH IN AUSTRALIA[33]

celebrated by the Australian press. Daily News of Perth published a report about the enlistment of Gurbachan Singh on 25 January 1915.

The Gallipoli connection of Gurbachan Singh, was corroborated on 20 October 1914, as the 3rd Infantry Battalion later on found itself fighting against the Turks along with the Sikhs, as part of ANZAC. Though the above news report was published on 25 January 1915, as stated in records, Private Gurbachan Singh, was discharged from service on 29 October 1914 as being, 'not of substantial European origin', implying that the individual did not go to Gallipoli with the 3rd Infantry Battalion. The individual has been recorded to have been able to speak Persian and at least three other Indian languages. Though the initial attempt of Private Gurbachan Singh to enroll himself was not successful and he was discharged very shortly afterwards, the individual is said to have re-enlisted himself in the Australian Imperial Force in April 1916, after which he served with 56th and 54th Infantry Battalions in France. He ultimately was discharged from active service in June 1918, due to the reasons of being medically unfit and being overage. The linkage of Gurbachan Singh with ANZACs and Indians troops fighting at Gallipoli does not end here.

Despite having not been able to go with the 3rd Infantry Battalion to Dardanelles, Private Gurbachan Singh has also been documented, to have claimed that he had two nephews who were fighting against the Turks at Dardanelles. The subsequent reference of Gurbachan Singh of ANZAC and his apparent link with the Indian troops at Gallipoli manifests during the time, when the Indian troops were battering the aftermath of deadly rain and squall during the ultimate days of their stay at Dardanelles. Though the ANZACs were equally affected by the sudden turn of weather, the terrain obtained in the defences of the 14th Sikhs had made them particularly vulnerable to the storm water. There has been a mention of a clean-shaven Sikh, serving in ANZAC, who along with other Australian troops, helped the troops of the 14th Sikhs after the destruction and misery caused by the rains and hail of November 1915. There is a recorded mention of an individual named Gurbachan Singh belonging to ANZACs, who helped the troops of 14th Sikhs.

It was the end of November 1915, clouds gathered and a sudden heavy downpour over the steep hillsides turned the Nullah into a mighty rivulet, rushing into our trenches and soon we were waist deep in heavily silt laden icy cold water. We braved the dark night and heaved a sigh of relief when next morning the ANZACs came to our rescue with plenty of warm clothing. Among the Australian soldiers, a clean-shaven Sikh Gurbachan Singh – his name tattooed on his forearm in Punjabi was most helpful to both sides.[34]

Whether the Gurbachan Singh mentioned by Major Dhanna Singh in his letter to Gallipoli Association and Gurbachan Singh, who enrolled in the 3rd Infantry Battalion of the AIF are the same, is a matter of further research. Alternatively, the co-incidence can also be explained by a possibility of a connection between the two nephews of Gurbachan Singh of the 3rd Infantry Battalion with the Gurbachan Singh as mentioned by Major Dhanna Singh.

FIGURE 77: GURBACHAN SINGH, A VETERAN OF THE
SOUTH AFRICAN, CHITRAL & TIRAH CAMPAIGNS[35]

Before arriving on Gallipoli, Indian troops interacted with their British officers in the battalions, but on Gallipoli, when they met Australians, for most of them there were no apparent differences between the two. However, for Australians, interacting with the Indian troops, for the first time by most of them, was altogether a different experience. Out of the 16,000 plus Indian troops on Gallipoli, belonging to different battalions / regiments, only the Mountain Artillery and the Mule Corps had an intimate and close working relationship with the Australians, due to the peculiarities of the mandated operational role.

The association between the Indian gunners and Australians at Gallipoli had developed due to a deep sense of camaraderie and a common sense of purpose between the two. The two Indian Mountain batteries had landed with the ANZACs on 25 April 1915 and for most of their stay at the peninsula, provided close support to the operations of ANZAC. These two batteries of Indian Mountain Artillery Brigade were the first one to land at Gallipoli. The CO of the 21st (Kohat) Mountain Artillery Battery had landed with his battery at Gallipoli on 25 April 1915 and the battery withdrew from the peninsula on the last day of the evacuation, 19 December 1915. The other Indian Mountain Battery, 26th (Jacob) had also landed on the same day and throughout the campaign supported the operations of the Australian and New Zealand Infantry. Except for the GOC of the ANZACs, General Birdwood who belonged to the Indian Army, only Indian component of the ANZACs, comprised solely of the elements of these two Indian Mountain Artillery batteries, in the form of Sikhs and PM troops.

As the guns of these batteries were in close support of the Australians, a close association between the troops of the two countries developed as a natural course. The Indian batteries were deployed in the defences of Australian Division; hence unfolding of a sense of bonding between the two was only a matter of time. In spite of incompatibility in the languages spoken and understood, the universal language of human companionship expressed by signs was widely used by both and the Australians, 'were always hanging around chatting to our fellows, though how they communicated was a marvel'.

For the Indian troops of the Mountain Batteries, the Australians were at times difficult to handle. With distance between the Allied held troops and the enemy being very minimal, any sign of movement by either, was countered strongly by the other. Any movement in the open was a sure shot invitation for an Artillery salvo or a rifle or a sniper opening up from somewhere. There were occasions of friendly banter between the Indians and ANZACs, during the course of these artillery duels with the Turks. 'The Australians were a nuisance sometimes, sitting in the open when the guns were firing and giving the show away, and we had on occasion to have armed sentries to keep them out.'[36]

The troops of Indian Infantry Brigade did not get an opportunity to develop the closeness with the troops of ANZAC, at levels of what existed between the Indian Mountain gunners and ANZACs. A relatively extended period of association between the Indian Mountain gunners and ANZACs was clearly responsible for the same. As part of this association, the drivers and mules of the Indian Mountain Batteries, immediately after the landings ferried the ammunition and essentials for the Australians. 'During the first three months our men were out every night carrying up stores for the ANZACs, and only once did I have a complaint of one being hit or ill-treated, and that was by a man who had too much rum on the beach and who got six months for it.'[37]

The Indian drivers of the Mountain batteries over a period of time had developed an excellent and an enviable knowledge of the terrain. The dead spots and vulnerable points along the route from the beach to the gun positions and beyond were fully marked by the Indian mule drivers. With this intricate knowledge of terrain, it was not uncommon to see Indian drivers being requested by one odd Australian or a New Zealander to lead them to their trenches. The CO of the 21st (Kohat) Battery was himself witness to few such incidents. 'I have many a time seen a driver whom I knew had been up all night, start off again up the hill to show an Australian the way to his unit. I have also seen our followers quite on their own initiative carrying water up the hill for Australians who looked done.'[38]

These and other incidents of extremely friendly and helpful nature of Indian drivers and gunners have not gone unnoticed and have achieved a status of folklore, 'In fact, I never realised before what perfect nature's gentlemen the average Sepoys were. The Australians treated our men absolutely as equals and would take orders from our NCOs probably better than from their own.'[39] These warm and cordial

AUSTRALIAN WAR MEMORIAL   C01461

FIGURE 78: INDIANS AND AUSTRALIANS AT THE HEAD OF A
VALLEY ON THE GALLIPOLI PENINSULA[40]

relations between the Indians and the ANZACs on the peninsula, fighting for a common cause were duly covered by the press of the time. Warrnambool Standard had reported on 9 August 1915:

The camaraderie and good feeling existing at the Dardanelles between the Australians and the soldiers of the Indian mountain batteries, who fought side by side in the famous landing at Gaba Tepe. The batteries did so well and gallantly that the Australians have metaphorically taken them to their heart. All are the greatest pals imaginable and the political effect of this entente cordiale should be good for both India and Australia.[41]

The scarcity of water at the peninsula was a perpetual cause of concern for the allied troops. In the initial phases of the operation, the limited numbers of wells were not able to take on heavy pressure of the exceptional number of troops and animals. The situation in the later phases of the operation had relatively eased out, due to a greater number of wells being identified and dug up. At the site of deployment of Indian Mountain Artillery Batteries, the situation was no different.

FIGURE 79: AN UNIDENTIFIED INDIAN DRIVER GUIDES HIS
PAIR OF MULES AND ARTILLERY TRANSPORT CART UP A
SLOPE NEAR Anzac COVE[42]

The troops of the Indian Mountain Batteries were dependent on a
single source of water. A well with limited quantities of fresh water
was under the charge of 21st (Kohat) Mountain Artillery Battery. The
story of the management of that well by a NCO of the Battery, Lance
Naik Satar Mohammed, as told by the CO is worth replicating:

After a bit, water began to get scarce so I put my men on strict ration and
told Satar Mohammed to give any surplus water to Australians. They soon
got to know this and came by the dozen to get water. They used to arrive
long before opening time and stand about in the open. The well was in full
view of the Turks, so Satar Mohammed would go out and make them get
into communication trench in a queue. He then went off to fetch his pump
and came back with our own men. When they were nearly finished the
ANZACs would start to get up, but Satar Mohammed would wave them to
sit down again and shout across the valley to any of our men who had not
drawn water. When they had been supplied, he signaled the ANZACs up.
After a bit he would open the trap to see how much water was left and hold
up his fingers to show how many more he could supply, when the tail of the
queue would fade away, not knowing where they could get a drink. When
all was over he unshipped his pump, said '*Goonait*' and pushed off. This went

on twice a day for three months, and never a complaint of an ANZAC trying to force him to give more than he wanted to, or not doing as he was told.[43]

FIGURE 80: ANZAC SOLDIERS WAIT TO DRAW WATER FROM THE TRENCHES[44]

The senior officers while moving along these tracks to visit the forward trenches were very vulnerable to enemy sniping activities. As most of these senior officers were part of the Indian Army and had some experience in serving with the Indian troops earlier in the subcontinent, they had developed an immediate affinity with Indian troops. During one such routine visit, General Birdwood, GOC of the ANZACs followed a small convoy of Indian mules transporting water on the peninsula. General Birdwood, with an experience of serving with the Indian troops, back home in India, greeted the Sikhs in chaste Punjabi, to the great astonishment of the Sikhs.

Once it so happened in July 1915; while following a mule carrying Pakhals full of fresh water, led by a *jawan* on an unbeaten track along the sea shore a shell from across the straits swept the mule lock & stock right away into the deep sea, where it disappeared after struggling for a while for her dear life. It was a miracle that beyond badly shaken, we were unhurt and hurriedly took shelter in a ravine close by, and stirred out cautiously to resume our march to the firing line. We had gone only a short distance when we heard from behind sound of heavy steps with long strides. We brought our rifles from 'sling to ready' and on looking back we found to our greatest pleasure, Field Marshal Lord Birdwood -- the heart & soul of the Gallipoli Campaign, surprisingly, all alone. His quick approach & his hand on my shoulder with the Sikh Salutation '*Sat Sri Akal*', gave us no time to pay our respects by presenting arms or otherwise. He spoke to us in chaste Punjabi '*Khalsaji ki hal hai, ate kithe challe hon*' – How are you and where are you going.[45]

REINFORCEMENTS: SUSTAINING THE CAMPAIGN

While the battalions of Indian Infantry Brigade were fighting the enemy and elements on the peninsula, the question of reinforcements was nibbling the mind of commanders. All four Indian battalions had suffered very heavy casualties. The reinforcements for the Gurkha battalions of the Indian Brigade were being organised under the arrangements with Nepal. On the other hand, the reinforcements for 14th Sikhs were being scrounged from the hinterland of Punjab. A very feverish pace of correspondence between Ian Hamilton and the War Office was underway for an urgent requirement of reinforcements for the 14th Sikhs. As part of an effort to immediately replenish the beleaguered 14th Sikhs, the War Office initially offered to Ian Hamilton, the two battalions of 51st and 53rd Sikhs. Though, Hamilton had serious reservations about the composition of these two 'Class Company' Regiments, the situation of the 14th Sikhs was so desperate that it required an immediate redressal. In spite of having serious apprehensions about the troop composition of the offered reinforcements, he Ian Hamilton reluctantly agreed, 'a few days ago were offered the 51st 53rd Sikhs who, despite their titles, are half Mohammedan. After consulting Cox and other Indian officers, I cabled back saying we would gladly have them, as soon as transport can be arranged.'[46]

However, the dynamics of the overall war effort in the region precluded any possibility of reinforcements for 14th Sikhs from 51st and 53rd Sikhs. Though initially offered, War Office in another cable, confirmed to Hamilton, negating any possibility of further reinforcements. The competitive requirements of additional Indian troops, both at Gallipoli / canal defences and the Western front were playing up in the minds of decision makers in the War Office. The War Office, giving priority to the canal defences over the requirement of reinforcements for the peninsula, had informed Hamilton about the non-availability of these two battalions for Gallipoli. As per the War Office, the immediate urgency was to reinforce the canal defences, as the troops deployed there badly needed reinforcements.

Both the 51st and 53rd Sikhs have already been disembarked. They had better remain off ship as long as possible, I think since they are reported to be feverish. The troopship can wait at Port Said. The men on the canal, I should like to point out, barely get two nights in bed per week.[47]

With the overriding priority being given to the canal defences over the peninsula, by the War Office, Hamilton was quite perturbed and his dejection over the loss of anticipated reinforcements from Sikh battalions was evident. For Hamilton, there was no need for additional troops at the canal defences and the existing troops stationed there were sufficient to ward off any possible threat. Hamilton's primary concern was Gallipoli and he was strong proponent for the cause of an immediate provisioning of reinforcements for Gallipoli by the War Office. 'The Sikhs meant for Gallipoli are gone; we shall never see them more; they mount guard by night against the ghosts of the Suez Canal.'[48] The conditions as obtained along the Canal defences, though out of the purview of this book, may have precipitated the decision of the War Office to deny Hamilton additional troops from the two Sikh battalions. Hamilton, being in command of the troops at Gallipoli was naturally not in sync with the thought process of stationing additional troops in Suez.

In spite of not getting any additional troops, Hamilton's faith in the capabilities of Sikh troops was unshakeable. This confidence of Hamilton stemmed from the exploits of the Sikhs on Gallipoli during the past three months. Taking a cue from the earlier missive of Kitchener, regarding the troops of 51st and 53rd Sikhs being not well, Hamilton wrote back that 'Sikh' troops would not have fallen ill, had the priority been given to at Gallipoli over Canal defences.

Our defeat is a foregone conclusion. All the same, I am determined to press the matter to an issue, if only to have a clean-cut precedent as to whether we do have a first call on troops in Egypt or whether it is the other way about. We want these men so badly. They don't get sick here and are worth four European battalions at present.[49]

Hamilton had also reached the conclusion that the only way to salvage the situation obtained at the peninsula in September 1915 was to get more Indian troops. The experience of the Indian troops in the frontier warfare had the potential of changing the situation completely.

Imagine had we been sent Indian Divisions for Suvla and if the New Army Territorial's and Yeoman had been sent instead to France. Each category would have given double value. The heat, the thirst, the scrub, the snipers, all so disconcerting to our fresh contingents would have been commonplaces of frontier warfare to our Indian troops and see what have we achieved here.[50]

In view of Hamilton, the situation in Suez did not demand additional troops. Fresh troops, if any available, were required on Gallipoli. 'In vain do we try to get our own two battalions through the Egyptian morasses; they are going to stick and do sentries over nothing. I could land a whole division there within four and a half days.'[51] The demand of additional Sikh troops was turning into desperate attempts by Hamilton to seek reinforcements. To the plea that no additional trained troops were available with the War Office for Gallipoli, at one point of time, a very desperate Hamilton was even ready to train them at Gallipoli.

Yet in vain do I write and cable my personal entreaties to Beauchamp Duff, the all-powerful Commander-in-Chief in India, and a very old friend, for two hundred Sikhs. Again, I beg for 200 recruits for the 14th, saying I will train them myself; I am refused – very politely and at great length – refused, because it would be politically inexpedient to send them.[52]

In spite of all the above-mentioned correspondence between the two most powerful anchors of British operations at the Gallipoli, the War Office was still not convinced about the priority of Sikh troops between Gallipoli and Suez. The continued pumping in of troops on the peninsula during the recent past might have triggered this caution. War Office was by this time had also come to terms about the priority of Suez defences over Gallipoli and as a compensation, agreed to provide Hamilton with a Double Company of Patiala Sikhs, with a caveat that nothing from the 51st and 53rd Sikhs should be expected by Hamilton:

from the GOC, Egypt's telegram of 15th September, it is understood that he can send you another Double Company of Patiala Sikhs to reinforce the 14th Sikhs. Possibly this will suffice for your requirements in the meantime, and the 51st and 53rd Sikhs will be left at the disposal of GOC, Egypt.[53]

Hamilton by this time was so desperate of additional reinforcements for the 14th Sikhs, that he had no choice but to agree with the proposal of additional troops in the form of a Double Company of Patiala Infantry and had reconciled with the fact that no additional troops were forthcoming:

In accordance with your telegram of 11th September, I am asking General Officer Commanding, Egypt, to send here, at once, the 51st and 53rd Sikhs, as I cannot do without them. I shall be very glad to receive the Patiala Sikhs as well, as the 14th Sikhs are badly in need of reinforcements.[54]

With severe depletion in the strength of 14th Sikhs after the third battle of Krithia on 4 June, two companies of Patiala State Infantry, were mobilised as reinforcements for the 14th Sikhs and 'A' Company of the Patiala State Infantry joined the 14th Sikhs in July 1915 at Imbros.

As a result of the latest decision, in Sep 1915, 'C' Company of Patiala Sikhs too, reinforced 14th Sikhs at Anzac Cove. The two companies of the Patiala Infantry, while in support of 14th Sikhs gave an excellent account of themselves. In addition, the reinforcements from Burma Military Police were also provided for the 14th Sikhs. The loss of SS *Ramazan* on 19 September 1915 resulted in the death of 277 Indian soldiers, who were primarily being sent as reinforcements for the Indian battalions at Gallipoli. In this incident, 14th Sikhs lost 48 soldiers of Burma Military Police which were to join the battalion as reinforcements. Similarly, 2/10 Gurkhas also lost 173 soldiers, which were meant as reinforcements for the battalion.

On the mobilisation of twenty Infantry battalions in October 1914, the battalions had been directed to make up their respective deficiencies from certain nominated Infantry battalions. For the 29th Indian Infantry Brigade, as per the initial composition, the four battalions were to make up the deficiencies from the following:

FIGURE 81: THREE INDIAN OFFICERS OF 14TH SIKHS AT IMBROS:
SUBADAR MAJOR SHAM SINGH (14TH SIKHS), SUBADAR KISHAN
SINGH (BURMA MILITARY POLICE) AND SUBADAR BHAGAT SINGH
(PATIALA INFANTRY) (*LEFT TO RIGHT*)[55]

14th Sikhs - 45th Sikhs
89th Punjabis - 90th Punjabis
69th Punjabis - 67th Punjabis
1/6 Gurkhas - 2/6 Gurkhas

The battalions on embarkation for Suez had catered for deficiencies
to be made up from these nominated battalions. Though, both 89th
and 69th Punjabis were withdrawn from the peninsula on 15 May
1915, the casualty analysis of both 14th Sikhs and 1/6 Gurkhas
indicate the fair share of 45th Sikhs and 2/6 Gurkhas in the overall
casualty figures as shown in Table 39.

TABLE 39: CASUALTIES OF 45TH SIKHS AND 2/6 GURKHAS
ON GALLIPOLI[56]

Unit	Attached with	Dead	Missing	Wounded	Total
45th Sikhs	14th Sikhs	15	4	48	67
2/6 Gurkhas	1/6 Gurkhas	12	-	69	81
Total		27	4	117	148

Despite an intense research, it was not possible to locate any definite source, hinting at dispatch of reinforcements for 14th Sikhs and 1/6 Gurkhas from 45th Sikhs and 2/6 Gurkhas respectively. It can be fairly assumed that there were no organised reinforcements from these two battalions to the 14th Sikhs and 1/6 Gurkhas and it is more likely that the deficiencies of 14th Sikhs and 1/6 Gurkhas were made up by these two battalions respectively.

The first organised reinforcements for the embattled Indian battalions on Gallipoli from India, could only be organised in August 1914. The rate of provisioning of reinforcements was simply not being able to cope with the rate of casualties being incurred by the Indian battalions on the peninsula. The peculiar class composition of the battalions on the peninsula enforced additional logistical qualifications. It was therefore, endeavored to have the similar caste composition of the reinforcements as of the receiving battalions. 648 Indian Officers, Rank and File and Followers as reinforcements, meant for the various units and sub units on Gallipoli, sailed from India in the month of August 1915 as shown in Table 40.[57]

The further dispatch of these reinforcements from Alexandria to Mudros met with a tragedy when the hired transport SS *Ramazan* was sunk on the early morning of 19 September 1915, by a German U Boat. The incident resulted in the drowning of 277 Indian troops. The Secretary of State for India had informed the Viceroy (Army Department) on 7 October 1915 regarding the tragic loss of SS *Ramajan* along with the loss of approximate '145' Indian troops only, a figure which was revised later on.[58] The issue has been discussed in detail in the next section of the book.

Similarly, in September 1915, the stream of the reinforcements continued for the Indian battalions at Dardanelles. This batch comprising 11 Indian Officers, 528 Indian Rank & File and 16 followers had sailed from India on 16 September 1915 as shown in Table 41.

For the month of October 1915, the reinforcements which sailed from India, were primarily meant for 14th Sikhs, 2/10 Gurkhas and 1/4 Gurkhas. The Ports of Embarkation for the troops embarking were either Bombay or Karachi. The ships carrying the following

TABLE 40: REINFORCEMENTS FOR 29TH INDIAN INFANTRY
BRIGADE IN AUGUST 1915[59]

Unit	Indian Officers	Indian Rank & File	Followers	Total
2/10 Gurkhas	-	77	1	78
1/10 Gurkhas for 2/10 Gurkhas	2	97	2	102
14th Sikhs	-	38	-	38
Burma Military Police for 14th Sikhs	1	72	2	75
1/5 Gurkhas	1	83	2	86
2/5 Gurkhas for 1/5 Gurkhas	1	30	1	32
1/6 Gurkhas	-	91	-	91
21st Mountain Battery	-	03	1	4
7th Mountain Artillery Battery	-	85	-	85
Supply & Transport Personnel	-	20	38	58
Total	5	596	47	648

TABLE 41: REINFORCEMENTS FOR THE 29TH INDIAN INFANTRY
BRIGADE IN SEPTEMBER 1915[60]

Units	Indian Officers	Indian Rank & File	Followers	Total
1/10 Gurkhas for 2/10 Gurkhas	4	176	10	190
Details of 14th, 15th Sikhs and BMP for 14th Sikhs	6	245	4	255
1/5 Gurkhas	-	23	-	23
7th Indian Mountain Artillery Brigade	-	83	-	83
21st Mountain Battery	-	1	-	1
Postal	1	-	2	3
Total	11	528	16	555

reinforcements for the battalions of the 29th Indian Brigade had sailed from India on 16 October 1915 as shown in Table 42.

TABLE 42: REINFORCEMENTS FOR THE 29TH INDIAN INFANTRY
BRIGADE IN OCTOBER 1915[61]

Unit	Indian Officers	Indian Rank & File	Followers	Total
Indian Mountain Artillery	-	1	-	1
1/10 Gurkhas for 2/10 Gurkhas	2	98	3	103
1/4 Gurkhas	-	92	2	94
14th Sikhs	1	47	2	50
15th Ludhiana Sikhs for 14th Sikhs	-	35	2	37
Army Depot for 7th Indian Mountain Artillery Brigade	-	75	4	79
1/7 Gurkhas for 2/10 Gurkhas	2	94	3	99
Total	5	442	16	463

An analysis of the reinforcements which set sail in October 1915 reveals the desperation for finding the drafts for the Indian battalions on Gallipoli. The desperation might have been further compounded by the loss of hired transport S.S. *Ramajan* in September 1915, in the Sea of Aegean. It was for the first time that reinforcements for the 14th Sikhs and 2/10 Gurkhas were being made up from 15th Ludhiana Sikhs and 1/7 Gurkhas respectively. Besides, these organised reinforcements from the 15th Ludhiana Sikhs, some Burma Military Police reinforcements already with the 15th Ludhiana Sikhs in Egypt had also been redirected to the 14th Sikhs.

Though a serious thought was being given to the notion of withdrawal of the allied forces from the peninsula, but the process set in motion for the provisioning of reinforcements for the 29th Indian Infantry Brigade from India, continued unabated. The magnitude of the losses being suffered by the Indian battalions were much beyond the available pace of reinforcements. In November 1915, following additional troops had set sail for Dardanelles from India.

A combination of twin factors of proposed de-induction of MEF from Dardanelles, coupled with the loss of SS *Ramazan* in the month

TABLE 43: REINFORCEMENTS FOR THE 29TH INDIAN INFANTRY BRIGADE IN NOVEMBER 1915[62]

Unit	Indian Officers	Indian Rank & File	Followers	Total
Supply & Transport Corps	-	-	1	1
82nd Punjabis for 14th Sikhs	2	98	3	103
1/7 Gurkhas for 2/10 Gurkhas	2	98	2	102
2/6 Gurkhas for 1/6 Gurkhas	2	96	2	99
14th Sikhs	-	1	-	1
Porter Corps	4	7	610	621
Total	10	300	618	928

of September 1915, had inculcated a sense of caution and it is very likely that no additional troops meant for Indian battalions on Gallipoli were reaching the concerned battalions. But the process of recruitment and subsequent dispatch of these drafts from India was continuing. In the month of December 1915 also, even when Indian troops were

TABLE 44: REINFORCEMENTS FOR THE 29TH INDIAN INFANTRY BRIGADE IN DECEMBER 1915[63]

Units	Indian Officers	Indian Rank & File	Followers	Total
1/5 Gurkhas	2	98	3	103
Medical Personnel	-	3	-	3
2/4 Gurkhas for 1/4 Gurkhas	2	98	3	103
1/6 Gurkhas	2	278	1	281
2/6 Gurkhas for 1/6 Gurkhas	1	48	1	50
1/5 Gurkhas	1	200	1	202
14th Sikhs	1	22	-	23
7th Indian Mountain Artillery Brigade	-	56	-	56
1st Labour Corps	13	61	995	1,069
Total	22	864	1,004	1,890

actually withdrawing from Dardanelles, another tranche of reinforcements had set sail from India, meant for Indian battalions on the peninsula.

Thus, it can be seen that over a period of five months, from August 1915 to December 1915, a total of 4,485 troops including combatants and non-combatants had been dispatched from India for the deployment on Gallipoli. A dearth of historical records has dampened all initiatives to delve more into this aspect. As a result, it is slightly difficult to accurately predict the numbers of reinforcements, which actually reached the respective battalions on Gallipoli. This strength includes the Porter Corps, which was dispatched from India for the deployment on Gallipoli but ultimately was not employed. Therefore, taking out strength of 17 Indian Officers, 68 Indian Rank and File and 1,605 followers, from the total number of reinforcements, it can be fairly assumed that approximately 2,793 combatants and non-combatants were dispatched from India as reinforcements for the battalions and sub-units of the 29th Indian Infantry Brigade, till 31 December 1915, when the 29th Indian Infantry Brigade along with its battalions was in the process of deinducting from the peninsula.

TABLE 45: SUMMARY OF TOTAL REINFORCEMENTS FOR
DARDANELLES DISPATCHED FROM INDIA:
AUGUST 1915 TO DECEMBER 1915[64]

Unit	Indian Officers	Indian Rank & File	Followers	Total
14th Sikhs	11	563	13	587
1/5 Gurkhas	5	434	7	446
1/4 Gurkhas	2	190	5	197
1/6 Gurkhas	5	513	5	523
2/10 Gurkhas	12	640	21	673
7th Indian Mountain Artillery Brigade	-	304	4	308
Indian Mule Corps	-	20	39	59
Porter Corps	17	68	1,605	1,690
Total	52	2,732	1,701	4,485

UNKNOWN AND UNDER THE SEA:
THE TRAGEDY OF SS *RAMAJAN*

The requirement of reinforcements for the Indian Expeditionary Force was never ending. As long as troops stayed on the peninsula, the requests for additional troops never ceased. With the serious depletion in the rank and file of the battalions of the 29th Indian Infantry Brigade, it was imperative that continuous supply of troops belonging to that particular regiment in the form of reinforcements is maintained. With little or no reserves available with the home depots of the battalions, all possible sources of the reinforcements were being explored.

In July 1915, due to a very poor bayonet state of the 14th Sikhs, as a result of the quantum of casualties, reinforcements of one Indian officer and 78 rank and file from Burma Military Police had reported to the depot of the Battalion at Multan. The command and control structure devised for the incorporation of these troops in Battalion envisaged that these additional troops will not be merged in the existing companies of the 14th Sikhs, but rather a separate company will be created, which will be posted with a regular Indian officer and non-commissioned officers to this company will be side stepped from the 14th Sikhs.

The details having been worked out, it was in the month of August 1915, that reinforcements had sailed from different Ports of Embarkation in India. All these troops, coming from different units and sub-units were to reinforce the battalions of the 29th Indian Infantry Brigade. With a shortage of weapons and equipment to equip these reinforcements, a case was taken up by the Director General of Ordnance Services in India with the GOC Egypt that all these reinforcements will be dispatched without any rifles and personnel equipment. The telegram dated 20 August 1915 mentions about the additional reinforcements planned for dispatch in the month of September also. 'I have the honour to inform you that the total number of men constituting the August drafts for the Dardanelles who proceeded unequipped were 633. The number of men under orders to proceed unequipped during September is 522. The total number of rifles and sets of equipment to be provided in Egypt is thus 1,155.'[65]

The drafts meant for different battalions of the Indian Brigade were drawn from totally different units but had the similar caste composition of the battalions for which these reinforcements were meant. The War Diary of IEF 'G', for the month of September 1915, makes a mention of dispatch of a total of 809 Indian troops including followers who were dispatched from India. The breakdown of the reinforcements included the following, as shown in Table 46.[66]

TABLE 46: REINFORCEMENTS IN AUGUST 1915 FOR
THE 29TH INDIAN INFANTRY BRIGADE[67]

Unit	British Officers	British Troops	Indian Officers	Indian Rank & File	Followers
2/10 Gurkhas	1	-	-	77	1
1/10 Gurkhas for 2/10 Gurkhas	2	-	2	97	2
14th Sikhs	2	-	-	38	-
Burma Military Police for 14th Sikhs	-	-	1	72	2
82nd Punjabi for 14th Sikhs	1	-	2	98	5
1/5 Gurkhas	2	-	1	83	2
2/5 Gurkhas for 1/5 Gurkhas	-	-	1	30	1
1/6 Gurkhas	-	-	-	91	-
2/6 Gurkhas for 1/6 Gurkhas	2	-	1	40	2
21st Mountain Battery	-	-	-	3	1
7th Mountain Artillery Battery	-	-	-	85	-
S & T Personnel	1	2	-	20	38
Total	11	2	8	734	54

Bombay was designated as the Port of Embarkation for the details comprising Companies of 2/10 Gurkhas, 1/10 Gurkhas and Supply and Transport personnel. 189 troops of these three sub units along with three British Officers, two Indian Officers and 33 followers had boarded the HT *Aronda* on 14 August 1915 and the vessel had set sail on the next day. Similarly, 407 Indian troops belonging to the Companies of 14th Sikhs, Burma Military Police, 1/5 Gurkhas, 2/5 Gurkhas, 1/6 Gurkhas, 7th Indian Mountain Artillery Brigade and Supply and Transport had embarked from Karachi on board HT *Chilka* on 16 August 1915 and sailed on the same day. The vessel also had on board six British officers, three Indian officers and 14 followers belonging to these sub units.

Though the War Diary of IEF 'G' for the month of August 1915 mentions the dispatch of the two subunits of the 82nd Punjabis as reinforcements for the 14th Sikhs and 2/6 Gurkhas for 1/6 Gurkhas, the same has been further explained in the War Diary for the month of September 1915 belonging to the force. In a telegram dated 6 September 1915, the Chief of General Staff had informed GOC Egypt that, 'owing to unsettled conditions company for the 14th Sikhs from 82nd Punjabis and company for 1/6 Gurkhas from 2/6 Gurkhas could not be sent'.[68] Taking out the strength of the 82nd Punjabis and 2/6 Gurkhas from the table given above, one finds that a strength of five Indian Officers, 596 Indian Rank & File and 47 followers had embarked as reinforcements in the month of August 1915 for Dardanelles as against the strength of eight Indian Officers, 734 Indian Rank and File and 54 followers, originally mentioned. Considering the actual strength which embarked for Dardanelles, the concerns for equipping of these reinforcements, expressed by the Ordnance Services as discussed earlier, appear to be a bit more realistic.

Templating the time taken by the battalions of the 29th Indian Infantry Brigade from Karachi to Alexandria, it can be fairly assumed that these reinforcements had reached Alexandria by the first week of September 1915. There was a time lag of about eight to ten days, before the troops embarked for the forward journey to Mudros, during which the troops earmarked for the battalions of the 29th Indian Infantry Brigade, were equipped with kits and weapons, which were available at the base at Alexandria. Balance of the kitting was supposed to be carried out on the peninsula itself, by the battalions receiving these reinforcements. The reinforcements for 2/10 Gurkhas, 14th Sikhs and certain logistic elements at the peninsula were allotted the hired transport SS *Ramazan* for the journey of almost 650 miles from

Alexandria to Mudros. The ship with 300 plus Indian troops along with the 28 members of the crew had set sail for Mudros on 15 September 1915.

The transport carrying these reinforcements, SS *Ramazan*, was a British steamer of 3,477 tons, constructed in 1905 at Middlesbrough and was owned by Liverpool Shipping Company Limited. The steamer had a crew of 29 persons and was being commanded by Captain C.J. Legget. The name of S.S. *Ramazan*, had earlier cropped up for the first time in relation to the mobilisation of the Indian Mule Cart Train. The ship had docked at Marseilles on 27 March 1915. That time, as the ship was being used for transportation of mules, the necessary fittings had to be resorted to make the transport suitable for carrying mules.

No.1 Corps was to sail as soon as ships could be made ready, and on March 27, SS *Ramazan* and another steamer arrived in the docks, and work was immediately put in hand to fit up these ships for carrying mules. I spent a good deal of time advising on the arrangements, and planning the disposal of my command on board. It was decided that the whole of No. 1 Corps and one troop of No. 2 should sail in these two ships. 577 mules were allotted to the *Ramazan* and 620 to the other vessel.[69]

Just as in March 1915, when the same ship had bare minimum accommodation for the mules being transported, this time the ship was again suffering from a serious space crunch and possessed bare essential accommodation for the number of troops on board. As a result, with the available space being very cramped, a large number of troops were accommodated in the forecastle of the ship. Most of the troops on board were very young, having just been recruited from the villages of Nepal and Punjab. These young men having just been recruited, and with a first step towards a relatively secured financial future, were eagerly looking for participation in the 'Active Service'.

For most of them, however, this was going to be the first and last journey outside their villages. In the early hours of 19 September 1915, when except for few sentries, most of the troops on board the ship, SS *Ramazan* were still in slumber, a German U boat was also prowling in the waters of Aegean Sea searching for the next victim. This U Boat had been responsible for the sinking of almost 10,577 tons of allied shipping in the 22 days of its patrolling in the Aegean Sea. The boat under the command of Kapitänleutnant Waldemar Kophamel had left Cattaro harbour on 31 August and was patrolling the South Aegean Sea till 22 September.[70] Having already knocked off, the French steamer *Ravitailleur*, an Austrian vessel captured by the French, two days before on 17 September near the south-west end of Crete, the German U-35, had homed down to its next victim carrying Indian troops.

At about 04:30 hours on 19 September 1915, with its lights absolutely dimmed, the British transport vessel, SS *Ramajan* was silently steaming towards Mudros. In the general area of west of Crete, with wind almost still and the atmosphere being clear, the visibility was very good. It was under these conditions, when the German U Boat locked onto the British steamer. The log book of the German U Boat mentions that;

Dived at dawn in front of dimmed vessel and drove attack. Steamer lies so high out of the water that torpedo may pass under her. Surfaced and fired a shot across the bow. Steamer does not set flag, turns away and tries to escape; therefore, opened gunfire on her.[71]

As if the torpedo shot was not enough, the subsequent gunfire from the U Boat was too much for the steamer. After taking six to eight hits, the steamer was not able to move ahead and stopped. The number of boats available vis-à-vis the number of troops on board was hardly a match. Limited number of boats on board and the relative inexperience of Indian troops in swimming did not help the situation either. For the strength of almost 400 personnel on board, including the crew, there were only seven boats. With the serious damage to the hull and the gun fire, the ship had taken too much impairment and was doomed to drown.

By 0630 hours all the seven fully manned boats had been launched from the steamer and slowly the boats had started moving away from the ill-fated steamer. The log book of the German U Boat identifies the troops on board the boats being as Indians, 'people wore brown and yellow turbans and tropical hats'.[72] Assuming that the last troop on board the stricken steamer had left, the Captain of the U-35 ordered to hit the steamer with the gunfire in the waterline of the forward hold. To the astonishment of the German crew, as the ship began to sink, a horde of troops started appearing on the deck. Either because no more boats were available on board or because the command elements of these troops had departed earlier, these young, innocent and brave men were destined to be buried in a watery grave. The log book of the German U boat succinctly captured this poignant moment:

As the ship began to sink, a large number of people suddenly came running up on deck from the forecastle, but they did nothing to save themselves. The actual crew of the steamer had already disembarked. In total, the transport must have been about 500 men strong. The number of lifeboats on the ship was far from sufficient. Unfortunately, it was not possible to think of rescuing the people by submarine because of the excessive number.[73]

Thus went down the British steamer SS *Ramazan* along with 277 Indian troops on board. Surprisingly, out of a crew of 29, only one fatality has been listed in the records, whereas out of almost 380 Indian troops on board, 277 perished in the watery graves of the Aegean Sea. This loss has generally been lost in the plethora of other losses of Indian troops in the overall contribution of Indian troops in the First World War. As far as the number of casualties are concerned, the loss of 277 Indian troops on 19 September 1915 is the major single day loss (killed) even surpassing the losses suffered by the Indian Brigade during the ill-fated third battle of Krithia on the peninsula of 4 June 1915. On 4 June, 14th Sikhs had suffered 133 fatal casualties, 1/5 Gurkhas-25 and 1/6 Gurkhas had 12 fatal casualties, thereby adding to a total of 170 fatal casualties.

The individual details of the loss being very farfetched, even the mention of the losses has generally been found wanting in the works on the subject so far. This section of the book is dedicated to the memories of these troops and attempts to do justice to their contribution. The casualty figures of the Indian troops, from the sinking of SS *Ramazan* have been analyzed by taking inputs from the CWGC database, which was then templated upon the details of casualties obtained from the Casualty Appendices of War Diaries of IEF 'G'. As all the troops on board the ill-fated steamer were going as reinforcements for the Indian battalions of the 29th Indian Infantry

Brigade, the sheer severity of the loss would have been implacable for the Indian Brigade.

As per details available on CWGC portal, 292 fatal casualties of Indian troops have been listed against the date of 19 September 1915. While maximum casualties of Indian troops due to sinking of *Ramazan* occurred on 19 September 1915, the entire 292 casualties on the portal against the date of 19 September cannot be attributed to sinking of the ship as on that date casualties from reasons other than sinking of ship also are possible, as the Indian troops were engaged in a long-drawn campaign against the Turks on the peninsula. As a corollary, the casualties due to the sinking of ship might also have been registered after 19 September 1915. Irrespective of the above, the fact remains that almost one Double Company of 2/10 Gurkhas and a half Double Company of Sikhs perished in the tragedy. The breakdown of the casualties, belonging to the different battalions and regiments, as per CWGC database includes as shown in Table 47:

TABLE 47: DETAILS OF CASUALTIES OF *SS RAMAJAN* AS PER CWGC DATABASE[74]

Unit & Rank	Number of Casualties
10th Gurkha Rifles	**173**
Colour Havildar	1
Follower	1
Havildar	5
Jemadar	1
Lance Havildar	2
Lance Naik	1
Naik	4
Rifleman	158
14th King George's Own Ferozepore Sikhs	**30**
Bugler	2
Drum Major	1
Follower	2
Lance Naik	2
Sepoy	23
15th Ludhiana Sikhs	**1**
Sepoy	1

Assam Military Police	1
Rifleman	1
Burma Military Police	48
Havildar	1
Jemadar	1
Lance Naik	13
Rifleman	33
Gwalior Transport Corps	1
Artisan	1
Indian Mountain Artillery	4
Driver	3
Gunner	1
Indore Transport Corps	1
Driver	1
Mule Corps	11
Driver	8
Follower	1
Lance Naik	2
Supply and Transport Corps	22
Follower	22
Grand Total	292

As far as public knowledge of the casualties of Indian troops due to the sinking of SS *Ramazan* is concerned, it can be claimed that the common public was not aware of the incident till as late as 9 November 1915, when the *Daily News* (London), published an article about the monumental loss, referring to the information provided by the Press Bureau of London. In a letter to the editor, under the headline of 'Suppression of Bad News', it has been alleged that there was an ostensible, cover up to withhold the news of the sinking of the ship from the common people. In the same tone, the letter goes on to further allege that though the news has been suppressed from release for seven weeks, the information about the losses had already been covered by the *New York Evening Post* of 29 September 1915. In fact, while this was an alleged cover up by the British Military planners, the news was covered by at least five American newspapers on 29 September 1915 itself to include the following:

- *The Evening World* (New York), 29 September 1915, p. 2.
- *The Evening Post* (New York), 29 September 1915, p. 1.
- *The Daily News* (Batavia), 29 September 1915, p. 1.
- *The Advertiser-Journal* (Auburn), 29 September 1915, p. 1.
- *The Evening Gazette* (Port Jervis), 30 September 1915, p. 1.

Athens, Greece, Sept. 28, via London, Sept. 29, 10.25 a.m.—The Greek Government has released the Sikhs and Gurkhas who were survivors of the British transport Ramazan, which was sunk by a submarine. They were sent immediately to Malta on the Messageries Maritimes steamer Siboni. Many of them had no opportunity even to obtain clothing.

FIGURE 82: IMAGE OF THE NEWS CARRIED BY *THE NEW YORK EVENING POST* OF 29 SEPTEMBER 1915[75]

While the news was adequately covered in the press of the USA, the apparent censorship over the release of the news in the local press of Britain was quite evident and more importantly when the news in the American press was routed through London. The concern was impressed upon by the editor of the *Daily News* (London).

You will not overlook the significance of the fact that this cablegram from Athens to New York was transmitted via London. That is to say, the news was passed by the British censorship for publication in America, though it was withheld from the knowledge of the British public.

H.

FIGURE 83: EXTRACT OF THE NEWS CARRIED BY THE *DAILY NEWS* (LONDON), 9 NOVEMBER 1915[76]

The issue of suppression of news about the sinking of the ship and the tremendous loss of life was also raised in the British Parliament. On 11 November, in the House of Commons, the Home Secretary was asked in no uncertain terms that whether the Press Bureau had deliberately permitted American press to cover the incident, whereas the same was not allowed for the British press.

Whether the Press Bureau refused to pass for publication in the British Press until November 06, the news of the sinking of the transport 'Ramazan', although it had permitted a cable announcing the fact to pass through London for publication in the American press of September 29.[77]

While it remains a fact that the news of the sinking of ship was not shared with the British press, a number of reasons for the same also have been circulated in the press of that time. For instance, Army and Navy Gazette of 13 November 1915, attributed the reason for non-sharing of the details of the incident with the possibility of, 'getting the names of those lost, to India before the news was published seeing that most of the people drowned were Sikhs and Gurkhas'. Assuming the credibility of the above for the time being, analysing the Casualty Appendix of the IEF 'G', for the month of October 1915, one comes across a telegram dated 20 October 1915, initiated by the 3rd Echelon Alexandria, addressed to the Central Casualty Bureau, in which the details of the casualties occurred on 19 September 1915 have been forwarded.[78] Prior to the details of casualties being forwarded, another telegram of date 7 October 1915 was forwarded by The Secretary of State for India to the Viceroy (Army Department) intimating him about the sinking of the ship. 'On 20 September, a Submarine sank a transport carrying the following from Alexandria for the Dardanelles. British Officers: 5, Indian Officers: 02, Other Ranks (Indian): 338, About 200 survivors were conveyed to Greece and Malta and thence to Alexandria.'[79] In a further explanation to the above, the next telegram on the same subject amplifies the casualties amongst the British and the Indian officers. Out of a total of five British and two Indian officers on board, one British and both the Indian officers were reported to be drowned. The Indian Officers included Jemadar Kishen Singh of Burma Military Police attached with the 14th Sikhs and Jemadar Sankhaman Limbu of 2/10 Gurkhas. Balance of the four British officers were saved in the incident. Three days later, may be for some sort of clarification on the exact details of casualties, the GOC, Canal Defences intimated to the C-in-C in India that the casualties have been reported due to the sinking of the transport. 'Drowned September 19th, British Officers One, 2nd Lieutenant 14th Sikhs name requires verification and cannot be traced; native officers 2/10 Gurkhas Sankhaman Limbu, Jemadar, Burma Military Police attached to the 14th Sikhs, Kishen Singh, Jemadar and Rank and File approximately 290, mostly 14th Sikhs.'[80]

The list of casualties forwarded on 20 October may be taken as authentic and corroborated as the details have been forwarded to the Central Casualty Bureau for intimation to the respective battalions and subsequently to the next of kin. In addition, as the details have been forwarded almost one month after the incident, the credibility of the details may be assumed on the basis of the assumption that all possible details must have been co-related and authenticated from different sources. But the question of allowing the information about the loss to pass through London to the American press and withholding the information from the British public largely went unanswered.

As part of my research and in an attempt to unravel the mystery of details, hitherto uncovered, the details of each and every casualty were matched with the details available on the CWGC portal, almost 3,260 data points of the details were analysed and a reconciled detail of the Indian troops who drowned on 19 September has been prepared. A summary of the breakdown of the casualties, belonging to the different battalions and regiments, is as given in Table 48, whereas the detailed description of the casualties of the Indian troops due to the sinking of SS *Ramazan* are appended in the end of the book.

Casualty Analytics

Attempting to fix the exact number of Indian troops which served on the peninsula in 1915 is indeed a very difficult proposition. War Diaries of the respective units do provide some information on the casualty figures, but the minor units, particularly the Indian Mule

TABLE 48: BREAKDOWN OF CASUALTIES OF SS *RAMAZAN* AS
PER CASUALTY LIST OF THE 3RD ECHELON ALEXANDRIA
(DATED 20 OCTOBER 1915)[81]

Units	Numbers
1/10 Gurkhas	84
14th King George's Own Ferozepore Sikhs	28
15th Ludhiana Sikhs	1
2/10 Gurkhas	84
26th Mountain Battery	4
Assam Military Police	1
Burma Military Police	45
Gwalior Transport Corps	1
Indore Transport Corps	1
Mule Corps	10
Supply and Transport Corps	18
Total	277

Corps, which has almost equal contribution in number of troops as the Infantry units combined, if not more; largely do not have respective War Diaries which can provide some inputs with respect to the casualties suffered. The research gets further impeded by the fact that turnover of troops in all the units and sub units of the Indian Army on the peninsula due to the massive number of casualties was a constant affair. Coupled with this, in spite of the intense efforts to determine the details of the reinforcements being dispatched from India, the granular details of the troops dispatched did not materialise and hit dead end multiple times. Peter Stanley in his book on Gallipoli has referred to this adversity in the efforts, when he writes;

While it is possible to be reasonably certain of some members of infantry or artillery units who died of wounds in Egypt and Malta, it is almost impossible to identify men of Supply and Transport or medical units, or to identify men serving on attachment with units on Gallipoli. Sorting out the confusion is possible, but only by laborious crosschecking of casualty lists against memorial records.[82]

The confusion referred to by Peter Stanley pertained to the fatal Indian casualties of the campaign. In addition, as corroborated by various historical records, the Indian troops suffered almost 4,000 plus casualties in terms of wounded, a number of them getting wounded multiple times and a number of them later on died also due to the wounds sustained during the various battles of the campaign. This faceless lot of injured Indian soldiers on the peninsula has been particularly unfortunate. The system of reporting of casualties as discussed earlier was not yet geared up to be able to handle the surge in the casualties and was getting matured on a daily basis. With no precedents of the reporting of casualties from multiple units and sub units to a location 3,000 miles away, complicated by the number of depots and the rudimentary system of records keeping, keeping a track of the casualties was indeed an arduous task.

In the ultimate chapter of the book, I have attempted to make a sincere effort to recognise the efforts of these unknown and faceless Indian soldiers who got injured on the peninsula, by providing them with recognition. The task was complicated and difficult. The cross checking of the casualty lists of the IEF 'G' as available with National Archives of India, was an elaborate and intricate exercise. The multiple sources of origin of the casualty intimations from Egypt to the multiple sources in India, coupled with multiple entries of a single person in multitude of sources appeared to be a dampener initially. The issue turned into a more baffling one, when one considered the magnitude of the attached troops from different units with the units at Gallipoli.

In order to resolve the imbroglio and to arrive at a near exact number of Indian casualties, both fatal and non-fatal, a data base of 86,679 data points in respect of 7,209 number of Indian casualties at Gallipoli has been created. The inputs for the same were taken from 165 casualty lists prepared by IEF 'G'. The next action in line was apparently and absolutely unfathomable. The task involved segregating all the 7,209 casualties into killed in action, died of wounds, severely and slightly injured and further classify them as per dates of casualties. The duplicate entries, reported by multiple channels needed to be checked against the details of Regimental Numbers and units, as there were 1103 entries with more than one name. Out of these there were

18 entries, whose names were repeated 20 or more times. Some of the details are as given in Table 49.

TABLE 49: ENTRIES WITH MULTIPLE NAMES /
DUPLICATE ENTRIES[83]

Name	*Number of Entries in Various Telegrams (More than 20 Entries)*
Amar Singh	20
Arjan Singh	21
Bir Singh	29
Bishan Singh	30
Chanan Singh	28
Gajjan Singh	22
Harnam Singh	71
Indar Singh	35
Jagat Singh	21
Jiwan Singh	28
Kehar Singh	27
Kishan Singh	21
Kishen Singh	22
Manbahadur Gurung	22
Mangal Singh	24
Narain Singh	25
Phuman Singh	26
Prem Singh	23
Puran Singh	22
Ram Singh	41
Santa Singh	31
Sham Singh	23
Sundar Singh	37

Each casualty was mapped against a specific casualty list to include Telegram Number, date of Telegram, Number of appendices in the respective telegram and the respective diary numbers. The data points within these 165 Telegrams were further found segregated into 96 Appendices and 186 Diary Entries. In addition, the details were collated by three different agencies, with each agency sending on an average of 44 details, on each day over a period of 12 months. The details of casualties, both fatal and non-fatal have been compiled, but the granularity and quantum of data was getting covered in additional 230 pages of the book, thereby making it logistically difficult to include the details in the present work. Some of the peculiarities of the analysis with respect to the casualties suffered by the Indian troops on the peninsula have however been analysed in the subsequent parts of the section.

Units and Sub Units

Starting with two Batteries of the Indian Mountain Artillery which landed on the peninsula on 25 April 1915, the composition of the Indian participation was witness to a continuous and constant change. The men and animals of the Mule Corps kept on arriving till August 1915. This process further continued as the replacements of casualties of Indian drivers continued to land on the peninsula. The composition of the Indian mainstay at Gallipoli, the 29th Indian Infantry Brigade also was subject to constant changes. After the departure of the 69th and 89th Punjabis from the peninsula on 15 May 1915, at one point of time three British battalions also came under command of the 29th Indian Infantry Brigade.

With each Indian battalion on the peninsula having reinforcements/ deficiencies made up from different units/sub units, the analysis of casualties was a difficult task. In the absence of a reliable communication system, existence of a multitude of agencies, the magnitude of casualties and a totally rudimentary system of reporting, it must have been a very arduous task; 109 years back to report the exact status and details of the casualties. With almost 2,700 duplicate and 7,029 cumulative entries in the three forwarding and receiving lists, the task of segregating and collating details was almost an impossible task. Each unit was having a large number of persons attached from other units. The task of the reporting agency to identify each casualty for the original or the current units was a difficult task. In the casualty returns, the 14th

Sikhs alone had reinforcements belonging to seven different units. Other units to include the Mountain Artillery Batteries similarly had a large number of attachments from the other units and sub units. On an average each Indian unit had attachments from six to eight different units/ sub-units. Starting from 25 April 1915 till 19 December 1915, the following Indian units and subunits represented the Indian Army on the Gallipoli Peninsula.

TABLE 50: MAJOR AND MINOR INDIAN UNITS ON
GALLIPOLI PENINSULA[84]

Formations/ Groups	Major Units	Minor Units/Detachments
7th Indian Mountain Artillery Brigade	21st (Kohat) Mountain Battery, 26th (Jacob's) Mountain Battery,	Headquarters 7 IMAB, MA Section, Divisional Ammunition Column
29th Indian Infantry Brigade	14th Sikhs, 69th Punjabis, 89th Punjabis, 1/6 Gurkhas, 1/5 Gurkhas, 2/10 Gurkhas, 1/4 Gurkhas	Headquarters 29th Brigade, 2 Double Companies Patiala Infantry
Hospitals	108th Indian Field Ambulance (with the 29th Brigade) 110th Indian Field Ambulance (with Convalescent Depot)	C Section (Indian) 137th Combined Field Ambulance (with 7 IMAB), C Section (British), 137th Combined Field Ambulance (on a transport)
Transport	1st, 2nd, 9th, 11th, 15th, 28th, 31st and 32nd Mule Corps	Detachments from 3rd, 6th, 7th, 8th, 10th, 12th, 14th, 18th, 19th, 20th, 21st, 22nd, 23rd, 24th, 25th, 27th, 29th, 33rd, 34th, 35th, 36th and 37th Mule Corps. Detachments from Gwalior, Bharatpore and Indore Imperial Service Transport Corps.

Though the above details represent only the details of the major and minor Indian units which were there on the peninsula, the Indian troops who were posted or attached with these units, belonged to a number of other major or minor Indian units. The casualty appendices

TABLE 51: INDIAN UNITS/ SUBUNITS AT GALLIPOLI[85]

1/10 Gurkhas	2/2 Gurkhas	27th Mountain Battery	69th Punjabis
1/2 Gurkhas	2/4 Gurkhas	28th Mule Corps	7th IMAB & Divisional Amn Column
1/4 Gurkhas	2/5 Gurkhas	28th Mountain Battery	7th Mule Corps
1/5 Gurkhas	2/6 Gurkhas	29th Mountain Battery	87th Punjabis
1/6 Gurkhas	2/9 Gurkhas	29th Mule Corps	89th Punjabis
1/9 Gurkhas	20th Mule Corps	2nd Mule Corps	8th Mule Corps
108th Indian Field Ambulance	21st Mountain Battery	30th Mountain Battery	90th Punjabis
10th Mule Corps	21st Mule Corps	31st Mountain Battery	9th Mule Corps
110th Indian Field Ambulance	22nd Mule Corps	31st Mule Corps	Assam Military Police
11th Mule Corps	23rd Mountain Battery	32nd Mule Corps;	Bharatpur Transport Corps
12th Mule Corps	23rd Mule Corps	33rd Mule Corps	Burma Military Police
137th Combined Field Ambulance	24th Mountain Battery	34th Mule Corps	Darrang Police Battalion
14th Mule Corps	24th Mule Corps	35th Mule Corps	Gwalior Transport Corps
14th Sikhs	25th Mule Corps	36th Mule Corps	Indian Subordinate Medical Dept
15th Ludhiana Sikhs	26th Mountain Battery	36th Sikhs	Indore Transport Corps
15th Mule Corps	26th Mule Corps	37th Mule Corps	Lakhimpur Military Police
18th Mule Corps	27th Mountain Battery	38th Mule Corps	Myitkyina Military Police
19th Mule Corps	28th Mule Corps	3rd Mule Corps	Naga Hills Military Police
1st Mule Corps	28th Mountain Battery	45th Sikhs	Patiala Infantry
2/10 Gurkhas	29th Mountain Battery	54th Sikhs	Lushai Hills Military Police

of the Force 'G' provide a mention of the original units of the Indian casualties along with the units with whom these troops were attached. Drawing from the detailed analysis of the casualty appendices, one comes to a categorical conclusion that the Indian troops who fought on the peninsula were drawn from at least 80 major and minor units and subunits, as mentioned in Table 51.

REPORTING PERIOD OF CASUALTIES

As discussed earlier, the system of reporting of casualties was still at its infancy even during the latter half of 1915, when the IEF 'G' was evacuated from the peninsula, though, by the time IEF 'G' was pulled out of the peninsula, the system of reporting of casualties to India had matured up to a reasonable extent. The system during the latter part of the Great War was able to keep pace with the quantum of scale of casualties. Even while the Indian Mountain Batteries had landed on 25 April 1915 and the casualties had started occurring immediately, the first official casualty return was initiated by the GOC, Canal Defences only on 17 May 1915 comprising of one serial. With the number of casualties being incurred by the Indian troops, some sort of delay was expected. The delay was further accentuated by the involvement of a multitude of agencies in the reporting chain of the casualties. The magnitude of the casualties was also directly related to the tempo of the operations. An analysis of the casualties included in the telegrams clearly identifies with the surge of casualties incurred by the Indian battalions during the conduct of the major battles on the peninsula. The details of the telegrams with the maximum number of casualties are as given in Table 52.

TABLE 52: REPORTING OF CASUALTIES IN
THE MAJOR BATTLES ON GALLIPOLI[86]

Telegram Number	Date	No of Casualties			Major Preceding Operation
		Killed	Wounded	Total	
K-17	30 August 1915	109	291	400	Sari Bair
MC-107	24 June 1915	106	252	358	Follow up Operations of Third Battle of Krithia

Reporting and Receiving Agencies

In the initial period of the operations at Gallipoli, two agencies were primarily responsible for reporting of the casualties amongst the Indian troops, namely the Third Echelon, Alexandria and the GOC, Canal Defences Ismailia. There has been a continuous repetition of the entries of casualties forwarded by both of these agencies. With a sprinkling of singular entries in the Casualty Appendices forwarded by both of these agencies, the challenge of sifting through each entry, continued to overwhelm the research for this section of the book.

With a cumulative total of 9,057 entries of the Indian casualties in the campaign in the appendices and the 14 parameters associated with respect to each entry, the cumulative data which required analysis amounted to a massive data base of 1,26,798 data points. During the latter part of the campaign, starting from November 1915, a third entity of Deputy Assistant Adjutant General, 3rd Echelon, Indian Section Suez, had also started forwarding the details of the casualties to the various agencies in India. An analysis of the Casualty Appendices forwarded by this 'Indian Section' also had multiple duplications, leading to same entry being reflected three times at least.

As far as receiving agencies were concerned, two agencies predominantly worked to receive and collate the details of casualties of IEF 'G' in India. The office of the Chief of the General Staff in India and the Commander-in-Chief in India received bulk of the details of the casualties of Force 'G'. In the later part of the campaign the Central Casualty Bureau also had started receiving the details of casualties of Force 'G' and further disseminating the details to the respective Depots.

Involvement of Depots

Every Indian battalion which was on Gallipoli, had a base Depot in India. The Indian battalions were in regular contact with the respective Depots for the issues pertaining to dispatch of reinforcements, details of invalids dispatched from Alexandria and dispatch of personal belongings of the deceased. The Depots while receiving all these details also acted as an interface with the office of the AG in India and the

Central Casualty Bureau to ask for any clarifications with respect to the details of the casualties. The Depot also acted as an interface between the relatives of the Indian troops on active service and the Indian battalions on active service. For the relatives, respective Depots were the sole source for any information with respect to their relative who was on active service.

The issues like mismatch of the regimental numbers, names and ranks were regularly raised by the Depots with the respective battalions. Besides the routine casualty reports being forwarded by the agencies as mentioned above, in some cases the Indian battalions engaged in the operations were also publishing the Battalion Orders reporting the fatal casualties. The Depot being the repository of all the details of the troops of the battalion usually asked for clarifications in these cases from the respective battalions. In one such instance, the OC of the depot of 2/10 Gurkhas had asked the Central Casualty Bureau that, 'Battalion Order from the front reports' death of Number 234 Bhimraj Rai, Darrang Battalion on 7 August. No trace of this casualty in reports received from you. Kindly confirm.'[87]

The frequent turnover of troops accentuated due to the quantum of casualties, in many cases resulted in the incorrect details being published. The Depots played a crucial role in reconciling the details of the casualties with the manifest of the troops proceeding from India or from the parent units as reinforcements to the units at Gallipoli. To resolve any such mismatches, the Depots were very prompt in seeking clarifications from the Central Casualty Bureau, who in turn asked clarification from the GOC, Canal Defences, Ismailia. In one such case, the Central Casualty Bureau asked the GOC, Canal Defences, 'Please verify Lahore 185 Weighman Ram Saran, Supply and Transport Corps, reported M-449, 1 November 1915. He did not proceed on service from Lahore Division.'[88]

The relatives of the Indian troops serving on Gallipoli, in many cases, repeatedly approached the Depots for seeking any information about the well-being of the soldiers. The Depots in such cases approached the Central Casualty Bureau or the respective battalion on active service to seek additional inputs. In one such the OC Depot of 87th Punjabis had asked the Casualty Bureau:

I have the honour to ask that you may make further enquiries regarding Number 2435 Sepoy Uttam Singh attached to the 14th Sikhs as some men and a Havildar of this Regiment, who have lately returned from the 14th Sikhs wounded, state that this man died in their presence as they were being taken from Dardanelles to Alexandria. They state that he received a bad bomb wound in the Dardanelles and died from the effects in the ship. The man's father has been told this story by some men in his village and so he is very anxious to find out whether it is correct.[89]

The similar situation subsequently became more complex as the reinforcements from different units and sub units started getting attached with the major units at Gallipoli. Relatives of the soldiers thus dispatched as reinforcements, when approaching the Depots of the parent units, were redirected to the Depots of the units which had received these reinforcements, with maximum of such cases belonging to the 14th Sikhs. The OC of the Depot in such cases, besides redirecting the relatives to the depot of the unit receiving these reinforcements, himself also took up the case with the OC Depot of the receiving unit. In the case of Number 242, Reservist Bhagat Singh of 26th Punjabis, the OC Depot of 87th Punjabis had asked the OC Depot of the 14th Sikhs:

I have heard from the men, 87th Punjabis attached to 14th Sikhs on Field Service, who returned from Field Service that Number 242 Reservist Bhagat Singh, 26th Punjabis (who proceeded on Field Service with the draft 87th Punjabis) has been drowned on the voyage to the Dardanelles in August last, will you please know if you have had any information? This information is required about his accounts etc, and especially for his relative's information who are asking repeatedly about him.[90]

With a multiple case of common names of the casualties, except for Regimental Numbers, there were virtually no other means to corroborate the details of the casualty. As the different agencies were reporting the units of the casualties as attached from or attached with, therefore the sanctity of the details of units was also not very accurate. An analysis of the Indian casualty lists of the Dardanelles, reveal that there were 16 individuals named *Bostan*, who belonged to different units. Out of these three were reported as killed and 13 were reported as wounded. With 16 entries in the single name of *Bostan*, and almost

16,000 Indian troops on the peninsula, the quantum of confusion was expected.

TABLE 53: MULTIPLE INDIVIDUALS WITH COMMON NAME
(*BOSTAN*)[91]

Unit/ Sub-unit	Died of Wounds	Killed	Severely Wounded	Slightly Wounded	Wounded	Total
11th Mule Corps	2	-	1	-	-	3
15th Mule Corps	-	-	-	-	1	1
1st Mule Corps	-	1	-	-	-	1
26th Mountain Battery	-	-	1	-	2	3
33rd Mule Corps	-	-	1	1	1	3
7th Mule Corps	-	-	-	-	2	2
9th Mule Corps	-	-	-	-	3	3
Total	2	1	3	1	9	16

To resolve some of the confusion associated with the individual named *Bostan*, the GOC, 1st Peshawar Division had written to the office of AG in India:

With reference to your Number 23867-2, dated 23 Feb. 1916, intimating the death of Number 2104 Driver Bostan, 1st Mule Corps, I have the honour to inform you that the wife of this man received a letter from him dated 24th February 1916, so that it appears doubtful whether he has been killed. Will you kindly cause enquiries to be made in this case.[92]

As the case was very peculiar and warranted immediate response, the Central Casualty Bureau made further enquiries from the 3rd Echelon regarding the details. 'Please verify the following. Your MFC – Indian 11 dated 22nd Feb, Driver 2104 Bostan. 1st Mule Corps killed 30th Dec. 1915. Wife received letter from him dated 24th Feb. 1916.'[93]

CLASSIFICATION OF CASUALTIES

The existing research on the subject of the Indian participation in the Gallipoli campaign has been restricted to the Indian troops who were killed in action on the peninsula. The CWGC portal commemorates the following Indian soldiers who sacrificed their lives for the cause of the *Raj*. A summary of the Indian troops killed or Died of Wounds as listed by CWGC include the following as shown in Table 54:

TABLE 54: INDIANS KILLED IN GALLIPOLI: CWGC DATABASE[94]

Commemorated Place/ Cemetery (Only Indian Officers, Troops and Followers)	No. of Indian Soldiers Killed
Helles Memorial (SS Ramajan not included)	1,181
Heliopolis Memorial, Egypt	25
Pieta Military Cemetery, Malta	6
Ari Burnu Cemetery, Anzac	3
Chunuk Bair Cemetery, Anzac	1
Manara Indian Mohammedan Cemetery, Egypt	1
Redoubt Cemetery, Helles	1
Skew Bridge Cemetery	1
Turkish Military Cemetery, Malta	1
Total	1,220

With multiple sources of data, the cross referencing of the casualties was a laborious and monotonous exercise. The quantum of data included in the CWGC database needed to be matched/ corroborated with the Casualty Appendices of the War Dairy of Force 'G'. To cater for the details of the soldiers who died due to wounds additional casualty appendices of 1916 (till April 1916 only) were also analysed. A comparison of the analysis of killed; Died of Wounds and deaths due to natural causes have been compiled. In the research, an additional 218 number of Indians were found to have killed / died due to wounds / died due to natural causes.

When the total number of 1,438 fatal casualties were plotted against the respective months of 1915, one comes across the twin bumps parallel against the months of June and August 1915, which is aligned to the massive quantum of casualties suffered by the Indian troops during the Third Battle of Krithia and the August offensive respectively.

TABLE 55: DIFFERENT DATA SETS OF THE INDIAN FATAL
CASUALTIES ON GALLIPOLI[95]

Total number of Indians who were killed / died due to wounds / died due to natural causes	CWGC Data Base (Less Casualties of SS *Ramajan*)	Details as per Fresh Analysis (Less Casualties of SS *Ramajan*)
	1,220	1,438

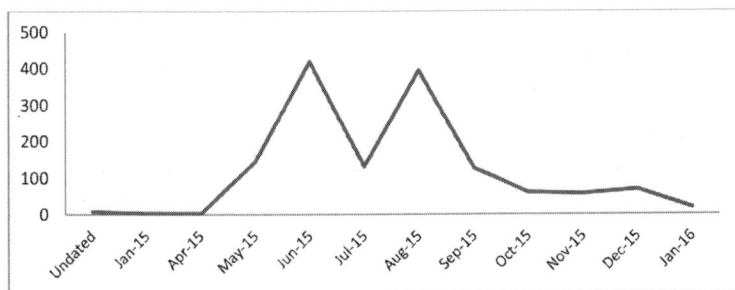

FIGURE 84: MONTH-WISE MANIFESTATION OF FATAL CASUALTIES
OF INDIAN TROOPS ON GALLIPOLI[96]

The number of Indian troops who were wounded on the peninsula was much more than the fatal casualties. Unfortunately, no credible research exists on the subject of the Indian troops who were wounded on the peninsula. With most of these soldiers being taken to different hospitals in Egypt / other nominated places, for treatment, there is no definite authority on the number of Indian troops wounded. Based on the database created from the Casualty Appendices, an approximate fix on the number of Indian troops wounded on the peninsula has been attempted. The wounded have also been classified into three distinct categories. For the Indian troops classified as wounded and for whom no specific details were available have been classified as wounded. Depending upon the degree of severity, for which details were available, other casualties have been categorised as Slightly Wounded or Severely Wounded. Though the extensive research has also brought to fore the individual details of the 3,407 Indian combatants and non-combatants who were wounded while on the peninsula, the paucity of space in the book has precluded the possibility of inclusion of these names in the Appendix. Catering for the wounded

Indian soldiers whose dates of getting wounded were not available in the casualty appendices (these casualties have been clubbed in the category of undated), the month wise analysis of the casualties (wounded only) of Force 'G' manifests in the following graphical description. The Battles of Krithia and the Sari Bair in June and August respectively glare out prominently, in terms of Indian casualties of wounded.

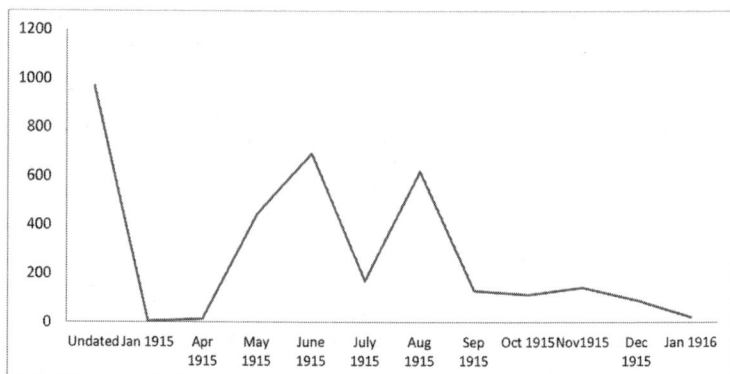

FIGURE 85: MONTH-WISE CASUALTY (WOUNDED)
MANIFESTATION AMONGST INDIAN TROOPS ON GALLIPOLI[97]

Casualties amongst Indian Officers

Indian officers were a crucial link between the British officers and the Indian rank and file in the colonial army. At Gallipoli also, the Indian officers had their fair share of casualties. An analysis of the casualty appendices of the Force 'G' brings forth the pattern of casualties amongst the Indian Officers of the various units and sub units of the Indian army. A total of 97 Indian officers belonging to 18 different units and sub-units suffered casualties in the campaign, the summary of which is as given in Table 56.

The details of Indian officers, who suffered casualties on the peninsula, are attached in the Appendix to the book. As everywhere else, the 14th Sikhs here also had an enviable proportion of casualties as far as Indian officers are concerned. A BlogSpot, The Great War

TABLE 56: CASUALTIES AMONGST INDIAN OFFICERS OF
FORCE 'G' AT GALLIPOLI[98]

Unit	Killed/ Died	Wounded	Total
1/10 Gurkhas	1	2	3
1/4 Gurkhas	–	1	1
1/5 Gurkhas	9	10	19
1/6 Gurkhas	3	10	13
14th Sikhs	4	11	15
2/10 Gurkhas	11	11	22
2/4 Gurkhas	–	1	1
2/5 Gurkhas	1	–	1
21st Mountain Battery	–	1	1
26th Mountain Battery	1	2	3
54th Sikhs	–	1	1
69th Punjabis	–	1	1
7th IMAB	2	–	2
89th Punjabis	–	5	5
Assam Military Police	–	1	1
Burma Military Police	–	1	1
Divisional Ammunition Column	–	1	1
Patiala Infantry	2	4	6
Total	34	63	97

(1914-18), hosts a picture of the British and Indian Officers of the
14th Sikhs which has the names of British and Indian Officers, who
became casualties on the peninsula. This section as an obituary to
these brave British and Indian officers would not have been complete
without the reference to the picture.

TOTAL INDIAN CASUALTIES

As the total number of Indian troops who served on the peninsula
had never been approximated, till Peter Stanley came up with his

FIGURE 86: BRITISH AND INDIAN OFFICERS OF THE 14TH SIKHS[99]

detailed narrative on the subject in 2015, the numbers of Indian casualties on the peninsula have similarly been relegated to the universe of unknown. As discussed earlier, attributed to the relative dearth of resources, Indian contribution in the Gallipoli campaign has never been the focus of attention of researchers.

The severe weather induced diseases and injuries took a heavy toll of the Indian soldiers. A total of 62 Indian troops had died due to the various diseases and injuries related due to non-operational reasons. A month wise analysis of these casualties' manifests into a surge in November-December 1915, reflecting the casualties due to the freak weather phenomenon on the peninsula in November 1915, with almost all casualties being attributed to frost bites and pneumonia.

With a detailed database on the subject, duly corroborated by the entries in the corresponding Casualty Appendices of the War Diaries, an approximation of the Indian casualties on the peninsula, supplemented by the details has been achieved. Considering all the available sources, it has been definitely ascertained that the total Indian casualties on the peninsula were not less than 4,843, accounting for both the fatal and non-fatal injuries. This figure also includes the Indian troops who while on Gallipoli peninsula died due to natural causes as given in Table 57.

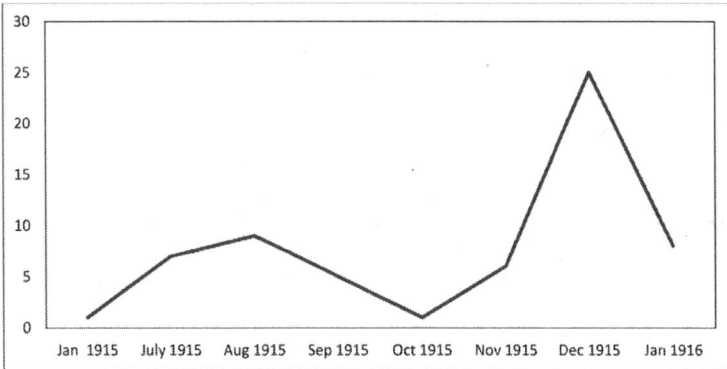

FIGURE 87: MONTH-WISE MANIFESTATION OF INDIAN TROOPS'
FATAL CASUALTIES DUE TO NATURAL CAUSES[100]

Determining the Details: The Summation

The Indian battalions at Gallipoli sustained a continuous and never-ending cycle of casualties and reinforcements during their deployment of almost eight months on Gallipoli. The cycle ensured a regular turn-over of troops from the Indian units and sub units. This turnover was so rapid that to match the reinforcements with the casualties is almost an improbable proposition. Having got a near fix on the day and month wise occurrence of casualties, both fatal and non-fatal, this section attempts to recreate the available combat strength of each Indian battalion at Gallipoli on a month-wise basis. The evaluation of the casualty data of the Indian troops at Gallipoli has been restricted only to the Indian Infantry and Artillery units on individual basis, whereas for Mule Corps the analysis is on the basis of a combined figure for the entire Indian Mule Corps.

In order to arrive at the near exact figures of the available combat power of each Indian unit, a number of sources have been exploited. The first source in the series has been the War Diary of the 29th Indian Infantry Brigade. Based on the daily entries in the War Diary of the Brigade, it can be summarised that there were 637 fatal casualties (killed in action) and four casualties who died of wounds later on, in respect of major units of the Indian Brigade. This does not include the units and sub-units of Indian Mountain Artillery and the Indian

TABLE 57: SUMMARY OF INDIAN CASUALTIES ON GALLIPOLI[101]

Rank	Died	Died of Wounds	Killed	Missing	Severely Wounded	Slightly Wounded	Wounded	Total
Followers	17	59	127	–	167	51	375	796
Indian Troops	43	199	959	30	838	453	1,426	3,948
Indian Officers	2	4	28	–	19	7	39	99
Total	62	262	1,114	30	1,024	511	1,840	4,843

Mule Corps along with the two Indian Field Ambulances. In addition, there were 2,638 wounded Indian troops and 160 were missing, which brings total number of Indian casualties to 3,439 in respect of these major units.

Taking the above-mentioned data as the starting point of the analysis, the strength of the units and subunits of the 29th Indian Infantry Brigade when it mobilised from India on 2 November 1914, comes to a cumulative total of 4,589 persons. Some component of 23rd Mule Corps mobilised from India, has also been included in the total strength. These details do not include the strength of the Indian Mountain Artillery Batteries, Medical units and the Mule Corps, which though operated on the peninsula but did not mobilise from India during the same time frame.

TABLE 58: THE STRENGTH OF THE 29TH INDIAN INFANTRY BRIGADE AS ON 2 NOVEMBER 1914[102]

Units	Indian Officers	Indian Troops	Followers	Total
14th Sikhs	18	818	40	876
2/10 Gurkhas	18	803	62	883
69th Punjabis	19	813	75	907
89th Punjabis	18	808	60	886
1/6 Gurkhas	18	808	80	906
23rd Mule Corps	6	9	116	131
Total	97	4,059	433	4,589

After having been deployed on the Canal Defences of Suez, the Indian Brigade was mobilised for Gallipoli and the units had embarked the assigned transports from Port Said on 27 April 1915. Though the complete complement of the 29th Indian Infantry Brigade had landed on the peninsula on 1 May 1915, the 2/10 Gurkhas was not part of the Brigade. Therefore, the total strength of the Indian Brigade and its units, when they landed at Gallipoli (less British Officers) was 3,212. This also does not include the details of Mountain Artillery Batteries and the Mule Corps as they had landed on the peninsula, in the initial waves on 25 April 1915.

TABLE 59: THE STRENGTH OF 29TH INDIAN INFANTRY BRIGADE
AS ON 1 MAY 1915[103]

Unit	Indian Officers	Indian Troops	Followers	Total
14th Sikhs	18	735	35	788
2/10 GR	–	–	–	–
69th Punjabis	18	735	38	791
89th Punjabis	17	735	33	785
1/6 Gurkhas	17	737	66	820
23rd Mule Corps	–	28	–	28
Total	70	2,970	172	3,212

With authenticated details of strength of 29th Indian Infantry
Brigade not available for the months of June and July 1915, the existing
strength as on 1 May 1915 has been reduced by the number of
casualties suffered by the Indian units in the month of May, June and
July 1915. The details of casualties have been collated from the sources
as described in the previous section of the chapter. As on 1 May 1915,
only four Indian battalions were part of the 29th Indian Infantry
Brigade, out of which two, 69th and 89th Punjabis had been deinducted
on 15 May, leaving only 14th Sikhs and 1/6 Gurkhas. The analysis of
casualties vis-à-vis the available strength has been carried out for the
14th Sikhs as shown in Table 60.

TABLE 60: CASUALTY FIGURES OF THE 14TH SIKHS[104]

Strength as on 1 May 1915	Casualties in May 1915 (All Types)	Casualties in June 1915 (All Types)	Casualties in Jul 1915 (All Types)	Total Casualties
788	136	412	92	640

Thus, it can be seen that in the case of the 14th Sikhs, out of a
strength of 788 Indian troops as on 1 May 1915, a massive proportion
of 81.22 per cent had suffered casualties (all types). Out of this share,
if only the fatal casualties are included, the matrix assumes a different
proportion. It is also worth mentioning here that during this period
there were no reinforcements received by the battalion from any source.
Working on a hypothetical construct that except for slightly wounded

and wounded all other category of Indian casualties were evacuated / died on the peninsula, during the first three months, the available strength of the 14th Sikhs as on 1 August 1915 is generally aligned with the calculations of the hypothesis, making it plausible that out of 788 number of Indian troops from 14th Sikhs, available with the battalion as on 1 May 1915, 380 numbers were not available with the battalion by 31 July 1915. Thus, it can be seen that on 1 August 1915, the battalion had 379 troops effective with it, which is largely aligned with the available strength as on 1 May 1915 and the casualties suffered by it during the period of those three months (408).

TABLE 61: MATRIX OF AVAILABILITY OF EFFECTIVES OF THE 14TH SIKHS[105]

Strength as on 1 May 1915	788
Casualties in May 1915 (Less Wounded/ Slightly Wounded)	103
Casualties in June 1915 (Less Wounded/ Slightly Wounded)	219
Casualties in July 1915 (Less Wounded/ Slightly Wounded)	58
Total Casualties (Less Wounded/ Slightly Wounded)	380
Effective Strength as on 1 August 1915	379 (788-380 =408)

The turnover of Indian troops on the peninsula, both in terms of magnitude and frequency was so much that it is practically impossible to get an exact fix on the number of Indians which served on the peninsula. In the final reckoning of the Indian troops on the peninsula, the strength of 69th and 89th Punjabis is generally excluded as they were on the peninsula only for initial 15 days. But on the other hand, the troops which were received as reinforcements by the Indian units on the peninsula even in December 1915 are included, bringing an imbalance to the calculations. To arrive at a near accurate estimate of the Indian troop's participation in the campaign, I have taken the strength return of 7 December 1915 as a baseline.

This return was forwarded by the GOC, Egypt to the C-in-C in India vide Appendix no. 31 on 7 December 1915. As the last Indian troops deinducted from the peninsula on 19 December 1915, the return is very realistic in order to calculate the Indian strength on the peninsula. To the strength forwarded by the GOC Egypt, the strength

480 *We Too Were There*

TABLE 62: EFFECTIVES AVAILABLE WITH THE INDIAN UNITS
ON 7 DECEMBER 1915 ON GALLIPOLI[106]

Units	Indian Officers	Indian Troops	Followers	Total
14 Sikhs	16	729	41	786
Patiala Infantry	4	182	18	204
1/4 Gurkhas	20	651	40	711
1/5 Gurkhas	19	637	39	695
2/10 Gurkhas	21	1019	47	1087
69th Punjabis	18	735	38	791
89th Punjabis	17	735	33	785
1/6 GR	7	727	47	781
7 IMAB	–	19	2	21
21st Mountain Battery	3	261	18	282
26th Mountain Battery	4	263	18	285
Artillery Reinforcements Enroute	–	103	4	107
Indian Mule Cart Train	12	223	3,462	3,697
137th Field Ambulance	3	8	124	135
110th Field Ambulance	4	24	173	201
108th Field Ambulance	7	10	169	186
Medical Reinforcements Enroute	–	–	45	45
Total	155	6,326	4,318	10,799

of 69th and 89th Punjabis as on 1 May 1915 has been added as these two battalions also served on the peninsula, which brings to a total of 10,799 Indian troops, both combatants and non-combatants who were on the peninsula as part of the Gallipoli campaign.

As the above state was compiled on 7 December 1915, and the state has been underscored with a caveat that, 'in continuation on my H-367 (Diary Number -27588) of 16th Nov., statement of effectives present with and enroute to join Force G', it can be assumed that all reinforcements dispatched to Gallipoli till November 1915 have been included in the subject state. The reinforcements meant for Force 'G' in the month of December 1915 were dispatched on 14 December 1915 and 17 December 1915 from Bombay and Karachi respectively. Therefore, it will be fair to assume that these reinforcements were not included in the strength return of 7 December 1915. As Indian Labour Corps meant for Gallipoli, though dispatched from India never reached Gallipoli, deducting the strength of Indian Labour Corps from the strength return of December 1915 and adding the balance reinforcements, the strength of the Indians which is likely to have served on the peninsula comes to 11,617 Indian Officers and Rank and File.

TABLE 63: MATRIX OF INDIAN TROOPS ON GALLIPOLI
(INCLUDING WHO WERE WOUNDED LIGHTLY & JOINED BACK
WITH RESPECTIVE UNITS)[107]

	Indian Officers	Indian Troops	Followers	Total
Strength Return of 7 Dec. 1915	155	6,326	4,318	10,799
Reinforcements dispatched from India on 14 and 17 Dec. 1915 (Less Indian Labour Corps)	9	800	9	818
Total	164	7,126	4,327	11,617

The official figures of the Indian troops which were sent to the peninsula, however, are different from the calculations arrived at above. Two figures quoted in the official publication on India's Contribution in the Great War, happen to be only one third of the figures arrived after extensive research. The official publication has included the following details as shown in Table 64:

TABLE 64: TOTAL INDIAN TROOPS ON THE PENINSULA
(AS PER OFFICIAL RECORDS)[108]

Indian Officers & Warrant Officers	Indian Other Ranks	Non-Combatants	Total	Remarks
30	3,003	1,335	4,368	Up to 31 October 1918
90	3,041	1,819	4,950	Up to 31 December 1919

The Gallipoli Peninsula was evacuated in December 1915. With a very rudimentary type of system of reporting existing at that time, a correction in the figures was not abnormal. There is no definite system to corroborate or negate the possibility of inclusion or exclusion of the subsequent reinforcements in these figures. It can be assumed that these figures do not include the reinforcements, which were later on dispatched to the Indian units. In spite of this assumption, the fact remains that the total number of Indian troops who served on peninsula, as provided in the official figures are only 42 per cent of the figures provided by the research carried out during the course of writing of this book.

As discussed earlier, the extensive database of the casualties amongst the Indian troops on Gallipoli, belonging to IEF 'G' have been calculated up to 1 April 1916. Analysing the casualty database, the unit wise summary of killed, died of wounds, died due to other causes and wounded (wounded, slightly wounded & severely wounded) when mapped against the reference points of Indian officers, Indian troops and followers, provide the following matrix as shown in Table 65:

TABLE 65: TOTAL INDIAN CASUALTIES ON GALLIPOLI[109]

Unit	Follower	Indian Troops	Officers	Grand Total
1/10 Gurkhas	5	139	3	147
1/2 Gurkhas	–	5	–	5
1/4 Gurkhas	1	59	1	61
1/5 Gurkhas	7	583	36	626
1/6 Gurkhas	10	744	22	776
1/9 Gurkhas	–	1	–	1
108th Indian Field Ambulance	50	7	–	57
10th Mule Corps	7	3	–	10
110th Indian Field Ambulance	2	1	–	3
11th Mule Corps	37	6	–	43
12th Mule Corps	–	1	–	1
137th Combined Field Ambulance	13	4	–	17

14th Mule Corps	3	1	–	4
14th Sikhs	20	851	23	894
15th Ludhiana Sikhs	–	12	–	12
15th Mule Corps	31	5	–	36
18th Mule Corps	7	–	–	7
19th Mule Corps	1	–	–	1
1st Mule Corps	65	22	–	87
2/10 Gurkhas	13	619	37	669
2/2 Gurkhas	–	4	–	4
2/4 Gurkhas	1	13	1	15
2/5 Gurkhas	1	78	1	80
2/6 Gurkhas	–	51	–	51
2/9 Gurkhas	–	1	–	1
20th Mule Corps	–	1	–	1
21st Mountain Battery	75	78	2	155
21st Mule Corps	1	1	–	2
22nd Mule Corps	1	–	–	1
23rd Mountain Battery	2	5	–	7
23rd Mule Corps	1	–	–	1
24th Mountain Battery	–	1	–	1
24th Mule Corps	1	1	–	2
25th Mule Corps	1	–	–	1
26th Mountain Battery	75	71	8	154
26th Mule Corps	10	5	–	15
27th Mountain Battery	13	7	–	20
28th Mule Corps	26	16	–	42
28th Mountain Battery	12	8	–	20
29th Mountain Battery	–	1	–	1
29th Mule Corps	1	–	–	1
2nd Mule Corps	43	10	–	53
30th Mountain Battery	11	6	–	17
31st Mountain Battery	1	–	–	1

31st Mule Corps	18	2	–	20
32nd Mule Corps	25	2	–	27
33rd Mule Corps	44	10	–	54
34th Mule Corps	4	3	–	7
35th Mule Corps	3	–	–	3
36th Mule Corps	3	2	–	5
36th Sikhs	–	26	–	26
37th Mule Corps	2	–	–	2
38th Mule Corps	1	–	–	1
3rd Mule Corps	9	4	–	13
45th Sikhs	1	46	–	47
54th Sikhs	–	12	1	13
69th Punjabis	–	31	1	32
7th IMAB	5	3	2	10
7th Mule Corps	5	1	–	6
87th Punjabis	–	8	–	8
89th Punjabis	–	110	7	117
8th Mule Corps	3	–	–	3
90th Punjabis	–	1	–	1
9th Mule Corps	50	18	–	68
Army Bearer Corps	9	–	–	9
Assam Military Police	–	4	1	5
Bharatpur Transport Corps	25	9	–	34
Burma Military Police	1	59	1	61
Darrang Police Battalion	–	19	–	19
Divisional Amn Column	–	2	1	3
Gwalior Transport Corps	5	–	–	5
Indian Subordinate Medical Dept	–	2	–	2
Indore Transport Corps	15	1	–	16
Lakhimpur Military Police	–	7	–	7
Lushai Hills Military Police	–	7	–	7
Myitkyina Military Police	–	6	–	6

Naga Hills Military Police	–	4	–	4
Patiala Infantry	10	128	14	152
Supply and Transport Corps	10	–	–	10
Total	796	3,948	162	4,906

Just like the discrepancies between the official figures and the research in the book, on the aspect of the total strength of the Indian troops on Gallipoli, the casualty details also suffer from the similar anomaly. The casualty details of the Indian troops, with IEF 'G' as on 31 December 1919, as contained in the official figures provide the following insights:

TABLE 66: TOTAL INDIAN CASUALTIES ON GALLIPOLI (AS PER OFFICIAL RECORDS)[110]

Status	Indian Officers & Warrant Officers	Indian Other Ranks	Followers	Total
Dead	33	1,591	127	1,751
Wounded	72	3,518	1	3,591
Missing	-	101	1	102
Total	105	5,210	129	5,444

The higher number of total Indian casualties on the peninsula as contained in the official figures can be attributed to the difference in the datum line taken by the author during the research. The Indian casualties on the peninsula as provided by the research are based upon a self-imposed cut off of 1 April 1916, whereas the cut off for the official data has been taken as 31 December 1919, a clear difference of additional 45 months or 1,350 days. In spite of the substantial time differential, the difference in the total number of casualties provided by research and the official figures is only of about 10 per cent (additional total number of casualties included in the official figures).

A careful examination of the official figures of the Indian casualties amongst the followers of the IEF 'G' provide certain very interesting insights. As discussed earlier, the documentation of followers of Indian Army of the time was below par, with IEF 'G' being no exception. A detailed research on the aspect of details of casualties amongst the followers of IEF 'G' has resulted in manifesting of exact details in terms of names, type of casualty, date of casualty and other ancillary details. With an immense differential in the details of the casualties amongst the followers, the current research can be assumed to be more realistic.

TABLE 67: DIFFERENTIAL IN THE TOTAL INDIAN CASUALTIES ON GALLIPOLI (AS PER OFFICIAL RECORDS & RESEARCH)[111]

Casualties as per:	Indian Officers	Indian Other Ranks	Followers	Total
Official Records	105	5,210	129	5,444
Research by Author	162	3,948	796	4,906
Differential per centage	+ 35 per cent	- 24 per cent	+ 84 per cent	10 per cent

With an approximation of the total strength of Indians, both combatants and non-combatants having been achieved and assuming that the slightly wounded troops/followers had joined back their respective units/ sub units on the peninsula, the next exercise was to map the above strength with the detailed casualty database, as discussed in the earlier section of the book. By carrying out this exercise, one comes to an approximate figure of 4,385 troops which did not join their respective battalions back and either died in action or were evacuated from the peninsula. Based on the above supposition and after transposing the summary of casualties (all types, less slightly wounded) amongst the Indian officers, Indian troops and Indian

TABLE 68: TOTAL NUMBER OF INDIAN TROOPS ON GALLIPOLI[112]

Indian Troops	Indian Officers	Indian Troops	Followers	Total
Total Indians served on Peninsula including unwounded / wounded who joined back	164	7,126	4,327	11,617
Total Indians Casualties (Less Slightly Wounded)	145	3495	745	4,385
Casualties of SS Ramajan	02	258	19	279
Total Indians on Peninsula	311	10,879	5,091	16,281

followers against the total strength of the Indians on the peninsula, it can be inferred that approximately 16,281 Indian troops served on the Gallipoli Peninsula.

HONOURS AND AWARDS

The grant of awards to the Indian troops during the Gallipoli Campaign has not been a very pleasant issue. As such, the Indians were not eligible for the award of Victoria Cross prior to the outbreak of the Great War. During the Gallipoli Campaign, almost 38 VCs were awarded to the Allied troops,[113] but no Indian troop was found fit for the award of VC. On the other hand, there is a very interesting background to the case for initiation of awards to the Indian troops during the Gallipoli operations.

Secretary of State for India on 20 July 1915, in an official communiqué addressed to the Viceroy of India had promulgated that Ian Hamilton has been conferred with the powers to award the Indian Order of Merit and the Distinguished Service Medal.[114] With the increasing acknowledgment of the role played by the Indian troops at Gallipoli, it was felt that the corresponding acknowledgment by the Government, of the sacrifices and bravery by the Indian troops was lacking. The communiqué did not specify the number of awards but instead had left the decision on the number of awards to be granted on to the discretion of Ian Hamilton.

Further amplifying on the conferment of powers to grant awards, the C-in-C in India in a detailed note to Ian Hamilton on 25 July 1915, further clarified that Government of India has granted him the power to confer 'limited' number of Indian Orders of Merit (IOM) and Indian Distinguished Service Medals (IDSM) at his discretion. A brief note about the awards was also forwarded for the information of Ian Hamilton.

IOM now consists of two classes vide Army Regulations, India Volume One Para 1006 and Volume Two Paras 363 & 364. Second Class is awarded for first conspicuous act of personal gallantry in the field while First Class of the Order can only be obtained by promotion of a man for similar service who is already in possession of a Second Class. On promotion from Second to First Class of the Order, the insignia in possession before promotion is returned to the Government of India and the allowance attached to the higher class only can be drawn.[115]

The advisory also provided a broad guideline on the ratio of awards to be conferred for the Indian troops at Gallipoli. It was advised that the proportion of IOM to IDSM should not exceed one to two or three. The advisory also requested that the brief account of particular set of gallantry for which award has been conferred should be published in the Field Force Orders and the extracts to be furnished for the publication in the Gazette of India.

The so called 'limit' of awards turned into a subject of concern. Though the initial correspondence which conveyed the decision of king for the conferment of awards had left the decision on the number of awards on to the discretion of Ian Hamilton, the frequency of correspondence on the subject suggest that 'limit' of awards was being indirectly being hinted to the office of Ian Hamilton. In another correspondence of 30 July 1915, the Secretary of State in India again asked the Viceroy (Army Department), whether he has, 'arranged with the GOC, Mediterranean Force regarding the "limit" of number of awards'?[116]

The tales of bravery of the Indian troops on the peninsula have been celebrated across the world by various military historians but have been sadly left unacknowledged and have been mentioned in passing only in the existing Indian literature. These acts of bravery and sacrifices were performed by these Indians under very challenging circumstances as have been brought up in the book. In the last section of the book, I have attempted to recreate these heroic actions of the Indian gunners and soldiers.

The Indian gunners of the Indian Mountain Artillery Batteries were engaged in an intense combat on the peninsula, since the day they had landed on the peninsula. Handling vintage equipment, while providing very crucial support to the MEF Infantry and keeping the Turkish Artillery silent, talks about the professionalism of the Indian gunners. Though every day on the peninsula was exciting, 19 May 1915 was quite an eventful day for the 21st (Kohat) battery. The battery was deployed in three sections. In the right section, Subadar Mit Singh was brilliant in his handling of his 10 pounder gun. Subadar

Mit Singh, from an open position was engaging a Turkish field battery of four guns. The dexterity and the swift handling of the gun by the Subadar had resulted in the silencing of the Turkish guns and the guns were manhandled by the enemy to a different location, bringing a much-needed relief to the MEF Infantry in defences. The display of extreme professionalism of Subadar Mit Singh in the face of enemy was recognised with the award of a Distinguished Service Order (DSO) for his actions of the day.

In the same section of the Kohat Battery, Lance Naik Karm Singh was passing orders from the position officer to the guns. During the process, Karm Singh was hit by shrapnel from an enemy shell. As the shell had landed at the parapet of the gun position, Karm Singh was blinded in both eyes from the hit. In spite of getting blinded, Karm Singh with blooded bandages around his eyes, continued to pass orders to the guns of the section. When asked by a gunner about his condition, Karm Singh reportedly told him that he was absolutely fine and can carry on. Subadar Mit Singh, himself being wounded, when asked about his condition, Karm Singh in the true sense of bravery and camaraderie told him, *Bilkul Tagrah, Sahib* (In high spirits, Sir!) and had continued to pass orders till evacuated. This extreme sense of devotion of Naik Karm Singh was also duly recognised and he was awarded IOM for this unparalleled bravery.

This was not the end of awards for the 21st Battery. The artillery shelling by the enemy and the rifle fire from the enemy Infantry was taking a toll on the gunners of Battery. The numbers of the wounded and dead of the Battery were slowly over taking the active personnel of the unit. Hospital Assistant Daulat Singh of 'C' Section of the 137th Combined Field Ambulance was one of the medical orderlies attached with the Battery. The shelling by the enemy Artillery was so intense that it was not possible to extract the wounded personnel of the Indian Battery. One of the wounded of the Battery was lying in open and was in the need of immediate medical care.

Hospital Assistant, Daulat Singh, without caring for his personal safety had continued to provide medical attention to the wounded and did not withdraw himself to safety, without getting the wounded back to the safety of the trenches. Daulat Singh was also one of the proud recipients of IOM on the same day. While only three individuals of the battery were awarded on that day, the stories of individual bravery and professionalism of the Indian Mountain gunners was definitely restricted to three.

The whole section did wonderfully well and every man deserved something for that day's work, but of course there are limits to the recommendations one can send in. One of the gun shields had four direct hits and fifty shrapnel bullets on it. The section had seven men reported wounded, one died of wounds, but there were a good many other slight wounds unreported.[117]

The third section of the battery also happened to be deployed just behind the right section. The day was momentous for this section as well, not from the opportunities point of view but from the casualties suffered. The maximum number of casualties suffered by this section resulted from the overshoots from the right section. As the section was deployed immediately behind the right section, all the targeted shells of right section found their targets in the third section due to overshooting. Though tactically unsound position, the position was offering fire support to the ANZACs deployed in the Quinn and Pope's post and Walker's ridge from an angle.

With dispersed allied positions without any continuous defensive line and allied posts almost hugging the Turkish defence lines in the area, the discipline and professionalism of the section called for a highest order, which the section very ably provided. The guns of the Battery had fired a total of 613 rounds, a no mean feat when considering the slow firing rate of the guns and the overwhelming preponderance of the Turkish Artillery.

This section got a chance at a later stage in the battle to prove its worth. The section's role was very crucial as it was the only gun position offering some sort of fire support to the embattled Quinn's post. Two Turkish Mountain guns in particular were troubling the post off late. With a distance of only 350 yards between the section and the Turkish gun positions, the task of silencing the Turkish guns fell upon this section. The gun layer of the section, Jan Mohamed carried on the task of pounding the enemy gun position, in spite of Gun Position officer of the section getting injured by an enemy shell. 'Jan Mohamed carried on, in spite part of the emplacement being knocked down by a High Explosive and had loosed off 22 rounds, 17 of which went into one or other of the enemy gun ports. Jan Mohamed got an IOM for this and the enemy guns never spoke again.'[118] Australians in the Quinn Post were very grateful to the Indian Mountain Battery for destroying the enemy guns. The holding of Quinn's post by the Australians was possible absolutely due to the Indian gunners silencing the Turkish twin guns on that day.

Narain Singh, a lineman in the 21st (Kohat) battery was another dare devil, who without caring for his personal safety was always out repairing the lines damaged by the enemy shelling. 'We had one lineman only, who managed to keep alive during the whole war in some wonderful way. He was always out repairing lines in dangerous places, and two or three times brought back chits from Australian officers to say they had seen him repairing lines under heavy fire.' The individual was later on awarded the IDSM for his conspicuous bravery and display of professionalism of highest order. Overall the tally of awards and recognition for the gunners and drivers of the Indian Mountain Batteries did justice to the sacrifices and hardships endured by these men. The honours and awards for the two batteries of the 7th Indian Mountain Artillery Brigade[119] included the following:

21st (Kohat) Mountain Battery

Subadar Mit Singh - Order of British India (2nd Class) (Twice Mentioned)
Subadar Chanda Singh - Indian Order of Merit (Twice Mentioned)
Three other awards of Indian Order of Merit (Indian Other Ranks)
Five awards of Indian Distinguished Service Medal
Driver Naik Ali Ahmed - Twice Mentioned-in-Dispatches
Eight Indian Other Ranks - Mention-in-Dispatches
S.A.S. Daulat Singh - IDSM, Indian Order of Merit and Mention

26th (Jacob's) Mountain Battery

Subadar Jowala Singh - Indian Order of Merit and twice mention
Subadar Hem Singh - IDSM and mention
Jemadar Mahomed Baksh - Indian Order of Merit and mention
Havildar Gurditt Singh - Indian Order of Merit and mention
Driver Havildar Inder Singh - Indian Order of Merit and mention

Gunner Fazl Illahi - Indian Order of Merit and mention
Shoeing Smith Sahib Singh - Mention-in-Dispatches
Seven Indian Other Ranks - Mention-in-Dispatches
Two Indian Other Ranks - Indian Order of Merit
Three Indian Other Ranks - IDSM

After Ian Hamilton was empowered to confer a 'limited' number of awards, in September 1915, a series of these awards were also awarded to the troops of the Indian Infantry battalions. All four awards conferred on the day pertained to actions during the Third Battle of Krithia, which was the epitome of sacrifice by the Indian battalions on the peninsula. Sepoy Bhagwan Singh of the 14th Sikhs was awarded IDSM for his conspicuous and selfless act of bravery on 5 June 1915. The citation of Number 4675, Sepoy Bhagwan Singh succinctly captures his action on the day.[120]

For exceptional bravery on June 5th during operations on the Gallipoli Peninsula, in the defence of a barricade which had been erected across a trench and which was being heavily attacked by bomb throwers. He showed great pluck and coolness, holding together the remnant of his company and eventually leading them into safety when a retirement was ordered.

Echoing almost similar sentiments as far as action on the day was concerned, Number 3693, Naik Bir Singh of the 14th Sikhs was also conferred with IDSM in September 1915. The citation of Naik Bir Singh outlines the bravery of the individual in the face of enemy.[121]

He showed exceptional pluck and coolness on June 4th during the attacks and counter attacks south west of Krithia. In the severe hand to hand fighting in the trenches he was invariably the first round the traverses in the attack and the last to retire when forced back.

The sheer number of casualties suffered by the 14th Sikhs, had resulted in the intense pressure on the attached Ward Orderlies of the Field Ambulances. Provisioning of the immediate first aid to these casualties and subsequent evacuation in the face of enemy called for an out of normal grit and determination. No. 3550, Ward Orderly Gurdit Singh of the 14th Sikhs, attached to 108th Indian Field Ambulance was one such medic, whose services during the third battle of Krithia were recognised.[122] 'For exceptional service in care of wounded under great difficulties. He showed remarkable intelligence and forethought.'[123]

The role of Indian medical assistants in managing the casualties during the course of the Gallipoli Campaign had come under very high appreciation by the senior military hierarchy of the time. Like Gurdit Singh, S.A.S. Bhagwan Singh, who has been earlier referred to in the previous chapter was another brave heart, whose medical skills and professionalism saved many lives, both Indian and allied during the campaign. The citation for the award for S.A.S. Bhagwan Singh, forwarded by the 14th Sikhs mentioned the single-handed initiative of the individual after the third battle of Krithia in the absence of the Regimental Medical Officer.[124]

On 28th June 1915 after Lieut. Cursetjee the RMO received wounds in action, Jemadar Bhagwan Singh single-handed carried on the medical duties until the new RMO arrived. At Anzac, he attended to casualties from other units in addition to his own. Recipient was a Sikh from Gujarwal in the Ludhiana district of Punjab. His is an exceptional service of an ISMD cadre with a single regiment.

For this exemplary professionalism under the enemy fire on Gallipoli, though S.A.S. Bhagwan Singh was awarded IOM, but his abilities and expertise were further recognised in during the battle at Sherqat in 1918 and was awarded MC. The citation of S.A.S. Bhagwan Singh read,

2nd Class Senior Sub Assistant Surgeon Bhagwan Singh, IOM, Ind. Med. Dpt. Mesopotamia. For conspicuous gallantry and devotion to duty at Sherqat, on 29th October 1918. When the regimental aid-post came under heavy fire, he displayed the utmost coolness in appeasing the wounded and alleviating their sufferings. Throughout the action his conduct was a fine example to his subordinates.[125]

1/6 Gurkhas was the second Indian Battalion after 14th Sikhs which had suffered a high quantum of casualties. The selfless service of No. 1108, Rifleman Danbir Thapa of 1/6 Gurkhas on 4 June 1915 was given due recognition by the award of IDSM.[126]

For conspicuous gallantry under fire on June 4th south west of Krithia. He remained within 10 yards of a Turkish trench after all his comrades had been killed, wounded or had withdrawn. He dug a hole under fire to protect a wounded man and brought him safely in after nightfall.

As part of mobilisation for the First World War, the 1st Patiala Rajindra Sikhs had left Patiala for Bombay on 12 October 1914. The battalion had set sail from Bombay on 29 October finally reaching Ismailia on 21 November 1915. The battalion as part of the Brigade was deployed on the defences of Suez Canal. As part of the Suez Canal defences, though the battalion was in no way involved in the operations at Gallipoli, but due to the very high casualty rates at Gallipoli suffered by the 29th Indian Infantry Brigade, 'A' Company of the battalion, with 180 troops, under command of Major Hardam Singh, had moved to Gallipoli on 7 July 1915. Due to the continued attrition being suffered by the 14th Sikhs, 'C' Company of the battalion with Major H. Campbell had also moved to Gallipoli on 25 September 1915.

Both the companies performed excellently while at Gallipoli and earned very high praise from the 14th Sikhs and 29th Indian Infantry Brigade. The troops of the battalion on 22 August 1915 had faced the enemy with tremendous courage and did not withdraw even under tremendous pressure from the enemy.

Patiala Company did very well this day under Subadar Kahla Singh. They were on an exposed flank along with a few of the 14th Sikhs and stood firm when the other troops in the line were taken back by the remnants of the other Battalion, which retired through the line after they had been cut up and failed in an attack losing 500 out of 800.[127]

The higher formation of the 14th Sikhs, the 29th Indian Infantry Brigade, also placed on record the conduct of the two companies of the 1st Patiala while in service at Gallipoli. 'Please inform the Patiala Darbar that Major Ishar Singh has been reported on by General Officer Commanding 29th Indian Infantry Brigade as having rendered good service in the field.'[128]

The account of services rendered by the two companies of the 1st Patiala Infantry at Gallipoli, in the assistance of 14th Sikhs has been eulogized in the annals of history. Three Sikh officers of Patiala Sikh Infantry, namely Major Ishar Singh, Subadar Bhagat Singh, and Subadar Kahla Singh have been specially mentioned in the dispatches

FIGURE 88: PATIALA DETACHMENT ON FAREWELL
PARADE FROM THE 14TH SIKHS[129]

TABLE 69: AWARDEES OF THE PATIALA INFANTRY ON GALLIPOLI[130]

Name	Unit	Award
Subadar Kahla Singh	1st Patiala Infantry	IOM (Second Class)
Subadar Kahla Singh	1st Patiala Infantry	OBI (Second Class) Bahadur
188, Sepoy Mit Singh	1st Patiala Infantry	Silver Medal (Serbia)
268, Sepoy Sampuran Singh	2nd Patiala Infantry	Gold Medal (Serbia)

from the battlefield. The Sikhs of Patiala Infantry due to their bravery and sacrifices were rewarded with the awards and as decided earlier these awards were separately promulgated and not mixed with the awards of the 14th Sikhs, the battalion with which the Patiala Sikhs had been attached.

The bravery and professionalism of the Patiala Infantry was also commended by the CO of the battalion, with whom these troops were attached during operations at Gallipoli. Major Earle, the Commanding Officer of 14th Sikhs in his letter of 11 January 1915, had commented, 'Of the Indian Officers, Major Isher Singh, Subadar Kahla Singh and Subadar Bhagat Singh were especially good.'[131] The services and sacrifices rendered by the 1st Patiala Infantry were also recognised and congratulated upon by the Lieutenant Governor

Michael O'Dwyer, when he reviewed the parade of the troops on 23 February 1919.

Officers and men, this morning, I desire to take this opportunity so kindly afforded me by His Highness of offering to you, on behalf of the British Government my congratulations on your return and my appreciation of the military sacrifice you have rendered to India and the Empire. You have within the last few weeks received a hearty welcome from your soldier Maharajah and his people on your return from four and a half year's arduous campaigning against the enemy in Europe, Asia and Africa. The Patiala Imperial Service Troops were among the first to take the field against the enemy and you did not leave it till the enemy were completely crushed. You have worthily upheld the splendid traditions of the Patiala state and the Sikh race. The infantry has done gallant service in Gallipoli, in the defence of Egypt for which they received special praise from General Allenby and in the final attack of September and October which led to the complete rout and surrender of Turkish Army.[132]

As an incentive and an instrument of motivation, the Special Order of the day also provided graded financial aid to the troops who served in the Great War, as per the length of the field service. The bonus and concessions granted to the soldiers were quite advantageous to the troops in those times. The Special Order granted half month of additional pay and allowances, which came under the category of pay (prewar scale) with three months of leave to all ranks who have been on field service for one year or under. For troops who had served in the field from over one year up to two years, the Special Order of the day provided for additional one month's pay and allowances as specified with four months of leave. For field service rendered between two years up to three years the financial concessions included two months of additional pay and allowances at specified scales with five months of leave. For all the troops who had served in the field for more than three years, the most beneficial concession included three months of additional pay and allowances at specified scales with six months of leave.

The Indian Mule Corps with its continued deployment and tasking on the peninsula for the entire duration performed a great role. A detailed discussion on the same has already been carried out in the previous sections of the book. Like other Indian troops, the bravery of soldiers of the Transport Corps was also awarded and recognised. Compounder Ganpat Rao[133] of Indian Animal Transport was awarded with IDSM for his distinguished service on the peninsula. Driver Dasharat Singh[134] of Indian Mule Corps was also awarded IDSM for his bravery and professionalism under the enemy fire on the peninsula.

A multitude of sources related to the grants of awards to the Indian troops, while serving on the peninsula makes the task of identification and collation of data with respect to these awards very challenging. A publication by the Government of India, titled India's Contribution to the Great War, makes a mention of awards conferred upon the Indian troops of IEF 'G'. As per the statistical abstract, as discussed in the book, a total of 219 awards were bestowed upon the Indian troops during the active service on the peninsula.[135] Based upon my research, a total of 263 awards were proffered upon the Indian troops. The details of the 263 awards are appended towards the end of the book; however, the statistical abstract for the same has been given below:

TABLE 70: HONOURS AND AWARDS TO INDIA TROOPS[136]

Award	Number of Indian Troops Awarded (Government of India Publication)	Number of Indian Troops Awarded (Research by the Author)
Military Cross	2	2
Order of British India	14	17
Indian Order of Merit	43	49
Indian Distinguished Service Medal	104	95
Indian Meritorious Service Medal	56	32
Mention-in-Dispatches	–	68
Total	219	263

Battle Honours are an established means to recognise and officially acknowledge the achievements of the Military Units in specific battles of a military campaign. It is a matter of pride and honour for the battalions / Regiments to be conferred with the Battle Honours. The Indian battalions had displayed courage and bravery against heavy odds in different battles as part of the Gallipoli campaign of the First World War. Following Battle Honours were awarded to the battalions of the Indian Army in Gallipoli.

Gallipoli 1915

21st (Kohat) Mountain Battery (Frontier Force)
26th (Jacob's) Mountain Battery
14th King George's Own Ferozepore Sikhs
69th Punjabis
89th Punjabis
1-4th Gurkha Rifles
1-5th Gurkha Rifles (Frontier Force)
1-6th Gurkha Rifles
2-10th Gurkha Rifles
Bharatpur Imperial Service Transport Corps
Indore (Holkar's) Imperial Service Transport Corps

Helles

14th King George's Own Ferozepore Sikhs
69th Punjabis
89th Punjabis
1-5th Gurkha Rifles (Frontier Force)
1-6th Gurkha Rifles
2-10th Gurkha Rifles

Krithia

14th King George's Own Ferozepore Sikhs
69th Punjabis
89th Punjabis
1-5th Gurkha Rifles (Frontier Force)
1-6th Gurkha Rifles
2-10th Gurkha Rifles

Anzac

21st (Kohat) Mountain Battery (Frontier Force)

26th (Jacob's) Mountain Battery

Landing at Anzac

21st (Kohat) Mountain Battery (Frontier Force)
26th (Jacob's) Mountain Battery

Defence of Anzac

21st (Kohat) Mountain Battery (Frontier Force)
26th (Jacob's) Mountain Battery

Suvla

21st (Kohat) Mountain Battery (Frontier Force)
26th (Jacob's) Mountain Battery
14th King George's Own Ferozepore Sikhs
1-5th Gurkha Rifles (Frontier Force)
1-6th Gurkha Rifles
2-10th Gurkha Rifles
Bharatpur Imperial Service Transport Corps
Indore (Holkar's) Imperial Service Transport Corps

Sari Bair

21st (Kohat) Mountain Battery (Frontier Force)
14th King George's Own Ferozepore Sikhs
1-5th Gurkha Rifles (Frontier Force)
1-6th Gurkha Rifles
2-10th Gurkha Rifles

Landing at Suvla

Bharatpur Imperial Service Transport Corps
Indore (Holkar's) Imperial Service Transport Corps

Scimitar Hill

Bharatpur Imperial Service Transport Corps
Indore (Holkar's) Imperial Service Transport Corps

NOTES

1. S. Tharoor (2018), *Inglorious Empire: What the British Did to India*, Penguin, London.
2. Ibid.
3. L.C.P.G. Bamford (1948), *The Sikh Regiment, The 14th King George's Own Ferozepore Sikhs*, Gale & Polden Limited, Aldershot.
4. R. Savory (2016), *A Subaltern of the Sikhs*, Abhishek Publications, Chandigarh.
5. Ibid.
6. Ibid.
7. Ibid.
8. Ibid.
9. Courtesy Prof (Dr) Charanjeet Thandi Sohi.
10. R. Savory (2016), *A Subaltern of the Sikhs*, op. cit.
11. Ibid.
12. Report of State Gazetteer, Jullundur, 1904.
13. Major B. & M. Gillott, eds. (2017), *Gallipoli Diaries: Headquarters 29th Indian Infantry Brigade.1915*. Great War Diaries Ltd.
14. Courtesy, Dr Tajinderpal Singh.
15. As narrated by son of Sepoy Nanak Singh.
16. Ibid.
17. Ibid.
18. Embarkation Statement, May 1915, War Diary, Army Headquarters, IEF 'A', vol. 10, 1st May to 31st May 1915, National Archives of India.
19. Telegram dated 2 May 1915 from the Secretary of War Office in London to the C-in-C in India. War Diary, Army Headquarters, IEF 'A', vol. 10, 1st May to 31st May 1915, National Archives of India.
20. Courtesy Ms Sukhpal Kaur Brar.
21. War Diary, Army Headquarters, IEF 'A', vol. 11, 1st June to 31st June 1915, National Archives of India.
22. Courtsey Ms Sukhpal Kaur Brar.
23. Ibid.
24. Bamford, *The Sikh Regiment*, op. cit.
25. Ibid.
26. Ibid.
27. Ibid.
28. Ibid.
29. Courtesy Ms Sukhpal Kaur Brar.

30. *The Daily News* (Perth, WA: 1882-1955), 23 April 1915, p. 5, *Helping Our Boys in Turkey.* https://trove.nla.gov.au/newspaper/article/811749 72?searchTerm=HelpingPer cent20ourPer cent20boysPer cent20inPer cent20Turkey
31. Ibid.
32. Reginald Savory.
33. *The Daily News* (Perth, WA : 1882-1955), 25 January 1915, p. 9, National Library of Australia.
34. Major Dhanna Singh, 14 Sikhs, *Gallipoli Journal*, Autumn 1978, p. 22.
35. Australian Sikh Heritage.
36. C.H.T. MacFetridge (1974), *Tales of the Mountain Gunners. An Anthology, Compiled by Those who Served with Them*, Blackwood.
37. Ibid.
38. *Tales of the Mountain Gunners,* op. cit.
39. Ibid.
40. Australia War Memorial.
41. Australians and Indians: Cordial Relations at Gallipoli (9 August 1915). Warrnambool Standard. Retrieved 14 May 2022, from https://trove.nla.gov.au/newspaper/article/73455621/7131999.
42. Australian War Memorial.
43. *Tales of the Mountain Gunners,* op. cit.
44. Australian War Memorial.
45. Major Dhonna Singh (1978), 'Sikh Seeks Sikh', *Gallipoli Journal*, Autumn 1978, 20–27.
46. I. Hamilton (2022), Ian Hamilton / *Gallipoli Diary*, 2 vols. 1920.
47. Ibid.
48. Ibid.
49. Ibid.
50. Ibid.
51. Ibid.
52. Ibid.
53. Ibid.
54. Ibid.
55. 14th Sikhs Album.
56. Telegram no. M-181, dated 15 June 1915. National Archives of India.
57. Ibid.
58. Casualty Appendix to War Diary, IEFG, Appendix 26, vol. 4, 1 to 31 October 1915, National Archives of India.

59. War Diary, Army Headquarters, IEF 'G', vol. 3, 1 to 30 September 1915, National Archives of India.

60. War Diary, IEF 'E' & 'G', vol. 12, 1 to 30 September 1915, Army Headquarters, National Archives of India.

61. Ibid.

62. War Diary, IEF 'E' & 'G', vol. 14, 1 to 30 November 1915, Army Headquarters, National Archives of India.

63. War Diary, IEF 'E' & 'G', vol. 15, 1 to 31 December 1915, Army Headquarters, National Archives of India.

64. Collated by the author.

65. IEF 'G', War Diary, vol. 2, 1 to 31 August 1915, Army Headquarters India, National Archives of India.

66. Ibid.

67. War Diary, Army Headquarters, IEF 'G', vol. 3, 1 to 30 September 1915, National Archives of India.

68. Ibid.

69. H.M. Alexander (2017), *On Two Fronts, Being the Adventures of an Indian Mule Corps in France and Gallipoli*, Van Haren Publishing, The Netherlands.

70. Australian Navy Monographs, vol. VIII (pub. 1923).

71. Translated Version of German U-35 War Diary.

72. Ibid.

73. Ibid.

74. Details extracted from CWGC portal.

75. Accessed from the url https://nyshistoricnewspapers.org/lccn/sn84031374/1915-09-29/ed-1/seq-1/, on 4 February 2023.

76. *The Daily News* (London), Suppression of Bad News, 9 November 1915. Available at https://www.britishnewspaperarchive.co.uk/search/results? basicsearch.

77. 'The Sinking of *Ramazan*', British Newspaper, 19 November 1915, British Newspaper Archives, https://www.britishnewspaperarchive.co.uk/search/results, accessed on 4 February 2023.

78. Casualty Appendix to War Diary Army Headquaters, India (F.S.R., Part II, Section 140; and Staff Manual, War Section 20), IEF 'G', National Archives of India.

79. Casualty Appendix to War Diary, IEF 'G', Appendix 26, vol. 4, 1 to 31 October 1915, National Archives of India.

80. Ibid.

81. Telegram no. M-419, dated 20 October 1915 from the 3rd Echelon Alexandria to the Central Casualty Bureau (Appendix 64, Diary

Number 24852), Casualty Appendix to War Diary, Army Headquarters, India (F.S,R., Part II, Section 140; and Staff Manual, War Section 20) IEF 'G'.

82. P. Stanley (2017), *Die in Battle, Do Not Despair: The Indians on Gallipoli, 1915*, Helion, Warwick.

83. Prepared by the author from different sources.

84. Drawn from different sources by the author.

85. Ibid.

86. Adapted from casualty database by the author.

87. Telegram no. 11299-X, dated 15 December 1915. From the OC, Depot, 2/10 Gurkhas to the Central Casualty Bureau, National Archives of India.

88. Telegram No. G-113, dated 9 December 1915. From the Central Casualty Bureau to the GOC, Canal Defences, Ismailia. Central Casualty Bureau, National Archives of India.

89. Telegram No. 183 - IDC, dated 28 January 1916. From the OC, Depot, 87th Punjabis, Dera Ismail Khan to the Central Casualty Bureau, National Archives of India.

90. Telegram No. 334-1-D.C, dated 4 March 1916. From the OC, Depot, 87th Punjabis, Dera Ismail Khan to the OC Depot, 14th Sikhs, Multan.

91. Adapted from casualty database by the author.

92. Telegram no. 6075-51-A, dated 1 April 1916. From the GOC, 1st (Peshawar) Division, to the Adjutant General in India, Simla, National Archives of India.

93. Telegram no. G-24, dated 4 April 1916. From the Central Casualty Bureau, Simla to the 3rd Echelon, Suez, National Archives of India.

94. Details extracted from CWGC portal.

95. Drawn from different sources by the author.

96. Ibid.

97. Ibid.

98. Adapted from casualty database by the author.

99. 14th (King George Own) Sikhs, Courtesy: The Great War (1914-1918) Forum, Available at https://www.greatwarforum.org/topic/139785-14th-king-georges-own-sikhs/, accessed on 31 May 2023.

100. Adapted from casualty database by the author.

101. Ibid.

102. Ibid.

103. Ibid.

104. Ibid.

105. Ibid.
106. War Diary, IEF 'E' & 'G', vol. 15, 1 to 31 December 1915, Army Headquarters, National Archives of India. Appendix 31, Diary No. 29800, National Archives of India.
107. Ibid.
108. Leigh. (1923). *India's contribution to the Great War.*
109. Adapted from casualty database by the author.
110. Leigh. (1923). *India's contribution to the Great War.*
111. Adapted from casualty database by the author.
112. Ibid.
113. VCs of Gallipoli and the Dardanelles, Gallipoli Association, Available at https://www.gallipoli-association.org/campaign/victoria-crosses/, accessed on 23 September 2023.
114. War Diary, Army Headquarters, India, IEF 'G', vol. I, 21 to 31 July 1915, National Archives of India.
115. Ibid.
116. Ibid.
117. *Tales of the Mountain Gunners*, op. cit.
118. Ibid.
119. *Tales of the Mountain Gunners*, op. cit.
120. War Diary, Army Headquarters India, IEF 'G', vol. 3, 1 to 30 September 1915, National Archives of India.
121. Ibid.
122. Ibid.
123. Ibid.
124. S. Talwar (2017), *Indian Recipients of the Military Cross*, vols. 1 & II, K.W. Publishers, New Delhi.
125. Ibid.
126. Ibid.
127. Punjab State Archives (1920), *Records Patiala State, Ijlase Khas*, File No. 1556, Part I (vol. 120).
128. Ibid
129. 14th Sikhs Album.
130. Punjab State Archives (1920), *Records Patiala State,* op. cit.
131. Ibid.
132. Ibid.
133. Supplement 29344, dated 29 October 1915 of London Gadget.
134. Ibid.
135. India. (1923), *India's Contribution to the Great War*, op. cit.
136. Compiled by the author.

Conclusion

The Great War, as it is commonly known has largely been a Great European war, with manifold reasons attributed to the didactic shift. The primary reason being that the war was predominantly a European one, was initiated by the European powers of the time and was primarily meant to be fought on European soil which later on spread to the other parts of the world. The Indian connect to the Great War manifested due to India being part of the colonial empire. The reasons for Indian participation in the Great War have also been discussed and debated during the past hundred plus years. Large volume of research exists on the subject. This aspect of the Great War has, therefore, deliberately not been discussed in detail in the present work.

Almost 1.3 million Indian soldiers were part of the various Indian army formations, which fought in the various theatres across the globe. It has also been historically researched that out of these 1.3 million, 74,000 Indian troops sacrificed their lives while fighting under the British flag. Gallipoli, in comparison was a very small but significant military 'misadventure', which was responsible for a serious setback to the political and military prestige of the British during the times. In the overall perspective, and in light of the findings of the research as discussed in the last chapter of the book, the Indian losses (killed) during the eight months of the campaign were 2.31 per cent of the total losses (killed) suffered by the Indian troops during the Great War. As far as participation proportion was concerned, Indian troops on the peninsula comprised of 1 per cent of the total Indian participation in the Great War. The industrial scale of death and destruction on the peninsula had witnessed loss of 1,30,000 men, out of which 87,000 were Ottoman and 44,000 allied troops, to include

British, ANZACs, French and Indians and other dominion troops. Juxtaposing the analytics as obtained in the final chapter of the book, in relative terms, Indian losses (killed) comprised of 4 per cent of the total allied losses (killed) on the peninsula.

On the surface of it, the relatively miniscule figures of 1 to 4 per cent across various parameters of Indian contribution in the Gallipoli campaign vis-à-vis the entire canvas of the Great War, appear to be almost irrelevant. But, herein lies the contraindication. The Gallipoli Campaign has been unique in terms of being the initial amphibious landing operations against the well-entrenched enemy, the magnitude of casualties and the repeated offensives of Indian troops against the very well-fortified Turks. The significance of the campaign though very well researched and documented by the Western military historians however, failed to generate enough traction with the Indian public conscience, the reasons for which were again were manifold.

The popular public perceptions with respect to the Indian connect with the Gallipoli campaign was attempted to be captured by the author with the help of a questionnaire. The results of the survey were not very surprising and were found to be generally aligned with the common knowledge and perception. With the major campaigns of the Great War, in which Indian troops fought, not being given due recognition, the treatment meted out to the aspect of Indian contribution in the Gallipoli campaign was expected. The situation, however, changed for better when Rana Chhina, started researching on the Indian connect with the Great War. Peter Stanley further authenticated the contribution of the Indian troops in the Gallipoli campaign with his seminal work in 2015.

The mobilisation of the Indian Expeditionary Forces for the active duty overseas in October of 1914 was preceded by a massive recruitment drive which was primarily led by the Martial Race concept. The concept was also predominantly manifested in the Punjab province of the time. The incentives for recruitment and retaining were unparalleled. The Infantry battalions of the time, which were being raised and nurtured by this recruitment drive, had recently undergone changes in the composition of sub units, Machine Gun sections had lately been introduced and the follower system both public and private was in the process of being institutionalised. Similarly, both the

Artillery and Mule Corps had also, not long ago sustained organic and systemic reformations, whose impact was yet to be observed in a full-blown operation. The 29th Indian Infantry Brigade when left India for the Western Front also comprised of these reformed Indian Infantry battalions. The 21st and 26th Indian Mountain Artillery Batteries had also landed on the shores of Gallipoli in the initial waves on 25 April 1915, with the latest tactics of employment of vintage Mountain Guns held in the inventory. The Gallipoli Campaign was, therefore, the first major active operation which was witness to the new organisation, newer tactics and latest employment philosophy of weapons by the Indian Army.

The significance of the campaign from the Indian perspective was further accentuated by the singular and unique eating habits of the Indian troops. The logistics of the campaign from the point of view of supply chain from India, almost 3,000 miles away to Alexandria and further to the peninsula to the last Indian soldier standing in the trenches was an indeed very long and arduous trail. The cooking of meal by the Indian troops under the conditions as obtained on the peninsula under observed Artillery and sniper fire deserves to be brought into public contemplation. In addition, the trials and tribulations of the Indian soldiers on the peninsula with their weapons, ammunition and equipment have until now been unperceivable.

Water was a precious source on the peninsula. The manner in which Indians handled the scarcity of water during those eight months, by improvising the carriage of water in the *Pakhals* along the two sides of a mule was a wonder for the ANZACs. To demonstrate the process of carriage, the Indian Mule Corps had reportedly showcased the entire workflow to the ANZACs. As far as logistics were concerned, though the concept of Martial Races was feeding the embattled Indian battalions on the peninsula in form of reinforcements, the supply chain for the reinforcements was very long. Similarly, the return chain of casualty evacuation was also very torturous. The Indian troops suffered on both sides of the chain. The massive number of casualties suffered by the Indian battalions triggered the dispatch of reinforcements and the corresponding evacuation chain of casualties.

The distances involved along with the availability of limited sea transport, due to demand in the other theaters of war, further compounded the misfortunes. S.S. *Ramazan*, the sea transport carrying Indian troops as reinforcements for Gallipoli was torpedoed by a German U Boat and sunk resulting in the drowning of 279 Indian troops. The services of the Indian Mule Corps, the Field Post Office and the Indian Medical Service on the peninsula have been till now shrouded in the cloak of archival history. The book attempts to bring to the fore, the sacrifices of the brave men of these lesser known units and sub-units and provide them with due recognition. The Indian Labour Corps, though conceptualised for employment on the peninsula, was never utilized for the purpose. The book retraces the journey of the raising of the Labour Corps and has attempted to provide a holistic view of the raising and dispatch of the Corps from India.

During the eight months on the peninsula, Indian troops developed a very close interpersonal relationship with the ANZACs. The Gunners and Drivers of the Indian Mountain Batteries had landed with ANZACs on 25 April 1915 and were one of the last troops to be deinducted from the peninsula. This military connect between India and Australia has since then witnessed an upward trajectory and also been alluded to in my previous book. While on the peninsula, the Indian units and sub units were reinforced by an astounding 136 per cent of reinforcements. On 1 May 1915, when the Indian troops landed on the peninsula, the strength of the Indian Infantry Brigade was 3,312 Indian Officers, Indian Troops and Followers, against which starting from August 1915 onwards till December 1915, strength of 4,485 Indian Officers, Indian Troops and Followers had been dispatched from India to Gallipoli. These statistics talk about the magnitude of the effort involved in drafting, dispatching and receiving these freshly recruited troops or attachments from other units as reinforcements by the Indian Army. During these eight months on the peninsula, the Indian troops suffered 1,438 fatal casualties and 3,468 wounded, combining a total of 4,906 casualties, a strength which was 108 per cent more than the total reinforcements dispatched from India for the beleaguered Indian battalions on the peninsula and 147 per cent more than the strength of the Indian troops which landed on the peninsula on 1 May 1915.

The Indian troops on the peninsula suffered insurmountable sufferings in terms of casualties, supply of water and rations, casualty evacuation and travel back to India. Each of the 16,281 Indian soldiers, who served on the peninsula had a story attached to him. The life story of each soldier revolved around his recruitment, mobilisation from India, travails on the peninsula and the evacuation and back to India after retirement, if one was lucky enough to survive.

Almost a century later, it was an extremely difficult proposition to retrace the life story of each soldier due to the non-availability of relevant records. I consider myself very fortunate, in that I was able to connect with the descendants of three Sikh soldiers who served on the peninsula as part of IEF 'G'. The service lives of Sepoy Udey Singh, Sepoy Nanak Singh and Subadar Gurmukh Singh followed different trajectories before and after Gallipoli, which merged on the peninsula and represent all 16,281 Indian soldiers who were on the peninsula. This book is an attempt to provide due recognition to the sustenance, service and sacrifice of these unsung braves.

APPENDICES

APPENDIX 1: COMPOSITION OF BURMA MILITARY POLICE OVER THE YEARS

S. No.	Year	Bengal							Madras	Bombay	Total	% Sikh of Total	% Gurkhas of Total
		Punjabis	Sikhs	Gurkhas	Others	Total	% Sikh of Bengal	% Gurkhas of Bengal					
1	1888	3,546	3,937	0	7,766	15,249	25.82	0.00	0	0	15,249	25.82	0
2	1889	4,181	4,743	0	6,407	15,331	30.94	0.00	0	0	15,331	30.94	0.00
3	1890	3,086	4,406	1,287	6,349	15,128	29.12	8.51	8	256	15,392	28.63	8.36
4	1891	0	0	0	0	0	0.00	0.00	0	0	0	0.00	0.00
5	1892	2,602	3,860	1,365	4,820	12,647	30.52	10.79	6	145	12,798	30.16	10.67
6	1893	2,134	3,426	1,328	4,634	11,522	29.73	11.53	1	52	11,575	29.60	11.47
7	1894	2,085	3,385	1,332	4,818	11,620	29.13	11.46	2	71	11,693	28.95	11.39
8	1895	0	0	0	0	0	0.00	0.00	0	0	0	0.00	0.00
9	1896	2,031	3,125	1,462	4,623	11,241	27.80	13.01	1	33	11,275	27.72	12.97
10	1897	2,225	4,154	1,616	5,760	13,755	30.20	11.75	2	154	13,911	29.86	11.62
11	1898	2,413	3,978	1,557	5,570	13,518	29.43	11.52	1	142	13,661	29.12	11.40
12	1899	2,449	4,012	1,423	5,665	13,549	29.61	10.50	2	137	13,688	29.31	10.40
13	1900	2,509	4,059	1,430	5,623	13,621	29.80	10.50	8	120	13,749	29.52	10.40
14	1901	2,475	4,248	1,695	5,814	14,232	29.85	11.91	2	111	14,345	29.61	11.82

(contd.)

APPENDIX 1 (*contd.*)

S. No.	Year	Bengal							Madras	Bombay	Total	% Sikh of Total	% Gurkhas of Total
		Punjabis	Sikhs	Gurkhas	Others	Total	% Sikh of Bengal	% Gurkhas of Bengal					
15	1902	2,468	4,166	1,325	6079	14,038	29.68	9.44	1	102	14,141	29.46	9.37
16	1903	0	0	0	0	0	0.00	0.00	0	0	0	0.00	0.00
17	1904	0	0	0	0	0	0.00	0.00	0	0	0	0.00	0.00
18	1905	2,375	4,144	1,267	6786	14,572	28.44	8.69	1	109	14,682	28.23	8.63
Total		**36,579**	**55,643**	**17,087**	**80714**	**1,900,23**	**29.28**	**8.99**	**35**	**1,432**	**1,91,490**	**29.06**	**8.92**

Source: From multiple sources.

APPENDIX 2: CASUALTIES OF INDIAN TROOPS DUE TO SINKING OF SS *RAMAJAN*

S. No.	Service Number	Rank	Name	Regiment	Unit	Secondary Regiment	Date of Death	Next of Kin
1	3538	Rifleman	SINGBAHADUR LIMBU	10th Gurkha Rifles	1st Bn.	-	19/9/1915	Son of Samsher Limbu, of Parwadin. Chhathar. Dhankuta, Nepal.
2	3548	Rifleman	ASRAJ LIMBU	10th Gurkha Rifles	1st Bn. attd 2nd Bn.	-	19/9/1915	Son of Gumansing Limbu, of Yansingok, Yangrup, Dhankuta, Nepal.
3	3070	Rifleman	ASRAM RAI	10th Gurkha Rifles	1st Bn. attd 2nd Bn.	-	19/9/1915	Son of Shembarna Rai, of Pakribas, Chainpore, Dhankuta, Nepal.
4	3115	Rifleman	BAGSING LAMA	10th Gurkha Rifles	1st Bn. attd 2nd Bn.	-	19/9/1915	Son of Chatursing Lama, of Chitre, Bijulakote, No. 3, East, Nepal.
5	3577	Rifleman	BALARAM LIMBU	10th Gurkha Rifles	1st Bn. attd 2nd Bn.	-	19/9/1915	Son of Manbahadur Limbu, of Tangkhua, Chhatar, Dhankuta, Nepal.

(contd.)

APPENDIX 2 *(contd.)*

S. No.	Service Number	Rank	Name	Regiment	Unit	Secondary Regiment	Date of Death	Next of Kin
6	3501	Rifleman	BALBAHADUR RAI	10th Gurkha Rifles	1st Bn. attd 2nd Bn.	-	19/9/1915	Son of Mandhoj Rai, of Luring, Gangtok, Sikkim, Nepal.
7	2765	Rifleman	BALDHOJ LIMBU	10th Gurkha Rifles	1st Bn. attd 2nd Bn.	-	19/9/1915	Son of Puransing Limbu, of Kasua, Chainpore, Dhankuta, Nepal.
8	3202	Rifleman	BHAGIMAN RAI	10th Gurkha Rifles	1st Bn. attd 2nd Bn.	-	19/9/1915	Son of Kulupatti Rai, of Damku Irawadumre, Okhaldhunga, Nepal.
9	3272	Rifleman	BHAIMANE RAI	10th Gurkha Rifles	1st Bn. attd 2nd Bn.	-	19/9/1915	Son of Rajbure Rai, of Sondel, Rawadumre, Okhaldunga, Nepal.
10	2646	Rifleman	BHAKTABAHA-DUR LIMBU	10th Gurkha Rifles	1st Bn. attd 2nd Bn.	-	19/9/1915	Son of Asamia Limbu, of Kumaru, Phedap, Dhankuta, Nepal.
11	3191	Rifleman	BHOJBAHADUR RAI	10th Gurkha Rifles	1st Bn. attd 2nd Bn.	-	19/9/1915	Son of Jitbahadur Rai, of Parpe, Chainpore, Dhankuta, Nepal.

12	3349	Rifleman	BHOJMAN RAI	10th Gurkha Rifles	1st Bn. attd 2nd Bn.	–	19/9/1915	Son of Tekbir Rai, of Punekhu, Talawa, No. 3, East, Nepal.
13	3080	Rifleman	BIRDHOJ SUNWAR	10th Gurkha Rifles	1st Bn. attd 2nd Bn.	–	19/9/1915	Son of Tirpane Rai, of Buji, Ramechhap, No. 3, East, Nepal.
14	3134	Naik	BIRKHABADUR LIMBU	10th Gurkha Rifles	1st Bn. attd 2nd Bn.	–	19/9/1915	Son of Panbir Limbu, of Lingbang, Phedap, Dhankuta, Nepal.
15	3509	Rifleman	BOMBAHADUR RAI	10th Gurkha Rifles	1st Bn. attd 2nd Bn.	–	19/9/1915	Son of Dhanparsad Rai, of Baspani, No. 3, East, Okhaldhunga, Nepal.
16	3591	Rifleman	BUDHIMAN RAI	10th Gurkha Rifles	1st Bn. attd 2nd Bn.	–	19/9/1915	Son of Chandrasor Rai, of Chhapgaun, Hatuwa, Bhojpore, Nepal.
17	3520	Rifleman	CHAKRABAHA-DUR RAI	10th Gurkha Rifles	1st Bn. attd 2nd Bn.	–	19/9/1915	Son of Ganjaman Rai, of Bosikhora, Hathuwa, Bhojpore, Nepal.

(contd.)

APPENDIX 2 (*contd.*)

S. No.	Service Number	Rank	Name	Regiment	Unit	Secondary Regiment	Date of Death	Next of Kin
18	2437	Naik	DAMBARSING LIMBU	10th Gurkha Rifles	1st Bn. attd 2nd Bn.	-	19/9/1915	Son of Parasing Limbu, of Lungja, Mewakhola, Dhankuta, Nepal.
19	2772	Naik	DAMBARSING RAI	10th Gurkha Rifles	1st Bn. attd 2nd Bn.	-	19/9/1915	Son of Parasing Rai, of Lungja, Mewakhola, Dhankuta, Nepal.
20	2870	Lance Naik	DATAHANG LIMBU	10th Gurkha Rifles	1st Bn. attd 2nd Bn.	-	19/9/1915	Son of Jasnand Limbu, of Sunthokra, Mewakhola, Dhankuta, Nepal.
21	3532	Rifleman	DAULATMAN RAI	10th Gurkha Rifles	1st Bn. attd 2nd Bn.	-	19/9/1915	Son of Jasnanda Rai; of Santhakra, Mewakhola, Dhankuta, Nepal.
22	3584	Rifleman	DHANBAHADUR RAI	10th Gurkha Rifles	1st Bn. attd 2nd Bn.	-	19/9/1915	Son of Ransur Rai, of Dilpa, Siktel, Bhojpore, Nepal.
23	3543	Rifleman	GANJAMAN RAI	10th Gurkha Rifles	1st Bn. attd 2nd Bn.	-	19/9/1915	Son of Tauman Rai, of Chachalung, Okhaldhunga, Nepal.

24	3537	Rifleman	HAIKAMSING RAI	10th Gurkha Rifles	1st Bn. attd 2nd Bn.	–	19/9/1915	Son of Akalman Rai, of Dilpa, Siktel, Rhojpore, Nepal.
25	2082	Havildar	HARKABIR THAPA	10th Gurkha Rifles	1st Bn. attd 2nd Bn.	–	19/9/1915	Son of Barnasing Thapa, of Malbanse. Ilam, Ilamdanda, Nepal.
26	1529	Colour Havildar	HARKAJIT LIMBU	10th Gurkha Rifles	1st Bn. attd 2nd Bn.	–	19/9/1915	Son of Hedal Limbu, of Libong, Mewakhola, Dhankuta, Nepal.
27	3371	Rifleman	HASTABAHA-DUR RAI	10th Gurkha Rifles	1st Bn. attd 2nd Bn.	–	19/9/1915	Son of Jagandhoj Rai, of Basa, Chisankhu, No. 3, East, Nepal.
28	3404	Rifleman	INDRABAHA-DUR GURUNG	10th Gurkha Rifles	1st Bn. attd 2nd Bn.	–	19/9/1915	Son of Maniraj Gurung, of Pakribas, Sabhayautar, Dhankuta, Nepal.
29	3507	Rifleman	INDRABAHA-DUR LIMBU	10th Gurkha Rifles	1st Bn. attd 2nd Bn.	–	19/9/1915	Son of Barnasing Limbu, of Chinim, Mewakhola, Dhankuta, Nepal.

(contd.)

519

APPENDIX 2 (contd.)

S. No.	Service Number	Rank	Name	Regiment	Unit	Secondary Regiment	Date of Death	Next of Kin
30	3581	Rifleman	INDRADHOJ LIMBU	10th Gurkha Rifles	1st Bn. attd 2nd Bn.	–	19/9/1915	Son of Atbir Limbu, of Birmanganj, Chaubis, Dhankuta, Nepal.
31	3522	Rifleman	INDRAMAN RAI	10th Gurkha Rifles	1st Bn. attd 2nd Bn.	–	19/9/1915	Son of Dhanganja Rai, of Kuksi, Chainpore, Dhankuta, Nepal.
32	3395	Rifleman	ISTAMAN RAI	10th Gurkha Rifles	1st Bn. attd 2nd Bn.	–	19/9/1915	Son of Maulidhan Rai, of Sasarka, Rawadumre, No. 3, East, Nepal.
33	3583	Rifleman	JAIBAHADUR RAI	10th Gurkha Rifles	1st Bn. attd 2nd Bn.	–	19/9/1915	Son of Hajurman Rai, of Khamare, Bhojpore, Nepal.
34	3571	Rifleman	JAIKAKNA LIMBU	10th Gurkha Rifles	1st Bn. attd 2nd Bn.	–	19/9/1915	Son of Hangsir Limbu, of Songopo, Phedap, Dhankuta, Nepal.
35	3582	Rifleman	JAINE RAI	10th Gurkha Rifles	1st Bn. attd 2nd Bn.	–	19/9/1915	Son of Suklal Rai, of Kaspakhalu, Menglung, Dhankuta, Nepal.
36	3661	Rifleman	JANCHBIR LIMBU	10th Gurkha Rifles	1st Bn. attd 2nd Bn.	–	19/9/1915	Of Phedap, Panthar, Dhallkuta, Nepal.

37	2874	Rifleman	JANGDHOJ	10th Gurkha Rifles	1st Bn. attd 2nd Bn.	–	19/9/1915	Son of Bale Rai, of Hathuwa, Chhatar, Dhankuta, Nepal.
38	3560	Rifleman	JASPAL RAI	10th Gurkha Rifles	1st Bn. attd 2nd Bn.	–	19/9/1915	Son of Dasrath Rai, of Sumlikha, Khotang, Bhojpore, Nepal.
39	3103	Rifleman	JITBAHADLTR LAMA	10th Gurkha Rifles	1st Bn. attd 2nd Bn.	–	19/9/1915	Son of Satasing Lama, of Sorakpo, Chaubisya, Dhankuta, Nepal.
40	3316	Rifleman	JITHARKA RAI	10th Gurkha Rifles	1st Bn. attd 2nd Bn.	–	19/9/1915	Son of Asman Rai, of Necha, Chisankhu, No. 3, East, Nepal.
41	2596	Rifleman	JITMAN LAMA	10th Gurkha Rifles	1st Bn. attd 2nd Bn.	–	19/9/1915	Son of Kadhane Lama, of Rawakhola, Rawadumre, No. 3, East, Nepal.
42	3539	Rifleman	KABIT RAI	10th Gurkha Rifles	1st Bn. attd 2nd Bn.	–	19/9/1915	Son of Dalbir Rai, of Santha, Yangrup, Dhankuta, Nepal.
43	3514	Rifleman	KALUMAN RAI	10th Gurkha Rifles	1st Bn. attd 2nd Bn.	–	19/9/1915	Son of Jangdhoj Rai, of Khana, Siktel, Bhojpore, Nepal.

(contd.)

S. No.	Service Number	Rank	Name	Regiment	Unit	Secondary Regiment	Date of Death	Next of Kin
44	3505	Rifleman	KARBIR LIMBU	10th Gurkha Rifles	1st Bn. attd 2nd Bn.	-	19/9/1915	
45	3245	Rifleman	KARNABAHA- DUR RAI	10th Gurkha Rifles	1st Bn. attd 2nd Bn.	-	19/9/1915	Son of Ariman Rai, of Sursipa, Chisankhu, Okhaldhunga, Nepal.
46	3007	Rifleman	KHARKABAHA- DUR LIMBU	10th Gurkha Rifles	1st Bn. attd 2nd Bn.	-	19/9/1915	Son of Bajahang Limbu, of Paireni, Chainpore, Dhankuta, Nepal.
47	3527	Rifleman	KRISHNAMAN RAI	10th Gurkha Rifles	1st Bn. attd 2nd Bn.	-	19/9/1915	Son of Gajbir Rai, of Khowa, Bhojpore, No. 4, East, Nepal.
48	3536	Rifleman	LACHHMAN LIMBU	10th Gurkha Rifles	1st Bn. attd 2nd Bn.	-	19/9/1915	Son of Ganwape Ilimbu, of Parwadin, Chhathar, Dhankuta, Nepal.
49	3528	Rifleman	LACHHMAN LIMBU	10th Gurkha Rifles	1st Bn. attd 2nd Bn.	-	19/9/1915	Son of Ranbahadur Limbu, of Gidange, Chaubisya, Dhankuta, Nepal.

50	3513	Rifleman	LACHHMAN RAI	10th Gurkha Rifles	1st Bn. attd 2nd Bn.	–	19/9/1915	Son of Kisorman Rai, of Husbo, Siktel, Bhojpore, Nepal.
51	3546	Rifleman	LALBAHADUR GURUNG	10th Gurkha Rifles	1st Bn. attd 2nd Bn.	–	19/9/1915	Son of Ranbir Gurung, of Pakhribas, Dailekh, Nepal.
52	3155	Rifleman	LALBIR RAI	10th Gurkha Rifles	1st Bn. attd 2nd Bn.	–	19/9/1915	Son of Ramdat Rai, of Likhkharka, Chisankhu, No. 3, East, Nepal.
53	2824	Rifleman	MAHAKMAN RAI	10th Gurkha Rifles	1st Bn. attd 2nd Bn.	–	19/9/1915	Son of Sirman Rai, of Dilpa, Siktel, Bhojpore, Nepal.
54	2888	Rifleman	MAHASER LIMBU	10th Gurkha Rifles	1st Bn. attd 2nd Bn.	–	19/9/1915	Son of Chhatrasing Limbu, of Tinglabo, Mewakhola, Dhankuta, Nepal.
55	1610	Rifleman	MAHENDRAD-HOJ LIMBU	10th Gurkha Rifles	1st Bn. attd 2nd Bn.	–	19/9/1915	Son of Wardare Limbu, of Tauka, Chhathar, Dhankuta, Nepal.
56	3572	Rifleman	MAIDANE LIMBU	10th Gurkha Rifles	1st Bn. attd 2nd Bn.	–	19/9/1915	Son of Mareke Limbu, of Songaupo, Phedap, Dhankuta, Nepal.

(contd.)

APPENDIX 2 (*contd.*)

S. No.	Service Number	Rank	Name	Regiment	Unit	Secondary Regiment	Date of Death	Next of Kin
57	2299	Havildar	MAITAHANG LIMBU	10th Gurkha Rifles	1st Bn. attd 2nd Bn.	–	19/9/1915	Son of Kalu Limbu, of Mandria, Ilamdanda, Ilam, Nepal.
58	3043	Rifleman	MANBAHADUR LIMBU	10th Gurkha Rifles	1st Bn. attd 2nd Bn.	–	19/9/1915	Son of Phaudabir Limbu, of Nandari, Chainpore, Dhankuta, Nepal.
59	3482	Rifleman	MANBAHADUR NEWAR	10th Gurkha Rifles	1st Bn. attd 2nd Bn.	–	19/9/1915	Son of Parbharam Newar.
60	2982	Rifleman	MANDHOJ LIMBU	10th Gurkha Rifles	1st Bn. attd 2nd Bn.	–	19/9/1915	Son of Bhartasing Limbu, of Nandari, Chainpore, Dhankuta, Nepal.
61	3700	Rifleman	MANTARE LIMBU	10th Gurkha Rifles	1st Bn. attd 2nd Bn.	–	19/9/1915	Son of Dalkarna Limbu, of Thepang, Panthar, Dhankuta, Nepal.
62	3529	Rifleman	NAIKSING LIMBU	10th Gurkha Rifles	1st Bn. attd 2nd Bn.	–	19/9/1915	Son of Makisor Limbu, of Gidange, Chaubisya, Dhankuta, Nepal.

63	3531	NANDLAL LIMBU	Rifleman	10th Gurkha Rifles	1st Bn. attd 2nd Bn.	-	19/9/1915	Son of Manparsi Limbu, of Gidange Chaubisya, Dhankuta, Nepal.
64	3512	NANDLAL RAI	Rifleman	10th Gurkha Rifles	1st Bn. attd 2nd Bn.	-	19/9/1915	Son of Hurno Rai, of Siktel, Bhojpore, Nepal.
65	3469	NARBAHADUR RAI	Rifleman	10th Gurkha Rifles	1st Bn. attd 2nd Bn.	-	19/9/1915	Son of Dhanbir Rai, of Patika, Rawadumre, No. 3, East, Nepal.
66	2703	NARMAN LIMBU	Rifleman	10th Gurkha Rifles	1st Bn. attd 2nd Bn.	-	19/9/1915	Son of Mandraj Limbu, of Parwadin, Dhankuta, Nepal.
67	3517	PANCHASOR RAI	Rifleman	10th Gurkha Rifles	1st Bn. attd 2nd Bn.	-	19/9/1915	Son of Singman Rai, of Khena, Siktel, Bhojpore, Nepal.
68	2767	PARMA RAI	Rifleman	10th Gurkha Rifles	1st Bn. attd 2nd Bn.	-	19/9/1915	Son of Puransing Rai, of Laketung, Memting, Nepal.
69	3503	PARTAPSING RAI	Rifleman	10th Gurkha Rifles	1st Bn. attd 2nd Bn.	-	19/9/1915	Son of Jukhman Rai, of Dilpa, Siktel, No. 3, West, Nepal.

(contd.)

APPENDIX 2 (contd.)

S. No.	Service Number	Rank	Name	Regiment	Unit	Secondary Regiment	Date of Death	Next of Kin
70	3256	Rifleman	PHARSAMAN RAI	10th Gurkha Rifles	1st Bn. attd 2nd Bn.	-	19/9/1915	Son of Adijang Rai, of Khwa, Dilpa, Bhojpore, Nepal.
71	3480	Rifleman	PREMSING GURUNG	10th Gurkha Rifles	1st Bn. attd 2nd Bn.	-	19/9/1915	Son of Jasbahadur Gurung, of Kopu, Kuncha, Lamjong, Nepal.
72	3160	Rifleman	RAJBAL RAI	10th Gurkha Rifles	1st Bn. attd 2nd Bn.	-	19/9/1915	Son of Darmaraj Rai, of Godel, Aselukharka, No. 3, West, Nepal.
73	3533	Rifleman	RAJDHAN RAI	10th Gurkha Rifles	1st Bn. attd 2nd Bn.	-	19/9/1915	Son of Jamansing Rai, of Warang, Siktel, Bhojpore, Nepal.
74	2660	Rifleman	RAJNANDA LIMBU	10th Gurkha Rifles	1st Bn. attd 2nd Bn.	-	19/9/1915	Son of Gothar Limbu, of Obrai, Yangrup, Dhankuta, Nepal.
75	2908	Rifleman	RAMBAHADUR LIMBU	10th Gurkha Rifles	1st Bn. attd 2nd Bn.	-	19/9/1915	Son of Asbahadur Limbu, of Angon, Chainpore, Dhankuta, Nepal.

No.	Number	Name	Rank	Regiment	Battalion		Date	Remarks
76	3592	RANAHANG LIMBU	Rifleman	10th Gurkha Rifles	1st Bn. attd 2nd Bn.	–	19/9/1915	Son of Dhanrath Limbu, of Gidange, Chaubisya, Dhankuta, Nepal.
77	3218	RANGALAL RAI	Rifleman	10th Gurkha Rifles	1st Bn. attd 2nd Bn.	–	19/9/1915	Son of Janbir Rai, of Kalbote, Ilam, Ilamdana, Nepal.
78	2911	SAIBAHADUR RAI	Rifleman	10th Gurkha Rifles	1st Bn. attd 2nd Bn.	–	19/9/1915	Son of Panche Rai, of Hathuwa, Chainpore, Dhankuta, Nepal.
79	1157	SANJAPATI LIMBU	Rifleman	10th Gurkha Rifles	1st Bn. attd 2nd Bn.	–	19/9/1915	Of Yemason, Yangrup, Dhankuta, Nepal.
80	3497	SANKHABIR LIMBU	Rifleman	10th Gurkha Rifles	1st Bn. attd 2nd Bn.	–	19/9/1915	Son of Nardhoj Limbu, of Tunbet, Mewakhola, Dhankuta, Nepal.
81	3542	TIRTHASOR RAI	Rifleman	10th Gurkha Rifles	1st Bn. attd 2nd Bn.	–	19/9/1915	Son of Rabiman Rai, of Baspani, Rawakhola, Okhaldhunga, Nepal.
82	3109	UDAIBAHADUR LIMBU	Rifleman	10th Gurkha Rifles	1st Bn. attd 2nd Bn.	–	19/9/1915	Son of Kancharaj Limbu, of Samite, Chaubisya, Dhankuta, Nepal.

(contd.)

APPENDIX 2 (contd.)

S. No.	Service Number	Rank	Name	Regiment	Unit	Secondary Regiment	Date of Death	Next of Kin
83	3579	Rifleman	BHOTABIR LIMBU	10th Gurkha Rifles	1st Bn. attd 2nd Bn.	–	19/9/1915	Son of Dalbahadur Limbu, of Sanglep, Phedap, Dhankuta, Nepal.
84	1575	Driver	BURHAN ALI	Indian Mountain Artillery	26th Jacob's Mountain Battery	–	19/9/1915	Son of Madad Khan, of Nala Musalmanan, Kahuta, Rawalpindi, Punjab.
85	1235	Gunner	KADIR BAKSH	Indian Mountain Artillery	26th Jacob's Mountain Battery	–	19/9/1915	Son of Faujdar Khan, of Sang, Gujar Khan, Rawalpindi, Punjab.
86	1387	Driver	LAL KHAN	Indian Mountain Artillery	26th Jacob's Mountain Battery	–	19/9/1915	Son of Haidar Khan, of Mehra Khurd, Rawalpindi, Punjab.
87	1717	Driver	WALI MUHAM-MAD	Indian Mountain Artillery	26th Jacob's Mountain Battery	–	19/9/1915	Son of Samand Khan, of Katha, Khushab, Shahpore, Punjab.
88	1162	Rifleman	AITABIR LIMBU	10th Gurkha Rifles	2nd Bn.	–	19/9/1915	Son of Dirgasing Limbu, of Thumithap, Mewakhola Dhankuta, Nepal.

No.	Number	Rank	Name	Regiment	Battalion		Date	Remarks
89	1086	Rifleman	AJIRMAN RAI	10th Gurkha Rifles	2nd Bn.	-	19/9/1915	Son of Kibalsing Lama, of Gairi, Solo, Okhaldunga, Nepal.
90	1129	Rifleman	BAGTABIR RAI	10th Gurkha Rifles	2nd Bn.	-	19/9/1915	Son of Yasball Rai, of Yubu, Cheme, Okhaldhunga, Nepal.
91	1116	Rifleman	BAHADUR LIMBU	10th Gurkha Rifles	2nd Bn.	-	19/9/1915	Son of Bakte Limbu, of Orokma, Mewakhola, Dhankuta, Nepal.
92	1085	Rifleman	BALBAHADUR RAI	10th Gurkha Rifles	2nd Bn.	-	19/9/1915	Son of Narandhoj Rai, of Bairag, Dhankuta, Nepal.
93	1151	Rifleman	BHAGTE SUNWAR	10th Gurkha Rifles	2nd Bn.	-	19/9/1915	Son of Purne Sunwar, of Som, Darjeeling, Bengal.
94	1147	Rifleman	BHIMBAHADUR RAI	10th Gurkha Rifles	2nd Bn.	-	19/9/1915	Son of Ambersing Rai, of Nirang, Siktel, Bhojpore, Nepal.
95	2638	Havildar	BHOWRAJ LIMBU	10th Gurkha Rifles	2nd Bn.	-	19/9/1915	Son of Dalbir Limbu, of Angsingbe, Yangrup, Dhankuta, Nepal.

(*contd.*)

APPENDIX 2 (*contd.*)

S. No.	Service Number	Rank	Name	Regiment	Unit	Secondary Regiment	Date of Death	Next of Kin
96	579	Rifleman	BHUDIMAN RAI	10th Gurkha Rifles	2nd Bn.	-	19/9/1915	Son of Tule Rai, of Palisampang, Bhojpore, Nepal.
97	1077	Rifleman	BIDHIMAN LAMA	10th Gurkha Rifles	2nd Bn.	-	19/9/1915	Son of Yakto Lama, of Rangbang, Phedap, Dhankuta, Nepal.
98	1093	Rifleman	BIMAN RAI	10th Gurkha Rifles	2nd Bn.	-	19/9/1915	Son of Sirdal Rai, of Tangdam, Chainpore, Dhankuta, Nepal.
99	1114	Rifleman	BIRDHOJ RAI	10th Gurkha Rifles	2nd Bn.	-	19/9/1915	Son of Methhang Rai, of Magdi, Pawa, Dhankuta, Nepal.
100	1164	Rifleman	BIRU LAMA	10th Gurkha Rifles	2nd Bn.	-	19/9/1915	Son of Kusang Lama, of Jhaku, Khotang, Charrikote, Nepal.
101	1165	Rifleman	CHANDRABA-HADUR RAI	10th Gurkha Rifles	2nd Bn.	-	19/9/1915	Son of Harilal Rai, of Dowa, Bhojpore, Nepal.

102	1156	Rifleman	CHANDRABIR RAI	10th Gurkha Rifles	2nd Bn.	–	19/9/1915	Son of Bakhtawar Rai, of Tekhutang, Gangrok, Sikkim, Nepal.
103	1110	Rifleman	CHANDRABIR RAI	10th Gurkha Rifles	2nd Bn.	–	19/9/1915	Son of Rajahan Rai, of Birgaon, Dhankuta, Nepal.
104	1094	Rifleman	CHANDRAMAN RAI	10th Gurkha Rifles	2nd Bn.	–	19/9/1915	Son of Randal Rai, of Dingding, Chainpore, Dhankuta, Nepal.
105	1154	Rifleman	CHATURMAN RAI	10th Gurkha Rifles	2nd Bn.	–	19/9/1915	Son of Madhil Rai, of Solo, Majuwa, Okhaldhunga, Nepal.
106	1983	Havildar	CHIRMAN THAPA	10th Gurkha Rifles	2nd Bn.	–	19/9/1915	Son of Dachi Thapa, of Muriabar, Chaubina, Phankuta, Nepal.
107	1128	Rifleman	DALBAHADUR RAI	10th Gurkha Rifles	2nd Bn.	–	19/9/1915	Son of Phipkarm Rai, of Suwachi, Panthar, Dhankuta..
108	1182	Rifleman	DALMARDAN RAI	10th Gurkha Rifles	2nd Bn.	–	19/9/1915	Son of Ramdhan Rai, of Damdi, Okhaldhunga, Nepal.

(contd.)

531

S. No.	Service Number	Rank	Name	Regiment	Unit	Secondary Regiment	Date of Death	Next of Kin
109	1157	Rifleman	DESBIR RAI	10th Gurkha Rifles	2nd Bn.	-	19/9/1915	Son of Yakansing Rai, of Oyenang, Siktel, Bhojpore, Nepal.
110	1145	Rifleman	DHARAMDHOJ RAI	10th Gurkha Rifles	2nd Bn.	-	19/9/1915	Son of Pirkilal Rai, of Binpa, Khamthing, Okaldhunga, Nepal.
111	2631	Rifleman	DHOJBIR RAI	10th Gurkha Rifles	2nd Bn.	-	19/9/1915	Son of Utpannu Rai, of Katta, Udaipore, Okhaldhunga, Nepal.
112	1198	Rifleman	DHOJE LIMBU	10th Gurkha Rifles	2nd Bn.	-	19/9/1915	Son of Jaiman Limbu, of Tofrek, Tamarkhola, Dhankuta, Nepal.
113	3282	Rifleman	GANJAMAN RAI	10th Gurkha Rifles	2nd Bn.	-	19/9/1915	Son of Jiooman Rai, of Salabo, Amchok, Bhojpore, Nepal.
114	931	Rifleman	GANJAMAN RAI	10th Gurkha Rifles	2nd Bn.	-	19/9/1915	Son of Jitiharka Rai, of Nembang, Ilam, Nepal.
115	1090	Rifleman	GORE RANA	10th Gurkha Rifles	2nd Bn.	-	19/9/1915	Son of Aike Rana, of Gogal, Alampore, Ramechhap, No. 2, East, Nepal.

No.	Regt. No.	Rank	Name	Regiment	Battalion		Date	Remarks
116	690	Rifleman	HARKABAHA-DUR LIMBU	10th Gurkha Rifles	2nd Bn.	–	19/9/1915	Son of Lakhrup Limbu, of Maidane, Chainpore, Dhankuta, Nepal.
117	1109	Rifleman	HARKABAHA-DUR RAI	10th Gurkha Rifles	2nd Bn.	–	19/9/1915	Son of Chhatarman Rai, of Birgaon, Dhankuta, Nepal.
118	169	Rifleman	HARKABIR RAI	10th Gurkha Rifles	2nd Bn.	–	19/9/1915	Son of Haikamsing Rai, of Pewang, Dhankuta, Nepal.
119	1142	Rifleman	HEMBAHADUR RAI	10th Gurkha Rifles	2nd Bn.	–	19/9/1915	Son of Sirilal Rai, of Bardu, Phikal, Ilam, Nepal.
120	1136	Rifleman	JAGATSING LAMA	10th Gurkha Rifles	2nd Bn.	–	19/9/1915	Son of Cheku Lama, of Liste, Chautara, No. 1, East, Nepal.
121	1123	Rifleman	JAHAJIT RAI	10th Gurkha Rifles	2nd Bn.	–	19/9/1915	Son of Bartiman Rai, of Tamring, Chainpore, Dhankuta, Nepal.
122	1161	Rifleman	JITBAHADUR RAI	10th Gurkha Rifles	2nd Bn.	–	19/9/1915	Son of Hazarman Rai, of Mukli, Chisankhu, Okhaldhunga, Nepal.

(contd.)

APPENDIX 2 (*contd.*)

S. No.	Service Number	Rank	Name	Regiment	Unit	Secondary Regiment	Date of Death	Next of Kin
123	1075	Rifleman	KANCHALAL RAI	10th Gurkha Rifles	2nd Bn.	-	19/9/1915	Son of Siamlal Rai, of Mardin, Chaubisya, Dhankuta Nepal.
124	255	Rifleman	KARBIR THAPA	10th Gurkha Rifles	2nd Bn.	-	19/9/1915	Son of Bahadursing Thapa, of Dehlunga, Tansing, Nepal.
125	1207	Rifleman	KARNABAHA-DUR RAI	10th Gurkha Rifles	2nd Bn.	-	19/9/1915	Son of Hajarman Rai, of Makhiya, Yangrup, Dhankuta, Nepal.
126	1186	Rifleman	KARNASING LIMBU	10th Gurkha Rifles	2nd Bn.	-	19/9/1915	Son of Dhanrup Limbu, of Yanguom, Panchthar, Dhankuta, Nepal.
127	1199	Rifleman	KHARKSING ALE	10th Gurkha Rifles	2nd Bn.	-	19/9/1915	Son of Kamarsing Ale, of Kharpu, Rawakhola, Okhaldhunga, Nepal.
128	1139	Rifleman	KRISHNADHOJ THAPA	10th Gurkha Rifles	2nd Bn.	-	19/9/1915	Son of Sherbahadur Thapa, of Alampore, Nepal.

534

129	384	Rifleman	LACHHIRAM CHETTRI	10th Gurkha Rifles	2nd Bn.	–	19/9/1915	Son of Narsing Chhetri, of Malgaon, Almora, United Provinces.
130	1144	Rifleman	LALBAHADUR RAI	10th Gurkha Rifles	2nd Bn.	–	19/9/1915	Son of Suba Rai, of Deosa, Rawakhola, Okhaldhunga, Nepal.
131	1102	Rifleman	LALBAHADUR SUNWAR	10th Gurkha Rifles	2nd Bn.	–	19/9/1915	Son of Kisnabahadur Sunwar, of Sije, Likukhola, Okhaldhunga, Nepal.
132	865	Rifleman	LILAMANJ RAI	10th Gurkha Rifles	2nd Bn.	–	19/9/1915	Son of Krisne Rai, of Sale, Rawadumre, Okhaldhunga, Nepal.
133	1152	Rifleman	MAHABIR LAMA	10th Gurkha Rifles	2nd Bn.	–	19/9/1915	Son of Doger Lama, of Kalikhola, Kalimpong, Darjeeling, Bengal.
134	2673	Naik	MAHABIR LIMBU	10th Gurkha Rifles	2nd Bn.	–	19/9/1915	Son of Bhagwansing Limbu, of Dingla, Dhankuta, Nepal.

(*contd.*)

APPENDIX 2 (contd.)

S. No.	Service Number	Rank	Name	Regiment	Unit	Secondary Regiment	Date of Death	Next of Kin
135	2126	Rifleman	MAKHARDHOJ LIMBU	10th Gurkha Rifles	2nd Bn.	-	19/9/1915	Son of Asnande Limbu, of Sunghongpe, Newakhola, Dhankuta, Nepal.
136	832	Rifleman	MANBAHADUR RAI	10th Gurkha Rifles	2nd Bn.	-	19/9/1915	Son of Birbahadur Rai, of Audrung, Dhankuta, Nepal.
137	1036	Rifleman	MANBIR LIMBU	10th Gurkha Rifles	2nd Bn.	-	19/9/1915	Son of Haibir Limbu, of Phedap, Dhankuta, Nepal.
138	2407	Rifleman	MANDHOL LIMBU	10th Gurkha Rifles	2nd Bn.	-	19/9/1915	Son of Jasbir Limbu, of Kuretar, Mewakhola, Dhankuta, Nepal.
139	1132	Rifleman	MOBIDHAN RAI	10th Gurkha Rifles	2nd Bn.	-	19/9/1915	Son of Ranman Rai, of Mamatem, Rawakhola, Okhaldhunga, Nepal.
140	56	Rifleman	NANDALHO KAMI	10th Gurkha Rifles	2nd Bn.	-	19/9/1915	Son of Mahabir Kami, of Menglung, Phedap, Dhankuta, Nepal.

No.	Number	Rank	Name	Regiment	Bn.		Date	Details
141	1213	Rifleman	NARBAHADUR LIMBU	10th Gurkha Rifles	2nd Bn.	-	19/9/1915	Son of Bhimraj Limbu, of Hamrok, Yangrup, Dhankuta, Nepal.
142	1193	Rifleman	NARBAHADUR THAPA	10th Gurkha Rifles	2nd Bn.	-	19/9/1915	Son of Kalu Thapa, of Pornagwikha, Pokra, Bilari, Nepal.
143	1130	Rifleman	PADAMBAHA-DUR SUNWAR	10th Gurkha Rifles	2nd Bn.	-	19/9/1915	Son of Tulachand Sunwar, of Khukse, Tamarkhola, Dhankuta, Nepal.
144	1134	Rifleman	PADAMBAHA-DUR THAPA	10th Gurkha Rifles	2nd Bn.	-	19/9/1915	Son of Ramdhan Thapa, of Khatte, Rawakhola, Okhaldhunga, Nepal.
145	1097	Rifleman	PAHALMAN RAI	10th Gurkha Rifles	2nd Bn.	-	19/9/1915	Son of Dhoje Rai, of Dingding, Chainpore, Dhankuta, Nepal.
146	1197	Rifleman	PANCHIAL LIMBU	10th Gurkha Rifles	2nd Bn.	-	19/9/1915	Son of Ulahang Limbu, of Hasing, Tamarkhola, Dhankuta, Nepal.
147	1105	Rifleman	PANJBAHADUR RAI	10th Gurkha Rifles	2nd Bn.	-	19/9/1915	Son of Rupabung, of Nigale, Panchthar, Ilam, Nepal.

(contd.)

537

APPENDIX 2 (*contd.*)

S. No.	Service Number	Rank	Name	Regiment	Unit	Secondary Regiment	Date of Death	Next of Kin
148	1160	Rifleman	PARSIE RAI	10th Gurkha Rifles	2nd Bn.	-	19/9/1915	Son of Sudarman Rai, of Muwi, Chisankhu, Okhaldhunga, Nepal.
149	1138	Rifleman	PARTABSING RAI	10th Gurkha Rifles	2nd Bn.	-	19/9/1915	Son of Daulat Rai, of Pabong, Gangtok, Sikkim, Nepal.
150	2038	Rifleman	PURANDAJ LIMBU	10th Gurkha Rifles	2nd Bn.	-	19/9/1915	Son of Tilbhoj Limbu, of Wareni, Panthar, Dhankuta, Nepal.
151	1214	Rifleman	PURNABIR LIMBU	10th Gurkha Rifles	2nd Bn.	-	19/9/1915	Son of Tilbaj Limbu, of Wareni, Panchthar, Dhankuta, Nepal.
152	1104	Rifleman	RAGHOBIR RAI	10th Gurkha Rifles	2nd Bn.	-	19/9/1915	Son of Senalal Rai, of Damku, Chisankhu, Bhojpore, Nepal.
153	1153	Rifleman	RAJBAHADUR RAI	10th Gurkha Rifles	2nd Bn.	-	19/9/1915	Son of Raguman Rai, of Sambin, Gangtok, Sikkim, Nepal.
154	1200	Rifleman	RAJMAN RAI	10th Gurkha Rifles	2nd Bn.	-	19/9/1915	Son of Gajesman Rai, of Damucha, Khotang, Ramechhap, Nepal.

No.	Number	Rank	Name	Regiment	Bn.		Date	Remarks
155	1187	Rifleman	RANBAHADUR SARKI	10th Gurkha Rifles	2nd Bn.	–	19/9/1915	Son of Jaswante Sarki, of Rawakote, No. 1, West, Nepal.
156	77	Lance Havildar	RATNE RAI	10th Gurkha Rifles	2nd Bn.	–	19/9/1915	Son of Jangnan Rai, of Pangnam, Dhankuta, Nepal.
157	1137	Rifleman	SAGUNE RANA	10th Gurkha Rifles	2nd Bn.	–	19/9/1915	Son of Subane Rana, of Manjal, Lanjung, Pokhra, Nepal.
158	1155	Rifleman	SANMAN SUNWAR	10th Gurkha Rifles	2nd Bn.	–	19/9/1915	Son of Birdhoj Sunwar, of Rasnalu, Charikote, Ramechhap, Nepal.
159	1149	Rifleman	SARBADHOJ RAI	10th Gurkha Rifles	2nd Bn.	–	19/9/1915	Son of Dalge Rai, of Surma, Majuwa, Okhaldhunga Nepal.
160	1073	Rifleman	SETALAL RAI	10th Gurkha Rifles	2nd Bn.	–	19/9/1915	Son of Rupman Rai, of Habu, Khesang, Bhojpore, Nepal.
161	1195	Rifleman	SINGDHOJ GURUNG	10th Gurkha Rifles	2nd Bn.	–	19/9/1915	Son of Gange Gurung, of Madi, Dhankuta, Nepal.

(*contd.*)

S. No.	Service Number	Rank	Name	Regiment	Unit	Secondary Regiment	Date of Death	Next of Kin
162	1091	Rifleman	SRIMAN RAI	10th Gurkha Rifles	2nd Bn.	-	19/9/1915	Son of Ajoinlal Rai, of Didung, Chainpore, Dhankuta, Nepal.
163	1117	Rifleman	SUKHMAN LAMA	10th Gurkha Rifles	2nd Bn.	-	19/9/1915	Son of Bhagsu Lama, of Ibum, Charkhola, Ramechhap, Nepal.
164	1225	Rifleman	SURABIR RAI	10th Gurkha Rifles	2nd Bn.	-	19/9/1915	Son of Suban Rai, of Apsora, Chisankhu, Okhaldhunga, Nepal.
165	353	Rifleman	SURJAMAN RAI	10th Gurkha Rifles	2nd Bn.	-	19/9/1915	Son of Panchabir Rai, of Nathuwa, Chainpore, Dhankuta, Nepal.
166	1579	Havildar	TILOKSING LIMBU	10th Gurkha Rifles	2nd Bn.	-	19/9/1915	Son of Birkasing Limbu, of Ilamke, Mewakhola, Dhankuta, Nepal.
167	46	Lance Havildar	UTTAMSING CHETTRI	10th Gurkha Rifles	2nd Bn.	-	19/9/1915	Son of Daulatsing Chetri, of Neansi, Pithoragarh, Almora, United Provinces.

168	1098	Rifleman	BAHADUR RAI	10th Gurkha Rifles	2nd Bn.	-	19/9/1915	Son of Sirdal Rai, of Dingding, Chainpore, Dhankuta, Nepal.
169	1121	Rifleman	KHAMBASING GURUNG	10th Gurkha Rifles	2nd Bn.	-	19/9/1915	Son of Nagisore Gurung, of Kalingo, Athrai, Dhankuta, Nepal.
170	1184	Rifleman	MANDHOJ RAI	10th Gurkha Rifles	2nd Bn.	-	19/9/1915	Son of Abirsing Rai, of Binpa, Okhaldhunga, Nepal.
171	1204	Rifleman	MANIRAJ SUNWAR	10th Gurkha Rifles	2nd Bn.	-	19/9/1915	Son of Late Sunwar, of Sabralu, No. 2, East, Ramechhap, Nepal.
172	1188	Rifleman	AGANSING LIMBU	10th Gurkha Rifles	-	-	19/9/1915	Son of Harkadham Limbu, of Hangpang, No. 5, District, Dhankuta, Nepal..
173	4751	Sepoy	BAGA SINGH	14th King George's Own Ferozepore Sikhs	-	-	19/9/1915	Son of Mastan Singh, of Farwahi, Barnala, Patiala, Punjab.
174	4844	Sepoy	BARA SINGH	14th King George's Own Ferozepore Sikhs	-	-	19/9/1915	Son of Rattam Singh, of Malla, Jagraon, Ludhiana, Punjab.

(contd.)

APPENDIX 2 (*contd.*)

S. No.	Service Number	Rank	Name	Regiment	Unit	Secondary Regiment	Date of Death	Next of Kin
175	4747	Sepoy	BARA SINGH	14th King George's Own Ferozepore Sikhs	-	-	19/9/1915	Son of Nanak Singh, of Dablan, Nabha, Punjab.
176	4743	Sepoy	BASANT SINGH	14th King George's Own Ferozepore Sikhs	-	-	19/9/1915	Son of Narain Singh, of Bhanra, Patiala, Punjab.
177	4757	Sepoy	BHAN SINGH	14th King George's Own Ferozepore Sikhs	-	-	19/9/1915	Son of Ditta Singh, of Khudi, Barnala, Patiala. Punjab.
178	4116	Sepoy	CHANAN SINGH	14th King George's Own Ferozepore Sikhs	-	-	19/9/1915	Son of Hamir Singh, of Ladbanjara, Dhode, Patiala, Punjab.
179	4756	Sepoy	GAJAN SINGH	14th King George's Own Ferozepore Sikhs	-	-	19/9/1915	Son of Fateh Singh, of Kanech, Pail, Patiala, Punjab.
180	4171	Sepoy	GANDA SINGH	14th King George's Own Ferozepore Sikhs	-	-	19/9/1915	Son of Prem Singh, of Lehra Mahabat, Moga, Ferozepore, Punjab.
181	4732	Sepoy	GHICHAR SINGH	14th King George's Own Ferozepore Sikhs	-	-	19/9/1915	Son of Partap Singh, of Kambarwal, Bassi, Karnal, Punjab.

182	4762	Sepoy	HARI SINGH	14th King George's Own Ferozepore Sikhs	–	19/9/1915	Son of Hira Singh, of Ghandawana, Ludhiana, Punjab.
183	4441	Bugler	HARNAM SINGH	14th King George's Own Ferozepore Sikhs	–	19/9/1915	Son of Phuman Singh, of Khiali, Ludhiana, Punjab.
184	4764	Sepoy	HARNAM SINGH	14th King George's Own Ferozepore Sikhs	–	19/9/1915	Son of Gujjar Singh, of Sandaur, Ludhiana, Punjab.
185	4834	Sepoy	JAGAT SINGH	14th King George's Own Ferozepore Sikhs	–	19/9/1915	Son of Sadhu Singh, of Ubewal, Sunam, Patiala, Punjab.
186	4267	Lance Naik	JAMIT SINGH	14th King George's Own Ferozepore Sikhs	–	19/9/1915	Son of Puran Singh, of Gholia Kalan Moga, Ferozepore, Punjab.
187	1679	Drum Major	JASWANT SINGH	14th King George's Own Ferozepore Sikhs	–	19/9/1915	Son of Ganda Singh, of Lopoke, Ajnala, Amritsar, Punjab.
188	3558	Sepoy	JIWAN SINGH	14th King George's Own Ferozepore Sikhs	–	19/9/1915	Son of Sadda Singh, of Changali, Dhode, Patiala, Punjab.

(contd.)

S. No.	Service Number	Rank	Name	Regiment	Unit	Secondary Regiment	Date of Death	Next of Kin
189	4526	Sepoy	KAPUR SINGH	14th King George's Own Ferozepore Sikhs	-	-	19/9/1915	Son of Diwan Singh, of Bhani Sahib, Ludhiana, Punjab.
190	4746	Sepoy	KARTAR SINGH	14th King George's Own Ferozepore Sikhs	-	-	19/9/1915	Son of Jiwan Singh, of Rangian, Dhuri, Patiala, Punjab.
191	4633	Sepoy	KHUSHIYA SINGH	14th King George's Own Ferozepore Sikhs	-	-	19/9/1915	Son of Ralla Singh, of Munak Kalan, Dasuha, Hoshiarpore, Punjab.
192	4442	Bugler	MADAN SINGH	14th King George's Own Ferozepore Sikhs	-	-	19/9/1915	Son of Jawahar Singh, of Mahori, Dhanaula, Nabha, Punjab.
193	3315	Sepoy	MAIHMA SINGH	14th King George's Own Ferozepore Sikhs	-	-	19/9/1915	Son of Kahan Singh, of Hironbadi, Bhikhi, Patiala, Punjab.
194	4738	Sepoy	MEHR SINGH	14th King George's Own Ferozepore Sikhs	-	-	19/9/1915	Son of Nand Singh, of Ladda, Dhuri, Patiala, Punjab.
195	4839	Lance Naik	NARAIN SINGH	14th King George's Own Ferozepore Sikhs	-	-	19/9/1915	Son of Dhian Singh, of Bhatian, Ludhiana, Punjab.

No.	No.	Rank	Name	Regiment			Date	Remarks
196	4660	Sepoy	PURAN SINGH	14th King George's Own Ferozepore Sikhs	–	–	19/9/1915	Son of Mangal Singh, of Kauloke, Phul, Nabha, Punjab.
197	4753	Sepoy	RALA SINGH	14th King George's Own Ferozepore Sikhs	–	–	19/9/1915	Son of Badal Singh, of Changli, Dhuri, Patiala, Punjab.
198	4727	Sepoy	SAPURAN SINGH	14th King George's Own Ferozepore Sikhs	–	–	19/9/1915	Son of Sowar Singh, of Dakhe, Ludhiana, Punjab.
199	4748	Sepoy	SEWA SINGH	14th King George's Own Ferozepore Sikhs	–	–	19/9/1915	Son of Hira Singh, of Sultanpore, Dhuri, Patiala, Punjab.
200	2874	Sepoy	SEWA SINGH	14th King George's Own Ferozepore Sikhs	–	–	19/9/1915	Son of Hazara Singh, of Hiron, Bhikhi, Patiala, Punjab.
201	1121	Sepoy	PHUMAN SINGH	15th Ludhiana Sikhs	14th King George's Own Ferozepore Sikhs	–	19/9/1915	Son of Dewa Singh, of Abuwal, Jagraon, Ludhiana, Punjab.
202	491	Rifleman	JASBAHADUR LIMBU	Assam Military Police	10th Gurkha Rifles	–	19/9/1915	–

(contd.)

545

S. No.	Service Number	Rank	Name	Regiment	Unit	Secondary Regiment	Date of Death	Next of Kin
203	1605	Rifleman	AMAR SINGH	Burma Military Police	-	14th King George's Own Ferozepore Sikhs	19/9/1915	Son of Khem Singh, of Garrihan Singh, Gujranwala, Punjab.
204	1442	Lance Naik	AMAR SINGH	Burma Military Police	-	14th King George's Own Ferozepore Sikhs	19/9/1915	Son of Nand Singh, of Mahalkhurd, Barnala, Patiala, Punjab.
205	1879	Rifleman	ATAR SINGH	Burma Military Police	-	14th King George's Own Ferozepore Sikhs	19/9/1915	Son of Teja Singh, of Chachowali, Kathunangal, Amritsar, Punjab.
206	1277	Rifleman	BACHAN SINGH	Burma Military Police	-	14th King George's Own Ferozepore Sikhs	19/9/1915	Son of Dhian Singh, of Soorewala, Mukhtsar, Ferozepore, Punjab.

207	1550	Lance Naik	BALA SINGH	Burma Military Police	14th King George's Own Ferozepore Sikhs	–	19/9/1915	Son of Narain Singh, of Begewal, Kathunangal, Amritsar, Punjab.
208	1642	Rifleman	BANTA SINGH	Burma Military Police	14th King George's Own Ferozepore Sikhs	–	19/9/1915	Son of Sundar Singh, of Viring, Jullundur, Punjab.
209	541	Lance Naik	BHAGAT SINGH	Burma Military Police	14th King George's Own Ferozepore Sikhs	–	19/9/1915	Son of Rala Singh, of 473, Chuk, Lyallpore, Punjab.
210	1764	Rifleman	BHAJAN SINGH	Burma Military Police	14th King George's Own Ferozepore Sikhs	–	19/9/1915	Son of Khazan Singh, of Jodhpore, Sahna, Ludhiana, Punjab.

(contd.)

S. No.	Service Number	Rank	Name	Regiment	Unit	Secondary Regiment	Date of Death	Next of Kin
211	1703	Rifleman	BHAN SINGH	Burma Military Police	-	14th King George's Own Ferozepore Sikhs	19/9/1915	Son of Kharak Singh, of Tharoo, Taran Taran, Amritsar, Punjab.
212	784	Lance Naik	BIR SINGH	Burma Military Police	-	14th King George's Own Ferozepore Sikhs	19/9/1915	Son of Maija Singh, of Nurpore, Khatra, Lahore, Punjab.
213	1020	Lance Naik	BISHN SINGH	Burma Military Police	-	14th King George's Own Ferozepore Sikhs	19/9/1915	Son of Prem Singh, of Chappe, Sherpore, Patiala, Punjab.
214	1504	Rifleman	BUDH SINGH	Burma Military Police	-	14th King George's Own Ferozepore Sikhs	19/9/1915	Son of Kehar Singh, of Jikhapal, Sanam, Patiala, Punjab.

215	1602	Rifleman	BUR SINGH	Burma Military Police	–	14th King George's Own Ferozepore Sikhs	19/9/1915	Son of Maggar Singh, of Dadupura, Kathunangal, Amritsar, Punjab.
216	1725	Rifleman	BUR SINGH	Burma Military Police	–	14th King George's Own Ferozepore Sikhs	19/9/1915	Son of Rur Singh, of Bhagthari, Dehranank, Gurdaspore, Punjab.
217	1246	Rifleman	CHANAN SINGH	Burma Military Police	–	14th King George's Own Ferozepore Sikhs	19/9/1915	Son of Phula Singh, of Paranah, Khalra, Lahore, Punjab.
218	1515	Rifleman	DAN SINGH	Burma Military Police	–	14th King George's Own Ferozepore Sikhs	19/9/1915	Son of Man Singh, of Kishanpura, Balwali, Sangñer, Punjab.

(contd.)

APPENDIX 2 (contd.)

S. No.	Service Number	Rank	Name	Regiment	Unit	Secondary Regiment	Date of Death	Next of Kin
219	1573	Rifleman	DEWA SINGH	Burma Military Police	-	14th King George's Own Ferozepore Sikhs	19/9/1915	Son of Santa Singh, of Gajal, Gandasinghwala, Lahore, Punjab.
220	5824	Rifleman	GAIL SINGH	Burma Military Police	-	14th King George's Own Ferozepore Sikhs	19/9/1915	Son of Sawan Singh, of Ranika, Ajnala, Amritsar, Punjab.
221	1510	Rifleman	GANDA SINGH	Burma Military Police	-	14th King George's Own Ferozepore Sikhs	19/9/1915	Son of Ram Singh, of Jikhapal, Sanam, Patiala, Punjab.
222	1712	Rifleman	GUJAR SINGH	Burma Military Police	-	14th King George's Own Ferozepore Sikhs	19/9/1915	Son of Dewa Singh, of Batorla, Bhadson, Nabha, Punjab.

223	1341	Rifleman	GURDIT SINGH	Burma Military Police	–	14th King George's Own Ferozepore Sikhs	19/9/1915	Son of Battan Singh, of Khothala, Pajjgran, Malerkotla, Punjab.
224	1836	Rifleman	HARNAM SINGH	Burma Military Police	–	14th King George's Own Ferozepore Sikhs	19/9/1915	Son of Sawan Singh, of Sadhanwali, Derababananak, Gurdaspore, Punjab.
225	1389	Lance Naik	INDAR SINGH	Burma Military Police	–	14th King George's Own Ferozepore Sikhs	19/9/1915	Son of Massa Singh, of Udat Bhagatram, Boha, Patiala, Punjab.
226	1166	Rifleman	JAGAT SINGH	Burma Military Police	–	14th King George's Own Ferozepore Sikhs	19/9/1915	Son of Dya Singh, of Nurpore, Khalra, Lahore, Punjab.

(contd.)

APPENDIX 2 (*contd.*)

S. No.	Service Number	Rank	Name	Regiment	Unit	Secondary Regiment	Date of Death	Next of Kin
227	1401	Lance Naik	JAIMAL SINGH	Burma Military Police	-	14th King George's Own Ferozepore Sikhs	19/9/1915	Son of Natha Singh, of Dair Mandin, Bagan Wala, Ambala, Punjab.
228	1212	Rifleman	JASSA SINGH	Burma Military Police	-	14th King George's Own Ferozepore Sikhs	19/9/1915	Son of Bur Singh, of Bal, Kathunangal, Amritsar, Punjab.
229	1185	Rifleman	JAWAHIR SINGH	Burma Military Police	-	14th King George's Own Ferozepore Sikhs	19/9/1915	Son of Kesar Singh, of Khatrakhurd, Ajnala, Amritsar, Punjab.
230	1622	Rifleman	JAWAND SINGH	Burma Military Police	-	14th King George's Own Ferozepore Sikhs	19/9/1915	Son of Dhyan Singh, of Kotsewian, Lahorimal, Amritsar, Punjab.

231	1595	Rifleman	JHANDA SINGH	Burma Military Police	-	14th King George's Own Ferozepore Sikhs	19/9/1915	Son of Santa Singh, of Gunuwal, Guruka Jandiyala, Amritsar, Punjab.
232	1605	Rifleman	KALA SINGH	Burma Military Police	-	14th King George's Own Ferozepore Sikhs	19/9/1915	Son of Sundar Singh, of Pandoni Ransinghdi, Taran Taran, Amritsar, Punjab.
233	1173	Rifleman	LABH SINGH	Burma Military Police	-	14th King George's Own Ferozepore Sikhs	19/9/1915	Son of Bhag Singh, of Dhanoe, Gharinda, Amritsar, Punjab.
234	1488	Rifleman	LAKHA SINGH	Burma Military Police	-	14th King George's Own Ferozepore Sikhs	19/9/1915	Son of Basant Singh, of Masorawal, Dhilwan, Kapurthala, Punjab.

(contd.)

APPENDIX 2 (*contd.*)

S. No.	Service Number	Rank	Name	Regiment	Unit	Secondary Regiment	Date of Death	Next of Kin
235	1505	Rifleman	MUKANDH SINGH	Burma Military Police	-	14th King George's Own Ferozepore Sikhs	19/9/1915	Son of Jita Singh, of Jikhapal, Sunam, Patiala, Punjab.
236	1596	Rifleman	MULA SINGH	Burma Military Police	-	14th King George's Own Ferozepore Sikhs	19/9/1915	Son of Kala Singh, of Bhitewash, Ajnala, Amritsar, Punjab.
237	1238	Lance Naik	MUNSHA SINGH	Burma Military Police	-	14th King George's Own Ferozepore Sikhs	19/9/1915	Son of Artar Singh, of Salempore, Morinda, Ambala, Punjab.
238	1077	Lance Naik	NAND SINGH	Burma Military Police	-	14th King George's Own Ferozepore Sikhs	19/9/1915	Son of Rur Singh, of Mannan, Batala, Gurdaspore, Punjab.

239	1527	Lance Naik	NAURANG SINGH	Burma Military Police	–	14th King George's Own Ferozepore Sikhs	19/9/1915	Son of Ganda Singh, of Pendori Sidwan, Taran Taran, Amritsar, Punjab.
240	1223	Lance Naik	PAL SINGH	Burma Military Police	–	14th King George's Own Ferozepore Sikhs	19/9/1915	Son of Gurmukh Singh, of Makhi Kalam, Patti, Lahore, Punjab.
241	1149	Lance Naik	RATAN SINGH	Burma Military Police	–	14th King George's Own Ferozepore Sikhs	19/9/1915	Son of Ganda Singh, of Khara, Serali, Amritsar, Punjab.
242	1204	Rifleman	SANTA SINGH	Burma Military Police	–	14th King George's Own Ferozepore Sikhs	19/9/1915	Son of Chanda Singh, of Kheyala, Lopoke, Amritsar, Punjab.

(contd.)

APPENDIX 2 (contd.)

S. No.	Service Number	Rank	Name	Regiment	Unit	Secondary Regiment	Date of Death	Next of Kin
243	1645	Rifleman	SANTA SINGH	Burma Military Police	–	14th King George's Own Ferozepore Sikhs	19/9/1915	Son of Dewan Singh, of Reru, Jullundur,Punjab.
244	1492	Rifleman	SANTA SINGH	Burma Military Police	–	14th King George's Own Ferozepore Sikhs	19/9/1915	Son of Gurdial Singh, of Gago Baba, Taran Taran, Amritsar, Punjab.
245	794	Rifleman	TEJA SINGH	Burma Military Police	–	14th King George's Own Ferozepore Sikhs	19/9/1915	Son of Gurdit Singh, of Gagobowah, Lahorimal, Amritsar, Punjab.
246	1463	Rifleman	THAKAR SINGH	Burma Military Police	–	14th King George's Own Ferozepore Sikhs	19/9/1915	Son of Sher Singh, of Ghanieke, Dehrananak, Gurdaspore, Punjab.

247	1403	Lance Naik	UJAGAR SINGH	Burma Military Police	-	14th King George's Own Ferozepore Sikhs	19/9/1915	Son of Nand Singh, of Bhakhana, Thekriwala, Lyallpore, Punjab.
248	686	Artisan	GANGA RAM	Gwalior Transport Corps	-	-	19/9/1915	Son of Chokharia, of Gird, Gwalior, Central Provinces. (Name wrongly shown on the Memorial as GANDA RAM).
249	177	Driver	RAMANATH	Indore Transport Corps	-	-	19/9/1915	Son of Devidin, of Kasipore, Gusai Ganj, Lucknow, United Provinces.
250	1359	Driver	ABDUL HAMAD	Mule Corps	-	-	19/9/1915	-
251	552	Driver	HAYAT MUHAM-MAD	Mule Corps	-	-	19/9/1915	Son of Sahib Din, of Nangiran, Rawalpindi, Punjab.
252	506	Driver	HUSAIN KHAN	Mule Corps	-	-	19/9/1915	Son of Jamal Din, of Jhathi, Abbottabad, Hazara, Punjab.

(contd.)

APPENDIX 2 (*contd.*)

S. No.	Service Number	Rank	Name	Regiment	Unit	Secondary Regiment	Date of Death	Next of Kin
253	1325	Driver	MUHAMMAD ABDULLAH	Mule Corps	-	-	19/9/1915	Son of Muhammad Cassim, of Karkhana, Secunderabad, Madras.
254	919	Lance Naik	MUNASWAMI	Mule Corps	-	-	19/9/1915	Son of Mooniah, of Karkhana, Secunderabad, Madras.
255	2066	Follower	SALAM DIN	Mule Corps	-	-	19/9/1915	-
256	461	Driver	SHAMSHER	Mule Corps	-	-	19/9/1915	-
257	447	Driver	SHANKARDAS	Mule Corps	-	-	19/9/1915	-
258	1956	Driver	WALAYAT KHAN	Mule Corps	-	-	19/9/1915	Son of Fetteh Khan, of Baran. Suddan Hotel, Poonch, Punjab.
259	Lucknow/ 829	Follower	ABDUL AZIZ KHAN	Supply and Transport Corps	-	-	19/9/1915	-
260	831	Follower	ABDUL HAMAD	Supply and Transport Corps	-	-	19/9/1915	-
261	830	Follower	ABDULLAH	Supply and Transport Corps	-	-	19/9/1915	-
262	Bombay/ 132	Follower	AZIM KHAN	Supply and Transport Corps	-	-	19/9/1915	Of Shahpur, Shahpur, Belgaum, Bombay.

263	187	Follower	KARM SINGH	Supply and Transport Corps	-	19/9/1915	-	
264	264	Follower	NARAIN SINGH	Supply and Transport Corps	-	19/9/1915	-	
265	807	Follower	NUR MUHAM-MAD	Supply and Transport Corps	-	19/9/1915	-	
266	186	Follower	PARTAP SINGH	Supply and Transport Corps	-	19/9/1915	-	
267	805	Follower	PAULA	Supply and Transport Corps	-	19/9/1915	-	
268	Jhansi/117	Follower	RAM LAL	Supply and Transport Corps	-	19/9/1915	-	
269	802	Follower	SAKHA RAM DIPA	Supply and Transport Corps	-	19/9/1915	-	
270	804	Follower	WAZIR	Supply and Transport Corps	-	19/9/1915	-	
271	1152	Driver	NURASANNA	Mule Corps	-	19/9/1915	-	Son of Mulliah, of Tawaipura Tarband, Secunderabad, Madras.
272	Jhansi/12	Follower	AMIR BAKSH	Supply and Transport Corps	-	19/9/1915	-	Son of Kalloo, of Orcha Gate, Jhansi, United Provinces.

(contd.)

APPENDIX 2 (contd.)

S. No.	Service Number	Rank	Name	Regiment	Unit	Secondary Regiment	Date of Death	Next of Kin
273	Jhansi/6	Follower	FATEH CHAND KANNA	Supply and Transport Corps	-	-	19/9/1915	Son of Muckand Ram, of Chandausi, Bilari, Muradbad, U.P.
274	Jhansi/9	Follower	JAMAN LAL	Supply and Transport Corps	-	-	19/9/1915	Son of Ganeshi Lal, of Kairawa, Muzzaffarnagar, U.P.
275	-	Follower	KHAIRUDDIN	Supply and Transport Corps	-	-	19/9/1915	
276	10	Follower	NANU	Supply and Transport Corps	-	-	19/9/1915	Of Lahera, Esanagar, Bundelkhand, Central India.
277	Jhansi/11	Follower	RAMBARAN	Supply and Transport Corps	-	-	19/9/1915	Of Khajuri Purri Bhaktavar Ahir, Bikapur, Fyzabad, United Provinces.

Source: From multiple sources.

560

APPENDIX 3: CASUALTIES OF INDIAN OFFICERS ON GALLIPOLI

S. No.	Rank	Name	Unit	Nature of Casualty	Date of Casualty
1	Subadar	Ajit Rai	2/10 Gurkhas	Wounded	28-06-1915
2	Jemadar	Amarsing Thapa	1/6 Gurkhas	Killed	08-07-1915
3	Subadar	Amrit Mal	1/5 Gurkhas	Wounded	18-05-1915
4	Jemadar	Anandahang Limbu	2/10 Gurkhas	Killed	07-08-1915
5	Subadar	Anokh Singh	14th Sikhs	Severely Wounded	06-04-1915
6	Subadar	Asbir Rai	2/10 Gurkhas	Severely Wounded	08-10-1915
7	Jemadar	Bakhshish Singh	89th Punjabis	Slightly Wounded	05-11-1915
8	Subadar	Balbir Chatri	Assam Military Police	Severely Wounded	27-10-1915
9	Subadar	Balsing Thapa	1/6 Gurkhas	Wounded	12-12-1915
10	Jemadar	Barkabahadur Rai	2/10 Gurkhas	Killed	28-06-1915
11	Jemadar	Bir Singh	14th Sikhs	Killed	06-04-1915
12	Jemadar	Biraj Gurung	1/5 Gurkhas	Severely Wounded	08-07-1915
13	Jemadar	Budhibal Rana	2/5 Gurkhas	Died	19-12-1915
14	Jemadar	Budhiman Gurung	1/5 Gurkhas	Wounded	08-07-1915
15	Jemadar	Budibal Rana	1/5 Gurkhas	Wounded	08-07-1915
16	Jemadar	Bur Singh	14th Sikhs	Wounded	06-06-1915
17	Subadar	Chhetradhoj Limbu	2/10 Gurkhas	Slightly Wounded	23-08-1915

(contd.)

APPENDIX 3 (*contd.*)

S. No.	Rank	Name	Unit	Nature of Casualty	Date of Casualty
18	Jemadar	Dalbahadur Thapa	1/6 Gurkhas	Wounded	08-07-1915
19	Subadar	Dalbir Rana	1/6 Gurkhas	Killed	21-07-1915
20	Subadar	Dhanbir Thapa	1/6 Gurkhas	Killed	22-05-1915
21	Subadar	Dhandhoi Rai	2/10 Gurkhas	Wounded	28-06-1915
22	Jemadar	Dhanlal Gurung	1/5 Gurkhas	Severely Wounded	18-12-1915
23	Jemadar	Dhanraj Pun	1/6 Gurkhas	Wounded	06-07-1915
24	Subadar	Dhansingh Gurung	1/5 Gurkhas	Wounded	21-08-1915
25	Jemadar	Dhiyan Singh	14th Sikhs	Killed	07-05-1915
26	Jemadar	Dulla Khan	26th Mountain Battery	Wounded	Undated
27	Jemadar	Gainda Singh	54th Sikhs	Wounded	08-09-1915
28	Jemadar	Gajadhar Singh	69th Punjabis	Wounded	29-05-1915
29	Subadar	Gajarsing Thapa	1/5 Gurkhas	Killed	07-11-1915
30	Subadar Major	Gambirsing Pun	1/6 Gurkhas	Wounded	21-08-1915
31	Jemadar	Gangasing Karki	2/10 Gurkhas	Severely Wounded	08-07-1915
32	Jemadar	Gobinda Pun	1/5 Gurkhas	Killed	28-06-1915
33	Jemadar	Gopal Gurung	1/5 Gurkhas	Severely Wounded	06-04-1915

34	Jemadar	Gopi Chand	Divisional Amn Column	Severely Wounded	18-07-1915
35	Jemadar	Gore Limbu	2/10 Gurkhas	Killed	08-07-1915
36	Jemadar	Goro Limbu	2/10 Gurkhas	Killed	08-09-1915
37	Subadar	Hansarup Limbu	2/10 Gurkhas	Killed	28-06-1915
38	Jemadar	Harishankar Gurung	1/5 Gurkhas	Killed	18-05-1915
39	Jemadar	Harjit Gurung	2/4 Gurkhas	Severely Wounded	18-10-1915
40	Subadar Major	Harkabir Thapa	1/5 Gurkhas	Severely Wounded	06-04-1915
41	Subadar	Jaimal Singh	14th Sikhs	Severely Wounded	08-07-1915
42	Subadar	Jamal Singh	Patiala Infantry	Killed	08-08-1915
43	Subadar	Jawala Singh	26th Mountain Battery	Wounded	05-09-1915
44	Subadar	Juthia Gurung	1/5 Gurkhas	Killed	18-05-1915
45	Jemadar	Kahn Singh	Patiala Infantry	Wounded	08-07-1915
46	Jemadar	Kandhara Singh	Patiala Infantry	Slightly Wounded	16-11-1915
47	Jemadar	Karbir Thapa	1/5 Gurkhas	Killed	07-08-1915
48	Jemadar	Kharak Bahadur Rana	Burma Military Police	Wounded	Undated
49	Jemadar	Khuda Baksh	7th IMAB	Killed	07-05-1915
50	Subadar	Kirpal Singh	14th Sikhs	Killed	04-06-1915
51	Subadar	Kulia Thapa	1/6 Gurkhas	Wounded	05-04-1915

(contd.)

APPENDIX 3 (*contd.*)

S. No.	Rank	Name	Unit	Nature of Casualty	Date of Casualty
52	Subadar Major	Lal Singh	14th Sikhs	Killed	04-06-1915
53	Subadar	Lilaram Gurung	1/6 Gurkhas	Killed	06-07-1915
54	Jemadar	Makhansing Limbu	2/10 Gurkhas	Died of Wounds	29-06-1915
55	Subadar	Mandhoj Lama	2/10 Gurkhas	Wounded	Undated
56	Jemadar	Manrup Limbu	2/10 Gurkhas	Killed	08-07-1915
57	Subadar	Mit Singh	21st Mountain Battery	Slightly Wounded	20-05-1915
58	Jemadar	Mukunsing Lombu	2/10 Gurkhas	Wounded	28-06-1915
59	Subadar	Narain Singh	14th Sikhs	Slightly Wounded	06-04-1915
60	Jemadar	Narprasad Limbu	2/10 Gurkhas	Wounded	21-08-1915
61	Jemadar	Nemansing Thapa	1/6 Gurkhas	Wounded	28-06-1915
62	Jemadar	Panchahng Limbu	1/10 Gurkhas	Slightly Wounded	21-08-1915
63	Jemadar	Panchasing Rai	2/10 Gurkhas	Killed	07-08-1915
64	Jemadar	Parsad Thapa	1/5 Gurkhas	Wounded	21-08-1915
65	Jemadar	Partab Singh	14th Sikhs	Wounded	Undated
66	Jemadar	Partab Singh	Patiala Infantry	Severely Wounded	08-08-1915
67	Jemadar	Pemnarain Thapa	1/5. Gurkhas	Killed	08-10-1915
68	Subadar	Pharsaldhoj Rai	2/10 Gurkhas	Wounded	08-09-1915

564

69	Jemadar	Phuman Singh	14th Sikhs	Wounded	06-04-1915
70	Jemadar	Prem Singh	14th Sikhs	Severely Wounded	06-04-1915
71	Jemadar	Premnarain Thapa	1/5 Gurkhas	Killed	08-08-1915
72	Subadar	Premsing Thapa	1/4 Gurkhas	PoW	Undated
73	Subadar	Punjab Singh	Patiala Infantry	Wounded	27-11-1915
74	Subadar	Rabi Gharti	1/5 Gurkhas	Wounded	02-07-1915
75	Subadar	Rajbahadur Limbu	2/10 Gurkhas	Died of Wounds	08-07-1915
76	Jemadar	Rajman Rai	2/10 Gurkhas	Died of Wounds	02-07-1915
77	Jemadar	Rala Singh	14th Sikhs	Wounded	06-04-1915
78	Jemadar	Ram Singh	7th IMAB	Killed	12-08-1915
79	Jemadar	Ran Singh	26th Mountain Battery	Died of Wounds	08-12-1915
80	Jemadar	Ranbahadur Gurung	1/6 Gurkhas	Severely Wounded	Undated
81	Jemadar	Sabarmukhi Limbu	1/10 Gurkhas	Slightly Wounded	16-11-1915
82	Subadar	Sahabir Thapa	1/6 Gurkhas	Severely Wounded	08-08-1915
83	Subadar	Saida Khan	89th Punjabis	Wounded	18-05-1915
84	Jemadar	Sankaman Limbu	1/10 Gurkhas	Killed	19-09-1915
85	Jemadar	Sant Singh	14th Sikhs	Severely Wounded	06-04-1915
86	Jemadar	Santbir Gurung	1/6 Gurkhas	Wounded	08-07-1915
87	Subadar	Santbir Ale	2/10 Gurkhas	Wounded	08-07-1915

(contd.)

APPENDIX 3 (contd.)

S. No.	Rank	Name	Unit	Nature of Casualty	Date of Casualty
88	Subadar	Santhbir Ale	1/6 Gurkhas	Wounded	28-06-1915
89	Subadar	Sayad Khan	89th Punjabis	Wounded	18-05-1915
90	Subadar Major	Sham Singh	14th Sikhs	Wounded	08-06-1915
91	Jemadar	Sherbahadur Gurung	1/5 Gurkhas	Killed	01-07-1915
92	Subadar	Sobha Singh	89th Punjabis	Wounded	16-05-1915
93	Jemadar	Sukhman Rai	2/10 Gurkhas	Wounded	28-06-1915
94	Subadar Major	Sundar Singh	89th Punjabis	Wounded	18-05-1915
95	Subadar	Tejganje Limbu	2/10 Gurkhas	Killed	28-06-1915
96	Jemadar	Tota Singh	Patiala Infantry	Died	21-08-1915
97	Subadar	Trilok Singh	14th Sikhs	Wounded	23-05-1915

Source: From multiple sources.

S.No.	Regtl No.	Rank	Name	Unit	Award
1	3243	Lance Naik	Amar Singh	14th Sikhs	Indian Distinguished Service Medal
2	4098	Havildar (Now Jemadar)	Amarsing Pun	1/4 Gurkhas	Indian Distinguished Service Medal
3	256	Rifleman	Anbir Gurung	2/10 Gurkhas	Indian Distinguished Service Medal
4	4295	Sepoy	Bachan Singh	14th Sikhs	Indian Distinguished Service Medal
5	3694	Havildar	Bahadur Sing Gurung	1/5 Gurkhas	Indian Distinguished Service Medal
6	4878	Rifleman	Balbahadur Gurung	1/5 Gurkhas	Indian Distinguished Service Medal
7	42	Havildar	Balbir Rana	3/5 Gurkhas	Indian Distinguished Service Medal
8	4538	Lance Naik	Bhag Singh, attd 14 Sikhs	45th Sikhs	Indian Distinguished Service Medal
9	4675	Lance Naik	Bhagwan Singh	14th Sikhs	Indian Distinguished Service Medal
10	4575	Lance Naik	Bhagwan Singh	14th Sikhs	Indian Distinguished Service Medal
11	4769	Naik	Bhairab Sing Gurung	1/5 Gurkhas	Indian Distinguished Service Medal
12	4386	Sepoy	Bharpur Singh	14th Sikhs	Indian Distinguished Service Medal
13	3100	Lance Naik (then Drummer)	Bir Singh	14th Sikhs	Indian Distinguished Service Medal
14	3693	Havildar	Bir Singh	14th Sikhs	Indian Distinguished Service Medal
15	–	Jemadar	Biraj Gurung	1/5 Gurkhas	Indian Distinguished Service Medal
16	4557	Sepoy	Bogh Singh	14th Sikhs	Indian Distinguished Service Medal

(contd.)

APPENDIX 4 (contd.)

S.No.	Regtl No.	Rank	Name	Unit	Award
17	4159	Havildar (Now Jemadar)	Budh Sing Gurung	1/5 Gurkhas	Indian Distinguished Service Medal
18	4539	Bearer	Budhi Ram. 108 Ind Fd Amb	Bengal Establishment, Hospital Assistants Branch (Army Bearer Corps)	Indian Distinguished Service Medal
19	-	Jemadar	Budhichand Bura	1/5 Gurkhas	Indian Distinguished Service Medal
20	4232	Sepoy	Chaman Singh	14th Sikhs	Indian Distinguished Service Medal
21	35	Havildar	Chambel Singh. Attd 108 ind Fd Amb	82nd Punjabis	Indian Distinguished Service Medal
22	4506	Sepoy	Chanan Singh	14th Sikhs	Indian Distinguished Service Medal
23	4393	T/Naik (then Sepoy)	Chanan Singh	14th Sikhs	Indian Distinguished Service Medal
24	4144	Drummer	Chanda Singh	14th Sikhs	Indian Distinguished Service Medal
25	-	Jemadar	Chintaram Bura. (Chintaram Burathoki). Hony Lt	2/5 Gurkhas	Indian Distinguished Service Medal
26	4766	Havildar	Dalbir Chand. Hony Lt	1/5 Gurkhas	Indian Distinguished Service Medal
27	128	Driver	Dasharat Singh	Indian Mule Corps	Indian Distinguished Service Medal
28	4818	Naik	Debiram Thapa	1/5 Gurkhas	Indian Distinguished Service Medal
29	128	Driver	Desharat Singh	Indore State Transport, Imperial Service Troops	Indian Distinguished Service Medal

No.	Number	Rank	Name	Unit	Award
30	4263	Lance Naik	Dhami. No 4 coy Attd 108 Ind Fd Amb	Bengal Establishment, Hospital Assistants Branch (Army Bearer Corps)	Indian Distinguished Service Medal
31	-	Subadar	Dhan Singh Gurung	1/5 Gurkhas	Indian Distinguished Service Medal
32	1108	Rifleman	Dhanbir Thapa	3/5 Gurkhas	Indian Distinguished Service Medal
33	830	Havildar	Dhane Gurung	3/5 Gurkhas	Indian Distinguished Service Medal
34		Jemadar	Dhanraj Thapa	3/5 Gurkhas	Indian Distinguished Service Medal
35	4567	Naik	Fateh Muhammad, No. 4 Coy Attd 108 Ind Fd Amb	Bengal Establishment, Hospital Assistants Branch (Army Bearer Corps)	Indian Distinguished Service Medal
36	4159	Lance Naik (then Sepoy)	Gajjan Singh	14th Sikhs	Indian Distinguished Service Medal
37	4573	Sepoy	Gajjan Singh	14th Sikhs	Indian Distinguished Service Medal
38	4614	Bearer	Ganga Singh. 108 Ind Fd Amb	Bengal Establishment, Hospital Assistants Branch (Army Bearer Corps)	Indian Distinguished Service Medal
39	226	Compounder	Ganpat Rao	Indore State Transport, Imperial Service Troops	Indian Distinguished Service Medal
40	4627	Rifleman	Gopal Sing Pun	1/5 Gurkhas	Indian Distinguished Service Medal
41	2860	Sepoy	Gujar Singh	14th Sikhs	Indian Distinguished Service Medal
42	3550	Ward Orderly	Gurdit Singh, Attd 108 Fd Amb	14th Sikhs	Indian Distinguished Service Medal

(contd.)

APPENDIX 4 (contd.)

S.No.	Regtl No.	Rank	Name	Unit	Award
43	3738	Lance Naik	Harnam Singh	14th Sikhs	Indian Distinguished Service Medal
44	–	Subadar	Hem Singh	21st Kohat Mountain Battery	Indian Distinguished Service Medal
45	3246	Drummer (T/Naik)	Indar Singh	14th Sikhs	Indian Distinguished Service Medal
46	4146	Sepoy	Indar Singh	14th Sikhs	Indian Distinguished Service Medal
47	1793	Naik	Indar Singh	88th Carnatic Infantry	Indian Distinguished Service Medal
48	724	Naik	Indrajit Gurung	3/5 Gurkhas	Indian Distinguished Service Medal
49	4118	Sepoy	Jagat Singh	14th Sikhs	Indian Distinguished Service Medal
50	4330	T/Naik (then Sepoy)	Jagindar Singh	14th Sikhs	Indian Distinguished Service Medal
51	4505	Sepoy	Jiwan Singh	14th Sikhs	Indian Distinguished Service Medal
52	2248	Lance Naik	Jiwan Singh	14th Sikhs	Indian Distinguished Service Medal
53	706	Rifleman	Kabiraj gurung	3/5 Gurkhas	Indian Distinguished Service Medal
54	4361	Sepoy	Kala Singh	14th Sikhs	Indian Distinguished Service Medal
55	2648	T/Naik (then Sepoy)	Kala Singh	14th Sikhs	Indian Distinguished Service Medal
56	4649	Rifleman	Kaman Sing Gurung	1/5 Gurkhas	Indian Distinguished Service Medal
57	604	Rifleman	Kesar Rana	3/5 Gurkhas	Indian Distinguished Service Medal
58	3903	Sepoy	Klem Singh	14th Sikhs	Indian Distinguished Service Medal
59	–	Subadar	Kulbahadur Thapa	3/5 Gurkhas	Indian Distinguished Service Medal

No.	Service No.	Rank	Name	Unit	Medal
60	3712	Havildar (Now Subadar)	Kulbahadur Thapa, SM & Hony Capt	1/5 Gurkhas	Indian Distinguished Service Medal
61	4019	Sepoy	Lakal Singh	14th Sikhs	Indian Distinguished Service Medal
62	56	Rifleman	Lal Sing Thapa	3/5 Gurkhas	Indian Distinguished Service Medal
63	4453	Sepoy	Lal Singh	14th Sikhs	Indian Distinguished Service Medal
64	4151	Sepoy	Lal Singh	14th Sikhs	Indian Distinguished Service Medal
65	4332	Havildar (Now Jemadar)	Lokbahadur Thapa	1/5 Gurkhas	Indian Distinguished Service Medal
66	4620	Havildar (Now Jemadar)	Lokbir Ale	1/4 Gurkhas	Indian Distinguished Service Medal
67	3807	Rifleman	Mahabir Gharti	1/5 Gurkhas	Indian Distinguished Service Medal
68	4220	Rifleman	Manbir Roka	1/5 Gurkhas	Indian Distinguished Service Medal
69	4540	Sepoy	Mangal Singh	14th Sikhs	Indian Distinguished Service Medal
70	-	Subadar	Mansa Ram Pun	2/5 Gurkhas	Indian Distinguished Service Medal
71	-	Risaldar	Muhammad Shah	Indian Mule Corps	Indian Distinguished Service Medal
72	4252	Sepoy	Munshi Singh	14th Sikhs	Indian Distinguished Service Medal
73	4548	Havildar	Nandasing Gurung	3/5 Gurkhas	Indian Distinguished Service Medal
74	-	Sepoy	Narain Singh	21st Kohat Mountain Battery	Indian Distinguished Service Medal
75	1489	Havildar	Narbahadur Gurung	2/5 Gurkhas	Indian Distinguished Service Medal
76	4324	Naik	Narbahadur Thapa	1/5 Gurkhas	Indian Distinguished Service Medal

(contd.)

APPENDIX 4 (contd.)

S.No.	Regtl No.	Rank	Name	Unit	Award
77	285	Havildar	Narbir Thapa	3/5 Gurkhas	Indian Distinguished Service Medal
78	1239	Naik	Nikka Singh	26th Jacob's Mountain Battery	Indian Distinguished Service Medal
79	-	Subadar	Patiman Rana	1/5 Gurkhas	Indian Distinguished Service Medal
80	4147	Sepoy	Phuman Singh	14th Sikhs	Indian Distinguished Service Medal
81	6529	Kot Dafadar (then Naik)	Pir Khan. 10th Mule Corps	Bengal Establishment, Hospital Assistants Branch (Mule Corps)	Indian Distinguished Service Medal
82	4388	Havildar	Puran Sing Gharti	3/5 Gurkhas	Indian Distinguished Service Medal
83	3657	Lance Naik	Ram Singh	14th Sikhs	Indian Distinguished Service Medal
84	-	Subadar	Ram Singh Burathoki	2/10 Gurkhas	Indian Distinguished Service Medal
85	4544	Lance Naik	Ratanbir Thapa	1/5 Gurkhas	Indian Distinguished Service Medal
86	3756	Rifleman	Rattan Sing Gurung	1/5 Gurkhas	Indian Distinguished Service Medal
87	980	Naik	Sahib Din, 33rd Mule Corps	Bengal Establishment, Hospital Assistants Branch (Mule Corps)	Indian Distinguished Service Medal
88	723	Rifleman	Saimdhoj Rai	2/10 Gurkhas	Indian Distinguished Service Medal
89	4292	Lance Naik (then Sepoy)	Sarmukh Singh	14th Sikhs	Indian Distinguished Service Medal
90	-	Subadar Major	Sham Singh,Hony Lt	14th Sikhs	Indian Distinguished Service Medal

91	4929	Rifleman (now Naik)	Shamsher Gurung	1/5 Gurkhas	Indian Distinguished Service Medal
92	898	Rifleman	Siriman Rai	2/10 Gurkhas	Indian Distinguished Service Medal
93	3658	Lance Naik	Sucha Singh	14th Sikhs	Indian Distinguished Service Medal
94	3171	Sepoy	Sundar Singh	14th Sikhs	Indian Distinguished Service Medal
95	948	Sepoy	Sundar Singh, attd 14 Sikhs	45th Sikhs	Indian Distinguished Service Medal
96	896	Rifleman	Amarsing Rana	1/6 Gurkhas	Indian Mertorious Service Medal
97	4683	Naik	Anaram Pun	1/5 Gurkhas	Indian Mertorious Service Medal
98	374	Havildar	Bahadur Pun	1/6 Gurkhas	Indian Mertorious Service Medal
99	443	Rifleman (now Naik)	Bahadur Thapa	1/6 Gurkhas	Indian Mertorious Service Medal
100	2629	Rifleman	Bhanbir Rana	2/5 Gurkhas	Indian Mertorious Service Medal
101	4057	Havildar	Bhimlal Thapa	1/5 Gurkhas	Indian Mertorious Service Medal
102	4799	Naik	Birbahadur Thapa	1/5 Gurkhas	Indian Mertorious Service Medal
103	1684	Lance Naik	Chanda Singh	89th Punjabis	Indian Mertorious Service Medal
104	2701	Lance Naik	Chandarbir Ale	2/5 Gurkhas	Indian Mertorious Service Medal
105	627	Lance Naik (now Naik)	Chandrasing Bura	1/6 Gurkhas	Indian Mertorious Service Medal
106	4785	Naik (now Havildar)	Dalbahadur Rana	1/6 Gurkhas	Indian Mertorious Service Medal
107	284	Rifleman	Dalbir Thapa	1/6 Gurkhas	Indian Mertorious Service Medal
108	2306	Lance Naik	Fateh Ali	89th Punjabis	Indian Mertorious Service Medal

(*contd.*)

573

APPENDIX 4 (contd.)

S.No.	Regtl No.	Rank	Name	Unit	Award
109	528	Rifleman (now Naik)	Gajasing Gurung	1/6 Gurkhas	Indian Mertorious Service Medal
110	1074	Lance Naik	Garbasing Gurung	2/6 Gurkhas	Indian Mertorious Service Medal
111	4345	Lance Naik	Harka Bahadur Thapa	1/5 Gurkhas	Indian Mertorious Service Medal
112	1122	Colour Havildar	Janki Singh	89th Punjabis	Indian Mertorious Service Medal
113	589	Rifleman	Jire Gurung	1/6 Gurkhas	Indian Mertorious Service Medal
114	1050	Lance Naik	Kansirma Thapa	2/6 Gurkhas	Indian Mertorious Service Medal
115	4693	Rifleman	Kesar Pun	1/5 Gurkhas	Indian Mertorious Service Medal
116	4307	Naik	Khambasing Thapa	1/5 Gurkhas	Indian Mertorious Service Medal
117	4290	Havildar	Kharak Singh Pun	1/4 Gurkhas	Indian Mertorious Service Medal
118	515	Rifleman (now Havildar)	Mame Gurung	1/6 Gurkhas	Indian Mertorious Service Medal
119	757	Havildar	Mandrabahadur Gurung	1/6 Gurkhas	Indian Mertorious Service Medal
120	345	Havildar	Mane Thapa	1/6 Gurkhas	Indian Mertorious Service Medal
121	678	Rifleman	Nalbahadur Gurung	1/6 Gurkhas	Indian Mertorious Service Medal
122	1178	Rifleman	Narsuba Gurung	2/6 Gurkhas	Indian Mertorious Service Medal
123	4362	Naik	Nepa Ghirth	1/5 Gurkhas	Indian Mertorious Service Medal
124	265	Rifleman (now Naik)	Panchabir Gurung	1/6 Gurkhas	Indian Mertorious Service Medal
125	4927	Rifleman	Shamsher Mal	1/5 Gurkhas	Indian Mertorious Service Medal

126	4563	Havildar	Singhir Thapa	1/4 Gurkhas	Indian Mertorious Service Medal
127	4889	Havildar	Tilbere Thapa	1/5 Gurkhas	Indian Mertorious Service Medal
128	1106	Naik	Bahadur Shah	Indian Mule Corps	Indian Order of Merit
129	–	Subadar	Bajirdhoj Rai	2/10 Gurkhas	Indian Order of Merit
130	–	Jemadar	Bal Singh Thapa	1/6 Gurkhas	Indian Order of Merit
131	851	2nd Class Sub-Assistant Surgeon	Bhagwan Singh	Indian Subordinate Medical Department	Indian Order of Merit
132	2775	Gunner Naik	Bir Singh	26th Jacob's Mountain Battery	Indian Order of Merit
133	1350	Lance Naik	Bir Singh	Indian Mule Corps	Indian Order of Merit
134	4799	Naik	Birbahadur Thapa	1/5 Gurkhas	Indian Order of Merit
135	–	Jemadar	Brij Gurung	1/5 Gurkhas	Indian Order of Merit
136	–	Lance Naik	Budhiram Rana	1/6 Gurkhas	Indian Order of Merit
137	–	Subadar	Chanda Singh	21st Kohat Mountain Battery	Indian Order of Merit
138	29	Rifleman	Chanrabir Singh Gurung	1/6 Gurkhas	Indian Order of Merit
139	–	Subadar	Chettradhoj Limu	2/10 Gurkhas	Indian Order of Merit
140	–	Subadar	Chhetradhoj Limbu	2/10 Gurkhas	Indian Order of Merit

(contd.)

APPENDIX 4 (*contd.*)

S.No.	Regtl No.	Rank	Name	Unit	Award
141	–	Jemadar	Chintaram Bura. (Chintaram Burathoki). Hony Lt	2/5 Gurkhas	Indian Order of Merit
142	–	Subadar Major	Chittahang Limu	2/10 Gurkhas	Indian Order of Merit
143	–	Jemadar	Dalbahadur Thapa	1/6 Gurkhas	Indian Order of Merit
144	4130	Havildar	Dandabir Thapa	1/5 Gurkhas	Indian Order of Merit
145	2131	Sepoy	Dasunda Singh	89th Punjabis	Indian Order of Merit
146	–	1st Class Sub-Assistant Surgeon	Daulat Singh	21st (Kohat) Mountain Battery (137th Combined Field Ambulance)	Indian Order of Merit
147	–	Subadar	Dhanji Gharti	1/5 Gurkhas	Indian Order of Merit
148	–	Subadar Major	Dhanraj Gurung	1/5 Gurkhas	Indian Order of Merit
149	2811	Gunner	Fazal Ilahi	26th Jacob's Mountain Battery	Indian Order of Merit
150	–	Gunner	Fazl Illahi	26th Jacob's Mountain Battery	Indian Order of Merit
151	–	Subadar Major	Gambir Singh Pun	1/6 Gurkhas	Indian Order of Merit
152	–	Subadar Major	Ganbir Singh Pun	1/6 Gurkhas	Indian Order of Merit
153	4485	Naik	Gangaraj Thapa	1/5 Gurkhas	Indian Order of Merit

No.	Number	Rank	Name	Unit	Award
154	880	1st Class Sub–Assistant Surgeon	Ghaus Muhammad	Indian Subordinate Medical Department	Indian Order of Merit
155	1096	Havildar	Gurdit Singh	26th Jacob's Mountain Battery	Indian Order of Merit
156	1088	Rifleman	Harka Gurung	1/6 Gurkhas	Indian Order of Merit
157	–	Risaldar	Hashmat Ali	Indian Mule Corps	Indian Order of Merit
158	3760	Lance Naik	Hazara Singh	14th Sikhs	Indian Order of Merit
159	343	Lance Naik	Hembahadur Rana	1/6 Gurkhas	Indian Order of Merit
160	1125	Driver Havildar	Indar Singh	26th Jacob's Mountain Battery	Indian Order of Merit
161	–	Driver Havildar	Inder Singh	26th Jacob's Mountain Battery	Indian Order of Merit
162	1115	1st Class Sub–Assistant Surgeon	Ishar Singh	Indian Subordinate Medical Department	Indian Order of Merit
163	435	Havildar	Jan Muhammad	21st Kohat Mountain Battery	Indian Order of Merit
164	–	Subadar	Jawala Singh	26th Jacob's Mountain Battery	Indian Order of Merit
165	–	Subadar	Kala Singh	1st Patiala Imperial Service Infantry	Indian Order of Merit

(contd.)

APPENDIX 4 (*contd.*)

S.No.	Regtl No.	Rank	Name	Unit	Award
166	424	Lance Naik	Karam Singh	21st Kohat Mountain Battery	Indian Order of Merit
167	-	Subadar	Kulbahadur Thapa	1/6 Gurkhas	Indian Order of Merit
168	-	Subadar	Man Bahadur Rai	2/10 Gurkhas	Indian Order of Merit
169	546	Pay Havildar	Muhammad Baksh	21st Kohat Mountain Battery	Indian Order of Merit
170	562	Lance Naik	Naharsing Gurung	1/6 Gurkhas	Indian Order of Merit
171	-	Jemadar	Nandlal Gurung	1/6 Gurkhas	Indian Order of Merit
172	-	Subadar	Pharsaldhoj Rai	2/10 Gurkhas	Indian Order of Merit
173	-	Subadar Major	Sahabir Thapa	1/6 Gurkhas	Indian Order of Merit
174	4813	Havildar	Santbir Gurung	1/6 Gurkhas	Indian Order of Merit
175	-	Subadar	Satalsing Thapa	1/6 Gurkhas	Indian Order of Merit
176	-	Jemadar	Tejbir Thapa	1/5 Gurkhas	Indian Order of Merit
177	-	Driver Naik	Ali Ahmed	21st Kohat Mountain Battery	Mention in Dispatches
178	3243	Lance Naik	Amar Singh	14th Sikhs	Mention in Dispatches
179	4098	Havildar (Now Jemadar)	Amarsing Pun	1/4 Gurkhas	Mention in Dispatches
180	256	Rifleman	Ambir Gurung	2/10 Gurkhas	Mention in Dispatches

181	4295	Sepoy	Bachan Singh	14th Sikhs	Mention in Dispatches
182	4575	Lance Naik	Bhagwan Singh	14th Sikhs	Mention in Dispatches
183	4386	Sepoy	Bharpur Singh	14th Sikhs	Mention in Dispatches
184	3100	Lance Naik (then Drummer)	Bir Singh	14th Sikhs	Mention in Dispatches
185	3693	Havildar	Bir Singh	14th Sikhs	Mention in Dispatches
186	4557	Sepoy	Bogh Singh	14th Sikhs	Mention in Dispatches
187	4159	Havildar (Now Jemadar)	Budh Sing Gurung	1/5 Gurkhas	Mention in Dispatches
188	4539	Bearer	Budhi Ram. 108 Ind Fd Amb	Bengal Establishment, Hospital Assistants Branch (Army Bearer Corps)	Mention in Dispatches
189	4506	Sepoy	Chaman (Chanan) Singh	14th Sikhs	Mention in Dispatches
190	4232	Sepoy	Chaman Singh	14th Sikhs	Mention in Dispatches
191	35	Havildar	Chambel Singh. Attd 108 Ind Fd Amb	82nd Punjabis	Mention in Dispatches
192	4393	T/Naik (then Sepoy)	Chanan Singh	14th Sikhs	Mention in Dispatches
193	4144	Drummer	Chanda Singh	14th Sikhs	Mention in Dispatches
194	-	Jemadar	Chintaram Bura. (Chintaram Burathoki). Hony Lt	2/5 Gurkhas	Mention in Dispatches

(contd.)

579

APPENDIX 4 (contd.)

S.No.	Regtl No.	Rank	Name	Unit	Award
195	4766	Havildar	Dalbir Chand. Hony Lt	1/5 Gurkhas	Mention in Dispatches
196	4263	Lance Naik	Dhami. No 4 coy Attd 108 Ind Fd Amb	Bengal Establishment, Hospital Assistants Branch (Army Bearer Corps)	Mention in Dispatches
197	830	Havildar	Dhane Gurung	3/5 Gurkhas	Mention in Dispatches
198	–	Jemadar	Dhanraj Thapa	3/5 Gurkhas	Mention in Dispatches
199	4567	Naik	Fateh Muhammad, No 4 Coy Attd 108 Ind Fd Amb	Bengal Establishment, Hospital Assistants Branch (Army Bearer Corps)	Mention in Dispatches
200	4159	Lance Naik (then Sepoy)	Gajjan Singh	14th Sikhs	Mention in Dispatches
201	4573	Sepoy	Gajjan Singh	14th Sikhs	Mention in Dispatches
202	2860	Sepoy	Gujar Singh	14th Sikhs	Mention in Dispatches
203	3550	Ward Orderly	Gurdit Singh, Attd 108 Fd Amb	14th Sikhs	Mention in Dispatches
204	3738	Lance Naik	Harnam Singh	14th Sikhs	Mention in Dispatches
205	3246	Drummer (T/Naik)	Indar Singh	14th Sikhs	Mention in Dispatches
206	4146	Sepoy	Indar Singh	14th Sikhs	Mention in Dispatches
207	724	Naik	Indrajit Gurung	3/5 Gurkhas	Mention in Dispatches
208	4118	Sepoy	Jagat Singh	14th Sikhs	Mention in Dispatches

209	4330	T/Naik (then Sepoy)	Jagindar Singh	14th Sikhs	Mention in Dispatches
210	4505	Sepoy	Jiwan Singh	14th Sikhs	Mention in Dispatches
211	2248	Lance Naik	Jiwan Singh	14th Sikhs	Mention in Dispatches
212	706	Rifleman	kabiraj gurung	3/5 Gurkhas	Mention in Dispatches
213	4361	Sepoy	Kala Singh	14th Sikhs	Mention in Dispatches
214	2648	T/Naik (then Sepoy)	Kala Singh	14th Sikhs	Mention in Dispatches
215	604	Rifleman	Kesar Rana	3/5 Gurkhas	Mention in Dispatches
216	3903	Sepoy	Klem Singh	14th Sikhs	Mention in Dispatches
217	-	Subadar	Kulbahadur Thapa	3/5 Gurkhas	Mention in Dispatches
218	3712	Havildar (Now Subadar)	Kulbahadur Thapa. SM & Hony Capt	1/5 Gurkhas	Mention in Dispatches
219	4019	Sepoy	Lakal Singh	14th Sikhs	Mention in Dispatches
220	56	Rifleman	Lal Sing Thapa	3/5 Gurkhas	Mention in Dispatches
221	4453	Sepoy	Lal Singh	14th Sikhs	Mention in Dispatches
222	4151	Sepoy	Lal Singh	14th Sikhs	Mention in Dispatches
223	4620	Havildar (Now Jemadar)	Lokbir Ale	1/4 Gurkhas	Mention in Dispatches
224	4220	Rifleman	Manbir Roka	1/5 Gurkhas	Mention in Dispatches
225	4540	Sepoy	Mangal Singh	14th Sikhs	Mention in Dispatches
226	-	Subadar	Mansa Ram Pun	2/5 Gurkhas	Mention in Dispatches

(contd.)

581

APPENDIX 4 (*contd.*)

S.No.	Regtl No.	Rank	Name	Unit	Award
227	4252	Sepoy	Munshi Singh	14th Sikhs	Mention in Dispatches
228	4548	Havildar	Nandasing Gurung	3/5 Gurkhas	Mention in Dispatches
229	1489	Havildar	Narbahadur Gurung	2/5 Gurkhas	Mention in Dispatches
230	4147	Sepoy	Phuman Singh	14th Sikhs	Mention in Dispatches
231	6529	Kot Dafadar (then Naik)	Pir Khan. 10th Mule Corps	Bengal Establishment, Hospital Assistants Branch (Mule Corps)	Mention in Dispatches
232	4388	Havildar	Puran Sing Gharti	3/5 Gurkhas	Mention in Dispatches
233	3657	Lance Naik	Ram Singh	14th Sikhs	Mention in Dispatches
234	-	Subadar	Ram Singh Burathoki	2/10 Gurkhas	Mention in Dispatches
235	4544	Lance Naik	Ratanbir Thapa	1/5 Gurkhas	Mention in Dispatches
236	3756	Rifleman	Rattan Sing Gurung	1/5 Gurkhas	Mention in Dispatches
237	980	Naik	Sahib Din, 33rd Mule Cps	Bengal Establishment, Hospital Assistants Branch (Mule Corps)	Mention in Dispatches
238	-	Shoeing Smith	Sahib Singh	26th Jacob's Mountain Battery	Mention in Dispatches
239	723	Rifleman	Saimdhoj Rai	2/10 Gurkhas	Mention in Dispatches
240	4292	Lance Naik (then Sepoy)	Sarmukh Singh	14th Sikhs	Mention in Dispatches

241	–	Subadar Major	Sham Singh, Hony Lt	14th Sikhs	Mention in Dispatches
242	898	Rifleman	Siriman Rai	2/10 Gurkhas	Mention in Dispatches
243	3658	Lance Naik	Sucha Singh	14th Sikhs	Mention in Dispatches
244	3171	Sepoy	Sundar Singh	14th Sikhs	Mention in Dispatches
245	–	Jemadar	Dhanlal Gurung	1/5 Gurkhas	Military Cross
246	–	Subadar Major	Ganbir Singh Pun	1/6 Gurkhas	Military Cross
247	–	Subadar	Bagbir Yakha	Burma Military Police	Order of British India
248	–	Subadar Major	Bhagat Singh	1st Patiala Imperial Service Infantry	Order of British India
249	–	Subadar	Chhetrandhoj Limbu	2/10 Gurkhas	Order of British India
250	–	Jemadar	Chintaram Bura. (Chintaram Burathoki). Hony Lt	2/5 Gurkhas	Order of British India
251	4766	Havildar	Dalbir Chand. Hony Lt	1/5 Gurkhas	Order of British India
252	–	Subadar Major	Ganbir Singh Pun	1/6 Gurkhas	Order of British India
253	–	Sirdar	Gurbuksh Singh	1st Patiala Imperial Service Infantry	Order of British India
254	–	Risaldar	Hashmat Ali	Indian Mule Corps	Order of British India
255	–	Lieutenant Colonel	Ishar Singh	1st Patiala Imperial Service Infantry	Order of British India

(contd.)

APPENDIX 4 (*contd.*)

S.No.	Regtl No.	Rank	Name	Unit	Award
256	-	Subadar Major	Jagandar Singh	69th Punjabis	Order of British India
257	-	Subadar	Jawala Singh	26th Jacob's Mountain Battery	Order of British India
258	-	Subadar Major	Manbahadur Thapa	1/6 Gurkhas	Order of British India
259	-	Subadar	Mit Singh	21st Kohat Mountain Battery	Order of British India
260	-	Major	Narain Singh	1st Patiala Imperial Service Infantry	Order of British India
261	-	Subadar Major	Sham Singh	14th Sikhs	Order of British India
262	-	Subadar Major	Sham Singh,Hony Lt 01.07.20, French Medaille Militarie 361/1916	14th Sikhs	Order of British India
263	-3	Subadar Major	Sundar Singh	89th Punjabis	Order of British India

Source: From multiple sources.

Bibliography

ARCHIVAL

War Diary, Army Headquarters, India (F.S.R., Part II, Section 140; and Staff Manual, War, Section 20), I.E.F.G. 1915, National Archives of India.

War Diary, Army Headquarters, India (F.S.R., Part II, Section 140; and Staff Manual, War, Section 20), I.E.F.G. 1915, WWI/343/H, National Archives of India.

War Diary Army Headquarters, India (F.S.R., Part II, Section 140; and Staff Manual, War, Section 20), I.E.F.G. 1915, WWI/343/H-4, National Archives of India.

War Diary Army Headquarters, India (F.S.R., Part II, Section 140; and Staff Manual, War, Section 20), I.E.F.G. 1915, WWI/344/H-4, National Archives of India.

WAR Diary, I.E.F.G. 1915 WWI/342/H, National Archives of India.

War Diary, Army Headquarters, India (F.S.R., Part II, Section 140; and Staff Manual, War, Section 20), I.E.F.G. 1916, WWI/354/H-3, National Archives of India.

War Diary, Army Headquarters, India (F.S.R., Part II, Section 140; and Staff Manual, War, Section 20.), I.E.F.G. 1916, WWI/354/H-7, National Archives of India.

Casualty Appendix to War Diary Army Headquarters, India (F.S.R., Part II, Section 140; and Staff Manual, War, Section 20), I.E.F.G. 1915, WWI/342/H-3, National Archives of India.

Casualty Appendix to War Diary Army Headquarters, India (F.S.R., Part II, Section 140; and Staff Manual, War, Section 20), I.E.F.G. 1915, WW1/343/H-3, National Archives of India.

Casualty Appendix to War Diary Army Headquarters, India (F.S.R., Part II, Section 140; and Staff Manual, War, Section 20.), I.E.F.G. 1916, WWI/355A/H-3, National Archives of India.

Casualty Appendix to War Diary Army Headquarters, India (F.S.R., Part II, Section 140; and Staff Manual, War, Section 20.), I.E.F.G. 1916, WWI/355/H-3, National Archives of India.

Casualty Appendix to War Diary Army Headquarters, India (F.S.R., Part II, Section 140; and Staff Manual, War, Section 20.), I.E.F.G. 1916, WWI/358/H-3, National Archives of India.

Casualty Appendix to War Diary Army Headquarters, India (F.S.R., Part II, Section 140; and Staff Manual War, Section 20.), I.E.F.G. 1916, WWI/356/H-3, National Archives of India.

Casualty Appendix to War Diary Army Headquarters, India (F.S.R., Part II, Section 140; and Staff Manual War, Section 20.), I.E.F.G. 1916, WWI/357/H-3, National Archives of India.

Casualty Appendix to War Diary Army Headquarters, India (F.S.R., Part II, Section 140; and Staff Manual War, Section 20.), I.E.F.G. 1917, WWI/360/H-3, National Archives of India.

Casualty Appendix to War Diary Army Headquarters, India (F.S.R., Part II, Section 140; and Staff Manual, War, Section 20.), I.E.F.G. 1917, WWI/359/H-3, National Archives of India.

Casualty Appendix to War Diary Army Headquarters, India (F.S.R., Part II, Section 140; and Staff Manual, War, Section 20.), I.E.F.G. 1915, WWI/344/H-3, National Archives of India.

Punjab State Archives (1920), *Records Patiala State, Ijlase Khas,* file no. 1556, pt. I (vol. 120).

Punjab State Archives (1920), *Ijlase Khas* (file no. 1556, pt. I, vol. 120). Patiala State.

Selected Published Works

Official Histories

A Brief History of the Canakkale Campaign in the First World War (June 1914-January 1916), 2004.

Ancestry (1915), *War Diary, 69th Punjabis* (No. 4272). Ancestry.co.uk. https://www.ancestry.co.uk/search/collections/60380/

Aspinall-Oglander, C.F. & Sketches (1992), *Military Operations Gallipoli.*

Aspinall-Oglander, C.F. (1929), *Military Operations, Gallipoli (History of the Great War Based on Official Documents by Direction of the Historical Section, Committee of Imperial Defence)*, W. Heinemann Ltd.

Battery, G.B. (1886), *The Historical Record of the No.1 (Kohat), Mountain Battery, Punjab Frontier Force.*

Douie, J.M. (1916), *The Panjab: North-West Frontier Province and Kashmir.* Library of Alexandria.

Major, B. and M. Gillott, eds. (2017), *Gallipoli Diaries: Headquarters 29th Indian Infantry Brigade 1915*, Great War Diaries Ltd.

Moharir, V. J. (1979), *History of the Army Service Corps.*

Nash, A. (2014), *Sowars and Sepoys in the Great War 1914-1918, Cavalry and Infantry Regiments of the Indian Army: Being a Record of Their Regimental Iconography, Services, Battle Honours and Ethnicity.*

Unit Histories

Australian War Memorial (1915), *Australian Imperial Force Unit War Diaries: 4th Infantry Brigade* (23/4/1, pt. 2).

Haltof, M. (1993), 'In Quest of Self-Identity: Gallipoli, Mateship, and the Construction of Australian National Identity', *Journal of Popular Film & Television.* https://doi.org/10.1080/01956051.1993.9943973

War Diary. (1991), 'Jacob's battery', *Gallipoli Journal*, 66.

Webster, C.D. (1916), 'The Supply of Followers on Active Service for a Battalion of Indian Infantry', *Journal of the United Service Institution of India, XLV*, 272-6.

Official Documents

Beatson, S. (2022), *A History of the Imperial Service Troops of Native States with a Short Sketch of Events in each State 1903*, Generic.

Bingley, A.H. (1900), *Handbooks for the Indian Army: Sikhs*, Government Central Printing Office, Simla.

Bonarjee, P. D. (1899), *A Handbook of the Fighting Races of India.*

Commission, G. B. C. W. G. (1927), *The Helles Memorial Register, Containing the Names of Certain Sailors, Soldiers and Marines from the United Kingdom, Australia and India who Fell in the Gallipoli Campaign and*

Have No Known Graves: Pt. 8, Soldiers who Fell on Land: Marriage-Paterson.

———, (1877), *Report of Settlement Operations in the Shahpur Kandi Tract of the Gurdaspur District.*

———, (1917), *Army Tables of a Battalion of Indian Infantry.*

Elly, E.B. (1893), *Military Report on the Chin-Lushai Country.*

Falcon, R.W. (1896), *Handbook on Sikhs for the Use of Regimental Officers.*

Gazetteer of the Jullundur District, 1904 (2000).

Government Gazette: Punjab and its Dependencies. 11 Oct. 1894-7 Aug. 1936 (1894).

Hamilton, I. (2019), *Sir Ian Hamilton's Despatches from the Dardanelles, etc.,* Good Press.

Maclagan, E. (1990), *Gazetteer of the Multan District.*

McFetridge, C.H.T. and J.P. Warren (1973), *Tales of the Mountain Gunners.*

National Archives of India [NAI], (1915), War Diary [Dataset], in IEF 'G' (vol. 15), National Archives of India.

———, (1914), War Diary [Dataset]. In IEF 'F' & 'G' (vol. 1).

———, (1915a), Casualty Appendix [Dataset], in *Indian Mediterranean Ex Force* (vol. 1).

———, (1915b), Casualty Appendix [Dataset], in *Indian Mediterranean Ex Force* (vol. 2).

———, (1915c), War Diary [Dataset], in IEF 'F' & 'G' (vol. 2).

———, (1915d), Casualty Appendix [Dataset], in IEF 'G' (vol. 1).

———, (1915e), War Diary [Dataset], in IEF 'G' (vol. 1).

———, (1915f), Casualty Appendix [Dataset], in IEF 'G' (vol. 2).

———, (1915g), War Diary [Dataset], in IEF 'G' (vol. 2).

———, (1915h), Casualty Appendix [Dataset], in IEF 'G' (vol. 3).

———, (1915i), War Diary [Dataset], in IEF 'G' (vol. 3).

———, (1915j), Casualty Appendix [Dataset], in IEF 'G' (vol. 4).

———, (1915k), War Diary [Dataset], in IEF 'G' (vol 13).

———, (1915l), Casualty Appendix [Dataset], in IEF 'G' (vol. 5).

———, (1915m), War Diary [Dataset], in IEF 'G' (vol. 14).

———, (1915n), Casualty Appendix [Dataset], in IEF 'G' (vol. 6).

———, (1916a), Casualty Appendix [Dataset], in IEF 'G' (vol. 7).

———, (1916b), Casualty Appendix [Dataset], in IEF 'G' (vol. 8).

———, (1916c), Casualty Appendix [Dataset], in IEF 'G' (vol. 9).

———, (1916d), Casualty Appendix [Dataset], in IEF 'G' (vol. 10).

Parkin, H. and B.M. Police (1901), *Manual for the Burma Military Police: Containing Orders and Rules for the Burma Military Police Issued the Sanction of the Lieutenant-governor of Burma*. Compiled by Major H. Parkin. Printed by Order of the Local Government.

Patiala. (1923), *Patiala & the Great War. A Brief History of the Services of the Premier Punjab State*. Compiled from Secretariat and Other Records [with Plates, including Portraits].

Police Administration of Burma for the Year 1898 (1899), Rangoon, Government Printing.

Punjab District and State Gazetteers: Part A] (1907).

Punjab District Gazetteers: Gurdaspur. Gazetteer of India. Hauptbd, (1979).

Punjab, P. (2015), *Report on the Administration of The Punjab and Its Dependencies*, Palala Press.

Punjab. (1870), *Report on the Census of the Punjab Taken on 10th January, 1868*.

Punjab. (2007), *Gazetteer of the Gurdaspur District, 1891-92*.

Report on the Administration of the Punjab and its Dependencies (2015), Patiala Press.

Report on the Police Administration of Burma (1919).

Singh, S.N. (1970), *Maharaja Ranjit Singh*, Languages Department, Patiala.

Statistics of the Military Effort of the British Empire During the Great War 1914-1920. (2015).

The Imperial Gazetteer of India (1907).

The Indian Army List (1915).

3 Indian (Lahore) Division Divisional Troops Royal Army Medical Corps 112 Indian Field Ambulance: 1 January 1914 - 29 December 1915 (First World War, War Diary, Wo95/3920/4) (2015).

Tyquin, M.B. (1993), *Gallipoli: The Medical War: the Australian Army Medical Services in the Dardanelles Campaign of 1915*. University of New South Wales.

War Diary, National Archives of India (1915), Army Headquarters, India, 14 (1915).

Weekes, C.H.E. (2011), *History of the 5th Royal Gurkha Rifles: 1858 to 1928*, Andrews UK Limited.

Wikeley, J.M. (1913), *Handbooks for the Indian Army: Punjabi Musalmans*. Superintendent Government Printing, Calcutta.

Newspapers and Journals

'In Enemy Hands' (1916), *The West Australian* (Perth, WA : 1879-1954), 7.

'India, U.S.I.O.' (1916), *Journal of the United Service Institution of India*.

'Indian Muslims'. (1914, November 4), *Observer*.

'The blizzard: Some experiences of field ambulance' (1997), *Gallipoli Journal*, 84.

'Turkey and Indian Muslims' (November 1914). *Jhang Siyal*.

Alymer, G. (n.d.), 'Lecture on Supply and Transport', Rawalpindi, 14 April 1917, *Journal of the United Services Institute of India*, *XLVI* (207), 297-311.

Atancanli, S. (2017), 'Kemel Attaturk and the Foreign Soldiers who Died in Gallipoli', *Gallipoli Journal*, 146.

Bricknell, M. (2002), 'The Evolution of Casualty Evacuation in the British Army in the 20th Century (Part 2) -1918 to 1945', *Journal of the Royal Army Medical Corps*, 148(3), 314-22. https://doi.org/10.1136/jramc-148-03-21

Chenevix, C. (1988), 'The Indian Army and the King's Enemies', *Gallipoli Journal*, 57.

Cooper, J. (2002), 'Animals in War', *Gallipoli Journal*, 99.

Fergusson, A.C. (1998), 'Indian Mountain Batteries', *Gallipoli Journal*, 86.

Greenhut, J. (1984), 'Sahib and Sepoy: An Inquiry into the Relationship between the British Officers and Native Soldiers of the British Indian Army', *Military Affairs*, 48(1), 15. https://doi.org/10.2307/1988342

Hargrave, J. (2005), 'The Indian Transport Train', *Gallipoli Journal*, 109.

Harrison, M. (1996), 'The Medicalization of War: The Militarization of Medicine', *Social History of Medicine*, 9(2), 267-76. https://doi.org/10.1093/shm/9.2.267

Hunter, C.W. (1918), 'Lice Borne Diseases and Disinfection', *The Lancet*, 378-81.

Jenner, H. (2003), 'The Indian Mule Corps', *Gallipoli Journal*, 102.

Lewis, J. (1993), 'Some Mules', *Gallipoli Journal*, 78.

Major, A. (2017), '"Hill Coolies": Indian Indentured Labour and the Colonial Imagination, 1836-38', *South Asian Studies*, 33(1), 23-36. https://doi.org/10.1080/02666030.2017.1300374

Martin, G. (1986), Financial and Manpower Aspects of the Dominions' and

India's Contribution to Britain's War Effort, 1914-19. https://doi.org/10.17863/cam.20128.

Mott, G.R. (2019), '1/6 Gurkhas and 6th bn South Lancers Regt in the battle of Sari Bair', *Gallipoli Journal*, 25,147.

Nicholls, B., P. Malins and C. McFetridge (2003), 'The Military Mule in the British and Indian Army', *Gallipoli Journal*, 101.

Omissi, D. (1994), 'The Indian Voices of the Great War', *Gallipoli Journal*, 74.

_____. (2007), 'Europe Through Indian Eyes: Indian Soldiers Encounter England and France, 1914-1918', *The English Historical Review, CXXII* (496), 371-96. https://doi.org/10.1093/ehr/cem004

Pearn, J. (1990), 'The Pivot: The First Australian Casualty Clearing Hospital at the Gallipoli beachhead — the first seven days', *The Medical Journal of Australia*. https://doi.org/10.5694/j.1326-5377.1990.tb126274.x

Phipson, C.E.S. (1970), 'With the Gurkhas on Sari Bair', *Gallipoli Journal*, 03(1970), 15-19.

Ross, W. Stewart (77 CE), 'To a Gurkha', *Gallipoli Journal, 77*.

Roy, K. (2001), 'The Construction of Regiments in the Indian Army: 1859-1913', *War in History*, 8(2), 127-48. https://doi.org/10.1177/096834450100800201

_____. (2002), 'Feeding the Leviathan: Supplying the British Indian Army, 1859-1913', *Journal of the Society for Army Historical Research, 80*(322), 144-61.

_____. (2010), 'From Defeat to Victory: Logistics of the Campaign in Mesopotamia, 1914-1918', *First World War Studies, 1*(1), 35-55. https://doi.org/10.1080/19475021003621051

_____. (2018), 'Indian Army and the First World War', in Oxford University Press eBooks. https://doi.org/10.1093/oso/9780199485659.001.0001

Saunders, D. (2017), 'A Subaltern of Sikhs', *Gallipoli Journal*, 146.

Savory, R. (1971), 'Gallipoli Memories', *Gallipoli Journal*, 6, 9, 10, 13-16, 18, 19, 21.

Shaheed Soherwardi, S.H. (2009), 'Punjabisation in the British Indian Army 1857-1947 and the advent of military rule in Pakistan', *Edinburgh Papers in South Asian Studies*, 24.

Singh, M.D. (1978), 'Sikh Seeks Sikh', *The Journal of the Gallipoli Association*, 27, 20-7.

Strachan, H. (2010), 'The First World War as a global war', *First World War Studies*, *1*(1), 3–14. https://doi.org/10.1080/19475021003621036

Thandi, H.S. (1982), 'A Profile in Courage', *Gallipoli Journal*, 34.

Tyquin, M. (1992), 'Medical Evacuation During the Gallipoli Campaign— An Australian Perspective', *War and Society*. https://doi.org/10.1179 /072924792791198904

Wingfield, M. (2004), 'Boats vs Horses', *Gallipoli Journal*, 108. www. abhilekh-patal.in. (n.d.).

OTHER SECONDARY WORKS

Books

Alexander, H.M. (2017), *On Two Fronts, Being the Adventures of an Indian Mule Corps in France and Gallipoli*, Van Haren Publishing.

Allen, C. (2015), *Plain Tales from The Raj: Images of British India in the 20th Century*, Hachette UK.

Andrew, Tait Jarboe (2013), *Soldiers of Empire, Indian Sepoys in and beyond the Imperial Metropole During the First World War 1914-1919*, North-Eastern University Boston, Massachusetts.

Anonymous, A. (2018), *The Works of John Ruskin: The Crown of Wild Olive*. Palala Press.

Atia, N. (2015), *World War I in Mesopotamia: The British and the Ottomans in Iraq*, Bloomsbury Publishing.

Bamford, L.C.P.G. (1948), *The Sikh Regiment, The 14th King George's Own Ferozepore Sikhs*, Gale & Polden Limited, Aldershot.

Basu, S. (2015), *For King and Another Country: Indian Soldiers on the Western Front, 1914-18*, Bloomsbury Publishing.

Beckett, I., T. Bowman and M. Connelly (2017), *The British Army and the First World War*, Cambridge University Press.

Beeston, J.L. (2016), *Five Months at Anzac (WWI Centenary Series)*, Read Books Ltd.

Bidwell, D. and D. Graham (2004), *Fire Power: The British Army Weapons & Theories of War 1904-1945*, Pen and Sword.

Birdwood, W.R.B. (1957), *Khaki and Gown, an Autobiography*.

Bradley, P. (2014), *Charles Bean's Gallipoli: Illustrated*. Allen & Unwin.

Broadbent, H. (2015), *Gallipoli: The Turkish Defence: The Story from the Turkish Documents*, Melbourne University.

Bruce, G. (2020), *Six Battles for India: Anglo-Sikh Wars, 1845-46 and 1848-49*, Sapere Books.

Burness, P. (2015), *The Nek: A Gallipoli Tragedy*. Exisle Publishing.

Candler, E. (2020), *The Sepoy*, Writat.

Carman, W. Y. (2021), *Indian Army Uniforms Under the British from the 18th Century to 1947*, Hassell Street Press.

Chambers, S. (2003), *Gully Ravine: Gallipoli (Battleground Europe)*, Pen and Sword Military.

Charles Hemphill Townsend McFetridge, C. H. T. M. W. M. (1974), *Tales of the Mountain Gunners. An Anthology, Compiled by Those who Served with Them, and Edited by C.H.T. McFetridge and J.P. Warren*. Blackwood.

Chasseaud, P. and P. Doyle (2005), *Grasping Gallipoli: Terrain, Maps and Failure at the Dardanelles, 1915*, Spellmount, Limited Publishers.

Chhina, R. (2001), *The Indian Distinguished Service Medal.*

Chowdhry, M.S. (2018), *Defence of Europe by Sikh Soldiers in the World Wars*, Troubador Publishing Ltd.

Chowdhury, S.R. (2019), *The First World War, Anticolonialism and Imperial Authority in British India, 1914-1924*, Routledge.

Clarke, G.R. (2021), *The Post Office of India and its Story*, Prabhat Prakashan.

Cohen, S.P. (2001), *The Indian Army: Its Contribution to the Development of a Nation*, Oxford University Press, New York.

Corrigan, G. (2015), *Sepoys in the Trenches: The Indian Corps on the Western Front 1914-15* (Reissue), Spellmount.

Crawley, R. (2014), *Climax at Gallipoli: The Failure of the August Offensive*. University of Oklahoma Press.

Creighton, O. (1915), *With the 29th Division in Gallipoli*, Longmans Green, London.

Crew, F. a. E. (1956), *The Army Medical Services: Campaigns.*

Cunningham, J.D. and A.C. Banerjee (1949), *Anglo-Sikh Relations*, A. Mukherjee.

Cunningham, J.D. and J.D. Cunningham (1990), *History of the Sikhs; From the Origin of the Nation to the Battles of the Sutlej [Aug 01, 1990], Joseph Davey Cunningham and J.D. Cunningham* (1915 edn.), Low Price Publications.

Dardanelles: Evacuation of Sick and Wounded (2017).

Davidson, L. (2005), *Scarecrow Army: The Anzacs at Gallipoli*.

Deshpande, A. (2005), *British Military Policy in India, 1900-1945: Colonial Constraints and Declining Power*, Manohar, New Delhi.

Dickmann, N. (2017), *The Horrors of World War I*, Capstone.

Doherty, S. and T. Donovan (2014), *The Indian Corps on the Western Front: A Handbook and Battlefield Guide*.

Edwardes, H.B. (1851), *A Year on the Punjab Frontier in 1848-49*.

Errington, P. W. (2008), *John Masefield's Great War: Collected Works*, Casemate Publishers.

Farwell, B. (1991), *Armies of the Raj: From the Mutiny to Independence, 1858-1947*, W. W. Norton & Company.

Fleischer, W. (2017), *Military Technology of the First World War: Development, Use and Consequences*.

Ganachari, A. (2020), *Indians in the First World War: The Missing Links*, Sage, New Delhi.

Gariepy, P. (2014), *Gardens of Hell: Battles of the Gallipoli Campaign*, Potomac Books, Inc.

Gaylor, J. (1992), *Sons of John Company: The Indian and Pakistan Armies 1903-91*, Spellmount.

George's and F.E.G. Talbot (1937), *The 14th King George's Own Sikhs: The 1st Battalion (K.G.O.) (Ferozepore Sikhs)*.

Gleichen, L.E. (2014), *Memoirs from the British Expeditionary Force: 1914-1915*, Pen and Sword.

Graham, C.A.L. (2014), *The History of the Indian Mountain Artillery*, Naval & Military Press Ltd.

Grehan, J. (2014), *Gallipoli and the Dardanelles, 1915-1916*. Pen and Sword.

Griffin, L. (1892), *Ranjit Singh; and the Sikh Barrier Between Our Growing Empire and Central Asia*.

Griffith, P. and P.G. Griffith (1994), *Battle Tactics of the Western Front: The British Army's Art of Attack, 1916-18*. Yale University Press.

Gudmundsson, B. (2005a), *The British Expeditionary Force 1914-15 (Battle Orders)* (First), Osprey Publishing.

Gulati, Y.B. (1972), *History of the Regiment of Artillery, Indian Army*, Leo Cooper Books.

Gupta, H.R. (1978), *History of the Sikhs: The Sikh Lion of Lahore, Maharaja Ranjit Singh, 1799-1839*.

Gupta, P. S. and A. Deshpande (2002), *The British Raj and Its Indian Armed Forces, 1857-1939*, Oxford University Press, New York.

Gürcan, M. and R. Johnson (2017), *The Gallipoli Campaign: The Turkish Perspective*, Routledge.

Hargrave, J. (2015), *At Suvla Bay: Being the Notes and Sketches of Scenes, Characters and Adventures of the Dardanelles Campaign*, Sagwan Press.

Hart, P. (2011), *Gallipoli*, Oxford University Press.

Hayward, J.B. (n.d.). *Honours and Awards Indian Army: 1914-1921* (1931st edn.), J.B. Hayward and Son.

Head, R. and T. McClenaghan (2013), *The Maharajas' Paltans: A History of the Indian State Forces, 1888-1948*.

Helles Memorial and World War One Indian Soldiers (2020).

History of the Great War, Military Operations Gallipoli (1st edn., vol. 1, Inception of the Campaign). (1935), William Heinemann Limited, London.

Holland, B.S. (2009), *How Europe is Indebted to the Sikhs? The Role of the Sikhs in the Europe During the Word War I (1914-18)*.

———. (2013), *Sikhs in World War I*. https://www.awm.gov.au. (n.d.).

Imy, K. (2023), *Faithful Fighters: Identity and Power in the British Army*. Bloomsbury Publishing.

James, L. (1898), *The Indian Frontier War*.

James, R.R. (2018), *Gallipoli* (1st edn.), Uniform Press.

Jarboe, A.T. (2015), *War News in India: The Punjabi Press During World War I*. Bloomsbury Publishing.

Jeffreys, A. (2022), *Indian Army in the First World War: New Perspectives (War & Military Culture in South Asia)* (rpt.), Helion and Company.

Kaul, C. (2003), *Reporting the Raj: The British Press and India, c. 1880-1922*. Manchester University Press.

Khan, Y. (2015), *The Raj at War: A People's History of India's Second World War*, Random House.

Khanduri, C.B. (1997), *A Re-discovered History of Gorkhas*.

King of Battle: Artillery in World War I. (2016), BRILL.

Laffin, J. (1980), *Damn the Dardanelles! The Story of Gallipoli*, Osprey Publishing.

Leask, I.D. (1989), *The Expansion of the Indian Army During the Great War*.

Leigh, M.S. (1997), *The Punjab and the War*.

Liddle, P. (1988), *Men of Gallipoli*.

Lockyer, C.B. (2009), *Gallipoli, Cape Helles, April 1915, the Tragedy of the Battle of the Beaches Together with the Proceedings of H M S Implacable Including the Landin.*

Lovett, A.C.I., and G.F.S. MacMunn (2016), *Armies of India.* Wentworth Press.

Lunt, J. (2017), *From Sepoy to Subedar: Being the Life and Adventures of Subedar Sita Ram, a Native Officer of the Bengal Army, Written and Related by Himself,* Routledge.

Lyster, M. (2011), *Among the Ottomans: Diaries from Turkey in World War I.*

Macdonald, J. (2019), *Supplying the British Army in the First World War,* Pen and Sword.

Mackenzie, C. (1930), *Gallipoli Memories.*

MacMunn, G.F. (1979a). *The Martial Races of India.*

Marshall, W.R. (1960), *Memories of Four Fronts.*

Mazumdar, R.K. (2003), *The Indian Army and the Making of Punjab,* Orient BlackSwan, New Delhi.

McCutcheon, C. (2015), *Hospital Ships & Troop Transport of the First World War,* Amberley Publishing Limited.

McGilvray, E. (2015a). *Hamilton and Gallipoli: British Command in the Age of Military Transformation,* Pen and Sword.

McGreal, S. (2009), *The War on Hospital Ships, 1914-1918,* Casemate Publishers.

McGregor, A. (2006), *A Military History of Modern Egypt: From the Ottoman Conquest to the Ramadan War,* Greenwood Publishing Group.

Mitcham, J.C. (2016), *Race and Imperial Defence in the British World, 1870-1914,* Cambridge University Press.

Monash, J. (2015), *War Letters of General Monash,* Black Inc.

Moorehead, A. (2015), *Gallipoli,* Aurum.

Moreman, T. (1998a), *The Army in India and the Development of Frontier Warfare, 1849-1947,* Springer.

Mortlock, M.J. (2015), *The Landings at Suvla Bay, 1915: An Analysis of British Failure During the Gallipoli Campaign,* McFarland.

Morton-Jack, G. (2018a), *Army of Empire: The Untold Story of the Indian Army in World War I,* Hachette, London.

Mullaly, B.R. (1957), *Bugle and Kukri: The Story of the 10th Princess Mary's Own Gurkha Rifles.*

Murphy, A. (1949), *To Hell and Back.*

Natwar-Singh, K. (1998), *The Magnificent Maharaja: The Life and Times of Bhupinder Singh of Patiala, 1891-1938*, books catalogue.

Nevile, P. (2012), *The Raj Revisited.*

O'Dwyer, M. (1988a), 'India as I knew it, 1885-1925', in Mittal Publications eBooks. http://ci.nii.ac.jp/ncid/BA42327361

O'Dwyer, M.F. (2016), *War Speeches*, Palala Press.

Omissi, D. (1998), *The Sepoy and the Raj: The Indian Army, 1860-1940 (Studies in Military and Strategic History)*, Palgrave Macmillan.

_____. (1999), *Indian Voices of the Great War: Soldiers' Letters, 1914-18*, Palgrave Macmillan.

_____. (2016b), *The Sepoy and the Raj: The Indian Army, 1860-1940.* Springer.

Pati, B. (1996), *India and the First World War*, Atlantic, New Delhi.

Perry, F.W. (1988), *The Commonwealth Armies: Manpower and Organisation in Two World Wars*, Manchester University Press.

Pradhan, S.D. (1978), 'The Sikh Soldier in the First World War', in De. C. Ellinwood (ed.), *India and the World War 1)*, Manohar, New Delhi, pp. 213-25.

Prakash, O. (2004), *History of Anglo-Sikh Wars.*

Prime, A.J. (2018), *The Indian Army's British Officer Corps, 1861-1921.*

Prior, R. (2009), *Gallipoli: The End of the Myth*, Yale University Press.

Raghavan, S. (2016), *India's War: The Making of Modern South Asia, 1939-1945*, Penguin, London.

Rance, P. (2015), *The Struggle for the Dardanelles: The Memoirs of a German Staff Officer in Ottoman Service*, Pen and Sword.

Roy, K. (2008), *Brown Warriors of the Raj: Recruitment and the Mechanics of Command in the Sepoy Army, 1859-1913*, Manohar, New Delhi.

_____. (2012), *The Army in British India: From Colonial Warfare to Total War 1857-1947*, A&C Black.

_____. (2015), *Military Manpower, Armies and Warfare in South Asia*, Routledge.

Savory, R. (2016a). *A Subaltern of the Sikhs*, Abhishek Publications.

Sharma, G. (1990), *Valour and Sacrifice: Famous Regiments of the Indian Army*, Allied Publishers.

Singapore's Early Sikh Pioneers: Origins, Settlement, Contributions, and Institutions (2017).

Singh, A. (2015), *Honour and Fidelity: India's Military Contribution to the Great War 1914-18*, Roli Books, New Delhi.

Singh, B.K.K. (2013), *Indian Military Thought Kurukshetra to Kargil and Future Perspectives*, Lancer Publishers.

Singh, F. (1964), *Military System of the Sikhs: During the Period 1799-1849*.

Singh, P. and J.M. Rai (2008), *Empire of the Sikhs: The Life and Times of Maharaja Ranjit Singh*, Peter Owen Publishers.

Singha, R. (2019), *The Coolie's Great War: Indian Labour in a Global Conflict, 1914-1921*, C Hurst & Co., London.

Smith, D. (2019), *The First Anglo-Sikh War 1845-46: The Betrayal of the Khalsa*, Bloomsbury Publishing.

Smith, T. (2020), *Comrades in Arms: Military Masculinities in East German Culture*, Berghahn Books.

Stanley, P. (2005), *Quinn's Post: Anzac, Gallipoli*, Allen & Unwin.

Stanley, P. (2021), *Die in Battle, Do Not Despair: The Indians on Gallipoli 1915*, Helion.

Steel, N. and P. Hart (1994), *Defeat at Gallipoli*, Trans-Atlantic Publications.

Stowers, R. (2005), *Bloody Gallipoli: The New Zealanders' Story*.

Talbot, I. (1988), *Punjab and the Raj, 1849-1947*.

Tan, T.Y. (2005), *The Garrison State: The Military, Government and Society in Colonial Punjab 1849-1947*. In Sage eBooks. http://ci.nii.ac.jp/ncid/BA73345812

Tennant, E. (2017), *Royal Deccan Horse in the Great War*, Naval and Military Press.

Tharoor, S. (2018), *Inglorious Empire: What the British Did to India*, Penguin, London.

Thursby, G.R. (1992), *The Sikhs*, BRILL.

Travers, T. (2016), *Gallipoli 1915*, The History Press.

Trench, C.C. (1988a), *The Indian Army and the King's Enemies, 1900-1947*. Thames & Hudson.

Tyagi, V. P. (2009), *Martial Races of Undivided India*, Gyan Publishing House, New Delhi.

Ulrichsen, K.C. and K. Ulrichsen (2014), *The First World War in the Middle East*, Hurst & Company, London.

Uyar, M. (2015), *The Ottoman Defence Against the ANZAC Landing - 25 April 1915*. Simon and Schuster.

Van Hartesveldt, F. R. (1997), *The Dardanelles Campaign, 1915: Historiography and Annotated Bibliography*, Greenwood Publishing Group.

Westerman, W. & N. Floyd (2020), *Clash of the Gods of War: Australian Artillery and the Firepower Lessons of the Great War*. Simon and Schuster.

Articles

'Alī, I. (1979), *The Punjab Canal Colonies, 1885-1940.*

'Alī, I. (2014), *The Punjab Under Imperialism, 1885-1947*, Princeton University Press.

Asghar, M. (2015), 'Forgotten Gunners of Gallipoli', *Royal Australian Artillery Historical Company.*

Barua, P. (1998), *The Army Officer Corps and Military Modernisation in Later Colonial India.* Hull University Press.

Beyerchen, A. & F. Sencer (2019), *Expeditionary Forces in the First World War*, Springer Nature.

Callahan, R. (1972), *The East India Company and Army Reform, 1783-1798*, Cambridge: Harvard University Press.

Das, S. (2014), 'Indian Sepoy Experience in Europe, 1914-18: Archive, Language, and Feeling', *Twentieth Century British History.* https://doi.org/10.1093/tcbh/hwu033

French, D. P. (1983), The Origins of the Dardanelles Campaign Reconsidered. *History, 68*(223), 210-24. https://doi.org/10.1111/j.1468-229x.1983.tb01405.x

Gerwarth, R. and E. Manela (2014), *Empires at War.* Oxford University Press eBooks. https://doi.org/10.1093/acprof:oso/9780198702511.001.0001

Greenhut, J. (1983), 'The Imperial Reserve: The Indian Corps on the Western Front, 1914-15', *The Journal of Imperial and Commonwealth History, 12*(1), 54-73. https://doi.org/10.1080/03086538308582650

Kumar, A. and C. Markovits (2020a), *Indian Soldiers in the First World War: Re-visiting a Global Conflict.* Taylor & Francis.

Macleod, J. (2001), 'General Sir Ian Hamilton and the Dardanelles Commission', *War in History, 8*(4), 418-41. https://doi.org/10.1177/096834450100800403

Yadav, K. (2016), 'Army Recruitment in Punjab, 1846-1913: An Evolutionary Study', *USI Journal*, July 2016-Sept. 2016.

Ziino, B. (2006), 'Who owns Gallipoli? Australia's Gallipoli Anxieties 1915–

2005', *Journal of Australian Studies*, *30*(88), 1-12. https://doi.org/10.1080/14443050609388071.

Electronic Sources

Australians and Indians: Cordial Relations at Gallipoli (9 August 1915), *Warrnambool Standard*. Retrieved 14 May 2022, from https://trove.nla.gov.au/newspaper/article/73455621/7131999

Simpson, C. (2010), 'From Ruthless Foe to National Friend: Turkey, Gallipoli and Australian Nationalism', *Media International Australia*, 137(1), 58–66. https://doi.org/10.1177/1329878x1013700107.

Thesis

Hingkanonta, L. (2013), 'The Police in Colonial Burma', PhD thesis. SOAS, University of London.

Tate Jarboe, A. (2013), 'Soldiers of Empire: Indian Sepoys in and beyond the Imperial Metropole during the First World War 1914-1918', PhD Thesis, North-Eastern University.

Zafar, F. (2017), *Canals, Colonies and Class: British Policy in the Punjab 1880-1940*.

Index

Index

Australians, close and intimate relationship 426; Anzac Cove and the Sikh troops of the Artillery Batteries 166; availability of sea shore at 'W' beach 171-2; Cape Helles in the Gallipoli Peninsula 163; casualty returns of 29th Indian Infantry Brigade Headquarters 185; catering for a lot of reorganisation and artillery support 173; communication trenches 181-2; complete complement of the 29th Indian Infantry Brigade 174; composite division with the Headquarter of Royal Naval Division established 172; continuous assaults being initiated by the MEF 175; continuous shelling by Turkish artillery 172; Coolie and Labour Corps from India, deployment of 305; disembarkation orders for the troops 165; dispositions of the battalions of the Brigade 184; Double Companies of the 69th Punjabis 165; Double Company of the battalion 180; Double Company of the Gurkhas 177; flat-bottomed boats 159; French Division 170; gap in defences between 'B' Company of the 14th Sikhs and the Royal Fusiliers 182; GOC of the 29th Indian Infantry Brigade 180; Gurkha Battalion moved as reserve on the "Y" Beach 184; in the Gallipoli campaign 32-3; Indian and British Battalions,

camaraderie and the integration between 183; Indian Field Ambulances, role played during the campaign 305; Indian Field Post Offices, functioning of 305; Indian Infantry Brigade, arrival at southern end of the peninsula 164; Indian Infantry Brigade, deeply involved in the digging 185; Indian Mountain gunners, professionalism and determination of 160-1; logistics of 303-6; massive artillery tirade launched against Turkish defences 177; No Man's land 181; no previous precedence of time-tested system of reporting of casualties 304; Observation Post (OP) of the section 180; of the Mountain Batteries 433; on Gallipoli 153-86; Operation Order for the formation 163; Operation Order Number 7 179; Order of Battle of the 29th Indian Infantry Brigade 179; 'Order of March' 161; Qantara, mobilisation of the battalions of the Indian Brigade to Port Said 161; reorganisation of defensive positions 176; responsibility delegated by the Indian Brigade to the 89th Punjabis 165-6; second battle of Krithia, non-utilisation of the Indian Brigade 173; Sikhs launched a ferocious counterattack on to the Turkish line 183; Sikhs proved every apprehension of the Turks 168; Supply and Mule Corps 305; sustained operations

Units 134; General Service
Units 134-5; later-half of 1897,
impending outbreak of a war on
North-West Frontier 131;
recruiting personnel for the war
132; Sardar Ala Singh, founder
130
Pay and allowances 378-83: 1/4
Gurkha and Indian Mule Corps
denied the grant of additional
pay 379; 1/4 Gurkha joined the
IEF 'G' from IEF 'A' in France
379; clothing allowance and
disposal of kit and personal
belongings of the deceased
Indian soldiers 380-1; IEF 'D'
378-9; EF 'G', deinduction of
379; of 1915 378, 379; Indian
army soldiers, entitled for *batta*
(allowance) 378; Indian Medical
Service (IMS) 381; Indian ranks
and permanent followers,
clothing allowance in peace time
381; Indian troops of IEF 'A',
increase of pay for 378; office of
the Adjutant General in India
379; rates of active service pays
and field allowance 381-2;
redeployment of 1/4 Gurkha
from the IEF 'A' to the IEF 'G'
379; soldiers of the Indian
battalions on the peninsula 383;
troops in France being granted
allowance 380; uninterrupted
continuance of the field
allowance to the troops of IEF
'A' 380; various IEFs in August
1914, mobilisation of 378;
withdrawal of the subject

allowance, strictly not
recommended 380
political leadership 87
political lessons 87
Postal arrangements 366-70: 34
Indian FPO 366; 65th FPO,
66th FPO and 325th FPO 367;
Advance Base Office of the 33rd
FPO at Mudros 367; Advanced
Base Office for the four FPOs
367; Expeditionary Forces 370;
Force 'G', operational command
of 367; Force "E" 370; free
postage to India, sanctioned by
the C-in-C in India on 25
November 1914 370; IEF 'G',
establishment of 367; Indian
FPOs to update the list on a
daily basis 369; Indian troops of
Force 'G', coordination of postal
facilities for 367; non-
availability of these orderlies
367; requirements of the
censoring, mails from India 368;
reverse process, mail initiated
from the peninsula by the
Indian units 368; 'W' beach
366
Practice of religion 383-6: 14th
Sikhs, extensive pace of
operations being conducted
385; facial hair, maintenance of
384; initial arrival of Sikhs on
the peninsula in May 1915 383;
reetha and the *sarson* oil, must
for a Sikh to take care of the
facial hair 384; *sarson* oil,
limited availability of 384; Sikh
being a devoted disciple of his

reduction of authorised scales of water per man per day 333-4; Regimental Bazaars 324; Regimental Gardens 324; religious beliefs of Sikhs 331; remoteness of the locations 325; scales of ration for the Indian troops 326; severe water scarcity 335; supply of water to the front-line troops 333; system of Commissariat 324; tobacco ration, utter shortage of 331

Recruitment and retention, incentivising of 102-9: 14th Sikhs, Lt F.A. Jacques 106; Canal Colony scheme 106; considerations of 'Martial Races' theory, cumulative effect 108; development of canals for irrigation 105; enhancing the social status of soldiers 104; executive order granting precedence to the soldiers 104; grant of 'Good Conduct Pay', 1837 103; Indian Army Order of 19 December 1914 107-8; Indian Army, social composition of 108; individual awards though recognised bravery and sacrifice 104-5; pension regulations of 1864 103; Punjab Government between 1919 and 1939, prime irrigated land to military grantees 107; Punjabi soldier, enlistment strategy of 105; rank of Indian officer, promotion to 104; recruitment post the mutiny of 1857 103; recruitment strategy, caste factor

in 109; senior Indian soldiers, pay scales of 103; seniority-based principle 104; stewardship of Major General Peel, Secretary of State for War, Commission appointed in July 1858 108-9; system of grant of land parcels to the soldiers 106

Redbreast 295

Regimental Commanders 107

Regimental Number 1414, Private Gurbachan Singh 429

Reinforcements, sustaining the campaign 438-47: August 1914, rate of provisioning of reinforcements 443; August 1915 to December 1915, troops dispatched from India for the deployment on Gallipoli 447; Hamilton provided with a Double Company of Patiala Sikhs 440-1; Hamilton's faith in the capabilities of Sikh troops 439; October 1914, mobilisation of twenty Infantry battalions 441-2; October 1915, reinforcements primarily meant for 14th Sikhs, 2/10 Gurkhas and 1/4 Gurkhas 443-5; possibility of reinforcements for 14th Sikhs from 51st and 53rd Sikhs 438-9; proposed de-induction of MEF from Dardanelles 445-6; reinforcements from Alexandria to Mudros 443; reinforcements from Burma Military Police provided for the 14th Sikhs 441; September 1915, 'C' Company of Patiala Sikhs reinforced 14th

mules 347; end of July, plans to launch another offensive on to the Turkish defenses 345-6; experience of the experimental move taught invaluable lessons to the Corps 342; first week of August, Indian Infantry Brigade started concentrating at Anzac for the August offensive 347-8; food, affected by the fly menace 343-4; Indian mule carts, limited availability of existing tracks 341; Indian Mule Corps on the peninsula, strength of 337; Indian Mule Corps, deployed on the peninsula 337; Indian Mule Corps, distribution into components 338; Indian Mule Corps, supervisory and conductor staff 343; Indian Mule Transport on the peninsula 337; Indian muleteers on board ship for landing at Anzac 338; interpersonal relationships among different ethnic groups 352; interpreter billets 345; Mudros, firm orders received for the Indian Mule Corps 337-8; Mule Corps, consist of 337; Number 2 outpost, manned by the troops from Otago Mounted Rifles of New Zealand Mounted Brigade 346; Number 3 Mule Corps, troops of, landed at Anzac 342-3; post the August offensive, Indian Mule Corps, divided into four groups 349; post the August offensive, situation at the Anzac changed

349; understanding of Hindustani by the frequently changing British staff 344-5; use of mules in pack role only 340; Zionist Mule Corps 339

Supply and transport corps 137-41: administrative planning 140; Indian Mule Corps 139; Indian Mule Train commanded by Col. C.H. Beville 140; restive North-West Frontier areas 138; saddlery modification 141; shipping requisitioned from trade for mobilization 138; sufficient animals of each variety 137

Suvla Bay 237-9, 247, 279, 351, 366: situation for the Indian Mule Corps 351

Suvla plan 237

tactical intelligence, restricted by the vicinity of the enemy 236

The Great War/Great European war 32, 37, 69, 89, 91-7, 102, 104-5, 107, 109-11, 113, 115, 119, 126, 130-2, 134, 136-7, 153, 187, 243, 308, 318-19, 323, 330, 366, 371, 373, 378, 402-4, 418-22, 465, 472-3, 481, 487, 496-7, 505: causes and consequences of 37; in Egypt 32; Indian Infantry on the Eve of 109-120; participation and contribution of the Indian troops in Europe 402; selective amnesia about the contribution of Indian soldiers 403

Third Battle of Krithia 132, 212,